CO-AUL-459

THE
DISCARDED
E & BALMORAL
PEG 2, MAN,   CANADA

A
DIARY OF
THE
FRENCH
REVOLUTION

VOLUME II

GOUVERNEUR MORRIS
From a painting by Thomas Sully, Philadelphia, 1808

DC
162
M6
1939
V. 2

A DIARY

OF THE FRENCH

REVOLUTION

BY

GOUVERNEUR MORRIS 1752–1816

MINISTER TO FRANCE DURING THE TERROR

———————— ◦ ————————

EDITED BY

BEATRIX CARY DAVENPORT

WITH ILLUSTRATIONS

II

HOUGHTON MIFFLIN COMPANY · BOSTON

The Riverside Press Cambridge

1939

COPYRIGHT, 1939, BY BEATRIX CARY DAVENPORT

ALL RIGHTS RESERVED INCLUDING THE RIGHT TO REPRODUCE
THIS BOOK OR PARTS THEREOF IN ANY FORM

The Riverside Press
CAMBRIDGE · MASSACHUSETTS
PRINTED IN THE U.S.A.

CONTENTS

ILLUSTRATIONS

VI

A VERY LONG DRIVE

THROUGH FLANDERS AND THE RHINELAND
IN QUEST OF IMMIGRANTS

SEPTEMBER 1790

Saturday 25. — Leave Dartford this Morning at five. The Inn is good. Arrive at the City of London Inn at Dover at three oClock. The Distance is not quite fifty five Miles and we are ten Hours in accomplishing it. After agreeing for my Passage and getting my Dinner I walk out and ramble to the Top of the highest Cliff. The View from hence is extensive but it is chiefly Water. I am told that the dreadful Trade, as Shakespear calls it, of gathering Samphire is still carried on in the same Way as formerly. A Man drives a Stake into the Ground above, to which he fastens a Rope and descends by that to the Spot where this Plant is found. The Price when gathered is 20^d per bushel, being quite as much as it is worth, and yet one would suppose that the Price is hardly worth the Risque. His Wife attends the Adventurer and draws up the full Baskets at a Signal agreed on. A fine Opportunity is afforded her of changing her Helpmate, should she be so inclined. A little before ten I go on board the Packet. According to Custom at this and every other English Port on the Channel (as far as I can learn) all Sorts of Claims and Impositions are made and practised. But we must in all Cases pay the Customs. At half past ten we get under Way in the Harbor of Dover, a fine fair Breeze from the North West and a charming Moon Light so bright that I see plainly in Mid Channel both the french and english Coasts. At three Quarters after one we are at the Key in the Harbor of Calais. The Master of the Packet being charged with Dispatches for the English Embassador, gets the Gates opened and we proceed to Mons.ʳ Dessein's.

Sunday 26. — Having given the needful Orders last Night, every Thing is ready to depart immediately after Breakfast this Morning. It costs me just eleven Guineas from London before I can clear out from this Spot. Leave the Gates of Calais about Noon. N. Westerly Wind and very fine Weather. We proceed for some Distance over a sandy Plain to a little Village, the Country on the right is evidently very good and so is that which we now get into & go thro to Gravelines, crossing once or twice a pretty meandring Stream which is I suppose dignified with the Name of a River. Two Hours and a Quarter bring us to this Place and about the same Time, thro a fine level Country, to Dunquerque, which is however in a very sandy Position as must be the Case with the Seaports, because the Shore from Calais to the Zuyder Zee is nothing but Sand. The Distance is five Posts, about twenty five Mile.

Monday 27. — This Morning wait upon Mons.ʳ de Bague and deliver a Letter from Mess.ʳˢ Bourdieu & Co?. We walk down to the Port, the Mouth of which is choaked with Sand. The Weather is very fine. Return from hence to the Exchange, where I see M.ʳ Gregory, to whom I present a Letter and we confer a little on Business. Dine with him and he promises to write to me after consulting his Father, and to inform me whether they will accept Bills upon Receipt of Bills of Lading, Invoice and orders for Insurance. They will come under Acceptance at the Rate of £10 St.ᵍ per Chest for Hyson Tea which they expect to sell at about £15, but they can sell a Quantity only to the India Company. The Commerce of this Place, which consisted chiefly in a Contraband with Great Britain, has been much injured by the lowering of the Duties in that Kingdom. At present they have got into the Whaling and West India Business. The Import of Tobacco is considerable also. Their Population is said to be ab.ᵗ 30000 and there is great Activity among them.

Tuesday 28. — This Morning I leave the Hôtel de Flandre where I found the Entertainment good and not dear. We go to the Sea Shore as it happens to be low Water, which is fortunate for it seems that the Road along the Dunes is very heavy, being

indeed a deep light Sand. When we arrive at the Beach the
View is fine. The Sun being upon our right shines brightly against
the Sails of Vessels in the Offing, which are numerous, of different
Sizes and at various Distances. It is nearly calm and the least
Surge which I ever saw on a Beach. On our right are the sandy
Hills called the Dunes, blown up into fantastic Irregularity, in
Part bare and white, in other Parts covered with such coarse dark
colored Vegetation as they admit of. I observe here a Kind of
Fishing which is novel to me and which is now carrying on in its
fullest Extent. A great Number of People are employed, some in
digging large Worms which are found between high and low
Water Mark. These are for Bait. Others in taking the fish from
off the Hooks; these are tied by Cords of about a Yard long to
Poles stuck in the Sand in Lines at right Angles to the Shore, so
that when the Tide is out the fish who take themselves are found
hanging at about a foot from the Shore. They are flat fish and
taken in great Numbers. After travelling some Time along the
Coast we turn to the right and get upon a Pavement which leads
to the Shore, and thence we go to a little Village called la Banque,
situated in the Middle of the Dunes upon a Plain of Sand. After
passing it a little Way we come into a fine Country. I am again
for the second Time strongly impressed with the Difference between austrian and french Flanders. The Appearances of Affluence in the former and Poverty in the latter are striking. Such
is the powerful Energy of Freedom even in a slender Degree.
We arrive at Furne after three Hours spent in going two Posts.
Here we are provided after long Delay with three miserable
Horses, with which we are to go all the Way to Ostend because
they are not strong enough to draw us to Nieuport, the usual
Route. This it seems is Part of the Way sandy, but by going farther round we have a Pavement. We pass thro a Village called
Previse or Pervise and stop at the Bridge of Scorback for our
Horses to be fed. Poor Devils, they want Food I believe, tho this
is not the best Mode of giving it. From hence we proceed to a
little Village called Ghistel where (as in some other Places) I observe there is a Kind of College for Education of the french and
english. I suppose Religion comes in for Something in this Business, and certainly those who desire that their Children should

imbibe the most blind and obstinate Prejudices which Superstition ever engendered upon Ignorance, cannot do better than send them to Flanders for Education. Here we stay as at Furne and at the Bridge of Scorback just half an Hour, and in an Hour and an Half we get to Ostend. Thus our Route stands to Furne 3 hours 2 posts, ½ an Hour to change, then to Scorback Bridge 1½ & ½ an Hour to feed, to Ghistel 1½ and ½ an Hour to feed, to Ostend 1½, being 4 posts tho short ones, which gives in the whole 6 Posts of scarce 36 Miles in 9 Hours. The Country is a rich Sand. The Weather is very fine. There is a great Deal of Tobacco raised in this Country but the most miserable I ever beheld. At fifty Paces Distance we could not tell whether a Field we saw was Tobacco or Turnips. Having omitted to enquire untill near our Journey's End for a Hotel we are directed to the Hôtel de Ville, which is I fear a bad one: from Appearances it certainly is. After Dinner I look at the Harbor which seems to be a very good one of the Kind. Return Home pretty well fatigued and go early to Bed. A very fine Day.

Wednesday 29. — This Morning after Breakfast I call on Mess.ʳˢ Robert Charnock & Co:. The Head of the House is gone to Hamburgh to be married to a Daughter of Mʳ Parish of the House of Parish and Thompson. Am received by the other Partner, Mʳ Parker. We converse upon Business and he is to write to me. I think we shall do Business together. Call on Mess.ʳˢ George Keith & Co? and deliver to Mʳ Keith a Letter from Phyn Ellices and Inglis; a polite Reception, a little general Conversation, News, Politics &c.ᵃ. I am not inclined to seize Openings here because I doubt a little of the Strength of the Parties. Call on Mess.ʳˢ Gregory Benquet & Co: and deliver a Letter from Mess.ʳˢ Gregory of Dunquerque. General Conversation. Speaking this Morning with Mʳ Parker of the smuggling Trade to London, He tells me that for 20 p% any Article will be delivered free of all Risques at any House which may be named in London. After Dinner I write, among others to Short & to Bouinville and Ternant for Letters of Introduction on my proposed Route. Mʳ Keith visits me and is very polite. I pay in the same Coin *et nous voilà quitte.* This Town is small and contains but ten or twelve thousand Inhabitants. The Commerce also is falling off. The flemish Mer-

chants have no Enterprize & there are few others who have the
needful Funds. It has however many Advantages for Traffic.
Sup with M.ʳ Gregory, and having nothing else to do or think of I
entertain the Party with pleasant Conversation; it consists of only
four besides myself, of which two are the Host & Hostess. A
Lady (her Sister I believe) and a Parson are the other two. They
tell me that I cannot get on without a Passport and I cannot get
that untill ten oClock ToMorrow. It has been a very fine Day.

Thursday 30. — This Morning I rise pretty early and write.
Dress and Breakfast, which last I cannot get till after nine. It
seems there is a Law prohibiting the Peasants from selling any
Thing before the Market Hour, which is nine oClock. This seems
to have been contrived by the indolent. I walk into the Market
which is well furnished. The Beef is not large but looks well and
the Vegetables of every Kind seem good, and there is a great
Plenty. I observe here what I have frequently seen in different
Places along this Route, small flat fish dryed apparently without
Salt, and tied up in Bunches for Sale. They seem to be of the
Kind which the People near Dunkirk were gathering. I wait till
ten oClock for M.ʳ Gregory to bring my Pass, but then call and
find he is not up. Call again a second Time and go with Mons.ʳ
Benquet, his Partner, to the Town House, and give my Name,
Country, Occupation and the Name of my Father; to this is added
a Description of my Person. Return again to M.ʳ Gregory's and
wait a considerable Time before the Pass arrives, for the Magistrates were occupied with Business when we were at the Maison
de Ville. By this Means I do not get off till half past eleven. I
get here very good Horses and my Bill is not extravagant, tho I
ought to have put up at the Couronne Impériale, that being the
best Hotel. Mine was not cleanly. We go again to Ghistel in an
Hour precisely. It is about seven Miles and our Stop there is just
a Quarter. Hence in another Hour to Yerbeke, about the same
Distance. After stopping again a Quarter of an Hour we go on to
Brugges & put up at the Hôtel de Commerce which is also the
Post House; the Distance is not quite so great as the last but the
Time to the Gates of Brugges is the same. I think the whole is not
less than 19 Miles. I pay three Posts. The Road is well paved,
which for the greater Part of the Way is indispensibly necessary.

The Country from Ghistel a deep poor Sand worth very little, and but little cultivated. Immediately on my Arrival I go down to the Bason which terminates the Canal from Ostend. Ships of 500 Tons can come up this Canal. There is now in it sixteen feet Water and the Rivers and Brooks are low at this Season of the Year. The Distance, I was told at Ostend, is about twelve Miles. It is a wonderful Effort of commercial Industry, but alas it now answers but little Purpose. There are however now in the Bason a Ship and a Brig. A Number of Fly Boats are discharging Sugars, Cotton and Coffee. I return to the Hotel and dine worse than I expected from its Reputation. After Dinner I ask for Tea and get some black Strap.

OCTOBER 1790

Friday 1 *October.* — This Morning I take some Tea and in the Sea Phrase clear out for Departure. The Hôtel de Commerce is very good I find *at making out a Bill*. The House however is clean & the Cook I believe pretty good. At half past seven I leave Bruges and proceed to Maldeghem in an Hour and three Quarters, the Distance about 9 Miles; we stop here a Quarter of an Hour and then go on to Eckelo in an Hour, Distance scarce 6 Miles. This is 2 Posts and an Half. The Country very poor & sandy. We are half an Hour in changing Horses and then we have two Posts of about twelve or thirteen Miles thro Warmstadt to Ghent, which is performed in two Hours. The Country about a League from Eckelo begins to mend and (chiefly by force of Culture) is beautiful and luxuriant. Near Ghent there are some fine Meadows. It is worthy of Remark that even in the poorest Soil the Houses are well built of Brick and there is throughout an Air of Neatness and Comfort not to be met with I believe in Great Britain. After Dinner I proceed to view the Cathedral which contains many Productions in Painting, Statuary and Architecture which merit

Attention. The Martyrdom of Saint Barbe appears to me the
finest Painting, altho there is a very fine one of Reubens. But
the Figure, Manner and Countenance of the young *Dévote* who is
endeavoring to draw out one of the Arrows with which the Saint
is pierced, seem to be the utmost Perfection which Art can arrive
at, and perhaps Nature herself could not go farther. Piety &
Humanity in the lowly bending of sedulous Attention, mingled
with all the Delicacy of female Tenderness, impress the Heart
most forcibly. There is a fine old Woman also, but there are many
such. In this Cathedral there are some modern Imitations of Bas
Relief by a Painter now living in this City. One must see them to
form an Idea of the Effect which can be produced by Light and
Shade. This Cathedral is dedicated to S.t Bavon and it is the
Saint's Day. While I am examining the Paintings &c.a a stout
Friar is roaring vehemently in Praise of his Saintship. Luckily I
do not understand Flemish. After viewing the inside of the
Church I come out & go round into the Steeple and mount up to
the Top, which they tell me is 310 flemish feet. The View from
hence is not so fine as I expected, for the Atmosphere is hazy,
which my Guide says is always the Case with a North or East
Wind. The Weather is nevertheless as fine as is possible. The
Country about Ghent is in general sterile and covered with what
appears from this Heighth like Forest, but is indeed chiefly
Bushes. After descending from this *Tour* my Guide leads me to
the Citadel of Charles the fifth, made to awe the rebellious Spirit
for which this City has always been remarkable. They are now
demolishing that Side which faces the City. A Number of Houses
in the Neighbourhood were destroyed by the Troops but my
Guide acknowleges that it was rather by the poor Inhabitants.
However, there was enough of Pillage & Ravage by the Troops.
We proceed from hence to the great Square and thence to the
Hôtel de Ville, which is quite a Janus, having one Face of Gothic
and one of Grecian Architecture. The former, like all such Buildings, looks like an oldfashioned Piece of Cabinet Work. The
latter is neither fine nor despicable. Return to Quarters well
tired. I find that the People of this Town are very much divided
in their Opinions. The Exclusion of the Tiers État works but
badly. They have received this Day the inflated Account of a

successful Action of the 28 Sep? to ballance a severe Defeat of the
15.th. But I think their Countenances are not bright. During my
Walk this Afternoon I find that I have been much deceived in the
Opinion I formed of the River Scheld. I did suppose that there
was Tide as far up as Mons, because in passing thro that City
there was the Appearance of a River at low Water, altho the Strait-
ness of it resembled more a Canal. I find now that the Flood goes
no farther than Ghent, where there is a Damm to confine the upper Waters to a certain Level. But it seems that the Navigation
in Canals is preferable to the other. One Horse draws a very large
Vessel and they go with Certainty a given Distance in the Time
allotted for that Purpose.

Saturday 2^d. — This Morning as soon as I have breakfasted I
go to the Church of the Recollets, in which are two admired Paint-
ings of Reubens, a dying Magdalen and a thundering Jehovah.
The Magdalen is a very fine Form and the Expression is good.
The other is considered as very fine. The Idea is that God the
Father raises his right Arm which grasps a Thunderbolt to strike
this sinful World. The holy Virgin catches his left Arm and in the
Style of a good Wife points to her Breast which had suckled his
Son, and Saint Francis, a faithful old Servant, covers the Globe
with his Mantle. According to the Mythology of the roman catholic Religion, both the Idea and Execution of this Piece are fine,
but I cannot admire the latter because the former is so absurd, and
so degrading to the Omnipotent, if indeed it were possible for Man
to honor or dishonor Him. From this Church we go to the Abbey
of St Peter, belonging to the Order of Benedictines. The Abbot
is well fledged. He has here a Palace, and his Income they tell
me is immense. The first Place we visit is the Refectory of the
Holy Fathers. In it are some fine Paintings. It is large, clean, and
just far enough from the Kitchin, so that they are not incommoded
either by the Heat or Smell, and yet the Victuals cannot get cold
in the Passage in Times of hard Frost. From hence we go to the
Library, which contains a great many Books and some very good
Paintings. From hence we go to the Church, in which they are
celebrating Mass so that we cannot examine the Altar, which is
of great Size and composed of massy Silver, partly gilt. There
are many fine Paintings in this Church, and among them two

very large Pieces bought lately of the Jesuits of Ypres. One of them is a Magdalen offering herself to an Infant Jesus. The Figure and Expression are prodigiously fine. The other is the Triumph of the Church in the Case of a young Monarch who turns Friar. He embraces the Cross and turns his Back upon the Pomp and Pleasure of the World, represented by two female Figures, both of which are fine. S.t Ignatius, to whom the young Devotee presents himself, is also an excellent Figure. The Expression of his Countenance dignified and majestic. There is also a good Assortment of Snakes and Thorns and Devils. — The Celebration of the Mass is an excellent Accompanyment to the View of these Paintings and it is not, I think, to be wondered at that a gloomy natural Temper, educated in the bigotry of Catholic Superstition, should after the Disappointments to which all human Plans and Wishes are liable, be at some melancholic Moment so impressed by the seeming Calm which reigns within monastic Walls, as to wish for that Retirement from the tumultuous and tormenting Solicitudes of Life. Such was the Fate of Charles, who first saw the Light in this City, and after vexing himself and his Neighbours during the Age in which he lived, threw himself at length into a Spanish Cloister. And thus he demonstrated by a lengthy Comment the solemn Declaration that 'Man walketh in a vain Shadow and disquieteth himself in vain.' I observe two well fed Novices who with Difficulty preserve the Tartuffe Visage during the Mass. I fancy they are not Novices in some of the monastic Mysteries. They are a Brace of as handsome young Dogs as ever enlisted in the Cuckold-making Corps. A View of such fine Paintings on religious Subjects and the solemn sounding Anthems thro long drawn Ayles of Gothic Architecture, seem well calculated to inspire reverential Awe. But when a little Familiarity has taken off the first Impressions, and the Youth, pampered with high and stimulating Food, sees female Beauty in the most enchanting Attitudes which the Painter could imagine or his Pencil express, will Nature, who speaks so expressively to all her Creatures, be silent only to him? I fancy not. — I think Charles the fifth in building a Fortress to bridle his fellow Citizens of Ghent, should have borrowed of S.t Peter the Ground on which stands this Abbey and Church; it is high, airy, healthy and commanding. Perhaps Leopold may by & bye do Something of this Sort. — At eleven oClock I leave Ghent and go in one Hour to Loochrist and in another to Lockeren, together two Posts of about six Miles each, over a sandy Plain. The Soil very poor but the Culture very good. It takes 20 Minutes here to change Horses. This is a pretty large Village lying on the River Durme, which we cross to come into it. From hence we cross again that River and go on the North Side of it to the Village of Waesmunster, and thence we go northwardly to the Star, a Post House; the Distance is one Post of about six Miles which with three Horses we accomplish in about seventy Minutes. There is no Pavement on this Part of the Road excepting thro Waesmunster, and the Sand is very deep. The Grounds along the River are fine but those at a little Distance from it very bad, and yet by Force of Culture they yield well. We change Horses here, which takes 25 Minutes, and go to St Nicolas, the Road for the first League lying thro the Sand, but then we get on a very fine Pavement. This is a very large Village. In going thro it Somebody throws a Brick against the Door of my Carriage, a Kind of Wit which I have been told is not uncommon in Flanders. At Beveren, another very large Village (indeed they might both be called Towns) we stop ten Minutes to give the Horses a little Bread and Water. We came hither in an Hour and forty Minutes, the Distance a Post and an Half, about nine Miles. In one Hour more we go another Post to the Ferry at Antwerp, the Distance about six Miles. The Scheld appears as wide here as the Hackinsack River in the Road from New York to Newark; I find the exact Width is 225 Yards. We cross in a Scow, and the Wind being contrary and partly with the Tide which runs here strongly, we are obliged to go a great Way down before we stand across. We are just an Hour from our Arrival at the Ferry to the Hotel of the Grand Laboureur in Antwerp, which lies indeed a considerable Distance from the Water Side where we landed. The View of Antwerp from the other Side of the River is fine. The most prominent Feature at a Distance is the Spire of the Cathedral, which to the Top of the Cross is said to be 466 feet, and that Part to which I ascended is said to be 400 feet, about 375 English. This Country throughout abounds with Churches and all along the Road there are Sancta Marias and Crucifixes for

the Convenience of itinerant Worshippers. My Guide of Ghent
(who had served a long Time in the french Army, which is not the
School of most rigid Superstition) pointed out to me in my Walk,
which he took Care should be thro the Streets where the Patriots
and Soldiery fought, the Marks of many Musket Balls in the Wall
of a House against which was an Image either of the Virgin or her
Son, I forget which, and *miraculously* not a Bullet had touched
that sacred Spot. Chance might have done this, was the first
Idea which entered the unbelieving Noddle of a Protestant, but
after passing I looked back and found that the Miracle would
have been to have hit it, for it stood on a Corner exactly out of
the Line of Fire. I might therefore very easily have explained
this Miracle, but if I should convince him of the Folly of the
Faith he has held for above sixty Years, 'tis ten to one if he could
now find a better and therefore it is best to leave him in Possession
of his present Property. The Weather has this Day been very
fine. The Distance we have come is about thirty to thirty three
Miles and we spent six Hours and three Quarters in doing it;
near one Hour of the Time was consumed in stopping and changing Horses. I find upon looking over my Route thro the Province
of Flanders and begining at Furne where we got the first imperial
Horses, that altho the Country is so level that Roads might be
run in almost every Direction, I have travelled about six Miles to
get a real Distance of five. The Time consumed in going a given
Distance is about the same as I have found it in France and the
Expence of the Post Horses is the same as nearly as may be, considering the Difference of Measures and Coins. There is however
the additional Expence of Tolls or Turnpikes in this Country.
Including the Money to Postillions, the Difference of Expence
between this and England is about as 3 to 4, or ⅓ more in England. The Turnpikes also are more expensive in that Country,
and the Inns infinitely dearer. My Expences from Calais till I arrive at the Hotel in this City are St⁵ £10, Distance about 112 to
115 Miles.

Sunday 3.ᵈ — After Breakfast this Morning I send to see if I
have Letters at the House of M.ʳ Wolfe, not having any at the
Post Office. About Noon M.ʳ Wolf calls on me and after some Conversation says he will call again this Evening. He has not yet

made Enquiries respecting the Sale of Lands. I dine at Home and
after Dinner walk along the Ramparts from the Middle of the
Town up to the Citadel. While near this latter Place a Procession
comes by. They make them every Day. I walk a little Way with
them but can hear nothing more than the tedious Repetition of
ora pro nobis Domine Deus. These good Folks seem to be of Opinion that the Omnipotent can be coaxed and flattered into their
Measures, but in this Idea I fear they are not singular. Voltaire's Observation is very just: '*Si le bon Dieu a fait l'homme
d'après son Image, l'homme le lui a bien rendu.*' I return Home
pretty well fatigued, take Tea and write till eleven. The Weather
has been very fine this Day.

Monday 4. — This Morning I dress and visit the various Persons from Whom I received Civilities when last in this City.
They are all abroad except M.̲ Cogels. I meet M.̲ Van Ertborne
in the Street, then go to a Coffee House where I see M.̲ Dubois,
thence to the Church of Saint Walburge, a Lady whose History
I am ignorant of. The Altar Piece is very noble, and particularly
famous for an Elevation of the Cross by Rubens. We go thence to
the Church of the Dominicans in which are many fine Paintings
and on the Outside is a Representation of Mount Calvary, such
as it exists at Jerusalem. The Monk who shewed it to me told me
that the Dominican who took the Dimensions of each Part at
the holy City omitted only one, and finding out this Omission
when he had got Home, he returned again. The Flagellation of
our Saviour by Reubens is not only an excellent Painting but it is
in high Preservation, and looks as freshly as if it had been finished
Yesterday. Dine at Home. Wolfe comes in the Evening. He has
sounded some Capitalists about Lands but they will not listen
to it. He is selling at 75 p% the Stock he bought of Parker &
Rogers. He calculates that it cost him about 50 p% and a Loss
of 5 p% on the Exchange, but with all this he makes between four
and five thousand Pounds Sterling by his Bargain. I find that he
grows a little more difficult than he was. Go to M.̲ Van Ertborne's to Supper. Conversation turns on the public Affairs of
this Country. It is said that the existing Government have left
themselves no Room to Retreat, but they are Priests and therefore they will find a Hole to creep out at whenever it shall be neces-

sary. There was a Raree Show this Day upon the Presentation of a Cannon by the Women of Antwerp, and the other Processions are going, it seems, every Day and all Day long. These Things will do to keep the People in Breath for a while but Something more will become necessary by & bye. The Weather has been very pleasant.

Tuesday 5. — This Morning write. M: de Wolf brings me some Letters and is curious to learn the News. I tell him they are Duplicates, and so some of them are and all of them appear, but I afterwards find that there are originals among them. M: Van Ertborne the younger calls and sits a little while, and M: Cogels comes shortly after and takes me up to go to his Country Seat. It is a very pretty Spot, indebted much to Art, because being a dead Level, Nature has given to no Part of this Country any particular Advantages of Prospect unless indeed it be the Banks of a River. I return to Town at six and go to the Church of the Dominicans where we have some fine Music. Return Home and converse with M: de Wolf a little farther about Business, then go to M: Van Ertborne's (the younger) to Supper, a good Supper and Wines and pleasant Conversation. The Weather has this Day been very fine. M: Cogels, who is an amateur of botanical Subjects, is now employed in the Culture of American Forest Trees. There are some young ones which are very promising, and there are some very fine Trees of the original Growth of this Country. It seems this *Terre* belonged formerly to the Jesuits. The Land Measure of this Country is the Bunder, which contains forty square Perch, the Perch is 20 feet long, consequently the Bunder contains 160000 square feet, but the Foot is about $11\frac{1}{4}$ Inches English and I find that the Bunder is about $3\frac{1}{4}$ Acres. The Medium Price of Land is about five to six thousand Florins per Bunder, say about five hundred Dollars per Acre.

Wednesday 6. — This Morning write. At one the younger M: Van Ertborne and his Lady call and take me with them to M: Cornelison's. On the Road I mention what I had understood to be the Price of Land but they tell me it is a Mistake, the Price is about ʄ2000 to ʄ3000 per Bunder except for the Low Land. This gives at the least $200 per Acre for the ordinary Soil. We have a pleasant Day. Return early and write. The Weather is very fine.

Thursday 7. — This Morning write. M! Wolf calls and is to come again this Evening. At one M! Van Ertborne calls again and takes me up to go into the Country and dine with M! Dubois; M! Cogels and his Lady are in the Coach with us. He is Son of M! Cogels, my Acquaintance, and has married a Woman who seems old enough almost to be his Mother, a Love Match on his Part, and turned adrift for making it by his Father. We have a pleasant Party at the House of Dubois. Walking with him after Dinner I take Occasion to observe that he has suffered for the Sins of his Youth in the Urethra, and then propose to him the Means of Cure, which he thankfully accepts. There has been a Man executed at Brussels by the Mob for insulting some Monks in a Procession. They gave him however Time to confess himself, and one of the holy Fathers was employed for that Purpose. It is a fine Thing to be a good Catholic. We return to Town early and I return Home, expecting M! de Wolf, who does not come. The Weather is still very fine. This Afternoon there were a few Drops of Rain.

Friday 8. — This Day I write. Dine at Home; in the Evening de Wolf calls and we come pretty near to an Agreement upon some Points. I then tell him that he must chuse whether to be jointly concerned with me in future Operations or leave me at Liberty to connect myself with others. He owns that this is fair, but it is what he don't like. He is to consider and give me an Answer ToMorrow. This has been a fine Day.

Saturday 9. — This Morning write. Receive a Letter from Paris which mentions a Negotiation now carrying on for the Debt due by the United States. Dine with M! de Wolf; we converse farther on Affairs and he proposes a Commission of 2 p% for his Trouble, and then that the Business be in thirds. I am to consider of this. We go to a Cabinet of Paintings, some of which are very fine. Afterwards walk to the Abbey of S! Michael, which we are to visit again ToMorrow, it being too late to see the Paintings. At my Return Home I find a dozen of Ortolans which I had ordered in the Feather. They are precisely the Reed Bird of America. Having been fatted in Confinement they are more oily than they are in America and have less Flavor. I but just taste them, having eaten a hearty fish Dinner. One of the Dishes was Sturgeon.

It is I find highly prized in this Country. It is good but dear, a florin per Pound. This Morning there was a little Rain but it is fair Weather in the Evening.

Sunday 10. — This Morning write till nine when M.ʳ de Wolf comes to Breakfast. Give him some Papers to examine. After Breakfast we go again to the Abbey of S.ᵗ Michael's where there is a Collection of fine Paintings. Leave him here and go out to the Seat of M.ʳ Dubois. We have here a pretty large Company and as usual Good Chear which is chearfully distributed. Return pretty early and read. It has rained a little this Day and looks like the Approach of Autumn. Two People were found in their House murdered this Morning. I took that Occasion to propose to Dubois a Society for the Purchase of Land in America.

Monday 11. — This Morning write. M.ʳ Werbroock calls and sits some Time. Presses me to go to his Country Seat, which I decline, having already many Engagements. Dubois calls, and finding de Wolf with me makes his Visit short. I give him however a Note of a Speculation in American Lands. De Wolf makes more Difficulties, however we get along a little. After Dinner I go to the elder Van Ertborne's to see from his Window a Procession. It is of Nuns who are to repossess a Convent suppressed by the late Emperor. My friend Mad.ᵉ Dubois assists at this Ceremony and after it is over I tell her that I will never forgive the Guilt of being Accessory to such a Sacrifice, and that for the Punishment of it I shall supplicate the Almighty to make her the Mother of all those Children which in the Course of Nature the Nun should have borne. — Madame Dubois is as yet childless. Take Tea with M.ʳ Van Ertborne and then return Home. M.ʳ de Wolf comes and stays to Supper. Mine Host gives me the best Snipes I ever tasted. They bear the same Proportion of Size to the Snipe of America that the Woodcock does to the same Bird on the other Side of the Atlantic. There are in the same Dish some smaller Snipes which are of the Size of the American. After Supper a Cart goes by and as I know the Gates are shut at half past six in the Evening I ask the Reason. He tells me that it is laden with Ordure and is to be emptied into a Boat from which it is afterwards sold in the Country. This Business is done it seems by Contract and the City receives about a thousand florins p? Ann? for the Excrement of its Inhabitants. He tells me farther that Gen! Dalton quarrelled with the Corporation of Bruxelles upon this Subject. He insisted on his Right to sell the Offal of his Troops, and obliged them to worship Cloacina in a Place prepared for the Purpose. The precious Offerings thus collected were sold by his Excellency, but the vigilant Agents of the City made a Seizure of it as contraband. This Matter was in Consequence brought forward by Appeal to the States of the Province, but before a final Decision the Gen! was obliged to quit the Country. This is one among many Grievances suffered under the former Government. It was a Violation of the Privileges secured to the Capital of the Province, if not by Charter, at least by long Usage, and I should suppose an uninterrupted Possession. It seems however to be but a whimsical Cause of Quarrel and I can't help telling my friend Wolf that if the History of the eighteenth Century should be written hereafter by a very merry Philosopher, he may be tempted to observe that towards the Close of it a War broke out in America for Tea and in Flanders for Turd. The Weather continues fair but is a little cooler than it was, this Evening.

Tuesday 12. — This Morning write. Dine with the younger Dubois in the Country. After my Return, write. De Wolf calls but makes his Visit short. We are to finish ToMorrow. I spoke to Cornelison about a Speculation in American Lands & told him that I had left a Note on the Subject with Dubois. He says that he is much more in a Situation to do a Thing of the Sort than Dubois. I enquire again about a Grass cultivated here for Pasturage which they call Spurry. It is sown after Grain is taken off, and having been fed, the Remainder is ploughed in as a Manure and other Grain sown. The botanic Name, they tell me, is Spartilla. This Morning the Weather was fine, at Noon cloudy and this Evening cold and blustering; about ten it begins to rain.

Wednesday 13. — This Morning write, and conclude Matters with M! de Wolf. Dine with M!s Dubois. He dines with the Bishop in Gala and leaves an Apology. The Count d'Otromonde also, whom I expected to meet, is in the same Predicament. The Countess presses me very politely to dine to Morrow. This is a charming Society and I quit them with great Regret. Return to

Town and write. Mʳ Wolf sups with me and stays till twelve.
The Wind was high last Night and this Morning from the Northwest, with Showers. This Evening it is again calm, and promises
fine Weather.

Thursday 14. — This Morning compleat my Letters and prepare for Departure. Mʳ de Wolf calls to take Leave and at ¼ past
eleven I step into the Carriage. My Expences at Antwerp amount
to £12..10 Sterling. From Antwerp we go to Walhem, at entering of which we cross the River Neethe, a Branch of the Scheld,
which is here between thirty and forty Yards wide. A Wooden
Bridge & a Drawbridge of Course, for this River is navigable
even with a Tide. We pass thro Maline without stopping, having
bated about a League short of it. Shortly after bating, the poor
Dog in following the Carriage gets his Foot much hurt by the
Wheel, and we are obliged to take him in. We are near six Hours
in going from Antwerp to Louvain and yet I do not think the
Distance is above 26 Miles. I have strong Horses, taken of Mʳ
Loos, mine Host at Antwerp. The Road from that City is very
fine, particularly from Malines to Louvain, a Strait Line of twelve
Miles. The Road wide, well paved in the Center, with fine Trees
on each Side. The Country very good, being less sandy than the
Route thro Flanders by a great Deal. At Louvain we put up at
the Ville de Cologne where I have but bad Fare; this is whole-
some. Mʳ Werbroock comes in after Dinner and gives me much
Conversation. It is very tiresome, but perhaps the Manner of
Listening to it may hereafter turn to Account. The Weather has
this Day been unpleasant. A high Southwest Wind which threatens Rain without Raining, but we shall probably have a little To
Night.

Friday 15. — This Morning at six I leave Louvain. The Inn is
bad and dear. The Town is large and surrounded with Works now
crumbling to Pieces. It is connected commercially with Maline
by a Canal which the Road crosses. It is situated in a Hollow,
having Hills to the Eastward and a rising Ground to the Westward. In two Hours we reach Tirlemont where we stop twenty
Minutes, the Distance about ten Miles. We then go on to Sᵗ
Tron where we arrive in two Hours and ten Minutes, Distance
about eleven Miles. We breakfast at the Sauvage Hotel. Dirty,

with a very civil, crooked old ugly Landlady. A bad Place enough.
About 4 Miles short of S⁺ Tron, at a little Village called Halle, we
leave Brabant and get into the Païs de Liège. In an Hour and
three Quarters from S⁺ Tron we arrive at a Post House in a Village, or rather Hamlet, called Oreye, the Distance about nine
Miles. This Village is on the Waters of the Meuse. We stay here
a Quarter of an Hour and then go on in two Hours and a quarter
to Liège, being about ten Miles, but a considerable Time is spent
in descending the Hill, examining Passport and going thro the
City to the Hotel de l'Aigle Noir. This last Stage is over a high
Plain, the preced⁵ Part of the Route thro a waving Country; on
the whole it is not unlike Picardy. The Soil is very good and it is
well cultivated but I think not quite so well as the flat Country.
Liège, altho the Soil is not worse than the adjacent Country of
Brabant, has Marks of great Poverty. I attribute this to a defective Constitution or imperfect State of Society, but it may have
arisen from political Combinations or Events. I am inclined to
think from what I see of this Country, that did the whole belong
to one Sovereign or State it would not be difficult to extend an inland Navigation from Malines to the Meuse, and the very many
Waggons which we meet laden with Coal would seem to shew not
only the Advantage but almost the Necessity of attempting it.
An Observation which strikes me very forcibly in this Day's Ride
is that if the Emperor can obtain from the Liegeois a free Passage
thro their Country, and comes this Way with twenty thousand
Men, while with ten thousand he watches Namur and pushes forward with ten thousand by the Route of Charleroy, it will
(humanly speaking) be impossible for the Patriots to make Head.
There is I think nothing from the Citadel of Liège to the Citadel
of Antwerp which could delay the Advance of good Troops well
commanded, for twenty four Hours. At Tirlemont there are the
Remains of very extensive and strong Lines but they would require a great Army to man them, and then it is I think questionable whether they would not be rather pernicious than useful.
Our Journey this Day is 40 Miles. The Road very good and the
Weather pleasant.

   Saturday 16. — This Morning before Breakfast I walk out to
see a little of the Town and call at an Armorer's. He shews me

some well finished Work and from his Manner of speaking I think
he understands the Business. The Difference in Price between
Work done here and in London is very great. He tells me that he
has now in hand an Air Gun, which being charged, will discharge
twenty Bullets in a Minute. That from thirty to forty Yards the
Shot is sure. The Price will be from four to five Guineas. In passing thro the Market I purchase a Hare, very large and fine, for
three Escalins of this Country, of which there are thirty nine in a
Louis. My Guide tells me that the Price of Beef is from 9 to 10
Sous per l^b, Veal and Mutton eight, Pork seven. There are ten
Sous in one of their Shillings, so that 13^d of this Currency is about
8^d Stirling, and a Penny is about equal to a Penny of the Currency of Pensilvania. This is I think the filthiest Town I ever yet
beheld, owing in some Measure to its Coal Trade. This Article
is dug all round the City they tell me, and in great Abundance.
The Price per Cart Load is I think ten of their Shillings, but perhaps ten Florins or twenty Shillings. Care would keep them clean,
for there is much Declivity to the Meuse, but they have not I believe any Concern on the Subject. According to Custom, Filth
and Beggary keep Company together. At every Step I am im-
portuned by squalid Wretchedness. This also I consider as arising from a vicious Government. The Insecurity of Property is
fatal to Industry, & Idleness must inevitably be productive of
Crimes and both of Misery. This is equally true applied to Individuals and to Nations. A large Abbey dedicated to the Patron
of the City will perhaps account in some Measure for the Poverty
of the People. The Liègeois appear to me to possess a Mixture of
German Steadiness and french Vivacity. Muscular, active, & a
Countenance of Enterprize. They are strongly attached to the
imperial Cause and opposed to the Brabançons. They say that
they have had already too much of priestly Authority not to oppose the Establishment of it. At ½ past nine I leave the Hotel of
the Black Eagle which is but indifferent and very dear. We are
half an Hour from hence to the Top of the Hill on the other Side
of the Meuse, which we cross on a good Stone Bridge; it is not
very wide here and is at present low. After ascending this Hill,
called according to Custom (from the poverty of Language)
Montagne, we go on thro Herve and Henri Chapelle to Aix la

Chapelle, over a waving Country of long Hills which we cross obliquely; they run about Northwest from the Mountains on our right and our Course is first East, then North East and afterwards more northwardly. I think this Country is without Exception the most beautiful I ever beheld. The Shape and Soil remind me of America but as it is more a pasture than grain Country and as the Fields are small and Cottages numerous, the View is more pictoresque. The Mountain, covered with Forest now grown brown by the Approach of Winter, forms a fine back Ground. It is a high even continued Ridge. Shortly before we reach our Journey's End we cross a Spur of it, if not the main Ridge. The Road is here unreasonably bad, having never been paved nor (from Appearances) otherwise taken Care of. Both the Ascent and Descent are steep and in a deep Gully so narrow that for the greater Part of the Way it is impossible for two Carriages to pass each other. We meet several Waggons and Carts but (luckily) in Places which admit of a Passage, tho with Difficulty. The Custom is to stop and look out for the next Reach of this winding miserable Route, which is a Reflection upon the Police of Aix la Chapelle, within whose Territory it is. Thro Limbourg and Liège the Road is very good, being paved. We have come about 27 Miles or at most 30, and including three Quarters of an Hour of Stoppage to refresh the Horses we are eight Hours and a Quarter on the Way. This gives seven and an Half of Movement, the first Half of which was employed in ascending from Liège and of the remaining seven two were consumed in the last four Miles. The Weather this Day is prodigiously fine. I put up at the Hotel of Dubich, which being full, Madame surrenders to me her own Appartment. If it be not clean it is at least scented, but alas! it is by a Close Stool. My Dinner would have been very bad but for Half a dozen of Grives which I bought in the Morning. Patience!

Sunday 17. — This Morning as soon as I have taken Breakfast, which from the Badness of the Butter is reduced to a Dish of Tea, I walk out to view this City, which within Walls of vast Extent is but small, containing I find about twenty thousand People. They are poor and likely to continue so from the Spirit of Gambling not barely tolerated but absolutely encouraged by the Magistracy. Call on M.ʳˢ Waller, who is not at Home. Then look into the Cathe-

dral and at the Town House. Take a Walk round a Part of the
Town, then come in again and see the Baths, the public Walk or
Watering Place and one of the Gaming Rooms, where a great
Circulation goes forward. Dine at Home, tho much prest by a
french Gentleman whose Name I forget, to partake of his Repast;
and I should have dined better had I accepted the Invit.ⁿ. After
Dinner read, and in the Evening visit again M.ʳˢ Waller from whom
I received a Note to take Tea. Here is a pretty considerable
Party, among whom are a beautiful Aunt of Madame de Chastellux. She tells me that she has been informed by her of my Intention to visit this Place. There is here an ancien Maître d'Hotel
of the King's, *réfugié*. M.ʳ Livingston, whom I had met at Gen.ˡ
Morris's, a sensible well informed Man. He as well as I stays Supper and we sit till about one. Return Home together & he in-
dicates to me the best Inns on my intended Route. The Weather
has been very fine this Day.

Monday 18. — This Morning I am detained above an Hour by
the sleepy Indolence of the Post Master and his People, so that I
do not get off till a Quarter after seven. The Grand Hotel Dubich,
once very good, is now very bad and very dear. The old People
are dead and their Son, who has been some Time in Paris, resides
here and his great fat Mistress superintends the Ménage, which is
in Consequence more like a Bagnio than an Inn. We go about
four Miles over a wretched Pavement, which like every Thing
else in and about this City bespeaks Indolence and Wretchedness.
I learnt last Evening a further Reason for the Neglect of the
Roads and other Objects of public Utility. There have been for a
long Time political Disputes in this City, and Commissaries have
been named by the Chamber of Wetzlaer to examine into and adjust the Differences. They have now been sitting for Years, receiving considerable Pay and Emoluments which consume the
Revenues, and therefore it is not likely that the Affair will be
speedily terminated. They have however committed one of the
antient Magistracy to Prison for Embezzlement of public Money
to considerable Amount, and such Delinquencies were it seems
among the primary Causes of Discontent, so that in examining
to the Bottom of the Business it may fairly be traced to the Spirit
of Gambling and Dissipation. After we get to the End of the *pavé*

we are on a gravelly Road and go thro a wretched Village called
Aldenham to Juliers. The Soil is all the Way gravelly and the
Country in that as in its Shape resembles the Neighbourhood of
London. It is in its natural State far more fertile but the Culture
is greatly inferior. We are half an Hour in changing Horses and
were three and an Half in coming hither, about fifteen Miles.
From hence we go in two Hours and an Half about 12 Miles over
a gravelly Plain to Bercheim, which lies on a small Branch of the
Rhine. The Grounds about it are cultivated as are those immediately adjacent to Juliers, all the Rest is in Forest except a
few Acres at the little Hamlet of Steinstraes, lying half Way between Juliers and Bercheim. The Trees in this Forest are small
and bespeak a Soil far from luxuriant. We are again Half an Hour
in changing our Horses and then proceed in three Hours about
fifteen Miles to Cologne over a gravelly Country. Immediately
after we set off we ascend a Hill of tolerable Elevation, after
which the Country is waving but without Streams in the Hollows
excepting in one or two Places. The Water bespeaks a similar
Country at their Sources, being clear and bright. At Keuning-
dorf we come to the gentle Declivity which leads to the Rhine at
about six to eight Miles Distance. It is a Plain but a little inclined. The Soil a gravel with a little Loam and if well cultivated
it must produce much, but I think from Appearances that there
is more Industry than Intelligence in the Husbandry of this
Neighbourhood. We have been ten Hours and an Half to get on
forty two Miles. After taking an Indifferent Repast, the greater
Part of which I give to my Dog, and drinking a Bottle of good
Rhenish, I (in the Sailor Style) turn in. The Weather has been
pleasant this Day but a high Wind at West threatens for ToMorrow.

Tuesday 19. — It rained hard last Night, and this Morning it
is fair. Upon Enquiry I find that (the Hour of nine being passed)
I must stay till three if I wish to view the Tomb of the three Kings
in the Cathedral. I determine therefore to make Use of the fine
Weather and depart. From the Chamber in which I am lodged I
have a View of the Rhine which is here about as wide as the Delaware at Trenton Ferry. It is crossed by what is called a flying
Bridge. This consists of two large Boats joined together by a

Stage which projects beyond the Sides considerably, and the Landing is on each Side a sloping Wooden Bridge, so that whether the River be high or low it can be used with equal Facility and Convenience. This Stage is large enough to hold many Carriages and Horses which are drawn in at one Side and come out at the other, the Whole being railed round with a Place apart for those on Foot and a little Gate to go into it. Between one Half and one third of the Distance from the Bow, but I think about one third, stands in each Boat a Mast tolerably high and these are strongly connected together at Top. Near the Top is a cross Piece below that which connects the two together, over which slides the Hawser, fastened a Midships near the Stern by a Capstern or Windlass. From each Mast there are Shrouds to the outside of the Stage, and from each a fore Stay to the Bow of the opposite Boat. The Bows are also connected together by a Piece of Round Timber. Each Boat has a broad Rudder, and I suppose the Tillers are connected by a Piece of Timber, but cannot distinguish. Each Tiller, however, has a Man at Helm. The Boats are neither flat nor sharp forward, but as it were between, both having a kind of double Stern joined at Top and diverging. I suppose they are built with two Keels so as to take the Ground occasionally. The Hawser goes a considerable Distance up Stream and is fastened to a Chain in a small Boat, that again to another and that to a third, and so on a sufficient Distance, to a Boat moored in the Middle of the Stream. In each of these Boats the Chain is raised a few feet by a kind of Mast standing far forward, and to each there are fixed at the Stern two Leeboards to operate as a kind of Rudders, which by keeping the Head to the Stream check the Rapidity of the Motion. Those nearest the Bridge have these Boards most perpendicular, and the upper Boat has none. One Effect of these Rudders is to give the Boats a considerable Heel, for evident Reasons, and would overset them if the little Mast were high. The Motion is acquired by steering the Bridge across the Stream in an Angle of $45°$; by encreasing or diminishing the Angle the Velocity is encreased or diminished. The greater the Length of the Chord, or in other Words the smaller is the Segment of the Curve, the easier is the Crossing performed. At a Quarter after twelve I leave the Hotel of the Holy Ghost at Cologne for Bonn.

We go along the Rhine, tho only once in Sight of it. The Distance
is about seventeen Miles which we go in three Hours and an Half,
including a small Stop for refreshing the Horses. The Soil is a
gravelly Loam cultivated in Corn and Vines. It resembles very
much the Soil of a Plain on my Farm formerly called Snake Rock.
It is level and I believe fertile. With good Husbandry it would
certainly yield well. After Dinner I wait on the french Minister
with a Letter from the Count de Montmorin, left for me at the
Post Office. He is at the Door when I enquire for him and takes
the Letter to deliver it. This is a little whimsical but I am rather
en déshabillé so that he does not I believe know what to make of
me. However, after reading the Letter he is very attentive, which
explains itself naturally enough by his urging me to stay ToMorrow, that he may comply with the Orders of the Count de Montmorin *qui sont très particulières*. Mad^e de Chastellux has also
mentioned me to him. This has been a very fine Day.

Wednesday 20. — This Morning the Count de Maulivier calls
on me in his Phaeton and we take a Ride together. He tells me
that the Elector pushes Œconomy to an Extreme which is ridiculous, and gives Instances; he says that at the same Time he is so
prone to laugh at the Foibles of Mankind that when he can find
no other Object he exercises his Talent on himself. He introduces
me to the Chief of the Finances here, as a Man of Talents and the
only one. I visit the flying Bridge and examine it. The Rudders
are not connected together by the Tillers as I supposed, neither
have the little Boats a Leeboard on each Side. These Leeboards
are made to rise and fall. The Masts have both a fore and back
Stay as well as a cross fore Stay. The Stays are not fixed, but on
boats, so as to present always the same Heighth with the Bridge.
To each Stage is affixed a short strong Rope with an Eye at the
End, this is taken up by a Boat Hook and put on a Pin in the
Capstern of the Boat of the Bridge which is nearest, and by turning of it they are made to approach more closely, and the Sterns
are pressed as closely by Means of the Rudders, to the Tiller
of each of which is affixed a Staff by which & by Means of
cross Pieces nailed aft on the Decks, it can be kept in any Angle desired. After viewing the Bridge I return to the Minister's
and dine. In the Evening there is an Assembly which is I find col-

lected on Purpose. The Arch Duke, late Governor of the Low
Countries, is here, to whom I am presented, and I converse with
him a little about the Affairs of Brabant. I have some Conversation also with the Minister of the Finances who is quick and sensible. He seems to consider the Situation of his Prussian Majesty
as critical. I asked of one who seemed likely to know, the Quantity
of Wine produced in this Country at a Medium from a given
Space. He tells me that their Land Measure is a Morgan of 150
Roude, each of which contains 108 square feet. This gives about
17.175 square feet English Measure, the Rhineland foot being
about 12.362 Inches English, so that the Morgan will be nearly
33/58 of an Acre. The Produce is from 30 Ahmes down to 2, but
usually from 10 to 15; and the Ahme contains 104 Pots which from
Description are about a Quart, so that the Ahme may be stated
as a Quarter Cask, and of course 16 Ahmes gives 4 pipes. Therefore the Medium Produce will be about 8 pipes to the Acre. Qu:
if there be not some Error in this Calculation. After the Company
are gone the Count takes me into his Cabinet to communicate a
Memoire he has written on the Claims of the German Princes to
feodal Rights in Alsace. On the whole I am perswaded that M.
de Montmorin's Letter has contained every Thing which I could
have wished. The Chancellor of the Exchequer or Minister of
Finance to the Elector, gave us a curious Account of the Ideas entertained by his Highness the Prince of Hesse Cassel. He considers the Attempt of a Nation to throw off the Yoke of Authority
as quite chimerical, and Disobedience in the Army as a Thing
impossible, so that if any little Disturbances should arise Nothing
more is necessary than to hang the Ringleaders. And indeed this
is a pretty good Method if you can catch them, but that is sometimes a little difficult.[1]

Thursday 21. — This Morning I cannot get off as I expected at
six oClock for Want of Post Horses. They are all engaged by
Travellers who spoke before me. One Set however, which went to

---

[1] To Luzerne Morris had written from Antwerp: 'The Flemings have, you
know, a little Spice of Obstinacy in their Character, and altho they have lately
adopted that fine french Fashion called *la lanterne* we must not from thence
too hastily conclude in favor of their Genius or Taste. It was a *lanterne* 'tis
true, but still it was *à la flamande*, and by awkwardly introducing a Confession
upon the Stage the whole Life and Spirit of the Scene were lost.'

Cologne at one oClock, return so early as that I depart with them at a Quarter before ten. We travel but slowly, which is pardonable as the Cattle are fatigued. In two Hours and three Quarters we reach Remargen, the Distance about 13 Miles thro a beautiful Country. We have the River on our left and almost constantly in View. The Mountains on our right, and beyond the River on our left also. These are in Part covered by Vineyards. The Valley tho narrow is very rich, the Road is good, the Weather fine. We meet at the Post House (or rather we are overtaken by) a british Messenger who left London last Sunday Evening. He tells me that not only the naval Armaments are pushed forward with Alacrity but that the Regiments are ordered to be compleated and (it is said) ten thousand new Troops to be raised. He gets Horses before me and promises to have a Set ready for me at Andernaught. We are a full Half Hour in changing Horses and our Postillion is determined not to redeem the Moments, but verifies what the Messenger observed to me: 'This is a terrible Country, Sir, to travel in; they are extremely slow and if you try to hasten them they are still slower.' My Servant gets quite out of Humor with his Countrymen, for his Perswasions are treated with silent Contempt. He observes very justly that such a People are not fit to be free, they must have a Master. In two Hours and three Quarters we arrive at Andernaught, which is but about 15 Miles if so much, and the Road excellent. The Horses are ready at this Place but yet we are detained a Quarter of an Hour to put them to, and when we get out of the City we go a considerable Distance upon a Walk, because the Road being here newly covered with Gravel he takes it in his Head that it is too heavy for three strong Horses tho quite level. Attempts to perswade him are ineffectual and my Wish to get to Coblentz before Night is of no Use either to him or me. About Half or indeed two Thirds of the Way towards that Place we meet another Post-Chaise and they change Horses in Spite of me. The Persons who are in it sit quietly and resigned. And yet it is they who have really Cause of Complaint, for my new Rider and Horses bring me on at a Rate which I have not known since I embarked at Dover. The Road is as fine as possible and the Valley begins here to enlarge, indeed it seems to me as if we had passed thro the Chain of Mountains, for those beyond us are shaped more like Hills. At entring Coblentz we cross the Moselle on a fine stone Bridge. The Distance from our last Post is about twelve Miles which, thanks to our first Postillion, consume two Hours and an Half. Thus we have been 8¾ Hours in coming 40 Miles, and as ¾ were employed in changing Horses our average Motion is 5 Miles an Hour with three Horses over an excellent Road nearly level. The Country is all the Way such as the first Stage but near Coblentz we went for some Miles over a Tract which swarms with Ground Mice. Indeed they seem to have destroyed that Part of the Country. I order Dinner immediately on my Arrival, which is half past six. It is to be ready immediately whereas the Table d'Hôte, which is spread, will not be furnished till eight. At Half past seven, finding no Appearances of Food, I offer mine Host a Bet that he will serve me as others have done, keep me waiting to spoil my Meat by over roasting it. He assures me that his Cook is excellent and that the Taste of People here is to eat Things with the Juice in. At eight oClock a Part of the Food designed for the Table d'Hôte is sent into my Chamber and the first Dish is a kind of Stew called Soup, made of greasy Crusts, which of course I do not touch, nor the Spinnage which accompanies it. To this succeeds a Piece of Veal which was ready dressed when I arrived, for my friend the Messenger dined off it a few Minutes after. This serves to stay the Stomach of my Dog. Then comes a sodden Partridge, not roasted to Rags but half stewed, half baked till it has neither Juice nor Taste. I complain in pretty severe Terms and they bring me a Shoulder cut from a Calf, but the poor Creature was I believe starved to Death. Hungry as I am the Sight excites a Nausea so that I cannot even see my Dog eat it. They had promised some Grives but luckily forgot it, wherefore I desire they may be roasted immediately, and a few Minutes after send down my Servant, whose earnest Supplications obtain them from the Cook while yet eatable, but as the Devil would have it they have eaten so many Juniper Berries that they are a Kind of solid Gin. There remains no Resource but salt Cheese made of Hog's Head which would have been very good had it been fresher (ie) newer. Mustard would have been a good Accompanyment to it but they have none. This Evening is if possible finer than the Day has been. A bright full Moon. The Wine here is good and a Bottle makes a good Night Cap for my short Bed, out of the foot of which however I can poke only one Leg, having left the other in America.

Friday 22. — This Morning after Breakfast I wait upon the french Minister, the Count de Vergennes, Son to the Minister of that Name. He is a young Man. He receives me *comme ça.* He has an Engagement which prevents him from paying me the Attention he would wish. His Secretary, however, shall accompany me &cᵃ, &cᵃ. Invites me to dine. I tell him that I want to get on and that I will either accept his Invitation or not, according as my Route of ToMorrow may render most proper. After I return Home I try to procure a Map of this Country but there is no such Thing in Coblentz. Monsʳ l'Abbé, the Secretary, calls and takes me to a Convent from whence there is a fine View of the City and the adjacent Country. Opposite to us is the Citadel, which is said to be impregnable, and indeed if the Garrison is sufficiently numerous and well provided I believe they are right enough. It is situated on a high Rock nearly perpendicular on every Side except one, where it joins to the Mountain, or rather Mount. This is narrow, not long, and very steep. We walk from this Convent down the Hill and ride to the Gardens of the Château, whence we walk to the River and stroll about conversing. I try to gather from the Abbé his Information for he seems to possess more than his Chief. Neither of them too much. Having in the Course of our Ride examined the Posts and Places of Rest I determine not to leave Coblentz till ToMorrow, because there is no good Place of abiding which I can reach till late and because by giving Notice this Day of my Route I can have Horses ready at the Posts on my Arrival, this being I find a customary Thing. Our Walk ended, we go to the Count's Hotel. The Family is numerous. Old Madame de Vergennes reminds me a little of Madame Grand. I eat for the first Time in my Life a Snail. It is tough, but I think that of Snails might be made a good Turtle Soup. The Conversation turns upon the Scioto Company which is treated very freely. I allow the Truth but correct many Errors, arising I presume from Misinformation. I wish to get away soon after Dinner but I feel that this would express itself too strongly and therefore stay till I can pretext my Departure properly. It is very fine Weather.

The Abbé this Morning pointed out to me three Châteaus belonging to the three different Ecclesiastical Electors, and he told me a remarkable Accident. A Prisoner confined for Life in the Citadel and in Chains, contrived to get to a Place where the Rock jutts out and gives a Perpendicular of above an hundred Feet to the next landing Place. Chained as he was he let himself fall, and proceeded from that Spot to Andernaught, but died the next Day from an inward Rupture. At Dinner Madame de Vergennes told me that she had eaten of Land-Turtles in the Levant which are of great Size and which are very good; from her Description they must go as far as fifteen or twenty Pounds. In this Electorate is the Seltzer Water, of which the annual Export is to the Amount of 100000 crowns of the Empire annually.

Saturday 23. — This Morning at six oClock we leave the Post House at Coblentz which is a pretty good Place, for the People are obliging and it is not excessively dear. We wait some Time for the Bridge to cross the Rhine and we go over it slowly. After passing thro a little Village we go up a Gorge of the Mountain and ascend for a considerable Distance. The Road is hard and good, our Horses are strong and our Driver is diligent, but yet our Progress is unavoidably slow. After going some Time along the waving Heighths we descend steeply to a little Village called Embs, situated on a pretty Stream of Water, the River Lahn. At this Village there are mineral Waters and two Châteauxs, one belonging to the Prince of Orange and one to the Prince of Hesse Darmstadt. I visit the Springs and Baths and feel and taste the Water. It is warm but not disagreable. We go hence to the Post House at Nassau, which is a pretty Village on the same Stream. By the bye, the handsomest Town I have seen in Germany is that of Neuwitt, built by the Count de Neuwitt on the Eastern Bank of the Rhine, between Andernaught and Coblentz, near to the former. We are four Hours in going to Nassau which is but a Post and an Half, the Distance from thirteen to fourteen Miles, but in this is included every Delay. We breakfast here, which consumes three Quarters of an Hour. Nothing can be more pictoresque than the Road to this Place. The Mountains covered to the North by Forest Trees and Bushes, to the South by Vineyards with abrupt Breaks of craggy Rock. The Stream meandring along among their Projections, in the Valleys some Meadows and Corn-fields. After leaving Nassau we cross the Stream in a Scow and shortly after ascend a High Hill or Mountain by an excellent Road but steep. It is built against the Side of the Declivity and the Wall is in many Places from twenty to thirty feet high. We have a very good Driver and good Horses but we are employed two Hours and an Half in getting to Nieustadt, which is but one Post and I think scarcely ten Miles. We change there in a Quarter of an Hour and proceed in three and a Quarter one Post farther to Schwalback. The Road is very bad. The Country consists rather of Hills than Mountains. The Soil is Clay, and the Culture being indifferent it seems rather exhausted. There are no Vineyards here, of course, Vines delighting in a warm gravelly Soil. Just before we reach Schwalback the Road is good; they are employed in making a very fine one. Schwalback lies in a deep Ravine so that we are almost on the Tops of the Houses before we see it. We arrive at the Golden Fountain Inn at five oClock, our Dis-tance in eleven Hours is about thirty three Miles. It is fifteen to Mayntz and therefore I determine to stop here. I visit the Foun-tains and taste the Water, which is very pleasant. The Wine at the Inn is very good and they give me a good Supper, which sur-prizes me tho not disagreably. The Weather has this Day been very fine. A little cool in the Evening. This is a watering Place of great Resort. I eat some Ziegen Cheese, very good but of bad Smell.

Sunday 24. — The Sabbath commences by a Dispute with the Post Master who obliges me to pay half Price for the Horses pre-pared Yesterday, before he will furnish any ToDay. It is in Con-sequence 7 oClock before I can get away & the Innkeeper says he dares not furnish Horses, so that I am obliged to submit to the Imposition. We go in two Hours and an Half to Wiesbaden, one Post of about ten Miles. The first Part of the Road is up the Hill from Schwalback and so by Degrees up to the Edge of the last Ridge, from whence the Prospect is very fine tho unfortunately the Morning is too hazy to see it distinctly. On our right and thence as far as we can see, the Rhine meanders thro a fine Valley; the Maine is directly before us and at the Confluence of those Rivers stands Mayence or Mayntz, so called from the Mayn, as

at the Junction of the Moselle and Rhine the City is called Con-
fluentia or Coblentz. A Number of Villages are scattered about
the Plain and I fancy if it were clear Weather we could see Francfort. After descending from hence we come to Wiesbaden where
we change Horses in less than a Quarter of an Hour. The Post
Master, to whom I mention what passed with his Confrère at
Schwalback, tells me it is a gross Imposition. The Price of Post
Horses is raised here for the present 25 p% on Acc.ᵗ of the Advance
in the Price of Forage by the late Coronation. We go to Hattersheim in 2¾, about fifteen Miles over a Plain of very good Land,
being a stiff Loam, but it is very indifferently cultivated. Not
only the System of Husbandry is bad, but the Tillage is slovenly,
the Earth not being duly pulverized nor yet ploughed to a sufficient Depth. All this arises I presume from the State of Society.
At Hattersheim we change Horses in ab.ᵗ ten Minutes and proceed
for Francfort. Just before we arrive at the little River Nidda our
Postillion changes Horses with a private Jobb, and we are thereby
detained; shortly after, our new Driver discovers that he has
lost something and goes back to look for it, but in Vain. About
Half Way from thence to Francfort a Passenger kindly stops us
to rectify an Accident to the lashing of a Pair of Shafts under the
Carriage, so that we are above two Hours & a Quarter before we
alight at the Red House Tavern, Inn or Hotel. The Country is
better this last Stage, being a richer and lighter Loam. I observe
in this Plain between the Mountain and Francfort, Orchards
like those of America, the Trees being large and vigorous. There
is on the Road from Hattersheim, a little to the Westward of the
River Nidda, an immense Château built by one Polingaro, who it
is said began with Nothing and accumulated an immense Fortune
by making Snuff of a particular Quality. The Secret of the Manufacture died with him. To judge of this Château by the Exterior,
it is fit for the Residence of a mighty Sovereign and must have
cost an immense Sum. In comparing this with the trifling useless
Article which enabled the Builder to misapply so much human
Labor, I cannot but consider it as one of the most striking Monu-
ments of human Folly that ever was erected. I get an indifferent
Dinner of Articles (*réchauffés*) and a Bottle of good Wine at the
Red House Hotel, which is the greatest Hotel I ever saw, there

being no less than 124 Chambers on these Premises belonging to
the Inn Holder himself, who is now building an additional House
for the Accomodation of Travellers. The Weather this Morning
was raw, but about noon grew very pleasant; at four this Afternoon it began to rain and continues, tho gently, for the Evening.
Our Distance this Day is about 35 Miles performed (all Stoppages included) in 8 Hours, being at the Rate of 4½ Miles per
Hour or one Half faster than our Route of Yesterday, altho the
Horses are not so good; but the Road is principally on a Level.

Monday 25.*th* — It rained all last Night. This Morning it looks
likely to clear but I am told it is impossible to get Horses before
Thursday. After Breakfast I wait upon Mess.*rs* Metzler Finguelin
and Volk, for whom I have a Letter from Mess.*rs* Le Couteulx et
Comp?. With their Aid I procure Horses which are to be ready at
one oClock. Return Home, write and prepare for my Departure.
I am ready at ½ past Twelve but it is ¾ after one before the
Horses are ready. This City is large and at Times populous. It
is a great Entrepot for the Distribution of Merchandizes throughout Germany. These are paid for principally in Coin but I cannot
learn the Means of obtaining that Coin. We go in five Hours and
an Half to Diebourg, at first thro indifferent Forest and afterwards, as long as Day Light lasts, over a miserable sandy Plain,
waste and wild. In some few Places it is cultivated but seems to
have been ungrateful for the Pains bestowed on it. A great Part
is low and wet, from whence I conjecture that the Means of amel-
iorating it lie near the Surface, a Stratum of stiff Clay. After
Dark we continue I believe thro the same Sort of Soil tho a little
more elevated. Dieborg is a very large Village, or rather it is a
walled Town. The Baron de Groshlaer and his Family receive
me very kindly. Shortly after the first Compliments and a Dish
of Tea we retire together. I ask him the Character of the Emperor. He confirms the Idea I had taken up of him, Heaven knows
how or why. He shares his Confidence between Manfredi, the Governor of his Children, and [Mercy d'Argenteau?] who was a long
Time Minister to the Court of France. The first is an artful, sensible sly fellow and his Turn of Mind is suited to the Temper and
Character of Leopold. The other is really a Man of Sense and a
Man of Business. There is a third, whose Name I do not dis-

tinctly hear, who is of great Genius but indolent and epicurean.
Shortly before he left Francfort, Leopold seemed to give much of
his Confidence to Colloredo, but this (as the others were gone
away) might have arisen as much from the Need of Counsel as
from any Preference to the Counsellor. The Baron is of Opinion
that both England and Prussia will try hard to gain the Emperor
and will offer him french Flanders, Artois and a Part of Picardy,
to desert the northern League. He says that Leopold is sore on
Account of the Insults offered to his Sister the Queen of France,
but he does not think the German Princes who have Claims on
Alsace and Lorraine will be able to obtain much Aid from the
greater Powers, if any. Indeed I think so too, for the Contest will
cost vastly more than the Object is worth. He imagines that the
Dutchy of Juliers will be the desired Object of his prussian Majesty, and this may be the Case, because he is not an able Man.
After Supper I happened to mention the Château of Polumgaro
and the Baron gave me an additional Anecdote. It seems that
there were two Brothers, one of which was established at Amsterdam and the other at Francfort. The latter, having some
Cause of Dissatisfaction with the Magistracy, applied to the
Baron, then Chancellor of Mayence, on the Subject of an Establishment in that Electorate. The Baron enquired into the
Means of confirming him in his good Dispositions, and after a
most flattering Reception, sent the handsomest Coach of the
Elector, with Servants in Gala, to take M.ʳ Polumgaro round
wherever he wished to go in Mayence. This compleatly turned
his Head and he forthwith established himself in that Electorate
and built the immense Château which I saw. By his Will he ordered ᶠ50,000 to be applied annually to the farther Extension of it,
but the Order is not it seems complied with.

Tuesday 26. — This Morning at six I leave Dieborg and go in
two Hours and an Half by a bad Road about 9 Miles to Darmstadt. The first Part of the Way was over a very indifferent Tract
of Country. We passed thro the Park where the Huntsmen were
employed in taking a wild Hog which is to be put into a smaller
Park, and there he will have the Honor of being hunted and perhaps killed by the Prince. The catching of these Animals is a
dangerous Business. As we approach Darmstadt the Soil is bet-

ter tho still sandy, but it is a rich Sand like Newark Neck in Color
and in every Respect; some very large Timber. The Grounds near
the Town are of good Quality on every Side but this is only for a
small Space, for our Driver says that the direct Road from hence
to Francfort is over such a sandy Plain as that which we passed
Yesterday. Indeed I suppose it is a Continuation of the same. We
go thro Darmstadt and there get on the Pavement; in an Hour and
a Quarter we reach a little Village called Eberstat. Here we bate
our Horses and ourselves, in which ¾ of an Hour are consumed.
The Distance from Darmstadt is about five Miles and the greater
Part of the Way the Soil is a poor Sand, some Pine Forest. From
Eberstat we go thro Zwingenborgh to Bensheim, where we employ an Hour and an Half in feeding the Horses. This last Stage
is ten Miles, performed in two Hours and an Half. The last four
or five, including Zwingenborgh, is fine Country. The Mountains on our left covered with Forest and Vineyards, on our right,
and all the Way from the Foot of the Mountains, a very rich
sandy Loam. Farther to the right it seems to be again poor Sand;
the Breadth of the good Land seems to be from a Mile to a Mile
and an Half. The Culture is also much better than I have met
with in Germany. From Bensheim we leave the main Road on
the left and go over a large Common which seems to be good
Meadow, and then thro a small Forest which shews by large
Trees and bad Roads a good Soil. Coming out of the Forest we
get upon a small Tract of what the Dutchmen on the Mohawk
River call Land. It is the only Spot I have seen in Europe that is
equal to the best Kind of American Soil. The little Town of Lorch
stands on a Sand Hill in the Center of it. The Houses here are all
hung round with Tobacco, but it seems to be the Suckers or second
Growth. If an intelligent Husbandry prevailed here the Grass of
these rich Lands would manure many hundred Acres of the adjacent Sands, which would by that Means yield more per Acre
than the Low Lands now do, and the Herds of Cattle would be a
pure Gain. I remember to have made the same Observation many
Years ago at Esopus in the State of New York, where indeed they
have the additional Advantage of Lime Stone in Abundance and
Perfection. I observed at Bensheim a Carpenter making Use of a
Screw Augre and I recollect that M.ʳ S.ᵗ Jean de Creve Cœur pre-

vailed on me once to buy at Philadelphia and bring with me to
New York some of the same Kind, which he sent to Paris as an
excellent American Invention. I observed another at Work with
a Mortize Axe which seems to be a very good Tool. It is like a
Pick Ax double; on one Side is an Axe about two Inches wide,
not half an Inch thick and about ten Inches long, on the other
Side is an Axe of the mortize Breadth and edged like a mortized
Chizzel. From Lorch the Soil is sandy and grows worse and worse
to Sanddorf. A Part of the Way is thro Pine Forest and the Rest
over miserable Fields where the Indian Corn Stalks are about the
Size of a Rattan and from two to three feet high, the Tops included. Sanddorf is about ten Miles from Bensheim and we are
two Hours & ten Minutes in performing it. We water the Horses
here and in one Hour & forty Minutes we arrive at Manheim, the
Distance five Miles. The first Part of the Way thro a Pine Forest,
afterwards over bad Sand as long as I can see, and by the Feel of
the Carriage it continues so. We have been twelve Hours and an
Half on the Road and our Distance is about 39 Miles. The Hotel
of the Cour Palatine is full and we are therefore obliged to go to
the Prince Charles, which seems to be very bad. They give me a
Supper which luckily I cannot eat and therefore I shall recover the
Tone of my Stomack, which was injured by unbaked Rye Bread
and bad Wine at Eberstadt. The Weather has been good this Day
but seems this Evening likely to rain.

Wednesday 27. — This Morning I am told that I cannot get
Horses because they are all bespoken by the King of Naples.
After Breakfast I walk out, and having looked at the Exterior
of the Château, go from thence to the Arsenal. In the Way is the
Play House. All these Buildings are in a Stile better suited to a
great Monarch than a German Elector. At Bonn the french Minister pointed out to me at a Distance one of this Elector's Châteaus which he says is unfinished but upon a Scale large enough
for the King of all Europe. From the Arsenal I go to the Gate of
the Rhine and walk thence round the Town. I think it might be
taken by a Coup de Main, altho said to be one of the best Fortifications in Europe. It stands well in a Plain with the Rhine on one
Side and the Necker on the other Side. It is regularly laid out, the
Streets are large and clean, but a large Half of its adult male In-

habitants are Soldiers. Indeed, the Existence of Manheim seems
to depend on the Presence of the Court and Army, for it has
neither Commerce nor Manufactures. The Elector is now at
Munich, and three out of five thousand Troops are down the
Rhine upon the Affair of Liège. The Population of this City is
about 20,000 Souls. It would make an excellent Frontier Town to
the french Monarchy. After Dinner I visit again the Baron de
Dolberg who was not at Home this Morning. Deliver him a Letter from the Baron de Groshlaer and we enter into Conversation.
He tells me that the Emperor is a domestic Man who loves his
Ease, and is good tempered. I ask if this last Trait may not be an
Appearance put on from political Motives. He thinks it may.
He says that the Viscount de Mirabeau had a long Interview
with Leopold at Francfort and pressed him to undertake a Counter Revolution in France, but he smiled and told him that it was
an impracticable Project. He thinks the Administration in
France was so bad as to occasion and justify a Revolution, but
quere. The Baron tells me that the Enmity of Austria to Prussia
is at the greatest imaginable Heighth. The Emperor has in his
Possession the original Correspondence for exciting a general Revolt in his Dominions the Instant a War should break out with
Prussia. I ask if this will not lead the Emperor to avenge the
meditated Injury. He says that it will probably fester inwardly
till a fit Occasion offers. He tells me that the Austrian General
says there are forty thousand Troops ordered to the Low Countries. He shewed him the List. This, with the Army already there,
will amount to fifty thousand Men. Too much if other Powers
stand neuter, and too little if they do not. Go from the Baron's
to the Post House and tell the Postmaster that the King of Naples
is not to go hence untill Sunday, wherefore I presume that he can
furnish me with Horses. He says that he can, undoubtedly, and
had not declined. He looks as if he spoke Truth and yet I am certain that he lyes, but I cannot guess the Motives of a Conduct so
unaccountable. It looks and feels as if foul Weather were brewing.
The Air is disagreable and tho not cold is very uncomfortable.
The Stove gives me a Head Ache and therefore I go early to Bed
to get Rid of my Troubles. A Frenchman in the adjoining Chamber, who is learning to play on the Violin, prevents me however
from taking too much Sleep.

Thursday 28. — This Morning I read. The Baron Dolberg, who was to call on me, does not come. I send therefore to know if there is any Mistake, and receive in Answer an Invitation to dine with him ToMorrow which of course I decline, probably to his Satisfaction, for the Seasons when Mankind feel hospitable are precisely those in which the fewest Objects present themselves for the Exercise of Hospitality. The late Coronation has rendered Visitors too numerous for all but public Houses. After Dinner I go to the Elector's Galery of Paintings and in a cursory View of his Palace from a Place where the Rear is partly discovered I feel amazed at the Extent of this Edifice, which is much larger than Yesterday I supposed it to be. His Galery of Paintings contains some fine Pieces, many good ones and many very indifferent. There are two Heads painted by a German whose Name I think is Balthazar Denner. These are very fine. After looking at Paintings till it is almost dark, I go into his Library, which is large and well filled. The Cieling is fine, an allegoric Painting by Krahe which represents Time discovering Truth; Virtue, Knowlege and the Arts are of his Party, and Minerva points out the Road in which to seek Truth. Ignorance and Vice are hurled into the Abyss. This Library is said to contain above 70000 Volumes, of course there must be many bad Books in it. I return Home and take Tea while my Bill is preparing, which proves, as elsewhere in this Country, an extravagant one. My Servant, who is a Native of Manheim, comes in and owns with Surprize that this City is dearer than Paris. I presume that the high Prices arise in some Measure from the usual Tricks of a Tavern. These are general and therefore pardonable, but the Market Prices of those Things which in many Countries are the Nourishment of the poor seem to me very great for a Country so far removed from Commerce, and at the same Time so fertile as this is said to be. Beef is about 3^d Sterling per pound at this the most plentiful Season, and it is far from being good; Mutton is about ⅛ less, Veal about ¼ more, being out of Season, and Pork about the same Price with Beef. The pay of a foot Soldier here is 3^d pensilvania Money and his Ration is two Pounds of Bread made of Rye Meal from which the Bran is not seperated. In the Dominions of the Prince of Hesse it is little better than half of that Sum, with the same Ration.

Supposing no Stoppages nor Accidents the Pay of the Hessian would amount to seven Spanish Dollars per Annum. The German Currency is the florin, containing sixty Creutzers (or forty Stivers) and the Rix Dollar, contain^g 90 Creutzers or 60 Stivers. 6^d pensilvania Money is worth 10 Creutzers, as nearly as I can establish the Value; which, by the bye, is no easy Matter because their Coin is so base as to circulate only at Home. The Value therefore must be found by the Rate at which other Coins pass, and as this is below their Value, that above stated is perhaps too high. But if it be right, we have for the florin 3/ and for the Rix Dollar 4/6. I believe, however, that the Rix Dollar is considered as worth only 2/6 Sterling, which gives 8 p% less. According to this last Valuation, five Pence Pen: Cur: will be equal to 6 Stivers or 9 Creutzers, but I incline rather to the former, which I believe to be very near the Truth. According to it 9^d pen: Cur: will be equal to 10 Stivers. One great Abuse in this Country upon Travellers is the Price of Lodging, which in the wretched Apartment where I am now placed & with Furniture suited to such an Apartment, is dearer than in most other Places. Indeed, the whole taken together, I think the Progress thro Germany more expensive per Mile than in England. It is true that a Horse goes about ten Miles for a florin, which gives 6 Creutzers per Mile, but then three Horses must be employed, which brings the Mile to 18 Creutzers or not quite 8^d Sterling whereas in England it is 1/, but the Barriers are more expensive than the Turnpikes & there is besides the Chaussée Gelt & Drinke Gelt or Pay of Postillions, a Bruck Gelt or Toll of Bridges, a Spuier Gelt or Fee for opening the Gates of fortified Towns, a Toll for return Horses laid on by the Magistrates, and above all a Tediousness which leaves longer Time for the Exercise of aubergistical Talents.

Friday 29. — This Morning I am prepared for Departure at a Quarter before six but it is just an Hour after when we get off, thanks to our Post-Master and his Post-Knights. Martin tells me that they spent Half an Hour by the Watch in greasing, and altho that was compleated by the Time I came out of my Chamber, yet the Horses could not be obtained untill an Hour after, for which they gave this good Reason: that Somebody who ordered Horses Yesterday at six and got them at seven did not de-

UNIVERSITY OF WINNIPEG
PORTAGE & BALMORAL
WINNIPEG 2, MAN.   CANADA

part till ten. — We go in an Hour and an Half to Shwetzingen ¾
of a Post, about 9 Miles over a good Road laid high. The Country
is a rich Sand well cultivated. We change here in a Quarter of an
Hour and go on to Waghousel, a Post of about eleven Miles,
in two Hours and twenty Minutes. The Soil Sand and for the
greater Part very indifferent, much of it in Pine forest; near
Waghousel is a large Bog or Quagmire. We change in a Quarter
of an Hour and go on over a better Road another Post of about
ten Miles to Graben in an Hour and three Quarters. The Soil is
of the same Kind but rather better. We change Horses here in
twenty Minutes and in two Hours and twenty Minutes more
reach Carlesruhe, a Post and a Quarter, about fifteen Miles, the
Soil light and indifferent the greater Part of the Way. We dine
here well and cheaply. Indeed it is a pretty general Rule that
good Taverns are less expensive than bad ones, and this seems to
be a very good one, the Post House. This Town is just 75 Years
old and contains about ten thousand Inhabitants. It is the Residence of the Prince of Baden whose Grandfather removed the
Seat of Government from Dorluch, which lies a few Leagues to the
Eastward. By the Extinction of a Branch of the Family which
dwelt at Rastadt, the whole of this Landgraviate is now united
and his Highness enjoys a Revenue of 1000000 Rix Dollars. He
keeps up about 2500 Men. The Streets of this Town are large and
clean and many of the Houses well built. We leave it in fifty
Minutes after our Arrival and proceed in three Hours over a very
good Road to Rastadt one Post and an Half, about 15 Miles.
The Country as long as I could see it was just the same indifferent
Sand which we had already passed. I observe this Day that the
whole Surface of the Earth (almost) is covered with Turnips and
those very fine ones. They pull them, cut off the Tops and bury
the Roots in Pitts which look afterwards like so many Graves.
In some Places I see they have spread the Tops over the Land and
ploughed them in. We were this Day twelve Hours and thirty
five Minutes in coming about 45 Miles. Deducting an Hour and
forty Minutes of Stoppage there remains eleven Hours less five
Minutes for that Space, which gives an average Motion of about
four Miles an Hour. The Weather has been lowering and sower.
At the Inn I enquire a little into the Culture of their Lands and

am told that the Harvest is cut early in July, then Turnips are
sown on the Stubble and next Spring the Turnip Grounds are
planted with Indⁿ Corn or Potatoes, sometimes sown with Spring
Grain. The artificial Grass is chiefly Luzerne and that for Pasturage, or rather, for soiling the Cattle. The Potatoes are planted in
April & gathered in September, and Wheat is sown after them.

   Saturday 30. — This Morning at half an Hour after six we
leave Rastadt. The Post House is a good Inn and what is remarkable here, it is clean. We arrive in two Hours at Stollhofen, one
Post of about ten Miles, the Soil sandy and variable but chiefly
poor, none very good. We change in ten Minutes, the quickest
Thing that has happened in Flanders or Germany. We go hence
to Bischoffsheim in two Hours a similar Distance. The Soil is
much better, it consists of a good Loam on a Basis of Gravel.
Many small Streams run thro it from the Mountains which lie at
no great Distance on the left, and these have good Meadows along
them. We come thro Leuichteren which is an old walled Town
which seems to have been of some Consequence in its Day. We
change Horses in a Quarter of an Hour and then go on to Kehl,
the last German Town in our Route. The Distance is about 8 to 9
Miles, being one Post. The Soil is perfect, a rich black Loam equal
to any Thing and the Husbandry seems equal to the Soil. This
Ride must be fine in the End of June but the Weather is this Day
cloudy and sour. It feels like Care and Sorrow, so that Fancy is
repressed and the Mind draws itself under its own Wings. We
change Horses here in twenty five Minutes and then proceed in
an Hour and an Half to the Hotel of the Holy Ghost at Strasbourgh. We cross the Rhine just as we leave Kehl over a long
wooden Bridge, it is very rapid tho now very low, it must in the
Season of Floods be impetuous indeed. The Soil is the same to
Strasbourgh. Germany is a mountainous Country, but yet from
the Mountain which lies on this Side of Schwalbach there is a
Plain for about 140 Miles southward up the Rhine on the East
Side of that River, and the Mountains lie along to the Eastward
of it at different Distances. I conjecture that the other Side is
similar to this; on the whole I cannot but regret that the Partition
of this Country among so many little Sovereigns, by destroying
Commerce renders the Bounty of Nature in a great Measure use-

less. It is a fine River for a Boundary, and should France be able to occupy that Space which lies West of the Rhine and Alps and North of the Mediterranean Sea and Pyranean Mountains, and obtain besides a good Constitution, she would not only be very happy in herself but contribute greatly to the Peace and Happiness of others; and in such Case I think it would be wise in her to abandon all foreign Possessions, for the Government of such a Territory would fully employ the ablest Minds. She would also be much stronger and much more formidable without them.

— After Dinner I visit the Mayor who is abroad at the Hotel de Ville; Mons.ʳ Dietrick and Mess.ʳˢ Weiss, Revel & Co:, who are also abroad. I then visit M.ʳ Brunck, Commissary at War, who seems to be a sensible honest Fellow. He tells me that the Count de La Luzerne has resigned and that most of the other Ministers will go soon. He tells me also that the Chevalier de Bart is a great Rogue. The Weather has this Day been lowering and disagreable and threatens Mischief for To Morrow; I determine therefore to postpone my Departure till Monday. Expences from Antwerp 31 louis d'ors.

Sunday 31 *Oct.*. — This Morning I visit again Mess.ʳˢ Weiss, Revel et Co:. See M.ʳ Revel & converse with him. He says, among other Things, that none but the Scum of this Country are disposed to expatriate themselves. Call on the Mayor, who is not visible. Dine with Mons.ʳ Brunck *en famille*. The Mayor is of our Party who is to give me this Evening a Passport. After Dinner return Home and receive a Visit from M.ʳ Revel who gives me a Note of the Houses fittest to stop at; I had taken one also at M.ʳ Brunck's. Go to the Comedy, where Chance places me next to Madame Revel. The Company is *comme ça*. From hence go to Supper at M.ʳ Dutrick's. They shewed me this Afternoon a Company of Children going to Exercise, and this Evening I am told that one of them, an only Son, was shot by one of the Militia whose Gun was accidentally loaded with Ball. I learn that the Affairs of France are what I supposed they about this Time would be. The People here are in general averse to the new System. The poorer Sort begin to suffer from the Want of Employment. The Weather this Day has been lowering and threatens Mischief.

NOVEMBER 1790

Monday 1 *Nov.* — This Morning at a Quarter after seven I leave Strasburgh. The Horses could not sooner be obtained. The Hôtel de L'Esprit is a good one and very clean. We go in one Post & an half to Sturzheim, between seven and eight Miles across the Valley; it is as rich as is possible, a deep black Mould. We go this Distance in an Hour and a Quarter and in a Quarter change Horses. We proceed to Wiltheim one Post, about five Miles, in an Hour and a Quarter. We were detained by an unwilling Horse. The Country is waving and very fertile, still a black Mold but of a looser Texture. We change Horses in a Quarter of an Hour and go two Posts to Saverne in an Hour and fifty Minutes, about ten Miles. The Soil and face of the Country is the same but the Soil grows lighter as we recede from the River. We change here and proceed in a Quarter of an Hour from Saverne. Nothing can be finer than this Valley and nothing more beautiful than the last fifteen Miles, where the Vineyards and Cornfields are scattered promiscuously together. In two Hours and thirty five Minutes we reach Phalsbourg which is but about six Miles, but the first three we ascend and the second, thro bad Road, descend a small Mountain. The Soil is not bad but it is kept in Forest, for over the Valley there are none but Nut and Fruit Trees. In a Quarter of an Hour we change Horses and go on for Homartin which we reach in forty five Minutes; it is a Post of about five Miles. We change in ten Minutes and proceed the same Distance in fifty Minutes to Sarburg. These last ten Miles are thro a Loam of good Quality and there is an Appearance of Ease among the People which is not common on this Side of the Atlantic, or rather, I should say there is an Appearance of Affluence in the Houses and Husbandry. The Weather has been dull but promises well for ToMorrow. The Mountains extending on our left from that which we crossed, and which are higher as

they recede, are covered with Snow. We put up at the Golden
Cross. The Mistress of the House seems to be a good Landlady
tho opposed to the Revolution. However, as I want more a Cook
than a Politician, I am content. My Supper vouches for her culi-
nary Talents and I freely submit the others to the Assemblée
Nationale.

Tuesday 2. — This Morning I leave the Croix d'Or, which is a
good House and not dear, at a Quarter after six. It rains and
seems likely to continue raining. In an Hour and five Minutes we
go a Post of about five Miles to Heming. It is a waving Country
almost hilly. The Soil is a good Loam with broken flat Stones,
and the Appearance of the Houses marks a People at Ease. We
change in ten Minutes and proceed over a thin Soil two Posts to
Blâmont in an Hour & fifty five Minutes, the Distance about ten
Miles over a hilly Country. We change Horses here in ten
Minutes and go two Posts farther of ab: eleven Miles to Beau-
mond. At leaving Blâmont we cross the little River Vezou and go
down on the left Side of it; on the right is a pretty large Abbey or
Convent. There are good Meadows along the River. The Soil is
here gravelly but pretty good. I see no Signs of the Culture of
either Turnips or Potatoes, both of which would succeed well.
We change Horses in ten Minutes and go on in eighty Minutes to
Lunéville over the same Kind of Soil, a Post and an Half, about
8 Miles. This is a good looking Town and in it is a Palace built
they say by the King of Poland. The Vezou falls here into the
Meurte. We change Horses in ten Minutes and go on to Dombale
in an Hour & a Quarter a Post and an Half, full 8 Miles. A fine
chocolate colored Soil mingled with a little Gravel. The Basis I
believe is Gravel. Here we cross the Salmon River, having
changed Horses in a Quarter of an Hour, and then proceed in an
Hour and fifty Minutes two Posts, ab: 10 Miles, to Nancy.
Shortly after leaving Dombale we crossed the Meurte to the Town
of S: Nicolas. The Soil is good to Nancy, which is a large and well
built Town; there is a very fine Place or Square in it with a Statue
of Lewis the Fourteenth which seems (if one may judge in
riding by) to be a very fine one. We change Horses here in ten
Minutes and go on to Vilaine, a Post House. At leaving Nancy I
observe a large Building which stands on the left. It is handsome.

The Postillion says it is a Maison de Force called Morinville. The Distance to Vilaine is a Post and an Half, about six Miles over a cold Clay. Hilly, and the Road very bad, having once been paved and the Pavement out of Repair. We get over it in an Hour and five Minutes, change Horses in ten Minutes and proceed in an Hour one Post and an Half, about seven Miles, to the Golden Lion Inn at Toul, where we cross the Moselle by two Stone Bridges, there being at this Place an Island in the River. The Soil is lighter the last Stage and the Road pretty good, but we can see but little as it is half after six when we arrive. The Weather has this Day been unpleasant. In the Morning it rained hard, and altho it cleared away at eleven, yet we had Showers at Times, tho not heavy, till our Arrival.

Wednesday 3. — This Morning at half past six we leave the Lion d'Or, a very good Inn and cheap. We proceed along a beautiful Valley, the Side Hills on both Sides covered with Vineyards, and Villages scattered about at the Foot of the Hills; we go in an Hour and a Quarter a Post and an Half about seven Miles; towards the End of it we cross a Hill. We change Horses at Void [Foug?] in ten Minutes and after leaving it about a Mile we cross the Meuse, which is here but a small Stream; we go along down it for some Time; there are good Meadows on the Banks. The Soil here is a pretty stiff Loam mingled with broken Stones. An Hour and a Quarter takes us another Post and a Half, about seven Miles, to Void where we change in ten Minutes and proceed for S! Aubin. The Soil is the same and the Road very bad. The Postillion says it has rained for three Weeks past but I think he must be mistaken, for the Streams shew no Swell equal to such raining. The Country for this last Post was hilly. In an Hour and twenty five Minutes we get on a Post and an Half, which is I think about eight Miles. This Town lies at the Head of the Ayre River, a Branch of the Oyse, so that in the last Distance we have crossed the Ridge which divides the Waters emptying northward from those which empty westward. We change as usual in ten Minutes and go in fifty five Minutes to Ligny-en-Barrois, a Post of about five Minutes, [sic]. We have the same Soil as before. At our Departure we ascend a high Hill, flat on the Top as they all are here, and we then proceed along it till we descend to the Town: it lies on the

River Omain, a Branch of the Marne. We change again in ten
Minutes and they give us five Horses, the Stages having Need of
more Cattle at Bar-le-Duc. We go thither two Posts, about ten
Miles, in an Hour and a Quarter thro a most delicious Valley.
The River meanders thro it and we cross it twice; the Sides are
high and steep, covered with Vines, the Bottom level, a good
light Loam, Corn Fields and Meadows. I enquire here for
Trout, this Place being famed for them, but there are only some
Pieces left; but they are majestic Ruins. We get fresh Horses
here in ten Minutes and with them climb the Hill (called Montagne) in our Way to Sandrupt. After we are up we go along a
hilly Road till we descend to that Village, which lies on the Sauxi
River, another Branch of the Marne. This is a Post & an Half
of about eight Miles, performed in an Hour and thirty five Minutes. At this Place I purchase a very fine Trout and depart in ten
Minutes after our Arrival. In an Hour and a Quarter more we
reach St Dizier, a Post and an Half, about seven Miles. At first
we ascend the Hill and the Rest of the Way, tho hilly, is chiefly
descending. The Soil is the same. We are now I think over the
hilly Country, being on the Banks of the Marne in Champaign.
We put up at the Soleil d'Or where in Addition to my Trout,
which proves a very fine one, they give me among other Things
a Wood Cock as fat as a Teal, which with good Wine to wash them
down make Amends for bad Roads and bad Weather. This Day
has been showery, cold and disagreable. This Evening the Horizon draws close round and it seems as if we were to have a settled
Rain. They tell me it has done nothing else but rain for three
Days past.

   Thursday 4. — This Morning at six we leave St Dizier. The
Soleil d'Or is a good House. In an Hour and ten Minutes we go
a Post and an Half, about seven Miles, to Long Champ, thro a
level Country and a good gravelly Soil. We change here in ten
Minutes and in an Hour and twenty five Minutes go two Posts,
about ten Miles, to Vitry-le-Français situated on the Marne; the
Country is the same. We change here in eight Minutes and proceed to La Chaussée. The Road is hilly, tho after the first Ascent
we go upon the Top of the Hill. We have here Vineyards and the
Soil is an ash-colored Loam with broken Stones. The Road is

good, Distance about 9 Miles, and every Inch of Land is cultivated, but I think the System of Agriculture is bad. The Village,
or rather Town of Vitry, for it is fortified in the modern Stile,
lies on the Marne and so does La Chaussée, I believe. We change
here in seven Minutes and go in one Hour and fifty Minutes to
Châlons-sur-Marne which like the two last Stages consists of
two Posts, but this is about eleven Miles. Our first Advance is up
the Hill and afterwards we proceed by a waving Descent to the
Plain. The Soil is gravelly but good and much cultivated. We
change here in five Minutes and proceed two Posts, about ten
Miles, to Jalons, in an Hour and fifteen Minutes. The Road lies
along the Marne, a fine gravelly Loam. We change here in ten
Minutes and go in an Hour and three Quarters to Épernay, two
Posts of about ten Miles. We are delayed by the Lameness of a
Horse, which is changed from under the Saddle &c.ᵃ. The Road is
good and pretty level till near our Journey's End when it is
hilly, but it presents us with a most beautiful View of Acᵗ. This
Village is at the Foot of the Hill producing the most excellent
Wine, and before it lies a Plain of good Land cultivated with vari-
ous Grain so as to form a beautiful Carpet bounded by the mean-
derings of the River, which on this Side runs close to the Hills.
We put up at the Hôtel de Rohan, which is very dirty, and mine
Host and his Wife look like Votaries of the jolly God, which au-
gurs ill for me. The Supper is but indifferent; the Wine, however,
is good of its Kind, indeed this is the Center of the finest Vineyᵈˢ.
The Crop has this Year been small but is accounted very good.
The best has been bought at 500# for 400 bottles which contain
each a Wine Quart.

Friday 5. — This Morning at Half past six I quit the Hôtel de
Rohan with the Intention never again to enter it. We proceed two
Posts, about ten Miles, over small Hills along the Marne, or
rather across the Points of Hills. We change here in ten Minutes
and proceed in fifty five one Post to Dormans; I was delayed by
permitting the Postillion to change Horses on the Road with another. The Soil is stiffer this Morning and without Gravel. We
change here in a Quarter of an Hour and ascend a long high Hill
which on the Top is a stoney barren; we descend it and arrive at
Parois. The Distance is a Post and an Half, scant seven Miles,

which we accomplish in an Hour and twenty Minutes. We
change Horses in a Quarter of an Hour and go a Post to Château
Thierry, about five Miles in fifty Minutes. This is thro a waving
Country of pretty good Loam. And as we have come all the Way
thro a Wine Country the Number and Size of the Villages is astonishing. We change here in eight Minutes and cross the Marne,
then go a little Way down it and turn up the Hill. The Soil is here
very rich and continues good on the Hills. We go to La Ferme de
Paris, a Post House, in an Hour and twenty Minutes, the Distance a Post and an Half, about eight Miles. We change here in
12 Minutes and go a Post and three Quarters to La Ferté-sous-
Jouarre in an Hour and thirty five Minutes, the Distance about
nine Miles. The 32 Mile Stone stands here opposite to the Post
House, which is 7½ Posts from Paris. 'We change Horses in ten
Minutes and in three Quarters of an Hour we go a Post, about
five Miles, to St Jean-les-deux-Jumeaux. The Road is paved and
the Soil pretty good. We change in ten Minutes and go in three
Quarters of an Hour a Post and an Half, about seven Miles, to the
Hôtel Royal in Meaux. The Road is excellent after we cross the
Marne about half Way. The Soil is a good gravelly Loam. Near
Meaux I observe large Fields of Turnips which shew that their
Husbandry is growing better.

Saturday 6. — This Morning at twenty five Minutes after six
I leave the Hôtel du Roi at Meaux which is a pretty good one; in
an Hour and forty Minutes we go two Posts, ten Miles, to Claye,
on a *pavé*. The Country consists of gentle Hills and is of a good
Soil; we change in a Quarter of an Hour and go in an Hour and
ten Minutes two Posts more, about nine Miles, to Bondy, which
is nearly level and the Soil good. We change here in five Minutes
and then an Hour and ten Minutes brings us one Post to Paris,
where I take up my Quarters at the Hôtel du Roi.[1] After I am
dressed I take a fiacre and visit at Madame de Flahaut's. She is
abroad but Monsieur presses me much to pass the Evening.
Go to the Palais royal and visit at Madame de Chastellux's.
She is also abroad. I go to Club where I find the Sentiment aristo-

---

[1] A successful tour in everything but its object. Morris had found the roads
encumbered with homing Kings after Leopold II's imperial coronation at
Frankfurt, but no sturdy Germans eager to settle the back lands of New York.

crat prevails not a little. Thence to Van Staphorst's whom I had met as I came into Town. Thence to the Restorateur's to Dinner; Van Staphorst tells me that Short is appointed to negotiate the Loans of the United States in Holland. I meet at the Restorateur's the Abbé Ronchon who tells me much of what is passing, and then I go to Le Couteulx's. I find them at Table; a very warm Reception. *Voilà ce que c'est que l'homme.* Laurent tells me after the Company are gone, how Affairs stand respecting the Negotiation. I get sundry Letters here which are on the whole *peu satisfaisantes.* Go hence to the Club de 89 where I just look in in Hopes of finding Short, and then go to the Louvre. Madame is at the Comédie. She returns and seems glad to see me. I find that Lord Wycombe is *un peu enniché ici.* The Weather has this Day been fine. My Friend, with Assurances of Fidelity, professes a Determination to be *sage.* I am obliged to doubt both a little. *Nous verrons.* Expences from Strasbourgh to Paris 17 Louis d'ors.

Gouverneur Morris to Robert Morris

Paris 16 Nov.[r] 1790

Robert Morris Esq[r]

Philadelphia

My dear friend.

I wrote to you from London on the twenty third of September and since that Period have had a long fatiguing Ride thro the Tract there ment.[d] In Flanders I found far less Probability of selling Lands than I imagined. The wealthy would be more likely to emigrate if the Emperor were less likely to succeed. After his Restoration it is very probable that many of them will be less pleased with their Situation than heretofore, because altho they were pretty generally in Favor of the Revolution when it began, they have long since grown heartily tired of it. This makes them forget their former Feeling and Conduct which the Government may, notwithstanding, be inclined to remember. The prevailing Party for some Time past has been the Clergy and their Dupes. They are looking for Victory to the Lord of Hosts, whose Good Will they hope to obtain by Processions and other Mummeries. The People must feel Oppression before they will incline to quit their Country. They are very different from other European Peasants. Frugal, sober, industrious, superstitious, steady in their Pursuits and Attachments, confined in their Ideas, and little desirous of changing their Condition or Situation, these People, should they once turn their Attention towards America, would become excellent Setlers and go thither in great Numbers and with much Property; but Events have not as yet prepared them to abandon their native Land. I offered to some very rich People of my Acquaintance a Speculation in American Lands and they seemed inclined to think of it in Case Things should continue in their then Situation, which by the bye was not probable. I caused an Offer to be held out to the Priests but they, whether they believed in the Efficacy of their own Prayers or found it most convenient to seem to believe I know not, but they declined also on the Score of Indigence. They are obliged to employ all the Funds of the Church to oppose the *impious* Emperor. Impious because his late Brother wanted to get hold of their Property, and for that Purpose to dissolve the Monastic Orders. They said however that if Things were a little more settled, it would be a good Thing to make Settlements in the Wilderness, for the Honor of God and to extend the Catholic Faith.

At Liege there is but little Wealth or Means among the People, who are in a Dispute with their Prince Bishop about some gambling Schemes which they dislike. Along the Rhine Nothing can be done except by the Soul Sellers who are hanged if they are discovered enticing the People to emigrate. All the Wealth *there* is in the Hands of Traders who enrich themselves by a Traffic with Holland and England, or of Nobles whose Privileges are so great at Home that they must loose by going abroad. These hold the Lands and the others possess the Money of Germany. In Alsace, one of the Provinces where the discontented of this Kingdom are most numerous, I found that these Discontents exist chiefly among two Classes of People. Those who were rich and expensive, and those who lived by that Expence. The former were chiefly such as held Employments, received Pensions or were possessed of Church Dignities. All these were in Debt and of Course are now Bankrupts. Of those who really had Estates and were discontented, there are very few who determine to expatriate themselves for any long Period. They do indeed expect a Change of Affairs, which Expectation must sooner or later be realized; first because all Things change and secondly because the present State is too monstrous and unnatural to endure. As to those who lived by the Expence of the rich they cannot be useful to us in any Way.

After giving this true Picture, I add that I have the Expectation of succeeding, and employ myself in Consequence. Mr Barlow you tell me has given Assurances that he can sell &c.ª &c.ª, but my dear Friend, this same Mr Barlow, after all his Sales, sends back under Protest a Bill for 100,000$^{\#}$ drawn for Account of the Scioto Company. If I do not realize your Expectations and Wishes, you may place it to the Account of this same Company, against whose Deceptions the Cry is general here, and whose Conduct will not I apprehend be agreable on your Side of the Water.

Mr de Chaumont has spoken to me about a Concern which he expects to hold in your great Purchase. Not having then received your Letter of the 31st of August, I told him that I was in hourly Expectation of receiving more accurate Information of your Intentions than at that Time I was possessed of. It seems to me that he may be very useful. He says that he declined any Concern in the Ouabache and Illinois Purchase but pointed out to you the Tract which Gorham and Phelps possessed. He observes very properly that if a Sense of Justice and Propriety did not oppose the Setling of his Countrymen beyond the Appalachian Mountains, a Regard to himself and his Prospects and Expectations in Life would prevent it; whereas the Tract you have lately purchased permits of that fair and honorable Proceedure which becomes Men of Character and Integrity.

I must mention here what I generally place at the Begining of my Letters, the Reception of yours hitherto unacknowleged. I have then two of the 8th one of the 14th and one of the 31 August. Mr Constable mentions Letters you was to write, and Mr Richard tells me that La Caze was to sail a few Days after the October Packet, and with him young Franklin *charged with your Land Speculations*. This I am very glad to hear.

VII

THE REVOLUTION MARKS TIME
LA FAYETTE LONGS FOR A *JOURNÉE*

NOVEMBER 1790

Sunday 7. — Richard calls this Morning and while he is here Staphorst comes to Breakfast. Have no interesting Conversation with either. Go to see M.ʳ Short as soon as my Carriage arrives and sit with him some Time. I find that ͟1500,000 are to be paid to the Ministry here from the Amsterdam Loan and that a Loan of $2.000.000 is to be opened for Speculations in the Debt. He joins in Reprehension of that Measure as not consistent with the great Principles of Right. Certainly France ought to be paid first. Short is strongly impressed with the Idea that he is to be continued at this Court and thinks this Holland Negotiation is an Evidence of it, but I own that I think otherwise. I tell him that I think it would be useful to contract for the Exchanges, which will have the double Effect of obviating any Suspicions in Regard to him and of obtaining in the long Run the most Money for the United States. After much Conversation on various Subjects I go to Le Couteulx's and they are all abroad. I leave a Card at M.ʳ Grand's. Call at Madame de Chastellux's. She is abroad. At the Louvre *denied*. At Mad.ᵉ de La Borde's and see Monsieur. Promise to come this Evening. At Mad.ᵉ de Ségur's. Stay and dine. They put me a little *au fait* of what is going. From thence go to the Count de Montmorin's; a very flattering Reception. Thence to Mons.ʳ de La Fayette's, who affects to be very well pleased to see me. I promise to dine with him ToMorrow. Thence to the Louvre. Madame receives me and tells of a *Dénonciation* of Mons: D'Angivilliers &c:, &c:. We just begin to quarrel when Capellis comes in. After him others, among them Montesquiou who says Cantaleu told him I was arrived. I leave them and call on Le Couteulx. See de Cantaleu and his Wife and speak to the former on Business. He and Laurent are to call on me ToMorrow Morning. Go to Mad: de Chastellux's and wait some Time for her Return from the Opera. At length come away without seeing her and go to Mad: de La Borde's. Receive many Compliments. Stay till near eleven and come Home. The Weather has been this Day pretty good.

Monday 8. — This Morning write. They say at the Post Office that I have no Letters which seems to me extraordinary. Swan calls and talks about his Plan for the Debt. I tell him that there are Reasons [1] which will prevent me from engaging in it but that I think it a good Thing and shall not object to the Interest proposed for M: Morris. That I will see M: Le Couteulx &c:, &c:. I wait for this last till one, who was to have been Here before twelve. Then go out and call on him. He is just gone abroad. I return and find him. We have a long and interesting Conversation on this Business. Agree on every Point now necessary. After he leaves me I go to the Louvre and stay till Madame returns. We have a pretty smart Conversation in which I am cold enough and sentimental enough. The Bishop d'Autun and M: S: Foi come in. The former seems still a little sore upon a certain Subject. *N'importe.* We converse freely enough. Stay pretty late and then go to Dinner at La Fayette's. He does not sit down till we have half dined and retires soon after, has not Time to hold the Conversation which he wished. This is according to Custom. From hence return to the Louvre and meet the Bishop coming down. I take him back and desire him to advise La Fayette to the same Conduct which I have done in a very delicate Circumstance. He has obtained from the King a Promise to chuse his Guard among the late Gardes Françaises and the Jacobins are violent on the Occasion. He says that he has a Right in talking to the King to give his Opinion as well as any other Citizen &c:. I tell him he should

---

[1] His semi-official mission to England.

put himself on different Ground, and say that he had earnestly
recommended the Measure to the King, it being a Tribute of
Gratitude to those brave Men who had so signally distinguished
themselves in Favor of Freedom &c.ª. The Bishop is entirely of
my Opinion and will speak, but he observes very justly that it is
much easier to convince La Fayette than to determine his Conduct. After this is over I go into the Salon and stay out the Company. The Comte de Luxembourgh has according to Custom
much to whisper. I tell him in plain Terms that the aristocratic
Party must be quiet unless they wish to be hanged. After he is
gone I have a reasoning Scene with Madame which would have
terminated unreasonably if I chose, but I am determined it shall
be all her own Act, so that there be no Ground for future bewail-
ings, which nevertheless I shall surely be exposed to. Go from
hence to the Palais royal and see Madᵉ de Chastellux and Lady
Tancred who is with her. The Dutchess comes in and we make
Tea &c.ª, &c.ª. Sup with the Princess. See Mʳ de Bouffler and the
Vicomte de Ségur. *Rien de marquante.* Get Home at a quarter
after twelve. Very fine Weather for the Season.

  Tuesday 9. — This Morning Mʳ Sayre ¹ calls upon me. His
Object is to get into the Affair of the Debt, which he knows I
find very little about. I tell him that I have just written a Letter
declining all Concern and cannot therefore serve him. I promise
however to mention his Application. Mʳ de Chaumont comes in
and after some Conversation respecting Holker's Affairs We converse on other Matters. First on Lands. He says that he suggested to R. M. the Idea of purchasing from Gorham, and that he
understood he, Chaumont, was to have an Interest therein. I
believe he will be interested for I think he can be useful. He mentions another Matter to me which if it can be brought about will
subserve much a Plan which I communicate to him. Go to Mʳ
Short's. Mʳ Sayre has been with him also. Converse with Short
on general Matters. He is going to see Montmorin and I tell him
that I have declined an Interest and assign in Confidence the
Reason. I find that his Mission is for the Purpose of borrowing

---

¹ Stephen Sayre (1736–1818), born on Long Island. Had been sheriff of London and banker there. Employed by Arthur Lee, constantly asking Congress
to repay his services to American cause.

the two Million of Dollars only. He agrees with me in Opinion that it will be useful to the United States that Individuals should contract for the French Debt, but thinks the french Government ought to be apprized of the true Situation of Things. I fully accord in this Sentiment and add that they should know also as nearly as possible what they have to depend on in Regard to the future. Visit Madame de Corney. Thence to du Molet's. Thence to the Count de Moustier's. Madame de Bréhan is violent in her Abuse of Monsieur de La Fayette. Go from hence to Le Couteulx's to Dinner. As they are abroad I say *bon Jour* to Le Normand. Montesquiou dines with us and after Dinner we go into Le Couteulx's Counting House and converse on the Business which brought us together. Go to Madame de Chastellux's and sit some Time with her. She is going to Mad? de Ségur's. I leave Word for Short to follow us thither. He does so and we converse about various Matters relating to America. I tell him that Morris's Contract with the Farm, which Jefferson considered as a Monopoly, was the only Means of destroying that Monopoly of Tobacco in Virginia by the Scotch Factors, which really existed. Give him some Reasons therefor. He seems surprized at this and is half convinced. He tells me that he fancies the Parties are pushing the Affair of the Debt for that Montmorin has applied to him on the Subject. We have a few Words on La Fayette's Subject. He expresses his Astonishment at this Man's Inaptitude & Imbecility. Poor La Fayette. He begins to suffer the Consequences which always attend too great Elevation. *Il s'éclipse au premier*. He tells me that La Rochefoucault is terribly puzzled about the Affair of Impositions. I reply that this is always the Case when Men bring metaphisical Ideas into the Business of the World. That none know how to govern but those who have been used to it and such Men have rarely either Time or Inclination to write about it. The Books, therefore, which are to be met with, contain mere Utopian Ideas. He begins to believe that there is some Truth in all this. I set him down at La Rochefoucault's and return Home. Le Couteulx has according to Custom neglected to send me what he promised. The Weather has been very fine.

Wednesday 10. — This Morning I write a little. Receive a Note from Mad.^e de Flahaut in Consequence of which I walk to the Louvre. Monsr is with her. I make her a Present of Buttons which she is permitted to shew to none but him untill ToMorrow. After some Time Monsr is called down and as I consider this to be a Rendezvous understood I am for proceeding immediately to the Object, but I find that she has formed her Plan too and it is now a Question to be meerly her friend. I tell her that this cannot be but if she wishes to get Rid of me Nothing is so easy, and immediately wish her a Good Morning. Of Course I am entreated back and Monsieur presently after comes in. He stays some Time and when he is gone we have a strange mingled Scene of Sentiments, Caresses and some Tears, which last do not come easily. At length she tells me that Matters are accomodated between her and the Bishop and so well accomodated that Nothing but the Entry of Monsr de Flahaut a few Days ago prevented him from doing the needful. Having told me this, she says I may if I please possess her. I agree to do so *pour la dernière fois.*... She says I am a Cheat in telling her it is for the last Time. We shall see. She says I must permit her to receive the Bishop and to deny herself to me, which I agree to readily, for I think I have a Secret which will insensibly tend to reverse this *belle Ordre des Choses.* The important Thing is that we mutually acquit each other of all Engagements. She keeps the Ring, to be delivered to me whenever she is *in Fact* unfaithful. So I think I have got out of this sentimental Scrape better than I expected. Return Home, dress and go to the Palais royal to dinner. Take with me a large Newfoundland Dog [1] which I bought in London and present him to her royal Highness who appears much pleased, and the Vicomte de Ségur *le prend en amitié. Cela s'entend.* Short is here. He tells me that he wishes the Contract for the Debt of America may not take Place, lest it should be suspected that he holds an Interest in it. After Dinner I take Short to Mad.^e La Borde's and then to

---

[1] After a six-weeks competition with post-horses, the large Newfoundland is thankful for a full stop in the palace of a fairy princess. The editor has come across a modern ultra-republican condemnation of Morris for the snobbishness of this presentation; but constant hospitality from a royal duchess was not easy to repay, a dog the classical gift from man to woman, a Terre-Neuve exotic and new.

Mad? de Ségur's, after which I set him down at the Palais royal.
We take a Turn round it together and then I go to Club where I
murder a little Time. It has been a fine Day. I think I had never
in my Life so many different Things agitating my Mind as at
present & I cannot commence one Affair because another is constantly obtruding.

Thursday 11. — This Morning I write a little. M? de Chaumont calls on me. He shews a Memoire to be presented by some
of Holker's Creditors. I make sundry Observations on it. He
then tells me that his Friend does not incline to part with his
Money unless on a Loan to the Congress. This he cannot certainly accomplish. The ultimate Object is to purchase Land. I
tell him that I will sell him Land to the Amount and tell him the
Place. He is to call again on this Subject. I go to the Manufactory and bespeak two Plateauxs for Gen! Washington. Thence
to visit Mons? de La Luzerne who is abroad. Thence return Home
and wait for M? Short who does not come. Go to Dinner at M?
Boutin's. Meet Mons? de Moustiers and Mad? de Bréhan who
say if the Troubles last she will go and live with me in America.
I of Course agree to the Arrangement. The Chevalier de Cubières
is here who reads us a Defence of Empiricism by a Quack. It is in
an Italian Jargon. It contains many good Strokes relative to the
Men and Things of the present Day and Generation. I go from
hence Home and then to Madame de Ségur's to whom I present a
Set of Buttons. After sitting a little while I go to M? Swan's.
He is very much indisposed and his sweet Help Mate is as sharp
as Vinegar, by Way of alleviating his Misfortunes I suppose. M?
de Valnais is here, whom I do not recognize, but his Name being
mentioned as he goes away I call him back and express my Surprize that he did not bring me the Proofs of the State of his Case
on which I had spoken to Mons? de La Luzerne. This brings on
an Explanation in which he is obliged to acknowlege himself in
the Wrong and make many Apologies, which I tell him are unnecessary. That if his Affairs have gone well I am satisfied, having had no other Object or Intention but to serve (not him) but
his Wife who is an American. Go from hence to Mad? de Chastellux's. She is abroad with the Dutchess. Leave my Name at Van
Staphorst's who is on a Party out of Town. Pass a little Time at

Club and then go to the Baron de Bezevald's where I meet again de Moustiers and Mad^e. The Baron is as usual on the high Ropes of royal Prerogative. De Mous.^{rs} is to send me ToMorrow his Plan of a Constitution for France. Take Leave here of Mad^e de Bréhan. This has been a fine Day.

Friday 12. — This Morning I write. Swan calls on me and complains that he can get no Answer from Le Couteulx. He thinks that my Refusal has discouraged him. After he is gone I continue my writing but Paul Jones comes in and I give him his Papers. He tells me he has been very ill. I receive a Message from Le Couteulx desiring to see me. Go there and he communicates the Answer given by Montmorin to Montesquiou. It would seem from this that the Money to be borrowed in Holland is to be paid to France. I do not believe that Fact. We converse upon another little incidental Subject, about which he is to write to me. Go from hence to the Pont Tournant and walk thro the Tuilleries. Thence go to visit Mad^e de Flahaut at the Lodgings of Capellis. My Deportment modest, tender, sensible. The Timidity of a young Lover who feels for the first Time. Monsieur is present, but yet I give her some touching Anecdote which I relate to him, and I think I have produced the intended Effect. Dine at the Count de Montmorin's. De Moustiers and his Sister and [sic] Law dine here. After Dinner I tell the Count de Montmorin that my Letter announcing his Intention to send Ternant to America has miscarried but that I sent a Duplicate from London and expect the Answer every Hour. After Dinner go to the Opera. I sit behind my late friend and as luckily the Music makes me always grave I keep still in the sentimental Stile. The Countess de Frize is here, to whom I pay my Respects in the adjoining Box. After the Opera luckily I meet Madame Foucault and luckily she receives me particularly well. I take Care for many Reasons that my Countenance shall beam with Satisfaction. Luckily she expresses herself to Madame in Terms very favorable to me. Le Couteulx tells me what he has been doing and I take him and Capellis up. At Capellis's I stay but a little while and am excessively gay and playful. My friend the Bishop is to be here and therefore I leave the Field free. She is mortified at this as I expected. Call on Madame de Chastellux and then as she is abroad

I return Home and read the Plan of a Constitution for France by de Moustiers. It has been a fine Day.

Saturday 13. — This Morning I write. A Person calls who wants to buy Lands in Virginia. I tell him that he will do wrong. Give him the best Information and Advice in my Power on that Subject. He is to call again. Has about 150000$^{\#}$ to dispose of. M.ʳ Short calls very late and offers me a Ticket to go to hear M.ʳ Condorci pronounce the Eulogium of Doctor Franklin. M.ʳ de Chaumont was with me to breakfast and shewed me a Memoire drawn for Mess.ʳˢ Robineau &c.ª which is quite right. I shew him the Map of the S.ᵗ Lawrence Lands and am at Dinner to give him a Map of New York on which I have protracted them. I decline therefore M.ʳ Short's proposal and he goes to dine at the Duc de La Rochefoucault's. I dine with Madame de Foucault and learn that the Populace are pilaging the Hôtel de Castres. The Occasion of it is that the duc de Castres has wounded their favorite Charles de La Meth in a duel which he had drawn upon himself by insulting the Duke. The History seems curious. M.ʳ de Chauvigny comes to Paris for the Purpose of fighting with Charles de La Meth, who (as he says) fomented an Insurrection in the Regiment to which he belongs. All this I learnt at M.ʳ de Boutin's where M.ʳ de Chauvigny, introduced by his Brother a Bishop, related what had passed on the Subject. He had called on M.ʳ de La Meth whose Friends at a Rendezvous given told him that M.ʳ de La M. would not fight till the Constitution was finished. The other replied that he must in that Case untill the Completion of it continue to assert on every Occasion that M.ʳ de La M. was a Coward. This Thing being again in Question at the Assemblée, de La M. declared that he would not have an Affair with Chauvigny untill he had settled with the Duc de Castres (Colonel of the Regiment) *qui m'a détaché ce Spadassin* [bully] *là*. De Castres of Course requires Satisfaction and they proceed to the Ground where the Friends of La Meth, who is an excellent Swordsman, object to his fighting with Pistols. De Castres, like a true Chevalier, agrees to decide the Matter *aux Armes blanches* and wounds his Antagonist. The Populace in Consequence destroy the Property of his Father. This is rare. I think it will produce some Events which are not now dreamt of. After Dinner I go to the

petit Dunkerque and thence to visit M.ʳ Swan in order to find out
M.ʳ Barlow's Lodgings. Go thence to the Louvre *chez* Capellis.
My fair Friend is just returned from Chaillot. She gives me a
great Deal of L.ᵈ Wycombe's History, who it seems was introduced
by Monsieur de S.ᵗ Foi in order to awaken the Bishop and bring
him back. After many sentimental Caresses we proceed with
Energy to the last Act which is forcibly impressed and as a natural
Consequence her Heart is opened. She declares that the Bishop
shall not have her. *Sed quere.* Go from hence to Mad.ᵉ de La
Borde's where there is a pretty large Society. The Assemblée (in
the Hands of the Jacobins) have it is said sanctioned the Doings
of the Day. This is rare. Mad.ᵉ de F—— asked me during the
Evening how Mad.ᵉ de Foucault had received me. I told her
wonderfully well &c.ᵃ, &c.ᵃ. She suspected as much. And in Truth
so did I, my Princess. The Weather has been fine this Day.

Sunday 14. — This Morning M.ʳ Richard calls and tells me that
Letters from La Caze have put Le Couteulx out of Humor. He
returns empty Handed and writes that R. M.'s Situation is very
disagreable. He says farther that young Franklin comes over
charged with his Land Plan. I am very glad of this for many
Reasons. Paul Jones calls on me. He has nothing to say but is so
kind as to bestow on me the Hours which hang heavy on his
Hands. I dress and the Count de Moustiers calls on me. We discuss his Plan of a Constitution together and he tells me that he
stands better at Court than ever he expected. He says he is personally in Favor with the Queen and he expects to be consulted
on Affairs by and bye. The King and Queen, he tells me, are
determined not to abuse their Authority if ever they recover it.
He tells me incidentally that both the King and Queen have mentioned me to him. The former twice, and that I stand well in
their Opinion. This may perhaps be useful to my Country at
some future Period. After he is gone I call on M.ʳ Short who was
to have breakfasted with me, but not being able to come has requested I would call on him. He had waited for me a considerable Time and is at length gone away but left Word he would
write from his first Stage.¹ I go to dine with Mess.ʳˢ Grand.

---

¹ To Holland to negotiate loans for the United States.

There is here a young Man whom I have frequently seen but
never conversed with before, a Mons.ʳ Pinson d'Arman who was
employed a little while in Holland and seems to be much *au fait*
of Affairs. He says that Mons.ʳ de S.ᵗ Priest is a Scoundrel of
moderate Talents and great Cupidity, sold to Russia &c.ᵃ, &c.ᵃ,
&c.ᵃ. I desire him to come and breakfast with me some Morning.
I set him down at the Place Louis Quinze and call on Madame de
Chastellux. She is gone to the Opera. I therefore visit at Mad.ᵉ
de Flahaut's. It seems to me from Appearances that L.ᵈ Wycombe
is expected and I tell her so, but she says it is the Bishop. Company come in immediately after me, Mesdames de La Borde and
de La Tour; after them Montesquiou, and while we are all here,
enter L.ᵈ Wycombe who is at once established as the Person to
whom a Rendezvous is given. We all go away but I presently after return and tell her *que je lui serai à charge pour quelques
momens de plus*. My Lord is more disconcerted than my Lady.
He seems not yet advanced to the Point which these Things tend
to. I go from hence to Club where I find there are some who justify the Populace for Yesterday's Business. It has been a fine Day
but this Evening is cold. De Moustiers told me that Montmorin
had asked for Carmichael as Minister at this Court, which might
excite Competition to M.ʳ Short and Madison, the present Com-
petitors. *Qu:* as to this Request of Montmorin.

Monday 15. — This Morning I write. M.ʳ Barlow calls and after a lame stammering Conversation I find that he has no Means
at Command to retire the Bill upon him. He talks to me of his
Expectation to make future Sales. I fear this Scioto Business will
turn out very badly. Dariell comes. His Heart is full and almost
broken. He enquires about Scioto Lands as a Retreat. I give
him Information and offer him my Rariton Tract, he to pay for
it as he can. He will think of this. I go to dine with Le Couteulx
according to an Appointment with Capellis. After Dinner go into
the Bureau and leave with Laurent some Papers. He is to call a
Meeting for Wednesday with Montesquiou. Go hence to Mad.ᵉ
de Chastellux's. An Abbé whose Name I recollect not expresses
the Wish of the Garde des Sceaux to converse with me. I promise
to wait upon him. The Dutchess of Orleans reproaches me for
absenting myself and I promise to dine with her ToMorrow. At 8

oClock I go by Appointment to Mad.^e de Flahaut's. She has not
returned from the Variétés but desires that I will wait. I am unluckily obliged to do so, having promised Capellis to spend the
Evening here. At half after eight she comes in and Mad.^{lle}
Duplessis with her. I shew more ill Humor than consists with
Good Sense or Politeness: at least such would be the Opinion of
most Observers. She is full of Apologies but I treat both her and
them like a Turk. This has the proper Effect. She feels the Necessity of Conciliation and proposes a Rendezvous for ToMorrow
Evening which I refuse to accept of. At length however she prevails but as we go in to Supper together I tell her that she will
probably fail if a new Comedy offers itself. I take Mad.^{lle} Duplessis to her Lodgings and then return Home. It is fine Weather but
a little sharp. At my Return Home I find a Map of Lands belonging to Alexander Macomb which Barlow has sent me.

Tuesday 16. — This Morning write. Chaumont calls. His
friend will not purchase a Part of the St Lawrence Tract. Paul
Jones calls. He has Nothing to say. The Abbé d'Andreselle [1]
calls and tells me that the Garde des Sceaux wishes I would dine
with him as he can then more conveniently converse with me. I
dine at the Palais royal and as the Princess is alone when I come
in I converse a little with her in a Manner to gain somewhat on
her Good Will. After Dinner we have a little Conversation with
the Chevalier de Bouflers; [2] *par Hazard* the Queen is our Subject.
Go from hence to Le Couteulx's; he was to have written to me but
has omitted it. He says he has not yet heard from Montesquiou.
From hence I go to Mad.^e de Flahaut's but the Count de Luxembourg is with her and before he goes Monsr de St Foi comes in and
after him Lord Wycombe, so that this Occasion also is lost. Go to
Mad.^e de Ségur's. See the Maréchal, who is just come Home.
Take Lady Tancred and Mad.^e de Chastellux to the Palais royal

---

[1] Barthélémy-Philibert Picon, Abbé d'Andrezel (1765–1825), Grand-Vicaire
de Bordeaux. When a refugee in Bath, 1795, Morris will feed him on cold
chicken and lobster.

[2] Chevalier de Boufflers (1738–1815) said to be just growing up after fifty
years' boyhood, his gay path sown with erotic fugitive verse, with airy cameos
in prose, with selfishness to his adorer, lovely Marquise de Sabran, his vows of
celibacy forbidding marriage. Good looks, courtesy, licentious wit, flippancy
and philosophy, prismatic brilliancy on froth.

and sup there. It has been a fine Day. I received Letters at Le Couteulx's which are not pleasant.

Wednesday 17. — This Morning write. M.ʳ Olive calls on me and gives some Ideas relative to Speculations in Lands. I hint the Plan which seems best to me. He approves of it much. I am to converse with Le Couteulx and again with him. I ask him if among his Friends there be Capitalists who would make a large Advance on a good Speculation. He thinks there are and is to see me in order to confer more fully on that Subject also. I dress and go at twelve to see Mad.ᵉ de F—— at her Request. She says on my Arrival that we cannot be sure of being alone. Without pressing her in any Manner to a Conclusion we get into my Carriage to take an Airing. In the Course of the Ride she avows that an Appointment with my Friend the Bishop induces her to wish that not having received my Caresses she may meet him with a Heart more at Ease. I take this Matter up very handsomely and tell her that we must come to a fair Understanding and break off all farther Connection. That this will cost me infinite Pain but I can accomplish it and will. My Proposition is by no Means agreable and we finish on the Road to Neuilly by turning back to visit her Religieuse and thence to her own Lodgings. Arrived at the Convent every Appartment for Reception of Visitors (*Parloirs*) is occupied except that of Madame l'Abbesse. We proceed thither and while Mad.ᵉ de Trant is sent for we sacrifice to the Cyprian Queen in the Retreat consecrated to Chastity: 'In those deep Solitudes and awful Cells where heavenly pensive Contemplation dwells and ever musing Melancholy reigns.'. . . return *chez elle* . . . and I leave her to receive her Bishop with all the Sentiment which he may desire. Going down Stairs I meet Monsieur le Mari who asks me to set him down in the Rue S.ᵗ Honoré. On the Road he expresses a Wish to go as Minister to America and desires me to prevail on his Wife to consent to such a Step, should it become possible to obtain the Place. I promise to speak to her on the Subject *gaiement et galamment*. It will afford a Pretext for keeping him sometimes out of the Way. Call on Mess.ʳˢ Le Couteulx. Abroad. Go to the Tuilleries to meet Laurent; find there the Abbé Ronchon to whom I praise Burke's Book.[1] I am high in his good

---

[1] *Reflections on the French Revolution.*

Opinion, which is well because it is an Opinion which will procure
many others. Find Le Couteulx who gives me Information and
says that Montesquiou will call at Montmorin's after Dinner.
Go to Montmorin's and sit some Time with Madame. She expresses her Conviction that La Fayette is below his Business,
which is very true. She says that the Queen will not consent to
make her Husband Governor of the Children of France, that the
Aristocrats abhor him. At Dinner Bouinville comes in. I request him to get me back the Memoire I wrote on their Affairs,
which he promises to do if he can. After Dinner we converse about
the Play of this Evening, *Brutus*,[1] which is expected to excite
much Disturbance. After six oClock, as Montesquiou does not
come, Bouinville and I go to the Play; at leaving the Room, as
it is supposed that there will be three Parties in the House I cry
in a Stile of Rant: *je me déclare pour le Roi et je vole à la Victoire!*
We cannot find Seats, wherefore I go to the Loge of d'Angivilliers
and find that I was expected, having promised to come and then
forgotten it. Lord Wycombe is established here next to my
Friend in the Place which I occupied formerly. S.t Foi is here a
cunning Observer. I determine therefore to play them all three
and I think succeed pretty well. Propose to her to make the old
Fox believe she is attached to the young Lord, which she ex-
claims against. She is, however, resolved I think to attach him
and may perhaps singe her Wings while she flutters round that
Flame. The Piece excites a great Deal of Noise and Altercation
but the Parterre, filled with Democrats, obtains the Victory
clearly and having obtained it roars for above ten Minutes *Vive le
Roy!* After the Play a Motion is made to place the Bust of Voltaire on the Stage and crown it, which is complied with amid repeated Acclamations. I write for the Amusem.t of our Party these
Lines:

> See France in Freedom's Mantle gay
>   Her former State disdains
> Yet proud her fav'rite Bard t'obey,
>   Tho dead his Spirit reigns.

---

[1] Voltaire (1694-1778) wrote his *Brutus* during an early three years' exile in
England, while still at the stage of imitating Corneille. First performed in
Paris, 1730, with but little success.

The common Road to Pow'r he trod:
Cried pull all Tyrants down!
And making of the Mob a God
Has gain'd from them a Crown.

I give them to Madame, desiring her to pass them to my Lor.
He is well pleased with them and this, as it enables her to magnify
her Merits by those of her Friends, must of Course please her.
She wishes to fix an Appointment with me for Friday Morning
but I desire her to write her Hour in Season for me to reply, so
that if there be any Thing to prevent my Attendance I can inform
her. — She is a Coquette and unfaithful, therefore I must recover
my Empire over her and then *reward her Sensibility*. It has been
a fine Day.

Thursday 18. — This Morning I write. Paul Jones calls and
gives me his Time but I cannot lend him mine. At three I call on
Le Couteulx who was to have been at Home but is gone abroad
according to Custom. Going away at near four oClock he meets
me and is to see Montesquiou and me at an Hour to be fixed by
the former for Saturday. I go to the Garde des Sceaux's.[1] His
Domestics know not what to make of me, a Thing which frequently happens at my first Approach, because the Simplicity
of my Dress and Equipage, my wooden Leg and Tone of republican Equality, seem totally misplaced at the Levée of a Minister.
He is yet in his Closet. I find in the Circle no one of my Acquaintance except DuPont the Œconomist who never took Notice of a Letter I brought from his Son & seems a little ashamed of
it. The Reception of the Minister is flattering and his Attentions
great, so that those who had placed themselves next him feel
themselves misplaced. After Dinner he takes me aside to know
my Sentiments. I tell him that I consider the Revolution as a
Project that has failed. That the Evils of Anarchy must restore
Authority to the Sovereign. That he ought to continue a meer

---

[1] Champion de Cicé (1735–1810), in 1781 Archbishop of Bordeaux, and since
1789 Keeper of the Great Seals, affixing them to the Assembly's acts against
the clergy, their civil constitution, the nationalizing of church property, au-
thorizing as Minister what he abhorred as prelate. Delightful picture, Morris's
wooden peg, plain as church-door beggar's, alighting from the severity of a
London-built chariot, a shock to supercilious lackeys.

Instrument in the Hands of the Assemblée &cᵃ. As to himself, the Minister, he should when he quits his Place go directly from the King's Closet to his Seat in the Assembly and there become the Advocate of royal Authority. He approves of my Ideas except for himself, and says he has Need of Repose. This is idle, and I tell him so. Ask him whether it be true that he intends to resign as of this Day (Madᵉ had told me so last Evening, having learnt it from her Bishop). He says that he knows Nothing about it; that he shall retire whenever the King pleases. After our Conversation the Abbé d'Andrezelle has a long *Entretien*. He tells me of a Society formed for a Correspondence with the Provinces to counteract the Jacobins. I give him some Ideas on that Subject for which he expresses himself to be much obliged, and asks me to be present at one of their Meetings, which I consent to. Go from hence to Madᵉ de Chastellux's. She is abroad. Thence to Monsʳ Millet's. He and his fair one are at Home. We commence a little Conversation together which the old Gentleman would not like if he understood it in all its' Latitude. I make my Visit rather short and then call on Madᵉ de Corney. The Abbé Sabatier is here and the Revolution is quite out of Fashion. Go from hence to Madᵉ de Ségur's and in the Course of our Tête à Tête tell her, or rather remind her that I advised her Husband to be quiet when he should arrive here. Her Countenance is not silent but Respect for him keeps her Lips close. She would otherwise say that she had communicated that Advice and that he had despised it. From hence I return Home (I had called on Madᵉ de La Borde who was abroad) and write. The Weather is still pretty good, but having been sharp all Day softens much in the Evening, which seems to augur a Change.

Friday 19. — This Morning write a little. Visit my fair friend at her Appointment and stay till late.... The Bishop d'Autun comes in. He says that the Garde des Sceaux and Sᵗ Priest [Minister of Paris or the Interior] go out on Sunday and that Duport is to replace the former. De Lessart is to be made Superintendant of Finance. He presses me to stay Dinner but I go to the Palais royal. We meet here the Duc de Laval. After Dinner I have some Conversation with him and the Count de Thiare, from whence I apprehend that a serious Plan is laid for introducing Troops of

the Emperor in order to liberate the King and Queen and restore
the former Government. After Dinner go to the Comédie Française and sit with the Dutchess to hear *Brutus*. Thence to Mad.^e
de Ségur's where I take up Mad.^e de Chastellux. They lament to
me that La Fayette has lost his Influence. In the Way Home she
tells me that she is perswaded there will be an Effort made by the
Emperor in favor of his Sister. I hinted to the Comte de Thiare
the Advantages that would result from putting the Dauphin into
the Hands of Governors and sending him upon his Travels. Return Home and read. This Morning it rains but is afterwards
fair and pleasant Weather.

Saturday 20. — This Morning I write very little for Mr Olive
comes in and keeps me a long Time. We make some Progress in
our Business. Just after he leaves me Van Staphorst and M.^r
Pinson visit me. The latter goes away and Staphorst tells me he is
un petit intriguant, which I am disposed to believe. Dress and go
to Dinner at Van Staphorst's. We have Nothing here *de marquante*. At ½ past five I go to Le Couteulx's and it is after six
when Montesquiou arrives. We discuss the Affair of the Debt
to France and in the Result Le Couteulx and Swan are to make a
Proposition ToMorrow which we are on Tuesday to discuss at
Montesquiou's. ToMorrow M—— and I are to meet at Montmorin's at Dinner. After He is gone Le Couteulx brings me back
to consider the Shares and having agreed on them I mention to
him the Sale of Lands, which opens up his Griefs. He complains
bitterly of R. M.. Go from hence to Mad.^e de Chastellux's. She
has desired that whoever calls would visit *chez la princesse*. I
go thither and stay Supper tho my Friend had pressed me much
to pass the Evening *chez elle*, but it is proper to shew Indifference
as that will stimulate a little the Desire to retain me. *Nous verrons*. The English Embassadress passes a few Minutes at the
Palais royal but I do not know her till she is gone. The Weather
this Day has been pleasant. Different Accounts from the Banks
of the Loire mention terrible Ravages committed by an Inunda-
tion of that River.

Sunday 21. — This Morning write. Mr de Chaumont comes to
converse on the Claims resulting from Holker's Gestion and afterwards he mentions the Intention of many Gentlemen having

Estates in S! Domingue to go the next Spring to America. Richard calls and wants to have some Talk but I dismiss him. My friend desires to see me this Morning, which I decline gayly, and that produces an urgent Request. I comply with it but keep myself upon the *Ton* of cool Indifference. The Bishop comes in and as my Carriage was sent away he is grave. She makes to him the most pointed Overtures and I smile at the Artifice. Go from hence to Club and then to the Count de Montmorin's. Before Dinner the Duc de Liancourt & Montesquiou being there, in the Course of Conversation on the Actings and Doings of the Assemblée I say that the Constitution they have proposed is such that the Almighty himself could not make it succeed without creating a new Species of Men. After Dinner I converse a little with Montmorin about his own Situation. He feels himself very aukward, not knowing whether to stay or go, or staying what to do. Montesquiou comes up and asks Information from me respecting the Debt from America to France. In the Result of his Enquiries it is agreed between him and Montmorin that no Proposition shall be accepted without taking first my Opinion on it. Go from hence to Mad? de Ségur's. A little Comedy is acted here by the Children, the Subject of which is the Pleasure derived to the whole Family by an Infant of which the Countess was lately delivered. The Play is written by the Father,[1] to whom I address in the Course of it these lines:

> For perfecting the comic Art
> Let others take a single Part
> While you my friend, with nobler Soul
> Embrace at once the mighty Whole;
> For here we see arise from you
> The Subject, Play, and Actors too.

As soon as the Piece is finished I slip away. Mad? de La Fayette, who was here, reproaches me a little for deserting them. Mons! has long been giddy from his Elevation, when he is a little sober I will see whether he can any longer be useful either to his Country or mine. I rather doubt it. Go to the Louvre. Mad?

---

[1] At St. Petersburg the Comte de Ségur had written many little comedies, acted before the Empress in the Hermitage, so his hand was in.

has quarrelled with her Bishop who is jealous of me, and therefore I treat her with a Tenderness not intended. Mons.͞ de S.͞ Foi comes in and after him Montesquiou, so that I cannot, as otherwise I should have done, pour Balm into her Wounds. Return Home early. The Weather has been tolerable since Noon. In the Morning it rained.

Monday 22. — This Morning I employ in writing. Dine with the Dutchess of Orleans & at the Hour agreed on visit my Friend. She is surrounded by Friends and Serv.͞ᵗˢ, being very ill. After some Time she tells me that her Quarrel with the Bishop has occasioned her Sufferings. My Sensibilities are awakened and dictate the Language which Artifice would have wished on such an Occasion to speak. Finally I tell her that I came last Evening to know simply whether she meant to break with me, but finding that she was distressed my Views were confined to the giving of Relief. That I loved but little Yesterday but feel now all that she can desire. She has a difficult Business, poor Woman. Go to Madame de Ségur's and sit but a few Minutes. Take Mad.͞ᵉ de Chastellux Home and sit with her until it is pretty late before the Dutchess comes, who insists on our going to Supper. The Chevalier de Boufflers and myself. While they sup he shews me his Report on the Encouragement of the Arts, which is well drawn. I make one or two Observations for which he is obliged &c.͞ᵃ. Return Home at Twelve. The Weather has grown very mild.

Morris to Washington

November 22

... This unhappy country, bewildered in the Pursuit of metaphisical Whimsies, presents to our Moral View a mighty Ruin. Like the Remnants of antient Magnificence, we admire the Architecture of the Temple while we detest the false God to whom it was dedicated. Daws and Ravens and the Birds of Night now build their Nests in its Nitches. The Sovereign, humbled to the Level of a Beggar's Pity, without Resources, without Authority, without a Friend. The Assembly at once a Master and a Slave, new in Power, wild in Theory, raw in Practise. It engrosses all

Functions tho incapable of exercising any, and has taken from
this fierce ferocious People every Restraint of Religion and of
Respect. Sole Executors of the Law, and therefore supreme
Judges of its Propriety, each District Measures out its Obedience
by its Wishes, and the great Interests of the Whole, split up into
fractional Morsels, depend on momentary Impulse and ignorant
Caprice. Such a State of Things cannot last....

Tuesday 23. — This Morning write. M.ͬ Swan calls on me and
shews a Plan of Association drawn by Le Couteulx. I tell him that
I have nothing to say to it and am too busy to examine it. As to
the Plan which may be proposed, I shall give the Count de Montmorin my candid Opinion of it. Continue my writing and at two
call on Mad.ͤ de Flahaut who expects the Bishop and desires for
once to meet him without having any Thing to reproach herself.
She is too weak just now or I would make her feel this Wish. No
Matter. Call on Le Couteulx and take him to Montesquiou's.
On the Way I reprimand him very sharply for his Conduct. He
takes it high, and I let him go on till he ends by begging my Pardon and promising Amendment. Mad.ͤ Dubourg dines with us
and we renew our Acquaintance with much Warmth. After
Dinner we retire to the Cabinet and consider the Proposition to
be made, which is at length concluded on, and then I leave them
together to discuss some other Money Plan. Go to Mad.ͤ de
Chastellux's. We have a pretty numerous Circle which I leave
at ten and go to Mad.ͤ Dubourg's. There is a large Party collected here, among them Mad.ͤ de Beaumont. Return Home at
twelve. The Weather has been damp this Afternoon. In the
Morning it rained hard and indeed till near five oClock in the
Afternoon.

Wednesday 24. — This Morning write. Receive a Message
from Mad.ͤ de F—— while I am dressing and in Consequence of
it call upon her. L.ᵈ Wycombe comes in soon after me. There are
some Circumstances which I do not like. Go hence to the
Palais royal and from thence with Mad.ͤ de Chastellux to Bellevue.[1] A very kind Reception from the Count and Countess. Im-

---

[1] Built by the Pompadour, but now lived in by the King's old aunts, on
whom Count and Countess de Chastellux were in waiting.

mediately on my Return I go to the Louvre to require an Explanation but my Lord is established here. I therefore make my Visit short. Go to Le Couteulx's. Laurent has not yet begun his Memoire. Return Home and write. Thence to Mad.ᵉ de La Borde's where I make a short Visit. Thence to the Baron de Bezevald's who is not visible. Return to the Palais royal where I take Tea with the Dutchess & stay the Evening. The Chevalier de Bouflers shews me the Décret he has prepared, on which I make for him some Observations. Retire at Twelve. The Weather this Day has been dull but not otherwise disagreable.

Thursday 25. — This Morning write and send my Letters to the Post Office. Mad.ᵉ Petit arrives to know when I will visit Mad.ᵉ. I write a short Note promising a Visit perhaps for the last Time. Go thither and find Monsieur there. Our Conversation, frequently interrupted, is harsh on my Part, on hers a bitter Sweet. We go together for her Convent but bodily Pain obliges her to return as she cannot bear the Motion of the Carriage. We have an Explanation. She cannot bear the Idea of loosing me entirely but cannot be wholly mine. I therefore, in the Stile of tender Heroics, express my deep Regret that I must see her no more. This being done, the Rest is all Tenderness from me. On our Return I accompany her Upstairs to take a last Adieu. Interruptions prolong too much this Scene but at length I leave her convinced that I love her to Distraction but yet will not see her. ToMorrow, however, she is to send to me to know my Determination. If she should omit this I shall be handsomely catched in my own Net, at least for the present. Go hence to Le Couteulx's. He has not yet commenced his Memoire but will set about it this Afternoon. Go to Mad.ᵉ de Foucault's. I find that my Constitution begins to feel the Life I have led. Drowsiness, Languor and Want of Appetite are the Result. To remedy this I eat little. She talks to me in a Stile of Invitation and I think it will be easy to forget in her Arms my lovely Countess. *Nous verrons*. After Dinner I go to La Fayette's. Mad.ᵉ receives me coolly enough. I stay some Time leaning on the Chimney Piece. He comes out and as soon as he sees me approaches. Asks why I do not come to see him. I answer that I do not like to mix with the Crowd which I find here. That whenever I can be useful I am at his Orders. He desires me to call ToMorrow at three. Go hence to Madame de Ségur's. Stay till a little after eight and then come Home. The Weather has been raw and damp this Day.

Friday 26. — Altho I went to bed at half past eight I do not rise till half past nine. My fatigued Nerves feel more composed. Write a little. Mad: Petit comes with a Note which is written guardedly. She brings some Books also which I had desired, and a Cup. The latter I send back and write a little Note full of Tenderness. Dress and go to Houdon's whose Wife receives me à la française. Go thence to de Corney's. He is upon the Look out for Something and complains of La Fayette. Go thence to Mons: Millet's. He and his fair Companion are at Dinner. Stay a while and go thence to La Fayette's. Converse about Half an Hour. He asks my Opinion of his Situation. I give it *sans ménagement* and while I speak he turns pale. I tell him that the Time approaches when all good Men must cling to the Throne. That the present King is very valuable on Account of his Moderation and if he should possess too great Authority might be perswaded to grant a proper Constitution. That the Thing they call a Constitution which the Assemblée have framed is good for Nothing. That as to himself his personal Situation is very delicate. That he nominally but not really commands his Troops. That I really cannot tell how he is to establish Discipline among them but that unless he can accomplish that Object he must be ruined sooner or later. That the best Line of Conduct perhaps would be to seize an Occasion of Disobedience and resign, by which means he would preserve a Reputation in France which would be precious and hereafter useful. He says that he is only raised by Circumstances and Events, so that when they cease he sinks, and the Difficulty now is how to excite them. I take Care not to express even by a Look my Contempt and Abhorrence but simply observe that Events will arise fast enough of themselves if he can but make a good Use of them, which I doubt because I do not place any Confidence in his Troops. He asks what I think of a Plan in Agitation with Respect to the protesting Bishops, viz to withhold their Revenues. I tell him that the Assembly must turn them out of Doors naked if they wish the People to clothe them. He says he is a little afraid of that Consequence. I reiterate to him the Necessity of restoring the Nobility, at which of Course he flinches and says that he should like two Chambers as in America. I tell him that an American Constitution will not do for this Country & that two such Chambers would not answer where there is an hereditary Executive. That every Country must have a Constitution suited to its' Circumstances, and the State of France requires a higher toned Government than that of England. He starts at this with Astonishment. I pray him to remark that England is surrounded by a deep Ditch and being only assailable by Sea can permit many Things at Home which would not be safe in different Situations. That her Safety depends on her Marine, to the Preservation of which every Right and Privilege of her Citizens is sacrificed. That in all possible Governments the first Care must be general Preservation. I mention de Corney and his Grievances. He tells me the intended Ministers, one of whom dines with us. They are all taken from among the People and thus without knowing it the People will find an additional Tie to the Great Envy of their Fellows. Go hence to Madᵉ de F—— and tell her that I will continue to visit her for a Month and then either accept her Cup or leave her entirely. She feels this a little but will feel it much more I think. A continued Scene of Interruption prevents us from doing what is proper. I go at eight to Madᵉ de Chastellux's and stay till near ten. She has a fever. The Dutchess is much agitated and distressed. Poor Woman. We have had a tolerably pleasant Day tho a little showery.

Saturday 27. — Write. Mʳ Richard calls and promises to favor me with another Visit to Morrow. Mʳ Olive visits me. His friends have already engaged in Speculations to the Isle of France which prevent them from undertaking any Thing in our Funds. Go to the Louvre and as Madᵉ is alone I seize the Moment to enjoy. Very soon after, some Visitors come in. We go to Madˡˡᵉ Duplessis and she being not ready we go to the Champs de Mars. Return and take her up. I find that my Plan with Madᵉ works pretty well. Call on Madᵉ de Chastellux and promise another Visit. Pass at Home to enquire if Le Couteulx has written to me, which he has not. Go to the Louvre and dine. She tells me this Morning that the Bishop is well with the Queen. *Cela s'entend.*

MARQUIS DE LA FAYETTE
From a drawing by Duvivier, Musée du Louvre

She tells me that De Moustiers spoke illy of me at Mad.ᵉ D'Angivilliers. He is wrong. Lord Wycombe calls after Dinner and is
seated à Côté comme d'usage. She offered the other Day not to see
him if I desired it but I refused. This I presume she expected in
making the Offer. I go to Le Couteulx's who is abroad. Thence
to Mad.ᵉ de Chastellux's. She is still indisposed. The Dutchess
is here. I go to Mad.ᵉ de La Borde's. She is abroad, wherefore I
come Home. It has been a very pleasant Day.

   Sunday 28. — This Morning M.ʳ Richard calls and before he is
gone M.ʳ Swan enters. He shews me a Plan of Memoire by Le
Couteulx which is very objectionable. At two I visit du Portail,
the new Minister at War, and go from thence to the Louvre.
L.ᵈ Wycombe is here and has had the whole Morning, say from
ten to two. He goes away, being pressed by Mad.ᵉ to return in
the Evening. She says he told her that she loved me, which at
first she laughed at but afterw.ᵈˢ seriously refuted. I do the needful Act immediately and presently after we receive Visitors. She
insists on my partaking of her Dinner. Mons.ʳ seems displeased.
After Dinner she sends me with Mad.ˡˡᵉ Duplessis to visit Mad.ᵉ de
Guibert who gives me an Eulogy on her late Husband by one of
his Friends. When we return my Lord is established à Côté. The
Marquis de Montesquiou is merry at having found them so situated. I tell him of Le Couteulx's Memoire and he promises to
call there To Morrow. I leave this Society and visit Mad.ᵉ de
Chastellux, then return Home. The Conversation at this last
Visit was quite high in the aristocrat Tone. The Idea of carrying
off the King is mentioned. My fair friend talk'd to me of presenting to L.ᵈ Wycombe the Cup formerly given to me and which I
had sent back. I think it probable that she has already bestowed
it on him. The Weather was pleasant this Morning but is grown
very cold this Evening.

   Monday 29. — M.ʳ Swan calls this Morning and shews me the
Draft of his Memoire which I correct. We then go together to
visit Le Couteulx who is gone out. This is quite in Style for him
and I think Business cannot prosper in his Hands. I return Home
and go from thence to Mad.ᵉ de Foucault's. Sit with Chaumont
and Hint the Idea of a Sale of the Delaware Works. He thinks
my Plan will probably succeed. Look over sundry Papers re-

specting Holker's Accounts. Go from thence to the Arsenal and visit Mad? Lavoisier and Madame de Caumont. From thence I pass at Home where I find a Billet from Mad? who wishes me to go to the Play. I go to dine at Mons? de Montmorin's. La Fayette comes in and Mad? de Montmorin observes that he does not seem very glad to see me. She asks the Reason. I tell her that I lately told him some Truths which differed so much from the Style of Flattery he has been accustomed to that he is not well pleased with it. Montmorin observes that La Fayette has not Abilities enough to carry through his Affairs. He says that within a Month past Things have appeared to him much worse than they were. He seems apprehensive of a Visit from foreign Powers and that the Count d'Artois and Prince of Condé may play a deep Game. *Nous verrons.* I go to the Play with Madame de Beaumont and am placed luckily opposite to my fair friend. I know not whether she observes me but if she does it will be useful. Go from the Play to Mad? de Chastellux's where I meet the Count de Ségur. I sit with them till eleven. This is a Republican Society. It has threatened Snow all Day.

Tuesday 30. — This Morning M? Richard calls to tell me of an Opportunity for Philadelphia. I give him a Letter and sit down to write. A Note from my Friend to which I do not reply. About three call there but she is abroad. Go to Le Couteulx's and leave with him another Letter. He says he wants to see me and I promise to dine with him one Day. Call on M? Grand who also presses me to stay Dinner which I decline. I ask him the Character of M? de Lessart.[1] He says he is a Man of good Sense but not a great Man. Le Couteulx seems to count upon him as a sure Friend. Go to the Palais royal but the Dutchess dines abroad, wherefore I go to Club. The Restorateur is not a good one. His Wine is very bad. Go from hence to Mons? Millet's where I find another *Entreteneur et Entretenue*. Make my Visit short. Call at Mad? de Ségur's. She is in Bed. Wishes to know the Purport of my Conversation with La Fayette. I tell her that I told him many serious Truths which were not to his Taste. I take the Vicomte

---

[1] De Lessart (1742–1792), Neckerist, Montmorin's successor for Foreign Affairs, accused for intriguing with Vienna, suppressing Austrian notes and his answers.

de Ségur to Madᵉ de Chastellux's where he reads a little Comedy
called *Le Nouveau Cercle* which is not without Merit, but he reads
too well to judge of it. For the Rest he has made himself the
principal Character of the Piece. Lady Cary is here, an Irish
Woman who has I believe the Merit of keeping a good House in
Paris. Leave this at a little after nine and go to the Louvre.
My Lord is here of Course. An Observation which I make on the
Assignats strikes him very forcibly. If I am not much mistaken
he will quote it. His Manner of seizing it shews a discerning
Mind. My friend apologizes for being abroad. Had I told her I
would call she would have staid at Home. I reply coolly that I
came late that I might not interrupt her Conversations with her
new Friend. She feels this cutting Sarcasm. She passed the Day
with the Bishop whose Leg is hurt. A Strain of the Ancle. I let
her make Enquiries about the Play where I believe she did not
see me, and my Answers will be a little disquieting I think. Get
Home at twelve. The Conversation of this Evening will make its
Impression.

DECEMBER 1790

Morris to Washington

Paris 1 December 1790

George Washington Esqʳ
private

Dear Sir
   I had the Honor to address to you a Letter on the twenty second
of last Month in the Close of which I mentioned the Intention of
saying at a future Period some few Words of the People who are
now on the Stage. To begin then with our friend Lafayette who
has hitherto acted a splendid Part. Unfortunately both for him-

self and his Country he has not the Talents which his Situation requires. This important Truth known to the few from the very Begining is now but too well understood by the People in general. His Authority depends on Incidents and sinks to nothing in a Moment of Calm, so that if his Enemies would let him alone his twinkling Light would expire. He would then perhaps raise Commotions in Order to quell them. This his Enemies have long charged him with, unjustly I believe, but I would not answer for the future. The King obeys but detests him. He obeys because he fears. Whoever possesses the royal Person may do what he pleases with the royal Character and Authority. Hence it happens that the Ministers are of Lafayette's Appointment. A short Description of their Use was given the other Day by Mirabeau. We make Ministers, says he, as we used formerly to send Servants to keep our Boxes at the Playhouse. I gave you the Explanation of this Jest while I was in London. Lafayette thinks that these his Creatures will worship their Creator, but he is mightily mistaken. You know du Portail, the Minister of War. He is said to be violent in favor of the Revolution. It is more than a Year since I have seen him, excepting a short Visit of Congratulation the other Day. My Judgment therefore should have little Weight, but I believe he is too much the Friend of Liberty to approve of the Constitution. For the Rest, he has as you know that Command of himself and that Simplicity of exterior Deportment which carry a Man as far as his Abilities will reach. He may perhaps remember his Creator in his ministerial Youth, in Order that his Days may be long in the Land of Office; but I venture to predict that his duteous Observance will not endure one Half Second beyond the Moment of Necessity. I believe I did not mention to you, about a year ago, the Intention to appoint him; but at that Time I endeavored to take his Measure. The Minister of the Marine I know nothing about. They say he is a good kind of Man, which is saying very little. The Keeper of the Seals, Monsieur du Port de Tertre, was a Lawyer of Eminence thrown up into Notice by the Circumstances of the Moment. He is said to possess both Abilities and Firmness. Monsieur de Lessart, the Minister of the Finances, is rather above than below Mediocrity, and possesses that kind of civil Assent which never compromises the Possessor, tho it seldom travels in Company with Greatness.

There is not a Man among them fitted for the great Tasks in which they are engaged, and greater Tasks are perhaps impending. I have no Proofs, but I have a well founded Opinion that the Leaders of one Party wish what those of the other fear and both expect, viz the Interference of foreign Powers. One previous Step would be to carry off, if possible, the King and Queen. The latter at least, for there is every Reason to apprehend for their Safety should violent Measures be adopted while they are here. . . .

Wednesday 1 *December.* — This Morning write. Dine with Madame de Guibert. She is disappointed in the Rest of her Guests. Mad.ᵉ de Flahaut sent an Excuse at half past three which produced no small Vexation. I had my Share. Visit Madame de Ségur and then go to the Louvre. She is just come Home and L.ᵈ Wycombe is with her. I stay but a little while and refuse to return. Come Home and take Tea. I find several Letters which are extremely disquieting.

Thursday 2. — I rise this Morning before Day after a Night of sleepless Anxiety. Sit down to write by Candle Light and get my Letters finished in Season. Receive a Note from Mad.ᵉ de Flahaut desiring me to come between ten and eleven as she is to visit Mad.ᵉ d'Angiviliers at Half past twelve. I find her ill and complaining. I have not the Disposition either to quarrel or enjoy. Mons.ʳ desires me twice to remind her at a quarter after twelve that she is to visit her Sister. I tell her that every Post since I have been here brings me afflicting Intelligence. She wishes to know what it is but I tell her that is unnecessary, I mention it in general that she may not be surprized at my Behaviour. At twelve L.ᵈ Wycombe calls and stays; I remind her repeatedly of her Engagement to her Sister and stay him out, for which I apologize to her. Go to M.ʳ Swan's in Consequence of a Note from him. He shews me the Memoire that is agreed on. Also the Draft of an Association. I do not approve of either but I shall not oppose. Call on the Bishop d'Autun and leave my Name. On Mad.ᵉ de La Tour the same and also on Mad.ᵉ de La Borde. Thence to Le Couteulx's. He is abroad. Mad.ᵉ is going

out and is Half stripped when I enter. During the few Minutes
which I stay she mentions a curious Anecdote of the Count de
Pilau. He is become devout to a most astonishing Degree and in
all the Bigotry of the romish Church. A Man who was driven by
the Priesthood from Spain on Account of his Religion or rather the
Want of it. A Man who abandoned an immense Fortune for the
Sake of avoiding exterior Ceremonies. O God! how weak, how
inconstant, how wretched is Man. Go to the Palais royal and
dine. After Dinner go to the Italiennes. A very good Piece is performed, *Euphrosine.* Go from thence to the Louvre. My Lord
comes out as I enter. She says he is to pass to Morrow Morning
with her. Owns a vast Friendship for him. — No Love. — This is
all very well. *Mais chacun à son Tour.* I stay the Evening and
take Mad.^lle Duplessis Home. Poor Thing, I believe I might make
a Progress with her if I would, but that is detestable. The
Weather has been pleasant this Day with high Westerly Wind.
My Bosom is torn with Anxiety and I find in my left Arm as well
as in my left Breast a phisical Sense of Grief.

Friday 3. — This Morning write, then go to Mad.^lle Martin's
and buy a Pot of Rouge for my Sister, afterwards to Dinner at
Mad.^e Foucault's. I arrive very late. Shew Chaumont after Dinner a Plan for the Sale of Lands combined with public Debt.
He is to consider of it. I have some little Conversation with Mad.^e
tending towards *Amitié.* Go from hence to the Louvre. Mad.^e de
Vergennes enters just before me. She gives us a pleasant Description of the last Arrest of Monsieur and Madame Necker during
their Retreat from France. To this she adds a Trait of Meanness
to their Conductors. In all Probability the Picture is highly
charged. After Mad.^e de Vergennes is gone we trifle but do nothing;
she declines on Account of bodily Pain and I do not press. I tell
her that she will soon love me violently; rally her on her Connection with My Lord who is to be here this Evening again, not
having had an Opportunity to converse as he wished this Morning.
She offers me a Present which he made her but I tell her I will
accept of Nothing but a Picture of her now in the Possession of
her Bishop and that I will have it. That if I continue in Paris she
will love me as much as ever but if I go away she will forget me.
She begins to feel the former Part of this Prediction and the latter

she has long known. Go to Mad.ᵉ de Chastellux's. We have here a Reading by the Vicomte de Ségur. The Piece is well imagined to produce theatrical Effect altho not strictly fitted for Representation. There is but little Merit in the Versification which shews a willing Muse but one whose Favors are not worth courting. From hence I go to Mad.ᵉ de La Borde's and between ten and eleven return, according to my Promise, to the Louvre. Support still the Gaiety which mingled with a little Sensibility charms. My fair one is delighted, perhaps in the Success of her Deceptions. *N'importe*. She says she has laughed much at her Lord who still holds his Resolution of going away next Monday. I think my fair friend you will try to prevent it. This has been a rainy Day. I take Home Mad.ˡˡᵉ Duplessis.

Saturday 4. — This Morning write a little and then go by Appointment to the Louvre. Mad.ᵉ is in a terrible fret. Has written a long Letter of Expostulation to her Bishop, who declined receiving a Visit from her because he would come out and call on her but yet he staid at Home and received two other fair friends. I laugh at her Resentment and tell her that if he goes on this Way my Affairs are desperate. L.ᵈ Wycombe enters and I leave them together which she is very glad of. I visit Van Staphorst who tells me Short has agreed for the first Loan of ᶠ2.500.000 at five p%. He is to allow 4½ of Charges. As I have received Propositions from them for the Purchase of Stock I am confirmed in the Opinion that this Loan is for a domestic Speculation. Visit Madame de Vannoise who is abroad. Thence to Mad.ᵉ de Corney's. Converse with her about her Situation. She asks if Short's Fate is determined as this House would suit him. I tell her not yet, but enquire into Circumstances relating to it for the Position is very good for an American Minister. Go hence to Mad.ᵉ du Moley's. She is not visible. Thence to Mad.ᵉ de Chastellux's with whom I stay some Time and then go to dine with Le Couteulx. After Dinner propose to him to make an Arrangement with the Farm about what Congress owe them. He desires me to call on him ToMorrow Morning. Go from hence to the Louvre. Mad.ᵉ is abroad. Thence to Mad.ᵉ de Ségur's. Sit with her some Time. Return to the Louvre. My fair one is returned and her Lord is with her. The Bishop comes in shortly after and is vexed to find us here. I mention to him the Idea that he ought to obtain if possible the Embassy to Vienna. I desire him to think of this. Sit some Time and then leave them (L.ᵈ Wycombe went out soon after the Bishop entered) much displeased with her Conduct and I let her see it. She has just now much the Advantage of me. This has been a very rainy disagreable Day.

Sunday 5. — This Morning I write and then call on Le Couteulx. The Memoire of Swan presented last Evening to the Assembly has been referred to the Committee of Finance. We discuss together my Plan relating to the Tobacco Debt of Congress. Laurent is well pleased with it and says he will get the Business done this Week. We take a Ride together in which he tells me somewhat of his own Situation and Intentions. He says that they have now a great Command of Money. After setting him down I go to dine with the Count de Montmorin. Ternant dines here. After Dinner Montesquiou comes in but I continue in Conversation with Madᵉ de Beaumont till he goes away. I think this will prevent a Suspicion which is rising. Go from hence to Madᵉ de Chastellux's and take Tea, then return Home and write. This has been a tolerably pleasant Day but it rained hard in the Morning.

Monday 6. — This Morning is employed in writing. At half past two Sir John Miller visits me and talks of Weights and Measures. Go to dine at the Palais royal and after Dinner visit Monsʳ de La Fayette. He is in a Peck of little Troubles. I make my Visit short. Madame's Reception is *à la Glace*. Return to the Palais royal and take Madᵉ de Chastellux to the Louvre. At coming away Madᵉ de F—— desires me to take her to Madᵉ de Corney's. On the Way she makes Approaches which I receive with perfect Coldness. On our Return she enquires the Reason. I tell her that my Reception when I last saw her was such that if Madᵉ de Chastellux had not asked me to bring her I should not have given the Trouble of my Visits. She hopes I will continue to see her as heretofore. I am silent. Arrived at the Louvre I hand her out and am about to return but she insists on my going up. Arrived there I take Leave but am perswaded to stay a little while. She attempts Explanation but I stop her by the Assurance that my Opinion is made up so that she may spare herself the

Trouble. Her Pride speaks a high Language but that cannot hold. She then either is or pretends to be ill. . . . What a Winter she must pass &c.. Mons!° comes up and after a few Words I again take Leave, but she begs me in English to stay. The Bishop comes in. I speak to him again on the Subject of an Embassy to Vienna, and mark out the Means of succeeding. I tell him that at present it is equally dangerous to be in or out of the Assembly. That a foreign Employ is the only Means of preserving himself *en évidence* and that if he can make himself the confidential Man between the Queen and her Brother he will be in the strait Road to Greatness whenever Circumstances will render it desirable. After he is gone I stay a few Minutes and then follow him, notwithstanding she presses me to stay. The Weather this Day has been pretty good.

Tuesday 7. — This Morning I sit down to write but a Letter from London renders me incapable of pursuing my Business. Dress. A Message from Mad.° de Flahaut desiring me to take her & Mad.ᵉ Duplessis to ride. Go thither and as she is alone I tell her that I must go to London and why. She bursts into Tears and offers me all the Money she has. She then assures me that I have misinterpreted her Conduct. Tells me how she parted with L.ᵈ Wycombe, who is I think much in Love without knowing it. We perform the Rites of the Cyprian Goddess. Go to the Bois de Boulogne and walk. Return. I set them down and go to dine with Mad.° Foucault who is vastly kind. Converse on Affairs with Chaumont. Call at the Louvre and take my Ladies to the Opera, thence to Supper at the Louvre. Much Satisfaction reigns this Day. There is reason to believe that my fair friend is pregnant. A very fine Day.

Wednesday 8. — This Morning I rise early and write. Go out at ten and visit Le Couteulx to whom I mention my intended Journey to London. Go from thence to M.ʳ Grand's and deliver him a Bill of Exchange from De Wolf for 2000#. I receive a Letter from Le Couteulx's Clerk brought by the English Mail urging my Departure. Go to the Louvre according to my Promise and find my fair Friend in Bed writing to her Lord. . . . We take up Mademoiselle Duplessi and visit Madame de Guibert. Return to the Louvre and dine. In the Evening go to the Palais royal and

attend the reading of a Tragedy written by Mons? de Sabran [1]
at fourteen Years of Age. It is very well written but before it is
finished I am called away by Mons? de Flahaut. Return to the
Louvre and sup.... We are just now well together but I have
said every Thing to Day which can affect a Woman who has
Pride, Sentiment or Affection, and she has a good Share of each.
We shall see how Things are at my Return. I lend her 1200# in
Paper to redeem so much Gold which she had pawned. I do not
expect to be repaid. This has been a rainy disagreable Day. At
my Return Home I write.

Thursday 9. — I did not get to Bed till after one and am up this
Morning at six. Dress and breakfast. At three Quarters after
seven I leave Paris and get in two Hours and an Half three Posts
and an Half to Luzarche where we change in five Minutes and go
in an Hour a Post and a Quarter to Chantilly.[2] The Loss of some
Screws detains me an Hour and twenty Minutes to get them repaired and then in an Hour and five Minutes we go to Lingueville a Post and an Half. We change in a Quarter and go in fifty
Minutes two Posts to Clermont en Beauvoisois, a Post and a
Quarter. Change again in a Quarter and go in an Hour and fifty
Minutes two Posts to S? Juste. Another Quarter is spent in changing and then fifty Minutes bring us a Post to Le Wavigny at six
oClock. Half an Hour is consumed by greasing our Wheels and
then in an Hour and twenty Minutes we go a Post and an Half
to Breteuil. Change in ten Minutes and go a Post and an Half in
an Hour and an Half to Flers. We are detained twenty Minutes
here in changing Horses and then in an Hour we go one Post to
Hebecourt. Change in a Quarter and then go in an Hour a Post
to Amiens, which we reach at five Minutes after twelve.

---

[1] Little Elzéar de Sabran, son of the widowed Marquise de Sabran who had
great artistic gifts, an out-size mop of curls, and a lifelong passion for Chevalier
de Boufflers not rewarded by marriage till they are both middle-aged refugees.

[2] The shiftiness of Parker and Rogers demands a breathless dash to London;
relays of horses and postillions work their allotted span, it is the passenger's
endurance which commands respect. Clattering watch in hand through the
night, sailing the Channel in three hours, it could have been sixty from door
to door if Gentlemen of the Road had not made sleeping at Rochester prudent.
Channel steamers only treble the sailboat's speed, but the train takes six hours
as against twenty-six of actual posting; the rest was greasing, watering and
changing horses, repairs, a hurried meal.

Friday 10. — At Amiens we are detained half an Hour and we consume one and twenty five Minutes in a Post and an Half to Picquigny. Another Half Hour is required to change and one and a Quarter to go to Flixcourt, one Post. We change Horses in a Quarter of an Hour and in an Hour and an Half go a Post and a Quarter to Ailly le haut Clocher. Change again in a Quarter and in one and a Quarter go to Abbeville. We enter it just at Daybreak and alight at seven o'Clock. Here we have the Carriage greased and take some Refreshment, which takes up an Hour and ten Minutes. As we go out I see a Carriage which we passed Yesterday while it was under Repair. A Gentleman in it with his Servant going the same Route. In an Hour and a Quarter we reach Nouvion where in ten Minutes we change and run the next Post to Bernay in Half an Hour, which is the most rapid Movement I have yet made in France or indeed in Europe. We change in five Minutes and go the next Post to Nampont in forty Minutes. Ten Minutes to change and one Hour and twenty Minutes, a Post and an Half, to Montreuil. Here I find the Landlord of a public House at Boulogne and send him forward to order Horses, prepare Dinner and engage a Passage Boat. We change Horses in ten Minutes and in an Hour and twenty Minutes go a Post and an Half to Cormont, where again we change in ten Minutes and go in fifty a Post to Samers. Ten Minutes more to change and an Hour and thirty five for the remaining two Posts bring us to the British Hotel in Boulogne at three Quarters after four. I wait Dinner till seven for Mr —— who does not get in till after eight, having broken down on the Road. After Dinner Morpheus, aided by a Bottle of Burgundy, takes full Possession of my Faculties. Indeed his restorative Balm is requisite both for Body and Mind. At half past eleven we go on Board of the Passage Boat & the Weather being dismal, dull, rainy and with but little Wind I get at once into my Birth [sic].

Saturday 11. — This Morning at three we come out of the Harbor of Boulogne and very shortly after we are out a Breeze springs up from the Westward which continues to freshen and blows smartly. We make the Folkestone Light House before six and run off the Mouth of the Harbor of Dover where we beat off and on, there not being Water enough to go in. At Day Light a Boat

comes off in which we embark with my little Baggage and at
eight o'Clock I am safe in the City of London Inn at Dover.
The Hotel at Boulogne is pretty good and cheap. The Boatman
made us pay a Guinea for his Aid, observing that his Price depended always upon the Weather, which is reasonable enough;
at least it contains what Candid calls the sufficient Reason.
When he took us on Board it was blowing pretty hard and rising
every Instant so that I had full Use for my only Leg in getting
from the one Vessel into the other. Luckily the Wind rather
ranges along than blows on the Shore so that under Cover of a
small jutting Point in the Beach we landed smoothly. An Hour
and ten Minutes are employed at Dover in getting my Breakfast
and in entering my Baggage. In two Hours and a Quarter I reach
the Fountain Inn at Canterbury, a little better than 16 Miles, for
which mine Host makes me pay 14^d per Mile. Thence we proceed
in ten Minutes and reach the George at Sittingburn in two Hours
and five Minutes, a like Distance of about 16 Miles, rather less.
We change here in five Minutes and in an Hour and an Half we
go eleven Miles to Rochester where we arrive at a Quarter after
three, and there I determine to put up because if I go on to London, which I should reach in about four Hours, it would expose
me at the worst Hours and in the worst Places to the Chance of
Highway Robbery and I think I can be in early enough Tomorrow, that is I can be dressed in London as soon as they are out of
Bed. Had I proceeded I should have been in sixty Hours from
Paris, say by this Route 260 Miles. The Weather this Day is dull
and disagreable.

Sunday 12. — At seven this Morning I leave Rochester and go
in two Hours and five Minutes over a Hilly Road 14 Miles to
Dartford. Stay there half an Hour and then come on in two Hours
and an Half 16 Miles to Mr Phyn's in Mark Lane. A cordial and
friendly Reception here but a very disagreable Account of the
State of M.r Rogers's Affairs. Parker has ruined him. After Dinner I visit M.r Rogers who acknowleges that he has treated me
very ill and is very desirous of making Reparation. He acknowleges the Justice of my Claim to a Preference on the Debt which
is entered in the Names of the Trustees. I desire him to state to
me the situation of that Debt, which he promises, also to call on

me ToMorrow Morning. Return Home and eat some Oysters.
I flatter myself, perhaps vainly, to struggle thro this Scrape.
The *Pigou* I heard this Morning is arrived. She sent up her Letters from Dover Yesterday Afternoon, having put them on Shore
about 4 o'Clock.

Monday 13. — This Morning I write. M.ʳ Rogers calls and
seems still desirous of doing all he can to repair the Wrongs he
has committed. After he is gone L.ᵈ Wycombe comes and speaks
about the Convention with Spain. It is of Course to be opposed
but I think they will be very feeble for certainly this Nation has
gained much by it. Go to Mess.ʳˢ Phyn, Ellices and Inglis's & give
Inglis the State of a Case I have drawn for the Opinion of Counsel
on M.ʳ Rogers's Affairs. Stay Dinner to meet the Attorney who
comes in about six oClock. We discuss the Affair together but he
is quite an Attorney, and endeavors to raise as many Objections
as he can. Receive a Note from Temple Franklin and go to look
for him at Osborne's Hotel. Find with him a female fellow Passenger, a french Woman who left her Husband on board the Ship
off Portsmouth. She is handsome. Receive from him many Letters and Packets which I bring Home and sit till near two reading
them. This has been a very rainy stormy Day.

Tuesday 14. — This Morning I call on M.ʳ Rogers and desire
him to make out a State of his Sales, which he promises. He
shews me an Assignment by Parker of Property in Puller's Hands.
He is to give me farther Particulars. I desire him to send out a
Power of Attorney to attach Parker's Property in the Hands of
Hasgill and others, which he sets about immediately. Go from
hence to visit the french and spanish Embassadors who are
abroad. Thence to R. Penn's and stay a few Minutes with the
Ladies. Thence to Lord Landsdowne's and the Dutchess of Gordon's — abroad. Thence to the Duke of Leeds' Office. He is not
yet come. Thence to M.ʳ Ogden's where I see Governor Franklin.
Thence to M.ʳ Low's. She is at her Toilette. Thence to M.ʳˢ
Church's. She is out of Town. Thence to Mark Lane to Dinner.
Converse after Dinner with Phyn, who tho he is sore under the
Situation to which we have reduced him tells me in a manly Manner that he will bear us out in it. Return Home about two oClock
in the Morning. The Wind is at Southwest and begins to blow

hard. The Day was fine. Andrew Elliot it is said is appointed Minister to the United States. [Only a rumor.]

Wednesday 15. — This Morning write a little. Mr Franklin calls and we go to see Mrs Church together. From thence I go to my Brother's out of Town and get Home Time enough to dress for Dinner at the Marquis of Landsdowne's. Ld Wycombe is at the House of Commons. I press the Marquis to go to France as I had promised that I would. He says he cannot without Leave from his Son. He repeats this after his Son joins us and it excites in him a Degree of Indignation and Contempt not feebly expressed in his Countenance. I return Home about ten. The Wind blew very hard all Night and was high from the Northwest all Day. It begins to lull this Evening. The Greenness of the Fields in this Season is highly pleasing.

Thursday 16. — This Morning I write a little and then go to the American Fund Office to have the Stock transferred out of the Names of Rogers and Parker; it is put upon the Names of two of the Trustees, subject to a Decision of the Claims made thereon by me and by his Creditors on private Account. We are detained here a long Time and must attend again on the Affair ToMorrow. Go from hence to Mr R. Penn's to Dinner and after Dinner visit the french Embassador. From thence to the Coffee House where I sup with Penn, Thornhill and a Mr Hat.(?) The Wine was bad at Dinner and the Spirit is bad at Supper. The Weather has this Day been dull drizly and disagreable.

Friday 17. — Mr Low calls on me and I take him into the City. Meet there the Assignees of Rogers to execute some Writings, which not being finished we are to call for the Purpose ToMorrow. I speak to Mr Henchman about the future Conduct of this Business and he seems inclinable to my Views. Call on Mrs Phyn who is dressing. Take up a Dog brought from Newfoundland for me. Go Home and write. Mr Franklin and his Father call. I take the young Man to dine with the french Embassador. After Dinner we have a long Conversation on the Affairs of France. Bring Franklin Home to eat Oysters. He gives me a curious Account of M.^{rs} Le Couteulx de Caumont who is it seems very much of a Whore. The Weather has this Day been wet with Westerly Wind. In the Evening it begins to blow.

Saturday 18. — This Morning I go into the City and execute the Writings agreed on. Thence to Mark Lane. M.ʳ Lane, Parker's Clerk, tells me that there is a Certificate pledged with Puller by Parker which prevents his final Settlement with Van Staphorsts from whom he is to receive Money and therefore he advises me to take it up by Way of securing myself. *Quere* however the Amount. M.ʳ Inglis asks me if they can rely on the Receipt of what I gave them Reason to expect in my Letter from Antwerp. I give him Information of what I have done on that Subject. M.ʳ Ellice tells me that News are arrived from Quebec of a large Army being in the Indian Country under the Command of Gen.ˡ S.ᵗ Clair who had sent to the commanding Officer at Detroit to desire that he would not furnish the Indians with any Arms or Ammunition, as that would be considered tantamount to a Commission of Hostilities. He says that this News excites much Alarm in the City lest it should induce Hostilities with America. I tell him that I have no such Apprehension. Sit a while with M.ʳˢ Phyn and then go to the Office of the Duke of Leeds. His Grace is in Council but that breaks up while I am here. M.ʳ Burgess comes to tell me that the Duke is very much engaged. He talks a great Deal but, stripping off the Compliment and Profession, what he says amounts to no more than that sundry Cabinet Counsels have been held on the Treaty with America and that a Reference has been made of the Affair three Months ago to L.ᵈ Hawkesbury whose Report has not yet been received. I answer to all this very drily that I have presented myself to let them know that I am alive. That I shall write from hence to America. That I leave Town next Week. That I will wait on the Duke at such Time as he may indicate. That if I learn nothing more than that Things are just as I left them, I shall meerly say so. That it may be worth their while to consider whether the Measures proposed last Session in Congress respecting the Commerce with this Country may not be adopted and what the Consequences would be. Go from hence to L.ᵈ Landsdowne's and leave Cards for him and L.ᵈ Wycombe. Thence to dine with M.ʳ Church. Sit late. The Weather has been wet and cold all Day. This Evening it is frosty.

Sunday 19. — M.ʳ Lane calls this Morning and tells me that Parker has not left a single Paper behind him. M.ʳ Thornhill calls and says he will try to get a Pointer for R. M. jun.ʳ. Dress and visit Mʳˢ Penn and Miss Masters. The latter says she would take £10.000 Stᵍ for her Estate near Phila?. I go to Genˡ Morris's where we dine *en famille* and I stay all Night. This has been a sleety nasty cold Day.

Monday 20. — This Morning I come to Town and stop at the House of Mʳ Rogers. Make a Sketch of the Account between us as it ought to be stated and desire him to compleat it. I find that he has kept the whole Account as a joint Concern with Parker, and that it is ballanced so as to leave the present Property a Profit. If to this be added the Sum they have received from it of the Trustees it can in no Point of View be considered as less than £10.000 Stᵍ gained. If I take the Remainder at its Value, about £10000, there will be a Ballance uncovered of £5000 and if Half of this be carried to the Credit of Parker in his Account with Rogers he will still be in Debt to the Amount of above £12000, which Sum he has wormed out of the other. I walk Home and dress. Go to dine with Bourdieu where I meet Mʳ Franklin. We sit till nine oClock and then visit at the french Embassador's. Abroad. I go to the Piazza Coffee House to eat Sprats which are very good, but they have it seems so bad a Smell that it is necessary to be in a Room by one's Self. My Supper, Small beer, Fire and Lights are charged 1/9, the cheapest Thing I ever met with in London. I pay however 3/6. This has been a very fine Day after Yesterday's Storm.

Tuesday 21. — This Morning I write. Lᵈ Wycombe calls with a young Gentleman whom he announces as a Lord but who seems by Look and Language to be a foreigner. I ask him carelessly if he has any News from France. He says he has recᵈ a Letter but it contains nothing particular. I call on Mʳˢ Low who is not at Home and on Mʳ Ogden who is going into the City. Dine with Mʳˢ Penn. We are to go to the Play. He returns about five oClock from his Election, being chosen for one of Lord Lonsdale's Boroughs. [Haslemere.] We go to the Theatre and see Mʳˢ Siddons [1] act very well in a very bad Piece *Isabella*.[2] Go from hence to the

---

[1] Too stately for light comedy, Sarah Siddons tore the hearts of her audiences.

[2] One of Mrs. Siddons's earliest emotional successes.

Dutchess of Gordon's where in one Room the Young are dancing and in another the Old are gambling — a faro Table. I stay but a very little while for the Party is to me vastly dull. The male Dancers are very indifferent. The Weather this Day has been pretty good.

Wednesday 22. — This Morning write and then go into the City to meet the Trustees. M.ʳ Lane has neglected sending a Letter to M.ʳ Baring at Bath so that he does not attend. I propose to them the being concerned with me in the Prosecution of this Business. They seem to doubt the Propriety of it and to this Point I say but little and only endeavor to shew the Profit, which seems evident enough. They are to think farther about it and I am to give them a Note of my Ideas. They ask me what Interest is to be paid on the Stock next January and I tell them at the Rate of six per Cent, for so I understood it. They ask me at what Price they shall sell and I answer that I think it best not to sell at present and give them my Reasons. They agree to suspend the Sales for a few Days. I receive from M.ʳ Rumsey a Letter from Parker, and Rumsey shews me a State Parker has made of the Accounts between Rogers and him which is of Course less unfavorable than that made by Rogers himself. I go to M.ʳ Phyn's and converse with him but Inglis is not at Home. Sit till after four and then go to M.ʳ Rogers who has sent me a State of his Account to shew my Share of Profit on the Transactions in which I ought to have been concerned. Go thence to dine with Lord Lansdowne where I meet a M.ʳ Morgan, formerly Secretary to Sir Guy Carleton, the present Lord Dorchester. We have a great Deal of Conversation this Day upon various Subjects. I give them my honest Sentiments respecting Britain and America which are not pleasing but I do not mean to please. Lord Landsdowne talks to me much about his Son after Dinner and as this Subject must be interesting to him I dwell on it in such Way as to unlock a little the old Reynard. He tells me that the present Administration cannot last. That he has no particular Reason to think or say so but that there are some general Indications which lead his Mind to that Conclusion. *Quere* whether he does not see thro the Medium of his Wishes. This Opinion, however, accounts for the decided Part he has lately taken against the Ministry. Go from hence to the french Embassador's. He is abroad and Madame is going out. Go to M.ʳˢ Church's who is vastly pleasant. I stay Supper with M.ʳˢ Low and take her Home. The Wind begins to blow hard from the Southwest after a very fine Day.

Thursday 23. — Last Night or rather this Morning we had a most violent Gale of Wind which has blown down the Chimneys of an adjoining House and which has I fear done great Mischief. God help and save the poor Mortals exposed to its perilous Fury. I go at twelve into the City & call on M.ʳ Inglis. I desire him to make a Proposition on my Part to the Creditors of M.ʳ Rogers or rather to his Assignees. He tells me that they have taken Counsel on a Case they have stated and he expects the Opinion will be such as to justify the Abandonment of the Property to me. Go to the Office and find I am too late, M.ʳ Henchman being gone. I tell Lane that I am determined to save Parker if he will secure me. Lane says that he can and will secure me. He says that in about two Months he will receive £3000 in Cash which will clear off all Demands upon him except mine. Call on M.ʳ Boehm and leave with him the Note intended for M.ʳ Henchman of my Plan for the future Conduct of the Fund Business. Call on M.ʳ Temple Franklin who is not at Home; I visit however his *Lady*. She is neither Handsome nor any Thing else but I think very much of a W——e. Call on his Father and leave my Card. Visit the Dutchess of Gordon who is abroad & then return Home. At six go to dine with the french Embassador. The Assembly have determined that Absentees shall loose all Rank and Emolument unless they return and take the civic Oath speedily. Go from hence to M.ʳˢ Penn's. She has a Card Party. I look on for about an Hour and then return Home and read. The Storm of this Morning has done much Mischief and seems to have extended widely. The Wind has been high this Day from the N.West, pretty clear and a little cold.

Friday 24. — This Morning I write. At five go to Dinner at M.ʳ R. Penn's. M.ʳ Boswell, M.ʳ Franklin and myself are the Guests. This M.ʳ Boswell is the Friend of the late Doctor Johnson. I get very nearly tipsy before I know what I am about. Go with M.ʳ Franklin to visit M.ʳˢ Church and then to the Piazza Coffee House where we sup together. He gives me some Account of his Gallantries both in France and in America. He shews a Note he has received from a young Inamorata in the same House with him. I think she will not prove so pure a Virgin as he imagines. The Weather has been pretty good this Day.

Saturday 25. — This Morning write and go at two to the Office of the Duke of Leeds. He was to meet me at half past two and I stay till after four. A little after three M.ʳ Burgess comes and we converse on various Subjects. His Grace has failed, for which M.ʳ Burgess makes many Apologies which I assure him are unnecessary. Go to M.ʳ Phyn's to Dinner. Meet there among others M.ʳ Shand who says he has been twice to see me. He will come again ToMorrow. I stay here to Supper also and return late. The Weather this Day has been fine.

Sunday 26. — M.ʳ Shand calls this Morning before I am up and stays till after three oClock. As soon as he is gone I dress and go to dine at M.ʳˢ Low's, thence to visit M.ʳˢ Penn and so return Home. The Weather is misty & cold.

Monday 27. — This Morning write, then call at Church's and leave a Present of Nuts and Apples for her. Go to the Office of the Duke of Leeds where M.ʳ Burgess tells me that he has just sent a Note to my Lodgings to inform me that the Duke is by sudden and severe Indisposition prevented from meeting me. Return Home and go from thence to Mark Lane where I urge M.ʳ Inglis to endeavor to bring Matters to a Decision with the Assignees of Rogers. He promises to set about it. Stay Dinner and pass the Evening here. Inglis comes in and says that some of the Creditors refuse to come in and sign, which may render it necessary to make Rogers a Bankrupt. If so I shall be delayed still longer here doing Nothing. A Letter from M.ʳ Wolf informs me that he cannot give a Credit which I had desired. The Weather this Day has been dull but grows pleasanter in the Evening.

Tuesday 28. — This Morning write. M.ʳ Franklin calls to postpone a Dinner Engagement and shews me the Love Letters of his Inamorata who I fancy understands Trap as well as he. Visit M.ʳ Shand who is abroad and then M.ʳ Rogers from whom I take some Minutes of Accounts. Then go to M.ʳ R. Penn's where I dine and spend Part of the Evening with him at the Mount Coffee House. The Weather tho dark and rather cold is not unpleasant.

Wednesday 29. — This Morning write and then go into the City
to attend a Meeting of the Assignees. It seems likely that we shall
be obliged to make M! Rogers a Bankrupt before any Thing effectual can be done. We are to meet on Monday and then they
are to give me their Sentiments on a Proposition I have made.
Visit M! and M!! Phyn. Return to the Piazza Coffee House where
I dine with Gov! and M! Franklin. We sit late and drink hard. . . .
The Weather has been pretty good this Day.

Thursday 30. — This Morning I am too much deranged by last
Night's Debauch for Business or for Amusement. Call however
on M! Rogers and desire him to make out Accounts for me. He
tells me that M! Parker is in Town and that Wadeson is to see
him on Sunday. Visit the two Franklins and M! Ogden, then go to
different Shops to get repaired the Damages of last Night. Dine
at the Piazza Coffee House and visit after Dinner at M! Penn's.
They have waited Dinner for me till near six. Take Tea here and
return Home. A wet disagreable Day. Peter Ogden consulted
me as to his future Prospects and as Andrew Elliott had informed
him of his Appoint! to be Minister and assured him of his Wish to
serve him, I advise him to hold fast of that Protection.

Friday 31. — This Morning write. M! Shand calls and afterwards M! Penn and his Son. I dine at the Piazza Coffee House
with Shand who comes Home and takes Tea with me and stays
till twelve oClock. This has been a tolerably pleasant Day

JANUARY 1791

Saturday 1 Jan! 1791. — This Morning M! Rumsey calls and
I send him in Pursuit of Parker. Write, then dress and call on
Rogers for Accounts. Afterwards visit Lady Tancred who is
abroad. Then call at a Jeweller's for my Watch Chain which is
not finished. Thence to Mark Lane to Dinner. Return between
eight and nine to meet Rumsey who does not get Home. The

Weather has been pretty good this Day tho rather wet for a Part of it.

Sunday 2. — This Morning about eleven M.ᵣ Rumsey calls. Could not get back in Season the last Evening. Will come again as soon as Wadeson the Attorney has left Parker. He comes after two and I then go to the Place and have a long Conference with Parker who seems inclined to come into my Measures, which are indeed the only just and proper Measures. I give Vent to as little Reproach as possible. I urge him to send for Wadeson again and to hold with him such Language as may prevent Attachments against his Property in America. I see he forms a Design to take some Advantage of me in the very Moment that I am trying to serve him. I do not blame him, for it is his Nature, and certainly I should see his Situation more composedly if my own Interest were not at Stake. Go hence to M.ᵣ Penn's to Dinner and stay till eleven. The Wind blew very hard this Afternoon but the Weather grows fine about ten oClock.

Monday 3. — This Morning go into the City to a Meeting of the Trustees of Rogers. They have not yet got the Opinion of Counsel and Nothing is done. The New York Packet is arrived and from what Inglis says I fear that the Bills of W.ᵐ Constable and Co: will be protested. Call at Mark Lane and have a long Conference with Phyn and Inglis. Dine there. Visited M.ᵣ Theluson who is not at Home. Stay late in the Family Way at Phyn's and come Home vexed and disquieted. My Letters from America are not pleasant and every Thing seems to be going badly. The Weather is good.

Tuesday 4. — This Morning M.ᵣ Franklin calls and we have some Conversation respecting the Sale of Lands and the Ways and Means of raising Money. I go into the City and am detained an Hour between Paul's and the Exchange by an *Embarras* of Carriages. Speak to M.ᵣ Wadeson and afterwards to M.ᵣ Maitland urging the Impropriety of the Attachment against Parker's Property while they hold the Funds liable for his Debt. I am detained untill it is so late that the Trustees have left the Office. Go to Mark Lane to Dinner. Phyn tells me that there is an Offer of Freight for our Sloop *Cato* to Canton. Converse with Inglis about this and other Matters after Dinner. Receive a Note from

Parker that he cannot see me this Evening, being indisposed. Stay the Evening here and get Home at two. The Weather was this Day stormy and disagreable. This Night it is clear and cold.

Wednesday 5. — This Morning at ten I visit Mᵣ Parker who is to see Mᵣ Rogers this Day for the Purpose of setling their Accounts. I give him some Notes I had made on that Subject and after talking the Matter over, with many fair Promises from him, I go into the City and wait a considerable Time at the Fund Office for the Trustees. At length Mᵣ Henchman comes but we cannot get Mᵣ Baring. He desires to see me ToMorrow at eleven. Mᵣ Wadeson sees me in the Street and stops me to shew Counsellor Mansfield's Opinions, which are favorable to my Claims. He takes me to Mᵣ Maitland's who assures me that when duly authorized he will relinquish those Claims which have been set up. I call on Rogers who is not at Home; leave a Message for him, then return and write. Go to the Piazza Coffee House to dine at six. Mᵣ Franklin keeps me waiting till seven. We dine together and I find that his Father cannot be perswaded to believe in the Solidity of American Funds. Return Home at ten. This was a fine Morning but a blustering Afternoon and wet.

Thursday 6. — This Morning I repair at eleven according to Promise to Mᵣ Baring's. Meet there Messʳˢ Boehm, Baring and Henchman and converse about the Stock entered in their Names. They agree to stand their present Advance for three or four Months and will consider of engaging with me after I am fully vested with the Rights of Parker and Rogers free and clear. Desire them to send out a Power to receive the Interest in America and subscribe it in the three per Cents. I mention to them a Loan on the Credit of this Stock but this they have not thought upon. I am to write to them and mention the Sum I am willing to let them dispose of and the Price. Upon my Offer of a Commission beyond the usual Interest they reject the Idea and declare that if they lend upon this Security it shall be at five per%. Go to Mᵣ Wadeson's and meet Mᵣ Rogers there. Mᵣ Walker assures me that he will readily relinquish all Claims upon the joint Property. Mᵣ Wadeson says I must render myself responsible for the Bills drawn on this joint Account and Rogers says they amount to about a thousand Pounds. I tell Wadeson that I will agree to become responsible to the Trustees for any just Claims which may exist against the Property transferred to me. With this Assurance Walker is satisfied. Go with Rogers to Rumsey's to find Parker in Order to settle with him, but I find that he is again gone out of Town. He says in a Letter to me that Rogers Yesterday alarmed him with the Fear of an Arrest. After severely reprimanding Rogers for this Conduct I write very urgently to Parker, and having desired Rogers to send out Letters to Craigie to deliver up the Powers sent to him by the Trustees, I go to look for Col? Walker, but my Coachman has neglected to provide himself with a Ticket from the Stamp Office. Turn about and call on Doctor (or M?) Cutting, who is abroad, and so is the Dutchess of Gordon. Go again into the City. Inglis stops me to desire that I will take Property of Parker's which is out of England, lest by the Operation of the Bankrupt Laws I should be entangled in a Dispute. I tell him that this Hint is so much the more useful as otherwise I should have tried to obtain Property here in Order to throw it into their Hands. Visit Mess?ˢ Pasley and M?Cullough who had left Cards at my Lodgings and then go to Mark Lane and dine. After Dinner Inglis comes in and speaks about a little Sloop which we have at Dunkirk and which it is proposed to send to India and to sell there. I tell him that if he thinks it worth while he may do so and in that Case take one Half of her to their Account at the Price fixed between Constable and Shand. He feels this to be a generous Offer and I think from his Countenance that it was very opportunely made. This being decided on we take Tea and I go to M? Penn's. The Family are all out and therefore I go to the Mount Coffee House and eat some Oysters and Olives. Stay till after eleven and then set down Penn and return Home. This has been a fine Day for the Season.

Friday 7. — This Morning I write and then call upon Col? Walker. He gives me a lamentable Account of the Agency of M? Barlow for the Scioto Com?. Go from thence to Gen! Morris's and make a Present of some Nuts and Apples which prove very acceptable. Return to Town and dine with M?ˢ Penn. After Dinner go to M?ˢ Low's and pass the Evening. The Company is composed of Refugees and after Supper they entertain me with the

Song of God Save the King and afterwards a ludicrous Account of a Connecticutt Election composed and sung by Gov: Franklin in the long Doggrel of *Derry Down*. I whisper to him and my other Neighbour M: Yorke a Stanza composed *Extempore* in Addition, which would have wounded them sorely had I have given it aloud, but tho they merited that and more I passed all off. Stay late and am disappointed at not receiving any News from M: Parker. He is a devilish slippry Fellow. The Weather has this Day been fine with light warm Showers and the Country looks more like Spring than Winter.

Saturday 8. — This Morning write. Dine at the Piazza Coffee House and after Dinner go in Pursuit of M: Parker, whom I find. He promises to give me Security for the Ballance of Accounts and ToMorrow will meet M: Rogers at my Lodgings. Call on him and desire him to come prepared with his Books and Papers. Get Home after eleven. The Weather has been fair this Day with high Wind from the West.

Sunday 9. — Employed all this Day in Settlement of Accounts between myself and Rogers and Parker. M: Wadeson is to draw an Assignment of all their Right, Title, Interest &c:, &c:. After the Settlements are made I converse with Parker about the Security he is to give me and at length propose to take *Facilities* at 7/6, and that he shall give his Bond with double Penalty conditioned for that Payment. He declares his Wish to make the Payment in that Way but fears that if the Facilities he has should be otherwise disposed of he may be ruined by the Rise. I press him hard, declaring constantly that I would rather have the Money. He stickles much and we are to see each other again. He wishes me also to become one of his Creditors on a general Assignment and I agree to do so, provided I be first secured. The Weather has been fine this Day tho I have not been able to enjoy it.

Monday 10. — This Morning write and then go into the City. M: Wadeson has not drawn the Assignment and will not do it. Dine with Church. In my Way thither visit Rogers and agree to some farther Articles of Account which he had omitted. After Dinner call on Rumsey to find Parker; he says I shall receive a Note from him ToMorrow Morning but he thinks I cannot see him till Wednesday. This is vexatious. He is alarmed by the

Pursuit of the Sheriff's Officers. The Weather has been tolerably good this Day.

Tuesday 11. — This Morning write. Mᵣ Rogers calls and gives me an Order for two Dividends on Stock, which I carry to Lockhart's the Bankers. He, on hearing my Name, enters into Conversation about it and desires to see me ToMorrow. Go into the City. R. Penn and his Son had called to ask me to dine, but I was obliged to decline. Go to Mᵣ Wadeson's for an Agreement delivered last Sunday, and he not being at Home I leave a tart Note. Call on Mᵣ Maitland and fix a Meeting for ToMorrow at twelve. He desires me to call on Mᵣ Smith, who had been enquiring the Price of Stock. I do so but it tends only to give them a good Opinion of the Funds, which they do not mean to purchase. Go to Mark Lane to dine. Stay till one in the Morning. Converse on Business after Dinner. I believe Things will yet go well. The Weather has been so so. About Noon it was fine and between one and two this Morning is clear and colder than it was, but still by much too mild for the Season. It is observed that this is the most stormy Season ever remembered and Inglis mentions that open winters are always bad for the Underwriters. The Reason of this is evident.

Wednesday 12. — Attend this Morning at a Meeting of the Trustees of S. Rogers. We do nothing. Discuss the Statement and Settlement of the Account between Parker, him and me. Maitland holds back from assenting to it. Walker offers me the Price stated for the Certificates if I will grant some Delay. I tell him that I will do nothing till I have had an Opportunity of enquiring. We are to meet again on Friday at twelve oClock. I get Rogers to sign the Account and am now if I can to get it signed by Parker. Go to sundry Booksellers and to the House of a Navy Agent to get the Forms of Accounts for Capellis. Go to Lockhart's. They are willing to make a Loan for me on the Credit of American Stock. They are to have one p% and to obtain the Money at 5 p% Int:. I am to write on this Subject when I am possessed of the Stock. I mention then a Speculation in the American Debt, which seems likely to answer. Am to write on this Subject also. Dine with R. Penn and call after Dinner on his Brother. Then return Home. I have sought in vain for Parker and am perswaded that he means to play me some Trick. It is this Evening a heavy Gale from the Southwest which began to rise at Noon. Shand comes in and sits with me till after one oClock.

Thursday 13. — This Morning write. M.ͬ Rumsey and —— endeavor to find M.ͬ Parker but he will not see me by Day Light. Call on Mess.ͬˢ Lockhart and leave a Letter on the Subject of Speculations in the American Funds. Converse with the elder about it a little. Visit M.ͬˢ Church. Call on young Franklin, then dine at the Piazza Coffee House. At the Table with me is an old Man who turns out to be 81 and who eats heartily; one of middle Age who seems to be acquainted with every Body, and a very young Man who seems both soft and green. There is Something remarkable in the History of the oldest and in the Manner of the others. At seven go to the Parliament Coffee House and there finally get M.ͬ Parker's Bond with a long Endorsement on it, intended by him to prevent the Effect of the Bond. He signs also the Account and I sign a Kind of Receipt purporting to be my Acceptance of his Assump.ⁿ for the Ballance. — Go to Gov.ˡ Franklin's. The Party are all gone but I step in to shew myself. Stay a little while and eat some pickled Oysters brought from New York, which are not so good as those they have made in the House. Return about one. The Wind blew hard all Day from the Westward but the Evening was calm and the Night is fine.

Friday 14. — This Morning write and then go into the City to attend the Meeting of M.ͬ Rogers's Trustees. It is put off because M.ͬ Parker could not meet them Yesterday. Call at Mark Lane and mention my Design to go to France immediately. Inglis does not seem to relish this. He thinks the Acc/ settled with Rogers and Parker should be left with them. I deliver it, desiring that a Copy may be made. He says he will speak to me about it ToMorrow. I fancy he means to ask some Concern for their Advance. Go to the Fund Office, and I find that Wolfe is disposing of his Stock. $32000 are transferring. Desire the Clerk, M.ͬ Lane, to mention to the Trustees the sending out of a Power of Attorney. He says they will not do it before the next Packet. Call on M.ͬ Rogers and I think M.ͬ Wadeson is with him. Ask him his News from America. He says that Craigie has not taken out the Interest and promises that if he does, it shall be carried to the

Names of the Trustees as ordered. He has rec.^d a Remittance. Call on Mr Rumsey to know if I can find Parker, but Rumsey is gone abroad. Go to dine with Mrs Church. Some American Ladies are here who go to a Rout after Dinner. When the Company are all gone I tell Church that the best Ground to hunt the Ministry on will be that of America. He seizes the Idea with Avidity and wishes that he had asked a few Friends to meet me on that Subject. I tell him that I would not discuss it with them. I think he will go to Work and I am sure that the more Stir is made on that Subject the better will it be for America. Return Home at ten and find that Rumsey has left a Message for me. Go in Consequence to his Lodgings. Parker is at the Black Bear in Piccadilly and wishes to see me. I call upon him but he has just left it. There was another Gentleman with him. Lane told me that an Attachment was laid on the Property of Parker in the Hands of the Trustees at the Suit of Tourton and Ravell. He has also Letters from Staphorst's House threatening to do themselves immediate Justice unless he satisfies them. This has been a tolerable Day and the Evening is very fine.

Saturday 15. — This Morning write, then go into the City. Call at Mark Lane and take Leave. Make an Offer of Interest to P. E. & I. in the Debt. As they do not at once accept I do not press it, but tell them my Prospects from it. Inglis tells me their Advance for us is £40000. Take Leave of Mrs Phyn, who from her good Heart gives me all good Wishes. Meet Franklin and ask him to dine. Call on Mrs Penn and say Adieu. On the french Embassador and Lady Tancred, no Body at Home in either Place. On Mrs Low. Thence return Home. Write, pay my Bills and then dine. After Mr Franklin leaves me I pack up. This has been a fine Day.

Sunday 16. — About half past eleven last Evening I got into Bed, but this being earlier than usual my Thoughts keep me awake. At four I rise and am off at half past four. Arrive at the City of London Inn at a Quarter before four in the Afternoon at Dover, about seventy Miles. I endeavor here to perswade some one to go off for France but in vain, as it blows a Gale of Wind and threatens to blow still harder. As I am obliged to stay I go to Bed at six.

Monday 17. — This Morning at seven the Master of a Passage Boat offers to take me to Calais. The Wind is a Head for Boulogne. We agree at three Guineas. We get under Way at ten Minutes after nine. The Wind is heavy and a high Surf going over the Bar, but we are so landlocked that our Vessel has very little Way. We strike in going out repeatedly and they consider themselves as Shipwrecked, but at length we get over the Bar without Injury. The Weather is very rough and just before we reach Calais it begins to rain & the Wind rises. At entring that Harbor we have a Hail Storm. The Wind was on our Beam all the Way and we are along Side of the Key in Calais Harbor at fifty five Minutes after eleven, so that the Totality of our Passage was but two Hours and three Quarters but from Harbor's Mouth to Harbor's Mouth not two and an Half. As we left Dover the Flag was struck, and so it was immediately after we crossed the Bar at Calais, so that we had not a Moment to spare. I leave Calais at fifty Minutes past twelve and in three Hours and thirty five Minutes reach the Inn at Boulogne where I left my Carriage, the Hôtel Britannique. Take some Refreshment while the Baggage is removing, Wheels greasing &cᵃ, and at half past five set off. A Supporter of the Carriage breaks in four Minutes which detains me two Hours. At half past nine we take a new Departure and at twenty Minutes after one reach the Post House at Montreuil, four Posts and an Half.

Tuesday 18. — At thirty five Minutes after twelve we leave Montreuil and at fifty five Minutes after eleven we reach Lingueville, twenty three Posts and three Quarters.

[After continuous driving from Boulogne, which he left at half past nine on Monday evening, Morris reached Paris at half past six on Wednesday morning, put up at a hotel in the since demolished rue du Carrousel, had three hours' sleep, dressed, and was at the nearby Louvre soon after ten, which does not look like diminished enthusiasm for the alluring Comtesse de Flahaut.]

Wednesday 19. — At five Minutes after twelve this Morning we leave Lingueville and at half past six arrive at the Hôtel du Roi, Rue du Carousel, six posts and a Quarter. The Weather during our Rout has been pretty good but for the greater Part very high Winds. Get to Bed at a little after seven and rise a little after ten. Dress and visit Madame de Flahaut who keeps me some time. We celebrate together but St Louis comes in so abruptly as to derange our closing moment. M.^r de F——, Mad.^{lle} Duplessis &c.^a. She complains to me of the Bishop's cold Cruelty. He is elected a Member of the Department of Paris and resigns his Bishoprick. He treats her ill. His Passion for Play is become extreme and she gives me Instances which are ridiculous. He comes in and I come away. Visit Mad.^e de Chastellux and go with her to dine at the Dutchess of Orleans's. Her R. H. is ruined, (ie) she is reduced from 450,000$^{\#}$ to 200,000$^{\#}$ p An.^m She tells me that she cannot give any good Dinners but if I will come and fast with her she will be glad to see me &c.^a. Return Home and at 8 o'Clock go to sup at the Louvre. The Bishop and St Foi with some others come in. Madame complains of being ill but continues at Play late. Capellis proposes on the Part of some of his Friends to deliver Window Glass at Nantes in Exchange for Potash. I tell him that this will not suit us but that it might be worth the Attention of his Friends to send out some Glass made in the Manner and of the Size of the British, to be sold on Commission, and to order some Potash, say each Commission of about 12000$^{\#}$ and then they could judge how far the Commerce might be worth their Notice. He wishes me to get the Models from England, which is to incur a certain Expence for nothing. The Weather has been tolerably good this Day but the Wind very high. This Night is less tempestuous, or rather this Morning, for till Midnight it has blown very hard.

Thursday 20. — La Caze calls this Morning and tells me how the Land lies here. He tells me also a Thing which I am sure is not true, viz that R. M. told him Jefferson had promised that I should be appointed to this Court. He gives me much of himself and his own Affairs according to Custom. While he is here a Message from Mad.^e de F—— that she is waiting for me. Go thither and do the needful. Afterwards in Conversation, replying to her Questions, I let her know that I am much less attached than I was &c.^a., &c.^a. She asks me what my Idea is of our Connection. I tell her that I have not yet considered that Subject. Finally she tells me that she supposes I have a regular Plan to give her Pain, but I assure

her I wish much to give her Pleasure. 'Tis strange but 'tis true
that the Pain arising from the Apprehension of loosing a Lover
is essential to the Pleasure a Woman finds in possessing him.
But with Man also, Objects derive their Value from the Hope of
acquiring or the Fear of parting with them. Go from hence to
Madame Foucault's and converse on Business with Chaumont;
we are to see each other ToMorrow. Thence go to see Madame de
Vannoise who disappoints me by being at Home; stay a few
Minutes. Thence to Mons.ʳ Grand's, they are abroad. Thence to
Messʳˢ Le Couteulx's, also abroad. To the Abbé Morelet's ¹ to
whom I deliver Letters at Dinner. Thence to Madame de Ségur's;
see the Maréchal who tells me that News are arrived from India
of a severe Check recᵈ from Tippoo Saib by Genˡ Mathews and
that the former is ravaging the Carnatic. Thence to Madame de
Guibert's at whose Instances I stay to Dinner. After Dinner
visit the Duc de La Rochefoucault. He is not at Home, wherefore
I leave a Letter from Rumsey with my Card. Thence to Monsʳ
de Montmorin's. It is the Embassadors' Day and of Course the
Salon is formally filled. Monsieur de Sᵗ Priest is here. I called on
Ternant in the Morning & should I suppose have found him here
at any other Time. Go from hence to Monsieur de La Fayette's;
both he and Madame are abroad. Thence to Madame de La
Borde's. She is also abroad. Thence to Madame de Capellis.
The Count D'Angivilliers is here and there is the Appearance of a
Party. I slip away and visit Madame de Chastellux where I find
the Countess de Ségur. Take Tea and at nine go to Madame
d'Houdetot's. Monsʳ de Bonnet wishes to know how Money can
best be remitted to England. I tell him all I know, which cannot
however be useful to him. The Object I find is to place in the british Funds and therefore I recommend the Funds of America. It
does not seem to strike and therefore I do not press it. Go hence
to Madame de Stahl's. I meet here the World. Stay some Time
in various Conversation, altogether of no Consequence, and then
return Home. This has been a very fine Day.

¹ Abbé Morellet (1727–1819), survival from salons of Madame Geoffrin and
Baron d'Holbach. His astringent tongue had delighted Franklin; Voltaire
had called him *l'abbé mords-les*, a simple effort for a Voltaire. Great worker
on *Encyclopédie* and *Dictionnaire de l'Académie*, whose manuscript he will save
with the Academy's archives and will hide them till quiet again walks the earth.

Friday 21. — This Morning Ternant calls and takes Breakfast.
He was appointed Minister plenipo: to the United States last
Sunday. We converse a little about his Mission. He wishes me to
be appointed here. I tell him that I understand from De Moustiers that Carmichael has been asked for. He says that if it be
not too late he will get that Matter altered. He will know more
about it and tell me. Write, and at two go to Madame Foucault's.
Chaumont proposes to confine our View to the Sale of the S!
Lawrence Tract and that this should go at 2$^{\#}$ per Acre. That it
should then be resold at an advanced Price and that I have Half
the Advance and he and his Friends the other Half. I agree to
this in the general but when we come to Particulars I think we
are not quite agreed. We shall see. He is to be with me To-
Morrow. Dine here and a Madame Pinié expresses much Attention to me *because my political Sentiments pleased her.* After
Dinner Chaumont's Wife [1] who is my Countrywoman comes in.
She looks very much like a Fool but she is glad to see an American.
Go from hence to the Louvre, having overstaid my Appointment
near an Hour. We proceed to Business. . . . Monsieur had desired
to see me so that we ring and send for him. I am thus disappointed and thereat a little vexed. He talks about sending Hardware to America for Sale, a Friend of his being at the Head of a
considerable Manufactory. I tell him his Friend may call some
Morning and I will speak to him. Go to Mad? du Bourg's. They
are here at Play and high Play too, in which I of Course take no
Part. Come away early. It has been a very fine Day and the
Evening is fine.

Saturday 22. — Chaumont comes and we spend the greater
Part of the Morning together in preparing for the Sale of the S!
Lawrence Lands. I go to dine with Capellis. It is four when we
sit down so that I leave them immediately after Dinner and go by
Appointment to the Louvre. After the genial Act we sit and chat
awhile. She is much distressed but tells me of a Gleam of Hope
in her Prospects. It is a distant and remote Dependence, however
I will try to bring it to some End. Go from hence to Madame de
La Borde's. She is abroad. Take some Apples &c? to Mad? de

---

[1] Born Grace Coxe of New Jersey.

Ségur. He is with his Wife, and the Conversation turning that
Way, the Pleasure a Man feels in speaking of himself leads him to
communicate the History of the War between Russia and the
Porte. From his Statement, England embroiled those Powers.
Having taken up the History a great Way back and brought
it to the Peace which concluded the former War between them, He
states that the Empress took on herself to be the liege lord (Suze-
raine) of Georgia. That the Afghis Tartars dwelling about the
Caspian Sea & who are constantly at War with the Georgians,
received Aid from the Pasha in their Neighbourhood and that the
Tartars of the Cuban made frequent Depredations on the Russian Territories and then crossed that fordable River into the
Turkish Territory. That Complaints having arisen on this Subject the Mediation of France was asked & accepted and he and
Mons! de Choiseul Gouffier [1] employed themselves efficaciously
in setling the Difference. It was agreed that the Pasha should no
longer give Aid to the Afghis Tartars and that those of the Cuban
should not be protected after their Inroads as before. That Prince
Potemkin having assembled a considerable Army to be reviewed
by the Empress in that Quarter and being informed that the
Cause of Complaint continued notwithstanding the Treaty, sent
immediately thro the Russian Embassador Baljakow a menacing
Message to the Turk. That this being communicated by the Reis
Effendi to Mons! de Gouffier he, much surprized, advised the
Turk immediately to arm and informed him, Ségur, of what was
done and doing. That he thereupon spoke in very high Terms to
the Russian Ministry who laid the Blame upon Prince Potemkin.
They agreed to submit to any reasonable Terms and altho those
proposed thro Mons! Gouffier by the Turk were conceived rather
haughtily, to his great Surprize they were acceded to. His Courier
however, charged with that Intelligence, was intercepted by
Turkish Robbers and murdered. That when he learnt that Accident he immediately sent another, but before that Messenger
arrived the English had been busy in dissuading them from all

---

[1] Choiseul-Gouffier (1752–1817), then Ambassador at Constantinople from
France, as Ségur was to St. Petersburg. As archæologist Gouffier had published an account of his excavations in Greece and had succeeded to d'Alem-
bert's chair in the French Academy.

Accomodation. Their Embassador M! —— told the Reis Effendi that he would be powerfully supported by Prussia and Poland. That if Austria should join Russia a powerful Diversion would be made by the Revolt of Flanders then in train. That they must not trust to France, whose favorite System was to support Russia, with whom she had lately formed very close Connections and of course could not be cordially attached to the Porte. The Reason of England was (says Ségur) that being vexed with Russia for forming a Treaty with France by which among other Things the Principles of the armed Neutrality are acknowleged, and for insisting on a like Acknowlegement in a proposed Renewal of her Treaty with England, she was in Hopes of making a Breach between France and her new Ally Russia or her old Ally the Turk. In Consequence of the british Intrigues the Porte refused to accede to the Terms which she had herself proposed, but sent others in a Style imperious and dictatorial. That he was much hurt at this, but to his very great Surprize the Empress acceded to those also; but by the Time that his Dispatches were cyphered and just as the Courier was about to depart, they learnt that the Turk had actually commenced Hostilities. —— He says that he long since informed his Court that Hertzberg had formed vast Projects menacing all Europe, but that no Attention was paid to his Information, and on the contrary he was represented as a Firebrand desirous of general Mischief. That he very early proposed the Triple Alliance of Austria, Russia and France, which was then rejected and has never been compleated because finally the french Revolution prevented a Ratification by France. He says the late Emperor Joseph told him shortly before his Death that the Empress of Russia had permitted him to make a seperate Peace, and that he might assure the King he would agree to give up Choizim and even Belgrade to effect it. We pass then to the Peace of Reichenbach and I tell him the Manner in which Van Hertzberg became the Dupe of his own Contrivances....

We learn this Day some News which if true will affect a little the Affairs of this Country. It is said that the catholic Militia of Strasburgh have all resigned and that a Petition is arrived signed by four thousand Persons, to which a much greater Number have adhered, desiring that all which has been done in Re-

spect to the Clergy and Nobility may be rescinded. That conciliatory Commissioners are named (three) to go thither. — From
hence I go to Madame de Chastellux's, who tells me that she is informed by a Person lately come from french Flanders that a general Apprehension is there entertained of a Visit from the Imperial
Troops. I do not believe in this Visit. The Dutchess comes in
and Mad⁹ de Ségur, the Vicomte also. I leave them and go to the
Louvre. I find Madame in Conversation with a Deputy from the
Islands who wishes a particular Person nominated to the Department of the Colonies, and that in the Demarcation of Limits with
Spain a Tract should be ceded in S⁹ Domingo for a Part of which a
Plantation will be given, of which she shall have one Half. I
sup here. She is very sad and it is in vain that I try to remove
that Sadness. The Weather has been very fine this Day. This
Evening thro the Negligence of my Coachman my Chariot gets
injured, he having left the Horses to do as they might think
proper, and I am well off that it is not torne to Pieces.

Sunday 23. — La Caze calls and gives me a Letter from Doctor
Jones. He repeats again that Jefferson had made R. M. a Promise
on my Subject, which is impossible. He tells me that he learnt
from Col⁹ Smith the only Objection to placing me in the Corps
diplomatique would be my other Pursuits. At half past three I
call on Mad⁹ de F——. The Bishop is with her. I take a Note of
the Person that the Colonists wish for their Minister and then go
to dine with Mons⁹ de Montmorin. Meet Ternant. Montesquiou
comes in after Dinner & says he wishes to see me. Ternant and I
come away together. In the Carriage he tells me that in entering
the Court at Montmorin's he took Occasion to observe on seeing
my Carriage that it would be a good Thing I were appointed the
Minister from the United States, to which Mont⁹ replied that he
should like it much. Ternant then told him it would be very easy.
to get it done, since nothing more would be necessary than to
signify a Desire of the Kind to M⁹ Jefferson. Mont⁹ then said
there was another Person desired it, viz M⁹ Carmichael. He asked
if it was he or his friends who desired it, but before any decisive
Answer could be obtained they entered the Salon. I set him down
at Rayneval's and then go to the Louvre. Take Madame to her
friend Mad⁹ de Guibert's and en route we embrace. Set her down

at her own Door, then take Tea with Mad: de Chastellux and sup
with the Princess. A very fine Day but drizly Evening. The
News of Strasburg Mont.ⁿ told me is unfounded.

Monday 24. — This Morning write. La Caze calls and delivers
me a Letter from Doctor Jones. At three I call at M.ʳ Grand's
where I stay Dinner and after Dinner call on Le Couteulx. Thence
to the Louvre but Mad: is abroad and has desired I would call at
eight. Visit Mad: de La Borde. Thence to Mad: de Corney's.
Thence to Mad: du Molet's. Thence to the Louvre where I stay
some Time with Company *toujours*. Thence to Mad: de Chastellux's, a short Visit, and return Home. This has been a prodigiously fine Day. An old Man called on me this Morning to whom
I had given an Introduction in America. He has made a Contract
with Duer who was to supply him with Money but he is here
without a Sous.

Tuesday 25. — This Morning Richard calls. He has Nothing
particular to say. I write. Ternant comes in. He tells me that the
Appointment of a Minister for the Colonies will experience considerable Delay. He wishes me to confer with the Committee of
Commerce. I promise to do so if they desire it. He wishes me to
tell Montmorin the Sum which I conceive to be needful for a
french Minister in America, which I will do when he tells me the
Appointment is actually made. At three oClock go to dine with
Mad: de Stahl who is not yet come in. I visit at the Louvre where
they are at Dinner. My friend is ill and goes to bed. Return to
Dinner. The Abbé Sieyes is here and descants with much Self
Sufficiency on Government, despising all that has ever been said
or sung on that Subject before him, and Mad: says that his Writings and Opinions will form in Politics a new Era as that of Newton in Phisics. Go from hence to Mad: de Bourg. She advises me
to pursue rather the *Attraits* of Society than any serious Attachment. Company come in which puts an End to that Matter.
Go to the Louvre and sit with my sick Friend to whom I administer all the little Consolations which I can. Thence to Mad:
de La Borde's. D'Angiviliers is very attentive. *Que veut dire
cela.*

Wednesday 26. — This Morning I am prevented from doing any
Thing almost. First Mons.ʳ de Flahaut presents to me by Ap-

pointment his Friend who is a Chief of the Works of Amboise.
He wants Vent for Hardware in the United States. I tell him the
pour and the *contre* of that Commerce and advise him to send out a
Parcell by Way of Sample. Before they leave me Col? Walker arrives and communicates a State of the Scioto Company's Affairs
which appear to be extremely perplexed. He asks my Advice but
I can give no Advice, not knowing sufficiently all the Facts; some
of the most important he remains ignorant of. Before he is gone
Col? Swan arrives and tells me that his Plan for the Debt has
fallen thro by the Mis Conduct of Cantaleu. He wishes me to
visit Montesquiou. I tell him that if Montesquiou wishes to see
me he can call on me. Write a little and then visit at the Louvre
in my Way to Dinner. Mad? is ill. Dine with La Fayette who is
tolerably well content to see me. Ternant is here. After Dinner
we have an interesting Conversation together. He tells me that
he had arranged a Plan for restoring Order by the Exertion of
Force, in which de Bouillie and La Fayette were to cooperate
but the latter failed while he was in Germany. He is now at
Work to bring about the same Thing. I see that he is desirous of
being in the Ministry here and would play at Heads for Kingdoms. They want some Person of this Sort of a Rank sufficiently
elevated to run no Risque unnecessarily and whose Temper will
not avoid any which may be necessary or proper. Go from hence
to the Louvre where I sit some Time. Visitors. The Bishop [1]
happening to be here I ask him what Kind of Place he has got,
what is the Income, whether it will support him &c.ª, and observe
that unless it will place him in an independent Situation he has
done wrong in accepting. He says that it is the only Door which
was open. Visit Mad? de Chastellux and then return to the Louvre
to take Home Mad.ˡˡᵉ Duplessis. The Weather this Day tho not
fair has not been unpleasant. On my Return Home I write till

---

[1] Talleyrand had resigned from his bishopric to become one of the several
Administrators of the Department of Paris, lately renewed with the Duc de
La Rochefoucault as President; Alexandre de Lameth, Admiral de Kersaint,
d'Ormesson, Thouin, Dumont, were fellow administrators; Mirabeau, du
Tremblay, Abbé Sieyès were among its directors. The ex-Bishop of Autun
does this work until the post is suppressed after Tenth August, 1792, except
for his absence on mission in England.

late. Ternant thinks a few Weeks will drive Things to a Decision.
I think not.

Thursday 27. — This Morning I sit down to write but Van
Staphorst comes in and makes Enquiry respecting Parker and his
Affairs. He tells me that the Agreement between Tourton and
Ravel's House and D. Parker was for a Million of Dollars at 50^s
each. At the Time this Agreement was made they could be purchased for about 25^s to 30^s. Gain at the highest Price if it was a
M^n of Dollars is 1,000,000$^\#$, but if as I conjecture $400,000 then
only 400,000$^\#$. I hint to Van Staphorst the forming of a Plan
for Sale of the American Debt here. He tells me that a Negotiation in Amsterdam for ^{f}1,200,000 ran off immediately and he
thinks at 75 p%. Call at the Louvre and then go to dine with the
Dutchess of Orleans. Go from thence to Mad^e Foucault's.
Chaumont will call on me ToMorrow or the next Day. Go from
hence to the Louvre. My Friend is better. Her Sister [1] comes
in who is arrived in great Penury at Paris and to whom her Sister has sent Money notwithstanding the Misery of her own Situation. Take Mad^{lle} Duplessis Home and then visit Mad^e de Stahl.
Return early and after drinking much weak Tea take a little
Medicine to counteract the Symptoms of Repletion which annoy
my Stomach. This has been a damp Day and indeed a rainy
Day, but warm.

Friday 28. — This Morning write. Mr Swan calls and shews
his Memorial to the Minister of the Marine on the Subject of
Salt Provisions. He offers me a Concern. I promise to consider
of it and give him an Answer. He leaves with me his Papers.
At four I go to Mr de Montmorin's. Sit and chat some Time with
Madame before Dinner. We speak a little of the Count de Ségur
who is I find in *mauvaise odeur* here. *Intriguant et faux*. But this
is general Character. Go from hence to the Luxembourg but
Madame du Bourg is abroad. Thence to the Louvre. Mad^e is

---

[1] Beautiful, perhaps semi-royal Julie Filleul, whose first husband, Marquis
de Marigny, brother of La Pompadour, had been Keeper of the King's Buildings
to Louis XV and as great a patron in his day as the present d'Angivillier.
After her adventures with Cardinal de Rohan, she had lived on a large pension
from the old King and had not long been the wife of the extravagant, impover-
ished, and extremely royalist Marquis de Boursac. The pension had doubtless
been reformed away.

much better and Mons.̠ very ill. Thence to Mad.ᵉ de Chastellux's. She is abroad. Thence to Mad.ᵉ de Ségur's. She makes some gentle Reproaches for my Neglect of her. Thence to Mad.ᵉ Foucault's and sup.... It can't be helped. Return Home at twelve. This has been a very fine Day. It is grown a little more seasonable (ie) a little colder.

Saturday 29. — This Morning write and at Noon take up Mad.ᵉ de Chastellux. We go together to Choisy and dine with Marmontel.¹ He thinks soundly. After Dinner he mentions his Mode of contesting the newfangled Doctrine of the *Droits d'homme* by asking a Definition of the Word *droit*, and from that Definition he draws a Conclusion against the asserted Equality of Rights. He admits however that all are equal before the Law and under the Law. I deny this Position and make him Remark that where there is great Inequality of Rank and Fortune this supposed Equality of legal Dispensation would destroy all Proportion, consequently all Justice. If the Punishment be a Fine it oppresses the Poor but does not affect the Rich. If it be a corporal Punishment it degrades the Prince but does not wound the Beggar. He is struck with deep Conviction at this Observation. I draw only one Conclusion, that in Morals every general Position requires numerous Exceptions, whereof [sic] logical Conclusions from such Positions must frequently be erroneous. I might have pursued (as I have sometimes done) my Remarks a little farther to the legal Compensation for Injuries where the Varieties are greater because the Party committing and the Party suffering wrong may each be of different Rank in Society. I might go farther and notice those Varieties of Sentiment which the Manners of different Nations introduce into social Life; for it is a Fact that 'the Ill we feel is most in Apprehension.' The Legislator therefore who would pare down the Feelings of Mankind to the metaphisical Standard of his own Reason would shew little Knowlege tho he

---

¹ Jean-François Marmontel (1723–1799), Academician, encyclopædist, permanent Secretary of French Academy. Had early raised a storm by asserting that pagan heroes of noble lives might enter Heaven; had championed Piccini against Gluck when Paris had been bitterly divided as to which was the greater composer, and had written libretti in free verse for operas composed by Piccini and by Grétry, notably *Didon*. Disciple of Voltaire, he writes periodical *Contes Moraux* in the *Mercure.*

might display much Genius. We return to the Palais royal where I sit down Mad.⁰ de Chastellux and then go to the Louvre. Visit Mad.⁰ and Monsieur, She pretty well, He very ill. Return Home and write. The Weather has been fine this Morning but in the Evening was damp.

Sunday 30. — M.ʳ Walker and M.ʳ Richard come in together. The Object seems to be at first how to manage with Barlow and Playfair against whom there is a Judgment in the Consulate and the different Summonses have been issued. There seems to be some feeble Chance of getting Money or Money's Worth from them. Richard tells me apart that the Assembly have determined to put the Tobacco en Regie under the Farm. *Quere.* Swan calls and I desire him to come ToMorrow. Paul Jones calls. He wishes me much to visit Little Page. I decline for the present. Go to the Restaurateur's to Dinner and thence to the Louvre where we celebrate the Recovery of Mad.⁰, but this added to the Fatigue she has had during the Day and some Irregularity of Diet brings on a violent nervous Affection. Monsieur is somewhat better but very ill. He has been smartly purged by an antimonial Medicine and they have applied a Blister. I think that ToMorrow he will be relieved or else from having been twice bled it will be necessary to give him Cordials. He is confoundedly frightened which is itself a bad Symptom. Return Home at six oClock, take Tea and write. The Weather has this Day been fine, but it grows warmer in the Evening, whence I augur Rain for ToMorrow.

Monday 31. — M.ʳ Swan calls on me this Morning and says he spoke to the Marquis de La Fayette and mentioned Robert Morris and Daniel Parker as being concerned with him in his Offer to supply the Marine. I tell him that he was not justified in this. I do not consent to any Concern as yet. Call on Le Couteulx and as he is not well I agree to come again on Wednesday. Visit at the Louvre. My fair friend is alone and in Sorrow. Complains of the cold Insensibility of her Husb.ᵈ'ˢ Relations. He is ill, very ill. The Baron de Montesquiou comes in and asks if her Dower is secured. It is not. D'Angiviliers has paid his Brother's Debts. *Qu:* whether he will pay this as a Debt *privilégiée*. Dine with La Fayette. Tell him Swan was not justified in what he said. Give him my Ideas of the Kind of Contract which should be made.

He says he will pay Attention to it and speak to the Minister of the Marine, Monsieur de Fleurieu. After Dinner I tell him that it would tend much to promote the Interests of America if a Minister of the Colonies were appointed. He says he will think of it. Go hence to the Louvre but Mad̶e̶ is not visible, the *parents* being here. Thence to Mad̶e̶ de Chastellux's where I sit some Time and return Home. M̶r̶ de Rouilliere is dead suddenly and as he was writing the History of the Times and was not friendly to the Powers which are, their Adversaries say that he was poisoned. This Morning it rained a little but cleared away and was fine about noon.

VIII

WHALES AND NICOTINE

FEBRUARY 1791

Tuesday 1 *Feb?* — This Morning write. Jones calls on me and wishes to have my Sentiments on a Plan for carrying on War against Britain in India should she commence Hostilities against Russia. At half past three go to dine with the Duke de La Rochefoucault. At half past five go to the Louvre and find that Mons. is better. *Les parents* begin to appear, of Course I leave them. Visit Mad? de Ségur and sit for some Time. She is just returned from attending on her Princess at Bellevue. The two old Ladies Mesdames Adelaide and Victoire ¹ are about to depart for Rome. Go to the Palais royal and spend the Evening. It has been a pleasant Day enough but cloudy and rainy this Evening. At Night a heavy Gale of Wind from the Westward.

Wednesday 2. — This Morning Richard calls about some Noth-

---

¹ These daughters of Louis XV, now sixty-eight and sixty-nine, are such back numbers, so pious, so unpolitical, that their emerging from their retreat at the Château de Bellevue (some nine kilometres out of Paris) might have been indifferent to the public had it not seemed to confirm a growing suspicion that the whole royal family meant to fly the country. The journey also seems like a protest against government treatment of the clergy, a burning topic of this winter's session. Their departure is a signal for fresh disturbances and angry debate. Scandal had it that filial obedience had caused one incestuous lapse in the saintly goodness of Madame Adelaide and that Madame de Staël's friend, the Comte de Narbonne, was a living proof, for what story could not be hung on the reputation of Louis le Bien Aimé. She had always befriended the young man, who now leaves everything he likes best to escort the old ladies to Italy. They will wander in Sardinia, Rome, Naples, Corfu, and Trieste before their nephew Louis XVIII gathers their bones to their fathers in the royal shrine of Saint-Denis.

ingness. I write. The Marquis de Montesquiou calls to speak about Swan's *Projet* for the American Debt. I tell him that the Offers hitherto made are not in my Opinion admissible. He goes away after some Discussion determined to cause a Proposition to be made to M.ʳ Swan. Ternant came this Morning and desired me to go to La Fayette's this Evening and thence to the Committee of Commerce. He said that he should have caused the Committee to write me a Note but that La Fayette, who chuses to seem (the *Omnis Homo*) to do every Thing preferred taking me along with him. I promise to meet at the Hôtel de La Fayette. Go to Le Couteulx's to dinner. He is not there. Capellis and another Marine Officer dine here and I must quit directly after. Desire Le Couteulx to call on me in the Morning that we may converse together. Make a short Visit at the Louvre and thence go to La Fayette's. Converse some Time with Ternant and when La Fayette comes up I tell him that I cannot go to the Committee but at their Request. That what I say will have less Weight. That I think it better for him to go this Evening with Swan and then if the Committee signify a Desire to see me I will wait on them To Morrow Evening. That in the mean Time he can signify to me what he wishes should be done. He agrees to the Propriety of all this in Words but I see that he is devilishly vexed. Be it so. Better he be vexed than carry me about in his Pocket. Go from hence to Mad.ᵉ de La Borde's. Abroad. Thence to Mad.ᵉ de Chastellux; stay some Time and take Tea with her and the Dutchess. Then return Home and write. A very fine Day.

Thursday 3. — This Morning write. Swan calls. He tells me that he has now the Contract in his Offer, provided he will admit certain Members of the Assembly to a Participation. There is he says a Knot of them who dispose of all Things as they list and who turn every Thing to Account. He speaks of their Corruption with Horror. He tells me that Sir Robert Herries is to supply the Farm with Tobacco when it is put *en Régie* and that he told him (Swan) last October that it would be put *en Régie* and that he should have the Contract. Ternant calls and tells me of what passed last Evening. He says that La Fayette agreed to the free Culture of Tobacco. That it is an Affair of Party entirely. He says that he proposed inviting me to the Committee but that M.ʳ Raymond ob-

jected as I was interested. This is the Man that Swan tells me is
Short's factotum. I dress and go to M.ʳ Mory's to Dinner. There
has been it seems a Mistake and instead of finding Chaumont I
meet two kept Mistresses. Chaumont and his Wife come in presently after. It is ridiculous enough. However, she goes Home.
We stay and dine late. Returning, Chaumont tells me that Mory
will not take Part in the Land Plan. He mentions another of his
Friends who will. *Qu?*. I go to the Louvre and find Mad.ᵉ with
her Husband. He is better. Stay some Time here, then come
Home and write. It has snowed the greater Part of this Day.

Friday 4. — This Morning I write. Call on M.ʳ Littlepage who
is abroad. See Van Staphorst, and go thence to the Louvre where
there is Company. The Husb.ᵈ is getting better. His Malady
arises from his Misconduct in pecuniary Affairs. He is a Wretch
and the best Thing he could do would be to die. Go to Monsieur
de Montmorin's and visit Mad.ᵉ de Beaumont. She is better in
Health. We have a numerous Collection at Dinner. After
Dinner our Conversation is more interesting to ourselves than to
the World. I tell the Count that England will send us a Minister
in the Spring. He says that Ternant is going out. As he himself must go to Council I have no Time for further Conversation. Mad.ᵉ de Montmorin shews me an Almanack from England
sent her by the Duke of Dorset in which among other Things is a
Table of Weights and Measures. She says that it is one among
many Things which will be useless to her. I write in a blank
Leave opposite to it:

> A Table here of Weight and Measure,
> In Times like these it is a Treasure
> For each one measures now the State,
> And what his Reasons want in Weight
> He makes up as a Thing of Course
> By the Abundance of Discourse.

Go from hence to the Louvre. Thence to Mad.ᵉ de Chastellux's
where we have Music. Thence to the Louvre and take Mad.ˡˡᵉ
Duplessis Home. Thence to Mad.ᵉ de Stahl's. Some Advances
are made to me by Mad.ᵉ ——. We shall see. This has been a
variable Day with some Snow and Sleet.

Saturday 5. — This Morning write. M: Swan calls and stays pretty long. He desires to know what Shares his Contract should be divided into. I tell him that I think one third should be enjoyed here in France, say three ninths, and four of the remaining six by Robert Morris. He is to consider of this. Paul Jones calls. I dine with Mad: de Stahl and go from thence to the Louvre. I find there Madame at Picquet with M: de S: Foi and the Bishop. Make my Visit short. Then go to Madame de Chastellux's. See there a M: Hodges who is in Pursuit of a Debt from France to a small German Prince. I give him some Hints respecting the Assemblée and desire him to obtain a List of the whole Amount. Spend the Evening here. The Weather is tolerably fair this Day and somewhat colder than it was. In Consequence of a Note from Swan I sent him 300# to pay petty Charges.

Sunday 6. — This Morning I write. Rich⁴ calls on me and afterwards Swan. Ruellan is arrived.¹ I tell Swan I will have Nothing to do with Ruellan. Go to Mons: Mory's to Dinner. We dine late. I did expect to have met a Person here who was to deal for Land but he is not present. After Dinner I go to the Louvre and perform the nuptial Rites, then return Home and prepare my Letters for ToMorrow's Post. I received many this Day from America. It has been very dirty Weather this Day. Snow and Sleet.

Monday 7. — Col? Walker calls. He had before written to ask my Interest with Le Couteulx; he wants the Advance of £300 St⁸. I promise to go to Le Couteulx's this Morning. Go thither. He is ill with the Gout in his Head, and asleep. Go thence to the Louvre. Detained late by a Reading so that Dinner is Half over when I arrive. Go from hence to Mad: de Boursac's and take her to the Comédie française where we have acted the Drama of the Vicomte de Ségur.² Fleury performs it admirably but it is a cold wretched Performance. The Idea is bad and yet requires the rich Genius of Shakespeare, which has not fallen to the Vicomte's Lott. Return to the Louvre and take some Tea. They keep me very late at Whist for six Pences. It has this Day been bad

---

¹ Robert Morris's broker at Havre.
² *Le Retour du Mari.*

Weather, raw and dirty. Col? Lynch, once Aid to Chastellux, called this Morning.

Tuesday 8. — This Morning I write. Marmontel calls. I go to the Louvre a little before three and stay a few Minutes. Thence to dine with Mad? Foucault. After Dinner go to the Louvre and celebrate.... I visit Mad? de Chastellux and say how dye you to the Dutchess. Then return to the Louvre and play six Penny Whist. My Friend is in bed but much better. The Weather has been foul this Day but rather foggy than wet.

Wednesday 9. — This Morning write but am constantly interrupted. Walker calls. Staphorst also calls and reads me Part of his Letters. Monsieur de Favernai came to breakfast between twelve and one, Richard before I was up. My only Means of getting free is to go out.... The Bishop and several others come in [at the Louvre]. I dine with La Fayette according to an Invitation of last Evening. I meet here Swan and Walker and a Man whom Chattelux formerly recommended. The Object is to know what System should be pursued respecting Tobacco. M? Raymond comes in. I am quite content to let them know my Sentiments on this Subject. First I state Facts whose necessary Result is evident. Secondly I lay it down that they must either pursue a Revenue on this Article in such Way as to make it a great one, or abandon the Idea of Revenue. That in the latter Case they must give every Body Leave to cultivate and to import that Article, but in the former they must either adopt an Excise or sell the Privilege to a Farm, or put it *en Régie* to the Use of the Nation. The first Plan is odious, the second unpopular and the third will countenance Fraud. As they have already excited much Discontent in the Tobacco Provinces it is dangerous to add new Cause of Alarm. I think it probable that they will begin by permitting the Culture and abandoning the Revenue, and that they will afterwards be obliged to have Recourse to the Tax and consequently to prohibit the Culture. M? Raymond is a sophistical cunning Fellow. Taking off the *Entrées de Paris* is another Point incidentally brought forward. Go from hence to Mad? de Chastellux's who is not at Home, thence to the Louvre and spend the Evening. It has been dirty Weather to Day.

Thursday 10. — This Morning write. La Caze calls with a M?

Ravara who is going to settle in Philadelphia and offers to take my Letters. I dine with the Dutchess of Orleans. After Dinner visit Mad? du Bourg who is in bed. I conclude that she is desirous of a little Recreation and accordingly propose it but she declines. I think however that she is sorry for having done so and that we shall come to a better Understanding. Call at the Louvre. Mad? is gone to the Bouffons [Opéra Comique], and I am much pressed to sup at Mad? D'Angiviliers. Return Home and write till ten, then go to the *soupé*. Stay till it is served (a little after eleven) and come Home. It has been a prodigious fine Day. The Aristocrats say that all Alsace is in league against the National Assembly and that some Districts of Brittanny are also come about.

Friday 11. — This Morning write. Swan calls. I open his Mind to some farther Prospects but refuse to give him pointed Information. Call on Le Couteulx who is too ill to be seen, and at the Louvre but Mad? expects Company, indeed they arrive. I go to the Baron de Bezevald's to dine and then again to the Louvre. We first quarrel and then embrace. Go hence to Mad? de Ségur's. She is abroad. Sit with him some Time and then return Home, take Tea and write.

Saturday 12. — Write. Col? Walker comes and stays with me till I go to Le Couteulx's. I ask Laurent to lend him the £300 which he wants. He does not chuse to do this. Go to Walker's Lodgings and write a Note to Grand & Co: on the Subject, thence to the Louvre where I dine with my friend and Mad!!e Duplessy. After Dinner while the latter is playing the fortepiano, as she is near sighted . . . almost perform the genial Act. . . . I lend Miss my Carriage and she goes to visit her Mother in Law. . . . As soon as she comes back I return Home and write. This has been a very fine Day and at Noon was very warm.

Sunday 13. — Richard calls and a Gentleman who wants to buy Lands in Virginia. I offer him Dover Estate.¹ He is to come again. I dine with the Count de Montmorin; visit at the Louvre after Dinner. Mad? has Company. Call on Mad? de Chastellux, then return Home and write. A pleasant Morning, in the Evening

---

¹ In Goochland, not far from Richmond, later sold by Morris to Madame de Ségur's brother, Count d'Aguesseau, and an endless source of worry. Part of Robert Morris's widely scattered investments.

a little Rain. The Assembly have abolished the Farm &c.ª, &c.ª, of Tobacco, permitted the free Culture and laid a Duty of 25# per Quintal on the Import.

Monday 14. — This Morning write. Swan calls and I tell him that I will not engage in his Provision Plan. He makes other Proposals &c.ª. Ternant calls. I go to the Restaurateur's and dine, having been favored with the Comp.ᵞ of Paul Jones for a long Time. After Dinner go to the Louvre. Mad.ᵉ is at Tric Trac. Go to the Tuilleries and visit Mad.ᵉ de Chastellux. Take up the Marquise and bring her Home. Go again to the Louvre where there is still Company. I come Home and write. This has been a very warm Day but a damp Atmosphere.

Tuesday 15. — This Morning write a little, then as it is a fine Day, go and take up my friend to ride; we make a short Turn together and upon our Arrival at the Louvre comply with the first Command. I dine with Mad.ᵉ de Foucault and go from thence to Mad.ᵉ de Chastellux's. Thence to the Louvre and my friend being gone for her Sister I am acquitted of my Promise and therefore return Home and write. This has been fine Weather to Day.

Wednesday 16. — M.ʳ Swan calls this Morning and tells me that the Assembly have decreed the Establishment of a *Régie* for the Manufacture and Sale of Tobacco on Account of the Nation. I walk with him in the Tuilleries & communicate a Plan respecting Tobacco which he highly approves of. He is immediately to set about the Execution. Take Madame de Chastellux to dine with her Niece. After Dinner set her down at the Palais Royale and return Home. Thence to the Palais royale and take Tea. We have Music. Thence to the Louvre. We are *sage*. ... Madame de Nadaillac sups here to see me. She is an Aristocrate *outré*, & has heard that I am of her Sect. She is mistaken. She is handsome and has a good dose of Esprit. Her Aunt my friend tells me she is virtuous and coquette and romantic. *Nous verrons*. This Day the Weather has been uncommonly fine.

Thursday 17. — This Morning M.ʳ Swan calls and gives me a Note of his Expences in Pursuit of a Provision Contract. We walk in the Tuilleries. He is to put a Stopper in the Hands of de Lessart on all other Contracts for Tobacco except the one. He is afraid that Le Couteulx will push for the Contract, and wishes me

to give him in such Case an Interest therein, which I refuse. Go
to the Louvre where I find the Bishop and feel that I am one too
many. He goes away, and I complain that she did not give me a
Hint to go off, but she says that I looked out of Temper. Go to
dine with Mons.̲ de La Fayette and speak to him about the
enormous Duty on Tobacco brought in American Vessels. He
wishes me to give him a Note about it. I tell him that I do not
chuse to meddle with Matters out of my Line. He says that Mirabeau has promised him to speak about it and he expects that both
the Tobacco and the Oil will be taken up by the Diplomatic Committee. I ask him whether it would not answer for the King to
suspend that Decree and give his Reasons. He says that he would
rather the Americans should be obliged to the Nation than to the
Prince. I tell him that I learn from some Persons well informed
that if he had spoken the Question would have been differently
decided. He says that on the contrary, it was so carried to spite
him, and that the Aristocrats in particular opposed it meerly on
that Ground. Go from hence to Mad.̲ de Ségur's. Thence to
Mad.̲ de Corney's who is moved. Thence to Mad.̲ du Moley's.
Thence to Mad.̲ de Boursac's whom I set down at her Sister's and
thence to Mad.̲ de Foucault's to Supper. We have here again
Mad.̲ de Nadaillac who assures me that there are many virtuous
and religious *young* Women in Paris. She says she will give me a
Supper with the Abbé Mauri.[1] I think if Time and Circumstances
serve she will take me *en Amitié*. Mad.̲ de Foucault wishes to
clear up some Doubts on the Score of my Constancy. I give her
all needful Assurances. Mad.̲ de Ségur confirms to me that the
Aristocrats lost the Tobacco Question. I think an additional Reason for their Vote is a Hatred to America for having been the
Cause of this Revolution.[2] It has been a fine Day but a little
colder than Yesterday.

---

[1] A Provençal of humble origin, Maury is the most fiery orator of the extreme Right in the Assembly, daring to stand up to Mirabeau. War, finance,
commerce, he embroiders with specious logic, but vigor and sense win him
some successes. Will advise the King to reject Constitution, 1791, and then
will emigrate to Italy.

[2] Whale oil and tobacco are putting the hero of two nations in a quandary.
While Short negotiates loans in Holland, American affairs are entrusted to La
Fayette, but as he is suspect to royalists as too Jacobin, suspect to extremists

Friday 18. — This Morning write. Dine with the Count de Montmorin and after Dinner mention to him the Decrees respecting Tobacco. He says he is doing every Thing in his Power relating thereto. I ask him if I shall write him a Letter on the Subject. He expresses a strong Wish that I would. Promise to do so. Ternant, who called on me this Morning, is here at my Request and is to be with me ToMorrow on this Business. Go to Madame de Chastellux's and take Tea. She recites some very extraordinary Things respecting the Vampires of Hungary and a German Conjuror. What I find extraordinary is that People of Credibility have avouched Facts which, being very much out of the Course of Nature and the Bounds of Possibility, demonstrate that they must have been great Liars or greater Dupes. Return Home and read. This has been a variable Day but the Evening is superb.

Saturday 19. — This Morning Ternant calls and we adjust in Part a Kind of Memoire respecting the Tobacco Decrees. I continue engaged in this till he returns at three oClock when I enclose it to Mons: de Montmorin, and give it to him to deliver. Swan came while I was at Work and I shewed it to him and he approved. He tells me that Delessart, the Comptroller, was engaged to the Merchants in England who formerly supplied the Farm, but his Friend has frightened him. He wishes some Estimate and Plan which I am to prepare. Dine with the Dutchess of Orleans and go after Dinner to see the Manufacture de la Reine with her R. H.; return to the Palace and thence Home to write. The Weather has been cold and raw this Day.

Sunday 20. — This Morning write. M: Richard calls and after him M: Swan who says that the french Party ask one Half of the Tobacco Contract, which is too much. He says that the Comptroller having been engaged to the English Houses holds himself high. He says also that one Person near the Comptroller insisted on knowing if I was engaged, and being told that I was, said there would then be no Difficulty. He desires me to have a Conference ToMorrow Evening, which I agree to. He is to call on me this Evening. Dine with Madame du Moley. She is very respectful and attentive. After Dinner I converse with him re-

as too aristocratic, and to both as too pro-United States, it is unfortunate that questions of importance to Franco-American commerce should have sprung up.

specting the Affairs of his Department and insensibly those of the
Finances, thence to those who administer them. He says Delessart is a Courtier, a Bachelor and very rich, with a good Deal of
Sense. Dufresne a noisy positive Fellow. If this Picture be just
it is easy to see which of the two will get the upper Hand. The
Weather is pleasant this Day. From Dinner I go to visit Madame
de Corney and then come Home and write, waiting for M.ʳ Swan
who instead of coming at seven keeps me till nine and then sends
Word he cannot come.

Monday 21. — This Morning write. A Man calls from M.ʳ
Grand to know whether by sending refuse Porcelaine to America
he can get Tobacco in Exchange. I give him all needful Information to shew the Folly of his Plan. M.ʳ Swan calls to tell me that
the Minister has given Orders to the Victuallers to lay in the
Stores for six Months, he being concerned with them and two
Members of the Marine Committee being also concerned with
them. I visit at the Louvre for a Moment after repeated Requests. Mad.ᵉ receives me with great Ability. I decline returning
after Dinner, at which she is not pleased but shews as little Mortification as may be. Dine at the Restaurateur's and return Home.
Write till nine when M.ʳ Swan comes in with a Monsieur Bre-
mont, who is Agent for the Coalition in the Assembly, to confer
on the proposed Contract for Tobacco. He wants I find for himself and his Friends one Half of the Concern and to furnish half of
the Funds, and he means I perceive to send this Half in Merchandizes, on which of Course there will be no small Advance
charged. He wishes to make himself Master of all my Knowlege
in the Tobacco Business, but he is a little deceived in that Matter.
We are to meet again. This has been a fine Day.

Tuesday 22. — This Morning write. Call on Mad.ᵉ de Flahaut
who has Capellis with her. I make a short Visit. She asks if I
will come again this Afternoon, and as this Request is in the Style
of Entreaty I promise to do so. Dine with Mad.ᵉ de Foucault and
meet there by Appointment the Abbé Ronchon. Mad.ᵉ is kindly
attentive. I bring the Abbé away with me and he tells me that in
the memorable Affair of Versailles, as it was known that the King
was that Day to hunt in the forest of Meudon, a Party of the
Populace in Number about a thousand, went thither, and among

them were some Assassins whose Object was to kill him, and that a Reward of a thousand Guineas was to be given to the Wretch who should perform that Deed. He says that the Count de S.t Priest being informed of this, sent to urge his Majesty to come immediately on important Business to Versailles. That this Message made the violent Party so much his Enemies as they afterwards appeared to be. The Abbé believes all this, which I must acknowlege that I do not. I think there is enough of little Villainy among them but I question whether there be such bold Criminality. Go to the Louvre. Stay but a few Minutes.... Return Home to write, having left my Name in the Way with Mad.e de Chastellux. Shortly after my Arrival M.r Ruellan and his Son come in: they take Tea and give me their Company till nine. This has been a pleasant Day. I mentioned to Chaumont the making Purchases of Debt; he is on the same Scent and says he will join with me.

Wednesday 23. — This Day I write and dine at Home lightly. The Marquis de Favernay called about one. He tells me that there is the Devil to pay in Languedoc. A Kind of religious War is there kindling between the Catholics and Protestants. He says that the latter, who are rich, have purchased over the national Troops and turned their Swords against the Catholics under Pretence of supporting the new Constitution. I suppose others give a different Account of the Affair, but it seems pretty clear that at Nimes and Usès they are actually come to Blows. I go at nine to the Louvre to take Mad.e to sup with Mad.e de Nadaillac; according to Custom she is not ready. We do not arrive till ten. Our Hostess is very pleasant. Insists that I shall be an Aristocrat whether I will or no. She gives me Assurances of her Religion and Morality &c.a, &c.a. But she is a Coquet and she is enthusiastic and romantic. What fine Materials for Seduction! I return Home at twelve. The Day has been rainy and very disagreable but at Midnight it is very fine.

Thursday 24. — This Morning write. At Noon walk till I am pretty well tired, then dress and go to the Louvre to dine. Mad.e is in Bed ill. When she got Home last Night she found in a blank Envelope a Will of her Bishop making her his Heir. In Consequence of some Things he had dropt in Conversation she concluded that he was determined to destroy himself, and therefore spent the Night in great Agitation and in Tears. Mͬ de Sͭ Foi, whom she roused at 4 oClock in the Morning, could not find the Bishop, he having slept near the Church in which he was this Day to consecrate two bishops lately elected.[1] At length it turns out that, pursuant to repeated Menaces, he feared that the Clergy would cause him to be this Day destroyed, and had ordered the Letter not to be delivered till the Evening, meaning to take it back again if he lived thro the Day. After Dinner she meets with a ridiculous Accident as I am seated near her in the Dusk of the Evening.... Go hence to Madame de Chastellux's. I learn that Paris is in great Tumult, of which I had indeed observed some Symptoms this Morning. At my Return from thence I go to the Louvre. The Bishop is here. I return Home and find the Place du Carousel full of Soldiers. This has been a very fine Day.

Friday 25. — This Morning write. Mͬ Swan calls and tells me that the Controlleur général has agreed to give a Preference in the Tobacco Contract to the Society of which he is to be a Member. I dine at the Palais royal. Called on my friend at the Louvre before and after Dinner but we are *très sage*. Return Home early and write. It is bad Weather.

Saturday 26. — This Morning I read, finding myself so much inflamed that I cannot sit up to write. Dine at Home. After Dinner visit my Friend and Madͤ de Chastellux. The Weather is but very indifferent and this Night blows hard.

---

[1] Civil Constitution of the Clergy was moved in May 1790; the King gave anguished consent 27 August, and 26 December sanctioned decree that all beneficed ecclesiastics must take civic oath to maintain it. Majority of clerical deputies solemnly refused to swear, sees and cures vacated by conscientious abstainers had to be filled. Out of seven juror bishops, three had no jurisdiction in France. So the Apostolic Succession is precariously continued by an unbeliever who, since his oath, is doubtfully qualified in the eyes of Rome, and since his formal resignation from his see in January to become a civil administrator of Paris, has signed his letters 'ex Bishop of Autun.' Dreading assassination if he refused and if he accepted, he spent the night close to the Oratory in Rue Saint-Honoré, the church vacated by Oratorians in protest at its 'sacrilegious' use for inauguration of civil system, the building surrounded by La Fayette with his Guards to ward off possible riot. Talleyrand, 24 February, consecrates the two first elected bishops, Abbé Expilly to Quimper, Abbé Marolles to Soissons, and will go through the ceremony once more to consecrate Gobel Bishop of Paris.

Sunday 27. — Richard calls this Morning. I write till four, then go to dine with the Count de Montmorin. He tells me that he is well pleased with my Reflections but he does not expect to do any Thing in the Tobacco Affair, the Assembly are so violent and ignorant. I mention to M. Dupont, who is here, my Plan, to which he gives but little Heed for the same Reason which M. de Montmorin assigns. This last tells me that a M. Pinchon, who it was said killed himself in July 1789, was murdered. That it was shortly after he had deposited his Portfeuille with the duc d'Orléans, which he had been perswaded to do on Acc. of the Troubles. That the duc de Penthièvre had been first proposed as his *Dépositaire* but this meeting with Difficulty his Son in Law was fixed upon. That the unhappy Man was brought Home and declared that he was murdered. He lived to sign several Papers. There was found in his House two Millions and his Estate is Bankrupt for 50 Millions. Mons. Dupont mentions that from a State of the Duke of Orleans's Affairs published by his Chancellor, it appears that he is arreared about fifty Millions more. Time will unravell these Things if the Suspicions be founded. I return Home and write.

Monday 28. — This Morning write. After my Letters are gone I call on Grand. None of them at Home. On Le Couteulx who is busy and begs I will dine with him. I see Swan who tells me that he and his friend are to visit me ToMorrow Evening at 7 oClock. I go to Mad. de Flahaut's. She is just going abroad. Dine with Le Couteulx, then call on Grand. I think I perceive that my Business with them bringing more Trouble than Profit, they begin to grow tired of it. Go to Mad. de Chastellux's. She tells me the Princess is much alarmed at what is passing in Paris.[1] There is a

---

[1] Paris excited by rumored discovery of a secret tunnel connecting the Tuileries with the stronghold of Vincennes, a crumbling disused *donjon* second only to the Bastille as an emblem of tyranny. La Fayette had advised the King to pull it down, but feels obliged to dispel a mob attempting its destruction. While marching his prisoners to the Conciergerie, he is fired at, Orleans agency suspected, which had threatened to end La Fayette supremacy. Unwounded, he hurries on to the Tuileries to quell a riot of a new color, armed royalists fuddling the castle guard with wine, forcing their way into the King's presence, to protect him or carry him off. News that their General was shot sobered the guard in time to manhandle the fine gentlemen out of the Tuileries. La Fayette arrives to find a puzzled King and a litter of abandoned weapons, mostly dag-

Deal of Riot conjured up but there seems to be no sufficient Object, so that it must waste itself. Go hence to the Louvre where I find Monsr de St Foi, & the Bishop is expected. I make my Visit short and return Home to read.

Extract from Letter of William Short to Morris [1]

Amsterdam. Jan. 30: 1791

... I lose all hopes of its ever being conceived by the American government how important it is to keep those employed here fully & minutely informed of their proceedings there – The activity & industry with which enquiries are made by those who are interested in our affairs mediately or immediately render this essential – whenever the person whom they suppose always freighted with intelligence from the government by whom he is employed, declares himself ignorant or uninformed, they suppose that he has something to conceal – their apprehensions are immediately agog – their alarms catch & spread from one to another – from nothing they create something & augur ill of any thing. — they think that the existence of the United States of

---

gers. He mocks at the '*Chevaliers du poignard*,' censures Duc de Villequier and Marquis de Duras, Gentlemen of the Bedchamber, as '*chefs de la domesticité.*' A courageous, dangerous day for La Fayette, but Paris titters.

[1] William Short is on one of his periodical visits to Holland, raising loans for the United States. Morris feels that better terms could be obtained if the Dutch money-lending monopoly could be broken, and persuades Short to place a loan in Antwerp. From Amsterdam, Short writes him: 'I have scarcely seen a man here ... who has not asked me after you – they all say you have *diablement de l'esprit* – that you are *bien aimable* &c. these are the Frenchmen who are here. – the Dutch say you have a long head – & well acquainted with business.' These letters are full of the classic moan of early American diplomats, lack of official news, when news affecting mercantile pockets manages to travel well enough. Jefferson had lately felt the inconvenience himself, but leaves his successors in the same plight; being Secretary of State involved far more than Foreign Affairs, and running his department with a staff of about three clerks perhaps made the commercial usage of duplicates and triplicates impossible. The system of friendly pockets, more trustworthy than the post, was yet vulnerable at wayside inns, and news of latest revolutionary liveliness often diverted volunteer postmen to other countries. There will be six months of total silence from his Government in the most critical year of Morris's mission to France.

America depends on a certain number of obligations at Amsterdam – & never can be persuaded that they have other more immediate & more pressing matters to attend to. – It would be worth while for government to sacrifice enough to the feelings of these people to employ a person on purpose in one of their bureaux, since they have not time themselves, to communicate on this side of the Atlantic the earliest & most authentic information – It would have another good effect also as it would tend to emancipate as well these people as the person supposed to have the first degree of the confidence of government, from the few who have a monopoly of the earliest & best information – Every possible means should be taken of unfolding the U.S. to the public eye here & of keeping them in constant view. We should make them believe if possible that the U.S. were on this side of the Atlantic – our distance, of which the idea is compounded of the number of leagues & the rare & scanty information received from thence, is a great detriment to our credit – the necessity of remedying this & the means of doing it appear to me so simple, that I cannot express my surprise at its not occurring to our government & particularly since one of its principal members has been a long time a witness of the evil. [A gentle thrust at Jefferson.]

[Morris reported the whale-oil and tobacco proceedings in full to Jefferson. The following extracts are from his letter to Robert Morris:]

Paris 7 March 1791

... You must already have learnt what they have done respecting Whale Oil and probably that they have given a Preference of six livres, five sous, per Quintal of Tobacco on the Importation by french Bottoms, which amounts to a Prohibition of others. Within these few Days they have determined that none but Vessels built in France shall be considered as french Bottoms.... the Idea of opening a Commerce between this Country and the Chesapeak by which Articles of the Growth, Produce and Manufacture of France should be exchanged for Tobacco, was visionary. Those who are acquainted with this Commerce know that such Hopes are vain. And yet the Perswasion that such an Intercourse might be effected has been at the Bottom of all those Plans and Propositions which have exercised the Attention of this

Government for Years. . . . I state this first because it is a Clue to guide thro the subsequent Labarynts. . . . After the heavy Duty that was laid upon American Oil and when the Tobacco Business came to be in Question, Col? Ternant, who took it into his Head that I might possibly know as much of the Matter as some other People and who had known me well in America, was desirous that the Committees should confer with me. He saw that the Business was going to the Dogs, and having a sound Head he foresaw the Consequences. . . . M! Raymond objected to my being consulted *because I was interes'ed.* To shew that Interest he mentioned your Contract, long since expired and in which you well know I had no Concern whatever. . . . Great Speculations had been made in Tobacco and many local Interests were engaged, so that the Decision was to be hurried thro during the Presidency of Mirabeau, while he could not take Part in the Debate. . . . When the Matter was taken up the Culture was permitted and such a heavy Duty laid as would secure an immense Profit to those who had purchased up the Tobacco on Speculation: then came the Difference of Duty on American Ships, without any particular Object except to punish La Fayette. This may seem a strange Reason but it is a true one. . . . The Exclusion of our Ships, also, from being admitted as french Bottoms arises from the same Desire to shew that his Support of America is useless, and at the same Time they have circulated the Idea that he prefers America to France, in Consequence of which he is afraid to do any Thing pointed lest he should loose his popularity. You will see from hence that our Affairs are in a very whimsical Situation.

[February 13 from Amsterdam Short sends some explanations to Morris:]

The heavy duty imposed on the American oil was much against the dispositions of the committees – In the beginning the committee of commerce were for prohibiting the American oils altogether & this because the Nantucketers [1] settled in France &

---

[1] The Nantucketers Short speaks of were nine families from that island who had in 1785 accepted a French Government invitation to settle at Dunkirk. The new duties would bear hard on those who had stayed at home, and who, by

of which one of the principals beseiged the committee day &
night & persuaded them that by this means they would come in
great numbers to settle in France & thus transplant that art to
that Kingdom & at the same time deprive us of it – they saw
immediately their national fisheries surpassing those of England
– & no rivalship to fear from us – This won them all & they expected in the next war to destroy the English fleet & domineer
all the seas – the honest Nantucketer not being a warring man
did not care much about this – he calculated on something more
immediate & more certain – that the prohibition would raise the
price of the oils he & his friends had on hand, & giving them
the monopoly in future would enable them to continue the high
price. – I found the committee devoted to this system & unwilling to reason about it, as is generally the case where we adopt
a system more from sentiment than from reason – After some
time however they became more moderate – I had several interviews with some of their most influential members & demonstrated the folly, absurdity & impolicy of the prohibition system
in the present state of the French fisheries, coasting trade & manufactures. – all I asked for was the continuation of the *Arrêt du
Conseil* of '87. – These same men instead of stopping there were
for granting much more, viz: for reducing the duties still lower –
for no other reason that I saw but from the law of the pendulum
which makes them vibrate at equal distances from the true point.
– It was not our business however to check these dispositions –
the committee of impositions had always been favorable on this
head – This was the situation of things when I last wrote to you
– At the time of fixing the tariff on the oils they found there
would be so much opposition in the assembly that they determined
to propose a duty higher than that of the *Arrêt du Conseil*, in
hopes by this means of succeeding – this either passed the house

---

the aid of a Massachusetts bounty, had built some forty new vessels to replace
the one hundred and fifty which the War of Independence had reduced to bat-
tered hulks. Averaging less than three hundred tons each they were working
the right-whale fishery in the north and fishing for sperm-whale off Brazil,
even working round the Horn and finding profitable sperm-whale fishing off
the coast of Chili. England was the largest market for sperm oil and France
for whale oil. Dunkirk Nantucketers will flourish in approaching war between
France and England.

or they were sure of passing it, when a member rose & by a long speech which satisfied *les honorables membres* proposed & carried the duty more than double what the committee had proposed. – The person in whose care I left my affairs at Paris writes me that there are great hopes of this being changed, but I own I do not count on it for the present although I think it very certain ere long.

What you say on tobacco makes me wish to make you acquainted with the progress of that business – I was fully convinced from the beginning that the assembly would not dare, on account of the Belgick provinces, to prohibit the culture – or if they did make a decree, that it would not be executed – the first report of the committee of impositions as you know, ended with the plan of permitting the home cultivation & manufacture – & of subjecting the importation to a *régie* – this was the worst possible system for us – – I did every thing I could, admitting the free cultivation, to facilitate the importation by rendering it free commerce subject to a light duty – with the right of *entrepôt* & facilities in paying the duty – I proposed another plan also of admitting it free of duty & this for a variety of reasons which it is useless to repeat here – this however I was sure would not be adopted. – Those of the committees with whom I had spoken (in all cases with M. de M[ontmori]n's knowlege & desire) were for the duty of 5. sous a pound or lower. – – My desire was of course that it should be as low as possible, & there was every reason to hope for a reduction. – The committee of imposition particularly, who had been our worst enemies, came over to the opinion of abandoning tobacco altogether as an article of revenue, as you will see in their report to the assembly of the 6th of December. – On the morning of the day that this subject was to be taken up, the committees, learning the opposition they were to have from Mirabeau &c., became alarmed as in the affair of oils & proposed against their principles the duty of ten sous in hopes of carrying it – such a duty on importation would be as bad as a *régie*, as the cultivation would be free. Of course I have desired those with whom I correspond to join Mirabeau rather than the committees at 10 sous. – I only know as yet that the subject was adjourned on the 4th & by the journal of the assembly there seems reason to believe that Mirabeau will abandon his system – if so I take it for granted he will oppose the high duty – The committee of imposition will propose a new plan favorable to their commerce with us, as they think. – It is however so complicated that it can be known only by time. – I suppose the question is decided before this – though it is as impossible to know when as what they will decide on any subject. – I cannot think with you that you would have played the part of a busy body in interfering in this business – on the contrary it seems to me that every American is in some measure bound to employ the talents he has & communicate the information he may be master of in such cases. I know not who you mean by 'those who seem to be particularly *charged* with the management of American affairs' – I only know that the only persons whom I have charged are the M[arqu]is de La F[ayette] – by the desire, & a Secretary by the authority, of those who ordered me here. – I cannot think that either of these can have insinuated what you mention – because the first esteems you – & the second probably does not know you. At any rate your reply by silent contempt is the best that can be made in this & all similar cases. – I do not understand the next sentence & still I should wish to do so – that you *think you see the end of many present men & measures & therefore let the world wag as it may* – If perchance you should not have heard the result of the Indian expedition it is that the object, which was to destroy certain towns & their crops, was effected – the army was returning when they were attacked by them – there was a skirmish & afterwards a bloody engagement – we lost 183 men – our army proceeded on their return without being further molested. – The latest letters rec.^{d} here are of Jan 6. – the winter extremely severe. – funds taking gigantic strides towards par. – the rise I fear too great to be natural – of course there may be again some fall. The State of Maryland has passed an act for doing full justice to their creditors injured by the late assumption of their debts by Congress – they have done this in a very wise & prudent manner, & which will be agreable to all parties. – Adieu my dear Sir & believe me

Y^{rs}

W Short.

Morris to William Short

Paris 20 February 1791

William Short Esq:
      Amsterdam

Dear Sir

Yours of the thirteenth reached me Yesterday Afternoon. I shall say no more at present about Loans but you may probably hear from me on the Subject some Time hence. You will observe that it is extremely difficult so to conduct Enquiry on a Subject of that Nature as not to communicate more than one would wish or learn less than one wants to know.

I think with you that there will be more Difficulty in getting Rid of the Oil-Duty than your Correspondents are aware of. Indeed I have observed in general, that those who foresee the fewest Difficulties meet with the most. I thank you for the Communications you have been so kind as to make on this Subject and that of Tobacco. By the bye, you seem to have taken from my Letter an Idea which was not in my Mind, but which has reached yours from an Expression which I must therefore explain. By those 'who *seemed* to be particularly charged with the Management of American Affairs' I meant the Persons who busied themselves therein as if they had an Authority which I suppose them not to have: and you know well that this kind of Men is very numerous in Paris.

You have seen the Decree which has been made respecting Tobacco and which gives to french Shipping a Preference of above 100$^{\#}$ per Ton over American. Previous to the Decision on this Business I was desired by a Note to dine with Monsieur de La Fayette in Order to confer on american Business. — And note that I had attended once before when he wished me to go with him to the Committee of Commerce but I declined untill the Committee should ask my Attendance, which they have not done. At the Conference to which I was invited were present Mr Swan and Col? Walker, and a little Man whom Chastellux formerly recommended to me as being a Disciple of Doctor Pangloss. In his Way to America he was Shipwrecked, got his Toes frozen off, and was afterwards I believe appointed to some subordinate Place in the consular Office. During the Conference another little Man came in whom I do not know but have been told that his Name is Raymond, and that he is from Alsace. After La Fayette had proposed the Question, I asked the Opinion of Walker and Swan which they gave, and the latter in particular observed that the Southern Provinces would soon supply the Kingdom if the Culture was allowed. I delivered my Sentiments to the following Effect. A Sacrifice of the Interest of France to that of America could not reasonably be expected. The first Question was or ought to be, whether they could dispense with the Revenue. If they could, then they should give it up entirely and consult the commercial Interest of the Country. That to this Effect, they should make the Article free to be imported and exported everywhere. That if on the contrary they should deem the Revenue necessary, then the following Modes of obtaining it occurred. 1. A Duty. 2. An Excise. 3. a Farm. 4. a *Régie*. That the first, if great, would be eluded. That the second, incompatible with their new principles, was not worth establishing on a single Article because of the Expence attending it. That the third was out of fashion and by the fourth they would be cheated. Respecting the free Culture, I gave it as my decided Opinion that in a short Time it would totally destroy the Tobacco Trade; and to this Effect I stated the Charges attending the Transportation of that Article which amount to about three Guineas on the Medium Produce of an Acre, and I have no Doubt that the South of France will produce as good Tobacco as Virginia. About this Time the Alsatian came in, and said a great Deal to prove what, if I can read the Countenance, he did not believe a Word of, viz that no Tobacco would be planted even if the Permission were granted excepting in Flanders and Alsace. I did not think it worth while to attempt an useless Confutation but told La Fayette that as they had already set Alsace on fire, I could not advise them to add more Fuel. That I had given him Facts from which he might draw his own Conclusions. That I would not pretend to advise, but would venture to predict. That the free Culture would be permitted, and thereby the Revenue be lost; but that afterwards the Culture would be prohibited thro all France and the Revenue be established. I could not but smile inwardly at the Conduct of the Business. The national Interests are every Way injured; those of America by no Means served; and Alsace is the Dupe. All this, Time I think will shew. — I cannot give you an Explanation of what is meant by the Words you underscore, but you may partly guess at it by what I have just now said. In Conversation hereafter we will take it up.

Finding that the Decrees bore so hard upon us, both in our Agriculture and Navigation, I have notwithstanding my previous Determination spoken to Monsieur de La Fayette, who (according to Custom) asked for *a little Note about it*. I spoke also to Monsieur de Montmorin, at whose Request I have really written a pretty large Note, which he will get translated and deliver to the diplomatic Committee. It purports to be Observations of sundry American Citizens. — I mean to keep out of Sight as much as possible, and do all the good I can; and for the Rest I repeat again, let the World wag as it may.

Your Friends here are well, and often ask me when you are to return. I answer that your Intention was for the End of this Month, but that you may be detained longer than you expected. I thank you for the Intelligence you communicate from America. The Indian Business seems to have been badly managed. As to the Rise of Funds, I am convinced that it was by Manœuvre. You have doubtless seen Hamilton's Plan of a Bank, which may have contributed to it. I presume with you that the Effects have again subsided. Such Variations will be rather injurious to credit, and if the Administration help to give those sudden Jerks they go on wrong Ground.

Pray find out whether the Empress of Russia is extending her Loans.

William Short to Morris

Amsterdam Feb. 28. 1791

Dear Sir

Of the interlocutors of the scene at M. de La F[ayette']s I know all except Col? W[alker] & the disciple of Pangloss. It is the M[arqu]is' *manie* to have this kind of comedy – & whoever gives into it with him is sure to lose much time & gain much *ennui.* The *Alsacien* of whom you speak is *Alsacien* I believe by birth but like several thousands, not to say millions, of his countrymen not particularly interested in any particular spot *ne possédant pas de terres.* – He & his family are settled in Paris & form a part of the recruits which the provinces constantly furnish to the capital, where they soon become naturalized, & often know or care no more about the province from which they came than about the *isle des lanternes.* – This is a sensible man & the *bras droit* of M. de La Fayette – for that reason I employed him on leaving Paris, as secretary – I well knew that any other that I could employ would never be able to see M. de La F. – which was the principal desideratum – – I think it possible enough that he believed what he said, notwithstanding his appearance, because he knew very little about the matter, viz the price & manner of cultivation of tobacco – & still less about the price & charges of importation – & none are so apt to believe as those who are ignorant. – He is however well informed in several respects & a man of uncommonly good character. — As to the decree they have made, & particularly the *coup fourré* of the 3/4 of the duty on French ships – it is like most of what they do, meer matter of chance – They did not know that they were passing a navigation act of a new kind since they exclude our vessels from the privilege of sharing the carriage of that part of our productions – the difference in the duty being more I suppose than the price of the freight. – I am glad of the note you made for M. de Montmorin & shall be happy if it produces effect – – Russia has lately made a loan here of 3. millions of guilders – & will very soon open another for the same sum – I suppose it probable you will have been informed by some of your correspondents here that the U.S. loan for 2¼ millions of guilders was taken up with an alacrity of which there are few examples. I was much pressed by all patriots to make use of the present favorable moment to extend it to 3. or 4. millions. – particular reasons prevented my doing it.

Yours

W Short

IX

THE FRENCH CONSTITUTION OF 1791

MARCH 1791

Tuesday 1 *March.* — This Morning write but meet with Interruptions. Go to the Court of the Tuilleries with Col? Walker who called upon me, but we are not permitted to walk in the Gardens. Try the Quay but the Mud is impassable. Return, dress and go to the Louvre. Send my Carriage from thence for Mademoiselle Duplessis. *En attendant* ... Go to Mad? Foucault's to dine. After Dinner visit Madame de Nadaillac. She and her Husband are Tête à Tête. We talk Religion and Morality. Monsieur observes with much Vehemence that the Man who, under pretext of the former, induces a Woman to violate the latter's Laws, is worse than an Atheist. Madame tries to mitigate a little this Denunciation. Now as Monsieur is of cold Temper and Temperament and Madame very enthusiastic, it seems to me that there is in this a remote Relation to the Abbé Maury, who is much considered by Madame. He is a *mauvais sujet* and she is very religious and duteous &ca^a, &ca^a. I part with her upon a pretty good *Ton* and Monsieur is also content. Return Home, and according to Appointment M? Swan and M? Barmont call on me. The Affair of the Tobacco is adjusted with the Comptroller so that we are to have a decided Preference. The Government are to furnish a Million and an Half, and the Interested on this Side of the Water are to make it up four Millions. The Business to be carried on on equal and joint Account. I go hence to the Louvre and spend the Evening there. Mad? de Guibert is of the Party, to whom I am a little more civil than usual, but maintain *un peu de dignité* at the same Time, for which I have my Reasons. Return Home pretty early. It has been a very fine Day.

Wednesday 2. — This Morning I read awhile and then go to the Louvre to take up my Friend and ride. She is under the Hands of her Hairdresser, which reduces our Minutes so much as only to permit a short Visit to Mad.e de Guibert. I set her down, return Home, dress and go to dine with Mons.r de La Fayette. I communicate to him some Hints respecting American Affairs and as he is desirous of taking them all up together I tell him that he had better in such Case get a Resolution or Decree empowering the Administration to act, for that otherwise he will have so many Interests opposed to his Plan that it must certainly fail. I think he will not follow this Advice because he wants to appear the Atlas which supports the two Worlds. I ask him to tell me what passed the other Day at the Château. He acknowleges that the Garde Nationale was drunk and himself so angry as to have behaved indecorously to the Gentlemen there, but he says at the same Time that Monsieur de Villequière was much in Fault, who, notwithstanding he had given his Word of Honor not to suffer any Persons to come into the King's Chamber except his usual Attendants, had suffered a Crowd to get thither, many of them of the worst Kind of People. Having heard his Story I tell [him], which is very true, that I am sorry for it, but as the Thing is done he must now bear it out with a high Hand and turn Mons.r de Villequière out of Office; assigning publicly as a Reason that he permitted certain Persons (to be named) to come into the King's Chamber on such an Occasion, contrary to the Promise made on his Honor. He finds this Advice very good. He must be preserved yet. I visit Madame de Chastellux and Mad.e de Ségur who are both abroad. I then return Home and write a little, afterw.ds read till near twelve. It has been a rainy Afternoon and Evening.

Thursday 3. — This Morning write by the Post and then go to the Louvre, where having consummated we go to take up Mademoiselle Duplessy, but she is not yet risen. We go to the Bois de Boulogne but as she takes some Scruples, very *mal à propos*, to walking there with me tête à tête, I immediately order the Coachman to return, and am very surly. She tries hard to remove this Humor but in vain. We walk about the Champs Élisées and then take up Mademoiselle. At our Return I propose to Monsieur de Favernay to go to the Restorateur's but Madame proposes that we should bring our Dinner to her. We go to the hotel des Américains and having made our Provision return and eat it there. After Dinner I come Home, read a little and dress. M: Barmont and Mons: de Bergasse come in. We have much Conversation on public Affairs, which form the Object of their Visit. They tell me that the Queen is now intriguing with Mirabeau, the Count de La Marc and the Count de Merci,[1] who enjoy her Confidence. They wish to visit me again. They tell me that Mirabeau, whose Ambition renders him the mortal Enemy of La Fayette, must succeed in ruining him by the Instrumentality of his Compeers in the Department [of Paris]. I incline to think, however, that La Fayette will hold a good Tug, being as cunning as any Body. Mirabeau has much greater Talents, and his Opponent a better Character. When these Gentlemen leave me I go to Mad: de Nadaillac's. We have here the Abbé Maury, who looks like a downright ecclesiastical Scoundrel, and the Rest are *fiers Aristocrats*. They have the Word *Valet* written on their Foreheads in large Characters. Maury is formed to govern such Men and such Men are formed to obey him or any one else. Maury seems, however, to have rather too much Vanity for a *great Man*. Mad: de Nadaillac is vastly attentive and insists that I must be an aristocrat *outré*. I tell her that I am too old to change my Opinions of Government but I will to her be just what

---

[1] Count Mercy-Argenteau (1722–1794) from 1766 until recently Austrian Ambassador to Court of Versailles. He had kept messengers galloping to Vienna reporting to Maria Theresa every act and word of her volatile young daughter, had bored Marie-Antoinette with constant advice. Since he had gone to govern and pacify revolted Flanders, she has sent through him to her brother Emperor Leopold secret letters urging military aid, and confides French military plans to the old diplomat, who with Count de La Marck constitutes the bugbear of the *Austrian Committee* against which there is loud clamor in the Assembly. She is trying to save a kingdom for her husband, but it means treachery to the new France. No letters have been found from the Queen to Mirabeau, but for eight months Mirabeau, in return for payment of his debts, has been sending letters of advice to the Tuileries while remaining in the Assembly the Revolution's man, never openly championing the King and Queen.

she pleases. Return about twelve. This has been a very fine Day.

Friday 4. — This Morning I write. Swan comes and by Way of saving Time I propose to him to walk in the Tuilleries. After discussing our Affairs and taking Exercise, I meet Mad.ᵉ de Flahaut, with whom I continue the promenade. Then go to the Restorateur's with Mons.ʳ de Favernay, where we dine dearly and badly. Thence to the Louvre and take Mad.ᵉ and Mademoiselle to ride. Set them down, return Home and write. It has been a prodigious fine Day.

Saturday 5. — This Morning write. The Count de Ségur calls on me. I ask him the Character of the Count de La Marck and the Count de Mercy. He tells me that the former is a military Man who understands his Business and that in the Affairs of Brabant his Plan was to raise a popular Party, which in Case of the Independence of that Country should be considered as the french Party, or at any Rate by sowing Dissention facilitate the Re establishment of imperial Authority. The Count de Mercy is, he says, one of the ablest Statesmen in Europe. While Ségur is here Chaumont comes in and stays some Time. He tells me of Dupont's Gallantries in America. After he is gone Van Staphorst comes, and before he leaves me Col.º Ternant arrives. Go to the Louvre and dine. After Dinner take Madame and Mademoiselle a short Ride. Return, and make the proper Use of a short Tête à Tête, then visit Mad.ᵉ de Chastellux who is abroad. Visit Madame du Moley who is very desirous of my Visits because she finds that I keep Company she cannot reach. Thence to Mad.ᵉ Le Couteulx's and sit a while with Laurent. Mad.ᵉ hints always a little at my supposed Galantries. I don't well know what this means. Go to the Palais royal and sup with the Dutchess. Mad.ᵉ de S.ᵗ Priest, who is here, wishes to know my Opinion of what has lately passed at the Louvre. I evade it handsomely, and Mad.ᵉ de Chastellux tells me so, being a little vexed because she says that they will quote against her what I have said and which they will understand very differently from the true Meaning. I ask her about the Count de La Marck & find that I am acquainted with him. He is intimately united with Mirabeau, is devoured by Ambition and of profligate Moral. *Nous voilà donc au fait.* Return Home by

twelve and take some Medicine, my Situation being very unpleasant. The Weather this Day has been raw and damp.

Sunday 6. — This Morning I write. I find myself much incommoded and feverish; go nevertheless according to Promise and
dine at the Count de Montmorin's. Swan was with me in the
Morning and shews a Letter announcing the Arrival of a Sample
of Salt Provisions from Boston. I speak to Ternant on this Subject and tell him that the Minister of the Marine is connected
with the Régisseurs and also that Mallouette is endeavoring to
obtain a Boon for his Mistresses Husband. He says that it is for
such Reasons he has long desired that all Supplies should be contracted for at Auction. I tell him that there is in that also an Inconvenience, for their Enemies might send them a Contractor
purposely to prevent the Supplies from being brought when most
needful. After Dinner I chat a long Time with Madame de Beaumont and Mad.ᵉ de Fersensac, which last is I think very well disposed. Monsᵣ d'Agout comes in. He is just arrived from Switzerland and brings me many civil Sayings from Mad.ᵉ de Tessé
who is become a Convert, she says, to my Principles of Government — There will be many more such Converts. I take Mademoiselle Duplessis to Mad.ᵉ de Flahaut's and then pay a short
Visit to Mad.ᵉ de Chastellux where I see Mad.ᵉ de Lostange; a very
handsome Aristocrate. Return Home and go early to bed. The
Weather has been this Day disagreable.

Monday 7. — This Morning I write, being still unwell. Swan
calls; I ask him to dine with me and send for Staphorst. I walk
with Swan for half an Hour in the Tuilleries, which fatigues me
much. At Dinner I take better than a Pint of Claret and we walk
afterwards. In the Evening Mad.ᵉ de Flahaut calls at the Door
and sends to know how I do. She will not come up, altho her Husband and Nephew are with her. I go early to bed. This has been
a prodigious fine Day.

Tuesday 8. — This Morning while I am writing Mᵣ Livingston
calls on me and I take him to the Bois de Boulogne where we walk
together. Return Home, dress and take Mademoiselle Duplessi
to the Louvre; go, after setting her down, to the Palais royal and
dine with the Dutchess. After Dinner visit Mad.ᵉ de Foucault
who is just going abroad and Mad.ᵉ de Nadaillac and the duc de

La Rochefoucault who are not at Home. Thence to the Louvre.
Madame says she expected me to dine with her and had sent to
ask me. This seems rather apocryphal. I make my Visit very
short as they are going to picquet. Visit Mad.ᵉ de Ségur who is
abroad and then go to Mad.ᵉ de Chastellux's where we take Tea.
A Trio of which the Dutchess makes the third. Go to the Louvre
and take Mademoiselle Duplessis Home. This has been a very
fine Day. The Evening is a little cold.

Wednesday 9. — This Morning I write and then pay a short
Visit at the Louvre where we do the needful. My friend tells me
that she has not slept last night, my ill Humor alarmed her and
made her imagine that I had some serious Cause of Offence. —
You are but at the Begining of this Carreer, my dear Adelle! and
you have probably a long Lane to go thro. Dine with Mons.ʳ
de Favernay where we drink a good Deal. After Dinner visit
Mad.ᵉ de Nadaillac. The Abbé Maury comes in. By Degrees I
advance. Call with Favernay at the Louvre. Thence go to Mad.ᵉ
de Chastellux's. Puisignieu and Mad.ᵉ de Ségur come in. I send
an Excuse to Mad.ᵉ Foucault and sit here till ten, then return
Home. It has been a delightful Day.

Thursday 10. — This Morning I write till one, then take up M.ʳ
Livingston and go to Lebrun's Galery. At 2 Mad.ᵉ de Ségur ar-
rives and I stay till near three, then go to the Hotel des Invalides.
We go to the Top of the Dome, from which we have a View of
Paris. Go to dine with Mons.ʳ de La Fayette and after Dinner he
sets me down at the Louvre where I amuse my Friend but Company coming in prevents me from participating in it. Call on
Madame de La Borde, M.ʳ & M.ʳˢ Walker and Col.º Swan and his
Wife, who are all abroad. Make a short Visit to Mad.ᵉ de Chastellux and then pass again at the Louvre where I still find Company
and therefore return Home. It has been a very fine Day.

Friday 11. — Write. Richard calls on me and after he is gone
Chaumont comes. Dress and go to the Louvre. Mad.ᵉ is not yet
up. She tells me she cannot take a Ride as she expects her Sister D'Angivilliers. I shew ill Humor and am going away. She
entreats my Stay. After she is up, Monsieur being out of the
Room, instead of embracing we are cold and at length quarrel notwithstanding her Artifices. In the Event she is taken ill. A ner-

vous Affection which a strong Dose of Œther removes in Season
to visit her Sister, who sends in Haste. After some Time she re-
turns and we ride together. They agree to give her 1000# per
Month but insist that she shall keep her Carriage. After setting
her down I go to Dinner at the Palais royal and thence to a new
Opera of which the Scenery is beautiful but the Words and the
Music only *comme ça*. Visit Mad.ᵉ d'Hudetot who is abroad, and
Mad.ᵉ de Chastellux. Then go to the Louvre where they are at
Supper. Take Mad.ˡˡᵉ Duplessis and Mad.ᵉ de Boursac Home. It
has been a very fine Day. I observe in an English Newspaper of
the 1.ˢᵗ of March that the preceding Friday Night and Saturday
Morning was a tremendous Snow Storm.

Saturday 12. — This Morning write. Swan calls but has nothing important to communicate. At three I go to dine with Mad.ᵉ
Foucault. After Dinner visit Mad.ᵉ de Nadaillac who has just
done spewing. We converse about her Malady. Afterwards upon
Religion, and she wishes to know whether I have the Virtue of an
American which she doubts, because she is pleased to say I have
the Amiableness of a Frenchman. I leave that Matter a little
doubtful but she seems a little displeased that her Husband
comes in, which is a good Sign. I make my Visit neither long nor
short and I perceive that both are content. Go to the Louvre
but the Baron de Montesquiou is here, who wants to get into Office, and then comes the Toilette and then Mademoiselle Duplessis. We make our Arrangement and I visit at Mad.ᵉ de Chastellux's who is abroad. Return to the Louvre. We take Made.ˡˡᵉ
Home and then stop at the Louvre in our Way to Mad.ᵉ d'Angivillier's. We do well the genial Act and then go on to Supper.
My Reception is very flattering here notwithstanding the Compliments of Mad.ᵉ ——. Drink a good Deal of Wine and then take
Mons.ʳ & Mad.ᵉ de Flahaut Home. It has been a very fine Day.

Sunday 13. — This Morning I write. Swan calls and tells me
what I had hinted to him, viz: that Rœderer's Motions and Resolutions have cut up the Régie by the Roots. Ternant calls, with
whom I converse a little on these Things. Dine with the Count de
Montmorin, and as Montesquiou comes in after Dinner I mention those Things to him. He wishes me to have a Memoire drawn.
Go Home and write till one in the Morning. It has been a very
fine Day.

Monday 14. — This Morning write. At Noon Mad.ᵉ de Flahaut calls and takes me up. We go to Mademoiselle Duplessis and then all together to the Bois de Boulogne where we walk. Return to the Louvre and dine. I lend my Carriage to Mademoiselle after Dinner to visit her Mother in Law and as Monsieur is called down by a Gentleman and M.ʳ de S.ᵗ Pres by some Ladies we seize the Occasion . . . I return Home and write. M.ʳ Swan and M.ʳ Bermont do not come as I expected.

Tuesday 15. — This Morning write. At one go to the Louvre and do family Duty. Dine there; go after Dinner to the Academy of Phisicians where Vic d'Azir pronounces the Eulogium of Doctor Franklin. Go thence to Mad.ᵉ de Chastellux's and spend the Evening at the Palais royal. It has been a very fine Day.

Wednesday 16. — This Morning write. Swan calls. Mad.ᵉ de Flahaut calls upon me but goes away before I can go down Stairs. I walk to Chaillot and say how dye do to Madame de Guibert. Return on foot and in the Tuilleries meet de Cantaleu who asks in Presence of another Deputy some Explanations respecting the Loan opened by M.ʳ Short in Holland. I tell him that I do not believe it is intended to pay it into this Treasury. Dress and dine with the Count Dillon. Call on Mad.ᵉ de Corney and then return Home. M.ʳ Swan and M.ʳ Bermont do not come till after eight. The Comptroller General is afraid to take any Step respecting Tobacco just now. We must wait a few Days. Perhaps a few Months. Go to Madame de Nadaillac's to Supper. A small Party and pleasant enough. It has been a very fine Day.

Thursday 17. — This Morning I write. Mad.ᵉ de Flahaut calls and takes me to ride. She is ill. I dine with her and play at Whist after Dinner. She goes to bed early and I visit Mad.ᵉ de Chastellux and the Dutchess of Orleans. Go afterwards to the Louvre, stay till my Carriage returns from Mad.ˡˡᵉ Duplessis and then go to Supper at Mad.ᵉ D'Angivilliers. Mad.ᵉ de Condorcet is here. She is handsome and has *une Air spirituelle* [sic]. Talk with Condorcet after Supper on the Principles of the Œconomists. I tell him, which is true, that once I had adopted those Principles from Books, but that I have since changed them, from better Knowlege of human Affairs and more mature Reflection; in the close of our Discussion I tell him that if the *Impôt direct* be heavy it will not be paid.

Friday 18. — This Morning I walk out to the Louvre. My friend is ill. I walk along the Quais till late, then dress and receive my Visitors who dine with me. Mons.ʳ & Mad.ᵉ de Flahaut, Mad.ˡˡᵉ Duplessis, Mons.ʳ de S.ᵗᵉ Foi and S.ᵗ Pardou; Chaumont, his Wife and Sister, Mesd.ᵐᵉˢ de Courcelles and Guibert. We drink well and I give the Ladies punch, which they like much, after Dinner. When the Rest are gone I go with Mad.ᵉ de Flahaut and Mad.ˡˡᵉ Duplessis to ride. My friend is taken ill en Route. We return, put her to Bed and play Whist at the Bed Side. This has been a very fine Day.

Saturday 19. — This Morning I walk to the Louvre but find my friend unprepared to receive me, tho I came by Appointment. Leave her. Walk, and when I return find M.ʳ Swan, who wishes me to take a Concern in his Timber Contract. I do not think his Offer is tempting, and give him my Ideas thereon. Crèvecœur calls and after him Paul Jones. I read to them sundry Observations on the State of Things here. Dress and go at four to Mad.ᵉ Foucault's. Dine, & after Dinner, in chatting on one Side, among other Things it is a Question as to the Causes why Children have or have not the Talents and Beauty of those who produce them. I tell her that I wish she loved me enough to let me give her a Child. She asks if I think myself able. I reply that at least I could do my best, and then as Monsieur is listening I change the Conversation. Go hence to the Louvre. Send my Carriage to Mad.ˡˡᵉ Duplessis and amuse Mad.ᵉ; in Consequence she resolves not to sup at Mad.ᵉ D'Angivillier's but only to visit. I call on Mad.ᵉ de Chastellux who is abroad. Then visit Mad.ᵉ du Moley and afterwards Mad.ᵉ de Corney. Then go to Mad.ᵉ D'Angivillier's and sup. Take Home Mad.ᵉ de Boursac and get to Bed before one. It has been a prodigious fine Day and the Evening is delightful. We hear this Day that there has been an Insurrection at Douay in which an Officer of the Militia has been hanged by the Populace. The Municipality would not proclaim the Law Martial. This is natural enough.

Sunday 20. — This Morning walk out and call by Appointment on my friend. She is not yet up. I leave her abruptly. Walk and return. Mons.ʳ is with her. Vic d'Azir comes in and we have a little Conversation respecting the Conduct to be pursued by the Court. I give him some Hints as to the past by Way of elucidating the future, and he is equally surprized at the Information and at the Force of my Reasons. I see this in his Countenance. After he and Mons.ʳ le Mari are gone we quarrel. It is necessary to do so. At a proper Moment I leave her abruptly. She asks if I will come back; I answer in the negative and take a pretty long Walk. At my Return S.ᵗ Louis brings a Note requesting me to come this Evening, to which I make no Answer. Swan and Walker are with me. The former wants an Answer to his Letter which I have not yet considered. The latter communicates the State of Affairs with Burton and Playfair. Dress, and as I am going out I receive another Note. Dine with M.ʳ Grand. After Dinner visit at Le Couteulx's. They are abroad. At Mad.ᵉ de Ségur's; stay some Time with her. Call on Mad.ᵉ de Chastellux who is abroad. Go to the Louvre. My friend thanks me for coming and her Voice is that of Pride breaking into Humility. Several Persons come in and go out; at length we divide into parties to see the Illumination of Paris for the King's Recovery. She goes with me, and on the Way solicits Explanation. After passing thro the proper Stages I consent to forgive and pass the Evening with her. This is received with Thankfulness as the greatest Obligation. Mons.ʳ de S.ᵗ Foi comes in between ten and eleven and tells us that the Pope has laid the Kingdom under an Interdict. This must produce some Movement as soon as it is known. Take Mad.ˡˡᵉ Duplessis Home. It is a dreadful Night. The Wind very high indeed from the Westward, with Rain. The Illumination this Evening was the poorest barest Thing immaginable.

Monday 21. — This Morning Col.ᵒ Walker breakfasts with me. At ten I call on Mad.ᵉ de Flahaut and we go to chuse a Silk and order it made up for M.ʳˢ Low. Set her down at the Louvre, and having embraced, I return Home on Foot. Read, then dress and dine with the Dutchess of Orleans who is so kind as to reproach me for absenting myself. After Dinner I visit Mad.ᵉ de Nadaillac. Her Reception is rather that of a Coquette than dévote. She gives ...[1]

... me on Friday. Go to the Louvre where my Friend is in Dis-

---

[1] Next page is torn out. Page 329 of original begins with end of entry for Wednesday 23.

tress, her Woman has a Child dying (as they suppose) in the House. I express tenderly my Satisfaction at seeing her take so sincere an Interest in the Sufferings of others. Visit the Child, who may yet I think recover. Go to Supper at Mad? de Nadaillac's. It was a cloudy Morning, rained a little after two oClock, and is a pleasant Evening.

Thursday 24. — This Morning a Note from Mad? de Flahaut informs me that the Child died a few Minutes after I left the Louvre. I call on her at her Request and satisfy the Sentiment. We then walk to her Sister's. Returning, we see the Bishop, and stop tho in a Carriage. So much for Appearances. Dine at the Restorateur's. After Dinner ride. Come Home early. Read and go early to Bed. It has been a fine Day.

Friday 25. — This Morning M? de Crèvecœur calls to enquire M? Short's Lodgings. Swan comes in; he has some Notes on my Calculations respecting his Wood Contract, but I cannot now examine them because my Servants want to clear my Chambers for the Reception of Company. I walk out and leave Swan at the Louvre. The Servants being out of the Way I announce myself. Madame is Tête à Tête with Monsieur de Ricy,[1] and sundry little Circumstances look very suspicious. She cries out with Suddenness and Alarm: '*Qui est-ce là?*' Upon naming myself: '*Je vai vous renvoyer toute suite!*' I turn round and leave them. She runs after me but I neither answer a Word to her Excuses nor give her a single Look. Return Home and dress. Mad? de Chastellux comes before I have quite finished. I have Mesd.?? de La Fayette, Ségur, Beaumont & Fersensac. The Gentlemen are Messieurs de La Fayette and Ségur, Ternant, Short, D'Agout & Abbé de Lisle. The Abbé Morellet comes in but he does not stay long; he finds that his Visit is much misplaced. After Dinner I walk to Mad? de Chastellux's and stay till ten oClock, then return Home and go to Bed. It has been a fine Day.

Saturday 26. — This Morning M? Swan calls and we examine

---

[1] De Ricie will have his uses. In an effort to guard her acquaintance with her future husband the Portuguese diplomat de Souza, then in its delicate springtime, against a concrete ghost of her past, Madame de Flahaut will in Hamburg, 1796, send this fellow refugee to meet the ship bringing Talleyrand from long American exile, with the modest request that he turn back without landing!

his Calculations. I offer to take his Application to Le Couteulx and to second it, but tell him that I am perswaded he will loose Money by his Contract if executed in the Manner he proposes. He tells me that the Contract for victualling the french Navy is soon to be put up at Auction. S! Louis comes to know if I expect Mad? &c? to dine with me, to which I answer in the affirmative, coldly enough. Call on Short who is just gone out. Return, and while I am dressing he calls on me. He tells me that he has but little Hope of being appointed to this Court. That Jefferson wishes him to return to America and says that the Appointment rests entirely in the General's Bosom. That it is to be made this Session. I shew him the Memoire and Notes I have made about Tobacco. Speaking about the Actings and Doings of the Assembly in this Regard, he says that the duc de La Rochefoucault is led by Roederer and Condorci, who are both Rascals. I remind him that I had judged the latter long since by his Countenance. I inform him of what can be done respecting Loans in Flanders. Shortly after he is gone, Monsieur and Mad? de Flahaut, the Child, Monsieur de S! Pardou and Mad!!e Duplessis come to dine. Our *abord* is un *peu froid*, and so continues. The Bishop D'Autun comes some considerable Time after, but Mad? de Boursac and Mons! de S!e Foi keep us waiting till near four. Mad? talks at me in Explanation and Pacification. After Dinner, Whist being proposed, she desires me to draw a Card, which I refuse, and she declares that unless I play she will never again set her foot in my House. I reply (*with all my Heart*) '*à la bonne heure.*' After the Party is over she asks if I will call on her before Supper; I answer dryly *no*. She had formed a Plan, I think, to wait upon Mad!!e Home and then on our Return to celebrate a Reconciliation, but this is premature. I visit Mad? de Chastellux. The Dutchess, to whom I mention the Reason why I did not ask her to Breakfast, expresses a great Inclination to come some Day or other. Go to Supper at Mad? D'Angivilier's. My friend receives me with a Coldness of wounded Pride very strongly marked. Luckily Mad? de Nadaillac is here, and I dress myself in Smiles and pleasantry. She choaks with Resentment. During Supper I am seated next to Mad? de Nadaillac and am *très aimable*, Countenance, Manner, all accord well. After Supper I ask Mad? de Flahaut if she con-

fides her young friend to me. She says that she cannot leave this
Company alone to go with me. I tell her she may arrange Mat-
ters as she pleases, and leave her. As I did not seize this Opening
I am to take Mad.ᵉ de Boursac Home. Get Home myself at a
Quarter after twelve. It has been a rainy, disagreable Afternoon
and Evening.

Sunday 27. — This Morning I rise late. Dress and call by Ap-
pointment on Mad.ᵉ de Fersensac. She is on the other Side of the
Way at Mons.ʳ de Montmorin's. I leave my Name and visit
Mad.ᵉ de Beaumont. Find them together, and am *très aimable*,
but a little cold to Mad.ᵉ de Fersensac who disappointed me.
Visit Mad.ᵉ de Montmorin who shews me the Letter of Gen.ˡ
Washington to the Assembly, printed in one of the public Papers.
It is not what the violent Revolutionists would have wished,
and contains a Hint respecting La Fayette which his Enemies
will not fail to notice. Go from hence to Mad.ᵉ de Ségur's who
presses me to stay and dine, which I refuse. Go and dine as I had
promised with the Dutchess of Orleans to see her Daughter.
It is a pretty little Princess and has an air *très fine*. Go from hence
to Mad.ᵉ Foucault's. The Conversation is immediately turned
upon Love. In the Course of it I observe that I have remarked
*deux espèces d'hommes. Les uns sont faits pour être pères de famille
et les autres pour leur faire des enfans.* She is delighted with this
Observation. — Chaumont reads me a Part of Laforet's Letter to
him, giving a very exalted Idea of the present Situation of America and counselling purchases of Lands and Stock. Call on Mad.ᵉ
de Nadaillac, D'Angivilier, Laborde, Le Couteulx and La Norraye. All abroad. Visit Mad.ᵉ du Molet and go from thence to
Mad.ᵉ de Chastellux's. Sit an Hour with her and the Dutchess,
then return Home. The Weather has been tolerably fair but approaches towards cold.

Monday 28. — This Morning write. M.ʳ Richard calls and after him M.ʳ Swan. I receive a Note from my friend desiring me to
spend the Evening. It is couched in Terms of more Humility than
her Looks portended at the last Interview. Go to Mad.ᵉ de Chastellux's where there is a Breakfast. The English Embassador
and his Lady are here. If I might judge from her Manner I have
made a little Progress in her Esteem. We shall see. Visit M.ʳ

Short and sit with him till near four; take him to La Fayette's
and go myself to dine with Mad.ᵉ de Stahl. After Dinner visit at
Monsieur de Montmorin's. I meet here *par hazard* the Baron de
Viosmenil. Go from hence to Le Couteulx's but they are not at
Home. Thence to the Louvre. Monsieur de Curt and Mad.ˡˡᵉ
Duplessis are here. He is a little tipsy and very full of amorous
Profession. Some more Company come in and I leave her, to her
great Disappointment. She gave Openings which I would not
seize, and she was in Spirits as having carried her Point, when my
Retreat convinced her that she had not gained the Victory she
supposed. I sit up late reading the Newspapers from America
which M.ʳ Short lent me. This has been a pleasant Day.

Tuesday 29. — This Morning walk and get a fall in the Street
which barks my Stump a little. Call in at the Louvre. My friend
comes to Explanation. Makes a thousand Vows and Protestations
and finally I give her my Hand. Leave her, and on my Return
Home, Swan calls. As I could not find Le Couteulx last Evening
he is to call again ToMorrow. Dress and dine with Le Couteulx.
He will not accept of Swan's Offer but says he will get a Friend to
do it for him. He urges me to obtain a Share in the Provision Contract. Says he would join in the Wood Business with me but not
with others. After Dinner chat a good Deal with Madame, who
is content to chat on Subjects of a leading Nature. Mad.ᵉ de
Troudaine comes in and reproves me justly for not visiting her.
Go to the Louvre and sit a long Time with my friend, who complains of being ill, and Mad.ˡˡᵉ Duplessis. The former feels very
happy at the Reconciliation and is now I think in the Situation
that she ought to be; apprehensive, and therefore feeling for what
she possesses and fears to loose. Visit Mad.ᵉ de Chastellux, who
tells me that the british Embassadress is much pleased with me.
I thought so. The poor Princess is very ill at Ease. Go to sup with
Mad.ᵉ de Nadaillac. I tell the Abbé Maury that I expect he will
get the Hat [1] which the Cardinal de Loménie has sent back. I

---

[1] The Cardinal's hat of Morris's jesting actually awaits Maury in Rome.
The Pope also makes him Ambassador to the Holy See from Comte de Provence, future Louis XVIII. Maury will be Napoleon's Archbishop of Paris,
1810–1814, against the Pope's commands, later expiating this disobedience in
Castle of St. Angelo.

tell him also that the holy Father has done wrong in not laying the Kingdom under an Interdict. He answers that Opinion is no longer with the Sainte Siège and that without an Army to support the Interdict it would be laughed at. That the Instance of England makes Rome cautious. I reply that the Cases are somewhat different, but further, as the Assembly have left the Pope nothing, he might play a sure Game since he can loose no more; and at any Rate he had better have done nothing than only one Half of what he might do, because Man may by Degrees be habituated to every Thing. He agrees to the Truth of this and owns that he should have preferred Extremities. I tell him that from the Moment when the Church's Property was seized I considered the Catholic Religion as at an End, because no Body would be a Priest for nothing. He agrees fully. This has been rather a dusky Day but not unpleasant. Mad: de Puinieu played extremely well on the forte piano this Evening.

Wednesday 30. — This Morning write. Swan calls and I tell him what passed Yesterday respecting his Affair. M: de S: Pardou calls and before he leaves me Admiral Jones comes in. I call on M: Standon who is abroad. Then call at the Louvre and go from thence to dine at Monsieur de Montmorin's. Immediately after Dinner go to the Théâtre de la Nation. There is here a dreadful Representation of monastic Vengeance and Guilt. Sup at the Louvre. Mad: d'Angiviliers comes in about eleven and we quit the Stage as there are Affairs in Agitation. This has been a tolerably pleasant Day.

Thursday 31. — This Morning write and after sending off my Letters, walk. Call at the Louvre. My friend is ill. Visit Mad: de Chastellux who is abroad. M: Short calls on me and we ride together. He tells me that he forwarded to Col? Hamilton the Offer of some Persons on the Part of the Genoese to pay the Debt of America to France. Dine with Mad: Foucault and advise the Count de Puinieu to turn a deaf Ear to the Solicitations of the expatriated french. Take Mad: de Foucault to the Bouffons and then visit at the Louvre. Perform the nuptial Act and then ride together. Visit Mad: de Chastellux afterw.ds who is again abroad. I return to the Louvre and spend the Evening.... It has been a fine Day.

APRIL 1791

Friday 1 *April.* — M.ʳ Standon calls and makes a very long Visit. After he is gone I go to the Louvre. Take my friend to ride. . . . I dine with the Dutchess of Orleans. After Dinner go to the Opera and leave it early to take Mad.ˡˡᵉ Duplessis Home and my friend to Mad.ᵉ de La Borde's. In the Way we call to enquire about Mirabeau's Health. Guards stop us lest the Carriage should disturb his Repose. I am shocked at such Honors paid to such a Wretch. On this Subject I quarrel with my friend. This is the second Time this Day. We make it up. I stay at Mad.ᵉ de La Borde's till eleven and then go to Mad.ᵉ de Stahl's. The English Embassadress is here and receives me very well. I return Home at one. This has been a very fine Day.

Saturday 2. — This Morning M.ʳ Standon with his Friend M.ʳ Fisher breakfast with me. They come late and M.ʳ Swan comes in, shortly after them, also M.ʳ Crèvecœur and after them Commodore Jones. I tell Swan that an Offer for the American Debt has been transmitted to Col.ᵒ Hamilton. Walk. Go to the Louvre. . . . Sit with her some Time and then go Home and dress. Visit Madame de Ségur who is abroad, Mad.ᵉ Le Couteulx who is in a *demi bain.* Call on Grand to know if he has any News from Franklin. He has not. Visit Mad.ᵉ de Chastellux and then Mad.ᵉ de La Fayette. This last tells me that I am in Love with Mad.ᵉ de Beaumont. I own it, tho it is not true. She says that her Company must be insipid after such agreable People. *Que veut dire cela.* Go to Monsieur de Montmorin's to dine. After Dinner visit with the Vicomte de La Luzerne at Mad.ᵉ de Trudaine's. She is abroad. Go to Mad.ᵉ de Chastellux's. Thence to the Louvre. Mirabeau died this Day. I tell the Bishop d'Autun that he sh.ᵈ step into the Vacancy he has made and to that Effect should pronounce his funeral Oration, in which he should make a Summary of his Life and dwell particularly on the last Weeks, in

which he labored to establish Order. Then dwell on the Necessity
of Order and introduce properly the King. He says his Thoughts
have run much upon that Subject this Day. I tell him he has
not a Moment to loose and that such Occasions rarely present
themselves. I spoke to the Count de Montmorin ab.ᵗ a Successor
to Mirabeau this Day, but he tells me that he cannot easily see
who shall be put in his Place. He owns that Mirabeau was
determined to ruin La Fayette and says that he had held him
back for some Time. He says that La Fayette is a Reed. Good
for Nothing. He thinks that there is no Chance now left but to
convoke the next Assembly as soon as may be, excluding the
Members of the present. And that the Meeting should be far
from Paris. The Theatres are shut this Day. The Weather is fine.

Sunday 3. — This Morning Richard calls and I tell him I am
going to Marli. Before I go he sends me a Note desiring on the
Part of Le Couteulx that I would call at Luciennes. I go to
Marli. Mad.ᵉ du Bourg receives me with the Joy of one who
wishes Something from a City to vary the Sameness of the Scene.
After Dinner we walk much about the Garden and see many
Scenes of rural Love. The Shepherds and Shepherdesses seem
to care but little for the Appearance of Strangers but pursue their
Gambols as freely as their Flocks and Herds. This furnishes the
Matter of our Conversation. On my Return I call at Luciennes.
Le Couteulx tells me that Lavoisier wishes to converse with me
about Tobacco, as a Company is forming to hire the Manufactory
&c.ᵃ, &c.ᵃ. We are to dine there To Morrow. I visit Mad.ᵉ de
Chastellux. Thence to the Louvre but Mad.ᵉ is abroad. I return
and spend the Evening with the Dutchess. Mad.ᵉ de Lostange
who is here, is I find the Daughter of Monsieur de Rouverie and
I dined with her at his House but have forgotten it. There is a
Violence of Aristocracy in her, as in many others, which is
diverting. She is handsome. This has been a wonderfully fine
Day.

Monday 4. — This Morning after Breakfast I walk out and call
at the Louvre. Mad.ᵉ is in Bed and complains of being unwell.
I make my Visit short. Walk in the Louvre, where Swan joins
me. He is to call ToMorrow Morning. Mons.ʳ Bermond has been
at my Lodgings and will be with me by and bye. Paul Jones

comes and tells me all he knows of what is going. After he is gone, Mons. Barmond comes with his Friend. Ternant enters immediately after them. He gives me a Copy of the Resolutions proposed for the Assembly. Some Conversation as to the Intention of calling soon a new Legislature. After he is gone the others mention a Treaty for purchase of the American Debt and offer me a Concern. They have employed a Person in America designated by M. Swan, who is empowered to distribute Douceurs to Amount of £16000 St. They have given 200000# to Rayneval and the same Sum to ——. I promise to read the Papers and consider the Subject. Swan is to receive Something for his Trouble. I dine with Mons. Lavoisier. Monsieur Moneron and Monsieur Le Couteulx go with Lavoisier and me into the Cabinet and there a Plan for Tobacco is discussed. It looks as if it would come to Something. After Dinner the Conversation is renewed. I take Le Couteulx and Lavoisier along the Boulevards as far as the Convoie of Mirabeau will permit. Sit them down and go back to the Marais, where I visit Monsieur and Madame de La Luzerne. They receive me *d'autant mieux* as that, being no longer Minister, my Attention cannot be suspected. Visit Madame de Nadaillac where I am led into an Altercation *un peu vive* with Monsieur, who, among other ridiculous Notions of aristocratic Folly, expresses a Wish for the Dismemberment of France. Go from hence to Mad. Foucault's; she is abroad, and I call on Mad. de Chastellux for a few Minutes. She is to inform me ToMorrow whether the Expedition to Sceaux takes Place the Day after. I cannot wait for her R.H. but make a short Visit to the Louvre. My friend is a little disappointed that I do not stay Supper. This Morning I gave her a Reason for not liking her Suppers which will I am sure dwell on her Mind. It has been a prodigiously fine Day. The Funeral of Mirabeau (attended it is said by more than 100,000 Persons in solemn Silence) has been an imposing Spectacle. It is a vast Tribute paid to superior Talents, but no great Incitement to virtuous Deeds. Vices both degrading and detestable marked this extraordinary Creature. Compleatly prostitute, he sacrificed every Thing to the Whim of the Moment. *Cupidus alieni prodigus sui*. Venal. Shameless; and yet greatly virtuous when pushed by a prevailing Impulse, but never truly virtuous because never under the steady Control of Reason nor the firm Authority of Principle. I have seen this Man, in the short Space of two Years, hissed, honored, hated, mourned. Enthusiasm has just now presented him gigantic. Time and Reflection will shrink that Stature. The busy Idleness of the Hour must find some other Object to execrate or to exalt. Such is Man, and particularly the french Man.[1]

Tuesday 5. — This Morning write. Swan calls upon me. He tells me that the Persons who proposed the Negotiation for the American Debt to Short have not employed any Person to negotiate the Matter in America. This seems a little strange, since Bermond told me last Night that Swan had himself employed a Person for that Purpose at their Request. I ask him if Bermond was concerned in that Proposition; he tells me, not to his Knowlege. This seems unaccountable. After I am dressed I visit M.r Short and go thence to dine with Mons.r de La Fayette. I ask him who is to replace Mirabeau in the diplomatic Committee. He says he thinks it will be the Bishop d'Autun. I come Home after Dinner, and Monsieur Bermond and his friend call on me. They offer me a fourth in their Plan and I accept. I tell them the Conversation with M.r Swan and from what they in Return tell me I find he has been compleatly a Double Dealer. He had perswaded them that he could bring Short to do whatever he pleased. This is truly ridiculous. They are to write to me ToMorrow offering a Concern. This Day has threatned with Rain but we had only a slight Sprinkling. The Weather is however very pleasant. The Trees in the Tuilleries are nearly out.

Wednesday 6. — M.r Swan calls. While he is here I receive a Message from my friend desiring to know whether I will call and

---

[1] The last remaining reverence of Parisians was for brains. Shuffling through heavy dust of a spell of fine weather, following the titan burnt out by overwork and overdissipation, someone complained that the streets had not been watered, a woman said the people would lay the dust with their tears. Mirabeau had left Talleyrand a fine speech to read to the Assembly, written by one of his loyal Swiss; this 'workshop' remains unsuspected till 1832, the moving effect is not marred. Mirabeau thought France needed a King, but also a Richelieu and that he, not La Fayette, was mentally equipped for the part; but this socialist-royalist, demagogue-aristocrat had played such a deep double game that no side could trust him; excessive in all things, in size and glitter of buckles and buttons, in splendor of clothes and words, in enormities of his pleasures.

when. Dress and go to the Louvre. The Screen is drawn, I find, so as to prevent a sudden View of the Bed by those who come in. I am cool. Shortly after my Arrival M.ʳ de S.ᵗᵉ Foi comes and I give him Room to converse. She begs me not to go away.... Says she was Yesterday several Times ready to burst into Tears when she thought of my going away. I think this is probable, for I had brought her to that State of Uncertainty and Apprehension which excites the strongest Emotions. I visit Mad.ᵉ de Nadaillac and by a rambling Conversation get more Ground than she is aware of. She talks of Religion, Duty and conjugal Vows before there is any Occasion, but to her Surprize I agree that these Vows should be held sacred. Tell her it is a happy Circumstance for her that she loves her Husband, because that otherwise she could not but entertain another Passion which would prove at length too strong. She likes still less my frank Acknowlegement of a Passion for my friend her Aunt. I think she is half determined to wean me, but she had better let it alone. Call on Mad.ᵉ Foucault who is abroad. Visit Le Couteulx on Swan's Business. Then go to dine at M.ʳ Short's Lodgings. M.ʳ Swan is here and a M.ʳ Shore, Brother to a Merchant of that Name in Petersburg, Virginia. The Decrees about Tobacco are the Subject of Conversation in some Measure. Go from hence to the Louvre and take my friend and Mad.ˡˡᵉ Duplessis to ride. Set them down at the Louvre. Visit Mad.ᵉ de Chastellux who is abroad. Take a Turn in the Garden of the Palais royal and come Home. Read till eleven. This has been a pleasant Day but windy, with slight Showers.

Thursday 7. — This Morning write. M.ʳ Brémond breakfasts with me. He has seen Rayneval and they have arranged their Plan. I call on my friend, who is ill. She desires me to visit her this Afternoon. I visit Mad.ᵉ de Beaumont. Dine with the Dutchess of Orleans. After Dinner visit my friend; during a Course of Blandishment she asks if I would in Case of her Widowhood become her Husband. I decline an Answer, but being much pressed, remind her that our Engagement no longer exists. She acknowleges this, but still urges for a Yes or No. I then ask her how she can think of putting such a Question to me after what she has told me of the Bishop's Influence, and after the Declaration that six Months' Absence had cooled her Affection &c^a., &c^a. She owns that I am in the Right, and is much affected. Monsieur comes in and I leave her. Go to Mad^e de Chastellux's. Short comes in and tells me that Payne is arrived. Brémond told me this Morning that Montmorin would not be long in Office. The Dutchess gives us this Evening the Relation of some new Horrors attending the Revolution. She has been this Afternoon to visit a sick Bishop. I return Home and read. The Weather has this Day been fine.

Friday 8. — This Morning Mr Bermond calls and I give him an Answer to a Letter received from him and Jeanneret & Co:. We discuss various Points and then I walk, having first read the Answer of Payne to Burke's Book.[1] There are good Things in the Answer as well as in the Book. I meet my friend in my Walk. Return pretty well fatigued. Payne calls on me. He says that he found great Difficulty in prevailing on any Bookseller to publish his Book. That it is extremely popular in England and of Course the Writer, which he considers as one among the many uncommon Revolutions of this Age. At four oClock I call on my friend who is alone to receive me. . . . She does not desire the usual Pleasure. This I consider as the Empire of the Mind. She chuses to appear afflicted. 'Tis very well. Dine with Monsieur de Montmorin. After Dinner I take him aside and express my Opinion that a speedy Dissolution of the present Assembly would be dangerous. Their Successors would be chosen by the Jacobins, whereas if some Months are suffered to elapse the Jacobins and Municipalities will be at War, because the latter will not brook the Influence of the former. He says that he fears the Municipalities will be entirely under the Guidance of the Jacobins. This is I think a vain Fear. He thinks that none of the present Members should be reeligible. I differ in Opinion, because he knows the Character and Talents of the present Set and can buy such as, after Reflection, may suit his Purpose. He says they are not

---

[1] Edmund Burke's *Reflections on the French Revolution* had been a European sensation in November, pleasing to courts who dreaded the 'French disease.' Thomas Paine had sprung to arms with his *Rights of Man* with even greater circulation, aided by Government efforts to suppress it. Considered the last word in political incendiarism, the reforms it demands become a commonplace of good government.

COMTE DE MONTMORIN
From the bust by Collet in the Musée de Versailles

worth buying and would for the most Part take Money to act as they please. That if Mirabeau had lived he would have gratified him to the Extent of his Desires. He says they must now work in the Provinces to secure the Elections, but I ask how he is to know the Inclination and Capacity of Members elect. He owns this to be a Difficulty. Speaking of the Court, he tells me that the King is absolutely good for Nothing; that at present he always asks, when he is to work with the King, that the Queen be present. I ask if he is well with the Queen. He says that he is, and has been for some Months. I am sincerely glad of this, and tell him so. Go from hence to Mademoiselle Duplessis and take her to the Louvre. Stay there some Time a Trio with my friend. Short comes in and we go together to the Palais royal. See Ternant there, to whom I return the Form of Resolutions which he gave me relative to the late Decrees respecting American Commerce, and to provide for a future Treaty. This last Point appears to me important. We go from Mad.ᵉ de Chastellux's to the Appartments of the Dutchess. She sets off to Morrow, under pretence of her father's being indisposed, to visit him, but in fact to bring about a Separation with her Husband whose Conduct is become too brutal to be borne. Poor Woman, she looks wretchedly. Go again to the Louvre to take up Mademoiselle Duplessis. Madame is become gay and *mocqueuse*; this is well. Set Mademoiselle down and call on Mad.ᵉ de Stahl who is not at Home. Return Home about eleven and read. This Day has been very warm.

Saturday 9. — This Morning Mons.ʳ Bermond calls on me. In the Course of Conversation I mention to him the Claims of the German Princes upon France for Supplies furnished a long Time ago. He opens this Matter up to me and says that he has Agreements already made with them and wants only about 1200000# to compleat the Affair, which will give at least twelve Millions. In the Course of Consideration he asks if I will propose the Matter to Monsieur de Montmorin. I am to consider of it and he is to call ToMorrow and furnish me with the proper Materials to converse upon. I visit my friend who is still in bad Health; I leave her and call on M.ʳ Short. We have a long Conversation on American Finance and I endeavor to shew him that the Proposition made in Name of Schweitzer Jeanneret and Co:

is a good one for the United States, provided they abate the Commission. This is my sincere Belief. I tell him also that from what the Parties have said to, and shewn to, me I am convinced that they have great Strength both with the Court and in the Assembly. That an Operation of this Sort would be so much the more useful as the United States might make Use of all their Credit to support their Domestic Operations. The Conversation is long, and he is a little changed in his Opinions. I tell him some Things which may render him a little cautious respecting M.ʳ Swan, who is I find in the Habit of using both of our Names for his particular Purposes. Go from hence to visit Madame de Troudaine. She is abroad. Return to the Louvre where I dine. Mad.ᵉ is taken ill after Dinner. She tells me during the Course of the Afternoon that she has not slept since the Conversation with me of Thursday last. '*Si jamais je vous ai fait de la peine, vous me l'avez bien rendu.*' I treat her with Tenderness. She says her Pride will not permit her ever again to mention the Subject, but I must have a wonderful Power over my own Mind to love only to a certain Point. I tell her that she well knows the Anguish which I felt at finding myself obliged to give up the Hope of Happiness with her, *et comme mon Cœur en étoit déchiré*. But it is accomplished. I appeal to herself. She owns that I am right, she cannot complain, but she is miserable. . . . She afterwards asks me whom I would recommend in Case of Widowhood to be her Husb.ᵈ. I tell her that I understand it is in Contemplation to permit the Marriage of the Clergy. She says she will never marry the Bishop because she cannot go with him to the Altar without mentioning first her Connection with me. I leave her and return Home. Read till it is late. This Day has been showery. One Storm of Thunder, Rain and Hail which is worthy of the Month of July. In Fact the Weather is very warm & even sultry. If it continues there will be no Lack of Spring Fever.

Sunday 10. — This Morning M.ʳ Bermond calls on me. He does not bring the Agreements he has made but gives me a long History of his Affair. It appears from hence that Mons.ʳ de Montmorin is acquainted with these Agreements. He is to have an Interview this Day with S.ᵗᵉ Foi who is to communicate what has passed with Rayneval, and he will let me know it. I decline in Consequence going this Day to Monsieur de Montmorin's. M.ʳ Short calls on me and shortly after him Payne comes, who turns the Conversation on Times of Yore; and as he mentions me among those who were his Enemies, I frankly acknowlege that I urged his Dismission from the Office he held of Secretary to the Committee of foreign Affairs.[1] He outstays Short, who seems to wish for his Absence. After they are gone I take Mad.ˡˡᵉ Duplessis to Mad.ᵉ de Flahaut's where we dine at her Bed Side. After Dinner we ride together. She touches repeatedly upon my Refusal, and I think we shall have more of this. Return Home and read till pretty late in the Evening, then go to the Louvre to meet M.ʳ Short who is to sup there, that is to pass an Hour or two. Nothing here very striking but several Things which I remark. Come away at half past eleven. Take Madem.ˡˡᵉ Duplessis Home and then come Home myself. The latter Part of this Day has been very fine. Swan called in the Morning while Bermond was with me and was to call again but did not.

Monday 11. — This Morning M.ʳ Bermond calls before I am up. He gives me a List of sundry Persons who form the Coalition in the Assembly, and tells me the various Things which have been done heretofore respecting the Rations. After he is gone I write, but am interrupted by Payne who brings with him a M.ʳ Hodges who was his fellow Traveller, and whom I had seen several Times in England: he is... As he seeks cheap Living also, it would seem likely that he is out at Elbows. To get rid of them I walk, hoping thereby to work off also a Pain in my foot which feels neither like Gout or Rheumatism but like a Sprain, which I do not recollect to have had. Return, and while I am dressing Bermond comes again to tell me that the Business treated Yesterday by the Coalition was one of his Affairs, and that they have decided to take it up. They will gain thereby 1800000#. They make him Overtures respecting the Rations. In the Conversation between Montmorin and Rayneval respecting the American

---

[1] Paine held this post from April, 1777, until dismissed in 1779 for making indiscreet disclosures about the French Alliance, or rather, about Louis XVI's anonymous helping of American cause while he was still at peace with England. The manuscript survives of the violent public attack Morris had made on Paine, who had to be disavowed because offending His Most Christian Majesty might mean the collapse of American hopes of victory and independence.

Debt, the former promised to mention it to me and arrange with me the Steps to be taken by the Court. Short dines with me and after Dinner I go to visit Monsieur de Montmorin. He is much engaged and I ask him a Rendezvous for ToMorrow but he cannot give it till the next Day, ToMorrow being devoted to his Embassadors. I see here the Chevalier de Bourgoyne who was long since introduced to me by Carmichael. He is now the King's Minister at Hambourg. Leave my Name for the british Embassadress and visit Madame de Nadaillac. Her friend the Abbé Maury is with her and I leave them together. She desires to see me again, which I promise. She is at Gros Caillou to attend the Innoculation of her Children. Go from hence to the Louvre. De Curt is here, tipsy, and is very amusing. I take him away between nine and ten and return Home. The Weather has been rainy in the Morning but afterwards pleasant. It continues very warm.

Tuesday 12. — This Morning M! Bermond calls and gives me some farther Developements of his System. I write and then walk out to the Louvre. Act with much Coolness towards my friend and give her at length a secondary Enjoyment without the least participation on my Part. She expresses a Regret at being happy alone but I reply that I had not the smallest Intention ... Go to the Palais royal to a Shop and return Home with Payne whom I met there. Dress and visit Madame de Troudaine who is not at Home. Dine with Mad? Foucault, then visit Madame de La Luzerne. Stay sometime and then call on Mad? de Stahl, who is just going out, Mad? de Ségur who is abroad, Mad? du Moley who wants to know why the Dutchess of Orleans is gone to the Town of Eu. I pretend Ignorance. Visit Mad? de La Borde where I see the *première Femme de Chambre de la reine.* She looks like a Procuress. They seem to be expecting Company and therefore I slip away. Return Home and finish my Letters for ToMorrow's Post. This has been a very hot Day. My Foot is excessively painful. I must give it rest.

Wednesday 13. — This Morning M! Bermond calls and gives me some further Information and at ten I call on Monsieur de Montmorin. Enter fully with him both into his Situation and that of the Kingdom; propose the Affair of the Rations and offer him the Interest agreed on. He declines being interested and after much Conversation agrees to push it on Acc. of the King, provided the Matter be secret. He says he can rely on me and that his Majesty will, he believes, have the like Confidence. I am to give him a Note this Day to be laid before the King. Go to M. Short's whom I afterwards meet in the Street and deliver Mad. de Stahl's Invitation for Saturday. Go to Jeanneret's and inform Bermond of Montmorin's Refusal; at the same Time give him to understand that the Business will be done. Prepare the Note for his Majesty. Then call at the Louvre, but my friend is abroad. Return Home and read. Go to dine with Monsieur de Montmorin and after Dinner give him the Note. He tells me that he must communicate the Affair to the Count de La Mark. Their *political* Connections are such that he cannot avoid the Communication. He will give me a definitive Answer on Monday Morning. Go from hence to the Louvre where I find de Curt making Verses on Madame. Just as I am coming away, M. Short enters. I go to Madame de Stahl's. Converse there with the Dutchess de La Rochefoucault. Madame de Stahl reads her Tragedy of *Montmorenci*. She writes much better than she reads. Her Character of the Cardinal de Richelieu is drawn with much Ability. The Society is small and we have no small Reprehension of the Assemblée nationale, who, it must be confessed, act weakly enough. *N'importe.* The Weather has this Day been very hot and in the Afternoon of course showery.

Thursday 14. — This Morning M. Bermond calls as usual and I give him an Account of the Delay which has arisen. Van Staphorst calls on me. I dress and visit Mad. de Nadaillac. Then pass at the Louvre without going in, but meerly leave some Books I had borrowed. Dine at the Restorateur's. Come Home after Dinner, when M. Bermond calls and we go together to M. Grefeuille's. He receives us I think too coldly and I find that he looks upon the Affairs which Bermond has in Hand very much in the Light of *Projets.* I find M. Bermond too sanguine and too credulous. Go hence to the Louvre. M. de Curt is here making Love. Mad. and I are rather Lukewarm and she enjoys the Advantage of her Position. I leave her therefore and come Home. The Weather has been very warm this Day.

Friday 15. — This Morning M! Bermond calls and presents M! Jobert, of whom he spoke to me Yesterday as a Man of very superior Talents. He gives me an Account of what he learnt from the younger Pellinc but I am perswaded that it is all Nonsense, and tell him so. After they are gone I dress and visit at the Louvre. A long serious Conversation in which I propose Arrangements for an eternal Separation as she cannot love me without the Hope of a future Union, and as I will neither give that Hope nor consent to visit her on the Score of meer Friendship. She is terribly agitated at this, which puts her out of her Play. At length in parting I refuse to come again in the Afternoon and kiss her Hand with much seeming Emotion when I bid her Adieu. She trembles and retires to lean on the Chimney Piece, telling me that if I am determined on her Ruin I am the Master. This brings Things back again and I agree to visit her this Afternoon. Call on Mad? de Nadaillac, whose Children begin to sicken with the Small Pox. We talk Religion and Sentiment but I am much mistaken if she does not think of Something else. Leave my Name for the british Embassadress and go to dine with Madame Foucault. She tells me that her Husband has abandoned his Project of going to England, which she was delighted with, and says that my Description of it has deterred him. I must endeavor to put this to rights. Her phisician also has agreed to advise the Jaunt as needful for her Health. Shortly after Dinner I go to the Louvre and we celebrate... We are presently after interrupted by Vic d'Azyr, with whom she has a Conversation about the bishop. I presume that it is to put him well with the Queen. After this, another Interruption by her Sister and a M! Dumas who brings disagreable Tidings respecting an Affair in which she was concerned.... and then comes M! de Curt full of amorous Declaration and Protestation. I leave this Scene at eight and go again to Mad? Foucault's. She tells me that her Husb? has taken it into his Head to go to Nantz, and in that Case she is resolved to go to England with one of her friends or with me. She says he is a very bad Fellow Traveller. At ten M! Stebell comes in. A Mademoiselle Chevalier, about fifteen, plays on the forte piano admirably well a Piece of her own Composition which has great Merit. Her Brother, younger than

herself, plays another Piece very well. After that M.ʳ Stebell,
who is wonderful. This Man makes from five to ten Guineas per
Day. He receives for his Visit here this Evening fifty livres.
It is said that he wastes with levity what he acquires with so
much Ease. The Weather continues fine and warm, or rather,
hot.

Saturday 16. — This Morning I visit at the Louvre, where we
are rather sentimental... I visit Payne and M.ʳ Hodges. The
former is abroad. The latter in the wretched Appartments which
they occupy. He speaks of Payne as being a little mad, which is
not improbable. I go from hence to return the Visit long since
made by M.ʳ Fisher, who is gone away. Call on Van Staphorst.
Visit at Mad.ᵉ de Ségur's but she is not visible; I presume that
she is abroad preparing for her Departure. Visit Mad.ᵉ de Troudaine, who being denied, I ask for Paper and commence a Note
to her, but before it is finished a Servant asks me up. She is
dressing and S.ᵗ André comes in. Nothing here. Mad.ᵉ receives
me well and we are to be *un peu plus liés ensemble*. Call on Short
and take him to Mad.ᵉ de Staahl's. After Dinner we have a fine
Scene of vociferous Argumentation between her and an Abbé.
I tell her that when she gets to Switzerland she must let her
Head cool and then digest her Ideas of Government, which will
become sound by her own Reflections. Go from hence to Madame
de Beaumont's where we make a long Visit and then go to the
Louvre, and after a while Mad.ᵉ goes into the Bath and the Society
wait on her there. I stay till after Supper and then take Mad.ˡˡᵉ
Duplessis Home. In the Way I am sprightly and she is pleased.
Ternant, whom I saw at Mons.ʳ de Montmorin's, tells me that
Fleurieu,[1] the Minister of the Marine, is about to quit his Post
and that he thinks he will be replaced by Mons.ʳ de Bougainville.
Montmorin reminded me that I am to call on Monday. The
Weather continues to be wonderfully fine.

Sunday 17. — This Morning M.ʳ Bermond calls and after he is
gone I dress and ride thro the Bois de Boulogne. Call on M.ʳ

---

[1] Comte de Fleurieu, hydrographer, sailor who drew up French naval plans
for War of Independence, will for a short time in 1792 be governor of the
Dauphin and will die full of honors under Napoleon.

Milne at the Muette but they are at Dinner. I dine with M.ʳ
Grand and go after Dinner to the Louvre, where we celebrate. . . .
We visit together Madame de Nadaillac whose Son is ill with the
Small Pox. Take up on our Return Mademoiselle Duplessis.
My friend takes again her Bath. I go to Madame de Staahl's.
A brilliant Society. The british Embassadress who is here, is
much *entourée* by the young Men of Fashion. At coming away
the Count de Montmorin, who is here, tells me that he cannot
give me an Answer ToMorrow, not having been able to speak to
the King this Day. It has been very fine Weather.

Monday 18. — This Morning M.ʳ Bermond calls and I send for
M.ʳ Swan. Payne calls on me. After he is gone, Swan comes. I
converse with him respecting the Supply of Rations to the french
Marine. We have this Day very much of a Riot at the Tuilleries.¹
The King intends for S.ᵗ Cloud but is stopped, not meerly by the
Populace but by the Milice nationale, who refuse to obey their
General. It seems that his Majesty, having sanctioned the Decree
respecting the Clergy and afterwards applied to one of the non
Jurors to perform the Ceremonies enjoined at this Season, has
incurred the Charge of Duplicity. I am a long Time in Expecta-
tion of a Battle, but am at length told that the King submits.
Call at the Louvre, where I find M.ʳ de Curt established. Go
away directly and visit Mad.ᵉ de Nadaillac. As she urges me to
prolong my Visit, and it is late, I send to the Guingette for a
Matelotte and dine in her Chamber. She makes many *façons*

---

¹ Sworn priest and patriotism being now synonyms, freethinking Paris was
rabidly determined that the King make his Easter communion and by means
of a Constitutional priest. Consumed by remorse for his sanction of Clergy's
Civil Constitution he wanted to attend Paschal Mass without communicating,
wanted this to pass without comment, longed for privacy of Saint-Cloud, for
ministrations of a man of God, old régime. Their Majesties' carriage is turned
back in Place du Carrousel, Danton in command of organized riot in which
well-known Orleanists move in disguise. A milestone in career of La Fayette
when National Guard flout his order to clear passage for royal coach, which
returns to Tuileries. His authority cut to pieces La Fayette reports to Commune, resigns his command, faints dead away in Hôtel de Ville, scene of his
first revolutionary triumph. Besieged in his house by hundreds of penitent im-
ploring Guards, on fourth day he is once again their Commander-in-Chief.
Baron de Staël says he should have broken his sword the instant the Guard
disobeyed. The sword seems intact — but not quite.

but we get along. We shall see how Things go by & bye. I
return to the Louvre but M.ʳ de Curt has also returned. She
expresses her discontent and I stay some Time for him to go
away. In vain. I therefore call on Mad.ᵉ du Bourg, who is not
at Home. Then on Mad.ᵉ de Ségur, also abroad. Visit my
Neighbour Madame de La Borde and then call on La Fayette,
who is gone out. Return Home, read a little while and go to
bed early. This Day has been very hot after a cloudy and cool
Morning.

Tuesday 19. — M.ʳ Bermond calls. After he leaves me I dress
and go to M.ʳ de Montmorin's but he has gone abroad, in Consequence I suppose of the Events of Yesterday. Go to Jeanneret's
and inform M.ʳ Bermond of this. In my Way call on Monsieur
de La Fayette who is abroad. Go afterwards to the Louvre and
quarrel with Mad.ᵉ. After proper Submissions on her Part we are
reconciled. Visit Mad.ᵉ de Ségur, who is abroad, then return
Home and read till M.ʳ Bermond calls. He tells me that he has
had a Meeting with S.ᵗᵉ Foi and another about the Rations, but
those who are to furnish the Funds cannot attend. There is to
be another Meeting this Afternoon. I dine at the Louvre. After
Dinner M.ʳ de Curt and M.ʳ Bertrand, who dine here also, accompany us to the Tuilleries. Go afterwards to the Dentist's and as
M.ʳ Bertrand and M.ʳ Curt have left us, the one before going to
the Dentist's and the other afterwards, we seize the Opportunity
... M.ʳ Vic d'Azyr the Phisician comes in and shews me the
Letter written by the Department to the King.¹ It is dictatorial
in the Extreme. My friend had already informed me of it, but
I am obliged to disapprove of it. After Vic d'Azyr is gone Mad.ᵉ
de Guibert comes in and after she is gone, a male Relation of my
friend. I return Home. It is still fine Weather and a little cooler
than it was.

Wednesday 20. — This Morning M.ʳ Bermond and M.ʳ Jobert

---

¹ Madame de Flahaut knew because it was Talleyrand who had composed
this address summoning the King to dismiss the enemies of the Constitution
by whom he is served, to announce to foreign nations that there has been a
glorious revolution in France, that he has adopted it and is King over a free
people. 'It is noticed with regret that you favor reactionaries... it is feared
that these marked preferences indicate the real inclination of your heart,' etc.

call. I set them to work to bring the Jacobins to the King's Relief in the Attack of the Department. I dress and visit the Count de Montmorin, to whom I shew the Form of a Letter I had devised as an Answer from the King to the Department. He tells me that this last were frightened into the Step they have taken. This is I know pretty true, but it is also true that the Step is bold and if successful, decisive. After conversing upon the present State of Affairs we have one Word on the Business. He has not been able to attend to it, from the Circumstances of the Moment. Visit Mad.ᵉ de Montmorin and sit some Time; she is much distressed by the Fear of Pillage and Insult, the baron de Menou having denounced her Husband last Night. I laugh at this Denunciation as ridiculous and endeavor to quiet her Apprehensions. Go from hence to Gros Caillou and visit Mad.ᵉ de Nadaillac, who disserts a great Deal upon Politics, with much Heat and Absurdity. It fatigues me. I go from hence to dine with M.ʳ Short. Ternant, who is here, tells me that he urged La Fayette to resign and that he agreed, but found afterwards various Reasons for not doing it. This is like him. Mons.ʳ de Châtelet has brought hither Lord Dare, who is the Son of Lord Selkirk, and who meets here by Accident Paul Jones. He acknowleges the polite Attention of Jones in the Attack on his Father's House last War.[1] Go from hence to the Louvre but Mad.ˡˡᵉ Duplessis is here which prevents all Act. She tells me that the *Entours* of the King have resigned. That those of the Queen will resign and that she has Hopes of being placed near her Majesty. I wish this may happen. She tells me that she has written to d'Angivilliers to travel, having obtained the Assurance that in such Case it shall be no Question of him. De Curt comes in, and after staying a little while I come Home and read till M.ʳ Bermond & Jobert call. The Jacobins are in Treaty with the Quatre vingt neuf for an Alliance. The Object is to prevent a Decree rendering the present Members ineligible for the succeed-

---

[1] One of John Paul Jones's earliest exploits in American service. Raiding the west coast of Scotland near the gardener's cottage of his birth, flying the flag of his adoption, pained to find that his crew had removed the Selkirk family plate, Jones had sent it back to Lady Selkirk, whose husband had escaped capture only by being away from home.

ing Assembly. After they leave me I go very sleepy to bed. The Weather is grown a little cooler but is still very fine.

Thursday 21. — This Morning M.ʳ Swan calls after M.ʳ Bermond is gone. Then M.ʳ Short, and before he goes away M.ʳ Bermond comes again, to tell me what had passed at the Jacobins &c.ᵃ. Dress, ride with M.ʳ Short, and then call on Mad.ᵉ de Flahaut with whom I have some Conversation on political Affairs. Go to dine with the british Embassadress. We are *en famille.* She is a very pleasing Woman. Go from thence to visit Mad.ᵉ de Nadaillac. Every Thing here is filthy. Go to the Louvre and spend the Evening. The Weather is rainy. La Fayette's Resignation makes much Noise. It is probable that he will reaccept, in which Case he will be worse than ever.

Friday 22. — This Morning as usual M.ʳ Bermond comes. I dress and visit at the Louvre. My friend has with her a Confidant of De La Porte who comes to communicate the Intention of the King to employ Mons.ʳ. But she will write a Letter to decline it, containing very good Advice for his Majesty. I tell her she must give me a Copy of it. The King's Intention arose from the Request of D'Angivilliers. She has still a Pain in her Side... We visit together Mad.ᵉ de Nadaillac. After returning to the Louvre I call on Mad.ᵉ de Ségur, who is abroad. Visit Mad.ᵉ de Troudaine, and when they go to Dinner, call on Mons.ʳ de La Fayette who is abroad. Go to Mons.ʳ de Montmorin's and sit some Time with Mad.ᵉ de Beaumont. Leave her with Mons.ʳ de Blacont and go to the Sallon, where a rising Thunder Storm induces Mad.ᵉ de Montmorin to express some Wishes not favorable to the Disturbers of the public Repose. As it is a Question whether La Fayette will reaccept, she expresses very just Opinions on his Subject. That his Weakness has done much Mischief and prevented much Good, but that it is better to be swayed by Weakness than Wickedness, and that his Successor would probably be one of those who mean most illy. After Dinner I speak to Montmorin, who has yet done Nothing in the Business. I communicate to him the Cause of the intended Coalition between the Quatre vingt neufs and the Jacobins. He tells me that he could have got the Exclusion Decree passed long ago if he would, but he was afraid of the four Years Decree, which has been nevertheless adopted. I tell him that if he can get the former now passed, it will be the Means of splitting the Jacobins and Quatre vingt neufs, after which they will both be more tractable. I give him further my Opinion that the King must endeavor to gain the Populace. He agrees in this. Go from hence to the Luxembourg, but Mad.^e du Bourg is in the Country. Thence to Mad.^e Foucault's and sit some Time with Monsieur & Mad.^e le Rey. Call at the Louvre but Mad.^e is abroad. Return Home and read. Go early to bed. This has been a showery Day with Thunder and Hail. This Day for the first Time since I am in Europe I saw a Dish of Frogs which are very good.

Saturday 23. — This Morning Mr Bermond calls and after he is gone I dress. In going to the Louvre one of my Wheels comes off and by that Means my Carriage gets much injured. When I reach the Louvre Monsr meets me and complains that Mad.^e is going to the Assembly with Mr Ricy. She tells me when I arrive that she is in a great Hurry, Mr de Montmorin is to read his Instruction to the foreign Ministers informing them that the King has put himself at the Head of the Revolution. I do not see that this can be a Matter of much Moment to her. She sets me down at my Door and tells me she hopes to see me this Evening. I write till three & then go to dine with Mad.^e de Troudaine. After Dinner Monsieur expresses himself in Favor of a Republican Government, which is growing now to be very fashionable. I endeavor to shew him the Folly of such an Attempt but I had better have let it alone. Go from hence to Mad.^e de Guibert's where of course I meet the Esprit jacobin. Thence to Mad.^e du Molet's where I make a short Visit, thence to the Louvre but Mad.^e is gone abroad. Thence to Mad.^e de Ségur's who is also abroad. Thence to Mad.^e de La Borde's. She complains much of the Republican Party and asks me why I do not express my Sentiments to the Bishop d'Autun. I tell her that they would have no Weight, which is true. Call on the duc de La Rochefoucault who is abroad as well as Madame. Visit Mr Short and sit with him some Time. He doubts much as to the political State of this Country but still thinks his Principles right. They may be very good but I am sure that in Practice they will never answer. Call on Mad.^e de Stahl who is denied to me, but her

Servants being in Gala I am sure she is to have Company, and Montmorency is admitted at the same Moment.[1] I return Home. The Weather is grown cool and is pleasant.

Sunday 24. — This Morning write. Go to the Muette and dine with M? Milne *à l'anglois*. After Dinner return to Town and visit the british Embassadress. They have had many English to dine and among them Gen! Dalrymple and his friend M? Davis. After awhile they go to Play and I take an Opportunity to ask her Ladyship when she is most visible. She says that Wednesday was her Day but she has none now in particular. I may however rely that I shall always find her at Home when she really is at Home. In this I am sure by her Voice and Manner she is sincere and I reply in according Accents. She is a charming Woman. Go from hence to the Count de Montmorin's and have a long and interesting Conversation with his Wife on public Affairs. Urge among other Things the Advantage to be derived from changing the *Entours* of the Queen. Leave my Name for Mons? and Mad? de La Fayette and return Home. It has been a very showery Day. Hail and Rain with some Thunder.

Monday 25. — This Morning M? Bermond calls. Nothing new. I write all the Morning. Payne comes and informs me that the Marquis de La Fayette has accepted. I receive a Note from my friend desiring among other Things that I would visit her at eight. I answer coolly enough. Dine with Mad? Foucault, and Cubières,[2] who is here, is taken in for a Dinner at the petits [sic] Écuries at Versailles. Visit Mad? de La Luzerne and after sitting some Time go to Mad? de Ségur's, who is just gone abroad. Thence to Mad? de Stahl's, also abroad. Leave my Name at Monsieur de La Fayette's and then go to the Louvre. Stay till

---

[1] Gala liveries may have expressed a mood. Narbonne is in Italy, the Baroness is a collector of emotions, a new one stands on her doorstep. Mathieu de Montmorency, tall, golden-haired, twenty-three, who had fought as a child in America, who had rocked Paris with lamentations at the death of Marquise de Laval, and who incidentally has a wife, will join Germaine's travelling troupe of brilliant young men, faithful for years of exile.

[2] Simon-Louis-Pierre, Marquis de Cubières (1747–1821), equerry or Master of the Horse with quarters at the King's Small Stables. Tact carries him through Revolution without emigrating, to resume his functions under Louis XVIII.

half past eight and then, as she does not come, I return Home leaving there the Marquis de Montesquiou and Monsieur Curt. This has been a fine Day. I left a Message for Mad.ᵉ that I had waited above Half an Hour and felt myself much obliged to her.

Tuesday 26. — This Morning M.ʳ Bermond calls as usual. I write, then dress and go to the Louvre. We quarrel a little. Afterwards we embrace which is the usual Course. M.ʳ de Ricy comes in and the Conversation turns on the Course to be pursued by d'Angivilliers. It is concluded that he should go to England. My friend has not declined the Place proposed for her Husband. The Bishop advises otherwise because the King may make such a Choice as that M.ʳ de F—— will not be unsuitable to the Rest and because the Refusal may offend a weak Mind, tho founded on Reasons which should attach. I add a Reason which had arisen in my Mind, viz that when once taken up the Court cannot again let them fall, so that it will be a Kind of Provision for her in all Events. Go from hence to Madame de Ségur's & sit with her some Time. She shews me the Letter from the Duke of Orleans to Mad.ᵉ de Chastellux with the Answer of the Latter. Go from hence to Mad.ᵉ de Stahl's where I find Lady Sutherland. She tells me that the Duke of Leeds has resigned. I express a Hope, should I stay some Time in Europe, to see her at the Head of the foreign Affairs. She says she should like it very much but Lord Gower ¹ is yet too young. I tell her that two or three Years hence he will have acquired the Tact, and then ——. He comes in just before I leave this Place and mentions also the Resignation of the Duke. I ask if L.ᵈ Hawkesbury is to succeed. He does not know. He seems so anxious to prove that the Duke's Health is the Cause of his Resignation that I cannot help assigning it in my own Mind to some Difference in the Administration. Return Home and meet M.ʳ Bermond and M.ʳ —— of the House of —— at Marseilles who wishes to open a Commerce with the United States, and comes to consult me thereon. The Weather has this Day been pleasant but very cool.

---

¹ George Granville, Earl Gower (1758–1833), eldest son of first Marquess of Stafford, succeeded Duke of Dorset as Ambassador to France 1790. Created Duke of Sutherland a short time before his death.

Wednesday 27. — This Morning M.ʳ Brémond calls. Tells me of the Offers made to the German Princes by Merville &c.ᵃ. I write and at two oClock call on Lady Sutherl.ᵈ who is abroad. Thence to Mad.ᵉ de Nadaillac's from whom I had received a Note complaining of Neglect. We laugh and chatter and toy and she complains of my Want of Respect, but I think I must be less respectful to be more agreable. We shall see. Go hence to Monsieur de Montmorin's to Dinner. After Dinner I have a long Conversation with him, partly on political Affairs. He promises to speak to the King on the Business in the Course of the Week. He has mentioned it to the Count de La Marck who approves. Among various other Things I suggest an Act of Oblivion by the Assembly and thereon another Revolution Letter. He approves much of this, telling me that he is now preparing a Letter from the King to the Prince of Condé. I come Home to meet M.ʳ Brémond and set him to work among the Jacobins to get the Decree or Act of Oblivion moved by them. Go afterwards to the Louvre but my friend is abroad. Visit at Mad.ᵉ de Troudaine's, who being also abroad I go again to the Louvre. She comes in late, wherefore I stay but a few Minutes. The Weather has this Day been cloudy and cool but very calm and pleasant.

Thursday 28. — This Morning M.ʳ Brémond calls. I write, then go to the Louvre. My friend is at her Toilette and complains of being indisposed. I make my Visit short. She wishes to see me this Afternoon and as I mention dining in the Marais it excites some Apprehension in her Mind. Go hence to the british Ambassador's. Mad.ᵉ is abroad. Visit Mad.ᵉ de Nadaillac who in the Course of a little amorous Conversation tells me that I must not expect she would capitulate for she tenders too much her religious and moral Duties. That if she should, however, be frail, she would poison herself next Morning. I laugh at this. Take Mad.ˡˡᵉ Duplessis to the Louvre, then go and dine with Mad.ᵉ Foucault. After Dinner call on my friend and we go to the Convent at Chaillot. Had the old Nun stayed away... Return to the Louvre, having taken up Mad.ᵉ de Guibert and called in our Way to take some Ices. Leave them at the Louvre and come Home early. The Weather has been cloudy and cool but not unpleasant.

Friday 29. — Mr Brémond calls as usual. After he is gone I dress and go according to her Desire to visit my friend.... We then ride together. We converse on Affairs and from what she says, but more from what she does not say, I find there is a Plan on foot to force all Power from the King into the Hands of the present Leaders of Opposition. After setting her down I visit Mad^e de Staahl who is abroad. Then take up Mad^{lle} Duplessis and leave her at the Louvre. Come Home and go from thence to dine with Mad^e Foucault. After Dinner call on Mad^e de Nadaillac, who being abroad desires I will wait. Informed of my Arrival she promises to come immediately, but I wait a long Time and then come away. Visit Mad^e de Ségur who is abroad. Mad^e de La Borde also abroad, and then go to the Louvre where I stay till near eleven. Montesquiou comes in and I remind him of what I had said respecting their Constitution. He begins to fear that I was in the right. He asks how the Evil is to be remedied. I tell him that there seems to be little Chance for avoiding the Extremes of Despotism or Anarchy; that the only Ground of Hope must be on the Morals of the People but that these are I fear too corrupt. He is sure they are. Mad^e told me this Morning that Monsr de Curt is to be Minister of the Marine if the Decree of *quatre ans* [1] is revoked. The Weather has this Day been cool and cloudy. It grows still cooler in the Evening and threatens Rain.

Saturday 30. — This Morning Mr Brémond calls. After he is gone Swan comes. He has been to Havre and been in Treaty with Ruellan to join in Execution of his Wood Contract. They have not quite agreed yet. I tell him again that I will have nothing to do with it. I write. Mr Monciel and Mr Brémond come in and

---

[1] The death of Mirabeau, at whom it had been aimed, makes more than ever foolish the decree excluding from public office for the next four years all deputies to the Constituent Assembly. The decree making these first deputies ineligible to the Assemblée Législative wastes some trained material, brings in cultivated lawyers from the Gironde, classical scholars whose ideals and gods belong to the great days of the Roman Republic. But Robespierre will get better listened to in Jacobin Club than by fine gentlemen of the States-General, bored by interminable harangues of the little cat-faced Arras lawyer, dapper, smug, implacable. Danton does his thundering from deserted monastery of the Cordeliers, until the Convention gathers in all firebrands, who stage the Terror that devours them.

THE COUNTESS OF SUTHERLAND
From the painting by Sir Joshua Reynolds

the former gives me an Account of what he has done with the Chiefs of the Jacobins. He is to have a further Conference. They think it will be best to act in Concert with the Court without appearing to do so, lest thereby they should loose their Popularity. I agree in the Propriety of this, & urge, conformably to what I suppose their Views to be, a Repeal of the *Décret de quatre ans* and the *Décret de Rééligibilité.* He is to propose this to them & to obtain if he can a List of the Articles they desire; also, if possible, of the Plans they aspire to. Go to dine at the british Embassador's. We are here *en famille.* Cubières comes with Robert [1] and they have a Collection of the Portraits of Petito in Enamel which are very fine. Go from hence to the Louvre. My friend is dressing. She tells me that she has good Hopes of succeeding to the Place she aims at. De Curt comes in who has much to say to her. Go from hence to visit Mad.ᵉ de Nadaillac who is abroad. Thence to Mad.ᵉ Foucault's where I sit a long Time with Mad.ᵉ Le Rey; afterw.ᵈˢ sup. When we get into the Salon we have a Deal of metaphisical Conversation. A Gentleman who has read Locke on the Human Understanding shews off. The Weather has been rainy and raw this Day.

---

[1] Hubert Robert (1733–1808), painter of romantic ruins, his work in violent contrast to the tiny enamels on disks of gold in which seventeenth-century Jean Petitot had reproduced every curl in the wigs, every stitch in the lace at courts of Charles I and Louis XIV, who seldom offered to a foreign ambassador a snuffbox ungarnished by a Petitot enamel reproducing in miniature portraits by Vandyke, Mignard, Philippe de Champagne. But Romney, Reynolds, and Hoppner show that this hostess was most worth looking at. Elizabeth (1765–1839), Countess of Sutherland, an orphan at two years old, bears in her own right a thirteenth-century title and owns the County of Sutherland. At fourteen raised regiment of 'Sutherland Fencibles,' at twenty married Lord Gower. The feudal state at Dunrobin was great. Every evening this young chieftainess had stood at her castle gates, east wind blustering off the North Sea, west wind sending rain from high moors, and had matriarchally settled her clansmen's disputes. In old age she will be called the Duchess-Countess who takes snuff. In 1793 she will raise Sutherland and Argyle Highlanders to defend her Far North against the French, kilties who win fame as the 93d Foot. Morris will write her delightful notes from Berlin, Dresden, Vienna. After Lord Gower's recall their continued friendship unlocks doors for Morris in England, as ex-American Minister to France.

MAY 1791

Sunday 1 *May* 1791. — M.ʳ Brémond visits me. He shews a new Proposition from La Merville respecting the german Rations. He gives me also the List of Articles desired by the Chiefs of the Jacobins. I visit the Count de Grippi who brought me a Letter from Carmichael and who is very much his friend. Go thence to the Louvre.... After she is drest I set her down at Mad.ᵉ de Guibert's and then go to Monsieur de Montmorin's where I dine. Bouinville is here, just returned from England. He tells me that Payne's Book works mightily in England, and he says that Pitt does not hazard a War with Russia, it is so unpopular. That he has again begun new Negotiations which will probably last till the Season is spent. After Dinner I have a long Conversation with Monsieur de Montmorin, in the Course of which I shew him a Note I have made on their Situation. He begs me to let him have it and I give it but with the Injunction that none but their Majesties shall know from whom it comes. He has not yet had an Opportunity to resume again the Affair of the Rations. I inform him of what has been done with the Chiefs of the Jacobins. He tells me how the Ministry stand in that Respect. He assures me that they can do Nothing with the King but thro him. He mentions a Wish to have Commissaries appointed by the Crown to keep the Peace in the different Departments &c.ᵃ. I reply that all Officers concerned in keeping the Peace should be appointed by the Crown but that it is too early to propose any Thing of the Sort. Experience must first demonstrate the Necessity. He tells me that he has indisputable Evidence of the Intrigues of Britain and Prussia. That they give Money to the Prince of Condé and to the Duke of Orleans. He says that he will resign the Place of foreign Affairs because he can now no longer act in it with Dignity. I advise against this, assuring him that his Letter will be viewed by foreign Nations in its true Light. He says that he would

if in Office bring on a War next Year. I tell him he should pro-
voke it as soon as possible, but that it should be a Land War.
He says that a Sea War with Britain is alone practicable and in
that Case they would be alone, for Spain will not act with them.
I ask him how the Emperor is disposed. He tells me that he is
feeble and pacific. That he will take no great Part for or against
any Body and if he interferes at all it must be to get his Share
of the Spoil. I tell him that I have a different View of Things
from him. That the War should be by Land and general. That
Poland should be tempted by the Country which lies between
her and the Baltic. Austria to have Silesia and in Exchange for
the Low Countries Bavaria. France to have the Low Countries
and to make an Incursion into Holland. Constantinople to be
given to the Order of Malta for the joint Use of all Christendom.
He starts at this, which is too great for his Mind, but I think it
may be brought about. It would cost France her Islands in all
Probability but I have a different Plan for them which I do not
communicate. He agrees on the Language to be held with the
Chefs des Jacobins. From hence I return Home and meet M.ᵣ
Brémond to whom I mention what is needful respecting the Rations and Jacobins. Go afterwards and visit Mad.ᵉ du Molet and
Madame de Corney. Make my Visits pretty long to each and then
go to the Louvre where I stay till past eleven. The Count de
Flahaut tells me as a Secret not yet communicated to his Wife
the Intention of d'Angivilliers to travel, by Way of avoiding the
Accusations against him. He thinks of Italy but I tell him that is
dangerous and that he had better go to England under Pretext
of visiting the Manufactures there. This has been a raw damp
Day.

Monday 2 May.—This Morning M.ᵣ Brémond and M.ᵣ Jobert call
on me. They communicate some Information of little Value and
ask my Opinion as to the Propriety of bringing the latter forward
to the Chiefs of the Jacobins. I tell them I think there is Danger
of alarming those Gentlemen. Shew how alone it can be done
without great Hazard. These People are too precipitate. I
write, then dress. Brémond calls again and tells me that he has
taken Measures to be employed in digesting the Decrees of the
Assembly and selecting those which are to form the Constitution

from the Mass. I approve of this. I go to the Louvre. M: de
Ricie is here and I make my Visit very short. Visit Mad: de Nadaillac who does not admit me for some Time. I perceive afterwards that she was in too sluttish a trim and has got into Bed to
conceal it. . . . We chat in such Manner as I think most fitting for
a little Coquet and such as leaves it always doubtful with her
whether she has or has not Possession of my Heart. If she does not
take Care she will in trying to catch me find herself caught. Call
on Mad: Foucault who is abroad. Then on Mad: Le Couteulx
who is in the Country. Then go to dine with Mad: de Troudaine.
After Dinner visit Mad: de Guibert. My friend comes thither and
tells me that her Brother in Law has resigned and is set off for
Italy. This is a cruel Stroke to her who has no Means of Existence but from him. I take her Home and stay a little while.
Then call at her Instigation to enquire if a Place about the Queen
will be acceptable to Mad: Le Couteulx. My friend Laurent
answers in the negative. He speaks to me about his Tobacco
Plan. Return Home early. This has been a cool Day but the Air
has grown drier and it promises to be fair.

Tuesday 3 *May.* This Morning M: Brémond calls and brings
with him the Plan of some Marshes near Arles which he proposes
to purchase and drain. Wishes me to mention it to Mons: de
Montmorin. I promise to consider it. I visit my Friend who is
still incommoded and very unhappy. I call on M: Short and after
a moderate Visit leave my Name for the british Ambassadress.
Then call on the Baron de Bezenvald and sit with him a while.
Go thence to the Dairy of the Enfant Jésus where Cream, Butter
and Eggs are to be had in great Perfection. Take some of each
and go to the Louvre where there is a Confidant of Mons: du
Port, the Minister of the Civil List, with whom Mad: has after
Dinner a long Conversation *à part.* During that Period Mons:
confides to me his Griefs, his Hopes and Fears. I then take my
friend to Mad:ˡˡᵉ Duplessis and we go all together to the Bois de
Boulogne and walk a little. Then return to the Louvre. My
friend is now in good Spirits and full of Fun. De Curt comes in
who is sick. I go to Mad: de Nadaillac's. Altho early she has a
Gentleman with her whose Presence prevents me from making
the Progress I intended. After some more Company come in I

ask in her Ear when she will be at Home. She is excessively confused and after some Consideration says Tomorrow. Afterwards she asks me why that Question. I tell her because she lives
a great Way from me and I do not like to come and meerly leave
my Name. She looks so disappointed that, putting all together I
must think that she had another Idea. She takes Occasion afterwards to ask me at what Hour I will come. I tell her about eight
in the Evening and she then talks of passing the Evening. That
she shall have some Company. I put that however out of the
Question for myself. Get Home at twelve. The Weather has been
fine this Day but is cool. Monsieur de Limon tells us that he is
well informed the Secretary of the Prince of Condé has taken a
large Bribe and come over with all his Master's Papers. He says
also that News just arrived from England shew that a War between that Country and this is unavoidable. His first News may
be true, his last must I think be false. I tell him so and add that in
a War between France and England single handed I would stake
my Fortune in Favor of France if tolerably governed.

Wednesday 4. — This Morning M.ʳ Brémond calls to examine
the Map left with me Yesterday. He says that his Friend Jobert
is better acquainted with the Subject than he is. In Consequence
of a Note from my friend I walk to the Louvre.... She presses
me to speak to Mad.ᵉ Le Couteulx notwithstanding the Refusal
of Monsieur. I return Home where Brémond and Jaubert are
arrived already. The latter gives me Information respecting a
Part of the Tract in Question. He then proceeds to communicate
the Topographic State of the Country but Payne comes in and
just after he leaves us the Count de Greppi who talks enthusias-
tically till three oClock. Dress and go to dine with Duportail
where I see after Dinner Gouvion & converse with him respecting
the future Commandant of the Gardes nationales. I think he
must be the Man. Go from hence to the Count de Montmorin's.
He has not yet ment.ᵈ the Affair of the Rations to the King. I
tell him there is another Affair dependent on it in which he may
with Propriety take an Interest. Ask him who is to succeed La
Fayette and observe that he should look round for a proper Character. He mentions Gouvion. I leave him and walk with Mad.ᵉ de
Beaumont. I find that her Father has communicated Something

of the Object if not of the Substance of my Conversation with him. Go to the Louvre where I receive a Note from my friend apologizing for her Absence. Thence to Mad.^e de Nadaillac's who comes to me from her Husband. She seems to be *un peu re-froidie* and a Sense of Duty has gained some little Strength. Company come in and I leave her. Soon after my Return Home Mr Brémond comes, who is vexed at Mr de Montmorin's Delay. He stays late, which I dislike, and at length begin to undress which is a broad Hint. The Weather has this Day been cool and looks lowering.

Thursday 5. — This Morning immediately after Breakfast I go to Luciennes. On the Way I observe that the Rye is univer-sally in the Ear, it has been so in a great Measure since the End of the last Month. I speak to Mad.^e Le Couteulx at the Request of my friend to know if she will accept of a Place near the Queen. She would like it much but is afraid it will not be agreable to her Husband and his Family. She is to write to me ToMorrow after consulting him. She wishes the Place for her Sister in Case she does not take it. I return to Town and dine with Mad.^e Foucault. After Dinner call at the Louvre but Madame is abroad. I come Home and write. The Weather is very cool and threatens Rain.

Friday 6 *May*. This Morning Mr Brémond calls and gives me a Note of the Offer made to him respecting the Rations. Receive a Message from my Friend to which I write an ironical Reply thanking her for what she has not done. While I am writing Mr Short comes and I quit Work to dress. Mr Swan calls while I am dressing. Neither of them have any Thing particular to say. I call on Le Couteulx who is abroad and then go to the Louvre. *Madame est très gracieuse.* She apologizes, which I assure her is unnecessary, then give her an Account of my Yesterday's Expedi-tion and then take Leave. She is astonished, begs Explanation and thinks it unreasonable that I should be out of Humor. I as-sure her very gaily that I am not and have not been out of Hu-mor, that all ill Temper is gone and I shall not again be liable to it. Where am I going to visit? Begs I would stay a little longer. Agree to do so. Tells me that Monsieur will be abroad at five oClock and wishes me to come then. I cannot. We talk about in-different Things on my Part indifferently but she is so strongly moved that she can scarcely speak. I leave her, and she pressing me again to come at five I decline and add: '*d'ailleurs, ma chère amie, on n'est jamais sûr de vous trouver.*' Go to Mad.ᵉ de Nadaillac's who reiterates to me the Assurance that she will never be frail. She swears every Day anew to perform her Duty. I advise her against this because in Case of Accidents she will be so much the more perjur'd. Dine with Mons.ʳ de La Fayette and after Dinner call on the british Embassadress who is gone abroad. Pass at my Lodgings and as I have not rec.ᵈ a Letter from Mad.ᵉ Le Couteulx I call on my friend and leave Word to that Effect. Visit Mad.ᵉ de Ségur who informs me that she has lately lost her youngest Child; I express a most animated Sympathy. Call on the Abbé Ronchon who is in the Country and then return Home and write. The Weather, which was cloudy in the Morning, has cleared off and the Evening is fine.

Saturday 7 May. — This Morning M.ʳ Brémond calls and tells me he is to meet on Monday at M.ʳ de S.ᵗ Levis's to confer about the Rations. After he is gone I write. He returns with a Deputy of Arles, M.ʳ Bonnemain, who gives me further Information respecting the Marshes near that City. I call on my friend, who is abroad. I then visit Mad.ᵉ de Nadaillac who is also abroad. Visit Mad.ᵉ de Lavoisier and sit with her some Time. Then go to dine with Mad.ᵉ de Foucault. After Dinner visit Monsieur de Montmorin who promises to speak about the Rations to the King To-morrow. He is afraid of the Things being known. I mention to him the Affair of the Marshes and also some political Points, particularly the Necessity of changing the Household of their Majesties. Go hence to the Louvre. Mad.ᵉ reproaches me for my Refusal of Yesterday. I communicate the Contents of a Note from Mad.ᵉ Le Couteulx. I stay till after nine and then come Home, where I find a Packet of Letters from America. The Weather has this Day been more pleasant but it is said that there was Frost last Night. They say there was Ice, which I do not believe.

Sunday 8 May. — This Morning I go to Luciennes. Mad.ᵉ Le Couteulx cannot decide on accepting a Place.[1] Communicate to

---

[1] Much significance and some pathos in all this reluctance. Before 1789, places near the Queen would have been beyond the eager reach of these cautious ladies.

him the Terms of Franklin's Bargain. After Dinner return early
to Town and go to the Louvre. Tell the Result of my Voyage to
my friend. There seems to be nothing new stirring this Day.
The Weather is grown still colder.

Monday 9. — Mr Richard calls this Morning and after him
Monsieur de Tubeuf who has made a large Purchase of Lands in
Virginia, in which I fancy he is much deceived and I tell him so.
Visit my friend whose Husb.^d is with her. She has hurt herself
Yesterday by a Fall. After he is gone she endeavors to excite me
but I am very cold. Nature presses me hard to comply but I am
determined, and she proceeds to enquire about the different Wo-
men she supposes me to be acquainted with. I answer in such
Manner as to obviate her Suspicions but not remove them.
She asks to see me this Evening but I decline. Visit the Count de
Greppi who seems willing to do Business. Call on the british
Embassadress who is not yet come Home from her Morning
Visits. Go to Monsieur de Montmorin's. Walk with Mad.^e de
Beaumont who says she would not like to be one of the Queen's
Women but will do whatever her father desires. After Dinner
converse with him. The King agrees to the Affair of the Rations
provided he can be sure above all Things of the Secret. In a few
Days he will reform his Household. Montmorin quits the foreign
Affairs. He is to be succeeded by Choiseul Gouffi[er] who is now
at Constantinople. He says he will continue in the Council but
will not have a Department. Every one who may now get into
Place he considers as an *Être éphémère*, and justly. Go to Mad.^e de
Nadaillac's. She has a Gentleman with her. She is very sorry that
she was denied to me the other Day. It was the Fault of her Servant and therefore she sent me a Message this Morning. We get
rid of our Companion with Difficulty and then from one Thing to
another we come very near to the Consummation but she is re-
fractory and talks much Religion and Morality. I leave her angry a little, but more I think because I did not persevere than because I went as far as I did. We shall see. Go to Madame Foucault's. Monsieur de Fauchet reads an excellent Comedy which
he has written. Bouinville is here. I take him Home and en route
he complains of Duportail's ingratitude to La Fayette. He says
that Montmorin was very low spirited this Morning. I tell him

what I had told Montmorin, that Things must grow worse be-
fore they can mend. The Weather is grown milder but during our
Walk this Morning I observe that the Vines have suffered by the
Frost. At Table they say that no Mischief was done in the open
Country owing to the Wind.

   Tuesday 10. — M͏ʳ Brémond calls and I tell him that I am in
Hopes of getting the Money which may be needful for the Rations.
He tells me that he is to be employed by the Jacobin Chieftains
to form a Selection of constitutional Articles and also to consult
on the Means of restoring Order &cᵃ. M͏ʳ de Tubeuf calls but cannot stay till I shall have written a Letter for him. I write and
send it by the penny post. When I am drest I call at the Louvre.
Mad͏ᵉ is in Bed so that I make a short Visit, it being near two
oClock. Visit Mad͏ᵉ de Ségur who gives me the Talk of the Society and that is very near the Truth. So much for the Secrecy of
this Court. Visit Mad͏ᵉ de Trudaine. Then go to the Hôtel des
Américains and thence to the Louvre where I dine. My friend tells
me that she expects soon to be placed as the first Woman of the
Queen who will reserve the Education of her Daughter, and the
Dauphin is to go into the Hands of a Man. This Place is I think
Montmorin's Object, for he told me that he would accept an Office in the Household. After Dinner we take a Ride with Mad͏ˡˡᵉ
Duplessis and walk in the Champs Elisées. Upon our Return . . .
contrary to my Custom I am extremely cold. She makes some Expostulation in broken Accents and then bursts into Tears. I tell
her that it is all her own Fault. I had apprized her that such would
be the Consequence of her Conduct &cᵃ, &cᵃ, &cᵃ. At length become somewhat more kind. We visit Mad͏ᵉ de La Borde and then,
having set her down, I return Home. Take Tea and M͏ʳ Short
comes in. He is terribly disappointed to learn from me that he is
not yet appointed. He has no Letters whatever. The Weather
this Day has been cloudy but the Temperature of the Air is
agreable.

   Wednesday 11 *May*. — This Morning M͏ʳ Brémond calls. After he is gone I write. Richard came while he was here and Swan
shortly after he went away. I visit Le Couteulx and speak with
him about the Disposition of Lands; am to give him a Note
thereof. I ask him in the Course of Conversation if from one to

two Millions could be readily commanded on a good Pledge. He says he would undertake it. I tell him that if the Thing I have in View takes Effect the most profound Secrecy must be observed. Dine at the Restorateur's and go thence to the Louvre. My friend wishes me to take her and Mad.^{lle} to ride which I decline. She asks where I am going, which I tell her and she is much alarmed. She retires to doze and I come away. Call on the british Embassadress who is denied for I see her afterwards at the Grille of her Garden when I return from Monsr de Montmorin's. I walk with Ternant and converse a little on Affairs. He speaks of my friend Short as being much below par, but I tell him that he will be appointed the Minister and that Jefferson considers him as one of the ablest Men in America. He is astonished at this. I ask Montmorin whether he has yet fixed a Meeting with Duport; he says it shall be done this Week and he will let me know. Go to Mad.^e de Nadaillac's. Little Interruptions of the Children prevent the free Course of Sentiment and just as it winds up to its Heighth the Abbé Mauri is announced. I stay but a little while after his Arrival. At the Restorateur's I saw the Count de Greppi who will I think call ToMorrow. The Weather continues cold and sour.[1]

... I kiss her with more Emotion and with less Respect. It goes against her Conscience but it gives her great Pleasure. Before we arrive I press her Hand gently to my Heart and sit her down in a Situation which will I think keep her from falling asleep before she has had Time to say her Prayers.[2] The Weather has this Day been very pleasant.

Sunday 15. — This Morning Mr Brémond calls and after he is gone I write. Go at three to Mad.^e de Guibert's and inform her that my friend cannot dine with her, being gone to Versailles. Swan came while Brémond was with me and staid him out to say absolutely nothing, but from hence resulted a great Loss of Time to me. I go to Monsr de Montmorin's to dine and com-

---

[1] Two sheets are here torn out, missing, 4 pages. The end of Saturday 14 apparently refers to the little Marquise de Nadaillac.

[2] One thing may be said for Lothario, that his Adèle was such a collector of men that she could command adulation, emulation, and exasperation but could not reasonably expect perfect constancy.

municate what I had learnt at Mad.^e de Guibert's from Monsr Toulangeon, viz that the Colonists are defeated in their View of excluding the Mulattoes from a Share in the Government. This will occasion much Heat among them. I find that it is very disagreable here. After Dinner converse with him apart. He fixes next Tuesday for a Meeting with Laporte about the Rations but expresses his Fear that the Assembly will not agree. I tell him that as he retires from the foreign Affairs he should secure the Civil List which is the only real Source of Authority. He says he is not fit to manage Money Matters. That he is weary of the State he is in. That if he could realize his Fortune He would go to America &c.^a. He says that Nothing would keep him near the Court but his Desire to serve, or rather, save the King and Queen. That he has already occasioned to them a vast Expence for an Object which has not succeeded. I tell him that the Attempt to buy the Members of the Assembly was a bad Measure. He says it was not in that that he occasioned the Expence. He is called away before we can go farther. I go to the british Embassador's and on entring she apologizes to me for being denied the other Afternoon. She says there are so many Frenchmen who break in upon her that she is obliged to give Orders for shutting her Door but I may depend that it will not happen again. I make a very long Visit and then go to the Louvre where I wait till the Return of my friend from Versailles. M.^r de La Porte is here and is disposed to talk with me. De Curt comes in and is outrageous about the Decree of this Morning. He says that the Deputies from the Colonies will all retire ToMorrow. They ought never to have gone into the Assembly and if they quit will become ridiculous. I come away early, leaving the two Sisters at picquet with the Bishop and Ste Foi. The Weather has this Day been very warm and pleasant.

Monday 16. — This Morning Mr Brémond calls. Immediately after Breakfast I dress & go to Versailles. Dine with Monsieur de Cubières who gives us an excellent Repast. He has a pretty large Society. He has a very pretty little Cabinet of natural History and many little productions of the fine Arts. I tell him that with his Knowlege of Chemistry and Mineralogy he would make his Fortune in America. I come away at five instead of walking in his Garden and go to visit Mad.^e de Nadaillac who persists in her

Design to leave Paris ToMorrow Morning. Monsieur de Limon is with her who tells me that he thinks the Separation of the Duke and Dutchess of Orleans will be amicably adjusted. Different Persons keep coming in so that we have not a Moment. She seems to be a little vexed at this and endeavors to get a few Words apart. She determines to postpone her Departure till seven oClock instead of five. I tell her I am engaged at nine and at one but if she will stay till eleven I will visit her. She cannot. I leave her with the Abbé Maury and Bishop de Condon. I learn that the West Indians have retired from the Assembly and that a Decree has been passed to prevent the Reeligibility of the present Delegates. I am well pleased with both of these Events for the West Indians have hitherto run into every Extreme to obtain popularity that thereby they might carry their favorite Measures, and being indifferent about France have contributed much to the Mischiefs which have been occasioned. Go to sup with Mad.ᵉ Foucault where there is a large Party. Bouinville who is here looks like a Lover and as I take him Home he owns that he *was* one, but he was not happy. I tell her that I will endeavor to see her at Spa; this delights her, less from any Interest in what concerns me than from the Sacrifice which that Step would imply to her Charms. The Weather has this Day been lowering and threatens Rain.

Tuesday 17. — M.ʳ Brémond calls. At one I go to Mons.ʳ de Montmorin's and meet there M.ʳ de La Porte. I find that Monsieur de Montmorin is or seems much disinclined to engage in the Affair of the Rations. He doubts much, he says, of the Success and adds that the King has great Repugnance to it. He had told me before that he was well inclined; this seems misterious. He says the principal Fear is the Fear of Discovery. I shew him that there is no Danger of that Sort. He desires to meet me on Saturday. I tell him I will but I cannot promise for the Patience of the Parties interested. He says they may do as they please. I tell him that the Thing will be done in Spite of any Opposition he can make. It is in itself a just Claim. This is a strange undecided Creature. De La Porte seems to be better inclined towards the Operation. Go to the Louvre and meet Mad.ᵉ at the Door. I do not go up for it is late and she is just come in with M.ʳ de Curt and

Mad.^{lle} Duplessis. Go to Mad.^e Foucault's and dine. After Dinner
visit Mad.^e de La Luzerne and then go to the Louvre. My friend
seems *triste*. She tells me that her Hopes are much damped. De
Curt is here who talks a great Deal and convinces me thereby that
he has a confused Head not worth a Farthing in Affairs. I come
away early tho the Bishop, who I saw at Montmorin's, exprest a
Desire to meet me at Supper. The Weather is lowering and cold.

Wednesday 18. — This Morning Mr Brémond calls and I tell
him that the Affair of the Rations is postponed till Saturday. He
is not at all pleased. I dress and at eleven go to the Louvre by Appointment. My friend in celebrating the hymeneal Rights [sic]
feels uncommon Pleasure and testifies it in various Ways. I go
to Le Couteulx's and converse with him on various Matters of
Business. Then visit Madame de Ségur, where the Conversation
turning on the Means of saving Property from the Confusions
now apprehended, I mention the Purchase of Lands in America.
The Count and his Brother in Law incline much to adopt that
Measure. I go to Hudon's and from thence to Mad.^{lle} Duplessis.
Take her to the Louvre and dine. After Dinner Monsieur goes
into the Salon according to Custom. I remain with the Ladies
some Time in the Salle à Manger. Mad.^{lle} joins Monsr . . . We
visit (all three) Madame de Guibert and then ride. I set them
down and come Home early. The Weather is sour and disagreable.

Thursday 19. — This Morning Mr Brémond calls again and tells
me that he has Information from Muller, the Confidant of the
Elector of Mayence, that the french Agents act as if they did not
wish to adjust Matters with the german Princes. He says that if
the Court do not mean to settle that Affair amicably he supposes
they will not adopt the Affair of the Rations. He is right in this
Conjecture, but I reply only by repeating what I had already said,
that the Affair is extremely delicate. The Count de Greppi calls
on me and tells me that Swan is in Treaty for the Debt to Spain.
Mad.^e de Chastellux's Servant comes and tells me that he goes to
Morrow to accompany her Son to the Ville d'Eu. I send for the
Child and write to its' Mother. At one I go to the Louvre where I
perform family Duty . . . I visit the English Embassadress who is
abroad and then sit awhile with the Baron de Bezenvald who in

the fervor of his Zeal for the Cause of Despotism tells me that all
the Princes of Europe are allied to restore the antient System of
french Government. This Idea is ridiculous enough but yet
there are thousands who believe it and who are not fools either,
but it is the Lot of Man to be forever the Dupe either of vain Hope
or idle Apprehension. We are too apt to forget the past, neglect
the present and misconceive the future. From hence I go to dine
with Mad⸢e⸣ de Trudaine and after Dinner Monsieur enters into a
Dispute with S⸢t⸣ André about the Rights of those Princes who held
Fiefs in Alsace. Monsieur is a very honest Man but he holds a
very dishonest Opinion, which is very common with weak Men
in Regard to public Affairs. This Controversy reduces itself to
one Point of Right and another of Fact. By various Treaties the
Princes have stipulated that the fiefs in Question shall be held as
heretofore of the German Empire. The Point of Right therefore
is whether this Tenure does not exempt them from the general
Decisions of the french Nation respecting that Species of Property. The Point of Fact is whether the Chief of the french or german Empire be by those Treaties and *quo ad hoc* the liege Lord.
This being Matter of Interpretation must be decided by publi-
cistes but the whole Question being between Sovereign Nations
it is probable that the Decision will depend on every Thing except
the real Merits. Go to the Louvre where *par hazard* we are left
alone ... I stay till her Company is assembled and then return
Home. The Weather continues sour and is the more extraordinary
as every Morning has been fine till towards nine oClock and then
grows disagreable.

Friday 20. — This Morning write. M⸢r⸣ Swan calls and stays
some Time, I know not for what. After he is gone Col⸢o⸣ Ternant
comes. He mentions Short's Absence from Paris as a very
extraordinary Thing under present Circumstances. He says also
that he possesses no other Information than what he derives thro
the Duc de La Rochefoucault who certainly can give him very
little. I dress and go to the Louvre. Mad⸢e⸣ is denied but I find it
is to sleep. She tells me that her Husband is gone abroad, she
invented that to be alone in order to receive the Bishop and another Person at Dinner, and was denied in Consequence of her
general Orders to that Effect. She is not inclined to receive my

Caresses but yet receives from them very great Pleasure. Afterwards I give her a Hint respecting the Bishop at which she is or pretends to be offended. Go to Monsieur de Montmorin's who tells me, as I expected he would, that the King will not agree to this Affair of the Rations. I am perswaded that there is some under Work in that Business. *Nous verrons.* Montmorin tells me that he considers the Assembly as finished and this gives me a very mean Opinion of his Sagacity. A few Days ago he was in Trepidation and now in a Kind of Security, both unfounded. He fears however yet for the Person of the King. He says that different People are urging him to do different Things but that he sees Nothing to be done. I tell him to remain quiet for the Assembly are now doing every Thing they can for the King with the Intention to do every Thing they can against him. I ask him whereabouts he is with the Claims of the german Princes. He says that he thinks the Emperor will become the intermediary. He says that he fears the Count d'Artois and Prince of Condé. I treat this lightly as supposing that they will only act in favor of the royal Authority but he says they will form a Party for themselves; by which I understand only that they will oblige the King to drive away all his former Advisors. Visit Mad.^e de Ségur who is abroad and Mad.^e de Guibert who says that I must court her for Years before I could make an Impression. I laugh and tell her that a few Days or even six Weeks might be reasonable enough but the Price she sets is really too high. This Remark furnishes a Deal of ridiculous Conversation after which I visit my friend, and finding Company stay but a little while. Return Home and read. A Fire is very pleasant for the Weather continues still very sour and disagreable.

Saturday 21. — Mr Brémond calls and I tell him that the Affair of the Rations is abandoned, at which he is of Course both mortified and disappointed. I write. Then go to the Louvre and sit a little while with my friend who is sick. Afterwards visit Mad.^e de Ségur. Then dine with the Baron de Bezenvald. After Dinner go again to the Louvre but I find a pretty large Company. Mad.^e goes to bed, being very ill. I sit with her some Time and then return Home, take Tea and read. The Weather is less sour than it was.

Sunday 22. — This Morning the Count de Luxembourg calls on me and makes a long Visit. Chaumont comes in while he is here. Brémond calls but retires. As soon as I get rid of my Visitors I write and then call at the Louvre. My friend is better, her illness, which was owing to fatigue, has been remedied by Rest. Go to M.ʳ Grand's and walk a while in his Garden with him, conversing on the State of public Affairs. The Kingdom of Poland has formed a new Constitution which will I think change the political Face of Europe by drawing that Kingdom out of Anarchy into Power. The leading Features of Change are an hereditary Monarch, the Affranchisement of the Peasants and a Share of the Government given to the Towns. These are the great Means of destroying pernicious Aristocracy. After Dinner go with Chaumont, his Wife, his Mother and Sister to see S.ᵗ Cloud. The Situation is fine and the Garden would be delightful if laid out in the Style of Nature, but it is a perfectly french Garden. The View from hence is very fine. We return along the Seine to the Bridge of Neuilly and thence to Paris. Go to the Louvre and find my friend recovered; I stay but a few Minutes. Come Home and go early to Bed. The Weather was but indifferent this Morning but the Afternoon and Evening are extremely fine.

Monday 23. — M.ʳ Richard comes this Morning. I write. Col.º Ternant dines with me. After Dinner I go to the Louvre and lend my Carriage to Mad.ˡˡᵉ Duplessis. We celebrate and when Mad.ˡˡᵉ returns we ride together. Stay till ten oClock at the Louvre. M.ʳ de Curt who is here finds that the french Monarchy is ruined because a Vote is given in the Islands to some free Mulattoes. The Weather was sour in the Morning but in the Afternoon pleasant.

Tuesday 24. — This Morning write. M.ʳ Richard calls and after him M.ʳ Van Staphorst who tells me that upon Col.º Hamilton's Motions it has been resolved not to borrow any more unless, all Commission included, the Loans can be made for five per Cent. *Cela s'entend.* Le Normand calls and complains. I offer him the S.ᵗ Lawrence Lands but he must pay part Money and this Idea almost distracts him. I dine with Madame de La Luzerne. M.ʳ de Mirepoix speaks very harshly of M.ʳ Necker and I defend that ex Minister. Go to Monsieur de Montmorin's and announce my

Departure for England. Same to the british Embassadress and Embassador. Then visit my friend and stay with her some Time but there is Company. This Day it has rained from about one oClock in the Afternoon. Small Rain and rather warm.

Wednesday 25. — This Morning write. M.ʳ Brémond and M.ʳ Richard give me some Interruption. At three I take Mad.ˡˡᵉ Duplessis to the Louvre and dine. After Dinner I write a Letter to the Count de Montmorin on the State of Affairs. Monsieur goes abroad and Mad.ˡˡᵉ takes my Carriage. In their Absence we do the needful. . . . As I inform her of my Departure she expresses much Regret of which I believe only a Share and let her see it. She weeps profusely. Stay the Evening here. It has rained all Day.

Morris to Montmorin

25 May 1791

Je désire, mon cher comte, avant de partir vous dire encore un mot sur la position des Affaires et je vous donne la peine de lire cette lettre plutôt que de vous prendre quelques minutes de plus par une Conversation. Vous m'avez très bien répondu l'autre jour en me demandant 'mais qui donc sont les personnes qui dans le moment sont bien vues du peuple.' Si c'étoit aussi aisé qu'il est difficile de répondre à votre question il restroit toujours à sçavoir pour combien de jours ces mêmes personnes conserveroient la bonne Volonté du peuple, ou pour mieux dire de la populace. Je ne me dissimule pas, comme vous voyez, la difficulté. Mais je vous prie en même temps de faire attention à une autre Chose qui est très claire. On connoit très bien les hommes, et les femmes aussi, qui sont détestés — très injustement, mais de bon cœur et en toute Vérité. Or c'est très possible qu'on ne choisira pas très bien, mais toujours ce sera très bien fait de changer. Quand les nouveaux venus seront dépopularisés il faut encore changer, puisqu'alors on se portera toujours contre les entours et non pas contre les chefs. Je suis très intimement persuadé que si les personnes que vous aimez conservent leur état pour quelques mois de plus la chose publique se rétablira. Déjà on commence à s'appercevoir que l'anarchie va bientôt tout détruire si on n'y porte pas bientôt un remède. Ce remède est l'autorité du chef, et comme tout dépend de l'opinion il faut le temps nécessaire pour bien faire sentir au peuple cette grande vérité. En attendant, je vous supplie en grâce de considérer que l'assemblée, que les départements, ont sollicités le renvois de plusieurs personnes, que les désordres inséparablement annexés à un numéraire fictif vont incessamment tomber sur les dernières Classes de la Société, qu'alors nous verrons naître une Sorte de procès entre les partisans de l'ancien et du nouveau régime, peutêtre entre le roi et l'assemblée; car il ne faut nullement douter que chacun cherchera de rejetter le blâme sur un autre. Si dans ce moment la cour se trouve entourée de ceux qui se sont attirés la haine très injuste de la populace, qui est ce qui répondra des conséquences? Surtout si la france est en même temps menacée en dehors? Vous sçavez bien les Combinaisons qu'ont faites depuis très long tems les mal intentionnés, et vous verrez que le *bon* père Duchene, que j'ai l'honneur de vous présenter, commence déjà d'endoctriner ses très chères ouailles. Adieu. Je me promets le plaisir de vous voir demain à votre Caffé et je vous prierai alors de me redonner celle ci avec deux autres petites pièces que vous connaissez.

Je suis avec un attachement très sincère

Mon cher comte

votre très humble Serviteur

G. M.

P.S. Il faut toujours se resouvenir que ce n'est plus question de liberté. C'est seulement de qui sera le maître. Si je pouvois me tranquilizer sur le Sort de la famille royale je serois très inquiet pour celui de la france si on s'avise (pour me servir de l'expression à la mode) de changer la dynastie.

[Translation:]

I wish, my dear Count, before my departure to say one word more on the position of affairs, and I give you the trouble of reading this letter rather than take up more of your time by a conversation. You answered me well the other day by asking 'but who then are the persons who are at the moment thought well of by the people?' Were it as easy as it

is difficult to answer your question it would still remain
to be seen for how many days these same men would retain
the goodwill of the people, or rather of the populace. I do
not, as you see, disguise the difficulty. But I beg you at
the same time to notice another thing which is very clear.
It is well known which men and also which women are detested, very unjustly, but heartily and in all sincerity. Now
it is quite possible that a good selection may not be made
but it will still be well to make a change. When the new-
comers become unpopular they must in turn be changed because the surroundings will then be blamed and not the
heads. I am most intimately persuaded that if the persons
you love [the King and Queen] can retain their status for a
few months longer, public affairs will right themselves. It is
already becoming evident that anarchy will soon destroy
everything if not speedily curbed. The remedy is the authority of the chief, and as everything depends on opinion, time
is needed to make the public sensible of this great truth.
Meanwhile I implore you to consider that the Assembly, that
the Departments, have solicited the dismissal of several individuals; that the disorders inseparably connected with a
fictitious currency will soon fall on the lowest classes of society; that we shall then see the birth of a sort of trial between
the partisans of the old and of the new régime, perhaps between the King and the Assembly, for it cannot be doubted
that each will try to throw the blame on the other. If at that
moment the Court is surrounded by those who have drawn
upon themselves the hatred, very unjust, of the populace,
who will answer for the consequences? Especially if France
should at the same time be menaced from abroad. You are
well aware of the combinations long since formed by the ill
intentioned, and you will see that the *good* Father Duchêne,[1]
whom I have the honor to present to you, begins already to

---

[1] *Good* 'Father Duchesne' was the anarchist newspaper started by Hébert
under the same title as a little royalist sheet, colloquially written by a post-
office employee called Lemaire to uphold the National Assembly's early ideal
of a constitutional monarchy. Very different was the teaching of the new
Father, whose double-distilled hatred of order and the decencies was to be
rivalled by Marat alone.

indoctrinate his very dear flock. Adieu. I promise myself the pleasure of seeing you tomorrow at your coffee and will then ask you to give me back the present, with two other short papers which you know of.

I remain with a very sincere attachment,

My dear Count,

Your most humble Servant

G. M.

P.S. We must always remind ourselves that it is no longer a question of liberty. Only of who shall be the master. Even if I could reassure myself on the fate of the royal family I should still be filled with anxiety for that of France if it is decided (to use the expression now in vogue) to change the dynasty.

Thursday 26. — This Morning both M.ʳ Brémond and M.ʳ Richard visit me. I write. M.ʳ Swan calls and I tell him my Surprize at Hearing that I am considered in America as speculating in the Debt to France. He assures me that he has never said or done any Thing to raise such Idea and that he will exert himself to remove it. I dine with the british Embassador and after Dinner we go together to visit Monsieur de Montmorin. He tells me that if he had 50,000 Men he would put every Thing to rights. I tell him that the *Enragés* are in Despair. He says he could give them the *Coup de Grâce* if he pleased for that he has Reason to believe they are in Pursuit of the Affair of the Rations. I tell him that I do not know but that I shall know. He asks me if I shall be back from London during the Month of June. I tell him that I shall. We have an interrupted Conversation and I promise to dine with him ToMorrow. Go to the Louvre. Embrace my friend and stay with her till Half past eight. Return Home. M.ʳ Short, who was to call at nine does not come till near ten and stays with me till one. We converse a good Deal about various Affairs but particularly Loans for the United States, and the Offers made for the french Debt. I give him my sincere Opinion that a Bargain in the Lump would be the best Mode of treating that Affair. The Weather has been very pleasant this Day.

Extracts from Letter of Morris to Washington

... In a Letter to Col? Hamilton of the 31 January 1790 I mentioned what had passed between M! Necker and me respecting the Debt due by the United States to France ... About this Time I received your Orders to communicate with the british Ministers, and altho I did by no Means consider that in the Light of an Appointment to Office, yet from Motives of Delicacy I determined to extricate myself from the Affair of the Debt as speedily as I could with Propriety.

I have ever been of Opinion that as we are not in Condition to pay our Debt to France, a Bargain by which the Period can be prolonged without Loss to either Party is desirable. I say without Loss, because the Conduct of this Nation has been so generous to us that it would be very ungrateful indeed to take Advantage of those Necessities which the Succor afforded to America has occasioned. Such Bargain must be either with the Government or with Individuals. But after the repeated Delays on our Part, to ask longer Time now would not look well. Indeed no such Treaty could be made without the Consent of the Assembly, and their Observations would not be pleasant. A Bargain with Individuals has the Advantage of bringing in the Aid of private Interest to the Support of our Credit, and what is of very great Consequence, it would leave us at Liberty to make use of that Credit for the Arrangement of our domestic Affairs. And on this Head I must mention to you my dear Sir that it has been my good fortune to prevent some publications which would have been particularly injurious to us. Their Object was to complain of the United States for speculating in their own Effects with the Funds of France; urging that while we owed heavy Installments already due here, all the Loans we obtain in Holland ought to be applied to the Discharge of them and therefore that the Speculations in our domestic Debt were a double Violation of good Faith &c? &c? &c?. The present State of Things here has occasioned so great a Fall in the Exchange that Money borrowed in Holland is remitted with great Gain, consequently Loans made there just now answer well & it is evident that the Parties who are endeavoring to contract, count on a considerable Profit from that Circumstance.

Much however is to be said on this Part of the Subject. First it is questionable whether our Reputation may not be a little affected, for you will recollect that about one third of our Debt to France arose from a Loan made on our Account in Holland of five Millions of florins, for which the King paid us here ten Million of Livres without any Deduction for Charges of any Sort. The Nation is now obliged to pay these five Millions in Holland, and for us to borrow that Amount there and then squeeze them in an Exchange which distresses both their Commerce and Finances, looks hard. There was a good Deal of murmuring about it when the last Operation of 'f1,500,000, Guilders took Place and I should not be at all surprized if some *Patriot*, by Way of shewing his Zeal, should make a violent Attack in the Assembly when the next Payment is made. There are many of these patriots who, if they can inculpate Ministers and distress those of different Sentiments, don't Care a Jot for Consequences. But supposing this not to happen, it is not possible for a Nation to make the Advantage which Individuals do in such Things because they must employ Individuals, each of whom will be too apt to look a little to his own Advantage. [27 May 1791.]

Friday 27. — Write. M.ʳ Brémond, M.ʳ Swan and M.ʳ Terrason call. I dine with M.ʳ de Montmorin and after Dinner call on Monsieur de La Fayette who is gone out. Go from thence to the Louvre. My friend has Company. Call on Mad.ᵉ de Ségur who is abroad. Then return Home and wait for M.ʳ Swan and M.ʳ Brémond who come after the Hour; agree with them on the Steps to be pursued respecting a Contract to supply the Marine. Then go to the Louvre and stay the Evening. The Weather this Day has been pleasant.

Saturday 28 May. — This Morning M.ʳ Short comes to Breakfast and we have again a long Conversation on public Affairs. M.ʳ Swan calls, for whom I write a Letter to the Count de Montmorin. Visit Madame de Ségur and confer with the Count and her on their Affairs and the Means of securing themselves by a Purchase of Dover Estate. Go from thence to see Col.º Ternant and deliver to him my Letters. Thence to visit Chaumont who gives me his News from America. Thence to the Louvre where

I dine Tête à Tête with my friend who has sent her Husband out of the Way, but lest he should suddenly return we are to go abroad at half past four; this leaves us but Half an Hour after Dinner and we employ it in the best Manner for we perform twice very well the pleasing act. We then ride, and return to the Louvre where I pass the Evening. This has been a pleasant Morning but rainy Afternoon.

Sunday 29 *May*. — This Morning M͇ͬ Brémond breakfasts with me. He tells me what passed Yesterday with M͇ͬ Short and I give him my Idea of what remains to be done. After he leaves me I prepare for my Departure and set off at Half past ten. In three Hours and forty Minutes we reach Chantilly and having ordered Dinner we go to view the Gardens. These have an Abundance of Water but from the too great Expansion of it there is a stagnant Scum and offensive Smell. I see nothing in this Garden worthy of Remark tho a great Deal of Labor has been expended upon it. At forty Minutes after four we leave Chantilly and in two Hours and five Minutes reach Clermont. I observe that there are Vines as far as this Village but they tell me that they were hurt by the Frost. The Inn I put up at (the royal Swan) has a good Reputation ill merited. I wait three Hours for a Couple of Eggs and a Plate of Pease, which indeed I had ordered for their Sakes and not for my own, having already an Indigestion from what I drank at Chantilly.

Monday 30 *May*. — After a sleepless Night with an uneasy Stomach I rise a little after three and we set off a Quarter before four, and a Quarter before seven we reach the Ville d'Eu, having spent besides a large Quarter of an Hour in getting Breakfast at Breteuil. The Distance 17¼ Posts which make about ninety Miles in fifteen Hours. I remember once to have observed that the first Vineyard I saw in going from Calais to Paris was at Écouen, but this Day I observe on the Hill we ascend between Breteuil and Flers some pretty extensive, and which look remarkably well. These are above sixty Miles from Paris. In coming out of Amiens we met a whimsical Accident. The Bidet on which the Postillion rode tumbled Head over Heels but as the Rider's Feet were at most eight Inches from the Ground he was landed in perfect Safety while poor Bidet got so far under the

Carriage that his Feet were engaged in the Splinter Bar. After leaving Abbeville to come to Eu we go thro a beautiful Country, the Distance something better than twenty Miles. The Villages are built in little Forests, about the Quantity needful for Firing with great Œconomy, but the Forest Trees are on the Exterior and among the little thatched Huts are small Gardens with Fruit Trees. The Scene is highly pittoresque. The Country also is fertile and as I observe in this Day's Ride a great Deal of Saint-foin, which seems to succeed even in the poorest Soil, I am led to enquire the Culture and find that it is sown either with Spring or Winter Grain like Clover, but instead of about six Pounds, a Bushel of Seed is necessary. This Grass is most used I am told in hot Climates but since it stands the Frost also I believe it would be a valuable Acquisition to America. It lasts in good Land five Years from one Sowing. The Weather has been very fine and they tell me, which is indeed very visible, that the Country begins to suffer from the Want of Rain.

Tuesday 31 *May.* — This Morning I wait upon the Dutchess of Orleans and breakfast in her Chamber with Madame de Chastellux. She sends to her Father to announce my Arrival and Desire of visiting him. The old Gentleman returns a very polite Answer and we agree that I shall dine with them. I find there is much Restraint and Etiquette here. After Breakfast she reads me her Letters to and from the Duke and then we walk till near Dinner Time. She tells me the History of their Branch from a long Time back and the Manœuvres used by him and those about him. He is a mighty strange Fellow. She tells me that what the World attributed to Fondness in her was meerly Discretion. She hoped to bring him to a more decent and orderly Behaviour but finds at length that he is to be governed by Fear only. She tells me of her Difficulties in bringing her Father to act. He is nervous and trembles at every Thing like Exertion. We have an excellent Dinner and in the Conversation at and after it I gain a little upon the old Gentleman's good Opinion. They embark after Dinner in a large Carriage to take an Airing and I go to my Hotel. Having nothing to do I order Horses and get off at a quarter past six. At a Half past nine I reach Dieppe over a high Plain intersected by a deep Ravine at Criel, a little Village lying on the small River ——, which is a good sized Brook. In descending to this Village there is one of the most beautiful Views of varied Culture that I ever beheld. The Distance from Eu to Dieppe is about eighteen Miles. The Soil very good of its Kind, viz a light Loam. The Culture is pretty good also. As soon as I get out of my Carriage I enquire if there be a Vessel for England, having understood that the Passage Boats are to go To Morrow Evening, but in this I was misinformed. She is just gone out, and as it is calm I get into a Boat and am rowed off to her. Our only Motion is that of rolling and as our Passengers are numerous, Vessel small and some of them have sick Stomachs, this with the Heat of the Weather renders the Position not a little disagreable. I get into Bed with my Cloaths on about eleven. The Weather has been very fine this Day.

JUNE 1791

Wednesday 1 June. — This Morning is perfectly calm and during the Day we have only light Airs so that our Progress is extremely slow. We do not loose Sight of the french Coast untill Darkness shuts up the View. As our Provisions are likely to fall short I get them to run on Board of a Fisherman, from whom I buy a pretty good Stock of Fish. The Weather is hot and calm.

Thursday 2. — The Weather is still the same and the Surface of the Sea is literally as smooth as Glass. Not the least Swell. Our Bread was nearly expended last Evening and we are this Morning upon Allowance. At four oClock we send off the Boat to a Sloop which lies about a League from us. She proves to be a Scotchman from the Port of London bound to Kildare, who for a good Price lets us have a small Supply of Ship Biscuit. We see Beachy Head a great Way off and this Evening we have a light Breeze from the Eastward which takes us on at near a League per Hour. Towards Midnight it grows more feeble, so that the Hope of getting on Shore this Night dies away with it. We have on Board a frenchman with his Daughter, just come out of a Convent, and I think I never saw a little Animal so salacious. Her Berth is under that of her Father but this Night they change because in the last the Master of the Boat was discovered going to Bed to her and the old Man was obliged to defend a Citadel which she was anxious to surrender to any Thing on Board in the Shape of a Man. This Scene amused me for I lay awake on Purpose, having as I thought observed that the 'connubial League' was agreed. At one o'Clock I lie down again for another fatiguing sleepless Night, and rise at a little after four as we are then well in with the Land. About seven we get on Shore and there is a fine Breeze.

- *Friday June* 3. — Having got thro the Ceremonies of the Custom House and taken our Breakfast I have at length the Pleasure of putting on clean Cloaths. A Mʳ Blunt, who was our fellow Passenger together with his Brother, and who lives at Horsham in this Neighbourhood, presses me to take that Route and to dine with him, which I decline as I am pressed to get forward. We leave Brighton at half past nine and in two Hours and a Quarter we get fourteen Miles to Cuckfield. The first six was over the Downs or rather by a winding Road thro them; we then from the Hill see expanded before us a beautiful Valey [sic] which contrasts well with the high brown Hills. The Downs are gravelly, the Valley sandy Loam, so that the Roads are made with broken Stone which seems to be very hard. We change in five Minutes and in an Hour and ten Minutes get on to Crawley, nine Miles. Within a Mile of this Place the Soil stiffens. We change again in five Minutes and go in an Hour and ten Minutes to Ryegate over a stiff clayey Loam; we change again in five Minutes and begin to mount the Ridge which lay before us when we were on the Downs. Indeed, we went over a small Spur of it in the last Stage. These Hills are sandy and barren with white Lime Stone in them. From Ryegate to Sutton, which is ten Miles, we go in an Hour and a Quarter over Walton Heath and Banstead Downs, a great barren of which a Part is cultivated and by Culture and Manure looks extremely well, but in the State of Nature this Tract must have been very wild. Antiently very fine Mutton

was supplied from hence to the City of London. We stay fifty
Minutes at Sutton for a very indifferent Dinner with excellent
Ale, and then get on in an Hour and three Quarters twelve Miles
to Covent Garden, which we reach at six oClock; so that, deducting the three Quarters expended in getting our Dinner, we have
been just seven Hours and three Quarters in going fifty five Miles
and the Expence exclusive of Dinner is £3..16.., about 15^d
and 8½ Minutes per Mile, or seven Miles an Hour. I take a
Hackney Coach and go to the french Embassador's where I
leave some Letters, he being out of Town. Thence to visit Lady
Tancred who is abroad, thence to Richard Penn's where I have
a most cordial Welcome. Happening on the Subject of going to
America to ask Miss if she would go along, she makes a little
consenting Hesitation which is very like Yes, and she understood
the Proposition more widely than I meant to make it. Take Tea
and go to Mr Franklin's. He is not at Home. Call on Mr Rogers
who says that his Trustees are prepared to make me Propositions.
Go to Lord Landsdowne's and deliver there a Letter. We have a
little Conversation and afterwards with Monsr Barthelemie who
comes in. Go from hence to Mr John Penn's but they are abroad.
Thence to visit Mrs Church where I sit a little while and then
return Home. Mr Franklin is waiting for me and stays till after
one oClock. The Weather has this Day been very pleasant with
a smart Breeze from the Eastward so that the Drougth is like
to continue. The Country I rode through is already suffering
much. The Hay is very short and thin, the Grain begins to look
sickly, and if this continue I fear they will suffer greatly. The
Russian Dispute is I find very unpopular but I do not see how
the Minister is to get out of the Scrape.[1]

---

[1] The Near East problem, forerunner of the Crimean War, whether to shed
Christian blood bolstering up the Turk as check on Slav expansion threatening
to Britain's communications with India. Russia planned the Dniester for boundary, annexing Ochakov district along Black Sea. Wishing to keep the Ottoman
Empire intact, Pitt sent ultimatum to Catherine. Split in Cabinet, resignation
of Duke of Leeds (which Morris had surmised was not all a matter of health),
siding of merchants and public with Fox and Burke, make Pitt withdraw ultimatum and Catherine triumphs in Peace of Jassy. Pitt loses prestige, keeps
his place; but sudden enforced change of policy has far-reaching effect on
European combinations, Prussia transferring friendliness from England to

Saturday June 4.th — This Morning M[r]. Franklin breakfasts with me and we consider sundry Things relative to M[r]. Morris's Affairs. I dress and go into the City; M[r]. J. Penn came while I was dressing. I visit at M[r]. Phyn's and speak on Business to M[r]. Inglis. Return from thence and leave a Note desiring an Interview with M[r]. Parker at his confidential friend's. Visit M[r]. Ogden and then go to dine with Lord Lansdowne. After Dinner take Tea with M[rs]. R. Penn and then return Home. The Weather has been hot this Day.

Sunday June 5.th — This Morning I visit the french Embassador and give him an Account of what is doing in France. Then go out to Gen[l]. Morris's where I dine. After Dinner take Major Barclay along, and visit Madame de La Luzerne. Call on my Return and leave a Card for Gen[l]. Dalrymple. Afterwards visit M[rs]. J. Penn and sit with them till eleven. The Weather has been very hot this Day and the Appearance of the Fields of Grain is very unpromising. The french Embassador tells me that the Ministry of this Country will go on arming and threatning till the Season for Action is past and then disarm in Part. I think this very likely.

Monday 6 June. — M[r]. Franklin calls on me this Morning to tell what has passed with M[r]. Pultney. I go into the City; M[r]. Inglis has not yet seen M[r]. Maitland; he is out of Town. I call on M[r]. Welsh who is abroad. On Eden and Court, also abroad. On Cazalet and Sons; converse a little with one of them and we agree to meet on Friday. Go to the Exchange. See again A. Wallace who called on me this Morning. Doctor Bancroft tells me he has a Certificate of Pensilvania to sell. Go to M[r]. Phyn's to Dinner and stay the Evening. The Weather is very hot.

Tuesday 7 June. — This Morning go early into the City. M[r]. Inglis has seen his Co trustees and we are to meet ToMorrow at one. I call on Messieurs Eden and Court and on M[r]. Wakelyn

---

Austria and Russia, which leads to her sharing in Second Partition of Poland, just now hoping so much from her new Constitution.

Winding up the Parker-Rogers muddle, working with Temple Franklin on sales of Robert Morris's great Genesee tract, make this the most busy, least social of Morris's London visits. News of the flight of the King and Queen of France sends him hurrying back, hopeful of a fresh crop of emigrants to American lands, but the market is held up by each new decree of the Assembly.

Welsh to receive Money. This last, who never noticed my
Introduction to him, asks of me Letters for his Son to my friends
in Paris. Call on M.ʳ Neave who is not at Home. Visit M.ʳ & M.ʳˢ
Lowe who are abroad, M.ʳ Franklin and M.ʳ Rogers, also abroad,
M.ʳˢ R. Penn and Miss Masters; sit with them some Time and
then go with Penn to dine at his Brother's. Call in our Way at
Ramsden's where I give six Guineas for a Glass. He is to send it
Home with a Stand and let me know the Price of that, should I
chuse to take it. After Dinner I tell Penn that I am authorized
to make them an Offer for the national Debt granted to them by
Pensilvania. He says they shall leave that to their Agents in
America. Call on R. Penn's Family in our Way Home and then
M.ʳ Franklin sits down with me to consider the Propositions to be
made to M.ʳ Pultney and Co:. The Weather this Day has been
very hot.

Wednesday 8 *June.* — This Morning M.ʳ Chalmers and his
Brother call. I go to M.ʳ Maitland's where after a long Alterca-
tion we agree to two Points needful for a final Adjustment of our
Affairs. Go from there to Bourdieu's. Dine with them and return
Home to receive M.ʳ Franklin who does not come till late. He
brings new Propositions from M.ʳ Pultney, who is a tight fellow
to deal with. The Weather has been cooler this Day, but the
Wind is still to the Eastward and of Course the Drought continues.

Thursday 9 *June.* — This Morning M.ʳ Franklin comes and we
go into an Investigation of the Proposals made by M.ʳ Pultney.
I make the needful Calculations and state the Payments to be
made. M.ʳ Parker comes and apologizes for not answering my
Letters &c.ᵃ, &c.ᵃ. I dress and call on young Penn to whom I
mention the Offer to be made for the Compensation granted to
them. He is to fix a Meeting with his Cousin and inform me of
it. I go to the City and dine at a Scotch Club where we have a
good Dinner and a good Society. Get Home at Half past ten,
where I find a Note from M.ʳ Franklin mentioning Objections to
my Statement. I go immediately to meet him at M.ʳ Colqhoun's;
and there I find in M.ʳ Colqhoun a very positive and opinionated
Man. I tell him finally that I will not agree to what he contends
for. M.ʳ Franklin comes Home with me and shews sundry Papers.
He does not like the Insertion of £1750 allowed to him in the

Deed as Part of the Compensation or Consideration. The Weather is pleasant but very dry.

Friday 10 *June.* — This Morning M.ʳ Franklin calls and I give him the Note of Payments calculated exactly on those formerly agreed to. He is to carry them to M.ʳ Pultney. M.ʳ Rogers brings me a State of the Account made out according to Prices I had agreed to with his Trustees. He is to fix a Meeting for this Day. M.ʳ Parker calls and makes a very lame Apology for neglecting to answer my Letters &c.ᵃ. He complains of Hubbard much. I go to M.ʳ Penn's and have a little Conversation with them about the Pensilvania Compensation. They are to see me ToMorrow Morning. Go into the City to attend the Meeting of Arbitrators but I find that it cannot take Place this Day. Speak to M.ʳ Cholett about the Discounting of Pultney's Payments. He says they must have Notes for this Purpose, as I supposed. Dine with Mess.ʳˢ Cazalett and after Dinner visit M.ʳˢ Low who is abroad. Then M.ʳˢ Penn with whom I stay a few Minutes. On my Return I find that M.ʳ Parker has been with me and is gone again. The Weather is still very dry and this Day has been warmer than the last. An Arrival from India brings Dispatches the Contents of which are not yet disclosed, it may therefore be concluded that they are unpleasant; indeed, it is evident from the India Gazettes that the Expence of the Campaign has been incurred and Nothing effected. Tippoo Saib was ravaging the Carnatic and consequently, without a Loss of Dominion, there must be a Loss of Value.

Saturday 11 *June.* — The Messieurs Penn breakfast with me this Morning and after some Conversation I make them a Proposal for their Compensation. They seem I think disinclined to it, being prejudiced in Favor of an Offer made to them by John Ross. I give them a Note in Writing for their Consideration. After they are gone I dress and go to visit my Brother; from thence I go to the french Embassador's and dine. He tells me that the Assembly have determined to form a new Treaty of Commerce with the United States and that Ternant is departed. Returning to Town I stop at R. Penn's and take Tea. The Weather has this Day been so cold as to make a Fire very agreable at least, if not absolutely necessary. The Grain looks blighted, and indeed it must have a very strong Constitution to resist Drought and the Alternative of great Heat and great Cold in so short a Period.

Sunday 12 *June.* — This Morning I employed in writing. Gen! Murray called on me to ask that I would get for him from America some dried Clams; Mr Prager to know if I had any American Debt to dispose of; Mr de Mezy on a Visit which he extended too much. At five I go to dine with R. Penn. His Brother and Wife and Col? Allen dine there. Mr Franklin has fixed with Mr Pultney agreably to my Proposals, nearly. John Penn tells me that his Cousin thinks it will be best to send my Proposals to their Agents in America. I take Mr Franklin to his Father's and visit M.^r and Mrs Low. The Weather has this Day been very cold. It is remarkable that a Week ago it was very hot, and it seems that it was snowing in Ireland. It is now very cold and the Accounts from Dublin are that the Weather is very hot.

Monday 13. — This Morning I am engaged in writing. Go at four to dine with Mr Chalmers and drink a great Deal too much Wine. Call on Mrs Phyn but make my Visit short as I perceive my Situation to be not over fit for female Society. The Weather is still cold and dry.

Tuesday 14. — This Morning Mr Franklin calls and endeavors to screw me down in the Price of American Debt. We have some Conversation respecting the Mortgage given by R. M. to Gorham and Phelps, and the Remittances to be made thereon to Paris &c.^a. I go into the City and sign Arbitration Bonds with the Trustees of Rogers. After which we state our Case &c.^a. Go from hence to Mr Phyn's to Dinner. Stay the Evening. The Weather is still dry and cold.

Wednesday 15. — This Morning I write a little and then ride out to Shooter's Hill to see the Children of the Count de Ségur. Return from thence over Blackfriar's Bridge and go to Highgate where I dine with Mr Cazalet and after Dinner we converse about Business. He is to give me a Note of what he will do. Return from thence by the Westward and visit at R. Penn's. The Weather has been this Day very cold. It looks likely to rain but the Wind is still Northeast.

Thursday 16 *June.* — Last Night or rather this Morning the

Wind blew very hard from the Northwest with Rain. It afterwards got back again to the Eastward and continues cold. Mr Franklin comes but we do Nothing for I find by a Note from Mr Rogers that there are Difficulties in the Way of dissolving the Trust Deed. Mr Henchman breakfasts with me as well as Mr Franklin. After Breakfast Mr Prager calls to shew a Letter from his friend fixing the Price he will give for American Stock. This refers to a former Letter and therefore proves Nothing; however, I cannot now go into the Discussion. After some Conversation with Mr Henchman we agree that, all Things considered, it will be best to dissolve the Trust Deed. The next Point is Payment to them of their Advance, and I tell him that I mean to provide for it but would rather do so from the Stock and that by borrowing on the 3p%. Finally offer to him the 3p% at 9/6 and the 6p% at 17/6 in the Pound. He talks of selling the Whole by Auction but this I disapprove of entirely. Dress and go to Eltham. Dine with Mr Gregory and am well received by Madame, which is I believe a principal Point in this Family. Return early and go early to Bed. The Weather has moderated much and this Evening is very pleasant and showery.

Friday 17 *June.* — Mr Rogers calls this Morning and shews me some Observations made by the Arbitrators on which it is necessary for me to remark. The Morning is consumed in this Business. Go into the City and offer to Inglis the 6p% Stock at 17/6. He tells me that Rogers and his Trustees have been trying to obtain from the Arbitrators a Decision which would oblige me to seek my Remedy for the Ballance due against Parker only, preventing him at the same Time from the Benefit of a Set off against Rogers. He is to set this Matter right. He tells me that Messieurs Gildart and Reed wish to see me about the Bonds which Truxton has given. I mention to him the Advantage of making Contracts for Wheat in America, should the Harvest here prove short, and as I am of Opinion that it will be short I recommend the making of Enquiry and sending out early Advices. Take Mr Phyn with me to Genl Morris's; we dine, and drink too much. He returns with me and takes Tea. After he is gone I eat part of a Supper I had ordered and by no Means want. The Weather has grown mild and the Wind tho still to the Eastward is more Southerly.

Saturday 18 *June.* — M: Franklin comes this Morning and mentions sundry Propositions which he has for the Sale of American Stock. I go into the City and visit M: Havard who communicates a State of the late M: Burgeois's Affairs. I give him my Opinion thereon and then ask whether the Award with Rogers's Trustees is made up, he being one of the Referees. He tells me that it will be finished on Monday and that the Ballance is somewhat less than is stated by the Account settled with Rogers and Parker. I visit Mess.ʳˢ Gildart and Reid who tell me of the Bonds given by Truxton and of their Contentment to find that our House are concerned, to whom they shall look for their Money. I give them the needful Assurances and then go to Mark Lane where I dine and stay the Evening. The Weather has this Day been raw and damp but has cleared up this Evening.

Sunday 19 *June.* — This Morning I rise late and dress immediately after Breakfast. Go to Salisbury Street to look for M: Parker and am to call ToMorrow. Then visit M: J. Penn sen: who is abroad. Go to Eltham and dine with M: Gregory. We walk before Dinner and I propose to him to be concerned with me in the Purchase of the Penn Compensation. Am to give him a Note, that he may enquire if a Loan can be obtained on it in Holland. Return to Town so as to get Home at Half after ten, having called on M:ˢ R. Penn who is not at Home. The Weather this Morning was very fine but the Evening is sour. The Wind all Day from the North East.

Monday 20 *June.* — This Morning I call on M: John Penn sen: and make him some Proposals respecting the Pensilvania Compensation; then leave my Card for Gen: Murray, Monsieur de Mezy, M: Knox & M: & M:ˢ Beckford. Look for M: Cutting, but in vain. Visit Lady Tancred and sit with her some Time. Miss Byron comes in. Call at the french Embassador's to enquire of his Health and then visit M: & M:ˢ Low. Return Home to Dinner. I called at M: Parker's and sent, but could not see him or hear of him. I saw M: Rogers and got a Note of Parker's Property in Holland. The Weather has this Day been very cold and disagreable. The Wind still at North East.

Tuesday 21 *June.* — This Morning I write. M: Franklin calls and tells me that he will take the 3p% Stock at 50p%. M: Prager

calls and I tell him it is sold; he wishes to know my lowest Price
for the six per Cents; I adhere to that formerly fixed of 90 p%
and tell him that I cannot strike even at that till I hear from those
who have it now in their Offer. Go into the City and meet M.ʳ D.
Gregory on Change. I tell him that the Gentlemen with whom
I was in Treaty for American Stock hang off. He informs me that
his Partner M.ʳ Forbes will not take a Concern in it and he tells
me that it is the House of Coudere, Brants and Changuion of
Amsterdam who have offered to procure Loans on the Credit
of American Stock and he thinks at four p%. I see on Change
M.ʳ Dearman of the House of Warder, Dearman and Co: who
tells me that he has sold the 6p% Stock at Par. Go to M.ʳ Phyn's
but M.ʳ Inglis is not there. Call on M.ʳ Havard, who tells me the
Award is not signed but he gives me the Heads of it and promises
to send to M.ʳ Wadeson to accelerate it. Dine with M.ʳ Phyn, and
as usual spend the Evening. This Day the Wind has got round
to the Westward and it is less cold. In the Evening with a Southwest Wind we have some refreshing Rain much wanted, but it
clears up again and the Night is dry and pleasant.

Wednesday 22 June. — This Morning I go into the City and
endeavor to obtain the Award of the Arbitrators, but to my great
Mortification find it will not be ready till Friday Morning. Ask
M.ʳ Inglis if he will take the Six per Cents at 17/6; he tells me that
he thinks he shall but must first consult M.ʳ Phyn. I call on M.ʳ
Donald who is not at Home. See M.ʳ Henchman who offers 14/
in the Pound for Omnium. This is ridiculous. I tell him what I
expect to do and what I wish from them, give him a Minute and
desire to meet at the Office on Friday at twelve. Dine with M.ʳˢ
Penn. Receive a Message from M.ʳ Parker whom I had called on
in the Morning, and in Consequence thereof return Home. He
comes at nine and stays till twelve. He expresses a Willingness
to do whatever I may think right respecting the Ballance which
will be due to me. The Weather has been tolerably pleasant
this Day but is still very cool with the Wind from the North East.

Thursday 23 June. — This Morning M.ʳ Knox calls on me and
has a great Deal to say about Nothing; he seeks for elegant Dic-
tion and forgets that there should be at least one Idea in Half
an Hour's Talk. After he is gone Doctor Bancroft arrives who

tells me that the Hon.^{le} Thomas Walpole has been applied to by
Lord Grenville to go out to America. I call on Mr Cutting and
then on Mr Rogers, both abroad; afterwards on Mr Franklin who is
gone out, and leave a Message for him. Then go to Genl Morris's.
Thence after a short Visit to the french Embassador. Call at
R. Penn's on my Return and get Home early. The Weather this
Day has been tolerably pleasant tho the fire is not disagreable.
It is calm almost.

Friday 24 *June.* — This Morning Mr Franklin calls and tells
me that he shall take to Amount of about £17,500 Sterling of
3p% Stock. We go into the City together and I learn that the
Award will not be compleated till ToMorrow at twelve. Go to
the American fund Office and after a great Deal of Difficulty
settle with the Trustees and obtain their Promise to give a Power
of Attorney to Mr Fox of Philadelphia to receive the Interest or
three per Cents &c.^a. Mr Franklin, R. Penn and I dine at the
Prince of Wales's Coffee House where we have but indifferent
Fare at a moderate Price. Take Tea at Penn's and come Home.
The Weather has this Day been pleasant with Wind from the
Westward.

Saturday 25 *June.* — This Morning I go into the City and
take up Mr Inglis. We go together in Pursuit of the Award which
is at last obtained and which is very far from satisfactory to me.
We go to Mr Maitland's and after much Conversation agree to
meet on Monday for the Purpose of carrying into Execution this
Award as well as we can. Mr Maitland gives me repeated Assur-
ances of a Disposition to do what is right on the Occasion. —
We hear that the King and Queen of France have effected their
Escape from the Tuilleries and have got six or seven Hours the
Start of their Keepers. This will produce some considerable
Consequences. If they get off safe a War is inevitable, and if
retaken it will probably suspend for some Time all monarchical
Government in France. I dine with Doctor Bancroft where is
Doctor Ingenhousz.[1] He mentions a late Discovery he has made

---

[1] John Ingenhousz (1730–1799), Dutch doctor pensioned by Austrian Court,
Maria Theresa having employed him to inoculate imperial family with small-
pox while Dimsdale did the like for Empress Catherine in Russia. Ingenhousz
discovered that vegetation gives off oxygen in sunlight, carbonic acid in shade.
Sir Joseph Banks (1743–1820), President of the Royal Society, had sailed round

respecting the Inflammability of Metals and offers to shew me a
Rod of Iron burning like a Candle. It is only necessary to place
it in vital Air. I set him down at Sir Joseph Banks's and return
Home early. The Weather is now grown warm, as the Wind is
got round to the Westward and stands at about West.

Sunday 26. — This Morning I write. M.ʳ Donald calls on me.
I dine with Gen.ˡ Morris and on my Return visit M.ʳˢ Penn. She
tells me that Butler has written to her Brother in Law John Penn
saying that he will get ten per Cent for his Money in America.
I examine their Accounts to see what is his Situation, which I
explain to him, but I dare say it will be forgotten before ToMorrow Morning. The Weather is this Day very pleasant and to my
great Surprize the Wheat seems to be in very fine Order after all
the Intemperature of the Climate.

Monday 27. — This Morning write. M.ʳ Franklin comes and
we go into the City together. After many Delays and Difficulties
I at length get thro the various Objects which I had in Contemplation. M.ʳ Franklin shuffles a little about the Stock he had
purchased, however he at length agrees to take it upon my signing
a Bond to secure the Entry of the Amount on the Treasury Books.
I dine with M.ʳ Phyn and after Dinner settle with them for the
6p% Part of the Debt. Visit M.ʳ John Penn sen.ʳ & tell him that
if he and his Cousin incline to sell their Stock and will write to
me their Terms, I will in Answer let them know whether I will
take it. The Weather is this Day very fine and warm.

Tuesday 28. — This Morning I rise at three and write. Mr.
Wadeson does not arrive till after twelve. Execute a mutual
Release with the Assignees of Rogers and having made up my
Letters I get off at one o'Clock. Arrive at Brighthelmstone at
eight and am astonished in my Route to see the Wheat look so
well. The Packet is already under Sail lying to. I get on board
by nine and find that Lord Sheffield with his Family are my
fellow Passengers. The Weather has been very fine this Day and
the Wind if it continues will soon waft us over, being at Southwest,
our Course Southeast.

---

the world with Captain Cook in *Endeavour* 1768–1771. On a later visit Morris
dines among the exquisite ornamentations of his Soho Square house, not rele-
gated to a museum for another 145 years.

Wednesday 29. — After a very uncomfortable Night from close Stowage and the Want of Air I find this Morning that the Wind has been ahead all Night so that we are not far from the Place of our Departure. It continues light and unfavorable. Make Acquaintance with L.ᵈ Sheffield [1] and his Family. He supposes me to be an Englishman and gives free Scope to his Sentiment respecting America, as all other Countries. Am attentive to his family, being a Wife and two Daughters, and the Attentions are well received. This Afternoon the Wind becomes favorable and promises well. We dine on some Mackarel taken this Morning. I hooked many and had them drawn up by others which is I think the only pleasant Way of Mackarel Fishing. Towards twelve the Lightning and Thunder which had appeared about Sunset in the Horizon approaches and gives us a Gust, succeeded as usual by a Calm.

Thursday 30. — This Morning being unable to sleep I turn out early. It is rainy and disagreable. About four the Wind springs up from the Southwest. We are still twelve Leagues from the Port at five when it freshens to a fine Breeze, and having the Tide at Flood with us we enter the Harbor of Dieppe between nine and ten, so that at ten o'Clock all is safe at M.ʳ LeRue's Hotel. He tells us that Passports are necessary and without them we shall be much molested and interrupted; this occasions a warm Walk to the Town House. On our Return I breakfast and pay my Respects to Lady Sheffield. His Lordship had already asked my House or Place of Abode in London and she reminds him of it again. I promise to see them at Paris and perceive clearly that the Attentions have been well received. At one I leave Dieppe and a Quarter after eleven arrive at Écouis, eleven Posts. I have Occasion to observe by the Mile Stones on this Route that the same Estimation I have made elsewhere holds good here, and that the Posts are about five English Miles each, for the 77 Mile Stone is a little beyond Totes, about an English Mile beyond it, and Totes is 18½ Posts from Paris. In our last Stage between Bourg Baudouin and Paris the *Bidet* came to the Ground and but for his great Boots the Postillion's Leg would

---

[1] John Baker Holroyd (1735–1821), first Earl of Sheffield, statesman, friend of Gibbon. This Lady Sheffield was first of three wives, born Abigail Way.

have been crushed. The Weather this Day has been very showery. The Country looks beautiful and the Crops are fine.

JULY 1791

Friday 1 *July.* — A bad Supper last Night and a worse Breakfast this Morning in a wretched Inn are followed of Course by a swinging Bill. The Reason why this always happens is very simple and clear. In such Places they never expect the Custom of the better Sort and of Course are indifferent to their good or evil Report. I take my Penn very coolly and correct this Bill but mine Hostess declares she will not submit, whereupon I take my Money and tell her that the Justice of Peace shall settle the Matter between us. Upon this she says she will rather take the Money than be at the Trouble of going before the Justice but I insist so much on his Interference that at length she accepts as a favor what she had refused. I leave this abominable House at a quarter before nine and reach Pontoise, which is 7½ Posts, at ten Minutes after two. The Inn here is pretty good. While Dinner is preparing I look at one of the Mills for which this Place is famous but I find nothing extraordinary in them. It is a common undershot Wheel moving in a Stone Trough. At five Minutes after four we leave Pontoise and shortly after see the first Vineyards. At Half past seven we reach Paris. This Road lies thro the beautiful Vale of Montmorenci which may be termed Cherry Valley. I observe here that the greater Number are Dwarf Cherry Trees so low that a Man may easily reach to the Top of many of them. The Country is beautiful and the Crops look vastly well.[1]

---

[1] Morris will hear a new note in the roar of Paris. Popular excitement has shifted from Palais-Royal to Tuileries; under the castle windows insults and counsels are shouted, a mushroom growth of news-sheets is cried; into the windows peer restless crowds making sure their royal captives are not again

Saturday 2 July. — This Morning I employ myself in reading the various Details which relate to the King's Flight and Arrest. Go to the Louvre where I find M.ʳ de Curt & Mons.ʳ de Flahaut. After they go away we perform the Rites and then I visit M.ʳ Short who is abroad. M.ʳ de La Fayette who is not at Home but I converse with his Wife who seems to be half wild. Then leave my Name at the british Ambassador's and dine with the Count de Montmorin. Return to the Louvre and repeat the Morning's Exercise. Stay till ten oClock. I visited this Morning the Count de Ségur also and saw the whole Family except the Maréchal. The Intention of the Assembly is I find to cover up if possible the King's Flight and cause it to be forgotten. This proves to me great Feebleness in every Respect and will perhaps destroy the Monarchy. The Weather lours and is cool but very pleasant.

Sunday 3 July. — M.ʳ Brémond calls and communicates what has been done respecting the Debt to France; he tells me also that he has had an Interview with Mons.ʳ de Montmorin respecting public Affairs and desires me to ask his Interference with Mons.ʳ Tarbet, the Minister of the Impositions, to give him some Material respecting the Finances. M.ʳ Richard calls while Brémond is here and according to Custom makes a thousand Questions and gives me a Deal of his Company. After he is gone Brémond gives me the secret History of many Things that have taken Place during my Absence. Visit M.ʳ Short, promise to dine

---

eluding them. The Queen had long resented La Fayette's policing of the Tuileries, knew he had staked his head on keeping her and the King from leaving it, but had outwitted him on the June night when she and her family crept out separately and disguised, to be driven by devoted Fersen to the great lumbering berline waiting ready horsed outside a Paris barrier. A time-table gone wrong, troops not at their post, a recognition and a capture, the failure of Varennes is too well known for a note. On the same night, by way of Valenciennes, the Comte de Provence had reached Belgium in safety.

26 June Morris had written to William Constable, N.Y.: 'The King and Queen of France have made their Escape but we do not yet know whether they got out of the Kingdom. This Event makes me very anxious to get back to Paris for I think the Confusion will work favorably to the Sale of American Lands. — 11 at Night, Intelligence is received that the royal fugitives are intercepted near Metz.' But back in Paris he writes again: 'The Evasion of the King and Queen has among other Things produced a Decree against Emigration which damps the Sale of Lands.'

together and then I dress and go to the Louvre where we join in our Devotions. Thence to visit Count d'Estaing who is abroad, then to Madame de Troudaine's. Stay with her awhile and then take up M.ʳ Short and we go together to Monsieur de La Fayette's to dinner. After Dinner call at Mad.ᵉ de Ségur's and the british Embassador's. Then go to Monsieur de Montmorin's. I apply to him for what Brémond wanted and he promises his Aid. I converse with him on the State of Affairs, observing that it appears to me almost impossible to preserve both the Monarchy and the Monarch. He says there is no other Measure can be attempted, and this leads us to discuss the different Characters who may be appointed either Regent or to a Council of Regency, and here I find insurmountable Difficulties; of Course they must go on with the miserable Creature which God has given. His Wisdom will doubtless produce Good by Ways to us inscrutable and on that we must repose. Set M.ʳ Short down. Visit Mad.ᵉ de La Borde who is abroad, then go to the Louvre and pass the Evening. My friend shews me a Letter of Mad.ᵉ de Nadaillac and makes herself very merry at the Expence of her Niece who seems to have written it for me. The Weather has been very pleasant this Day.

Monday 4 *July.* — I write for the Post. M.ʳ Swan calls and tells me what he has written to America respecting public Affairs. He says that Barrett goes out high charged about the Conduct of Affairs here. I take up Mad.ˡˡᵉ Duplessis at three oClock and leave her at the Louvre. Mad.ᵉ desires a Word. She cannot keep an Appointment made with me because of a previous Engagement to hear the Bishop read his Plan of Education.[1] This suits me very well. I dine at M.ʳ Short's with the Americans in Town and the Marquis de La Fayette. Payne [2] is here, inflated to the Eyes

---

[1] Talleyrand's ideas are the basis of France's splendid system of public education to this day.

[2] Revolutions make strange pen-fellows. Thomas Paine and Marquis du Chastellet, a colonel of the King's Chasseurs, English-speaking son of a duke, had with Marquis Condorcet inaugurated their five-membered Société Ré-publicaine July first and issued a short-lived journal. The day after the King's flight Paine and Chastellet had placarded all Paris with a trumpet call for a Republic, royalist Malouet tearing their manifesto off the very door of the Assembly and demanding their prosecution. Carlyle's whirlwind chapter should be read.

and big with a Litter of Revolutions. I go hence to visit Mad.ᵉ de Guibert and write for her some foolish Verses. Return Home early and read. The Weather is fine.

Tuesday 5. — This Morning I write. Afterwards call on Le Couteulx who is abroad. Take Mademoiselle Duplessis to the Louvre. Call on M.ʳ Chaumont who is arrived but gone abroad to dine. I then go to the british Embassador's where we have a very good Dinner. After Dinner she sits down to Hazard and I come away. Take my friend and her friend to Mad.ᵉ de Guibert's, then to her Sister's and afterwards to her own House, where I stay a little while. I learn this Day that about sixty of the Aristocratic Party have resigned and this under a Declaration which stipulates as a Condition of their future Agency those Things which had been communicated to them by the Committee of the Constitution as previously determined on. This is a poor Trick and the Measure is a dangerous one. The Weather has been fine this Day. Vicq d'Azyr says that the Queen's Hair is turned grey by her late Adventures. Paul Jones called on me this Morning. He is much vexed at the Democracy of this Country.

Wednesday 6. — This Morning arrange my Papers and sit down to write. Chaumont comes in and we consider a little the Plan for Disposal of S.ᵗ Lawrence Lands. He says it is unfortunate that just now Emigrations are inhibited but this is only momentary. In the Course of this Discussion I discover that the Exemplification of Macomb's Power ¹ to me is lost and I cannot account for it. After Chaumont is gone I dress and go to dine with Mad.ᵉ de Troudaine. Madame Lavoisier is here. After Dinner I go to the Louvre and take my friend and Mad.ˡˡᵉ to ride. We go to the upper End of the Isle S.ᵗ Louis from whence there is a beautiful View up the Seine, then we go on the South Side of the River and turn up till we get to the Boulevards above the King's Garden; we then pursue the Boulevards round to the Invalids. I set them down at the Louvre and return Home to write. The Weather is very fine. I saw this Evening a Part of

---

¹ For a year Morris had been impatient for its arrival; for want of it he felt that bargains had been missed in 1790, when emigration regulations had been less strict.

Paris which I had never seen before. It is not much inhabited
but there are many fine Gardens.

Thursday 7. — This Morning I write, having risen early for
that Purpose; after sending my Letters to the Office I dress and
call on Le Couteulx. Propose to him a Purchase of the Canada
Lands which he seems inclined to. I then go to the Louvre but
my friend is abroad. I visited first Lord Sheffield and M.̠ Short,
both abroad, then I go to Madame de Ségur's and sit with her
some time and return to the Louvre where I dine. Go afterwards
to the Bois de Boulogne and then come back and stay the Evening. The Weather is fine but warm.

Friday 8. — M.̠ Chaumont comes this Morning and we consider
the Means of vending the S.̠ Lawrence Tract. After him M.̠
Brémond. They consume so effectually my Morning that by the
Time I have taken Mad.̠ᵉ Duplessis to the Louvre it is half past
three. I dine with them and after Dinner go to the Coach
Maker's, or rather Wheelwright's (*le Charron*) to enquire what
is necessary to be done to my Carriage, and he proposes a Variety
of Things, among the Rest to have a new Hammer Cloth and new
Painting. These two Articles will cost above twelve louis. I
desire him to make me out a List of all that is needful to be done
and bring it with the Prices ToMorrow Morning. We take a
Turn to two or three Shops and then having set Mademoiselle
down I take Mad.̠ᵉ Home.... A Carriage stops at the Door. It
is Mad.̠ᵉ de Guibert. I stay a little while with them and then go
to Mad.̠ᵉ de La Borde's where I spend the Evening. I see here for
the first Time the Declaration signed by a Number of Members
of the Assembly declaring their Adhesion to the Cause of Royalty.
It is diffuse and weak. They might easily be caught in their own
Trap. I return Home early. The Weather has been warm this
Day but this Evening we have a fine moderate Rain which will
be very useful.

Saturday 9. — This Morning M.̠ Brémond calls and after he
is gone I write. Dress at four and dine with Monsieur de Mont-
morin. After Dinner converse with him. He desponds much.
Go to the british Embassador's and leave my Name, also at
La Fayette's and for Lady Sheffield. Sit a little while with
Madame de Ségur and then go to the Louvre. My Friend re-

ceives me with Reproof for what is unfounded; I immediately suppose the Reason and take my Leave. She is very angry at this. We shall see how it ends. The Weather has been pleasant this Day.

Sunday 10. — This Morning I write. M.ʳ Brémond brings me an Ac/ of what Otto has written from America respecting the Debt to France. He tells me that Bergasse has prepared his Work on the french Constitution which will be shewn to me and he proposes some Measures in Relation to it which I decline a Concurrence in till I shall have seen the Object they mean to pursue. M.ʳ Short comes after his Hour and we go together to the Mont Valérien. This Place has a very fine View. We return after Dinner, having walked up and down the Hill from & to Surenne which I find fatiguing. Dress and visit the british Embassadress. Thence to the Louvre. My friend is abroad but returns soon; I ask where we are to go to see the Procession of Voltaire and I find that she is disappointed in a Place which is disagreable. I leave her immediately and visit Mad.ᵉ de Ségur where I spend the Evening. Mad.ᵉ de Maubourg and Mad.ᵉ de La Fayette. The Chevalier de Bouflers and M.ʳ Short and M.ʳ Toulangeon.[1] As usual a political Conversation & I find the Opinions are getting round. The Weather this Day has been pleasant but it begins to rain now and threatens for Tomorrow.

Monday 11. — This Morning it rains hard. Brémond calls and desires me to go to see Bergasse. After I have finished writing I go thither, having previously called on Hudon the Statuary. The Treatise of Bergasse will be short, clear and eloquent, I think it will have great Merit, but I fear the public Mind will not be well prepared for it. Call on Le Couteulx. He is gone to see the Procession of Voltaire.[2] I go to Monsieur Simolin's for the same Purpose. It is so late that we return to the Louvre and eat a hasty Dinner, after which we go again to Simolin's and see

---

[1] Vicomte Thoulongeon (1748–1812), army colonel who dedicates himself to philosophy and the arts; early joined Tiers État, works to reorganize army, education and highroads; useful public servant, not gossamer like Boufflers.

[2] From Simolin's of the Russian Embassy they watch young Matthieu de Montmorency carry in procession the urn containing the ashes of Voltaire to deposit it in the Pantheon. The *char* drawn by four grays harnessed abreast, led by men in classical attire designed by David.

the fête. It is very poor and not at all bettered by the Rain. Return to the Louvre and seize an Opportunity for hasty Enjoyment. Spend the Evening here but return a little after ten oClock. It still continues to rain.

Tuesday 12. — This Morning I write. Walk out and call on my friend who complains of illness. Return Home and dine. Mons.ʳ de Flahaut, M.ʳ Swan, Paul Jones and M.ʳ Barret dine with me. After Dinner I visit the Maréchal de Ségur and then go to Mons.ʳ de Montmorin's. He is shut up with Company; I stay a good while with the Ladies. Short comes in and we get into a Dispute. He insists that Religion is both absurd and useless and that it is unfriendly to Morals. I hold a very different Opinion. Call on Mad.ᵉ de La Suze and condole with her on the Death of her friend the Baron de Bezenvald. His Death forms of Course a Subject of Conversation and her Connection with him enters as a Thing of Course. She is much afflicted. It is according to parisian Manners equivalent to the Loss of a Husband in America. Go from hence to the Louvre and there Madame informs me that L.ᵈ Wycombe is gone to America. Return Home very early. This Day has loured but the Weather is pleasant. It is cool.

Wednesday 13. — This Morning M.ʳ Chaumont calls. He has spoken to Grand who does not incline to purchase American Lands. He has not seen his friend Mory. He says that in conversing on this Subject he finds that the Scioto Comp.ʸ have done great Mischief. At eleven I go to breakfast with Lady Sutherl.ᵈ and afterwards attend her to M.ʳ Hudon's to see the Statue of Gen.ˡ Washington. She is a charming Woman. Call on Mad.ᵉ de Ségur. The Count is in Bed, ill with a Fluxion on his Jaw. Puisignieu and Berchini are here. The former has resigned but the latter holds his Regiment because he cannot afford to relinquish it. He has just left Count D'Affri who has received Orders from the Swiss Cantons to insist on Specie Payments to the Troops of that Nation. These Gentlemen declare that the Discipline of the Army is gone and that is I believe very true. I call on Le Couteulx who is abroad. I sent him this Morn.ᵍ a Message by Richard to which he seems to have p.ᵈ no Attention. Go to the Louvre. Mad.ᵉ de Guibert returns from the Assembly with my friend and offers to give me Dinner if I will take her

Home. I lend her my Carriage. Dine with my friend and after Dinner enjoy the private and secure Moment. . . . We ride and take up first Vicq d'Azyr who tells us that Mons.ʳ Pétion,¹ one of the three Commissaries dispatched by the Assembly to accompany the King, behaved in the most beastly as well as the most unkind Manner. Sitting in the same Carriage with the royal Family he permitted himself to . . . at his Ease and amused himself by explaining to Mad.ᵉ Elizabeth the Means of composing a Council of Regency. We take a Turn in the Bois de Boulogne, quarrel a little and then become very affectionate. Stay at the Louvre till ten and then come Home. I received a Note from Mad.ᵉ de Montmorin recommending an unfortunate Irish Gentleman. I gave him a Guinea and spoke to the british Embassador to send his Children to Dublin. It is a little extraordinary that an American Rebel should be instrumental in procuring the Return at his Majesty's Expence of those who descend from Irish Rebels: but such are the Vicissitudes of human Life. The Weather has been pleasant this Day. Rather warm about Noon.

Thursday 14. — This Morning shortly after Breakfast I walk out and call on M.ʳ Franklin, who is abroad. Then on M.ʳ Le Couteulx who is also abroad. Sit a little while with his Wife, then go to the Champ de Mars where there is a great Multitude assembled to celebrate by a Mass the Anniversary of the Capture of the Bastile. After walking about here a while and feeling the Approach of Fatigue I return. On my Way examine the Operation of a Water Screw which is more considerable than I expected. After I return Home and dress I go to dine with Madame de Troudaine. Thence to Mad.ᵉ de Guibert's, stay a little while and

---

¹ Handsome Pétion flattered himself he had fluttered the gentle heart of the King's sister on that interminable drive back from Varennes through the dust and heat; his vanity had made him not a little ridiculous. Next year as popular mayor of Paris he will do nothing to control attacks on the Tuileries, always turning up late, saying he had not been informed. In 1793 he falls with the Girondins, escapes imprisonment by flight, is found in a field half eaten by wolves, *le beau, le 'vertueux'* Pétion (or Péthion). La Fayette's friend La Tour Maubourg could be counted on for good manners on the drive; the third Commissary, Barnave, went further and was so impressed by the Queen's conversation that he will work in secret to repair the harm his generous young republicanism had already done to her, sympathetic letters in the King's Iron Cupboard discovered to his undoing.

then follow my friend to the Louvre. She has got Rid of her Husband and of Mr Bertrand.... We then ride. I stay till after eleven. In the Assembly this Day the republican Party have treated the King very harshly, but the Report which insists on his Inviolability will pass. Monsr de Troudaine ment.^d as having heard from young Montmorin that the King is by Nature cruel and base. An Instance of his Cruelty among others was that he used to spit and roast live Cats. In riding with my friend I tell her that I could not believe such Things. She tells me that when young he was guilty of such Things. That he is very brutal and nasty, which she attributes principally to a bad Education. His brutality once led him so far while Dauphin as to beat his Wife, for which he was exiled four Days by his Grandfather Louis XV. Untill very lately he used always to ... in his Hand as being more convenient. It is no Wonder that such a Beast should be dethroned.

Friday 15. — Mr Brémond calls this Morning and I tell him that I am much engaged. Write till after four and then dress. Dine with Monsr de Montmorin. Montesquiou is there who asks me whether I am not to be app.^d Minister here. I tell him no. That Mr Jefferson wishes much that Mr Short should be app.^d &c.^a. He says he is perswaded that he could bring the Treasury Board into any reasonable Measure respecting the Debt from the United States to France. I tell him that Difficulties would now arise on the Part of the United States. Go to the Louvre. Meet at the Bottom of the Stairs Capellis and Monsieur de Flahaut. The latter is so kind as to give us his Company. After the Toilette is finished and he departed we attempt to honor him but are interrupted. We ride together and then go together to Mad.^e de La Borde's. Paris is in Uproar this Evening on Account of the Decree passed almost unanimously by the Assembly declaring the Inviolability of the King. The Weather has been clear and very warm.

Saturday 16. — This Morning I write. Mr de Flahaut calls on me. There is a great Disposition for Riot among the People but the Gardes nationales are drawn out and so posted as to prevent Mischief. Paul Jones comes and after him Mr Franklin. He has had an Interview with Le Couteulx.... They have disclosed to him the State of R.M.'s Affairs as I suspected they would. I take M.ʳ Franklin to visit M.ʳ Barret who is abroad and having set him down go to Le Couteulx's. Laurent talks on a good Deal and I see that he is devilish angry but rather afraid to break out. I hear what he has to say with a calm Countenance on which Candor and Sincerity are painted; approve of his having written a Letter to Franklin, and thus, without touching at all upon the sore Points on either Side, I leave him half convinced that he is mistaken. Call on Count Greppi who is just packing up to depart in a few Days for Vienna. Go from hence to the Louvre where I dine. After Dinner I visit Ségur and leave with him the Map and Description of Dover Estate and Eden Park [near Wilmington, Delaware]. Then visit Mad.ᵉ de La Fayette and after a few Minutes of Entretien return to the Louvre. We go to the Bois de Boulogne and take a Promenade, thence return and spend the Evening at the Louvre. Get Home at ten and read. The Weather has this Day been very warm.

[Morris had seen the excitements only from afar but gathers reports together for Robert Morris.]

Gouverneur Morris to Robert Morris

Paris 16 July 1791

Robert Morris Esq.ʳ
                    Philadelphia
My dear friend,
    ... You will have heard thro various Channels of the King's Escape from the Tuileries. By the bye he was said to be in perfect Liberty there, but yet our friend La Fayette was very near being hanged because he got away, and his Justification tends to shew that his Majesty, besides his parole given, was so closely watched that he had but little Chance of getting off unobserved. This Step was a very foolish one. Public Affairs were in such Situation that if he had been quiet he would have soon been Master because the Anarchy which prevails would have shewn the Necessity of conferring more Authority, and because it is not possible so to ballance a single Assembly against a Prince

but that one must prove too heavy for the other or too light for the Business. The Assembly also, very strongly suspected of corrupt Practises, was falling fast in the public Estimation. His Departure changed every Thing and now the general Wish seems to be for a Republic, which is quite in the natural Order of Things. Yesterday the Assembly decreed that the King being inviolable, he could not be involved in the Accusations to be made against those concerned in his Evasion. This has excited much Heat against them. The People are now assembling on the Occasion and the Militia (many of them opposed to the King) are out. As I lodge near the Tuilleries it is far from improbable that I shall have a Battle under my Windows. The Vanguard of the Populace is to be formed by two or three thousand Women. A good smart Action would I think be useful rather than pernicious, but the great Evil arises from a Cause not easily removed. It will I think be scarcely possible to confer Authority on, or in other Words to obtain Obedience for, a Man who has entirely forfeited the public Opinion; and if they lay him aside, I do not see how they are to manage a Regency. His Brothers are abroad and so is the Prince of Condé. The Duke of Orleans is loaded with universal Contempt, and if they should name a Council of Regency they would be obliged to take either feeble or suspected Characters. Add to this the Struggle which must arise in a State where there is a King dethroned, and that for trivial Causes. At the same Time the State of their Finances is detestable and growing worse every Day. They have passed a Law against Emigrations, altho by their Bill of Rights every Man has a Right to go where he pleases, but this you know is the Usual Fate of Bills of Rights. How long the Restriction may continue is uncertain, but while it lasts no Lands can be sold in Detail, that is to Setlers, and of Course those who inclined to buy in large Tracts hang off. These Changes and Confusions have suspended (at least) the Object about which I formerly wrote to you and which I will explain hereafter.

Paris 20 July 1791

Robert Morris Esqr
                    Philadelphia
My dear friend
  My last was of the sixteenth. The Riot of that Day went off
pretty easily but the next Morning two Men were lanterned and
mangled in the parisian Taste. This occasioned some little Stir.
There had been a pretty general Summons to the friends of Liberty, requesting them to meet in the Champ de Mars. The Object of this Meeting was to perswade the Assembly by the gentle
Influence of the Cord, to undo what they had done respecting the
imprisoned Monarch. As the different Ministers and municipal
Officers had received it in Charge from the Assembly to maintain
Peace and see to the Execution of the Laws, they made Proclama-
tion and displayed the red Flag. In coming from the british Embassadors about seven in the Evening, I met a Detachment of the
Militia with the red Flag flying, and some of the civil Officers.
I went shortly after to a Heighth to see the Battle but it was over
before I got to the Ground, for as the Militia would not as usual
ground their Arms on receiving the Word of Command from the
Mob, this last began according to Custom to pelt them with
Stones. It was hot Weather and it was a Sunday Afternoon for
which Time, according to Usage immemorial, the Inhabitants of
this Capital have generally some pleasurable Engagement. To be
disappointed in their Amusement, to be paraded thro the Streets
under a scorching Sun and then stand like Holiday Turkeys to be
knocked down by Brick-Bats, was a little more than they had
Patience to bear, so that without waiting for Orders they fired
and killed a dozen or two of the ragged Regiment: the rest ran off
like lusty fellows. If the Militia had waited for Orders they might
I fancy have been all knocked down before they received any.
As it is, the Business went off pretty easily. Some of them have
since been assassinated, but not above five or six, as far as I can
learn. Lafayette was very near being killed in the Morning but
the Pistol snapped at his Breast. The Assassin was immediately
secured but he ordered him to be discharged. These are Things
on which no Comment is necessary. I think we shall be quiet here
a little while, but it is possible enough that seizing some plausible

Occasion a violent Effort will be made and then if the Militia succeed, Order will be established.

Adieu. I am ever very truly and affectionately yours.

Sunday 17. — This Morning I write. M.' Brémond calls and gives me Copies of the Letters of M.' Jefferson &c.ª. I dress and go to the Louvre. As soon as the Toilette of my friend is finished ... I go to M.' Grand's and dine. After Dinner return to Town and visit the british Embassadress who receives me with a charming Cordiality. Col.º Tarleton and Lord Selkirk are here and the Conversation accidentally falls on American Affairs, which is diverting as they do not know me. Tarleton says that once on the Outposts he obtained a List of Gen.¹ Washington's Spies and that Clinton, after putting them in the prevost, after a few Days let them all out from Weakness of Compassion. I blame this Weakness &c.ª. Go from hence to the Louvre and in my Way meet the Municipality with the *Drapeau rouge* displayed. At the Louvre we get into the Carriage of my friend and after stopping to take my Telescope go to Chaillot, but the Time lost there in taking up Mad.ᵉ de Courcelles brings us too late on the Heights of Passy to see what passed in the Champs de Mars. On our Return, however, we learn that the Militia have at length fired on the Mob and killed a few of them. They scampered away as fast as they could. This Morning however they massacred two Men and this Evening they have, it is said, assassinated two of the Militia in the Street. This Affair will I think lay the Foundation of Tranquility, altho perhaps a more serious Affair is necessary to restrain this abominable Populace. Go to Madame de Ségur's to pass the Evening. Her Company are all frightened and stay away except the Chevalier de Boufler. Ségur tells us what passed between the Queen and him and how he has been deceived by her. He desires me to dine with him on Thursday to meet the Count de La Marc at the Request of the latter. I think I guess the Reason, *mais nous verrons.* I think one of the finest Views I ever saw is that which presented itself this Evening from the Pont royal. A fine Moonshine, a dead Silence and the River descending gently thro the various Bridges between lofty Houses all illuminated (for the Sake of the Police) and on the other Side the Woods and distant

Hills. Not a Breath of Air stirring. The Weather has this Day been very hot.

Monday 18. — M.ʳ Brémond comes again this Morning. I sit down to write but reiterated Interruptions prevent my Progress. Dress and call on M.ʳ Franklin to whom I give a Note of the Answer to be made to Le Couteulx's Letter. Go to the Louvre and say how d'ye. My friend has Company so I go to M.ʳ Short's. Converse with him on public Affairs and particularly respecting the Loan he is desirous of opening in Flanders. M.ʳ Swan, who was with me this Morning, mentioned sundry Things as communicated by M.ʳ Short in some of which he appears to have been a little mistaken. Call on the Coachmaker's and at the Painter's. Then go to dine with Monsieur de La Fayette where I meet again Col.º Tarleton.¹ La Fayette gives me an Account of what passed Yesterday.² I return to the Louvre and send away my Carriage but a Shower has prevented our intended promenade. Madame contrives however to get Rid of her Visitors [4 lines inked out]. He is much out of Humor and after walking about a little while leaves us to our Meditations, which we pursue to mutual Edification. We then go together to Mad.ᵉ de Guibert's; after a short Visit return to spend the Evening. Monsieur de Curt who is here, reads us a Speech which was to have been spoken on the King's Inviolability. It is pretty well and the Publication will be useful by & bye. The Weather is very hot.

Tuesday 19. — This Morning M.ʳ Brémond calls and I give him the Information I have, in Consequence of which he departs immediately to have an Interview with M.ʳ Short. M.ʳ Chaumont

---

¹ All unwittingly Morris *may* have been meeting the 'Scarlet Pimpernel' in this British Colonel who at twenty-two had charmed Loyalist hearts in Philadelphia and at twenty-four, with his Legion mounted swiftly on a chance capture of Virginia thoroughbreds, had ravaged the Carolinas till he met his match in Daniel Morgan at the Cowpens. The thrill of smuggling condemned aristocrats out of France would be in character.

² This dinner sounds very calm. La Fayette had been shot at the day before, on his white charger had performed prodigies of valor. Hour after hour Paris had mounted the high altar of the Patrie to sign monster petitions for the abdication of a King who could not even run away successfully; Danton's idea, but he and Camille Desmoulins took care to spend Sunday 17 July in the country. The red flag meant a proclaiming of martial law, Mayor Bailly reading the riot act, followed by shots and confusion.

comes to Breakfast. M.ʳ Richard called early. Chaumont says
that the Scioto meets him every where and that he thinks the
Time for selling Lands will be in the next Winter &c.ᵃ. After he is
gone Brémond and Jeanneret come and tell me what has passed
with M.ʳ Short. I confer with them on the Steps to be taken and
then write; between four and five go to dine with Mons.ʳ de Montmorin and after Dinner shew him a Letter I have received from
Swan respecting American Salt Provisions for the french Navy.
He desires a Memoire to be prepared &c.ᵃ. Call on the british Embassadress who is abroad. Then on Madame de Ségur and after
sitting with them some Time, go to the Louvre. My friend does
not come Home till ten, wherefore I leave her in a few Minutes after her Arrival. She is a little hurt at this. The Weather is grown
somewhat cooler but is still very warm and calm.

Wednesday 20. — M.ʳ Brémond again this Morning, and M.ʳ
Franklin. M.ʳ Franklin breakfasted with me. I write, and having
finished my Letters carry them to M.ʳ Barrett's. Go to the Louvre.
My friend is going abroad but desires me to call again. Visit
Mad.ᵉ Lavoisier and then return to the Louvre; while my Carriage
is gone to wait of Mad.ˡˡᵉ Duplessis we enjoy. Dine with M.ʳ Short
and visit at the Duc de La Rochefoucault's. Then go to the Luxembourgh and make a very long Visit to Madame du Bourg.
When I return Home I receive a Request from my friend to visit
her as she does not, according to her former Intention, go abroad.
But it is too late. The Weather has been pleasant this Day.

Thursday 21. — This Morning at the Request of my friend I
call on her and we go together to the Hôtel Dieu. We afterwards
walk in the Champs élisées. We quarrel a little and on our Way
back I tell her that our Connection will soon terminate. We part
cooly enough. I promise however to call on her this Evening.
Dine at the Count de Ségur's where I meet Monsieur de La Marc
and Monsieur Pellin.¹ This last has I find nearly the same Ideas

¹ Few men can have been feeling so deflated as Mirabeau's secretary Pellenc
(nothing monotonous about Morris's Pellin, Pelling, Pilin), without the great
flame that had fanned his industry, preparing notes on every conceivable subject as it arose in the Assembly, to which Mirabeau had given life. He soon
begins to haunt Morris's breakfast table with the inevitable Brémond, rash
Provençal breathless with schemes. In 1787 Brémond had been sent to Paris
to adjust taxation on the tanning industry of his Province; Brienne then com-

of a Government that I have. Walk with Madame de Ségur after Dinner in the Gardens of the Palais Bourbon. She asked me this Afternoon (I presume with a View to judge for her Husband) whether if the Place of Minister was proposed to me I would accept it. I told her Yes if they would give me Authority. She asked then whether I would take the Chance of acquiring it if the King and Queen would promise to act according to my Advice. I told her that in such Case I would consider. Go to the Louvre where there is a large Company. I keep very much on my Center. Monsieur Ricie is among them and seems just arrived from Holland. Madame makes some Advances so as to preserve her own Dignity. I keep myself in a State of grave Indifference. I will play out this Game and then Good Night. Take Home La Borde and his Wife. The Weather is very warm.

Friday 22. — This Morning write. Carry my Letters to M.ʳ Barrett's and then go to the Louvre. We are, contrary to my Expectations, very happy together and I stay Dinner. After Dinner we go to see the *Intrigue épistolaire* which is a very good Piece, then take an Airing and sup with Mad.ᵉ de La Borde. The Weather is very warm. This Day the Inhabitants of the Gros Caillou have been disarmed.

Saturday 23. — This Morning I sit down to write but M.ʳ Short comes in and we have a long Conversation on the Affairs of the United States in which I communicate to him all the Information I can think of as useful to him. We fix the Terms of a Loan in Antwerp and he gives me the Assurance of a Preference to Operations by my friend [1] there in Case of his Success. I walk to the Louvre and find my friend much indisposed. Return Home and dress. She and her Husband, Mad.ˡˡᵉ Duplessis and Mons.ʳ de S.ᵗ Pardou, Laborde and his Wife with her friend O'Connell dine with me. After Dinner we go to the Bois de Boulogne and we quarrel a little but reconcile.... Spend the Evening at the

---

missioned him to prepare a complete review of national finances. It was to be ready to give every deputy to the States-General a copy; they were distributed June, 1789, Brémond long out of pocket for labors and printing. His delight is to ferret out secrets and serve them hot to Morris. This busybody is able enough, a little mad, perilously indiscreet. Improving the new Constitution and saving the King is their lay.

[1] Michael Dewolf.

Louvre and return Home early. The Weather has been very warm this Day.

Sunday 24. — This Morning I write and then call on my friend to accompany her to the Hôtel Dieu but she complains of being ill. I call on M.ʳ Short and shew him the Letter I have written to De Wolf, which he approves of. Go for Mademoiselle Duplessis but she is not yet dressed, wherefore I return to the Louvre and send my Carriage for her. Find here M.ʳ de Montesquiou and M.ʳ de Rici. The latter stays till after Dinner. I read in the Salon till the Company return and then take my Leave. Dine at Monsieur de Montmorin's and give him Swan's Letter; he promises to deliver the Memorial enclosed in it to the Minister of the Marine and inform me of his Answer. I tell M.ʳ de Montmorin of Bergasse's Work on the Constitution and that we will take an Hour or two when it is finished to read it together. Go from hence to visit Mad.ᵉ de Puisignieu, having passed at the Door of the british Embassador. Sit a while and then take Puisignieu to Mad.ᵉ de Ségur's. Spend the Evening here. Nothing remarkable. Short tells me that he left at the Louvre a large Society and that I was expected there.

Monday 25. — M.ʳ Brémond calls this Morning and desires permission to present M.ʳ Pelling. I write. Call on Madame de Lostange. Then go to the Louvre where I find M.ʳ de Rici. Make my Visit very short and refuse to come in the Evening. Call on M.ʳ Franklin and we go together to Mad.ᵉ de Lavoisier's to Dinner. As the Party is rather High-flying they conclude Haphazard that the Riot at Birmingham has been occasioned by the Government. This is ridiculous enough. I propose to Lavoisier a Speculation in the S.ᵗ Lawrence Lands. He says that if Le Couteulx adopts it he will think of it. Take the Abbé Ronchon to the Duc de La Rochefoucault's and sit awhile with Madame d'Anville. Then call on the british Embassadress and Mad.ᵉ de Ségur. Afterwards ride in the Champs Elisées. At my Return visit Mad.ᵉ de La Borde and then come Home and read. The Weather is very hot.

Tuesday 26. — This Morning write. M.ʳ Brémond calls and tells me that Pelling expects to dine with me Tomorrow. Swan calls and asks my Commands to Havre. I receive a Message from my Friend and call on her. Go to the Hôtel Dieu and thence to the

Opera House and hire a Box. She got a Fall in coming down Stairs.... She is very attentive to remove my Coldness but I tell her that our Connection must speedily end because that her Friends dislike me and of Course make an Impression on her Mind. That this being the Case each of us must seek Happiness his own Way. I stay and dine with her and then go to the Opera together, *Œdipe* followed by the *Ballet de Psiché*.[1] The Music of this Opera is excellent, by far the best I ever heard, and upon my expressing this Idea they tell me it is the best on the french Theatre. The ballet is prodigiously fine. Spend the Evening at the Louvre where I meet M.ʳ Short. Shew him a Letter I received from de Wolf. He tells me that the Agents of America at Amsterdam inform him the Credit of the United States declines; their Bonds, which were above par, having sold lately at 99. I tell him that there is some Underwork in this. Agree on what I am to write to De Wolf. The Weather continues very hot.

Wednesday 27. — This Morning write. Between one and two go to the Louvre. Brémond was with me this Morning and says that it is necessary to have Camus for sundry Affairs and desires me to contrive it. My friend tells me that she wants small Assignats for M.ʳ Bertrand and that she will gain by it. I of Course promise my Assistance. Call on Mad.ᵉ de Ségur and chat with him and her a while. He wishes me to fix a Day for dining with the Count de Montmorin in order to converse with him on the State of public Affairs. I promise to do so but avoid naming the Day. Dine with the Duc de La Rochefoucault. After Dinner go to the Louvre and stay there the Afternoon and Evening. My friend is ill, that is, weak. *Mais n'importe*, she will be better. I told her this Morning that I had always known how to appreciate the Conduct of her friend the Bishop respecting me. That his Manner, which she made me observe, is not therefore surprizing but I mention it to her now because hereafter it may become necessary to remind her of it. She tells me that Mons.ʳ de Montmorin is given up entirely now to Barnave and Lameth. This I am not at

---

[1] For Corneille's tragedy *Œdipe* Lully had written incidental music in honor of Cardinal Chigi's Paris visit, August, 1664. Lully's music for the ballet *Psyché* with its great scene in Hades, belongs to the radiant fêtes of the art-loving ostentatious youth of the Roi Soleil, before any Maintenon had made his soul.

all surprized at. Montesquiou and he have had *une Scène un peu
vive* on the Occasion. The Weather continues very warm.

Thursday 28 July. — This Morning Mr Brémond calls and tells
me that I may make what Terms I please in order to have Camus.
I write and at the Request of my friend call on du Moley who is
engaged and cannot be seen. Go to the Louvre and thence to
Mad.^e de Guibert's where we dine. After Dinner ride, and as M.^r
de Ricie seems desirous of being well with me I let him tell me the
Plans and Designs of his Friends. I find they are very desirous
of having Monsieur de Montmorin. And I find that they have
the proper Idea of some venal Characters. Stay till eleven at the
Louvre before Mr de Montesquiou comes on an Invitation from
my friend, to whom I have promised 100,000[#] if the Business
which she is ignorant of succeeds. I communicate to Montesquiou the Necessity of having Camus and he promises to try him.
I tell him that my friend is ignorant of the Business. He asks me
if I have mentioned it to the Bishop. I tell him that he has been
long acquainted with it but not from me, that I have never conversed with him neither do I mean to do it, on that Subject.
The Weather continues very hot.

Friday 29. — This Morning Mr Brémond calls and I tell him
what passed respecting Mr Camus, and the Promise I have made.
Write, then visit at Mr Montmorin's but he is abroad. At Mad.^e
de Ségur's, who tells me that Mad.^e Adelaide has been harranguing
the People of Rome on Occasion of the King's Escape, about
which she was under a little Mistake, having been informed that
he was at Luxembourg. Take up Mad.^{lle} Duplessis and go to the
Louvre where I dine. My friend receives an Invitation to go to
the Play which she accepts; I let her see that I am displeased;
she apologizes but I take no Notice of it. Sit down to play with
Mad.^{lle} Duplessis soon after she is gone, and in a little Time she
returns, having been disappointed. This is pleasant enough for
she cannot now recover one Thing and has missed the other. I
take the proper Advantages of this Situation and leave her doubting what are my Determinations. Go to Mad.^e du Bourg's where
there is a Table of rouge et noir. Chat with the british Embassadress and play for Trifles so as neither to gain nor loose. Tell
Mad.^e de Beaumont that Ségur and I shall dine with them Tomor-

row and that I want to see her Father before Hand. Tell Mad.^e
de Ségur that I will meet her Husband there, but that he must introduce the Conversation. Go to Mad.^e de La Borde's and sit a
while. The Company is numerous here as at Mad.^e du Bourg's
and the Weather excessively hot.

Saturday 30 *July.* — Mr Brémond brings me a State of the Case
of Château Trompette and a Note of the Sums to be distributed
for that, the India Business and the Rations. I receive a Message
from my friend desiring to see me. Call on Van Staphorst who is
abroad, and then go to the Louvre. Sit with them till Dinner is
served and go to dine with Monsieur de Montmorin. Converse
with him a few Minutes before Dinner to prepare him for a Conversation with the Count de Ségur who is to meet me here but he
does not come. Monsr de Montmorin says he has recommended
Swan's Memorial to the Minister of the Marine and endorsed
thereon that Recommendation, but I would bet that he has never
read the Memorial. Receive a Note from my friend urging me to
visit her about 8. I call on the british Embassadress and I find
that with Attentions I should gain the Confidence of her Lord,
who has more Abilities than People in general suppose. Go to the
Louvre, and being disappointed in the Expectation of a clear
Stage, Mad.^e is so well disposed that we take the Chance of Interruption and celebrate in the Passage while Mad.^{lle} is at the Harpsichord in the Drawing Room. The Husband is below. Visitors
are hourly expected. The Doors are all open. *N'importe.* Spend
the Evening here. The Weather continues to be excessively hot.

Note shown the 30 July 1791 to the Count de Montmorin. He
says that the King & Queen do not now talk to any Body about
the Constitution. I think he is mistaken. He says that he has already told La Mette and Barnave that he shall advise the King as
to his acceptance of the Constitution.

Ne seroit il pas utile que le Roi et la Reine défendissent à qui
que ce soit de leur parler de la Charte constitutionelle, et aux
Ministres de s'en mêler? Que cette défense soit connue de tout le
monde? La raison à donner est fort simple. '*Nous ne voulons en
rien ni influencer ni préjuger la question puisqu'il s'agit d'une convention solemnelle entre la Nation et son Chef.*'

Voici les Conséquences d'une telle démarche.

Dabord l'assemblée dans l'incertitude de la conduite que tiendra le roi aura un Motif de plus pour lui accorder de l'autorité. Ensuite les personnes qu'on soupçonne d'avoir influé sur sa Conduite et celle de la Reine seront écartées de la Chose, même dans l'opinion publique, et cela est nécessaire. Enfin sa Majesté se conservera les moyens d'agir ultérieurement avec plus de dignité. Il faut peutêtre qu'il se décide d'accepter, mais il ne faut pas que cette décision soit connue. Certainement il faut faire quelques observations sur les Articles, mais ce n'est pas la peine d'en parler avant qu'ils soient décrétés. Le Roi aura encore un beau Moment, et il lui sera possible de regagner, par une Conduite noble et sage, tout ce qu'il doit désirer. L'avenir présentera la moisson des grains qu'on seme aujourdhui.

[*Translation:*]

Would it not be advisable for the King and Queen to forbid everyone, no matter who, to speak to them about the constitutional charter, to forbid the Ministers to interfere in it and to let this prohibition be generally known? The reason to be given is perfectly simple: 'We do not wish in any way to influence or prejudice the question, as it is a solemn convention between the Nation and its Head.'

Here are the consequences of such a step.

To begin with, in the uncertainty of what line the King will take the Assembly will have an extra motive for granting him authority. Secondly, the persons suspected of having influenced his conduct and that of the Queen, will even in the opinion of the public be detached from the affair, and that is necessary. Finally his Majesty will preserve the means of acting later on with more dignity. He must perhaps decide to accept but this decision must not be known. Assuredly some observations must be made on the Articles but it is not worth while discussing them before they are decreed. The King will still have a fine moment and it will be possible for him to recapture by a wise and noble conduct all that he can wish for. The future will bring the harvest of the seed sown today.

Sunday 31. — This Morning send to M.ʳ de Montesquiou who calls a little before twelve. I propose to him Operations with Camus and offer him Interest therein; he startles at the Idea of selling his Vote but I observe to him that it is only disposing of that of M.ʳ Camus. He tells me (which I knew before) that he is in very great Want of Money and he promises to operate disinterestedly with Camus for the good of the Affair. I tell him that I intend to secure for him a Share of the Ration Business. Dine with M.ʳ Grand and as we all find the Weather to be very hot he places a Thermometer in the Shade, which mounts to 28 of Réaumur or 89 of Farenheit. This is pretty well. I visit M.ʳ Miln and leave them at seven. Go to the Louvre where I find Mons.ʳ. She tells me that he has been with her all Day. He lengthens out his Visit and she prepares to ride. I stay with him and he complains of her Conduct. Mons.ʳ de Ricie was here from one till half past three and talking always *Démagogie*. Go from hence to Mad.ᵉ de Ségur's. The Count de La Marck, who is here, seems desirous of being well with me and yet of concealing that Desire, a Sort of Male Coquetry. He communicated I find to Monsieur de Montmorin our Dinner at Ségur's; thus there seems to be a Thread of Design running thro the whole Web. Ségur tells me that he will buy the small Farm I offer near Wilmington.

AUGUST 1791

Monday 1 *August.* — This Morning M.ʳ Brémond comes to Breakfast. I write. Jones calls and I keep him to Dinner. Go to the Louvre but my Friend is abroad. Call on Mad.ᵉ de Ségur and wait till he comes Home, when I take the Papers to prepare an Agreement about Eden Park. Call on du Moley who is busy. On Mad.ᵉ de Lostange who is abroad. On Mad.ᵉ de Guibert with whom I sit a little while; on Mad.ᵉ de La Borde who is gone abroad. Again at the Louvre. My friend, who dined with the Bishop, returns Home immediately after my Arrival. She complains of Ill Treatment from him and has in Consequence a violent nervous Attack. About ten, there being Company, he comes in and I leave her. The Weather has been still very hot all Day but is cloudy towards Evening & at eleven is cooler.

Tuesday 2. — M.ʳ Brémond calls and tells me that Camus ¹ has been softened by the golden Tincture in the Affair of Malta so that there can be no Doubt of him in other Things if the Application be properly made. I call at the Louvre to know how my friend does. She is going to dine in the Country. Call on du Moley and ask him to exchange small Assignats for large ones; he tells me that he has not the Distribution of them. Go to Ségur's and shew him the Draft of an Agreement for Eden Park. He approves of it and says he will immediately take Measures to obtain the Money and we will then compleat the Business. Visit Mad.ᵉ du Bourg and then go to the Restaurateur's to dine. Meet M.ʳ Clifford and we converse a little about Speculations in American Lands. Go to the Opéra bouffe to see *Lodoiska*,² a Piece much celebrated but which I think very bad. Thence to the Louvre. Mad.ᵉ not yet come in. I wait for her and tell her what passed with Du Molley. Sit a while and then leave her, assigning as a Reason that her friends do not like me and I do not chuse to be one too many. The Weather is something cooler but still very warm.

Wednesday 3. — This Morning M.ʳ Brémond calls. At two, in Consequence of a Message, I visit my friend. Opportunity offers itself fully but I refuse ... This excites much Emotion of Course. I at length agree and we enjoy. I dine with her and go after Dinner to a Dentist's; on our Return we leave Mad.ˡˡᵉ Duplessis and go together to Chaillot; it is ab.ᵗ half past eight, of Course not

---

¹ So even the fervent Jansenist, Camus (1740–1804), could be bought; sincere as he was opinionated, it was partly to pay off old scores, old sufferings of old Jansenists, that he had urged the Assembly to decree civil constitution of the clergy.

² First performed in July *Lodoïska*, by Luigi Cherubini (1760–1842), is the musical sensation of 1791, which hears it two hundred times. The public puzzled, Haydn and Beethoven impressed by its interesting counterpoint. Plot romantic, Polish, Lodoïska imprisoned in castle of one admirer, escaping with another under cover of a Tartar raid. Too modern for the Paris Grand Opera established by Lully, 1672, which was clinging to mythology and the classics.

dark, but on the Quai between the Louvre and Tuilleries we again embrace. Had the Coachman turned his Head he must have viewed this edifying Scene. Spend the Evening at the Louvre. My friend tells me that the Chevalier de Coigny's Embassade to the Princes is meerly to communicate the Situation of Things. It is I think a very false Step in Politics. The Weather is somewhat more pleasant but still very warm.

Thursday 4. — This Morning M: Brémond calls again but has not yet got the India Papers. He tells me that the Baron de Cormeyré is going out as one of the Commissioners to the french Islands, having the Intention to invest his Property in a Plantation; and he says that he has very liberal Principles respecting the Commerce with the United States. He wishes to see me, which I agree to. M: Franklin calls and communicates his Intelligence from America. He asks me to introduce him at the british Embassador's which I decline, not being well enough there to take that Liberty. Go with him to visit Gen: Duportail who is abroad. Thence to the Louvre where I am told that Mad: has changed her Mind and gone to the Assembly. Return Home and write. Dine with the british Embassador. As I arrive too early and find Pen, Ink and Paper on the Table, I write for her:

> 'Tis said that Kings with wild Ambition fir'd,
> To Pow'r despotic always have aspir'd
> Like untam'd Coursers whose indignant Soul
> Spurns at Restraint and scorns all weak Control.
> Hence British Senators, with patriot Skill,
> Have strove to check and curb the Monarch's Will,
> But Gallic Statesmen take a wiser Course
> And make the Bridle stronger than the Horse.

Lord Palmerston [1] dines here, who is a very pleasant Companion. Go to Madame de Montmorin's and find there the Count de La Marck whose Countenance shews still, I think, the Desire of further Acquaintance. I observe that he and M: de Montmorin take different Routes to meet in the Cabinet of the latter. Call on Madame de Ségur who is abroad and then on Madame de La

---

[1] Second Viscount Palmerston, father of Queen Victoria's Prime Minister. Paris is full of British tourists this comparatively tranquil summer.

Suze where I see the Count de Berchini; he receives a Complaint from the Militia Camp in the Plain of Grenelle who find the Ground too hard and rough to sleep upon. This is quite in Character. He gives a Description of this Corps which resembles I find any other Corps of Militia with the single Difference that the Individuals here differ essentially from each other in Point of Fortune, and have in general the most profligate Manners. The Weather is less warm.

Friday 5 August. — M⁵ Brémond calls this Morning but M⁵ Catallan the Dentist coming shortly after, He goes away. M⁵ Swan comes and shews me the Letter he has received from the Minister of the Marine. Brémond returns and brings me the french Constitution. While I am reading it Jones comes in and interrupts me. Dress and call on M⁵ Franklin. We dine together at the Restaurateur's and as the Abbé Ronchon happens to be there we go together to visit a Manufactory of plated Ware and afterwards see the new Coinage of Half Pence. Thence I go to Madame du Bourg's and stay till near ten. From thence to Mad⁵ de La Borde's. My friend, who is here, is very cold and so am I. The Weather continues Hot and dry.

Saturday 6. — This Morning M⁵ Brémond calls. I promise to see Monsieur de Montesquiou ToMorrow. He has not been able to see M⁵ Rayneval who is sick. Write. M⁵ Short calls to know if I have yet received an Answer from Antwerp. I receive it while he is with me, but recommend waiting a while to see what Events will turn up. He asks my Opinion of the Constitution. I tell him it is a ridiculous one. He says several of his friends have asked his Opinion about placing Money in our Funds, and that he has recommended them to Bankers. The Bankers of this City know Nothing about our Funds. Dine with Monsieur de Montmorin & converse with him on Affairs. He has a pretty just Opinion both of himself and others. He repeats what has happened this Morning with the King. The Recital of the Scene brings Tears both in his Eyes and mine. Poor Man, he considers himself as gone and that whatever is now done must be for his Son. M⁵ de Montmorin communicates the State of Swan's Application and upon suggesting the Idea of empowering Ternant to contract for Supplies to the Islands he flies off and shews me that he is like every

other Frenchman I have met with on that Subject. He fears the
Merchants of Bourdeaux,[1] but seems further to be seriously of
Opinion that the Supply of their Islands from this Country with
Flour and salted Provisions is a Matter of considerable Consequence. Go from hence to the british Ambassador's and Madame
de Puisignieu's. The Ladies are abroad and I return Home. It
is excessively hot and from the Want of Rain one is almost suffo-
cated with Dust.

Sunday 7. — This Morning I write. At one call on the Marquis
de Montesquiou and converse with him on Business. He tells me
that a Bribe has been offered to Amelot who has communicated
the Matter to the Committee [of Finance]. That it was for the
Affair of the Rations. That Camus opened on the Subject and it
was decided to call a Meeting with the diplomatic Committee for
Tuesday. Call on M.ʳ Franklin and we go out to Auteuil where we
dine with Madame Helvétius.[2] A raving mad democracy forms
this Society. Return to Town and visit Mad.ᵉ de La Borde. Then
go to the Louvre where Mad.ᵉ receives me very coolly indeed.
M.ʳ de Montesquiou arrives just before me. I stay but a little
while and then go to Mad.ᵉ de Ségur's. The Constitution forms
now the general Subject of Conversation, in which I take the
least possible Part. The Weather continues excessively hot.

Monday 8. — This Morning Brémond brings with him Pellin
and as he is to be one of our Council I shew him the Observations
I am making as far as I have gone. He seems desirous that they

---

[1] For years the world's supply of sugars and rum had sailed from San Domingo in French bottoms and passed through the port of Bordeaux, a profitable
monopoly. Charges and months of ocean travel could be saved by shipping the
island products to the United States direct, taking back wheat, and as a patriotic free lance Morris works hard to further American commerce with the
French Islands and the plan of sending them supplies in part payment of
America's debt to France, an idea many men claim as their own. Bertrand de
Molleville as Minister of Marine supports it.

[2] A pious pilgrimage for Temple Franklin, whose grandfather Benjamin at
eighty had proposed to the *beaux restes* of this siren, then sixty-five, who had
soothed his days in neighboring Passy with her charm, combined with the
brains of her philosophic and masonic satellites. As an adolescent dandy with
red heels, leading a cat on a ribbon, Temple had known her hospitable rooms
at Auteuil. Were they still smelling like stables with ten birds and eighteen
cats? Widow of an epicurean farmer-general, Madame Helvétius (1719–1800)
was beautiful and good.

should be speedily compleated in order that such Part as Circumstances will permit may be adopted. Go to Pashe the Banker's and get a small Bill discounted, then call at the Louvre. My Friend is lying on the Bed and I find that her Mind has preyed upon her Quiet. I stay with her and dine quasi tête à tête, having only Mad.^{lle} Duplessis, so that our Conversation in English is quite free. The Bishop comes in who is a little attentive. After Dinner Mad.^e again lies down and Mad.^{lle} retires to the Window with a Book; she is near sighted so that after many little preparatory Caresses my friend gets so much animated as fairly to proceed to the Act which is fully accomplished in the Presence of Mademoiselle. Return Home and write. Sup with the british Embassadress where I meet Lord —— Fitzgerald. He is just returned from America, having made a long Tour thro the interior Parts of it. He is a pleasant, sensible young Man. Our Party, which has only the Addition of his Brother and Lord Gower, is one of the most pleasant I ever remember. The Weather is somewhat less warm about Midnight and in the open Air.

Tuesday 9. — This Morning write. At two visit my friend who has Company with her till three. Dine at the Restorateur's and then return Home and write. The Weather continues to be dry and very warm.

Wednesday 10. — This Morning write. Mr Jaubert comes and begins a Translation of my Work. Dine with the Vicomte de Ségur. Among others Monsr Rivaroll [1] is here who has a great Deal of Genius. Go to the Louvre where I find Monsr and Mad.^{lle} Duplessis. He goes down Stairs and as there is no other Means we perform the Act at Dusk in the Presence of Mad.^{lle}. The Weather is still warm. We had a Shower about two oClock with some Thunder. Spend the Evening at the Louvre.

Thursday 11. — This Morning write. Mr Jaubert calls with the

---

[1] Comte de Rivarol (1754–1801) had blazed from obscurity into the great world at twenty by a prodigality of epigram, caustic wit and inimitable storytelling. Nobody had ever mocked so many people in such small compass as his *Petit Almanach de nos grands hommes*, dedicated to unknown gods, which in alphabetical order eulogized all the worst French writers. His *Le chou et le navet*, a satire on Delille's fashionable *Jardins* in which the kitchen garden had been omitted, did not come off so well.

small Part which he has translated of my Work and it employs a long Time to correct it and bring it up to the Force of the original. Dine with M.ʳ Franklin and then go to the Louvre. My friend is in Distress and her Husband out of Humor. We ride and stop a Moment near the Champs Élisées. The Ladies walk and Gen.ˡ Dalrymple passes, with whom I have a few Words of Conversation. He seems as usual very desirous of getting a few Scraps of Intelligence. We return to the Louvre and set down Mademoiselle. Call on Mad.ᵉ de Corney who is abroad. Go to Mad.ᵉ de Boursac who is not yet ready. We take a Turn and in the Course of it perform the usual Ceremonies. I leave the Ladies at the Louvre and return Home. The Weather is still very warm. There was a pretty smart Shower this Day but without Thunder. The Regiment of Berwick has it is said gone over. This was reported before but is now confirmed.

Friday 12 *August.* — Write. Then go to the Louvre and having celebrated the nuptial Hour we converse on the Affairs of my friend who is distressed at the Bishop's Coldness on the Score of her Interests. I tell her that I am not at all surprized at this. Our Conversation leads me to give her his true Character. Dine with Mons.ʳ de Montmorin and in Consequence of what Brémond told me this Morning mention the Rations. He says that Affair is ruined in the Committee, which is directly the Contrary of what Brémond told me. Swan was with me also about his Provisions. I doubt much of his being able to do any Thing. Fix with M.ʳ de Montmorin a Meeting for Wednesday next to consider the Situation of public Affairs. Call on Mad.ᵉ de Ségur, having left my Name for the british Embassadress. At coming away Ségur tells me I shall have his Answer in a few Days, about the Estate he is to purchase. This looks, I think, like a Design to be off. Go to Mad.ᵉ du Bourg's and sit with her a while tête à tête. She expected me to pass the Evening and seems well disposed to make a little Connection but I do not press at all. I even tell her that I do not like *les bonnes fortunes* where the Heart is not interested. Spend the Evening at Mad.ᵉ de La Borde's. I find that Montmorin begins to be much mounted against the Constitution. The Weather is somewhat less ardent.

Saturday 13. — M.ʳ Bremond calls and I communicate what M.ʳ de Montmorin mentioned about the Rations. He tells me that Bergasse has compleated his little Performance which is in the Press, and that he will send me a Copy before Publication to examine. Send him for Jaubert who comes late and then has not compleated the Translation. I grumble indecently and frequently, too much indeed. Doctor Bancroft calls and tells me that young Knox is trying to sell the Lands on the S.* Lawrence notwithstand.* what I mentioned to him. I dine with M.* Short. After Dinner take my friend and Mademoiselle Duplessis to the Bois de Boulogne, afterwards set the latter down and go for Mad.* de Boursac; on our Way we embrace. Spend the Evening at the Louvre. It is diverting to hear some People complain that the republican Party are getting the upper Hand in the Assembly. It would seem as if their Opponents, the Makers of the Constitution, were a Monarchic Party. The Weather is less hot than it was.

Sunday 14. — Write all Day. M.* Jaubert dines with me and we compleat the Translation of my Work. In the Evening go to the Louvre and spend a little while with the Company there. Then go to Madame de Ségur's where I find the Count de La Marck and Puisignieu. Ségur speaks to me about Eden Park in point of Salubrity. I tell him the Truth and still urge him to purchase the Dover Estate. Return Home early. The Weather is again very hot.

Monday 15. — Write this Morning. M.* Franklin and M.* Bosville [1] call, also M.* Swan and M.* Brémond. Advise Swan to apply to M.* de Curt and promise myself to speak to him. Go to the Louvre. De Curt comes there and after a Conversation in which he complains of M.* Short's Conduct he promises to exert himself in order to effect the Object which Swan has in View. Dine here, ride after Dinner and embrace in the Carriage after setting down

---

[1] William Bosville (1745–1813) of Gunthwaite, Yorkshire, an estate he neglects for Paris and London. Fought against Americans as Lieutenant in Coldstream Guards. Rich hospitable bachelor, conservative, eccentric, dressing like a courtier of George II. He follows up his acquaintance with Morris in London, where in his front hall in Welbeck Street hangs a slate on which intimates inscribe themselves as dinner guests for the day, twelve his limit, five his hour, 'better never than late' his motto, so a footman shuts his door on stroke of five. On Sundays he drives his coach and four to Wimbledon to Horne Tooke's.

Mademoiselle Duplessis. I return Home early. The Weather is astonishingly warm.

Tuesday 16. — This Morning write. At three go to the Louvre. My friend tells me that her Husband has written to her a Letter insisting on his Rights. That she has in Answer refused and expects a Quarrel. I dine with the Count de La Marck who tells me that our Meeting at M.ʳ Montmorin's, intended for tomorrow, is postponed till Friday, at which Time Pelling will have prepared a Plan also. The Constitution, they tell me, has this Day been adopted. I go to the Louvre where Mad.ᵉ is at her Toilette with M.ʳ Short. I decline going with them to Chaillot but take an Airing and return Home. Brémond and Bergasse call. The latter stays late and corrects a Part of the Translation of my Work. The Weather still very warm.

Wednesday 17. — This Morning write. M.ʳ Brémond calls according to Custom. I dine at the Louvre. After Dinner call on the british Embassadress who is abroad. Return Home. M.ʳ Bergasse ¹ comes and finishes the Correction of my Work. Go to the Luxembourg and pass the Evening with Mad.ᵉ du Bourg. Ségur tells me that he daily expects the Credit asked for from his Correspondent, when he will compleat the Contract for Eden Park. The Prince de Poix [a Noailles] who is here, talks aristocratically in the most pointed Manner, and tho a weak Man, yet, as Doctor Franklin observes, Straws and Feathers shew which Way the Wind blows. The Weather has been less ardent this Day.

---

¹ Bergasse, a lawyer from Lyons, sent by its Tiers État as deputy to States-General; by October, 1789, he resigned, unable to subscribe to all the new ideas. Had made his name defending Korneman against Beaumarchais. Critical publicist, his able articles little attended to because they support the King, to whom he is now sending one of his memoirs full of advice. He is loyal to his author as a translator, does not make Morris's work his own, Adèle de Flahaut can still detect foreign turns of phrases. Identity of Jobert, Jaubert, Joubert, less sure. He may be Joseph Joubert, critic whose opinions create current literary opinion, his posthumous Maxims and Essays praised by Sainte-Beuve in same breath with La Rochefoucauld, Pascal, and La Bruyère. Before the King accepts the Constitution, royalist quills produce a shower of corrective memoirs rivalling the 1789 spate of finance plans. Morris's effort has been called by Theodore Roosevelt a very able state paper. As Montmorin does not show it all to Louis XVI until after the formal acceptance, Morris is exempt from responsibility. His aim was to make the King's acceptance conditional and critical, keeping a door open for discussion and amendment.

Thursday 18. — This Morning M! Brémond calls and I make
further Corrections in his Tables of Finance, the Effect of which
will be considerable I think. Swan calls also. I dine at the Restorateur's and then visit at the Duc de La Rochefoucault's, afterwards at Mad? de La Fayette's. Leave my Name for the british
Embassadress and then go to Mons! de Montmorin's. He imprudently quits a Circle of Embassadors to come to me and mention Tomorrow as the Day of Meeting. He says he has desired
Pelling to collect all the popular Traits of the King's Conduct
since he came to the Throne and put them into his Speech. This
is very wrong and I hint as much to him, but a foolish Vanity will
doubtless prevail on that Subject. Take an Airing and then go to
the Louvre where I wait for my friend; de Curt arrives, with
whom I have some Conversation. This Man has Genius and Information but his Judgement is not exact. He is however very
honest, at least he says so. He has spent in public Life his fortune with the Means of enriching himself had he pursued the Conduct usual in his Situation. *Qu:* does he regret this? On the Sentiment now excited depends I think his future Conduct. Stay the
Evening here. It is grown pleasant.

Friday 19. — This Morning M! Brémond calls with his Tables.
M! Bosville also. I go to the Louvre and shew my Work to my
Friend who tells me that it has much of the Foreigner in the
Stile. I dine with M! de Montmorin and after Dinner consider the
Report of M! de Beaumetz [1] on the Manner of presenting the Constitution to the King. I wish them to take up the great Question
as to his Majesty's Conduct, but in vain. We only go about it,
Goddess and about it. I find that feeble Measures will most
probably be adopted. I go hence to the Louvre. Mad? de Corney
is with my friend who has quarrelled this Day with her Husband
because she will not admit his Embraces. I take her (having first
celebrated) to Mad!!e Duplessis & thence we go to Mad? de La
Borde's where we spend the Evening. The Weather is still warm

---

[1] Chevalier de Beaumetz, deputy of noblesse from Artois, joined Constitutionalists, pushed through trial by jury, abolition of torture, publicity of
judicial debate, approved assignats, but voted against sale of Church property
and eligibility of Jews. Fundamentally a monarchist, will be accused 1792 of
trying to re-establish the King's power and will save his neck by emigrating.

tho not so much as it was. Our Conciliabule this Evening was La Marc,[1] Pellin, Beaumetz, Montmorin and myself.

Saturday 20. — This Morning M.ʳ Swan, M.ʳ Brémond and M.ʳ Corméré [2] call on me. M.ʳ Swan wants a positive Answer from Brémond and I desire them to take an Appointment together. After he is gone we go into the Discussion of the Question what Kind of Connection with her Colonies is suited to France and what Intercourse can she allow them with foreigners, particularly the United States. As we agree in Opinion on this Subject we next proceed to the Ways and Means of effecting our Object, and fix on a Plan of Operation in this Respect which will probably succeed. He is to prepare a Memoire which he is to shew me and in the mean Time to procure a Resolution referring generally to the Colonial agricultural, commercial and fiscal Committees to report on the Powers and Authorities to be given to the Commissioners who go out to S.ᵗ Domingo. These are to be induced to report generally an Authority to consult with the Colonial Assemblies and digest a Plan of Union, Connection and commercial Regulation with them, to serve as a Basis for future Determination. And then these Commissioners are to do the Rest. After fixing this Plan I converse with him on Matters of private Interest resulting from it and as he relishes them he will of Course work hard to accomplish the Object. Visit my friend, who is dressing to go out. Her Husband continues sulky. . . . we are sage. Dine with M.ʳ Bosville. Bancroft and his Mistress, Jones, a M.ʳ Crew and an Irish Officer are of the Party. After Dinner take Mad.ᵉ de La Borde to the Italian Comedy where *Paul and Virginie* is well acted and is I think a good Piece enough. After setting her down I go to the Louvre and stay there a few Minutes. The Weather has at last grown pleasant.

Sunday 21. — M.ʳ Brémond calls and brings me some Notes

---

[1] Count de La Marck, Belgian of princely House of Arenberg, commanded a French Regiment; had retained confidence of the Queen ever since he followed her to France after her marriage, and had tried hard to reconcile his friend and hero Mirabeau with Her Majesty and with La Fayette. Another foreigner who tries to influence France's destiny.

[2] Baron de Cormeyré, a brother of that unfortunate Marquis de Favras who was hanged as a scapegoat to shield the King's elder brother, Comte de Provence.

of Reflections on the State of the Finances which he says will
frighten Mons.r de Montmorin into the Adoption of my Measures.
I shew him that these Reflections would indeed frighten him if
just but it would be to a Purpose directly contrary to what I wish.
I write, then dress and call on M.r Franklin who shews a Disposition to be dealing in the Debt from America to France. Go to the
Louvre where at the Request of my friend I stay to dine and before Dinner indulge ourselves in the private Hour of Joy. After
Dinner visit the british Embassadress where Lord Mountmorres [1]
bores me. The british Embassador and prussian Minister tell
me that a Convention was signed between the Empress of Russia
and the Grand Turk on the twenty sixth of last Month upon the
exact Terms which she had always insisted on. Go from hence to
the Luxembourg and leave my Name for Mad.e du Bourg, thence
to Madame de Lostanges who is in the Country, and then to M.r
Bergasse who corrects what I had written this Morning. He says
he will write to the King Tomorrow on the State of Affairs and
tell him that having obtained the Communication of my Plan in
order to correct the Language, he communicates it to his Majesty,
but under the strictest Injunction of Secrecy. Go to the Louvre
where I stay but a Moment & then return Home. The Weather is
grown very pleasant.

Monday 22. — This Morning at twelve go with M.r Brémond to
Monsieur de Montmorin's and meet there Monsieur de La Marck.
We examine Brémond's Tables; and afterwards I give M.r de
Montmorin my Ideas on some Part of this Business and at the
same Time reproach him for not having made me previously acquainted with the Opinions of Monsieur de Beaumetz. Go from
hence to the Louvre where I meerly shew myself to comply with
my Promise and then dine at the Restorateur's. Return to the
Louvre. Ride. After our Return I agree to stay the Evening,
which is wrong for I wrangle with my friend. The Weather is
pleasant but rather warm.

Tuesday 23. — This Morning I write a little. M.r Brémond calls
and requests me to take Part in a Speculation in the Funds, which
I decline on the Principle that this Gambling, ruinous to some and

---

[1] Henry Redmond Morres, second Viscount Mountmorres, strong supporter
of Pitt in Ireland, writes on politics and shoots himself, 1797; born about 1746.

dangerous to all, becomes unfair when a Knowlege of Facts enables an Individual to bet with a Certainty of Gain. Chaumont
calls. He goes out of Town this Evening. I go to the Louvre &
Madame receives me very coldly. I make such Apologies as are
necessary to put her in the Wrong. She hints very dubiously an
Intention to confine our future Connection to that of pure friendship. I pass a sufficient Time to have the Air of mature Reflection and then I tell her that I think she is perfectly right. That
I shall not therefore attempt to change her Resolution but have
in Consequence made up my own, and so bid her Adieu. She begs
an Explanation, which after much Entreaty I give. That I shall
absent myself till I have formed another Connection. This is a
Stroke she did not expect. Begs me to try only a few Days, that
her Mind may change &c^{a}. I tell her no, that I approve much her
Decision and am far from desiring her to alter what she finds convenient. She begs me at Parting to come this Evening to the
Opera but I leave that Matter doubtful. Just after I get Home
Fontenille calls on me and presses me hard to dine with him. I
go and at Dinner he mentions the Arrival of Madame de Stahl.
I go in Consequence to the Opera and communicate that Cir-
cumstance as a Reason for not abandoning her in the present
Moment. The Weather is growing warmer.

Wednesday 24. — This Morning Mr Swan calls and makes a
Draft of Articles to form the Basis of an Agreement for furnishing
Provisions to the french Marine. Mr Brémond comes and while
he is here Lord Mountmorres and Mr Bosville. Then La Caze.
When the rest are gone Mr Brémond presses me again on the Subject of Stockjobbing, which I peremptorily decline. He then asks
my Opinion of his Plan for his own Government. We discuss it together and it appears to hold out a considerable Chance of Profit.
I dress and call at the Louvre. Madame tells me that she is convinced the King will soon commit another Folly, and gives me the
Reasons. I visit Mad^{e} de Stahl who receives me well. She is getting over the Illusions she was under about the Constitution.
Leave my Name for the british Embassadress and then go to dine
with Doctor Bancroft. An English Paper which Bosville shews me
mentions the Receipt of good News from India but it seems that
at the same Time the Stocks have fallen, that is the India Stock,

3 p%. Go from hence to Mad? de Guibert's where I spend the Evening. The Amusement is Colin Maillard or blind buck and davey or blind Man's buff. My friend seems desirous of coming round and I receive her Advances so as to leave the Impression doubtful. Come away early.

Thursday 25. — This Morning M? Brémond calls and after him the Count de Ségur; then M? Franklin about a Bill which R. M. has drawn on him. After he is gone, Ségur tells me that one Reason why he went into the Country is that he expected to be called on to advise the King, and then he tells me the Advice he would have given. I think he is mistaken in his Motive, for he has at different Times shewn a strong Disposition to be the Counsellor. When this is over we fix our Agreement for Eden Park, which is to be executed ToMorrow Morning. I then dress and go to the Louvre, having received from my Friend a Ticket for the Academy. We make an early Dinner and go thither. Nothing very extraordinary but I observe that among these Auditors there is more of Religion than I expected. This is a good Sign. Return to the Appartments of my friend who brings with her the Abbé de l'Isle and he recites to us some charming Verses. Go to Monsieur de Montmorin's and tell him that I have some Reason to apprehend that the King means to make another Coup de Théâtre. He says he thinks not. We then discuss pretty fully what he is to do and I find that he is getting a little up towards the right Point. He expresses much Anxiety about a Minister of the Finances. I tell him that whenever there is sufficient Authority I will give him a Plan for the Finances. Return Home early, having paid a Visit in my Way to La Borde. He is very melancholy about the King's Situation. I tell him that there is no Danger and point out in general the Conduct which his Majesty ought to pursue. He begs me to give it to him in writing; this I decline for the present. He says that the King understands English well and that he will be perfectly secret, of which I may be certain as he has been so many Years a Valet de Chambre to Louis the fifteenth.

Friday 26. — Compleat this Morning with the Count de Ségur the Sale of Eden Park and pay the greater Part of the Money to Le Couteulx and Company. Request them to pay Le Normand three to four hundred thousand livres, which Laurent promises to do. La Caze was with me and I told him that I intended to apply on this Subject to Le Couteulx. Call on Mad.ᵉ de Flahaut who is *pleine d'agaceries* but I receive every Thing very coolly. Dine with Mad.ᵉ de Stahl who requests me to shew her the Memoire ¹ I have prepared for the King. I am surprized at this and insist on knowing how she became acquainted with it. She tells me pretty nearly. I read it for her and the Abbé Louis ² thro whom she gained her Intelligence, and they as I expected are very averse to so bold a Tone. I am well perswaded that a poor Conduct will be adopted. The british Embassadress came in during our lecture which interrupted it, to me very agreably. Madame de Coigny was with her. Go from hence to Madame de La Borde's. Mad.ᵉ de Flahaut comes in pretty late and says that she waited for me. I tell her I am surprized at this for I neither promised nor intended to come. This touches Home. She is vastly attentive now but she is yet a great Way from her Journey's End. The Weather has grown at last to be very pleasant.

Saturday 27. — This Morning I walk out to the Louvre, my friend having promised to look over and correct my Work. She is ill. She begins, however, the Correction but is obliged from Weakness to quit it. She begs to renew our Connection. I tell her it cannot be. That I cannot submit to an Inferiority and will not ask her to sacrifice her Sentiment. After a great Deal of this Sort of Thing I at last consent to kiss her and then give Way to her Caresses.... Return Home and dress. Then go to the Manufacture of Angoulême and afterwards to dine with Monsieur de

---

¹ A bulky pocketful for paying evening calls, the fair copy of Morris's translated work, but to read it to Madame de Staël the moment the subject came up, in his pocket it must have been; doubtless on the way to his own Egeria for final touches and this chance of trying its effect on France's most intellectual and political woman seemed tempting, however indignant he might afterwards be at her trap.

² In Abbé Louis (1755–1837) Morris was up against an enquiring mind. After a brief spell of diplomacy this Abbé will spend his emigration studying English money methods and will become the great finance minister of the Restoration, Baron Louis.

Uninfluenced by Morris's plan, the King's acceptance of the Constitution is unconditional and their Majesties enter upon their last spell of popularity, cheers at theatres, illuminations in streets, and a general amnesty for all revolutionary offences, as suggested by La Fayette. This released all prisoners connected with the King's flight or the 17 July riots.

Montmorin where I arrive late. After Dinner retire into his Closet and read to him the Plan I have prepared of a Discourse for the King. He is startled at it. Says it is too forcible. That the Temper of the People will not bear it &c^a. We have much Discourse on this Subject. I leave the Thing with him. We are to confer farther on it and he is to shew it to the King on Monday. I give him Leave (which otherwise he would have taken) to shew it to his Daughter. I know that she will encourage such a Step, having previously mounted her Imagination to that Point. I go again to the Louvre, having so promised. My friend tells me that the Bishop has spoken to her of my Work, Mad^e de Stahl having told him that I had shewed it to her. She finds it very weak. My friend told the Bishop that this is false for that on the Contrary she feared only from its being too strong. A good Deal of this Sort of Chit Chat. I expected that Conduct from Mad^e de Stahl and am not therefore surprized. Go to sup with the british Embassadress. She and her Husband are sitting together. We have some agreable Conversation before the Arrival of Madame de Coigny. We have some little Compliments together, Mad^e de Coigny and I, and I think it possible that we may be pretty well together, but this depends on the Chapter of Accidents for she must be at the Trouble of bringing it about. Stay late here. The Weather is very pleasant.

Sunday 28. — Mr Brémond calls as usual. I write all the Morning. Mr Bosville, Doctor Bancroft and his friend Mrs Rose dine with me. After Dinner I take the two last to the Door of the Opera. My friend complains that I do not come to see her tho I had assigned before my Reasons to her Messenger; promise to visit her this Evening and after taking the Doctor and his Lady Home, go to the Louvre. En route I convinced myself that I may, if I please, receive the Kindness of the Doctor's friend. Mine is gone to pay a short Visit. I sit Half an Hour with Mademoiselle Duplessis and then return Home. It begins to rain and the Weather is very pleasant.

Monday 29. — This Morning Mr Brémond calls. I write. Mr Swan also calls. Go to the Louvre but I had made it too late and my friend is gone into the Country. Go to some Shops, then call on Mr Short, Ld Palmerston and Genl Dalrymple. Dine with M^r

Franklin. After Dinner visit at Mr de Montmorin's. Walk and converse with Madame de Beaumont. She tells me that Madame de Stahl has told her Father that she has seen my Work. She is a devilish Woman, but I tell Made de Beaumont the whole Story. It is clear that Mr de Montmorin cannot and will not make Use of my Draft. I go from hence to the Louvre and wait Madame's Return. Sit a while here and then go to Made de Stahl's; she is at her Toilette yet. I am disappointed here in the Expectation of meeting Lady Sutherland. The Conversation is dull. I have not an Opportunity of saying to Made de Stahl what I intended for she seems a little Conscience struck and avoids me; but I tell the Abbé Louis that I renounce all Interference in the Business and shall desire that my Plan may not be followed. The Weather has grown very cool indeed.

Tuesday 30. — This Morning write. I have Company¹ to breakfast at twelve. Among them the Abbé de Lisle to recite Verses. Mr Short, who is one of them, tells me that a further Loan has been opened in Holland and he will communicate to me the particulars. I go with my friend to the Louvre and thence to

---

¹ Among them Henry Temple, second Viscount Palmerston (1739–1802). By kind permission of the owner of his *Diary in France during July and August 1791* and of the Syndics of the Cambridge University Press (England), who published it in 1885, his entry for August 30 may be quoted: 'Went to a breakfast at Mr Morris's. He is an American, a gentlemanlike sensible man of property and estimation in America. He was concerned in the line of finance during the war. He has only one leg, having been obliged to undergo an amputation in Consequence of jumping from a window in an affair of gallantry. Made an acquaintance with Madame de Flahaut, a very sensible agreeable woman. Her husband and she have apartments in the Louvre, where they live much at home and have a small society most evenings. The chief purpose of the meeting was to hear the Abbé Delisle read some passages of his poem on the imagination, which he did. They were very beautiful, and from what I have heard the poem must be a delightful work. It is hoped it will be published this winter.'

L'Imagination will have prodigious success when published in the calmer Paris of 1806. Begun in Constantinople embassy of Choiseul-Gouffier, it is the very secular abbé's most original work, rich in imagery and episode. Lord Palmerston's startling explanation of the wooden leg smacks of Paris in the nineties, not of sober wartime Philadelphia; obviously imparted with sly twinkle by one of the fair guests and swallowed whole by this very socially minded traveller, who had for years been a Member of Parliament, lord of the Admiralty, 1766, lord of the Treasury, 1777, and well known as a writer of verses.

the Opera. She is much afraid of loosing me just now. I decline supping with her. Return Home early. It is very cold this Evening, for the Season, especially after such great Heat as we have had lately.

Wednesday 31. — This Morning write. Brémond calls and desires me to get him appointed one of the Commissioners of the Treasury. I call at the Louvre about two. Mad.ᵉ de Flahaut is in Bed, being ill of a Cold. I stay and dine with her and while Mons.ʳ de S.ᵗ Pré and Mad.ˡˡᵉ Duplessis play at Tric Trac I amuse her at another little Game. We propose one more serious but Vic d'Azyr comes in and, the Chances of Company being great, I go to Monsieur de Montmorin's. Give him a Memoire on the present State of Things. He tells me that Mad.ᵉ de Stahl once took him in as she did me and that her Father told him it was a common Trick with her to pretend to know in order to learn. I tell him that I have caused her to believe that I have given up the Idea entirely and desire him to speak of it lightly and as of a Thing which I had abandoned. He says that it is now in the King's Possession who found the Discourse prepared for him difficult to swallow because it acknowleges the Loss of the Crown : but he replied to this that it was only defective because he had not the Command of 150,000 Men. I return from hence to the Louvre at the Request of my friend but she has Company, wherefore I return Home. The Weather has a perfect autumnal Feel, and is rather cool even for Autumn.

Mémoire for King's Speech

27 Août. 1791.

Messieurs,

Ce n'est plus votre roi qui vous parle. Louis seize n'est plus qu'un particulier. Vous venez de lui offrir la couronne, et de faire connoître les conditions d'après lesquelles il doit l'accepter.

Certainement, messieurs, si j'étois étranger à la france, je ne monterois pas les marches glissantes du trône. Mais le sang qui coule dans mes veines ne me permet pas d'être insensible au sort des françois; descendu d'une longue suite de Rois, le souvenir de ceux qui ne sont plus, les droits des générations à venir, et mon amour fraternel pour le peuple que la providence divine m'avoit confié, tout enfin me défend d'abandonner mon poste. il faut bien que je le conserve pour vous garantir au moins de l'anarchie et de la guerre civile. dans cette position périlleuse, je n'ai pris conseille que de ma conscience, et c'est d'après elle que je me décide à accepter votre constitution. puisse-t-elle assurer le repos au royaume et contribuer à sa prospérité.

La france, en vous accordant sa confiance entière, vous a mise en possession de la toute puissance. Vous êtes donc devenus responsables devant le trône de l'éternel du bonheur de ce peuple immense dont le sort est entre vos mains — j'étois roi — il ne me reste plus aujourdhui ni autorité, ni influence. cependant j'ai un dernier devoir à remplir; c'est celui de vous faire part de mes réflections sur votre ouvrage. je vous prie de les écouter avec une attention sérieuse.

[Translation:]

Gentlemen,

It is no longer your King who speaks. Louis sixteenth has become a private individual. You have just offered him the Crown and made known the conditions under which he must accept it.

Most certainly, Sirs, if I were an alien to France I would not mount the slippery steps of the throne. But the blood which flows in my veins does not allow me to be indifferent to the fate of Frenchmen; descended from a long line of Kings, the memory of those who are no more, the rights of generations yet to come and my fraternal love for the People confided to my care by Divine Providence, all forbid my abandoning my post; I must retain it to guarantee you at least against anarchy and civil war. In this perilous position I have consulted only my conscience and it is in accordance with its dictates that I decide on accepting your Constitution. May it assure peace to the Kingdom and contribute to its prosperity.

France, in granting you her entire confidence has possessed you of complete power. You have thus become responsible before the throne of the Almighty for the happiness of this great People whose fate is in your hands. — I was King — today neither influence nor authority remain to me but I still have a last duty to fulfil; it is that of sharing with you my reflexions on your work. I beg that you will listen to them with serious attention.

[After this opening the King was supposed to assert the maxim that all Government must be instituted and exercised for the advantage of the people, and go on to say that as the Assembly have decided on hereditary monarchy they may rest assured that he will have no other object but the prosperity of France; that his own interest is inseparable from the strength, glory and happiness of the Kingdom; that other public functionaries may have personal ambitions but that the King can only elevate himself by increasing the riches and might of the country; that he may make mistakes or be misled by others but can never be bought; that it is certainly to his interest, as he can only act thro the hands and eyes of others, for his Ministers to be watched by the people's representatives, and be punished for malfeasance whether from incapability or any other cause; and that he cannot but wish that justice be well administered as his glory and the public welfare both depend on it.]

[Editor's translation:]
'Such are some of the advantages of hereditary monarchy. Have you ensured the good and guarded against the evils of which it is susceptible? This is a question of the utmost importance to France and to humanity.

'You begin by a Declaration of the Rights of Man; but such pronouncements having so far produced only metaphysical discussions a King need not comment on them, as his functions demand a knowledge of Man as he is, rather than as he ought to be. It would seem that there are disadvantages in such a preamble to a Constitution, because if the Constitution assures the rights of man the declaration becomes useless, and if there should be any divergence between the two acts disputes might arise and those who decide between them become the arbiters of the Constitution.

'To show that this difficulty is not imaginary it will suffice to remind you of the first article of your Declaration, that "men are born and remain free and equal in their rights." (*Les hommes naissent et demeurent libres et égaux en droits.*) You have however decided that "representatives shall be distributed among the 83 Departments according to the three proportions of territory, of population and of direct contribution." (*Les représentans seront distribués entre les quatre vingt trois départemens selon les trois proportions du territoire, de la population et de la contribution directe.*) It results that a certain number of men in one Department will have the right to elect more representatives than the same number in another Department and might therefore conclude they are not equal in the important right to choose the members of the legislative body.

'You have also declared that "the law is the expression of the general will," (*La loi est l'expression de la volonté générale,*) that "all citizens have the right to take part personally or thro their representatives in framing it," (*tous les citoyens ont droit de concourir personellement ou par leurs représentans à sa formation,*) and that "all citizens being equal in the eyes of the law are equally eligible to all public dignities, places and employments, without other distinction than those of their virtues and talents." (*Tous les citoyens étant égaux à ses yeux sont également admissibles à toutes dignités, places et emplois publics, sans autre distinction que celles de leurs vertus et de leurs talens.*)

'On the other hand you have ordained that "to be an active citizen a direct contribution must be paid somewhere in the Kingdom equal to at least 3 days labor" and that "nobody may become an elector if he does not unite to the qualifications of an active citizen that of paying a direct contribution of   days work." (*Pour être citoyen actif il faut payer dans un lieu quelconque du Royaume une contribution directe au moins égale à la valeur de trois journées de travail*) and that (*nul ne pourra être nommé électeur s'il ne réunit aux conditions nécessaires pour être citoyen actif celle de payer une contribution directe de   journées de travail.*)

'Looking at these two articles together it seems doubtful whether the first can be considered as an inalienable right, and in this hypothesis, whether the second is a fair modification of it.

'You have likewise declared that "for the maintenance of the public forces and for administrative expenses a general contribution is indispensable, and should be equally apportioned among all citizens according to their means;" (*pour l'entretien de la force publique et pour les dépenses d'administration, une contribution commune est indispensable, et qu'elle doit être également répartie entre tous les citoyens en raison de leur facultés;*) and yet by your Constitution you delegate exclusively to the legislative body the power of establishing public contributions and determining their nature, their quality and the manner of collecting them. Now as several taxes, especially indirect taxes, are assessed not according to the means of the people but according to their consumption and even according to their prime necessities, it is possible that your declaration might in the matter of taxation be subject to serious objection from a portion of our citizens.

'It will be well to examine the organization and distribution of the legislative, executive and judiciary powers. According to the Declaration of Rights "any society in which the separation of the powers is not defined has no Constitution." (*Toute société dans laquelle la séparation des pouvoirs n'est pas déterminée n'a point de constitution.*) Be that as it may, their distribution is of great importance. It must now be seen whether you have provided for this in such way that none can encroach upon the others. Beginning with the legislative power, you have decreed the following Articles:'

[Which Morris then dissects and criticizes in detail.]

SEPTEMBER 1791

Thursday 1 *Sep*.. — This Morning I write notwithstanding sundry Interruptions as Mr Swan, Mr Richard and Mr Brémond. Then go to the Restaurateur's to Dinner. Afterw.^{ds} to the Louvre where we pass together an Hour or two in Security.... I then go among the Booksellers and afterwards to the Luxembourg.

Thence to Madame de Boursac's. Bring her to the Louvre and spend the Evening there. The Weather is pleasant.

Friday 2. — This Morning M.ʳ Brémond calls, also La Caze who presses me much to meet him at two at Le Couteulx's in order to compleat an Arrangement respecting the Affairs of R. M. which cannot take Effect just now, I am perswaded. Go at one to M.ʳ Swan's to see his Salt Provisions which have been examined. They are very good. Thence to M.ʳ Le Couteulx's. Laurent says that he and La Caze will breakfast with me ToMorrow. Go to the Louvre and sit awhile with my Friend. Coldness on my Part which is un-pleasing to her as I make no Complaint but leave her to her own Reflections. Promise to see her in the Afternoon. Leave my Name with Mad.ᵉ de Stahl and go to the Count de Montmorin's. He tells me that the Peace between Russia and the Porte is concluded on and that he is well informed that different Bodies of Troops are now on their March, so that the Emperor and King of Prussia being in good Understanding together, it seems probable that Something will be attempted against this Country. I tell him that if this be so it appears to me the more necessary to make the King declare at least the Outlines of the Constitution he desires. He says the Emigrants will hear of Nothing but the antient System. If this be insisted on we shall I think have warm Work. Visit Mesd.ˢ de Puisignieu and Lascaze who are both abroad. Mad.ᵉ de Corney with whom I sit some Time, and then at the Hour ap-pointed go to the Louvre. My friend is not as I expected alone. She contrives to take Mad.ˡˡᵉ Duplessis Home that we may be alone in the Carriage afterwards but I decline the Advantage which this Situation presents. Wounded at this; and the more so as I decline Explanation. Leave her at Madame de La Borde's where I make a short Visit and then go to the british Embassa-dor's. Converse a little here with the Count de La Marck who either is or pretends to be of my Opinion respecting the Constitu-tion and the Conduct to be pursued by the King in that Regard. Mad.ᵉ de Stahl, who is here, is in violent Disputation with the Abbé de Montesquiou and the Bishop d'Autun is in Part the Sub-ject, to the great Edification of Monsieur de Narbonne who is just arrived from Italy. Montesquiou at Supper gives a Picture of the Finances of this Country which is very like the original and which of Course is not handsome. The Weather is very pleasant.

Saturday 3. — Write this Morning. M. Brémond brings me the Memoires of Monsieur de Corméré who is to call on me ToMorrow. I visit my friend and merely say how dye; call and leave my Name for Lord Mountmorres. Visit M. Franklin and converse with him on the Affairs of R. M. We dine together at the Restorateur's. I take him Home and then go to the Louvre. We ride to the Bois de Boulogne and on our Return Mademoiselle visits in my Carriage and we make Use of the Occasion. I go to the Luxembourg and sit a while with Mad. du Bourg but return Home early. The Constitution has been presented this Evening to the King who has promised to return an Answer speedily.

Sunday 4. — This Morning Brémond calls but Mons. de Corméré does not come. Brémond tells me what he supposes to be the Intention of Barnave, Lameth &c. respecting the King's Conduct. At two I take Mad.ˡˡᵉ Duplessis to the Louvre where we dine. Mad. has a nervous Attack after Dinner which she tells me arises from some harsh Expressions which I used. I convince her that she was mistaken as to the Expressions and this puts Things a little to rights. We ride after Dinner and she begs me to promise again a matrimonial Connection. Instead of rejecting this, as usual, I give her Hopes. Go to the british Embassador's and stay awhile at the Hazard Table in the Joys and Sorrows of which I do not participate. Go to the Louvre and stay a few Minutes, then return Home early and go to Bed. The Weather is quite autumnal and very pleasant.

Monday 5. — This Morning Le Couteulx and La Caze, who were to breakfast with me at Half past nine, do not come till after ten and bring with them Le Normand. After Breakfast Laurent talks a great Deal respecting the Debt of R. M. and throws out some Threats. I answer with great *Sang froid*, premising that he may do as he pleases. After much useless Chatter he proposes to me a Plan which I close with and send to M. Franklin to dine with me that I may procure his Assent. Write a little. M. Short comes and consumes the Rest of my Morning. M. Franklin agrees to my Plan after La Caze had talked to him a long Time so that he has the Merit of the Victory over Franklin's Repugnance. We call on Le Couteulx to let him know that it is agreed, and then ride in the Bois de Boulogne. I afterwards visit Madame de Stahl who is abroad. Mad? de La Suze with whom I sit a little while. Then call on Mad? de Puisignieu who is abroad. Mad? de Flahaut also abroad; Mad? de Guibert, Mons? Millet and Mad? de La Borde, none of whom are at Home. I return Home and read. The Weather is very fine.

Tuesday 6. — This Morning M? Brémond calls and after he is gone M? de Corméré. We examine together his Memoires on which I make to him sundry Observations & he takes Note to alter, correct and amend. I then dress and call at the Louvre.... I am quite cool towards her and make my Visit short. Return Home and make a light cold Dinner. Visit at Mad? du Bourg's who is abroad and then go to La Fayette's. Stop in my Way and view the Church of S? Sulpice, the exterior of which is disproportionate and fantastic, the interior immensely heavy. Sit and converse a long Time with La Fayette, then call at the Louvre, thence to Mad? La Borde's and leave my Name. Return to the Louvre and sit till near ten. Madame is abroad and I meet her as I go out. Go to Madame de Stahl's. Ask the Abbé Louis what News there is. He says, I think with a View to pumping, that the King's Discourse will consist partly of mine and partly of other Materials. I tell him there will be Nothing of mine in it, and I really believe so. I tell him further that I give up all Idea of directing his Conduct on the present Occasion, and so I do. I follow Lady Sutherland and Madame de Coigny out and M? Short follows me. Lady Sutherland, in getting into her Carriage, urges me to come more frequently to see them and expects me to dine on Sunday and send in the Morning to ask for Dinner. She takes no Notice of M? Short who stands next me, and in turning round to speak to him after she is gone I find both his Countenance decomposed and his Voice broken. Thus he will go Home with Illwill wrankling in his Heart against me because he is not taken Notice of. This is hard but this is human Nature. He is Chargé d'Affaires and I am only a private Gentleman. He therefore expects from all and more especially from the Corps diplomatique a marked preference and Respect. I wish him to receive it but that is impossible in this Quarter for the present. The Weather is still very fine.

Wednesday 7. — This Morning M.ʳ Franklin calls and we adjust together the Form of a Letter to be written by me to him respecting the Arrangement of R. M.'s Affair with Le Couteulx and Le Normand. After this I write; at two call on Mad.ᵉ de Flahaut who is abroad. Visit Mad.ᵉ de Guibert and then at her Request call again at the Louvre. Dine with Monsieur de Montmorin where Madame de Stahl and her Cortège also dine. I find that she and the Bishop d'Autun press him very hard upon some Subject or other. Go to the Louvre and give Pleasure there without Pain. Take up Madame de Guibert at her House and bring her to the Louvre. M.ʳ Short is here whose Countenance is not yet cleared up. I sup with the Count de La Marck who tells me that the Object of Madame de Stahl and her Bishop was to obtain a Revocation of the Decree which excludes him and others from the Ministry and thereby reduces him to the Rank of a *très petit intriguant.* We have here the Archbishops of Aix and Lyons, that is the ci devant Archbishops, and we have Madame d'Ossun, one of the Queen's Dames d'atours. The Archbishop of Aix tells me that he is engaged in drawing up a Protest against the Constitution on the Part of the Nobles and Clergy, the former of which desire to object against the natural Equality of Mankind because Kings are of divine Appointment, but the latter object to it. I suggest to him that it might be proper to render this Protest subordinate to the King's Speech, but he thinks differently. Madame d'Ossun is so attentive that I think a good Impression is made in my Favor. The Weather is very fine.

Thursday 8. — Write a little this Morning. M.ʳ Brémond and M.ʳ Swan take a considerable Part of my Time. At two I go to the Louvre and thence to the Salon ¹ to see the Exhibition of

---

¹ No traditional Salon with academicians comfortably hung, independents allowed to exhibit two morning hours of a single day and in the open, sun or rain, of Place Dauphine. D'Angivilliers, derided by artists as the Elephant, had emigrated; this new Salon is widely representative, the non-elect, even the non-French, admitted on equal terms with sacrosanct Academicians. Jacques-Louis David exults; freedom has come to art but he will guide it; will inspire the Revolution with his Brutus and Horaces; will commemorate Jeu de Paume, death of Marat, and other big moments; will design her triumphal arches and her feasts of Reason. He will sit on her Councils — he will also become Court Painter to Emperor Napoleon!

Painting and Statuary, not yet open to the public but which the Bishop d'Autun, charged with this Business by the Municipality, admits Strangers to see. There are some very good Pieces. Return to the Louvre where I dine and quarrel a little with my friend, but she is ill and of Course I sympathize. Madame de Corney comes in and stays the Afternoon. I leave them together, leave my Name with Mad.^{e} de La Borde and come Home. The Weather is warm again.

Friday 9. — Write. Go to the Louvre at two oClock and sit with my friend who is ill. She reproaches me for my Coldness of Yesterday notwithstanding her Sufferings. I give her a Reason which is not pleasant to her and leave her to judge for herself and conduct herself in future as she may think most proper. Dine at the british Embassador's where I meet M.^{r} and Mrs Villars who are returning from a ten Months Tour thro Italy, Switzerland &c.^{a}. After Dinner we go to the Palais royal and walk, stopping at the Booksellers' Shops. This is *bien à l'anglois*. Go from hence to the Louvre where I spend the Evening. My friend is still very much indisposed. The Weather is grown quite hot. Having set down Mad.^{lle} Duplessis I call a Moment at Mad.^{e} de La Borde's where I ought to have spent the Evening.

Saturday 10. — Monsieur Brémond calls to tell me his Observations on Mr de Montesquiou's Report. Mr Dariell calls to get his Money and I give him a Note to Le Couteulx to receive 6000$^{#}$. Call at the Louvre in Consequence of a Message from my friend ... Dine here.... I go to Monsieur de Montmorin's but have not an Opportunity to speak to him as he is engaged till he goes to Council. Leave my Name at Mad.^{e} de Stahl's, call for a Moment at the Louvre and return Home. The Weather is very warm.

Sunday 11. — Mr Bosville calls this Morning and consumes my Time. I go to the Louvre.... Of Course I indulge her. Dine at the Restorateur's and go after Dinner to the british Embassador's where I have a pleasing Reception from Madame l'Ambassadrice. Go afterwards to the Louvre where I stay the Evening tho very sleepy. The Weather is extremely warm. The Count de La Marck, whom I saw at the Embassador's, tells me that the King's Observations will be made ToMorrow or the next Day. He seems a little cool and shy on this Subject.

Monday 12. — This Morning Brémond calls and tells me that the King objected to the Speech prepared for him by Pelling in Consequence of a Memoire he had received in English. I write. A little before three take Mademoiselle Duplessis to the Louvre. Dine with the Vicomte de Ségur and then make a short Visit to the Embassadress of England. Go to the Louvre and sit some Time with my friend. . . . Go to Madame de Guibert's where I am to pass the Evening but I leave it early. M.ʳ Short tells me that on Friday last in Council M.ʳ de Montmorin produced Observations written by Pelling but the King preferred mine and on this he felicitates me. I lead him off the Scent but he tells me that he is informed of this in such Manner as admits of no Doubt and also that Monsieur de Montmorin is vexed at that Preference. He says that he was asked by what Channel I could get at the King and that he said if I had done any Thing of this Sort it must be thro Monsieur de Montmorin. The Weather continues very warm.

Tuesday 13. — This Morning M.ʳ Bosville calls and then M.ʳ Franklin. I write. Dine at the Louvre where I learn the Purport of the King's Letter which is meagre enough. It would seem that Intrigue has at Length succeeded and caused the poor Monarch to adopt a middle Party which is good for Nothing. Go to the Opera, which is execrable, but the ballet of *Télémaque* compensates for that Ennui. Return Home, read and take Tea.

Wednesday 14. — This Morning M.ʳ Brémond, Paul Jones, M.ʳ Swan and M.ʳ Franklin call. The King goes to the Assembly and accepts in form the Constitution. I call at the Louvre; dine with the Count de La Marck where we discuss the Declaration (about to be made public) of the Emperor and King of Prussia. Go to the Louvre after Dinner; as we are near to squabbling I leave my friend abruptly and come Home. The Weather continues very warm.

Thursday 15. — This Morning M.ʳ Brémond visits me. I write. Call on Le Couteulx who is not at Home. Dine at the Restorateur's. Go to the Louvre at four. We are alone and make good Use of an Hour. Take a Ride to the Bois de Boulogne, having taken up the Abbé Morelet and his Niece. Return to the Louvre. I come Home. The Evenings are cool and the Days very hot.

Friday 16. — Write. Call at the Louvre at three and then go to dine with Monsieur de Montmorin. I meet there the Spanish Embassador who leaves Town To Morrow. I tell him that I brought him a Letter of Introduction two Years ago. This touches him as I expected it would. He makes a World of Apologies but I cut them short by telling him with a Smile that it is of no Consequence as I have had the Pleasure of making his Acquaintance in the Houses where we have met. This ends by a Promise to be more intimate on his Return. I ask Monsr de Montmorin for the different Papers I have given him. He tells me that the last is in the King's Hands, being intended to regulate his future Conduct. On Enquiry I find that he did not deliver it till after his Majesty had accepted the Constitution. This is wrong, but it is too late to do any Good by saying so. The first Paper, being a Discourse intended for the King, He says the King has returned but as I gave it to him he wishes to keep it. I ask him what became of Pelin's Work; he says that was only a Memoire. I tell him what Short told me; he says it is a fabricated Story, but from what he afterwards tells me I find that Short's Account and Brémond's are different Editions of the same Thing and I am now pretty well perswaded that the poor King has been prevented by an Intrigue in which Mr de Montmorin is a Party from acting as he ought. I ask him if it is true that they are like to suffer for Want of Corn. He says there would be enough if there were Authority sufficient to cause an equal Distribution. I hint to him the Advantage of providing a Quantity of Flour to distribute gratis to the Poor of this City in a Moment of Distress, and point out both the Means and the Consequences. Desire him to think of this and be secret. I visit the british & Swedish Embassadresses, both abroad. Go to Madame de Guibert's and sit some Time. Mad.^e de Flahaut comes in and I come away. Go to Mad.^e de La Borde's where I sit a little while. My friend enters shortly before I come away and looks a little formal on my going up to speak to her, so this must take its' own Course. I spend the Evening at the Count de La Marck's where I meet the two Embassadresses. A very slight Circumstance leads me to a faint Hope that if Time and Opportunity serve — *mais nous verrons.* The Weather continues to be very cool in the Evening and very warm in the Day.

Saturday 17 *September.* — This Morning Brémond calls. He complains that he cannot get Montesquiou's Accounts and suspects that the Publication of them is stopped. He tells me that the King has had for some Days the intended Manifesto of the Princes. *Qu: de hoc.* Dine at Home. Bosville dines with me who is cropsick. After Dinner go to the British Embassador's where I see Lady Hamilton,[1] a very extraordinary Woman of the Town who went to Italy in keeping and there became so much the Passion of Sir William Hamilton that he has married her. She is a fine Creature to Appearance. Dalrymple, who is here, tells me that the Stocks in England have fallen by the selling out of Numbers who desire to place in the American Funds. Go to the Louvre where I stay but a little while. Tell Short what Dalrymple told me. Go to Mad.ᵉ du Bourg's where we have a small aristocratic Party. The Weather has grown much cooler. I went this Morning to Le Couteulx's to adjust R. M.'s Affairs. After some Conversation and Calculation we part; Laurent, who leaves Town Tomorrow, is to write to me on this Subject.

Sunday 18. — This Morning is introduced by Peals of Artillery. It is high Festival on the Adoption of the Constitution. As no Carriages can move I walk out at one and go to the Palais royal, thence to the Louvre. Stay and dine with my friend and at Dinner, having approved of a Sentiment of Mr. de Curt's, she opens with so much Warmth that I shew by a profound Silence my Displeasure. This introduces a Scene of Formality and *Bouderie.* At length, Mad.ˡˡᵉ Duplessis being at the Pianoforte, the third Person and Madame and I on the Sofa, as I find her Determination is taken I take mine and leave her abruptly. Return Home and having deposited my Purse, Watch and Pocket Book, walk thro the Rue St. Honoré to the Champs Élisées, thence to the Tuilleries. The Illumination of the Château [2] and Avenue is superb. Having had enough of the crowding

---

[1] Romney's Lady Hamilton, Charles Greville's Emma Hart (1761?–1815), with her auburn hair and her after-dinner accomplishment of Greek goddess attitudinizing, this year securely married to Sir William Hamilton (1730–1803), British Ambassador to the Bourbon Court of Naples, where she first sees Lord Nelson in 1793.

[2] From inside the Tuileries Madame Elizabeth describes the splendor to a *confidante*: 'The garden was superb, illuminated *tout en lampions et en petites*

and squeezing and walking I return Home and go early to Bed.
The Weather is grown cool and threatens Rain. While at the
Louvre a Balloon let off in the Champ de Mars passed over our
Heads.

Monday 19. — This Morning write. Madame de Montmorin
and her Daughter and M.ʳˢ Villars, together with M.ʳ Villars and
M.ʳ Franklin, breakfast with me; M.ʳ de Montmorin comes in and
gives me the Memoire I had written for the King. He shews me
at the same Time a Note in which he desires a Translation of it.
I ask him if he has thought of the Affair of the Flour; he says that
he has not, as I proposed that we should have some further Conversation about it. Wishes me to make a small Note on the
Subject to be delivered together with the Memoire. I promise to
do so. After our Ladies are gone I go to the Louvre where we
embrace. I then tell my friend of her Misconduct which she
acknowleges but retorts. We ride together and she communicates
her Views and Situation. I read to her my Memoire, telling her
that she is to assist me in the Translation in order that at a
future Day I may let the King know that she is in his Secret.
Promise to speak to Monsieur de Montmorin on her Subject.
Visit Mad.ᵉ du Bourg and Mad.ᵉ de Stahl, both of whom are
abroad. Sit a while with Mad.ᵉ de La Suze and then go to the
british Embassador's. The prussian Minister asks me whether
I was one of the *Faiseurs* of the King's Letter. I tell him no,
and tell him further what I would have written. The british
Embassador is present and tells me he did not believe the Story.
Gouvernay afterwards speaks to me on the Subject and says
that he defended me against that Imputation. I tell him in
general Terms what I would have done and then add that if at
last it should become necessary, from the despair of doing good
thro the Means of the King, to apply to the Princes, I have
thought of him as the proper Person to be employed therein.
Lady Hamilton sings, and acts in singing with a Degree of Per-

---

machines de verre que depuis deux ans on ne peut plus nommer sans horreur.'
All in fairy lights and little machines of glass which for the last two years one
cannot mention without horror. — Poor dim lanterns which at best made
darkness visible in the streets, now only associated with the dread cry '*À la
lanterne!*' and hasty clumsy hangings.

fection which I never yet beheld. She is truly a most charming Woman but she has a little the Air of her former Profession. The Weather has grown very cool. Lady Anne Lindsay [1] who is here, reminds me that we met at the Dutchess of Gordon's.

Tuesday 20. — This Morning write. Dine at Home. At five go to the Opera *Castor and Pollux*.[2] The King and Queen are here. They are received with vast Applause and the Parterre prohibit all Applause except to them. I see Mons. de Montmorin who tells me that it will be impossible to take Measures respecting Subsistence for a Sum greater than what may be furnished by the Civil List. We are to converse further about this. I go to the Louvre and thence to Fontenille's where there is much Company and Play. I read here the Letter to the King from his Brothers which is well written. Come Home about one oClock fatigued.

Wednesday 21. — Write this Day. Brémond tells me that S. Foi, Rayneval &c., &c., &c., have set on foot an Intrigue to detach the Emperor from the King of Prussia by the Means of Mons. de Metternich and that all the original Pieces have been communicated to him. At five I call at the Louvre and desire my friend to assist me by correcting my Translation ToMorrow Morning. She is engaged, and as this is a very paltry Engagement which nevertheless is to be kept, I testify in a short Manner my Dissatisfaction. Go to Mons. de Montmorin's. Speak to him about the flour Business. He is grown cold on this Scent. His Difficulties may be real but I grow tired of a Man who has always Difficulties. He tells me that the King is urgent for my Translation which he (Montmorin) supposes is in order to communicate it to the Queen. I call on Madame du Bourg and sit with her some Time. Talk with the Prince de Poix about Lands. Sup with the

---

[1] Lady Anne Lindsay (1750–1825), daughter of James, fifth Earl of Balcarres, had in 1771 written one perfect ballad, 'Auld Robin Gray,' keeping her secret till she acknowledges it to Sir Walter Scott two years before her death.

[2] Composed, 1737, by Jean-Philippe Rameau (1683–1764), one of the few French-born musicians of the French School, *Castor et Pollux* had held Grand Opera boards till supplanted by Gluck's *Orpheus*, the marvel of 1762. (As Morris never mentions *Orpheus* or *Armide*, perhaps they were seldom given after Gluck left France, 1780, Gluckistes routed by Piccinistes.)

Count de La Marck. *Rien de marquant* here. The Weather is grown so cool that a little Fire is not unpleasant.

Thursday 22. — This Morning write. Brémond tells me that de La Porte begins to gain an Ascendency over the King and Queen. I send for Bergasse to come and correct my Translation. Tell him what to write in Consequence. He dines with me. I go after Dinner to the Louvre and lend my Carriage to Mad.^lle Duplessis. In her Absence we embrace and my friend being in good Disposition for that Purpose, at our second Encounter she nearly faints away. Return Home and write. The Weather is such that I find this Evening a little Fire very agreable. Mr Franklin was with me this Morning to shew a Part of R. M.'s Letter to him.

Friday 23. — This Morning I write; send off Mr Brémond and at three, having finished the Copy of my Work, I go to the Louvre and submit it to the Perusal of my friend, consequent on which I make one or two Corrections. Refuse however to soften one Part which is very strong. Dine at Monsieur de Montmorin's and after Dinner give him the Translation as he goes out to go to the Council, having first ment.^d to him that the strong Traits are I fear dangerous just now as his Majesty has accepted in a different Manner from what I expected. He tells me that there is no such Danger. He promises to return me my Discourse. I go to the Louvre but as there is Company I go to Mad.^e du Bourg's after making a short Visit; stay here some Time. A Table of rouge et noir occupies this Society. Go hence to Madame La Borde's and spend the Evening. Speak to La Borde and set him to Work to give me the Facts respecting the King's Acceptance, and promise to give him a Letter for the King. Speak also to La Porte respecting a Purchase of Flour for Paris. The Weather is pleasant this Day.

Saturday 24. — Write. Go to the Louvre at three and get my friend to look over and correct my Work. Dine at the british Embassador's and go after Dinner to Monsieur de Montmorin's. Give him a Letter on the Flour Plan and ask for my *Discours*, which he will not yet give. I think he means to copy it and is so lazy that it will not be compleated in a long Time. Return to the Louvre where I pass the Evening. The bishop d'Autun who is here *me fait sa cour*, from whence I conjecture that he has learnt from some Quarter or other *que je suis un peu monté*. We shall see. I receive his Advances *ni bien ni mal*. The Weather grows cooler every Day.

[Endorsed by Morris:]

D:[aft] *Letter of 24 Sep*. *1791 to Monsieur de Montmorin about the Subsistence of Paris*

Il me paroît à peu près démontré, Monsieur le Comte, qu'au printems prochain on manquera du pain à Paris, si même la disette ne s'y fait pas sentir auparavent, soit par la rareté des grains, soit par l'abondance des assignats: ne sera-t-il donc pas utile de prendre dès à present les mesures convenables pour s'assurer d'un approvisionnement de farine? On pourroit, moyennant la somme de trois Millions, faire venir de l'Amérique à Paris (tous frais compris) environ douze millions livres de farine, ce qui vous mettra à même de faire une livraison journallière de deux cent mille livres de pain pendant l'espace de deux mois. Vous ne devez pas voux dissimuler que quand la disette se manifestera, il ne sera plus possible de contenir le peuple, et vous avez déjà vu les excès auxquels il peut se porter. il est donc de la dernière importance que le roi se procure les moyens de tirer parti d'une circonstance qui pourroit lui être dangereuse si on ne s'y prépare d'avance. il sera je crois utile de donner du pain aux pauvres en laissant monter le prix pour les autres au point qu'il voudra. Voici en peu de mots la manière d'opérer. le Roi fixera une somme quelconque qui sera déposée à Londres entre les mains des personnes qui j'indiquerai. Alors je donnerai les ordres de faire acheter pour le montant en farine, d'en faire l'expédition pour *falmouth* et d'y attendre des Ordres ultérieures. Ces farines commenceront à arriver de quatre à cinq mois d'ici et si alors on en manque à Paris, elles seront expédiées au Havre, mais si au contraire (et contre toute attente) l'abondance règne à Paris, alors elles seront envoyées aux marchés de l'europe qui offrent le meilleur débouché, et dans ce cas il est à croire qu'elles se vendront sans perte. Il pourroit très bien arriver que la prochaine législature se décidat à faire des œconcmies, et entre autres d'en vouloir à la liste civile, mais elle n'osera pas y toucher dès qu'elle scaura que le roi en fait l'usage dont il est question. Au reste l'objet que je vous propose est une grande affaire d'état, et non pas d'argent ni de commerce, ainsi je ne veux rien y gagner, et je n'y gagnerai rien; je n'ai d'autre désir que d'être utile à des personnes dont je respecte les malheurs.

J'ai l'honneur d'être

[*Translation:*]

It appears to me more than probable, Monsieur le Comte, that next spring Paris will lack bread, even if the dearth does not make itself felt sooner either from the scarcity of grain or the abundance of *assignats*. Would it not therefore be useful to begin at once taking appropriate measures to assure a provision of flour? One might for the sum of three millions bring from America, all charges included, about twelve million pounds of flour which would enable you to make a daily delivery of two hundred thousand pounds of bread in the space of two months. You cannot doubt that when the scarcity becomes manifest it will be impossible to restrain the people and you have already seen the excesses of which they are capable. It is then of the greatest import-ance for the king to procure the means of extracting good from a circumstance which might be dangerous to him unless guarded against. It will I think be useful to give bread to the poor, letting the price of it for others rise to what it will. Here is in brief the mode of operation. The king will decide on a given sum to be deposited in London in the hands of persons indicated by me. I will then give orders to have purchases of flour made to the amount, to have it sent to Falmouth and there to await further orders. This flour will begin to arrive four or five months hence, and if needed then in Paris it will be sent on to Havre, but if on the con-trary (and against all expectation) abundance should reign in Paris, it would be sent to the markets of Europe which offer the best opening, and in that case would presumably sell without loss. It might well happen that the coming

legislature should decide to make economies and have designs on the Civil List, but will not dare touch it when they
hear that the King is putting it to this use. Moreover, the
object I am proposing to you is a great affair of State, not
of money making or commerce; I therefore wish to gain
nothing and would gain nothing by it; I have no other wish
than to be useful to persons whose misfortunes I respect.

I have the honor to be ...

Morris to His Majesty Louis XVI

A Paris ce 24 Septembre 1791

Sire

j'ai eu l'honneur de vous addresser hier par Monsieur de
Montmorin la traduction du mémoire que je lui avais remis le
dernier d'août. Ce mémoire était fait avant que votre Majesté
eut pris son parti. Ainsi il s'y trouve des expressions un peu
fortes. j'ai cru pourtant de mon devoir de n'y rien changer, car,
dussai-je paraître sauvage, je serai toujours vrai.

Vous trouverez cijoint Sire une note confiée le 26 janvier 1790
à une personne qui devoit la remettre entre les mains de la reine.
je ne scai pas si sa Majesté l'a reçue; mais je vous en fait l'hommage à présent pour vous prouver que j'ai toujours eu le désir
de vous être utile, et aussi que ce n'est pas après coups que se
font mes prédictions.

Je viens d'écrire aujourdhui à Monsieur de Montmorin une
lettre sur l'approvisionment de paris, et je supplie votre majesté
de vouloir bien y faire attention. C'est par le peuple de cette
ville que se sont faites et la révolution et la constitution. il sera
toujours maître de tout pendant que les assemblées nationales
tiendront ici leurs séances, à moins que votre Majesté ne puisse
reprendre son autorité. il vous coûte cher Sire d'acheter les
députés, et cela ne sert à rien puis qu'ils ne sont que des instruments entre les mains du peuple. d'ailleurs ils ont trop peu de
consistance et même de fidélité pour qu'il vaille la peine de les
corrompre. Quand même on viendroit à bout d'en avoir les trois
quarts, ils n'oseroient rien faire contre le voeu de la populace;

et il est beaucoup plus aisé d'avoir la populace. j'ai eu dans une autre occasion l'honneur de remarquer à votre majesté que 'les hommes ne sont gouvernés que par la force ou par l'opinion, et que la force même ne dépend que de l'opinion: qu'ainsi entre les gouvernemens absolus et modérés, il n'y a d'autre différence que celle de l'opinion plus ou moins générale. dans le gouvernement absolu tout dépend de l'armée, et dans l'autre de la masse de bons citoyens qui s'appelle *peuple*. Quand il n'y a plus de gouvernement ce n'est plus le peuple, *c'est la populace qui domine, parceque c'est elle qui, ne pouvant rien perdre, espère tout gagner; et qui, devenant ainsi la seule force qui agit, inspire seule la terreur.'* plusieurs moyens se présentent pour s'assurer non seulement de la populace, mais aussi du peuple. je me borne dans ce moment à celui de leur donner du pain et cela d'une manière à montrer non seulement la bonté, mais aussi la sagesse et la prévoyance de votre Majesté. Alors vos bienfaits leur présenteront à la fois et l'idée de Munificence et l'idée de grandeur; et cette dernière émeut singulièrement la nation française. Elle s'occupe rarement du bien, elle s'extasie toujours du beau.

En tous cas, Sire, je dois insister pour vos propres intérêts sur le secrêt le plus absolu, parceque s'il étoit connu que votre Majesté s'occupe de cet objet, on ne manqueroit pas de dire que c'est pour corrompre le peuple, mais quand la nécessité arrivera tout le monde sera persuadé que c'étoit pour le secourir. Alors la méchanceté de vos ennemis au lieu d'être dangereuse ne sera que méprisable. d'un autre côté, si votre Majesté ne veut pas s'en occuper, il lui convient de paroître n'en rien savoir, parceque le peuple croit toujours que dès qu'on prévoit le mal on peut l'écarter.

[Translation:]

Sire,

I had the honor of addressing to you yesterday by Monsieur de Montmorin the translation of the memorandum I had given him last August. This paper was written before your Majesty had decided on a course of action. Therefore it contains strong expressions. I have however thought it my duty to alter nothing, for at the risk of appearing uncouth I will always be sincere.

You will find herewith, Sire, a note confided on 26 January, 1790, to a man who was to place it in the hands of the Queen. I know not whether her Majesty received it but I now offer it to you to prove that I have always wished to be of use, and also that it is not after things have happened that I make my predictions.

I have just written to Monsieur de Montmorin a letter on the provisioning of Paris and I implore your Majesty to give heed to it. It is by the people of this town that the revolution and the constitution have been made; it will always be the master while the National Assemblies hold their sessions here, unless your Majesty can resume his authority. It costs you dear, Sire, to buy the deputies and it serves no purpose, for they are instruments in the hands of the people; besides, they have too little consistency or even fidelity to be worth corrupting. Even if three quarters could be won over they would dare nothing against the will of the populace, and it is far easier to win the populace. I had on another occasion the honor to remark to your Majesty that 'men are only governed by force or by opinion' (Morris quotes from his letter of May 25 down to 'inspire terror.') Several methods present themselves for making sure not only of the populace but of the people. I limit myself for the moment to that of providing them with bread, and that in such way as to show not only the kindness but also the wisdom and foresight of your Majesty. Then your benefactions will suggest to them the idea both of munificence and of greatness; and this last is singularly moving to the French nation. It seldom notices the good but goes into ecstasies over the beautiful.

In any case, Sire, I must in your own interest insist on the most absolute secrecy, for were it to be known that your Majesty acts in this matter it would inevitably be said that it is as a bribe to the people, but when once the need begins to be felt everyone will be satisfied that it was for their good. Then the malice of your enemies will be despicable instead of dangerous. On the other hand, if your Majesty wishes to take no part in it he had better appear to know nothing of it, because the people always believes that ills foreseen might be prevented.

Sunday 25. — This Morning M.ʳ Brémond calls. I write. Call on La Borde and give him a Letter for the King which he promises to deliver immediately. Visit M.ʳ Ludlow who is not at Home. Go to the Louvre; the bishop d'Autun comes in shortly after me and tells us that the Consideration of his Report is postponed till the next Legislature. He is sore under this; my friend tells me some Time after that she is much hurt at this Circumstance and that she tells me because she will conceal Nothing from me. This (whether Art or Nature) is well done. I call on M.ʳ Short who is abroad. Dine at the Louvre. In the Evening we walk out to see the Illuminations which are very splendid, that is, the Château and Gardens of the Tuilleries, Place Louis Quinze and Champs Élisées. M.ʳ Windham,[1] who is with us, seems attentive to Mademoiselle Duplessis but I think he is too young and too old to be taken in. The Evening is prodigiously fine and the fire very agreable.

Monday 26. — This Morning write. M.ʳ Brémond calls and gives me Bergasse's Publication on the Finances. While he is here M.ʳ Short comes in and gives me Letters from the President and Secretary of State of the United States. I tell him that Brémond informs me, he Short, has paid the arreared Debt of the United States to France. Short tells me that this is not true. I go to the Louvre for a Moment & then dine at the Restorateur's, return to the Louvre and take my friend to some Shops to assist me in the Choice of Articles for America. Stay with her till after nine; she is ill. Spend the Evening with Mad.ᵉ de Guibert. The Weather grows cooler.

Tuesday 27. — This Morning write. M.ʳ Franklin calls. We dine together at the Restaurateur's. After Dinner I call at Mad.ᵉ de Guibert's to tell my friend that I cannot go with her to the Bois de Boulogne. Go to Mons.ʳ de Montmorin's to solicit him in favor of Brémond who called on me this Morning for that

---

[1] William Windham (1750–1810), M.P. for Norwich 1784–1802, one of the members in charge of Hastings impeachment. Secretary for War under Pitt, 1794–1801, and again under Lord Grenville, 1806–1807.

Purpose. Meet him at his Gate going to the *Spectacle*. Visit at the british Embassador's. They go also to the *Spectacle*. I go to the Louvre and sit awhile with Mad.^e, Mad.^lle, and Mr Short. Then visit at Madame de Vanoise's and Mad.^e de Lostange's. Both abroad. Return Home early and my Stomach deranged, I know not why. The Weather is very fine.

Wednesday 28. — Write. Brémond calls. I was ill last Night and therefore I walk this Morning; the Weather is very dry with high Wind from the North East. Dine with Mr Franklin. Go after Dinner to Monsr de Montmorin's who is just going to Council. I press him on Brémond's Subject. He tells me that he had another Person in Contemplation but at length he promises that if De Lessart names Brémond he, Montmorin, will not oppose. Sit a while with Mad.^e de Montmorin and then go to the Louvre where I find a Coxcomb of a Lawyer whose Name is Turpin. He stays a long Time. We have a Deal of English Company. Lord Holland, Lady Anne Lindsay &c.^a. The bishop d'Autun tells me that Demoutiers is appointed and asks if I am *lié* with him. I answer: tolerably well, which leads to a Discussion in order to know the Ground. I see that he is forming Design on him. Come Home to sleep, being much fatigued. The Weather is pleasant. Probably it is de Moustier's Appointment which brought the bishop d'Autun forward towards me. He tells me that Montmorin communicated it on Thursday last.

Thursday 29. — Write. Dine at Home. Brémond calls and says he saw Mr de Montmorin Yesterday and is much dissatisfied with him. After Dinner I go to the Louvre. We ride. On my Return lend my Carriage to Mademoiselle and make Use of her Absence. In going hence I take the Chevalier de Luxembourg with me and *en route* he tells me how far he was in the Affair of Favras. It seems that when it began to take Wind a little, Mirabeau and others endeavored to make him the Cat's paw that in Case of Need he might be converted into the Scape Goat. I sup with the Count de La Marck who is shortly to leave Town. I ask him whether he intends for Germany and as far as Vienna. He says that he does. He says that he means to go to his *Terre* and spend some Time in Hunting, and in meditating on what he has seen for the last three Years. He does not incline to buy

American Lands. The british Embassadress is here and complains a little of Neglect, which I assure her arises from Business. This is true, but besides, I think she is a little *préoccupé* [sic] just now. The Weather is very pleasant but very dry and grows daily colder.

Friday 30 *Sep.* 1791. — Write. The King goes this Day to terminate the Session of the Assembly, or rather, to bid them farewell. About four oClock I go to the Louvre. Send my Carriage for my friend but she misses it and they stay away so long that I accept of Dinner here instead of going to Monsieur de Montmorin's. Visit in the Evening at Madame de Staahl's and Madame de Vanoises's who are both abroad. Spend the Evening at Mad.ᵉ de La Borde's. The Weather is dry and grows cooler.

President Washington to Gouverneur Morris

Philadelphia July 28th 1791.

Dear Sir,

I have now before me your favors of the 22ᵈ of November — the 1ˢᵗ & 24th of December 1790 — and of the 9th of March 1791.—

The Plateaux which you had the goodness to procure for me, arrived safe; and the account of them has been settled, as you desired, with Mr. R. Morris. — For this additional mark of attention to my wishes, I pray you to accept my thanks. —

The communications in your several letters, relative to the state of affairs in Europe, are very gratefully received; and I should be glad if it was in my power to reply to them more in the detail than I am able to do. — But my public duties, which are at all times sufficiently numerous, being now much accumulated by an absence of more than three months from the Seat of Government, make the present a very busy moment for me. —

The change of systems, which have so long prevailed in Europe, will, undoubtedly, affect us in a degree proportioned to our political or commercial connexions with the several nations of it. — But I trust we shall never so far lose sight of our own Interest & happiness as to become, unnecessarily, a party in their political disputes. — Our local situation enables us to maintain that state with respect to them, which otherwise, could not, perhaps, be preserved by human wisdom. — The present moment seems pregnant with great events, but, as you observe, it is beyond the ken of mortal foresight, to determine what will be the result of those changes which are either making, or contemplated in the general system of Europe. — Although as fellowmen we sincerely lament the disorders, oppressions & incertitude which frequently attend national events; and which our European brethren must feel; yet we cannot but hope, that it will terminate very much in favor of the Rights of Man. — And, that a change there, will be favorable to this Country, I have no doubt. — For under the former system we were seen either in the distresses of War, or viewed after the peace in a most unfavorable light through the medium of our distracted State. — In neither point could we appear of much consequence among nations. — And should affairs continue in Europe in the same state they were when these impressions respecting us were received, it would not be an easy matter to remove the prejudices imbibed against us. — A change of system will open a new view of things — & we shall then burst upon them as it were with redoubled advantages. —

Should we, under the present state of affairs, form connexions, other than we now have, with any European Powers, much must be considered in effecting them, on the score of our increasing importance as a Nation; — and at the sametime, should a treaty be formed with a nation whose circumstances may not at that moment be very bright, much delicacy w^d be necessary in order to shew that no undue advantages were taken on that account. For unless treaties are mutually beneficial to the parties, it is vain to hope for a continuance of them beyond the moment when the one which conceives itself over-reached is in a situation to break off the connexion. — And I believe it is among nations as with individuals — the party taking advantage of the distresses of another will lose infinitely more in the opinion of mankind, & in subsequent events, than he will gain by the stroke of the moment. —

In my late tour through the Southern States, I experienced great satisfaction in seeing the good effects of the general Government in that part of the Union. — The people at large have felt the security which it gives, and the equal justice which it administers to them. — The Farmer — the Merchant — and the Mechanic have seen their several Interests attended to, and from thence they unite in placing a confidence in their Representatives, as well as in those in whose hands the Execution of the Laws is placed. — Industry has there taken place of idleness, and œconomy of dissipation. — Two or three years of good crops, and a ready market for the produce of their lands has put every one in good humour; — and in some instances they even impute to the Government what is due only to the goodness of Providence.—

The establishment of public credit, is an immense point gained in our national concerns. — This, I believe, exceeds the expectation of the most sanguine among us. — And a late instance, unparalleled in this Country, has been given of the confidence reposed in our measures, by the rapidity with which the subscriptions to the Bank of the United States were filled. — In two hours after the Books were opened by the Commissioners the whole number of shares were taken up, & four thousand more applied for than were allowed by the Institution; besides a number of Subscriptions which were coming on. — This circumstance was not only pleasing as it related to the confidence in Government; but as it exhibited an unexpected proof of the resources of our Citizens. ——

In one of my letters to you, the account of the number of Inhabitants which would probably be found in the U. States on enumeration — was too large. — The estimate was then founded on the ideas held out by the Gentlemen in Congress of the population of the several States — each of whom (as was very natural) looking through a magnifier would speak of the greatest extent to which there was any probability of their numbers reaching. — Returns of the Census have already been made from several of the States, and tolerably just estimate has been formed (now) in others: by which it appears that we shall hardly reach four Millions; but this you are to take along with it, that the *real* number will greatly exceed the *official* return; because, from religious scruples, some would not give in their lists; — from an apprehension that it was intended as the foundation of a tax, others concealed, or diminished theirs; — and from the indolence of the deputy Enumerators, numbers are omitted. — The authenticated number will, however, be far greater I believe, than has ever been allowed in Europe; and will have no small influence in enabling them to form a more just opinion of our present growing importance than has yet been entertained there. —

This letter goes with one from the Secretary of State, to which I must refer you for what respect your public transactions, and I shall only add to it the repeated assurances of regard and affection with which

I am Dear Sir

Your obed.^t & obliged

G.^o WASHINGTON

Morris to President Washington

Paris 30 Septr 1791

George Washington Esqr

Philadelphia

private

Dear Sir

Mr Short has delivered to me within these few Days your favor of the twenty eighth of July. I cannot express to you what I felt on reading it. The View which it gives of our Prosperity as a Nation swelled my Bosom with Emotions which none can know but those who have experienced them. The wonderful Change which has been effected in our Affairs by the Operation of the general Government has exceeded the Predictions of its warmest Friends. How great a Source of Joy is this to those who have been at all instrumental in its formation and Establishment, those especially to whom Providence in his Bounty has imparted a sincere Affection for their fellow Men. Yes, my dear Sir, Man is not meerly a selfish nor a material Being, and I attest your Heart to witness that Truth from the Conviction of its own Feelings.

The King has at length, as you will have seen, accepted the new Constitution and been in Consequence liberated from his Arrest.

It is a general and almost universal Conviction that this Constitution is inexecutable. The Makers to a Man condemn it. Judge what must be the Opinion of others. M.ʳ Short will doubtless forward all the public Documents respecting it, and therefore I shall not trouble you with any of them. His Majesty is to go in about an Hour hence to close the Session of the national Assembly, and then they leave the field to their Successors. His present Business is to make himself popular; indeed his Life and Crown depend upon it, for the Constitution is such that he must soon be more or less than he is at present, and fortunately he begins to think so, but unfortunately his Advisers have neither the Sense nor the Spirit which the Occasion calls for. The new Assembly as far as can at present be determined is deeply imbued with republican or rather democratical Principles. The Southern Part of the Kingdom is in the same Disposition. The northern is ecclesiastical in its Temper. The Eastern is attached to Germany and would gladly be reunited to the Empire. Normandy is aristocratical and so is Part of Brittainy. The interior Part of the Kingdom is monarchical. This Map is (you may rely on it) just, for it is the Result of great and expensive Investigation made by Government; and I think you will be able by the Help of it and of the few Observations which precede it, fully to understand many Things which would not otherwise perhaps be so easily unriddled. You doubtless recollect that the now expiring Assembly was convened to arrange the Finances, and you will perhaps be surprized to learn that after consuming Church Property to the Amount of one hundred Millions Sterling they leave this Department much worse than they found it. Such however is the Fact, and the Chance now is (in my Opinion) rather for than against a Bankruptcy.

The Aristocrats who are gone and going in great Number to join the Refugee Princes, believe sincerely in a Coalition of the Powers of Europe to reinstate their Sovereign in his antient Authorities, but I believe they are very much mistaken. Nothing of Consequence can be attempted this Year and many Things may happen before the Month of June next, were the several Potentates in earnest. I am led to imagine that their Views are very different from those which are now assigned to them, and it is very far from impossible that the Attempt (if any) will so far as france is concerned be confined to a Dismemberment. The weak Side of this Kingdom as Matters now stand is Flanders, but were the Provinces of Alsace, Lorraine, French Flanders and Artois rent away the Capital would be constantly exposed to the Visits of an Enemy. These Provinces were you know acquired at an immense Expence of Blood and Treasure and if Louis the fourteenth could have succeeded in making the Rhine his Boundary, from Switzerland to the Ocean, he would have obtained the Advantages almost of an insular Position. Indeed it is difficult to abstain from the Wish that the Countries included within that Boundary were united under a free efficient Government, since it would in all human Probability be the Means of dispensing the Blessings of Freedom in no distant Period to all Europe. But on this Subject it is now permitted to a rational Being to form rather Wishes than Hopes, much less Expectations. I will enclose herein a Note just now received of the latest Intelligence from Coblentz; it is written by the Prince de Condé to his confidential Friend here and is accompanied by the Request that all french Gentlemen capable of actual Service will immediately repair to the Standard of Royalty beyond the Rhine, or rather on the Banks of that River. To the Troops mentioned in this Note are added by the Counter Revolutionists here 15,000 Hessians and 16,000 French Refugees so that exclusively of what the Emperor may bring forward they muster an Army *on Paper* of 100,000 Men. The Emperor has about 50,000 Men in the low Countries. But all these Appearances, and the proposed Congress of Embassadors at Aix la Chapelle, do not in the least change my Opinion that Nothing serious will be attempted this Year of our Lord.

M.᷍ de Montmorin has resigned and the Count de Moustiers is named as his Successor, but whether he will accept seems to be very doubtful. He is now at Berlin, and as he is an intimate of Monsieur de Calonne who is one main Spring of the Counter Revolution he is I presume in the Secret of what may be really in Agitation. This on one Side, and on the other an Office the Power and Authority of which is just Nothing at all; for you will observe that by the new Constitution every Treaty and Convention whatsoever must be submitted to the Investigation of the Assembly, to be by them accepted or rejected.

You will have seen I suppose, ere this arrives, what has been done here respecting the Colonies. It is supposed that they will be perfectly satisfied because their internal Legislation is left to themselves; but I much doubt of this, for their Commerce, which involves their Existence, is left entirely at the Mercy of the Assembly which will not be over attentive to their Interests when they fall into Competition with those of the Mother Country. I send out to M! Morris a Bundle of Pamphlets written here by a M! de Comeré according to Hints and Observations which I furnished to him. M! Morris will give you one, and you will see that it was calculated to produce a liberal System of colonial Government beneficial to them and to us. In order to bring it about it was proposed that Commissioners should be sent out with full Powers to treat with the Colonial Assemblies, and could that have been carried this Pamphlet would have been the Ground Work of the Instructions to the Commissioners. The Proposition was rejected, but as it is more than probable that the Colonies will have had a full Taste of the Sweets of free Trade before the Troubles are composed, and as they will have learnt that Fear can produce what Reason could not, I do expect that at Length this Government must come into some such Measure, and thereby not only the Stumbling Block will be taken out of the Way to useful Treaty between France and the United States, but at the same Time and by the same Means the Road will be laid open for solid Connection with Great Britain. In all Cases we have the Consolation, that if the Powers of Europe by their excluding Principles deprive us of the needful Vent for our Produce, which becomes daily more and more abundant, we shall from the Cheapness of Living and of raw Materials which result from that Circumstance make great and rapid Progress in useful Manufactures. This alone is wanting to compleat our Independence. We shall then be as it were a World by ourselves, and far from the Jarrs and Wars of Europe, their various Revolutions will serve meerly to instruct and amuse. Like the roaring of a tempestuous Sea, which at a certain Distance becomes a pleasing Sound.

Farewell my dear Sir, may you be well and happy is the sincere Wish of   yours

Extract: G. Morris to Robert Morris

Paris 30 Sepr 1791

... The Count de Moustiers is appointed Minister of foreign
Affairs here. I know not whether he will accept but you will see
in this Appointment that our friend La Fayette has no Kind of
Influence. He is about to retire into Dauphiné [corrected later
to Auvergne] to spend the Winter on his Estate. The King and
Queen detest him. And the Princes and Nobles hold him in
Contempt and abhorrence so that his Sun seems to be totally
set,[1] unless he should put himself at the Head of the republican
Party who at present are much opposed to him. All this results
from Feebleness of Character and the Spirit of Intrigue, which
bring forward the Courtier but ruin the Statesman. I am very
sorry for him because I believe he meant well.

---

[1] Accurate as far as it goes. Morris could only gauge Paris feeling; he knew
nothing of La Fayette's triumphal progress to Chavaniac, his castle in the
foothills of Auvergne, where his adoring wife will have her first respite from
deadly fear for his bodily safety and from all the odd fish he brought to their
Paris house, and those civic priests who to her deep piety were no priests at
all. La Fayette abolishes his post as Commandant of National Guard; generals of division are to command in turn. He and Pétion are nominated to succeed Mayor Bailly; out of 80,000 electors only one-eighth vote, of these, two-
thirds elect November 16 the King's sworn enemy, republican Pétion. La Fayette cannot bear tranquillity for long; Girondists will declare war; he will soon
be commanding an undisciplined, ill-found army on the northern frontier.

X

LEGISLATIVE ASSEMBLY

OCTOBER 1791

Saturday 1 *Oct*.. — Write. Mr Brémond comes to Breakfast. He tells me that Mr Delessart has another Person in Contemplation for the Treasury Office. Mr Short calls and speaks to me about opening a Loan in Antwerp. I desire him to give me a Note of what he wants to do and what he will agree to do and that I will write in Conformity. I dine with Monsr de Montmorin. After Dinner ask him again for my Discourse. He promises on his Honor to give it me. I desire him to give the King my Letter ab.^t Subsistence. That I care Nothing for the Event but it is his Duty to lay the Matter before his Majesty. I ask him who made the King's Speech, which is excellent. He assures me that the Ground Work is by the King himself. I desire him to make the King observe the Difference of Effect between this and those long Stories which they made him tell heretofore. He says that he has already done so. I go to the Louvre, and having staid a little while visit Madame de Wit, then return to the Louvre to meet Short. He desires me not to write till some Days hence to Antwerp. The Bishop d'Autun, who comes in, takes him aside and holds a long Conference which I conjecture relates to the Debt from Am.^a to France, which the pious Bishop wishes to make Something out of. Return Home early. The Weather very pleasant with a little Fire.

Sunday 2. — Write. Dine at the Louvre. After Dinner visit Madame de Stahl who has a Motley Company which she says have partaken of a Coalition Dinner. There is Beaumetz, the

Bishop d'Autun, Alexander Lameth, the Prince de Broglio &c.ᵃ, &c.ᵃ. Malouet[1] comes in and also the Count de La Marck who converses with Madame, I observe, *en particulier*. As to the others who dined with her, their Coalition seems natural enough. Ségur is here, who tells me he has asked for the Ambassade de Londres and is told that it will meet with no Difficulty but must be left to the Successor of Monsieur de Montmorin. Go hence to the british Embassador's. Stay a little while and leave them at Play. Return Home and write. Fine Weather.

Monday 3. — Write. Dine at the Restorateur's; call on Grand et Comp: and sell a Bill of Exchange on London. Visit my friend. Spend an interesting Moment with her; she is in Distress and I administer Consolation. Sup at Madame de Guibert's where I am *ennuié jusqu'aux yeux*. Fine Weather.

Tuesday 4. — Write. Dine at the Louvre. Spend the Evening at Madᵉ de Witt's. Nothing.

Wednesday 5. — Write. Dine with Mʳ Short. Mʳ Franklin came in Consequence of a Note and had not yet written to London in Completion of the Agreement with Messieurs Le Couteulx. We settle this Matter for ToMorrow's Post. After Dinner I visit La Fayette who receives me very coldly. I am not surprized at this. Go thence to the british Embassador's and take Tea. Thence to Madᵉ du Bourg's who is abroad. Visit at the Louvre and then go to sup at the Count de La Marck's. He assures me that he is concerned in no Party or Coalition of Parties. That he despises every Man almost in the Country & means to enter into the Service of some foreign Prince. The Bishop d'Autun sups here and I cannot help thinking there is some Mistery in all this; but what I think I can perceive pretty clearly is that he is much disappointed in his Expectations. The Members of the late Assembly are all high toned in their Reprehension of this Day's Work of their Successors,[2] which is too little respectful towards

---

[1] Pierre-Victor Malouet (1740–1814) consulted by the King in secret. Wanted a constitutional monarchy on British model; had founded club of *Impartiaux*, 1790, soon dubbed *Club Monarchique*. Had spent five years in San Domingo as commissary.

[2] Paralytic Couthon, whining from his wheeled-chair, wishing to set the tone of the recently elected *Assemblée Législative*, had got it decreed that the King have no special seat, be not addressed as Majesty. Paris still had man-

the King. Are they hurt that any others should exceed them in Marks of Indignity? We spend on the whole a pleasant Evening. The Weather is very fine.

Thursday 6. — Rectify Errors in this Journal owing to a Neglect of two Days. Having slept very little I am incapable of Business. Read. Brémond brings me a Publication of Bergasse. Chaumont calls on me. I dine at the Restorateur's and visit after Dinner Mad.ᵉ du Bourg, who has been at the Salon and is at Dinner with Mons.ʳ de Laval. Go hence to Mons.ʳ de Montmorin's and thence to the Louvre, where my friend is just returned fatigued from Rainci. I tell her the Reason of the Coldness which she complains of on my Part. The national Assembly, which had Yesterday determined not to address the King by the Title of Sire or votre Majesté and to place him on a level with their President &c.ᵃ, &c.ᵃ, have this Day rescinded those Resolutions as they find the Current of Opinion in Paris to be against such Measures. Return Home early. The Weather is fine.

Friday 7. — Write this Morning. Call at the Louvre. My friend is in Distress for her Sister who has fled from her House to avoid the Pursuit of her Husband's Creditors. This Husband has it seems spent her Fortune and gone into all sort of vilainous Extravagance and Folly. I dine with the Count de Montmorin who has not yet presented to the King my Letter on Subsistence. This is ill done and I think he will live to repent it. Go again to the Louvre where I find M.ʳ Morris and Lord Holland.[1] They make a terribly long Visit and altho I stay two Hours I leave them there. Call at Madame de La Borde's and having staid a little while go to Mad.ᵉ de Staahl's and spend the Evening. *Rien de marquante* here except that from the Manner in which she mentions the King's Speech I am led to believe that it is not written by her particular friends. This Morning the Weather threatens and is dirty in the Evening with a Southerly Wind.

Saturday 8. — Write this Morning. Go to the Louvre and while my Carriage is gone for Mademoiselle Duplessis embrace my

---

ners; even the Funds were shocked, falling so low that the Assembly ate its words the following day. The King's tactless delay in visiting it had piqued it into a stupid vote.

[1] Second Baron Holland, brother of Charles James Fox.

friend. Go to the Salon, where I meet Mad. de Fontenille. Dine
with her and go after Dinner to Bergasse's. Read as much of his
Reply to Montesquiou as is already finished. Thence to the
Louvre where I spend the Evening. The Weather is damp but
agreable.

Sunday 9. — Write all the Morning. Dine at the Louvre; go
afterwards with my friend to Chaillot and thence into the Fauxbourg S.t Germain. We visit Mad. de La Tour and afterwards, she
being abroad, call on Mad. de La Borde where I get out. She asks
me what the Queen is to do to become more popular. I tell her,
after considering a little while, that she must write a Letter to the
Emperor and contrive to have it intercepted &c.ª. This is an excellent little Stroke if well executed but otherwise it is wretched.
Return Home. The Weather is mild and pleasant. Write till late.

Monday 10. — This Morning write. Brémond and Cormeré
call on me. Send off my Letters for America which M.r Franklin
promises to forward by the Cook who is going out. Dine at Home.
After Dinner visit Mad. de Flahaut and as she is by Appointment
alone we consummate but in a second Operation there is an
Alarm, which with the Expectation of Monsieur le Mari leads us
to quit this Scene. Go to the Couturière's, and to spend a Half
Hour while the Work is finishing, we walk in the Garden of the
Hôtel de Biron. Nothing worth looking at here but there is a
great Extent of Ground. Take up Mademoiselle Duplessis and
having left the Ladies at the Louvre I visit Mad. de Fontenille.
Sit awhile and then leave my Name with Mad. de Corney. Visit
Mad. de Vannoise and afterwards leave my Name for Mad. de
Cantalue. Go to the Louvre and thence to spend the Evening at
Mad. de Guibert's. M.r Short tells me that Col.º Ternant arrived
in America the 9 August. The Weather has been rainy last Night
and cloudy this Morning but this Evening it is pleasant.

Extract from Morris to Robert Morris

Paris 10 October 1791.

... this Morning I am told that it is in Contemplation to chuse
him for Mayor of Paris [La Fayette].

The People of this City are become wonderfully fond of the King and have a thorough Contempt for the Assembly, who are in general what used to be called at Philadelphia the blue Stockings. There is however this Difference between the two Capitals, that with you virtuous Poverty is respected but here Splendor is indispensible. Judge the Consequence. And to enlighten that Judgment know that at this Moment they stand on the Brink of Bankruptcy which can only be avoided by encreasing the Vigor of the executive Magistrate. This becomes daily more and more apparent and Paris exists as it were on the Interest of the national Debt. These Facts will enable you to understand why the other Evening at the Italian Comedy, as it is called, the Parterre or People cried out continually *Vive le roi! Vive la Reine! Vive la famille royale! Sire, vive votre Majesté!* These Words *Sire* and *Majesté* were you know proscribed by the Assembly, which was obliged by a strong Expression of the popular Sentiment to retract that Decree the very next Day. A patriot in the Midst of this Acclamation took into his Head to cry *Vive la Nation!* but the rest silenced him immediately. Now my dear friend this is the very same People which when the King was brought back from his Excursion whipt a democratic Dutchess of my Acquaintance because they heard only the last part of what she said, which was '*il ne faut pas dire vive le roi.*' She had the good Sense to desire the Gentleman who was with her to leave her. Whipping is you know an Operation which a Lady would rather undergo among Strangers than before her Acquaintance.

Tuesday 11. — This Morning I walk, being in great Want of Exercise. Go to the Louvre. My friend is dressing and Mʳ Windham comes in. She goes abroad on Business. I go to the Salon to look at the Paintings, thence to the Tuilleries. Dress, and dine with Mʳ Short. After Dinner go to Desnos the Geographer's, thence to visit at the Louvre and return Home to write. The Weather is very pleasant.

Wednesday 12. — Mʳ Brémond calls this Morning and tells me that he will bring Monsieur de La Sonde ToMorrow to communicate the Plan now in Agitation for detaching the Emperor from the Cause of the Princes. I go to Marly and dine with Madame du Bourg. We have a disagreable rainy Day. On my Return to Town I receive unpleasant Information respecting the Delaware Works in a Letter from R. M.. Of Course I spend alone a disagreable Evening.

Thursday 13. — M.ʳ Brémond calls this Morning and tells me that Monsieur de La Sonde cannot come till To Morrow. Chaumont calls on me. I dine with the british Embassadress. After Dinner, pretty late in the Afternoon, call at the Louvre but my friend is abroad. Visit Madame de La Borde where Mons.ᵉ de La Colombe arrives and talks a Deal of strange Things. *Bavardage.* I come Home and write. A rainy disagreable Day.

Friday 14. — M.ʳ Brémond and M.ʳ de La Sonde breakfast with me this Morning. I write. Go to the Louvre where I find Lord Holland. As he goes away the bishop comes and I decamp. Go to the Salon and thence to Monsieur de Montmorin's to dine. Tell him after Dinner that the Republicans mean to begin their Attack by the civil List and suggest to him the Means of preventing it. Go to visit Mad.ᵉ du Bourg. Thence to Mad.ᵉ de La Borde's. Leave this just as my friend enters; after exchanging the usual Compliments go to Mad.ᵉ de Stahl's where I spend the Evening. Mad.ᵉ de Vauban indulges herself in talking of her friend La Marc. Come away early. Monsieur de La Sonde gave me his Memoire to read and is to send me a Copy of it. S.ᵗ Foi has for three Days past been in Conference on this Subject with the Secretary of M.ʳ de Metternich. Montmorin tells me that de Moustiers has declined accepting but will come on soon to Paris. The Viscomte de Ségur told me that he thought Barthélémi would be appointed here and de Moustiers in Switzerland. He may have gleaned Something. Montmorin says he will give me my Memoire when he has had it copied and I must call some Morning. He says Nothing can be done for supplying Provisions to Paris. I tell him that I am very glad not to be charged with that Business. That Mischiefs will arise of which Neither he nor I will have any Thing to accuse ourselves *as we have done all in our Power.* I think he has not. The Weather has grown very cool this Evening.

Saturday 15. — Write. M.ʳ Franklin calls this Morning and I give him a Letter to send to R. M.. Dress and visit Le Couteulx who has rec.ᵈ Letters from America with which he is well content.

Converse with him about the Sale of Lands, which he begins to listen to with Attention. Call at the Count de Ségur's but he is not yet arrived. Dine at the Restorateur's and then go to the Louvre where to my great Surprize I find a numerous Company of English. Mad.ᵉ ought to have been alone. As soon as they have done Dinner I leave her and go to the british Embassador's. Lady Sutherland is not at Home. Call on Mad.ᵉ de Ségur again. She is just arrived. Visit Mad.ᵉ de Wit, leave my Name with Mad.ᵉ de Fontenille and then go again to the Louvre. Tell Mons.ʳ de La Porte what has passed with Monsieur de Montmorin respecting the Subsistence. Give him Hints also as to the Means of defeating the Republicans. The Weather is very pleasant.

Sunday 16. — This Morning walk out and go to the Louvre. Spend Half an Hour tête à tête with my friend and tho' exposed to Interruptions we consummate. I return Home and Mons.ʳ Seward calls upon me. I get from Van Staphorst and lend to him the *Federalist*. Go to Passy and dine with M.ʳ Grand. Return to the Louvre. Sit awhile with my friend and Mad.ˡˡᵉ Duplessis. This last is much distressed and my friend tells me that her Pension is stopped and she knows not what to do. Poor Girl, she spends her Days and Nights in Tears. We go together to Mad.ᵉ de Guibert's. I set them down on our Return and go to the Luxembourg. Spend the Evening here. Mad.ᵉ de Sardis seems to be a little en Train with Lord Robert Fitzgerald; this interferes with an Idea rather than a Plan of mine. There is a Pole here whom I saw at Mad.ᵉ de Stahl's. He was a principal Agent in their late Revolution. I converse with him a little and drop the Idea that perhaps an Opportunity may speedily present itself to possess the Country which lies between Poland and the Baltic. He shews on this Subject the Eagerness which I expected. Get Home a little after twelve. The Weather is grown colder. It was fair at Noon but Winter seems to be approaching.

Monday 17. — Write. Send in a blank Cover 500# to Mad.ˡˡᵉ Duplessis with Precautions of every Kind to prevent Discovery. Go to the Louvre and while my Carriage is gone for Mad.ˡˡᵉ we celebrate. Take up M.ʳ Franklin and we dine together at the Restorateur's. After Dinner I go again to the Louvre and while Mad.ˡˡᵉ gets her Head dressed ... We go to Mad.ᵉ de Damas' and

while Mad.^{le} pays a Visit there we remain in the Carriage ... Go
to Mad.^e de Guibert's where we spend the Evening. After Supper
I am *un peu aimable* and as I come away have a curious Conversation with Lady Anne Lindsay who is desperately in Love with M.^r
Windham and tortured by Jealousy. I tell her that if she wishes
to bring back a Lover she must alarm his Fears and if she chuses
to make Use of me I am at her Orders.¹ Tell her how she ought to
act, and she says that if it becomes necessary she will apply to
me. The Weather, which has been dirty, is grown very pleasant
this Evening.

Tuesday 18. — This Morning immediately after Breakfast I
dress and go to the Count de Moustier's. He appears very glad to
see me and we converse about the State of Affairs. He seems inclined to accept the Office of foreign Affairs. We go together in
my Carriage as far as the Count de Ségur's where he takes his own
and in the Way I communicate to him the Means of changing the
french Constitution and making at the same Time a considerable
Acquisition of Territory. He shews an Attachment to the Interest of Prussia. Pay a long Visit to the Count de Ségur. He is intriguing to the very Eyes while he declares his Determination to
be quiet. It is very possible, however, that he tells the Truth, for
Man deceives himself oftener than he deceives others. Go to the
Louvre where I stay Dinner. In my Way I left my Name at Lady
Sutherland's in coming from Monsieur de Montmorin's where I
declined staying as he was much engaged. After Dinner I pay a
Visit to Monsieur de Montmorin and find him much agitated.
After staying some Time in the Salon we retire together and he
gives me at last the Speech I had prepared for the King. He then
tells me that his Heart is full and he must unburthen it. That La
Marck being gone he has Nobody but me whom he can trust. He

---

¹ The lady having crossed the Rubicon of forty which Morris had not yet
reached, it is with gallant irony that he offers himself as runner-up in her flirta-
tion with Windham. Not all persiflage, for gossip Fanny Burney had reported
them engaged a year ago: 'I hear Lady Anne Lyndsay is going to be married
to Mr. Wyndham, the member for Norwich, the excentric Mr. Wyndham. His
choice suits that character.' Miss Burney thought him 'one of the most agreable, spirited, well-bred and brilliant conversers I have ever spoken with — a
very elegant figure, and an air of fashion and vivacity.' Lady Anne consoles
herself by marrying, 1793, Andrew Barnard, colonial secretary to Lord
Macartney at Cape of Good Hope.

then proceeds to tell me that the King, after appointing du Moustiers and after du Moustier's Acceptance, wishes to be off because
he fears his Reputation as an Aristocrat, and especially the incon-
sequent Conduct of Madame de Bréhan, both of which he, Montmorin, had apprized him of before. He tells me that De Moustiers is at the Hour we are talking in Conversation with the King
and Queen and he feels much wounded that he is not of the Party.
He says that he has proposed two Things, one to have a Council
formed of Persons devoted to the royal Interest who would pursue
the Constitution strictly but with the View to destroy it, and the
other to leave the Ministry as it is but with the Change only of
his own Place and to have a private Council to consist of himself,
Dumoustiers, Malouette and the Abbé de Montesquiou, or if he,
from Respect to his Patron *Monsieur*, should decline, then the
Archbishop of Aix. That they will do Nothing; that he finds his
Measures are disconcerted and he knows not what to count upon.
That he supposes this to come from the Count de Merci who gives
the Queen Counsels well calculated to serve the Interests of
Austria. I tell him that perhaps some Persons have done him ill
Offices at Court. He says No, that he is well received, perfectly
well but ——. He declares that he will quit, let what will happen.
I see however that he will not quit entirely if he can help it. He
tells me that he has not Force enough of Character to pursue the
Measures which he knows to be right. This I well knew. He gives
me a History of what passed respecting the *Cour plénière* in Regard to which, having first opposed the Plan as dangerous and
afterwards insisted on vigorous Measures to carry it thro as the
slightest Symptom of Retreat might prove fatal, he found a different Plan adopted, and then when the King was about to take M.
Necker he told his Majesty that he would give himself a Master
whom he must obey. That subsequent to this Appointment he
took a Course different from that which he had formerly pursued,
and adopted M. Necker's lenient Modes of proceeding. I remind
him that I had frequently pointed out the fatal Consequences of
those Half Way Measures. He acknoweges this and says that
he also saw them but he had not sufficient Vigor of Mind to pursue the Course which appeared to himself to be right. I ask him
what Situation the King and Queen are in with Respect to the

Princes. He says that there is no Understanding between them. I tell him that I am informed that the King receives Letters from his Brothers which he does not communicate. He says that this is true but he reads to him such Parts as relate to public Affairs. I tell him that the Queen, I understand, receives Letters from the Emperor respecting Affairs here. On this Subject he seems to be not quite clear & says again that he apprehends the late Change to arise from Austrian Counsels. He recommends to me the greatest Secrecy in a Style which seems to beg my Pity for so much of human Weakness. After leaving him I go to Mad? de Wit's and leave my Compliments, that I cannot spend the Evening here. Go to the Louvre. I had told my friend, upon observing that Mad.^{lle} Duplessis was still in Tears, that I was fearful she had not rec^d a Letter I had sent her, and communicating the Contents desire her to find out how that Matter is. She is much affected by this. She tells me that she fears it has miscarried. The Bishop d'Autun tells me that de Moustier's Character of Aristocracy is not well relished at Paris. The Weather is pleasant this Day.

Wednesday 19. — This Morning the Count de Moustiers breakfasts with me. He tells me what passed yesterday Evening with the King and Queen. He tells me that I stand high in their Opinion as well as in that of Monsieur de Montmorin. He says the King has offered him the Embassy to England and that he is to stay there untill a proper Opportunity shall offer of placing him in the Ministry, which would at present be dangerous. He wishes me to perswade Montmorin to stay longer, which I promise to attempt. He says he will urge the sending to America for a Supply of Provisions, or rather of Flour, according to my Proposal to Mr de Montmorin. He has some Scheme of Finance in his Head which I must discover if I can. Call at the Louvre and am cold towards my friend in Consequence of her Reception, which is not warm. She is hurt at this. I make my Visit short. Go to the Watch Makers and Petit Dunkerque, thence to Mr de Montmorin's where I dine. After Dinner I exchange a few Words with him but Mad? de Stahl being here and he being obliged to go to Council I promise to dine with him on Saturday next and consider together his Situation after Dinner. Take Mad? de Montmorin to the french Comedy and having set her down leave my Name at the Luxembourg for Mad.ᵉ du Bourg and at Mad.ᵉ de Guibert's, then return Home and write. The Weather is variable.

Thursday 20. — This Morning read and write. I was kept awake Part of last Night by a heavy Gale of Wind. I know not from what Quarter it came but it was very loud. This Morning it blows from the Southwestward with Showers. About three I call at the Louvre and then go to dine at the Restorateur's. After Dinner return to the Louvre and lend my Carriage to Mad.ˡˡᵉ Duplessis but Monsieur le Comte stays with us till Monsieur de Curt arrives. We continue at Play. I then, after Mademoiselle's Return, take my friend to her Sister's and en Route we embrace. She wishes to know why I am cold and serious but I refuse to tell her. Set her and Mad.ᵉ de Boursac down at the Louvre and then return Home and read. The Wind blows again very hard from the Southwest. This is dreadful Weather for the Channel.

Friday 21. — This Morning M.ʳ Brémond calls and tells me what passed yesterday with Monsieur de Montmorin. He says he hinted to him an Intention to attack the Ministry. I write. The Count de Moustiers calls and tells me that he asked an Audience of the Queen on the Subject of Flour. Her Majesty told him that she had never yet seen my Letter to Monsieur de Montmorin and she thinks it is of a Nature not to have escaped her Attention. He desires me to give him a Copy. He then tells me that the King of Prussia will furnish Money to assist in putting the Finances of this Country to rights. He tells me what passed with his prussian Majesty on that Subject and that he intended to head his Armies for re-establishing the french Monarchy. He communicates a Number of Queries which he put to Monsieur D'Urue respecting Finance and he tells me that D'Urue assures him there is not a Man in this Country capable of managing the Finances, there being no one who joins a Knowledge of Money Matters to that of State Affairs. He tells me what passed between the King of Prussia and the Emperor at Pilnitz, as related to him by the King. Leopold began to higgle but the King told him at once that however different their Dominions he would send an equal Force with the Emperor, which astonished the latter. I give him many Hints and Outlines of a Plan for the Finances of this Country and he desires me to write on the Subject. I tell him that a good Constitution is a previous Requisite. That this is the Moment for forming one so as to obtain the royal Consent and I give him some Ideas on this Subject. Tell him that my Plan is, at present, to perswade Monsieur de Montmorin to continue in Place untill he, Moustiers, can be properly admitted, and then to be made President of the Council. That the King must press Monsieur de Montmorin to continue and he must make the Removal of Duportail a Condition, by which Means, if Delessart can be brought about, there will be a Majority in the Council. I am to press this Plan on Monsieur de Montmorin and de Moustiers is on his Side to urge the Court. I dine at Mad.^e de Stahl's and say too much against the Constitution, to which she provoked me by fishing for the Praise of her Father. I did not swallow the bait. Go from hence to the Louvre and sit a while with my friend and Mad.^{lle} Duplessis to procure a pleasant Digestion and then return Home and write. The Wind has been high all Day from the Southwest with Showers.

Saturday 22.^d — Write. Go to the Count de Moustier's. He is not at Home but I sit a little while with Mad.^e de Bréhan and leave for him a Copy of my Letter to Monsieur de Montmorin about flour for Paris. Go to the Louvre and embrace. Dine with Monsr de Montmorin. Before Dinner I go into his Closet and there urge him to continue for some Time longer in Office, then to retire as president of the Council. He will not agree, first because it is impossible to manage the Department well and secondly because he has so pointedly declared his Determination to retire that he cannot retract. I think this last is the strongest Reason. I mention to him S.^{t(e)} Croix as being recommended by the Garde des Sceaux in the Name of all the Ministers. He says that if there were not particular Reasons against admitting him (and I find that these Bottom on pecuniary Foundations) he would be the fittest Person in the World in order to render the Ministry contemptible. He says that if Ségur will not accept, Barthelemi would answer. — Monsieur de Molleville,[1] the Min-

---

[1] Marquis Bertrand de Molleville (1774–1818) is now the King's most trusted Minister, so will not long be tolerated by the *Législative*; deprived of

ister of the Marine, gives us at Dinner the Account of a dreadful
Insurrection of the Blacks at St Domingo. I trust that the
Account (which is not official) is exagerated. After Dinner he
tells me that he had a long Conversation with Demoustiers about
me this Morning and wishes to know my Success with Monsieur
de Montmorin. This leads to a Conversation on the Subject with
Mad.^e de Beaumont in which I communicate the Plans of the
King's Enemies as they have been communicated to me. They
urge me to renew the Attack on Monsieur de Montmorin. I do
so, and he tells me that his Difficulties are insurmountable; that
the Affair of the Princes having Possessions in Alsace is ready
to be reported and he is perswaded that the Assembly will not
do what is right. That the Affair of Avignon ¹ also involves a
very disagreable Dispute with the Pope which he is certain will
be improperly treated by the Assembly. I tell him that these
Objections are trivial. He is only to communicate the whole
Truth to the Assembly and let them decide as they please. That
as to the Treatment of french Subjects in foreign Countries, which
forms a second Head of Complaint, he must remonstrate firmly
on the Part of the Nation and communicate the Result, which
will I acknowledge be unsatisfactory but for that very Reason
desirable. I then tell him that he has done so much to injure
himself with his Order as a Nobleman that he must continue in
Office till he can recover his Reputation with them, to which
Effect the sending of the Abbé de Montesquiou to the Princes
to know what Constitution they wish for will greatly operate.
I had opened this Chapter to him in the Morning, as well as the
Negotiation to be made with the Emperor. I find that this last
Idea of his Order works, I add therefore that he must stay and
thereby defeat the Designs of his Enemies. He recurs then to
his Declarations so publicly made that he would retire: I tell
him that these may be easily obviated because the King can

---

office he becomes head of a secret police to keep watch on republican extremists. His *Memoires* fill out some of Morris's entries.

¹ One of the Constituent Assembly's last official acts decreed that Avignon
be taken back from the Pope and reinstated as French territory. The for and
against became locally a competition in atrocities, sixty persons flung half
killed down disused ice-tower in Papal Palace to avenge revolutionary Le-
scuyer, murdered messily with scissors inside a church.

desire him to continue untill he can find a suitable Successor. The Weather is very fine this Day. As I am about to leave Monsieur de Montmorin's Madame takes me aside to know the Success of my Application to her Husband. I tell her that he does not absolutely agree but I think he will. I think however that he has at Bottom some Reason which he will not communicate as yet. Go from hence to the british Embassador's and the Count de Ségur's and leave my Name for the Ladies. Then visit Mad.ᵉ de Guibert and afterwards Mad.ᵉ de La Suze. At this last Place I am told that the Duke of Orleans has declared his Bankruptcy and put his Affairs into the Hands of Trustees, who allow him a Pension. I did expect to have met the Count de Moustiers here but am disappointed. Return Home and read. Mons.ʳ de Montmorin repeated to me this Morning what he had once mentioned before, viz that he considers it as indispensibly necessary that the Queen should be present at the Discussion of Affairs of the Cabinet, and that for this Purpose there should be a privy Council, to which Mallouette should be admitted. I do not see the Use of this, neither can I conceive his Reason. If he expects thro Mallouette to govern that little Council he mistakes his Man — at least I think so. I told Monsieur de Molleville that it appeared to me most fitting to remove du Portail at present and place there some brave honest Soldier without much Regard to his Abilities, and then when de Moustiers comes forward to place him, de Molleville, as Garde des Sceaux and Bougainville as Minister of the Marine. He approves of this but wishes to stay where he is untill he shall have gained some Reputation by putting the Affairs of that Department in Order.

Sunday 23 October. — This Morning write. M.ʳ Brémond and M.ʳ Richard call. I dine at the Louvre. Visit Lady Sutherland after Dinner. Call on Mad.ᵉ de Ségur, who is abroad, and then return Home and write.

Monday 24. — This Morning write. Brémond calls. Chaumont tells me that all the Lands in the State of New York are sold. That those about the Oneida Lake went off at 3/— per Acre for 60,000 Acres and the Rest at 8.ᵈ. This Rest is I suppose the Land lying between the Waters of the Hudson, Mohawk, Lake Ontario, River S.ᵗ Lawrence and the Lakes Champlain and

George, after taking out of it the Tracts already sold. The greater Part of this is I presume a rugged Mountainous Country. The Count de Moustiers comes and I propose to him a Disposition of the S! Lawrence Lands which promises him a great and certain Advantage. He catches at it and will I think work hard. We discuss many Points respecting public Affairs. I dine with Lady Sutherland. M: Rivarolle who is here entertains us after Dinner with much Conversation. It is pleasant. After Dinner I visit Madame de Ségur, Flahaut, La Borde, Vannoise, all of whom are abroad. Then go to see Le Couteulx who is ill of the Gout. He tells me he has lost 220,000# which a Broker has run off with. Go from hence to Madame de Guibert's where I spend the Evening. The Weather is vastly fine but very cool.

Tuesday 25. — This Morning write. Dine at the Restorateur's. Go to the Louvre and at the Request of my friend leave her for a while. Go to Mad? de Ségur's, who is abroad. To Mad? de Stahl's where I find Mess.ˢ de Malouette and de Moustiers. The former tells me that he has advised Monsieur de Montmorin to quit his Post. He says that the Garde des Sceaux keeps the King in constant Alarm and governs him by his Fears, so that M: de Montmorin has very little Influence left. He says that I am mistaken in my Idea that this Constitution will crumble to pieces of itself. That the Resources from the Assignats will hold out a considerable Time. That by delaying the Liquidation they can procrastinate the Moment of Distress, that the Taxes are tolerably well paid &cᵃ. I persist in my Opinion, notwithstanding that it is now evident that foreign Powers will do Nothing. Indeed I am perswaded that their Efforts would have tended rather to support than to destroy the new System because Mankind generally resist against Violence. De Moustiers shews me a Note he has made and transmitted to the Queen relative to Subsistence. He says he has Reason to believe not only in a Coalition of the different Parties which divided the last Assembly, but that they are interested in the great Speculations of Grain made in the Neighbourhood of Paris. Go to the Louvre and sit with my Friend who is alone, but we are sage.... Return Home and write.

Wednesday 26. — Write. M: Brémond calls and tells me that

the Republican Party count with Certainty upon an Attempt of the King to escape. That they mean to facilitate it and then, laying the Blame of all Events upon the Monarch and his Nobles, they will stop Payment and be ready to meet any Attack whatever. At twelve I go by Appointment to the Count de Moustier's where I meet Monsieur Tolozan. This Meeting is at his Request to confer on the Subject of Subsistence but from what passes I do not see what can have been his Object. Dine at the Louvre. After Dinner take Mad.^{lle} du Plessis to her Mother's and then visit Mad.^e de Ségur. I find that Ségur is ready to accept the Place of Monsieur de Montmorin altho he does not avow it. Return to the Louvre and celebrate while my Carriage is gone for Mad.^{lle}. Spend the Evening here but retire while the Company are at Supper. The Weather is very raw & disagreable.

Thursday 27. — Write. Mr Swan calls. Franklin and Paul Jones dine with me. After Dinner I visit Mr Bertrand de Molleville, the Minister of the Marine. He is denied. I go to the Louvre. My friend is abroad. Return Home and write. Spend the Evening with the Baron de Grand Cour. A very large Company and of Course no Society. Lord Gower tells me that he has quitted Play, on which Circumstance I very sincerely congratulate him. The Weather is pleasant.

Friday 28. — Write. Mr Swan calls and I tell him that I could not find the Minister Yesterday but shall see him to Day. Mr Brémond tells me that he has been to solicit the Interest of Alexander Lameth to get placed. This was by the Recommendation of Pelling. Lameth has promised him and while there he saw Duportail's Man come in with a List of Officers for his Inspection and Approbation, and as he was busied in the Examination Brémond asked to have a friend appointed sub lieutenant which was immediately promised. Mr Jones and Mr Sears call upon me; the former confirms the News of his Brother's Death.[1] I wait on Mr de Molleville and open Mr Swan's Business. I tell him that the making Contracts with the lowest Bidder will not answer in this Country as in England because there the Articles

---

[1] This must be the Philadelphia doctor, buried 24 June, an old friend and correspondent of Morris's who might have saved his leg had he not been away in May, 1780.

always exist within the Power of the Government and consequently if the Contractors fail in their Performance pecuniary
Damages set every Thing right, but here a failure may be of the
most dangerous Consequence and it would frequently be the
Interest of an Enemy to occasion that failure and to pay the
stipulated Penalty. Hence I infer that there should be a moral
Security in Addition to the pecuniary and conclude that any
Contract he may make should be conditional on the Approbation
of the Parties concerned in America by the Minister plenipotentiary there. I next suggest to him that it would be advantageous
to fix a Price for Provisions deliverable either in Europe, America,
the Isle of France or the West Indies, so that only an Order need
be given for the Quantities and Places. Shew him the Advantages
that would result therefrom. I then suggest that it would be
proper to have always on Hand sufficient for six Months Provisions to fifty Ships of the Line and to have every Month a
fresh Month's Supply, so that after deducting what was consumed, the Ballance of the Provisions in Store beyond six Months'
Supply should be sold. I tell him that if his Contract be on good
Terms it will be but a trifling Loss (if any) to the Marine and that
the Commerce will gain what the Marine looses, but that by this
Means they will always be prepared for War. I conclude by
telling him that I am before all Things an American and therefore
he must consider what I say accordingly, but that it may not be
amiss to consult de Moustiers. He is very well pleased with all
this and I think desirous of forming some such Plan. He desires
to have a Sample of the Provisions sent to him, which I promise
shall be done if any of them be left. Communicate to him the
Tricks of his Commis, who are sold to the *Régisseurs* &c.ª. He
tells me what passed this Morning with the King relative to
Monsieur de Montmorin. His Majesty is a little vexed with him
and says that he has been pestering him for six Months to name
a Successor &c.ª. M.ʳ de Molleville's Brother, who is just returned
from Coblentz, tells him that Monsieur de Montmorin is detested
there but that *his* Appointment is approved of. Go to the Louvre.
I find my friend in tête à tête with M.ʳ Stewart and therefore
I make a very short Visit. She desires me to come this Afternoon.
I go to Mad.ᵉ de Foucault's, Mad.ᵉ du Bourg's and Madame de

Ségur's, who are all absent, Mad.ᵉ de Foucault not arrived but
expected this Evening. Go to Mons.ʳ de Montmorin's to dine.
He shews me the Report he intends making to the Assembly. It
is wonderfully little considering the Time he has consumed in
making it. Propose to him some Amendments which I think he
will not adopt and he will repent it if he does not. He declares
War against the News Paper Writers, and these are sometimes
troublesome and sometimes dangerous Enemies. He says that
Ségur has been with him this Morning & accepted. He tells me
that the King has not asked him to stay. To this I reply that
it is his own Fault because he had declared so pointedly his
Determination that the King was exposed thereby to the Mortification of a Denial, but if he would have consented to stay on
such Application being made it would have been made. He says
that he does not know whether he shall continue in Council. He
has told the King that he will stay if he desires it but wishes his
Majesty to consider the Matter well beforehand because if hereafter he should find it convenient to send him away it would be
injurious to both of them. Mʳ Suart comes in to correct the
Style of the Count's Memoire and I leave him. Mallouette comes
during the Dinner and we converse afterwards; he confirms to
me that Monsieur de Montmorin is without Influence. Go to
the Louvre where I find my friend a little cold and vexed. We are
bored by a Duke de Xeres who gives us a Half Hour's Disserta-
tion to prove how disagreable it is to be pestered by *les ennuyeux*.
Never was Precept better supported by Example. He prevents
us from setling our Differences in a tête à tête. Go to Mad.ᵉ de La
Borde's and thence to Mad.ᵉ de Stahl's. Have a long Conversation here with Mad.ᵉ de Beaumont who suffers exceedingly at her
father's Removal from Office. The british Embassadress tells
me that both she and Lord Gower have quitted playing and that
she thinks I like them well enough to be pleased at it. I assure
her of my Attachment, more in Tone and Manner than by Words,
and I think the Seed is not sown on barren Ground. Come Home
early. The Weather is fine but cold.

Saturday 29. — This Morning Mʳ Swan calls and I tell him
what passed with the Minister. He is to send some salt Provisions
immediately. The Count de Moustiers comes in and I shew him

the Maps of the St Laurence Lands. Paul Jones comes in and
while they are here Brémond calls me out to tell me that the
Emigrants expect to enter in January next and that the Queen
is at length agreed to act in Concert with the Princes. This, he
says, is arrived direct from the Prince of Condé this Day. I am
afraid that the Court have some underhand Scheme and if so
they bet a Certainty against an Uncertainty. I go to Van Staphorst's who is abroad. Call on Mr Jones and take them to look
for Apartments in the Palais royal; fix them at the Hôtel de
Paris. We dine together at the Restorateur's. After Dinner I
go to the Louvre. They are just risen from Dinner and Madame,
the bishop and Monsr de Ste Foi set down to piquet. She receives
me with great Coldness. Is going to the Comedy. I stay till
the Party is over and in going down Stairs express ironically my
Thanks for the Reception I meet and bid her good Night in a
Style which implies my Determination not to come again. Call
on Mad.^e de Ségur and Mad.^e de Vanoise. They are both abroad
and I return Home and take Tea. Spend the Evening at the
Vicomte de Ségur's. The News from Hispaniola are very bad and
I think exaggerated, but the Negroes are in Revolt and employed
in burning the Plantations and murdering their Masters.   De
Moustiers says he imagines Mr de Montmorin has a Mind to
secure to himself the british Embassy and have him sent to
Switzerland. He is therefore determined to push the Queen on
that Subject. I advise him to let that alone and tell him the
News brought to me this Morning. He tells me that his friend
Durue seems inclined to make a Purchase of Land. The Weather
is very fine but cold.

Sunday 30. — This Morning write. Dine at Mr Grand's. Visit
Mad.^e de Ségur who tells me that her Husband has this Morning
resigned the Office of foreign Affairs which he had accepted
yesterday. I congratulate her on this Event. Spend the Evening
at Mad.^e du Bourg's where I learn from Monsieur de Blacon that
the Official Intelligence is arrived of the Revolt at St Domingo,
which is very serious. Monsr de La Sonde, who called this Morning with Monsieur Brémond, told me that he has further Intel-.
ligence from Mr Metternich and he tells me that Monsieur de La
Porte is this Evening to submit to the King a Plan sent at his

Majesty's Request by Mons? de Murier,¹ who he says is a little fellow of Sense, Information and unconquerable Spirit. I am to know whether his Majesty adopts it. Mad? de Ségur tells me that her Husband has grounded his Refusal on the Treatment the Ministers met with yesterday from the Assembly. The Weather this Day has been very fine but cold.

Monday 31 *October.* — M? de Corméré calls this Morning. Brémond breakfasted with me. De Corméré brings Half his Plan of Finance for S? Domingue but has forgot the other Half. He goes away next Week and I am to write by him. I drop the Idea that this Island will become independent. He seizes it and says that such is his Object. I write. A Message from my friend to dine with her. I go thither and find both Monsieur and Mad?ʰᵉ. My Reception is very formal. She is pale, thin, and complains of her Nerves. I ask what is the Matter. Nothing. Her Appetite is gone and I find that on the whole she is miserable. In the Evening I take her Hand in Token of Peace and as she is rather cold and formal I tell her it was not worth while to send for me if she meant to preserve that Behaviour. This leads to Explanation. I will not enter into Justifications one Way or the other but I tell her I will judge for myself, leaving her the same Liberty. She tells me that she was taken ill at the Theatre and continued so during the whole Piece. That she has been miserable ever since. Indeed this appears evidently enough. I forgive and promise to see her Tomorrow but advise her to take Care how she indulges in such Whims hereafter. Return Home and write. The Weather is very fine but cold. Last Night it froze Half an Inch of Ice.

---

¹ General Dumouriez, who will be Minister of Foreign Affairs after Morris's appointment, becoming later the hero of the French Republic's first great military successes.

NOVEMBER 1791

Tuesday 1 Nov. — M. de Cormeré comes this Morning with the other Half of his Plan and tells me that the Plan is already formed and tolerably well digested for establishing the Independence of S. Domingue. I call on Mad. Foucault but before she appears am obliged to go to Dinner. M. Jones was with me this Morning. I dine with M. Tolozen. The Count de Moustiers, Mons. de Mallouette, de Virieux, Mallet du Pin[1] and Mons. Gitet are our Company, all staunch royalists. At coming away Mons. —— follows me to desire I will stay and converse about the Subsistence. I tell him it is unnecessary. That I should ask for 6 M.ns which I am sure they cannot furnish. I learnt here that the Colonists are about to present a Petition to the King which will go just Half Way to the Mark and is of Course good for Nothing. Go to the Louvre and lend my Carriage to Mad.lle. We embrace cordially. I stay till 9 oC.k and then go to spend the Evening at Mad. De Witt's. Return Home at eleven. The Weather is raw, a damp Cold which feels half Way between Rain and Snow.

Wednesday 2. — M. Brémond brings me a Piece, or rather the Begining of a Piece which he is preparing on the Finances in Reply to Mons. de Montesquiou. I correct it. Swan calls. I go to the Louvre for an Instant. Then go to dine with Mad. Foucault. The Maître d'hôtel has shot himself this Morning so that we dine late. After Dinner Mad. gives me an Account of the Conduct of Mad. de Nadaillac at Aix la Chapelle and Spa which is ridiculous enough. Go to Le Couteulx's and sit with

---

[1] Mallet-du-Pan (1749–1800) edits newspapers; wants equal guaranty for rights of nation and of monarch. Sent by the King on secret mission to sovereigns allied against France he will try in vain to prevent intrigues of *émigrés* who dictate the insolent Brunswick Manifesto.

them some Time. Thence to the Louvre where I stay a little while with Monsieur de Ste Foi for Mad.^e to arrive, and then bid her good Night. Return Home and write. The Weather is raw and cold.

Thursday 3. — Write. At two go to Mr de Molleville's and speak to him about Swan's Application. He has not yet tried the Provisions sent. He says that many Objections are made against being supplied from America, such as the Distance, the Uncertainty &c.^a, &c.^a. He has desired that they should be detailed in writing and will place his Observations in the Margin. He tells me that he is determined not to wait for the Attack of the Assembly but will always find them in Work. For this Purpose he has already proposed to them a Number of Decrees and of such Nature that they will be in the wrong if they do not adopt them. He is to send me a Copy. He tells me that he proposed me the other Day at Monsieur de Montmorin's as Minister of Foreign Affairs. I laugh at this. Discuss with him the Manner of treating their Colonies if they mean to secure their Fidelity &c.^a. Go to Monsieur de Montmorin's. He is abroad. I visit Mad.^e and Mad.^e de Beaumont. There is over this Family an air *lugubre et très sombre*. Mad.^e de Beaumont tells me that her Father has Nothing and seems to be very uncertain about his future Destiny. Dine with the british Embassadress. The Princess de Tarente [1] is here who tells me that the Queen often talks to her of me when they are riding together. I reply only by a Bow. She repeats it and dwells on the Subject but I make only the same Reply. Call on Mesdames de Stahl and Dubourg who are both abroad. Go to the Louvre. My friend complains of having been alone all the Morning and Evening. It is not my fault. At nine come Home and write.

Friday 4. — This Morning I write. Visit Mr Jones, then go to the Louvre and dine. While my Carriage goes for Mad.^lle Duples-

---

[1] Princesse de Tarente, in waiting on Marie-Antoinette, becomes one of the Court's most heroic figures, her courage in the September massacres surprising the murderers into letting her go free, in spite of her scornful refusal to bear witness against her Queen. She had been appointed Dame d'Honneur, 1785, and her devotion knew no bounds. Her *mémoires* give in detail fatal days of 20 July and 10 August inside the Tuileries. Born Louise de Châtillon, daughter of Duc de La Vallière; wife of Charles de La Trémoïlle, Prince de Tarente.

sis we embrace. After Dinner go to the french Comedy and pass the Evening at Mad.̣ de La Borde's. The Weather is cold.

Saturday 5. — Write. Call a Moment at the Louvre and go to dine with Mad.̣ Foucault. Bougainville comes in and tells me that he conversed t'other Day with Monsieur de Molleville about the Provisioning of the Marine from America, and that there are some very extraordinary Circumstances which he will call and communicate To Morrow Morning. Go to the Louvre and sit awhile with my friend who has Company. Return Home and write.

Sunday 6. — Write. M.ͬ Short calls and stays a long Time. The Question is in Regard to Loans for the United States in Antwerp. He stickles much about the Commission and desires me to let Wolf know that I have no Share in it, because that in a Letter written to Grand's House from Genoa he observes that they count on having the Commission. M.ͬ Jones, M.ͬ Sears, M.ͬ Franklin and M.ͬ Swan dine with me. After Dinner I visit M.ͬ de Montmorin who tells me that no Successor is yet appointed to him nor has the King at all made up his Mind. I ask him what is to become of himself and tell him that if he has any Doubt of the King's Intentions I will write to his Majesty on the Subject. He says he should be ashamed both of the King and of himself if he thought him capable of neglecting him. Go to the british Embassador's where there is a large Party of English and give her some Verses which I think she will be pleased with. From thence I go to the Louvre and while Mad.ˡˡᵉ visits in my Carriage we embrace. Spend the Evening here reluctantly. The Weather is clear and cold.

Monday 7. — Write. Go to see Monsieur de Moustiers but meet him in the Way. Thence to Monsieur Tolozon's. He tells me that they have a Year's Supply of Grain for the Troops. I ask him how much Bread they give and of what Quality. He tells me that the Ration is a Pound and an Half, of which three Quarters Wheat and one Quarter Rye. The Bran is not seperated. He says this makes an excellent Bread which many of the Officers prefer to the Bread of fine Flour. It soaks well in Soup, which considering the Mixture of Rye is a little extraordinary. Go to Mad.̣ Foucault's. M.ͬ Franklin dines here and we go together

after Dinner to see Mad.^e Lavoisier where there are a Number of
Gens d'Esprit, who are in general but so so Company. I go from
this to the Luxembourg where I find Ld Robert Fitzgerald in
tête à tête with Madame du Bourg. After he is gone I propose
[5 lines inked out] I leave her, and as she desires me to come very
often it will I think depend on myself to do or not to do. Go
to Mad.^e de Ségur's who reproaches me for having absented myself a long Time. She tells me that they begin to apprehend the
Independence of St Domingue. Go to Mad.^e de Guibert's and
stay a little while till Mad.^e de Flahaut arrives, and then come
away. The Weather is very cold. I write till late.

Tuesday 8. — Write. Call at the Louvre. Mad.^e is abroad.
Go to Monsieur de Montmorin's and sit a while with him. He
tells me that the Objection to appointing de Narbonne Minister
of foreign Affairs is his Connection with Mad.^e de Stahl. I ask
him if the King is fully apprized of the Double Dealing of his
present Ministers; he tells me that he is. I give him some Hints
respecting a Constitution for this Country and the Means of
restoring its Finances. Visit Mad.^e de Beaumont & talk Poetry
and Literature instead of Politics. Just before Dinner I announce
myself and it to Madame de Montmorin. After Dinner Monsieur
de Rayneval comes in who is in much Choler against the Assembly. He says the Diplomatic Committee have it in Contemplation to address his Majesty for the Removal of the whole Department of foreign Affairs, Clerks and all. He is determined, he says,
to defend himself; that he cares Nothing for his Place but will
struggle for his Reputation.[1] Go to Madame de Ségur's and
promise to return and give her the News I shall collect. She is
in great Anxiety about the Colonies and with her is a Person
who declares himself to be totally ruined. His Spirits are quite
broken. Go to Mad.^e de La Borde's where the same Thing presents
itself in the Duc de Xeres who shews me the Copy of a Letter
from Messrs Pouash of the Cape to the House of Pouash at Havre.
Go again to Mad.^e de Ségur's and give her the News, which are
yet tolerable as to Port au Prince where her Husband's Property
lies. Go to the british Embassador's. Her Countenance shews

---

[1] This Alsatian diplomat had been for twenty years attached to the French
Foreign Office.

me that the Verses are not thrown away. Afterwards she tells
me that she was ashamed, flattered and delighted. *Tant mieux.*
I tell the Abbé de Montesquiou a Part of what I told Monsieur
de Montmorin this Morning of the Means of establishing a
Constitution for this Country. His Mind opens to these Ideas.
We have all the World and his Wife here. Madame de Tarente
tells me that she loves me because I love the Queen and her
Reception proves that my Conversation is not disagreable. I
make it short. During Supper I observe to the Embassadress that
she don't eat but is meerly a Dish at her own Table and that not
the worst, but that she has not the Politeness to ask one to partake of it. Mad.^{e} de Montmorin wants to know the Subject of
our Conversation, which is in English. Lady Sutherland tells her:
il me dit des Méchancetés. — Ah! il est bien capable. Mad.^{e} de
Stahl comes in late and Mad.^{e} de Tarente makes Mouths at her.
I read Monsieur de Blanchelande's Letter which contains a very
unfavorable Account of Things in Ste Domingue. Retire early.
The Weather is cold but clear and pleasant.

Wednesday 9. — This Morning Mr Swan calls on me and I correct his Letter containing the Offer of Supplies to the Minister of
the Marine. While I am dressing Mr Franklin calls to obtain my
Consent to a Proposition of Le Couteulx's which is unreasonable
and which of Course I decline. Mr Bouainville also calls to give
me some Information respecting Mr Swan's Plan which I knew
before. Go to the Minister's and meet there Monsieur de Montmorin and Monsr de Malouette. I tell Monsr de Molleville that
Mr Swan has been with me. He says that he wished to see me on
that Subject to request that he would make his Proposals. I
tell him that the Proposals are as I understand made this Day.
That the best Way is to make an Agreement, with a Clause providing that Communication shall be made of all Steps taken to
Monsr de Ternant, and that I will write such Letters as to secure
at any Rate the Supply. He likes this much. Take Malouette
with me to de Moustiers where we dine together. He tells me that
he has not seen Mr Durue since we last met &c.^{a}. Go to the
Louvre by Appoint.^{t} but Mad.^{e} de Boursac & Mad.^{lle} and Monsieur
arrive at my Heels. I make a short cool Visit. Thence to Mad.^{e}
du Bourg's and return Home at eleven. The Weather is very
pleasant.

Thursday 10. — This Morning Mr de Wolf calls and we converse on the Terms to be settled with Mr Short. Mr Swan calls and I send him to the Marine Office for Information. Mr Richard came on the Affair ment.^d yesterday by Mr Franklin and I send him back as he came. Mr Short comes and we agree on the Conversation to be held with Mr de Wolf. I dress and call a Minute at the Louvre. Then go to Madame Foucault's. She is abroad. Thence to Mad.^e de Ségur's. She is also abroad. Thence to Monsieur de Montmorin's. Urge him to prepare a Reply from the King to the Decree against the Emigrants, and leave him engaged in it. Spend a few Minutes with Mad.^e de Beaumont and then go to dine with the british Embassadress. Mr de Rivarolle and Monsr de Fontenille are here. After Dinner go to the Louvre and celebrate. Mr Short comes in, who tells me that he and de Wolf are pretty well agreed. He says he likes him very well. Return Home early and read. The Weather is pleasant.

Friday 11. — This Morning Mr de Wolf breakfasts with me and tells me what passed yesterday with Mr Short. Mr Swan calls and tells me what has been done by the Minister of the Marine. Mr Brémond brings me a Work to examine and correct. I write a little, then walk in the Tuilleries. Dine with Mad.^e de Stahl where I meet the Abbé Raynal.[1] He makes many Advances towards me. I receive them but coolly because I have no great Respect for him. Demoustiers tells me that his friend Durue declines a Concern in Land Speculations. After Dinner Madame de Stahl asks my Opinion as to the Acceptance of the Office of foreign Affairs by her friend de Narbonne. I give her my Opinion so as not to encourage the Idea but yet not to offend. Go to the Louvre but my friend who was to be alone has Company. Visit Madame de Guibert, de Fontenille, de Corney, all abroad; Mad.^e de Vanoise and then Mad.^e Le Couteulx, who is not at Home. Go to Mad.^e de La Borde's and thence to sup with the Baron de Grand

---

[1] Abbé Raynal (1713–1796), Jesuit, dismissed from Saint Sulpice, 1747. Weighty work on the Europeans in East and West Indies burnt by public prosecutor after ten years' free circulation. In United States, 1781, wrote history of unfinished War of Independence. Repatriated, 1788, his denial of his well-known opinions had made some noise. Philosopher, Encyclopædist.

Cour who has very excellent Claret. Stay late. Nothing *marquant*. The Weather this Day has been very pleasant.

Saturday 12. — This Morning M.ʳ de Wolf breakfasts with me and tells me that M.ʳ Short will not consent to the Extension of his Loan beyond three Millions of florins. M.ʳ Brémond comes and I correct and amend his Work to which I add a short Conclusion. At three Monsieur and Madame de Flahaut come to Dinner, the Minister of the Marine shortly after, Monsieur and Madame de Montmorin towards four and Madame de Beaumont, who was at the Assembly, at half after four when we dine. A pleasant Party and my friend exerts herself to please; of Course she succeeds. The Minister of the Marine mentions to me again an Affair which one of the Colonists mentioned at his Request the other Day and which I gave the Go by. It is to combine the Payment of the American Debt with the Assistance to be given to the Colony of S.ᵗ Domingue. Promise to attend to it. He tells me what he has done with Swan's Application and is to communicate the Reply of the Régisseurs. Mons.ʳ de Montmorin tells me that he wrote to the King his Opinion as to the Decree against the Princes and offered to prepare a Work for him on that Subject, that he went afterwards to his Council but he never opened his Lips. I find that my poor friend is dropt but he must not be abandoned. Madame de Flahaut takes me to the Comédie française and from thence I go to visit Mad.ᵉ de Vauban where I stay a few Minutes and go to the Louvre. Spend the Evening here *amicalement*. The Weather is pleasant this Evening but rained about Sunset.

Sunday 13. — This Morning M.ʳ de Wolf breakfasts with me. M.ʳ Swan calls to know the Fate of his Provision Affair. I tell him what passed yesterday on the Subject. He and M.ʳ Wolf, M.ʳ Short and M.ʳ Jones dine with me. I mention to M.ʳ Short the Plan of the Minister of the Marine respecting the American Debt and ask him whether it will suit the United States. He thinks it will and tells me that the Arrears are paid up within about 6,000,000# and that after paying the Arrears there will remain about 20,000,000#, but he doubts their Willingness to receive it. After Dinner go to the Louvre but my friend, who had sent for me between four and five, tells me now (at six) her Husband is returned. I leave her and go to the french Comedy to meet Madame Foucault. My friend does not like this, especially as I shew not the least Regret at our Disappointment but only Impatience to get away. She tries to keep me but I give her Reasons for going which have no Sort of Weight and which could not of Course influence me, so that she must conclude that there is Cause for jealous Apprehension. This will operate. Go from the Comedy to Mad.ᵉ du Bourg's. Ségur tells me that my Predictions respecting the Depreciation of the Assignats was one Cause of his Refusal. I converse here with the prussian Minister and give him my View of the American Finances. He is a *complaisant* but he has Ability. It was fine Weather this Morning but this Evening it rains.

Monday 14. — Write this Morning. Dine at Home. Call at half past four at the Louvre;... sit down to Cards while the Hair Dresser renews her Coiffure. She tells me that her nervous System continues to be agitated in every Fibre, accompanied with extreme Lassitude. Go to the british Embassador's. She is abroad and so is Mad.ᵉ de Ségur and so is Mad.ᵉ de Stahl. I return Home and write. Go to sup at Mad.ᵉ Foucault's *en petit comité*. It has rained this Day pretty plentifully but cleared up about 8 oClock. The Weather is much milder.

Tuesday 15. — M.ʳ de Wolf breakfasts with me and tells me that he wishes me to give him a Credit for £30,000 S.ᵗᵍ to be used in Case his Loan should stick on Hand, so as to compleat the Business with Honor. I tell him that this would just now be very inconvenient but that I will try to arrange Matters for that Purpose. M.ʳ Swan calls and tells me that the Régisseurs have made a vilainous Report on the Business which the Minister of the Marine submitted to them, and that his Secretary Dubois, who is their Creature, transmitted to them Observations which laid the Ground Work for it. M.ʳ Short calls and tells me he has received a Letter from Hamilton by which it appears that the Government of the United States mean to make up the Depreciation to France of the Debt they owe. I tell him that in such Case the best Way will be to give them Obligations in florins at 4½ or 4 p% at a Par Exchange. That I am to see the Minister of the Marine on the Subject of the West India Plan tomorrow. I call

a Moment at the Louvre and promise to return. Dine with M!
Short and after Dinner go to the Louvre. Play. Call and visit
Mad? de Stahl. She is angry with me. I told Mons! de Molleville
that she had consulted me relative to Narbonne's Acceptance
and he has used it as a Pretext against his Appointment. I tell
her that I see Nothing in this to make a Handle of. That Every
Body knows Monsieur de Narbonne has been in Contemplation
for that Office and therefore it is natural enough to ask the Opinion of different People whether in Case the Post is offered he
should accept. I then add that he had better not think of it.
That the Object is meerly to fill a Gap for a few Months and then
to drop the Person who may have been appointed. She tells me
that the Ministry is stronger than is imagined and is about to
give me her Reasons, which she delivers in Part, when M! de
S! Léon arrives and puts an End to the Conversation. After him
comes Monsieur de Montmorin and then Monsieur de Chapelier.
Mons! Pétion is it seems appointed Mayor of Paris and this alarms
a good Deal *la bonne Société*, but I think it is not amiss provided
other People are wise. The Weather is grown very mild. The
Wind hard from the Southward with Rain.

Wednesday 16. — This Morning write. M! Wolf calls at about
½ past one and I take him to Lépine's where he buys a Watch, a
Repeater, at 42 louis paper Money which accord! to the Rate of
Exchange on Antwerp and that between London and Antwerp
brings it to nearly the same Thing as 30 Guineas in London, but
according to the Exchange direct on London is just £31..13..6
Sterling. Set M! de Wolfe down and go to M! Bertrand's to Din-
ner. He communicates the Reply to M! Swan's Offer and then
gives me the Memoire presented to the King on Behalf of the
Colonists for the Transfer of the American Debt. I give him my
Ideas on that Business and he desires me to reduce the Plan to
writing, for which Purpose I take with me the Memoire. The
Letters from the Governor of S! Domingo contain very unfavorable Accounts. The Insurrection still rages. After Dinner I visit
Mad? de Ségur, having called at the British Embassador's, but
Lady Sutherland is just going out. Ségur wants to know how he
shall be placed in America, whether he can exist awhile on about
400 St! p? Ann?. I tell him that he can and I think it probable

that he may make the Attempt. Go to Mad? Foucault's and spend the Evening. *Rien de marquante.* The Weather is fine this Day.

Thursday 17. — This Morning write. M? Wolfe calls. I go to Le Couteulx's where I stay Dinner. Madame seems to receive every Advance well; *que croire?* He asks my Assistance to get an *Affaire* finished in Spain and thereupon I propose to him another Affair to be coupled with it. He is to call on me the Day after ToMorrow. I visit M? Franklin *pour affaire* and play Chess. Return Home and write. The Weather is damp and disagreable.

Friday 18. — This Morning write. M? Wolf calls and takes Leave. I have de Moustiers and Madame de Bréhan, Mad? Foucault and her Brother & Sister, Madame de Pignieu her Sister, and the Chevalier ——, Franklin and the Marquis de Cubières to dine with me. At half past seven I go to the Louvre where I preserve a Degree of Coolness which is edifying to my friend. Company come in and I go to Mad? du Bourg's where there is a large Party. Go to Mad? de La Borde's and spend the Evening. Here also there is a large Party. I leave them at eleven. De Moustiers prest me hard to write on the Finances, which I evade for the present, telling him that Things change too rapidly and too much. De Lessart, it is said, is to become Minister of the Marine. The Weather has been bad all Day; last Night the Wind blew excessively hard from the Southward and it is pretty brisk all Day.

[Consulted daily, hourly, by Ministers and diplomats, Morris might well feel himself of some weight; they were taking him seriously but the Legislative Assembly was not taking them seriously, power had shifted from Ministries to *Manège*, where minister-baiting delights the new deputies. In no frame of mind for leaving stones unturned, Morris on his own initiative sends this letter to the King:]

Dʳ.[aft] Letter of 18 Novʳ. 1791 to the King of France

18 Nov.ʳᵉ 1791

Sire,

Il y a déjà long temps que Monsieur de Montmorin a quitté son poste, et Monsieur de Ségur ne l'accepta que pour s'en démettre le lendemain. Les circonstances ne permettent pas encore à votre Majesté d'y placer une personne qui lui convient, et elle éprouve une grande difficulté a faire même une nomination provisoire; une indifférence aussi marquée pour les premières places de l'empire démontre par le fait les vices de la Constitution. Il faut qu'elle soit bien mauvaise puisque personne ne veut s'en mêler, et il faut qu'elle soit bientôt changée parcequ'on sentira bientôt qu'elle est inéxécutable. Le parti républicain s'en apperçoit et se promet tout de l'impatience où doit naturellement se trouver votre Majesté. Il est persuadé qu'elle prêtera l'occasion à ses Ennemis de s'élever sur les ruines de la Monarchie, et il se flatte que dans les secousses inséparables d'une anarchie aussi complette, le roi restera seul au milieu des décombres de son royaume.

Dans ce moment Sire, j'ose encore m'adresser à votre Majesté. Je n'examinerai pas si son ancien Ministre l'a bien ou mal servi, parceque même en supposant qu'il fut sans talent et sans zèle, il me paroit convenir au roi de se constituer en Obligation pour faire éclater sa reconnaissance. Des circonstances fâcheuses l'obligent de lutter contre une Assemblée représentative. Or, de telles Assemblées sont toujours ingrates, et en conséquence leurs adherens ne sont mus que par le Sentiment passager de l'enthousiasme. Mais un Roi, et surtout un Roi reconnaissant, commande a l'éspérance, c'est à dire au mobile universel des humains. Il en résulte que tout le monde abandonnera tôt ou tard la Cause de l'assemblée pour soutenir celle du Roi. Ainsi quand même la reconnaissance ne seroit pas une vertu, elle seroit toujours une qualité royale parcequ'elle est toujours un grand moyen de gouverner. Ce n'est pas pourtant à tout le monde ni à tout propos qu'il convient de faire des largesses. Dans une lotterie royale ce ne sont que les gros lots qui vaillent, parceque les petits hommes et les petits services sont rarement utiles aux Rois. En répandant des gratifications légères on dissipe des sommes immenses, pour

faire une foule d'ingrats. En accordant au contraire des Récom-
penses grandes, mais rares, on excite les Efforts de tous en ne
payant qu'un Seul, et on parvient ainsi à concilier l'économie
la plus sévère avec une grande magnificence.

Le moment s'approche, Sire, où les factions qui déchirent la
france déployeront toutes leurs forces. Si les émigrans restent
tranquilles jusqu'à ce que les républicains soient entièrement
brouillés avec ceux qui désirent la conservation de ce qu'ils ap-
pellent la monarchie, les derniers s'uniront insensiblement au
parti aristocratique, et alors les républicains recevront la loi.
Dans cette Union il sera question de l'autorité royale, et les
droits de votre Majesté ne seront soutenus que par ceux qui es-
pèrent en tirer parti. Je ne fais pas l'éloge de l'humanité, Sire,
mais un Tableau de la france. Puisse-t-il être utile à Votre Majesté. Je désire son bonheur, et celui de son auguste Reine, de
toute mon Âme; et c'est d'après ce Désir que j'ose leur faire part
de mes réflexions, persuadé qu'elles pardonneront un zèle peut
être importun.

[*Translation:*]

Sire,

It is some time since Monsieur de Montmorin quitted his
post, and Monsieur de Ségur accepted it only to resign the
following day. Circumstances do not yet allow your Majesty
to give the place to a person who suits him and he is even having great difficulty in making a provisional appointment. So
marked an indifference to the first offices of the Empire
demonstrates the vices of the Constitution. It must indeed
be bad if nobody will be concerned with it, and it will soon
have to be changed because it will soon be found inexecutable.
The republican party realizes this and hopes everything
from the state of impatience in which your Majesty must
naturally find himself. They are convinced that it will
furnish the occasion for the elevation of his enemies on the
ruins of the monarchy, and flatter themselves that the shocks
inseparable from such complete anarchy will leave the King
deserted amid the wreckage of his kingdom.

In this moment, Sire, I dare once more address myself

to your Majesty. I will not examine whether his former Minister served him well or ill because, even supposing he were without talent and without zeal, it seems to me becoming to the King to make a point of proclaiming his gratitude. Untoward circumstances oblige him to struggle against a representative assembly. Now such assemblies are ever ungrateful, consequently their adherents are moved only by the fleeting sentiment of enthusiasm. But a King, and above all a grateful King, has command of hope, that is to say, of the universal motive power of human beings. It results that everyone will sooner or later abandon the cause of the Assembly to uphold that of the King. Thus even if gratitude were not a virtue it would always be a royal quality because it is always a great means of ruling. It is not however to everybody nor on every occasion that it is desirable to bestow bounties. In a royal lottery it is only the big prizes which count because small men and small services are rarely of use to Kings. In multiplying slight gratuities immense sums are dissipated only to create a swarm of ingrates. In according on the contrary recompenses large but infrequent the efforts of all are stimulated by the payment of one, and thus the most severe economy can be combined with great munificence.

The moment approaches, Sire, when the factions that are rending France will deploy all their forces. If the emigrants keep quiet until the republicans are completely embroiled with those who wish for the preservation of what they call the Monarchy, these last will insensibly unite themselves to the aristocratic party and then the republicans will receive the law. In that union there will be a question of the royal authority, and the rights of your Majesty will be upheld only by those who hope to profit thereby. I am making no eulogy of humanity, Sire, but a picture of France. May it be useful to your Majesty. I desire his happiness and that of his august Queen with all my soul; and it is in accordance with that wish that I have made my reflections known to them, persuaded that they will pardon a zeal perhaps intrusive.

Saturday 19. — This Morning M.ʳ Brémond calls and brings
me the last Work of Bergasse. He has altered what I had added
and restored what I had altered. The Consequence is that his
Work instead of being genteel is vulgar and of Course will fail
much of its Effect. He tells me that under the Auspices of the
triumvirate Duport, Barnave & La Meth, he and others are
about to publish a Journal. I tell him not to connect himself too
much with them. Go to Mons.ʳ de Molleville's and give him a
Plan for procuring the needful Supplies for S.ᵗ Domingo. See
there de Marbois.¹ Go to Mad.ˡˡᵉ Duplessis and take her to the
Louvre. Stay Dinner there and as Mad.ᵉ is taken ill after Dinner,
stay the Evening. Mons.ʳ Vic d'Azyr tells me that he repeated to
the Queen the Conversation he had with me respecting the
Decree against the Princes & that she desired to have it in Writing,
telling him that she knew how to value every Thing from that
Quarter. He thinks that this contributed in some Degree to the
Rejection. I don't believe a Word of the Matter. He desires me
to give my Advice as to the Conduct they should pursue respecting the Decree against the Priests. I desire to have the Decree
and the constitutional Acts relating to those unfortunate Men
before I give my Opinion. The bishop d'Autun says that Mons.ʳ
de Lessart ² is Minister of foreign Affairs. I think from de Marbois'
Manner that he is in Pursuit of Office. The Weather is tolerably
clear and the Continuation of Southerly Winds has made it
very moderate.

Sunday 20. — Write. M.ʳ Brémond comes and shews me the
Form of an Account he is about to make in Confutation of
Clavière. M.ʳ Swan calls and I shew him what I had begun in
Reply to the Régisseurs but as he has not all his Materials ready

---

¹ François de Barbé-Marbois (1745–1837) Morris had known in Philadelphia
as Consul, as Chargé d'Affaires. He had married American Elizabeth Moore.
Will be mayor of his native Metz and member of Paris directory. As Consul-
General he had organized all French Consulates in the United States. Reorgan-
ized finances in San Domingo, made enemies. Has long public career ahead
of him with interval at Cayenne after 18 Fructidor.

² De Lessart (1742–1792), a Neckerist like Montmorin. Suspected of
intrigue with Court of Vienna the Abbé Fauchet denounces him 3 December.
Later sent to Orleans, the High Court for treason trials; brought back as far as
Versailles by Danton's orders, he will there be massacred without trial in September, 1792.

I desire him to compleat his Work and then bring it to me. Go to the Louvre.... I dine at Monsieur de Montmorin's and tell him the Purport of my Letter to the King on his Subject. Speaking again about his Continuance in Office he says that it was impossible, that he will tell me the Reason one of these Days. That the King ought to be obliged to him for concealing it. I tell him that I always supposed he had some Reason which he did not mention because those which he gave were insufficient. Call on the british Embassadress. He compliments me on the Verses given to his Wife. There is here one of the Queen's Women who desires to be acquainted with me. She turns the Conversation upon Politics. I make my Visit very short and go to the Louvre. Thence to Madame du Bourg's. Sit with her till near twelve.... Call at the Louvre in my Way Home to see M.ʳ Short who desired to speak with me this Evening, but he is not here. The Weather, which has been lowering for some Days, has grown quite clear and bright. The Wind still from the Southward and of Course mild.

Monday 21. — This Morning M.ʳ Brémond calls and tells me that M.ʳ Short has announced to the Treasury an Order to make up the Depreciation of the Assignat Money paid to France. He founds on this the Hope to do Something. I doubt it, but give him a Plan which he will follow and for that Purpose see Monsieur de La Porte toNight. I call at the Louvre but my friend has Company; I leave her and visit M.ʳ Short who is abroad. Call on Mad.ˡˡᵉ Duplessis who is not ready. Go to M.ʳ Le Couteulx's who is abroad. Look for Marbois but cannot find him. Call on Mons.ʳ Millet and sit with him a little while. Go to Mad.ᵉ Foucault's where I dine. Chaumont tells me that there is a Plan for giving Succor to the Colony of S.ᵗ Domingo by assigning the American Debt and he tells me that he caused an Offer to be made on that Subject of the Debt by S.ᵗ Iry when he went out fourteen Months ago. And this I find came from Grand and Co: of Amsterdam. It was very indigested. Return to the Louvre and lend my Carriage to M.ˡˡᵉ Duplessis.... She [Madame de Flahaut] tells me that she and the bishop have had an interesting Conversation this Morning in which they have agreed to be in future meerly friends without imposing any Restraint upon each other.

I visit Mad? de Ségur and Madame Tronchin, both abroad. Madame Fontenille, with whom I sit awhile and then go to Mad? de Guibert's to Supper. A mighty dull Evening. The Weather continues pleasant but threatens Rain.

Tuesday 22. — M? Brémond comes and seems to be pretty sure of Success in his Plan for the Debt. I doubt entirely. Call on the Minister of the Marine and explain fully to him my Plan for supplying the Colony of S? Domingo. Go to M? Short's & communicate the Result of this Conversation. Thence to the Louvre and dine. After Dinner take my friend to pay a Visit and while she is there I go to Madame de Ségur's. She takes me up and I return with her to the Louvre. Spend the Evening here. The Weather is grown very foggy and damp.

Wednesday 23. — This Morning write a little. M? Brémond comes and repeats his *Projet* which I cannot approve of but consent to his trying it, tho I think even that will have pernicious Consequences. Call on M? Franklin at the Request of Le Couteulx. He will not endorse the Notes altho Le Couteulx offers to guarantee him against the Consequences. He says they may fail. This proves that he is a very prudent young Man and one who will probably die rich. I go to Le Couteulx and tell him that Franklin will call to settle Matters with him. He makes, as usual, a great Deal of Talk for Nothing tho I tell him I am in a Hurry. Go from hence to Mad.^{lle} Duplessis and take her to the Louvre where I spend the Rest of the Day and Evening, my friend being ill. In the Afternoon her Cook nearly lost her Life by imprudently using Charcoal in a Stove in a close Chamber. There are some Accounts in Town that the People of Provence [1] are in actual War with each other; I fancy they are very exagerated. The Weather is very disagreable, damp cold fog.

Thursday 24. — This Morning write. Mons? de Marbois calls on me and after him Mons? de Moustiers. I take up Mad.^{lle} Duplessis who sets me down at M? Short's. Converse with him on the Plan which is in Agitation respecting the Colony of S?

---

[1] The new religious freedom had uncorked the enmities of centuries; Protestants who had worshipped secretly in mountain caves were now turning on their persecutors, paying off old scores in those hills they knew so intimately, killing Catholics with gusto.

Domingo, then go to the Louvre. Stay to dine on Condition that my friend, who is ill, will agree not to go abroad this Afternoon. Visit the british Embassadress who is not at Home and then return to the Louvre. The Weather has been very damp and disagreable all Day but clears up this Evening.

Friday 25. — This Morning M̃ʳ Swan calls and I employ myself in preparing his Memoire to the Minister. Monṣ̃ & Mad̃ᵉ de Flahaut, Monṣ̃ S̃ᵗ Pardou and Mad̃ˡˡᵉ Duplessis dine with me. It is whimsical enough that my little Dinner, consisting of three Things, is drawn from an immense Distance. Oysters from Colchester, Trout from the Rhine and Partridges from Querci. After Dinner visit with Madame at the Abbé Morelet's where I see Crevecœur who seems crusty. Return to the Louvre and thence to Mad̃ᵉ de La Borde's to pass the Evening. The Weather this Day has been very pleasant.

Saturday 26. — This Morning I compleat M̃ʳ Swan's Memoire and give it to him. M̃ʳ Tolozan calls and talks about the Situation of public Affairs. The Union of able and honest Men necessary to save the Kingdom. I agree to this but tell him that unless the King and Queen will give their full Confidence to such Men it will answer no Purpose. He proposes dining with him again to meet certain Persons, which I agree to. Brémond does not call as he promised and Monsieur de La Porte told me last Night that the Scheme he has in Agitation is impracticable. I call at the Louvre and dine at Monṣ̃ Monmorin's. [sic] Converse with him before Dinner. He says the King never answers his Letters and asks if he answers mine. I tell him no, and that I do not expect it because I wish nor want Nothing from him. He says he lately communicated the Assurances that one of the Provinces with all the Troops in it could be depended on as adhering to the royal Cause. He does not tell me which it is. He tells me that the real Cause why he quitted the Ministry was that he had not the full Confidence of their Majesties. That they were governed sometimes by Counsels from Brussels ¹ and sometimes from Coblentz.

---

¹ Mercy-Argenteau, for so many years Austrian Ambassador in France, is now at Brussels, so for Brussels read Vienna, the *Austrian Conspiracy*, so-called. Advice from Coblentz means the *émigrés*, the King's two brothers and the Prince de Condé.

That he urged them to adopt a privy Council to decide in all Cases, and endeavored to convince them that unless they fixed a Plan of Conduct they would be greatly injured, but in vain. Mons: Bertrand, who dines here, tells me that he has made great Changes and Reforms in his Bureauxs. He is determined to make a striking Example of some mutinous Seamen. I advise him to hang a few in each Port and keep some for the Purpose of an Execution at the Yard Arm of each Vessel going out of Port. I tell him the Conversation I have had with M: Short and that as soon as he is empowered to treat we can adjust Matters pretty nearly and conclude by Letter. Call on the British and Swedish Embassadresses and on Mad: de Ségur, all abroad. Go to the Louvre. My friend meets me by Appointment but her Husband comes in and I go out. Call on Mad: de Wit who is abroad, pay a short Visit to Madame Tronchin, then take up Mad:lle Duplessis and bring her to the Louvre. My friend reproaches me for being out of Humor, in Consequence whereof I take my Leave and go to the Luxembourg. Sit with Madame a long Time; we talk Politics and what is called Love and Sentiment, and I think she is inclined to capitulate but I incline to think that I had better let this Matter alone. The Weather this Morning was very pleasant but we have this Evening a thick cold fog.

Sunday 27. — This Morning write. M: Brémond calls, and tells me that he still hopes for Success to his Plan. I do not. Go to the Louvre. Thence to visit Madame Foucault and return to the Louvre where I dine. Go to the Théâtre de Monsieur where we see the *Club des bons Gens*, an excellent Piece perfectly performed. After the Play I visit Mad: de Vauban who is just going abroad. I come Home and read. The Weather has been very fine this Day but this Evening it lowers.

Monday 28. — Write by the Post. M: Jones calls and while he is here M: Swan comes. I go thro his Memoire, in which he has been obliged to make some Alterations. Brémond comes and I work with him at a Pamphlet on the Finances; I dictate and he writes. At four go to dine with the british Embassador. After Dinner, as there are none but the Family, we chat together very freely. He puts M: Short on the Carpet and she opens against him. I assure her that he is a very sensible, judicious young Man and very attentive to his Business. She asks me where he is that he has not appeared lately at Court. I tell her he was in the Country with the Duke and Dutchess de La Rochefoucault and is now gone on Business of the United States to Holland. She asks if he is Embassador to all the Nations of Europe and laughs heartily at the Idea. I tell her that the Business he is employed in there does not require an Embassador. She says he has not the Look and Manner which such Character requires. I reply that he might not do so well perhaps in Russia but at any other Court I do not conceive Figure to be very important. She puts an End to the Conversation by telling me that if I wish to give Foreigners a favorable Impression of my Country I must get myself appointed. A Bow of Acknowlegement for the Compliment is the only Reply which it admits of. She appeals to the Embassador and of Course he answers as usual upon such Appeals, in the affirmative. Go from hence to the Louvre, and there my friend, who is dressing, tells me of a Plan laid by her Husb.^{d} and Sister to take her in. We embrace and then I visit Mad.^{e} de Ségur who is abroad and Madame de La Suze who is in Bed. Sit with her awhile and Demoustiers and his Sister in Law come in. He tells me that he has been able as yet to get but one *Actionnaire* and him for only 100,000$^{#}$. Go from hence to Madame de Guibert's where I spend the Evening. The Wind has been very hard all Day from the Southward; it is indeed a heavy Gale.

Tuesday 29. — Mr Swan calls and gives me the fair Copy of his Memoire to be delivered to the Minister. Mr Brémond calls and I add a little to his Work but he has not the Materials for continuing it. Walk. Then dress and go to the Minister of the Marine to whom I deliver Swan's Memorial and add sundry Explanations and Informations. He is very forcibly struck with this and thanks me much. He promises to enquire into the Abuses complain'd of. Call an Instant at the Louvre and go to dine with Mad.^{e} Foucault. Leave this early to go to the french Comedy and see Préville but I am too late, the House is full. Call on Mad.^{e} du Bourg who is just gone out, and so is Mad.^{e} Le Couteulx. Visit Madame de Cantaleu and sit some Time with her. Call on Mesd.^{es} de Vanoise, de Fontenille and de Wit who are all abroad. On Mad.^{e} de La Borde with whom I sit a little while and then return Home. The Weather has been very pleasant this Day.

Wednesday 30. — Write. Paul Jones calls and while he is here Mr Franklin comes who is troublesome about his three per Cents. Monsieur Vic d'Azyr comes in and I send the others away. He talks to me about public Affairs in order to carry my Opinions to the Queen. Mr Swan comes in and I tell him what passed with the Minister of the Marine. Dress and call for a Moment at the Louvre, then go to Le Couteulx's and dine. After Dinner settle with him the Plan of Operation for a little Affair in Spain. He promises to write all the needful Letters so that I may have them next Saturday. I don't expect that he will do this. Go from hence to Madame du Moley and thence to subscribe for the *Logographe* for my brother. Call at the Louvre and sit with my Friend who is in ill Health and low Spirits; then return Home. The Weather has been pleasant tho lowering all Day, but this Evening we have a heavy Gale from the Southward with Rain.

DECEMBER 1791

Thursday 1 *Dec.* — Write this Morning. Dine at Home and go at four to the Louvre. Embrace my friend twice and then go to Mad.^e de La Borde's. Take her to the *Comédie française* where I have the Pleasure to see Préville [1] perform in the *Boureau bienfaisant.* He is truly an Actor. Nothing below and nothing above the Part, no false Ornament but '*the naked Nature and the living Grace.*' The Queen is here and is perfectly well received. I sit directly over her Head and Somebody I suppose tells her so, for she looks up at me very steadily so as to recognize me again; this at least is my Interpretation. My Air, if I can know it myself, was that of calm Benevolence with a little Sensibility. Go to the Louvre and spend the Evening. Portail has resigned this

---

[1] Morris was lucky to hit off a brief reappearance of the celebrated comedian Préville (1721–1799), retired from the stage of the Comédie Française in 1786. *Sosie* and the *Bourru bienfaisant* were, with *Figaro*, his most famous rôles.

Morning, at least so says the Bishop d'Autun. The Weather this Morning was very fine but it threatens again for the Night and towards twelve the Wind rises from the South.

Friday 2 Dec. — Write. At half past two take up Mad.^{lle} Duplessis and go to the Louvre where we dine *en trio*. After Dinner Mad.^{lle} goes out for a few Minutes and we make Use of the Occasion. Mr Catcherby[1] comes in at five to take the Ladies to the Opera. I follow them but arrive before them. Madame looks very coldly and scarce speaks. She tells me afterwards that I treated her roughly and with ill Humor and that Mr Catchooby remarked on it. She scarcely speaks to me while we are here. I take her Son to the Louvre and then visit Madame de Vauban. The Count de Ségur comes in and from his Conversation I find that he is again intriguing with Lameth & Co?. Go to Mad.^e de La Borde's & spend the Evening. Take my friend Home and our Conversation consists meerly of Replies to her Questions. It is bad Weather again to Day. The Wind blew very hard last Night. A Letter of the Empress of Russia to the Prince de Condé is shewn to us which is very encouraging to the Emigrants.

Saturday 3. — Write. Mr Brémond calls and tells me that the secret Council of the King consists of Mr de Molleville, M. [sic] de Fleurieu and Monsr de La Porte. He gives me an Account of his Situation with the Committee Barnave and Lameth &c.^a. After he is gone Mr Swan calls and after him Mr de Marbois; while he is here Brémond returns and brings several Materials on which to ground an Attack of the Republican Party. I dress and go to dine with Monsr Tholozan. De Moustiers, Malouette & Gitet are our Party. The Dinner is excellent. I call at the Louvre but my friend is as I expected abroad. Go to Mad.^e de Ségur's and the british Embassadress who are both abroad. Then visit at Monsr de Montmorin's and go afterwards to Mad.^e de Stahl's. While she is dressing we have some Conversation which is not unpleasing to her. We have here a large Company. Delessart has been denounced this Day by the Abbé Fauchet, and the bishop d'Autun who dined with him tells me that he was so sick he was obliged to leave the Table. I return Home early. The Weather is rainy and disagreable.

---

[1] This Prince Victor Kotchoubey attached to Russian Embassy in London.

Sunday 4. — This Morning I write a little. M.ʳ Brémond calls and after shewing me what he had written to Lameth and Laborde proceeds to give me all the Information in his Power. I send him to Lameth to advise that De Lessart retire, because he has not Firmness enough for the Situation in which he is placed. I go to the Louvre. My friend is not well. She wishes me to dine with her which I decline. I tell her that she behaved very ill on Friday and she seems to be sensible of it. Dine with Madame du Moley. Converse with Du Moley after Dinner and gather some Information respecting the Affairs of his Department. Go to the british Embassador's. Périgord the Banker tells me that there are very bad News from India. L.ᵈ Cornwallis has retired to Bangalore and has lost his Military Chest. If this last be true the Retreat was a Rout. Périgord says (par parenthèse) that he pays £1500 S.ᵗ p.ʳ Ann.⁹ postage. M.ʳ Crawford of Rotterdam is here. L.ᵈ Gower tells me that a young Oswald who is here inherits from his Uncle about £18,000 S.ᵗ p.ʳ Ann.⁹ I suggest the Idea which I had heard somewhere that he gambled successfully in the british Funds at the Peace. He gives me the following Anecdote. He went to see Fitzherbert to take Leave as he was going to London. M.ʳ Oswald was there, and being asked if he had any Commands said No. At Chantilly L.ᵈ Gower put up and M.ʳ Oswald passed him. At Calais he found M.ʳ Oswald waiting for a Wind and he left him there and announced to the Ministry the Peace which he had learnt from M.ʳ Oswald on the Road, tho not directly, but from the Report spread as he went thro. The Wind at Calais was fair enough for him tho not for M.ʳ Oswald. Go from hence to Mad.ᵉ Tronchin's to a *Thé*. Mention to him the Advantages which would result from the Purchase of Lands in America. Come away before Supper. The Weather is rainy and disagreable.

Monday 5. — This Morning write. Visit M.ʳ de Montmorin and while there prepare a little Paragraph for him contradicting the Report that he has absconded. Dine with Mons.ʳ de Marbois. The Duc de Castries is here. We converse a great Deal about the State of public Affairs, which Marbois appears to be very ignorant of both as to Men and Things. Go from hence to the Louvre but my friend being not yet come in I visit Mad.ᵉ de La

Borde who is abroad. Return to the Louvre. She overstays her Time half an Hour but apologizes because she dined tête à tête with the Bishop d'Autun to correct his Work, which is an Address to the King from the Department against the Decree inflicting Penalties on the non juring Clergymen. She thinks the Step improper and so do I. She says it is well written. I am cold and as she asks the Reason I tell her that it is improper to dine tête à tête. That as to any Connection between them I am convinced that there is none but the Appearance is injurious. I consent at last to embrace her and then we take up Mad.^{lle} Duplessis and go to Mad.^e de Guibert's where we spend the Evening. The Weather continues very wet and disagreable.

Tuesday 6. — This Morning Mr Brémond calls and I dictate to him a philippic against the Chef des Républicains. Dress and call on the Minister of the Marine. He shews me the Sketch of a Speech to be made by the King to the Assembly. We talk on public Affairs and the Means of establishing a Constitution in this Country which may secure the just Rights of the Nation under the Government of a real King. He promises to sound the King and Queen and I promise to sketch out some Hints. Go to the Louvre where I dine. In the Evening lend my Carriage to Mad.^{lle} and during her Absence and that of Monsieur we embrace. We have but just Time to recover our Seats when Mr de Ste Foi comes in. I come Home and write. The Weather is still wet and disagreable.

Wednesday 7. — This Morning employ myself in preparing a Form of Government for this Country. At half past four go to dine with Monsieur de Montmorin. Find him employed in reading the Address to the King by the Members of the Depart.^t of Paris. It is well written in many Respects but the Style is rather that of a popular Harangue than of an Address to a Monarch. In order also to excuse their Interference they inveigh much against the Emigrants and prove that while they talk big they tremble. Monsr de Montmorin tells me that the Bishop d'Autun pressed Péthion, the Mayor, to sign it who refused, saying that he approved of the Thing but would not fall out with the *Fous & enragées* because it is they and not the reasonable People who support Revolutions, and for his own Part he does not chuse to be hanged for the Sake of giving Triumph to Reason. I think he acts wisely and the other, who constantly places himself between two Stools, will never have a secure Seat. Visit Mad: de Ségur. He is in Bed for a Cold and tells me that Things go very badly so that he turns his Mind towards farther Investment in America. Go to the Louvre but my friend is not come in so I visit Madame de La Borde & as she is just going abroad I sit a little while with him and in Conversation we go from one Thing to another till at last he communicates to me a Journal he is writing and which is distributed at the King's Expence to all the Lodges of free Masons [1] in the Kingdom. He says that the King, the Queen, Monsieur de La Porte and he are the only Persons in the Secret. I tell him that by the same Means he may feel the Pulse of the Nation and determine from thence what can be attempted with a Prospect of Success. He prays me to give him a List of the Questions which I propose and I promise to do so. I leave him to repent of this Confidence, for that is the Nature of Man. Return Home and write. The Weather was very pleasant this Morning but this Afternoon it rains. M: de Narbonne [2] has been to the Assembly this Morning to announce his Appointment. I shall be surprized if he succeeds for tho he is by no Means deficient in Point of Understanding, I think he has not the needful Instruction, that he has not acquired the Habits of Business and that he is totally void of Method in Affairs. *Nous verrons.*

Thursday 8. — M: de Crèvecœur and M: de Brémond breakfast with me. Give the former a Certificate that his Son is an American Citizen. The latter shews me the Questions he has prepared to be sent to the Departments in order to discover the Temper of Men's Minds. I write after they are gone, continue preparing the Form of a Constitution for this Country, when a Person comes in who tells me that he sent in July last the Form of a Constitution for America to Gen! Washington. He says that he has made such Objects his Study for above 50 Years. That he knows America perfectly well tho he has never seen it, and is

---

[1] About the only mention of Freemasons. In common with nineteenth-century historians Morris seems oblivious of them as a cause and directing force of the Revolution, on which such stress is laid by the latest writers.

[2] New Minister of War, soon an *émigré*.

convinced that the American Constitution is good for Nothing. I get Rid of him as soon as I can but yet I cannot help being struck with the Similitude of a Frenchman who makes Constitutions for America and an American who performs the same good Office for France. Self Love tells me that there is a great Difference of Persons and Circumstances but Self Love is a dangerous Counsellor. M.ʳ Swan comes in and I quit my Work to dress. Go to the Louvre and send my Carriage for Mad.ˡˡᵉ Duplessis & Mad.ˡˡᵉ Beltz who dine here as well as me. While the Carriage is gone we embrace. The Dinner is excellent and a Carp of the Rhine is not the worst Part of it. This Fish is very good where the Waters are good and therefore would I think be a great Acquisition in our large Ponds in America. After Dinner I visit Mons.ʳ Boutin & Madame Tronchin and Mons.ʳ Le Couteulx and Mad.ᵉ de Vannoise who are all abroad. Call on Mad.ᵉ du Molet and make a short Visit. Then go to the Luxembourg where I find nobody; visit Mad.ᵉ de Ségur and then go Mad.ᵉ d'Houdetot's and excuse myself for not spending the Evening. Return Home and write. The Weather, with some few Intervals of fair, is very disagreable; Rain and Sleet.

Friday 9. — Write. Dine at the Louvre. After Dinner we retire into an AntiChamber & celebrate while Mad.ˡˡᵉ amuses herself at the Harpsichord (piano forte). Visit Mad.ᵉ Foucault and go from thence to the Luxembourg but there is nobody at Home. Return to the Louvre and go thence to Mad.ᵉ de La Borde's where I spend the Evening. Nothing remarkable. The Weather is very bad, alternately Rain and Snow with short Intervals of Cold. The Wind at Northwest.

Saturday 10. — This Morning write. Call at the Louvre and go thence to dine at the Restorateur's. After Dinner go to the french Comedy and see Préville. He is seventy five Years of Age and his Action is perfect. The best of the others may be said to act well their Parts but he represents his. I find that I had formed just Ideas on this Subject. For he is free precisely from those Faults which had struck me in the others. Return to the Louvre and spend the Evening. The Weather is bad, alternately Rain & Snow but more of the latter; it clears up for awhile and is very fine, then again becomes bad. At Midnight it is clear and moderate.

Sunday 11. — This Morning write. Paul Jones calls and after him de Moustiers. I dine with Mad? Grand. Call after Dinner at the british Embassador's, not at Home, sit a while with Mad? de Ségur, then return Home and write. The Weather is unpleasant. Cold with flights of Snow but not cold enough to freeze in the Day.

Monday 12. — This Morning write. The Count de Moustiers calls on me and tells me he has Expectations to sell the S? Lawrence Lands. I tell him that I must raise the Price on Account of the Exchange. M? Swan calls and tells me that the *Régisseurs* have contracted for Provisions till March 1793. Promise to visit the Minister of the Marine Tomorrow & converse on that Subject with him. Dine with the british Embassador. Return Home after Dinner and write. At ten oClock go to Mad? de Guibert's. My friend tells me that she staid at Home waiting for me all the Evening. Tis her own fault, she sent Word that she should go out soon. Come away early and sit down again to write. The Weather was very cold last Night but pleasant this Morning, raw and dull in the Afternoon, a high Wind from the Southward at Night with Rain.

Tuesday 13. — This Morning write; finish the Copy and Correction of a Plan of Government and of general Principles to accompany it. M? Brémond was here and I told him that his Offer for the American Debt is finally rejected. M? Swan comes and I tell him I will call on the Minister as soon as my Carriage comes home, but this is not untill late. I call however, and he is at Dinner. Go to Mad? Foucault's and dine. The Chevalier d'Orléans is here who was lately brought Home Prisoner by his Crew.[1] He tells me that they will not be tried, from a Conviction that if tried they will be acquitted. Stay here till every Body is gone away; Mad? desires it but when I propose to lie with her she tells me that Friendship suits her better. That Opportunities can never be had for those frequent and confidential Interviews which love requires and that therefore she must be content to lead a reasonable Life. I acknowlege that there is force in this Observa-

---

[1] A Foucault cousin, not a royalty, this naval officer whose letters had long been labelled 'Duke of Orleans' in catalogue of Morris's papers, a mistake lately cleared away by comparing handwriting, dates, and subject-matter.

tion and as I feel no very strong desire I practically adopt the System. Go to Mad.ᵉ du Bourg's where there is a *Thé*. Thence to the Louvre where my friend receives me with many Compliments which imply Reproach for having so long absented myself. At eleven take Mad.ˡˡᵉ home and en Route am tempted to be indiscreet. The Thing would I believe be possible enough but it would be wrong. The Weather has been fair this Morning and warm, rainy and dull this Afternoon, and in the Evening it blows hard from the Westward.

Wednesday 14. — This Morning write a little and then call on Le Couteulx who says he has attended to the Business which I recommended to him but I think he has not. Call at M.ʳ Grand's but there is no Body at Home; this is disagreable for I fear that the Exchange will take a Rise, tho it must again decline. I go to the Louvre and from thence with my friend, Mons.ʳ & Mad.ˡˡᵉ to dine with the Minister of the Marine. We have a good Dinner and as much Company as the Table will hold. The Count de Thiare, who is here, is rather sullen, which is extraordinary for he is one of the most pleasant Men I know. Speak to the Minister about M.ʳ Swan's Affair. He assures me that the *Régisseurs* have no Orders to purchase Provisions and if they have done so it is at their Peril. I tell him that I have prepared some Notes on a Constitution to shew him. He says he has sounded the King on the Subject who has commanded him to attend to it. He has recommended to his Majesty the most profound Secrecy and taken Occasion to inculcate the Necessity from seeing in a Gazette what had passed in Council. A Mons.ʳ l'Escalier is here, charged with the Adjustment of Affairs at the Isle of France and in India. Converse with him a little and on the Subject of his Mission with the Minister. Tippoo Saib, he tells me, has made superb Offers but unfortunately they are not in Condition to accept of them. Go from hence to Mad.ᵉ de Boursac's where I take up Mad.ˡˡᵉ Duplessis and go with her to Madame de Guibert's. Thence to her Mother in Law's where I leave her. Thence to Mad.ᵉ du Moley's, Fontenille's and de Corney's, all abroad. Thence to Mad.ᵉ de Witt's where I stay awhile, after she is gone out, with him. He tells me the Cause of the Dissolution of the Partnership of Hope and Hartzing of Amsterdam. I think I had heard it before. Call on Mad.ᵉ Tronchin who is abroad and then take Mad.ˡˡᵉ Duplessis to the Louvre where I stay the Evening. The Weather was unpleasant this Morning, fair at Noon and in the Evening again damp and cloudy.

Thursday 15. — Write. Call on M.ʳ Grand. Nobody in the Bureau. Dine at the Restorateur's and go at four to the Louvre but Monsieur has contrived to be at Home. My friend contrives to get into a little Dispute with him and to put him in such a passion that he goes down to his Chamber. We profit by his Retreat. Call on Madame de Ségur who is abroad. Leave my Name for the british Embassadress and visit at Madame de Montmorin's. Thence to Mad.ᵉ La Borde's whom I take to sup at Mad.ᵉ d'Houdetot's. The Weather is very disagreable, wet and raw.

Friday 16. — This Morning go to M.ʳ Grand's and negotiate a Bill for ᶠ1000, thence to Mons.ʳ de Molleville's where we read and consider the Plan of a Constitution &c.ᵃ, &c.ᵃ. Dine with Le Couteulx, then go to the Louvre. Thence to Mad.ᵉ de Ségur's and thence to Mad.ᵉ de Stahl's who is abroad. Spend the Evening with Mad.ᵉ de La Borde. The Weather is very damp and disagreable.

Saturday 17. — M.ʳ Brémond comes and keeps me employed all the Morning in the Corrections of his Letter under the Signature of Junius. Call an Instant at the Louvre and then go to dine at the Restorateur's with M.ʳ Swan who called on me this Morning. After Dinner we go together to the french Comedy. Préville acts the Part of *Sosie* in Molière's *Amphitrion*. It is wonderful. He would be considered as an excellent Actor his Age out of the Question, but all Things considered he is a prodigy. Sup at Mad.ᵉ Foucault's and converse with M.ʳ Franklin, to whom I shew a Letter just received from the Trustees in London about the three per Cent Stock. He tells me that Colqhoun's House is broke and I find that R. M. has borrowed of Pultney & his friend $100,000 which is I suppose the Negotiation he made with Col.ᵒ Smith. The Weather continues rainy and bad.

Sunday 18. — Write. Go to the Louvre. Dine here and before Dinner perform the needful Rites. After Dinner visit the british Embassadress and afterwards Mad.ᵉ Tronchin. Go thence to the Louvre and stay a little while with Mad.ᵉ, afterw.ᵈˢ return Home. The Weather still damp and disagreable.

Monday 19. — Write. Paul Jones comes in but I neglect him perforce so that he goes away. The Count de Moustiers comes in and when my Letters are finished we converse first on Business and afterwards on politics. Dine at the Restaurateur's and next to me sits a little Man who says he has seen all my Country, — *peut être*. He has been at Hudson's Bay but there is more Snow in the Country where he was born, for it is common there to enter at the Door in the Evening and go out at the Window in the Morning. I don't believe him but I don't tell him so. I ask however whereabouts this is and he tells me it is among the Montagnes des Vosges. I must enquire. Go to the Comédie française. I am above Half an Hour waiting before my Servant can get a Ticket and afterwards I get a very bad Place but still I think myself recompensed by Préville, who is truly formed to hold the Mirror up to Nature and shew to the very Shape and Body of the Time his form and Pressure. Franklin is here, who tells me that some Persons have been with him to purchase Lands &c.ᵃ. Spend the Evening at the Louvre. The Weather is very disagreable, cold and damp.

Tuesday 20. — Write this Morning a little and then go out. Call on Mʳ Le Couteulx who still neglects the Business he had undertaken. Go from thence to Madᵉ Vannoise's and afterwards to the Louvre where I stay only an Instant, Monsʳ de Ricé being there and Madᵉ in a Conversation which seems to be interesting. Go to Monsieur Millet where I dine. Monsieur de Bougainville ¹ is here who has served in Canada in the War of 59. He gives a very flattering Description of that Country and I put such Questions to him as draw forth a full Confirmation of the Accᵗ given by McᶜComb of the Sᵗ Lawrence Lands. We afterwards converse together on the public Affairs of this Country. He tells me that I am mistaken in my Idea that he is in Amity with Sᵗᵉ Foi, the Bishop d'Autun &c.ᵃ. That he considers them as a Pack of Rascals and the King views them in the same Light and detests them. He assured Bougainville that he accepted the Constitution meerly to avoid a civil War. I tell him that the King is betrayed by the

---

¹ Louis-Antoine de Bougainville (1729–1811), navigator, explorer, discoverer. With the versatility of France's armed forces this great sailor had fought the British in Canada as a captain of dragoons, A.D.C. to Montcalm.

Weakness if not by the Wickedness of his Councillors. He says that he is of the same Opinion. I ask him what he thinks of Fleurieu. He tells me that he is a poor Creature. Go to the Luxembourg to a *Thé* of Mad.^e du Bourg and thence to Supper at Mad.^e Le Couteulx's. The Weather is still very bad. What must it be in London.

Wednesday 21. — Write. Mr Tholozan and Monsr Giliet call on me; the former goes for Metz To Morrow Morning. Mr Crawford comes in. He appears to be very much out of Humor with R. M., who has not done what he ought in various Respects; at least, so says Mr Crawford. Go to dine with the Minister of the Marine. He shews me the Proof Sheet of his Address to the Assembly and will send me some Copies. He says that he expects to get the Decree passed. It is adjourned till next Tuesday. Go home with Mad.^e de Flahaut who dines here. Monsieur is ill with the Gout & has a high Fever. Visit Mad.^e d'Albani [1] and then return to the Louvre and spend the Evening. The bishop d'Autun observes to me that the Jacobins have not been able to raise a Riot about their Address. I tell him that since the frolic at the Champs de Mars there is little Danger of Riots because the People are not very fond of them when they find that Death is a Game which two can play at. He says that the King is in wondrous high Spirits since his Vetos have gone off easily, and says that he will apply them every now and then. Poor King. The Weather continues to be detestable. It is somewhat colder with an easterly Wind which may perhaps clear away the Damps we now endure.

---

[1] Countess of Albany (1753–1824), widow of Prince Charles Edward Stuart, the Young Pretender, whom she married secretly, 1772. Born Louisa, daughter of Gustavus Adolphus, Prince of Stolberg-Gedern. Her liaison with the poet Alfieri was already fifteen years old and lasts till his death; a *déclassée* princess, for she had more than once run away from her royal husband and his beatings when in his cups, and had been dragged back by her brother-in-law, Cardinal of York, whose profile figures with her husband's on Canova's bas-relief in Saint Peter's, Rome. Fair hair, dark expressive eyes, a graveness saved from pedantry by flashes of wit, she becomes a frequenter of Madame de Flahaut's little salon. Received at the British Court. Retires to Florence with her scholar-poet, labels the French *singes-tigres*, forbids their language, thinks no religion possible in a world so weighed down with war and revolution; but in Paris is not yet recluse and franco-phobe. Cousin of Madame de Tarente.

Thursday 22. — Write. Brémond calls and tells me that Mons.ʳ de Narbonne has secured Mons.ʳ de Condorcet and that he has got his friend Monciel appointed to Mayence. I dine with Madame Tronchin and meet here Madame de Tarente. Ask her to procure for me a Lock of the Queen's Hair. She promises to try. I think her Majesty will be pleased with the Request even if she does not comply with it, for such is Woman. Go to the Louvre. My friend is hurt that I did not come to see her or send to enquire about her Husband this Morning. I excuse my Neglect. At half past nine go to Mad.ᵉ La Norraye's. Here are a Number of very beautiful Women. A Daughter of Mad.ᵉ Cabarrus ¹ who is enchanting. The Weather continues to be very disagreable.

Friday 23. — Write. M.ʳ Swan calls. I visit M.ʳ Crawford who is abroad. Mad.ᵉ de Ségur, whose Husband went off this Morning with a sleeveless national Errand for Berlin. I think it is next to impossible that he should succeed. She is distressed about his Departure. Take Mad.ˡˡᵉ Duplessis to the Louvre and then go to dine with Mad.ᵉ Foucault. After Dinner return to the Louvre and sit with my friend who is in Distress. Her Husb.ᵈ has again run himself in Debt. Go to Mad.ᵉ de La Borde's and spend the Evening. Madame d'Albani who is here (and who by the bye is a sensible well informed Woman) tells me that the prussian Minister here is despised at Home and remains in this Country because he is deeply in Debt. She speaks contemptuously of the Conduct of Ségur. The Weather has been very bad this Morning, it snowed last Night and this Morning we have a cold Rain. Towards Midnight it clears up.

Saturday 24. — Write. Visit Mons.ʳ de La Fayette who is with the King. At Mons.ʳ de Montmorin's, all abroad. At Madame de Stahl's who is in bed. She is glad to see me & tells me all the News she knows. The Abbé Louis comes in who is *flagorneur au possible* (Hibernice) blaney. Dine at Home and go after Dinner to the Louvre. Pass the Afternoon with my friend and repeat my Caresses until she is satiated with the genial Joy. Go thence to

---

¹ This divinity, wife of self-styled Marquis de Fontenay, had already had the first and most legitimate of her many children, whose fathers will include Napoleon's army contractor Ouvrard and a real Prince de Chimay, after her revolutionary connection with Tallien of the Terror.

Madame de Witt's and spend the Evening. The Emperor has acceded to the Conclusum of the Diet of Ratisbon. The Weather continues bad.

Sunday 25. — Write. M.ʳ Swan calls. After he is gone I go to Mad.ᵉ Tronchin's. Thence to Mad.ˡˡᵉ Duplessis. Take her to the Louvre where we dine in Trio. After Dinner visit the british Embassadress and as she seems *très peu empressée* I keep aloof. This will I think operate a little but whether well or ill is doubtful. We shall see. Leave my Name with Mad.ᵉ de Ségur and then go again to the Louvre. The Weather is still bad. Mad.ᵉ d'Albani spends the Evening here and the Abbé de L'Isle repeats his Verses.

Monday 26. — Read and write. At four oClock go to the Louvre and sit awhile with Monsieur. Say *bon jour* to Mad.ᵉ and go to Mad.ᵉ de Stahl's where I dine. Thence to Mad.ᵉ de Ségur's. Sit with her a while and then go to the Louvre. My friend observes that I am out of Humor and I state to her the Cause which is in her Conduct. She endeavors to remove the Impression but I leave it with her. Sit a little while with Monsieur, then return Home and read. The Weather is still very unpleasant.

Tuesday 27. — Write. Go to the Louvre. My friend presses me hard to stay and dine, which I refuse, and as I place this Refusal to the Account of her Conduct she has in Consequence a nervous Affection. Dine with Mad.ᵉ de Montmorin. De Lessart, the Minister of foreign Affairs, is here and as we turn a great many Things over in Conversation after Dinner I conclude in going away by telling him that the King is the only Piece of Wood which will remain afloat in the general Ship wreck.[1] He says that he begins to think so. After Dinner I return to the Louvre and find my poor friend very ill. A little Kindness in Tone and Manner does her more Good than the Dose of Œther which she had taken. Take Mad.ᵉ de La Borde up to visit Mad.ᵉ d'Houdetot & then bring her to the Louvre but a Message from her Husband announcing some new Misfortune obliges her to return. The Weather continues bad. The Wind is high from the Northwest with heavy Showers.

---

[1] This myopia about the King's future will last more and more unaccountably up to the morning of August Tenth; critical months in which Morris's knack of prophecy is not functioning.

Wednesday 28. — Write. I have no News yet from Le Couteulx whom I called on Yesterday to tell him that it is just 40 Days since he agreed to do a Business which we had conversed about. Go to the Minister of the Marine and speak to him of Swan's Affair. He waits for a Decree of the Assembly. The West India Business. It has been suspensed with a View to receive News from S.t Domingue. Tell him of the Inconveniences attending this Delay. Recommend the bringing of the Swiss Troops to Paris under the Pretext that they are too aristocratic to be trusted on the Frontiers. They will preserve Order here in the general Confusion which may be expected. Recommend that under similar Pretexts the Cavalry be brought to an interior Circle. He approves of this. Go from hence to Mad.lle Duplessis and take her to the Louvre where we dine. After Dinner we perform the cyprian Rites and then go to Mad.e d'Albani's to a *Thé*. Afterwards I go to the Baron de Grand Cour's. De Moustiers tells me that the Proposals he had made in Berlin are laid aside because there is no sufficient Ground of Confidence in the Government of this Country. He says that his Enemies have prevailed in appointing him to Constantinople. I recommended to the Minister of the Marine to be employed as Chef du Département des Vivres Monsieur Bertrand, who was at the Head of the African Company at Marseilles. The Weather is still bad this Day but has cleared up in the Evening.

Thursday 29. — This Morning write a little. M.r Swan calls and consumes my Time. Go to the Louvre and perform the cyprian Rites, then take up M.r Catchubey and dine at the Restorateur's from whence we go to the Opera, where her Majesty makes her Appearance and is well received. From the Opera we go to Mad.e de Guibert's where I pass the Evening. Nothing remarkable this Day. The Weather less foul but not fair.

Friday 30. — This Morning write. Take Mad.lle Duplessis to the Louvre and then go to dine with Mad.e Foucault. After Dinner return to the Louvre. My friend is not well. Go to Mad.e de Stahl's and leave my Name. Thence to the Luxembourg where I sit awhile with Mad.e du Bourg. Call on Mad.e de Ségur who is abroad and then go to Madame de La Borde's where I spend the Evening. Recommend to Mad.e Tronchin the Purchase of R. M.'s

Dover Estate. Take my friend Home; we are cool en Route without being indisposed to each other. The Weather has this Day been very fine. I asked La Borde if he would take a Journey of ten or twelve Days. He answers affirmatively.

Saturday 31. — This Morning Brémond comes and presents Mons.ᵣ de Monciel,[1] the newly appointed Minister to Mayence, who wishes me to point out to him his Line of March. I tell him that it will be necessary to have a confidential Person at that Spot. Shew him how he may acquire useful Intelligence and point out the Insufficiency of the present Administration. Close by telling him that he will do well to have a Correspondence by which he will convey useful Intelligence to the King. He is very desirous of this and at his Instance I promise to sound his Majesty on that Subject. Dine with Mons.ᵣ de Montmorin and desire Mons.ᵣ de Molleville to mention this Matter to the King and let me know the Result. De Lessart communicated this Day to the Assembly a Message from the Emperor which is decisive of his Sentiments. He has ordered his General Bender to defend the threatened Electorate of Treves. Call at Madᵉ de Ségur's and Madᵉ de Stahl's, then go to the Louvre and thence to Madᵉ de Moley's. After Supper go to Madᵉ de Witt's. The Weather is again rainy and disagreable.

Extract: Morris to President Washington

Paris 27 Decʳ 1791.

As to the State of Things here I would convey it to you as fully as Propriety will admit but I know not yet by what Opportunity this Letter will go and the post office was never more abused under the most despotic Minister than it is at present, notwithstanding the Decrees to the Contrary. Every Letter I receive bears evident Marks of *patriotic* Curiosity. This anxious Spirit of pettifogging Villainy proves the fear of those who make Use of it, and truly they have Reason to fear for every Day proves more

---

[1] Terrier de Monciel (1757–1831) succeeds Girondist Minister Roland in the Interior. Becomes involved in plan with Morris to bribe troops to get the King safely out of Paris, just before August Tenth, 1792.

clearly that their new Constitution is good for Nothing. Those
whom I had warned in Season of the Mischiefs they were preparing endeavor now that it is too late to lay the Blame on others
by Way of excusing themselves, but the Truth is that instead of
seeking the public Good by doing what was right, each sought
his own Advantage by flattering the public Opinion. They dare
not now propose the Amendments which they perceive and
acknowlege to be indispensible. They have besides no Confidence
in each other for everyone feels a Reason against it and meets
moreover with daily Proofs that his Copatriots are no better than
himself. The Assembly (as you who know such Bodies will
naturally suppose) commits every Day new Follies, and if this
unhappy Country be not plunged anew into the Horrors of
Despotism it is not their Fault. They have lately made a Master
Stroke to that Effect. They have resolved to attack their Neighbors unless they dissipate the Assemblies of french Emigrants who
have taken Refuge in their Dominions. These Neighbors are
Members of the german Empire, and France threatens to carry
into their Country not fire and Sword but *la liberté*. Now as this
last Word does not in the Acceptation of german Courts mean
so much *Liberty* as *Insurrection* you will see that the *Pretext*
is given for Hostilities without violating the Law of Nations.
Add to this that three french Armies of 50,000 Men each are
ordered to assemble on the Frontiers. One under your old Acquaintance Rochambeau in Flanders, one under our friend La
Fayette in Lorraine so as to penetrate by the Moselle River into
the Electorate of Treves, and one under a Monsieur Lükner in
Alsace. This last I am told has but slender Abilities and the other
two you are acquainted with. Putting all other Things out of the
Question it is self evident that the Empire must bring Force to
oppose the Force thus ordered, and in Consequence it is not to be
doubted that 50,000 prussian and 50,000 austrian Troops will
make their Appearance as speedily as Circumstances can permit.
Now I am thoroughly convinced that if this Country were *united
under a good Government* and in Peace with England they could
set the Rest of Europe at Defiance, but you have no Idea my
dear Sir of a Society so loosely organized. America in the worst
of Times was much better because at least the criminal Law was

executed, not to mention the Mildness of our Manners. My Letters predicting their present Situation may perhaps have appeared like the Wanderings of exagerated Fancy, but believe me, they are within the coldest Limits of Truth. Their Army is undisciplined to a Degree you can hardly conceive. Already great Numbers desert to what they expect will become the Enemy. Their *Gardes nationales* who have turned out as Volunteers are in many Instances that corrupted Scum of overgrown Population of which large Cities purge themselves and which, without Constitution to support the Fatigues or Courage to encounter the Perils of War, have every Vice and every Disease which can render them the Scourge of their friends and the Scoff of their Foes. The Finances are so deplorably bad that the Bankruptcy which actually exists by the Depreciation of the Paper Money must soon be declared by stopping Payment in some Quarter or other, unless those effectual Remedies be applied which seem to be beyond the Power of the Government and beyond the Talents of those who administer it. The Discontent is general but it does not break out, partly because the Antipathy to the *Aristocrats* and the Fear of their Tyranny still operates and partly because no safe opportunity offers. Everyone is bewildered in his Meditations as to the Event and like a Fleet at Anchor in a Fog no one will set Sail for fear of running foul. If they come to Blows on the Borders a curious Scene will I think present itself. The first Success on either Side will decide the Opinions of a vast Number who have in Fact no Opinion but only the *virtuous* Determination to adhere to the strongest Party, and you may rely on it that if the Enemy be tolerably successful a Person who shall visit this Country two Years hence will enquire with Astonishment by what Means a Nation which in the Year 1788 was devoted to its Kings became in 1790 unanimous in throwing off their Authority and in 1792 as unanimous in submitting to it. The Reasons are given to you in my Letter of the 29th of April 1789 and my Fears exprest in that Letter seem now to be on the Eve of Reality. The King means well and may perhaps by his Moderation finally succeed in saving his Country. I hope much from this Circumstance but alas the Moderation of one who has been so wounded, so insulted, seems to be but a slender Dependence and yet I verily believe it to be the best and I had almost said the only Dependence.

31 Dec!

A Courier arrived last Night with Dispatches which are to be communicated to the Assembly this Morning. The Emperor informs the King that he has given Orders to Gen! Bender (who commands in the low Countries) to protect the Electorate of Treves with all his Forces. I did not mention, as I ought to have done, that the Courts of Berlin and Vienna have concluded a Treaty *for the Protection of the German Empire and Maintenance of its Rights*. You will have seen that the Emperor, having adopted the Determinations of the Diet respecting the Claims of those Princes who have certain feodal Rights preserved to them by the Treaty of Westphalia in Alsace and Lorraine, reminded the King that the Dominion of France over those Provinces is conceded by that Treaty. The Dutch Government has proposed a Treaty with the Emperor as Sovereign of the low Countries for mutual Aid and Protection in Case of Insurrections, which Offer is accepted. All this is explained by the Intrigues of France to excite Revolt in Holland and Flanders, and the Completion of such a Treaty will place the Emperor at Ease should he operate against this Country next Spring.

JANUARY 1792

Sunday 1 *January* 1792. — Another Year is gone — Write this Morning. M. Swan calls, being alarmed lest the Minister of the Marine should be turned out. Dress and visit Madame Le Couteulx. Leave my Name for different Persons. At Mad.º d'Houdetot's, Cantaleu's, Le Normand's, Grand's, Vannoise's, Boutin's, Moley's & Grand Court's. See Mons. Millet and Mesdames Guibert & Courcelles. Leave my Name for Madame Dewitte and Lavoisier. Visit Mad.º Foucault who is delighted with this Mark of Attention. Then go to the Louvre where I dine. We are twice interrupted ... At half past five I leave my friend, who is vexed at it, and visit Mad.ᵉ du Bourg. Go from thence to Mad.ᵉ l'Ambassadrice de l'Ångleterre who tells me that she was afraid I had forgotten her. This is well. Call on Mad.ᵉ de Ségur and sit awhile with her. Then go to a Thé at Mad.ᵉ Tronchin's and afterwards return to the Louvre where my friend receives me coolly. I return it by being very cold all the Evening. The Weather was fine at Noon but is grown bad again to Night.

Monday 2. — This Morning write. Dine at the Restorateur's and visit my friend after Dinner. . . . I pay a Visit to Monsieur who laments to me the Coldness and Neglect of his Wife. She sets me down at Home where I wait a while for Mons.ʳ Catchuby, but as he does not come I visit Mad.ˡˡᵉ Duplessis and then return.

Tuesday 3.ᵈ — M.ʳ Brémond and M.ʳ Monciel call on me and stay too long. After they are gone I write. At three go to the Louvre and thence to M.ʳ de Moutiers to dine. The Vicomte de Ségur talks more Nonsense in a given Time than I have yet heard from him. After Dinner de Moustiers shews me a Note he has prepared for Monsieur de Lessart respecting the present State of Affairs. He shews me a Model of one of the New York Pilot Boats, the Dimensions of which are 49 f.ᵗ Keel, 15 f.ᵗ Beam, 7 feet in the Hold, two feet breadth of Keel and two feet Heighth above the Water, the Rake aft is 3 feet and the Rake forward 8 feet. The Draft of Water forward 4½ feet and aft 7½ feet. The Price compleatly rigged, and built with live Oak and Red Cedar is N. Yk C.ʸ 569£. The length of the Deck is, from the above Dimensions, just 60 feet. Qu: would not a Schooner of double this Size, rising six feet out of Water, having a double Deck and five feet between Decks, be one of the fastest and safest Vessels in the World. Would she not be built and sheathed with Copper, compleatly fitted with Provisions for twelve Months, for £1000 S.ᵍ; would not such a Vessel be easily navigated by four Men and consequently with a Crew of ten be equal to any Weather or Season. These are Points worth examining for Packets. Go again to the Louvre but we have no Moment to ourselves. Pass a few Minutes with Mad.ᵉ Le Couteulx whose Society receives me with an Air of Strangeness not pleasant. Go to the british Embassador's where I stay late and have a little sparring with Mad.ᵉ de Stahl who is vexed at it. The Weather is fine at last.

Wednesday 4. — This Morning M.͏ʳ Crawford calls to ask my Opinion and Advice respecting some Points in his Marriage Contract with Miss Campbell. M.͏ʳ Chaumont also calls. I walk in the Tuileries where I meet Mad.͏ᵉ Foucault. She tells me she has drank Spa Water this Morning and is très . . . She goes to one . . . Place which is shut up and is obliged to look about for another. By Enquiry she gets at last what she wants. One of my Countrywomen would have suffered every Extremity rather than make known her Situation. Dress and call on my friend. We embrace and as soon as she is drest I take her to Mad.͏ˡˡᵉ Duplessis and thence all three go to dine with Mons.͏ʳ Bertrand. He tells me that the King is well pleased with the Idea of receiving Intelligence direct from Monsieur de Monciel. The Committee delays the Report on the Colonial Application. He thinks it best under the present Circumstances not to contract for Wood with M.͏ʳ Swan nor with any Body else. I am of the same Opinion. M.͏ʳ de Montmorin tells me he has received a Letter from Col.͏° Ternant but he has only run over it and can give me no News. Qu: what does this mean? I take the Ladies to the Louvre and then visit Mad.͏ᵉ de La Borde and Mad.͏ᵉ de Vannoise who are both abroad. Go to Mad.͏ᵉ de Witt's and spend Part of the Evening. Thence to Mad.͏ᵉ de Stahl's and pass the remainder. Mad.͏ᵉ de Valence [1] who is here seems very glad that I speak to her. This arises from my great Coldness the other Evening at the Louvre. Such is Woman, — and Man too. Everyone is taken at the Price he puts on himself, if taken at all, and the great Art consists in placing the Merchandize at as high a Value as it will bear. My Conversation this Evening with Mr de Witte on Money and Exchange has given him a very high Opinion of my Information on that Subject and I think he will speak of it again. The Weather this Day has been fine. The Wind has got round to the Eastward.

Thursday 5. — This Morning write a little. M.͏ʳ Brémond and M.͏ʳ Monciel call on me and I inform the latter that the King accepts of his Proposal. They are to shew me a Memoire upon Switzerland before it is presented. I visit my friend who is very formal so I leave her and ride. Dine with Count Dillon. Call on the british Embassadress who had asked me to Dinner but I

---

[1] Madame de Valence, daughter of the Genlis and wife of an Orleans Equerry.

am too late. Go to Mad.^e de Ségur's and thence to Mad.^e de La
Borde's and thence to Mad.^e de Guibert's where I spend the Evening. The baron de Grand Cour told me at Dinner that it is
published in the *Courier de l'Europe* that Col.^o Smith is appointed
Minister plenipô: from the United States to the Court of London.
This is strange and is I suppose a Part of what the Count de Montmorin had received. The Weather is clear and cold. Wind from
the North East.

Friday 6. — Write very little. Go to Breakfast with Mad.^e de
Vannoise. Thence to the Louvre where I sit a long Time with
Monsr. Mad.^e comes in and I tell her that I shall go out to America next Spring. This News distresses her not a little. She ex-
claims 'then I shall loose all my friends at the same Time.' She
says that the Bishop leaves her in a few Days but as yet she can-
not tell me whither he goes. I dine with Monsieur de Montmorin.
Ask him what Ternant says respecting the App.^t of a Minister
to this Country. He says that his Letter mentions Nothing of the
Matter but he will ask Rayneval and inform me. After Dinner I
go to the Louvre and sit with my friend the Evening. We of
Course embrace. Go to Mad.^e de La Borde's. Nothing here. The
Weather has been fine this Day but feels like what we call a
Weather breeder. The Air is light and seems to portend Snow.

Saturday 7. — This Morning write. Take Mad.^{lle} Duplessis to
the Louvre, then go to dine with Mad.^e Foucault. After Dinner
visit the Countess d'Albany. Thence to Mad.^e de Witte's where I
take Tea and then go to the Louvre and pass the Evening. The
Weather is foul again this Day; it snowed last Night and this
Morning, during the latter Part of the Day and the Evening it
rains.

Sunday 8. — This Morning I set about sorting some Papers
but Commodore Jones comes in and interrupts me. After I am
dressed I go to the Louvre where there is Company. We get rid
of them for a Moment and use it as we ought. Dine here. Mad.^{lle}
Duplessis is of Course one. The Bishop d'Autun comes in and eats
a cold Dinner. We play and the Women sleep. He observes to me
that the Assignats have reduced France to a deplorable Condition, which is true enough. Go to the british Embassador's; she
is abroad. Go to Mad.^e de Ségur's and sit with her some Time;

thence to the Luxembourg. Mad? du Bourg presses me to come
and see her to *converse* together. Mad? de Ségur told me that the
bishop d'Autun goes to England soon. I visit Mad? Tronchin but
I leave her speedily and go to Mad? du Moley from whence I return to the Louvre and pass the Evening. Mons? de Grand Cour
did not call on me as he promised, neither have I been able to
meet him. The Weather is grown cold again. It snowed last
Night and freezes pretty hard all Day to Day.

Monday 9. — Write. Brémond comes. He tells me that they
offer to make him Secretary to Mons? de Monciel. I tell him that
they wish to get rid of him. I take up Mad?lle Duplessis and leave
her at the Louvre. Dine with Mad? Foucault. Go afterwards to
visit Mad? du Bourg. Thence to the Louvre where I spend the
Evening. It has snowed the greater Part of this Day.

Tuesday 10. — This Morning M? Brémond and M? Monciel
call on me and Breakfast. After they are gone I read and write till
my Carriage is ready, then go to the Minister of the Marine's
with whom I have a Conference on the Bishop d'Autun's Mission
and on other public Affairs. He tells me that he has communicated to the Queen his Sentiments on the very impolitic Step now
taken and that she is sensible to this Confidence. He says the
King spoke of me in very favorable Terms the other Day when he
communicated to him the Plan of a Correspondence with Monsieur de Monciel. I tell him it is Time to arrange Matters with
the Emperor &c?. He says (and justly) that unless he were sure
that the King and Queen make no imprudent Confidences He
dare not risque himself. The Risque is indeed great. Go to the
Louvre but Monsieur is with my friend. Go to the british Embassador's where I dine. Converse with her after Dinner a good
Deal. She asks whether in London I favor the Ministerial or Opposition Party. I tell her that when a Measure is proposed my
Sentiment depends on the Thing and not on the proposer, consequently I am for or against according to my Judgment; but if
they will make L? Gower Minister of foreign Affairs I shall then
wish Success to his Measures for her Sake. Tell Madame de
Tarente to inform the Queen from me that Monsieur de Molleville is the only Minister in whom she ought to have Confidence.
Go to the Porcelaine & meet her there. We exchange little pres-

ents of *Amitié*. She shews me a great Deal and I find it more convenient to give China than Time. Go to the Louvre ... Stay till eleven and then return Home. The Weather is grown again less cold, the Wind having got round to the Westward. M.ʳ Bertrand tells me that he expects his Namesake every Day and that he is employed in arranging his Bureauxs. I tell him that the Assembly have I fear resolved to ruin him by suffering his Department to perish. He suspects the same Thing.

Wednesday 11. — This Morning M.ʳ Monciel and M.ʳ Brémond call. The former tells me that he has conversed with Mons.ʳ Barthélémi upon the bishop d'Autun's Errand to London. He informs him that the Object is to make an Alliance with England in order to counterballance Austria and the Offer to England is the Isle of France and Tobago. This is a most wretched Policy. Brémond tells me that the Jacobine Party have got hold of a Plan of their Enemies to work a violent Change in the Constitution, and brings me a Newspaper which contains it. There is Reason to believe that some such Thing was in Agitation. It is very absurd. I go to the Louvre where we have Company but Mad.ᵉ sends them away under the Pretext that she is going out and then we embrace. Go with her to take up Mad.ˡˡᵉ Duplessis. We dine together here and I stay the Evening, the Weather being bad. It has been wet and dirty all Day, this Evening it snows hard.

Thursday 12. — This Morning go out early, call on de Marbois who assures me that he is faithful to the King and considers that as being the only possible fidelity to the Nation. Go to the Baron de Grand Cour's and as he is abroad I go to the Count de Moustiers who is also abroad. Call on Monsieur Millet and then go to the Baron Grand Cour's again. Sit some Time with him and urge in such Manner the Land Speculation that he seems seriously disposed towards it. He is to call on me next Sunday. Go to the Louvre where my friend asks in a very serious Tone if I have advised M.ʳ de Molleville to oppose the Bishop d'Autun's Embassy. I tell her that I have. She is very angry at this and we have a tartish Conversation. Go to Madame de Guibert's to dine. Nothing here. Go to the Opera with Difficulty as the Horses slip at every Step. Thence take Mad.ᵉ de La Borde to Mad.ᵉ d'Albani's and afterwards to Mad.ᵉ d'Houdetot's. Go to the Louvre and am very easy and unembarrassed in a Conversation both with Madame and the bishop. She is cool and she will feel (I think) the Consequences. The Weather is clear and cold. Marbois told me that he was in Hopes the Bishop's Embassy would be stopped. The Embassador of Venice wished to know my Opinion of the State of Affairs. I tell him that I know very little about them and that I chuse to know but little. He seems much surprized at this. He tells me that De Stahl has Leave of Absence and he says that he thinks the Embassy to Britain will be stopped.

Friday 13. — This Morning Mr Brémond and Mr Monciel call on me. The former sent me last Night a Piece written by Duport against Mr Pitt. It is a very poor piece of Stuff. They (the Triumvirate) have given it to Brémond to get it printed and he wishes to correct some of its Badnesses but I tell him not to change a Letter. To have it printed immediately and to keep the Original, by which Means he will have the Authors in his Hands, for it is written by Duport and corrected by Lameth. Brémond and Monciel had a Conference with these Gentlemen Yesterday on the Subject of the Bishop d'Autun's Embassy and on mentioning the Terms to be proposed, Brémond asked how such a Treaty could be presented to the Assembly. The others answered that the Authors would be hanged, and really I think so too. De Moustiers comes in and Monciel tries to make Acquaintance but in vain till I tell de Moustiers in English that he must be acquainted. We discuss Land Matters and some political Points. He consumes my Morning. Take Mad^{lle} Duplessis to Mad^e de Flahaut's and stay Dinner as she is got into good Humor. After Dinner we go to the french Comedy and I take them Home. Go to Mad^e de La Borde's. La Borde consults me on a Proposal made to him by Beaumarchais to give his only Daughter (a most charming Girl) to La Borde's Son. He mentions to me Beaumarchais' Fortune which is very great and La Borde is ruined. I tell him that Beaumarchais has a very bad Reputation but that is Nothing to the Girl, seeing that she cannot help it. That in my Country such a Marriage would be detestable because we do not marry for Money, but in this Country where Money is every Thing, if his Son behaves well afterwards the World will not complain. On the whole I advise him to mention the Matter to some old Stagers here and know their Opinions. He says he has not yet mentioned it to his Wife and that he must ask the King's Consent. This last seems to me very unnecessary but I do not say so. The Weather is very cold Today.

Saturday 14. — Write. Go to Le Couteulx's. He has at length written to Madrid and is to give me Notes of his Letter that I may write in Conformity. Converse on the State of R. M.'s Account. He is to consider a little the Means of purchasing from Le Normand his Share. Console her a little for the Loss of her youngest Child. Not quite common Place and that is the most that can be said. Dine at the Restorateur's and go after Dinner to the Louvre. My friend is ill in bed so I stay here the Afternoon and Evening. The Bishop, who is here Part of the Time, goes off to Morrow. The Assembly have this Day, upon a Report of their diplomatic Committee, determined to attack the Emperor unless he begs Pardon by the tenth of February. The Bishop says the Nation is *une parvenue* and of Course insolent. He says their Situation is such that Nothing but violent Remedies can operate and these must either kill or cure. St Foi says the Emperor will be angry, but having more Fear than Anger, must submit. I ask them what is to become of their Finances. The bishop says that at a certain Day, to be fixed, the Assignats will be no longer a forced Currency and the Holders will be left to lay them out in Lands as they may. I think that I never heard more Absurdity from Men of Sense in all my Life. The Weather has changed and the Wind at South brings Rain and of Course Thaw.

Sunday 15. — This Morning the Baron de Grand Cour calls on me and I shew him various Maps of Lands and explain the Advantages of the Tract which de Moustiers had offered to him. De Moustiers comes in and we have a long Conversation on the Subject but the Baron does not know how to make up his Mind. He is to look about him and call again. I go to Mr Short's. He is much dissatisfied with Mr de Wolf. He says that he has told him different Stories on the Subject of his Loan &c.^a, &c.^a. He is very anxious about the diplomatic Appointments in America and complains that Mr Jefferson does not write to him. He mentions the Correspondence of the Commissioners of the Treasury here but only in a confused Manner. We are to have further Con-

versation. I leave him, as it is late. Go to the Louvre where I
dine. After Dinner visit the british Embassadress and meet there
Col? Cosmo Gordon. Call on Mad? de Ségur who is abroad.
There are sad News, it is said, from S! Domingue. The Town of
Port au Prince totally destroyed. Return to the Louvre but
Mons! de S! Pardou is here and means to continue all the Eve-
ning, which my friend regrets very much. Go hence to Mad? de
Pinieux's & spend the Evening. The Weather is grown warm but
it is very dirty.

　Monday 16. — This Morning M! Monciel calls on me and gives
me to read a Memoire on the Affairs of France with Switzerland,
made by Mons! de Salis, a Swiss. I write and then call on the
Minister of the Marine. M! Short was with me and Col? Gordon,
Brother to the late Dutchess Dowager. This last says that America ought to appoint me Minister to the Court of London. The
Minister of the Marine shews me the Answer he is preparing to
the Accusations of the marine Committee. It will be a good one.
Call on Le Couteulx who is abroad. Pay a Visit to my sick Dog
who is in the Hospital. Go to the Louvre but my friend is abroad.
Call on Mons! de Montmorin and converse on the strange State
of Affairs. Advise him to write a Memoire, the Heads of which I
mention. He promises to do it. He tells me that while the Duke
of Orleans was in England he tried hard to obtain an Authority to
offer a Treaty to England, which was of Course not granted. He
tells me the Conversation which he had on that Subject with the
Bishop d'Autun who hopes, as he says, to turn out Pitt and thinks
his Success certain if he could have the Aid of the Duc de Biron.
This is curious enough. After Dinner we go to the Theatre of the
Rue de Richelieu to see *Mélanie,* a Drama of Monsieur de La
Harpe which with many Beauties of Detail is in my Opinion a
very bad Piece. Go from hence to the Louvre and lend my Carriage to Mad!!e Duplessis after which we ... The Weather is
very warm with Rain.

　Tuesday 17. — M! Monciel does not come this Morning but
M! Brémond does and reads to me a Mémoire upon Switzerland
written by M! Sweitzer. I stay till two oClock waiting for M! Le
Couteulx. Then go to the Louvre and make my Visit very short.
Call on Le Couteulx and agree on the Letter he is to write enclos-

ing mine for M.ʳ Carmichael. He is to write to me also and I
promise to prepare a Mortgage on the Delaware Works. Dine
with the british Embassador and his Wife; we are quite snug,
being but four at Table, his private Secretary being the fourth.
We converse very freely. She again brings up M.ʳ Short (I know
not why she dislikes him so much) and asks if he will ever be a
great Man among us. I tell her that I think not as he is not a
public Speaker but he may notwithstanding be a very useful Man
here. I say this in a Tone which ends that Part of the Conversation. I find that in this House there is a profound Contempt
mixed with Abhorrence for my friend the Bishop d'Autun and I
think the Letters written from it will not facilitate the Object of
his Mission. Go hence to the Louvre where I pass the Evening.
My friend is confined to her Bed by a violent Cold. The Weather
is warm with Rain this Morning, clears up from the Southwest at
Noon and of Course is showery afterwards. I observe in Mad.ᵉ
Le Couteulx's Garden that there is a most perfect Verdure.

Wednesday 18. — M.ʳ Brémond and M.ʳ Monciel call on me and
read a Continuation of the Memoire on Switzerland. After they
are gone I write. M.ʳ Catchubey comes in and after him M.ʳ Short.
He tells me that by his Letters he finds that the foreign Appointments are undoubtedly made at this Moment in America. He
declares himself to be totally ignorant of the Persons to be named
but at the same Time he talks of buying Plate and employing a
Maître d'Hôtel, whence I conclude that he is pretty certain of
being fixed here. I tell him that I would bett ten to one against
my being appointed any where and I think it most probable that
if both he and I are named it will be to the Courts opposite to
those he has conjectured, and that, because the unlikely Events
are generally those which happen. He says he thinks it possible
that he may be appointed to Holland which would disappoint
him cruelly and he knows not whether he would accept it. Bravo!
Take Mad.ˡˡᵉ Duplessis to the Louvre and then go to dine with
Mad.ᵉ Foucault. Converse with Chaumont after Dinner on
MacComb's Purchase of Lands in America and the Means of
turning it to Account. Visit Madame du Bourg and then go to
the Louvre. Thence to Mad.ᵉ de Witt's and then again to the
Louvre. My friend is much hurt at hearing that I dine again

Tomorrow with the british Embassadress. She declares, however, that there is no Jealousy in the Case. The Weather is grown very warm. It is also rainy and disagreable.

Thursday 19. — M.ʳ Monciel and M.ʳ Brémond call on me. M.ʳ Chaumont comes and we come to a Decision on the Subject of Yesterday. De Moustiers comes and tells me that Grand Cour was to have called. I go to the Louvre and embrace my friend. Thence to Le Couteulx's and leave with him a Mortgage on Dover Estate. Thence to Monsieur de Montmorin's to announce my Departure for Saturday Morning. Thence to the british Embassador's to Dinner with the Corps diplomatique. Call on Mad.ᵉ de Ségur and after sitting awhile with her go to the Minister of the Marine's who is abroad. Thence to Mad.ᵉ d'Albani's and thence to the Louvre. The Weather is grown colder and promises to be fair.

Friday 20. — This Morning M.ʳ Brémond and M.ʳ Monciel call. M.ʳ Forsyth comes and brings Letters for Chaumont from Constable relative to MacCombe's Purchase. M.ʳ Short comes and presses me to go to Antwerp, he being very uneasy about M.ʳ de Wolf. I think with little Reason, and tell him so. M.ʳ Swan comes who has Nothing to say. De Moustiers calls and takes Leave; is to write to me in London. I dress and go to M.ʳ Bertrand's. Nothing is done. He is to speak in Council tonight about the American Debt and the Appropriation thereof to the Colony of S.ᵗ Domingo. Call on Col.ᵒ Gordon and Gen.ˡ Dalrymple, then take Mad.ˡˡᵉ Duplessis to the Louvre. Dine with Mons.ʳ Millet who has two or three kept Women. Go to the Louvre and thence to Mad.ᵉ de La Borde's. She consults me respecting her Son's Marriage with Beaumarchais's Daughter and I give her the same *No* Counsel that I did to her Husband. The Weather is cool and clear.

Saturday 21. — M.ʳ Chaumont comes and we fix the Terms on which I am to purchase if possible M.ᶜComb's Land. M.ʳ Brémond comes and tells me that de Lessart has sent an Express Yesterday to assure the Emperor that the Embassy of the Bishop d'Autun and the violent Speeches in the Assembly mean Nothing at all. Go to the Louvre and take a Ride with my friend. Dine here and pass the Day and Evening. M.ʳ de Molleville comes in and I tell him what I have heard of de Lessart. He says that it is true he

believes, because they have now no Hope from England. M!
Short comes in and tells me he has received a Letter from the
french Agent enclosing a Receipt for the Money de Wolf was to
pay, but yet he wishes to stop that Loan. I tell him I cannot
write further on the Subject till I hear from de Wolf. He asks my
Advice respecting Propositions from the Treasury here and I give
it fully. The Weather has been fine this Day; this Evening there
is a Fog.

Sunday 22. — This Morning I settle my Accounts with the
Coachmaker and prepare for my Departure. Take a Fiacre and
go according to my Promise to the Louvre. Vic d'Azyr comes in
immediately after me and tells me he has been to my Lodgings at
the Request of her Majesty to desire that if I learn any Thing in
England interesting to them that I would communicate it. While
he is here M! Short comes to desire I will get a Piece of Business
done for him with M! Parker. I desire him to write to me in London. When they are both gone I embrace my friend . . . and she
renews to me the Assurance that she will go with me to America.
Bid Monsieur Adieu and then call at the Hôtel des Américains
and purchase two Pâtés. At a Quarter before twelve leave Paris
and at ten Minutes after five arrive at the Pont S!e Maxence. The
Weather cold and disagreable, the last eight Leagues over a cold
Sand. This Tract extends to the Right and Left considerably.
At my Arrival the Hostess tells me that some Gentlemen of
Limoges were very ill treated here yesterday Evening by the
Volunteers. By the bye, they did me the Honor to call me Aristo-
crat, supposing no Doubt that I am going to Coblentz. It has
rained a little all Day.

Monday 23. — Leave Pont S! Maxence at ten Minutes after
seven this Morning and go up an inclined Plain to Bois Lehus, a
Post and an Half, good Land; thence to Gournay over a high
Plain. We descend to this Village or Town lying on a Stream
which runs into the Oise, a Post and a quarter, thence to Cuvilly
thro a Country a little hilly but the Road is level enough, thence
to Comtry les Pots thro the same Country a Post each, thence
thro a waving Country to Roye which lies on the Auregne, a
Branch of the Somme, this is a Post and an Half; thence to
Fonches a Post over the same Kind of Country, thence a Post

with very bad Horses to Marché le Pot over a high Plain; thence a Post and an Half rather descending to Péronne on the Somme. We get into the Hôtel du Grand Cerf at fifty Minutes after three, being eight Hours and forty Minutes for nine Posts and three Quarters. It has rained all last Night and all this Day with a high Wind from the Southwest.

Tuesday 24. — This Morning at six I leave Péronne; the Hotel is good but dear. We go a Post and a Half over a waving Country of long Hills and the Road a good Deal injured by the wet Weather, to Suilly; thence a Post to Bapaume over the same Kind of Country. This is a fortified Town but the Ground to the Northward is higher than that on which it stands. Thence we go a Post to Ervillers, the Country is a little waving and we descend a little. The Soil hitherto is but midling. From Ervillers we go two Posts to Arras over pretty long but not steep Hills. The Soil is light but good. Arras is a large City & fortified but it appears to me to be commanded by Ground near it. From Arras we go over the same Kind of Country a Post and an Half to Souchet and thence over a like Country but the Hills less high to Bethune, two Posts. From hence we go a Post and an Half thro a Country almost level and very rich to Lillers. We arrive here at five o'Clock and a Postillon tells us that we cannot get admitted into Aire. The Postmaster confirms this Account and in Consequence I determine to stay where I am and accordingly put up at the Tavern which they indicate. Here I discover that the Postillon is the Master of the House and Son of the Postmaster, but it is too late to retreat. I am entertained indifferently but with Zeal. I find that here as at Péronne the Gardes Nationales or *Volontaires* are *en très mauvaise Odeur*. They are out of Humor with the Inhabitants who neither like the Paper Money nor those who oblige them to receive it. The Weather is very bad, it has rained all Day; it cleared towards Evening but promises ill for Tomorrow.

Wednesday 25. — This House is clean but it is dear and poor. We leave it at twenty Minutes after five and go a Post and an Half to Aire, a fortified Town but not strong, the Country is level and very rich. From Aire we go two Posts to St Omer thro a very fine Country. The Fortifications of this Town are going to Decay and the best Wish I can form for them is that they were levelled, for at present they would just furnish to a cruel Enemy an Excuse for beating to Pieces a Number of very fine Buildings. From St Omers we go two Posts to Recousse over a hilly Country, or rather a waving Country, the Roads a good Deal cut. From thence we go to Ardres, a small walled Town but the Post House lies to the left so we do not go thro it; the last Distance is tolerably level but the Soil since we left St Omers is less good. From Ardres we go over a flat low Country and most of it but poor to Calais, two Posts. We arrive here at twenty Minutes after two so that our eight Posts and an Half consume just nine Hours and Yesterday ten Posts and an Half were performed in eleven Hours. From the Rate at which we went these Days I conclude that the Posts are rather longer than usual. The Weather is very bad, a high Wind from the Southwest and hard Rain. I find that the Packet cannot go out so I amuse myself as well as I may by a Walk round the Ramparts. This Town is much smaller than I imagined; it may be made just as strong as the Owner of it may think fit, for it is on a Plain adjoining to the Sea Shore where the Beach is very shelving.

Thursday 26. — It blew very hard all Night from the Southwest and continues to blow this Day a very heavy Gale of Wind with Rain. Visit Lord and Lady Fitz Gerald and Ld Robert. Reception polite but very cold, of Course I shall not trouble them again either here or elsewhere, at least I think not. I am indisposed and solitary, the Weather is very bad, and on the whole I find my Situation as tiresome as it need be. *N'importe*. It is the Means of acquiring Appetite for a better. Little Chance of a Change but tow.^{ds} Midnight the Wind becomes less violent.

Friday 27. — This Morning the Wind abates. Going out of my Chamber I see Mr John Francis. We walk together and become Society for the Journey. Ld Robert Fitz Gerald calls on me and while we are sitting together the Master of the Passage Boat comes to let me know that he shall set off immediately. We embark as soon as we can and are off at about three. A little after eight we get on Shore at the Beach of Dover and take a little Supper contentedly, having had a very pleasant Passage. It blew very heavily on this Coast Yesterday and there were some Vessels wrecked.

Saturday 28. — The Weather is grown bad again. Wind high from the Southwest with Rain. We cannot get off before eleven as the Custom House is not open till late. We reach Rochester ten Minutes before five, a rainy disagreable Day.

Sunday 29. — This Morning at a Quarter after nine we leave Rochester. I stop a little while on Shooter's Hill to see Mad.ᵉ de Ségur's Sons and then go on to Froome's Hotel, Covent Garden, at which Place we arrive a Quarter after two. After Dinner we visit M.ʳ & M.ʳˢ R. Penn and take Tea with them. Then go to Rob.ᵗ Morris's,[1] Jones's and Constable's Lodgings. Leave our Names for them. Return Home and eat some Oysters. The Weather this Day has been a little better but it rained in the Morning and rains again this Evening.

Morris to President Washington [2]

London 4 feb.ʸ 1792

George Washington Esq.ʳ

Philadelphia

Dear Sir

I wrote to you on the twenty seventh of December but there were many Things which I did not write and some of them I will now communicate. At the Close of the Session of the first national Assembly a Coalition was brought about between the *Jacobins* and the *Quatre vingt neufs*. It is proper to explain these Terms. The *Jacobins*, so called from their meeting at a Convent or Church of that Name, were then the *violent Party*. The others, who took their Name from a Club instituted in the Year 89, were those who termed themselves *moderate Men*, Friends to Order

---

[1] Robert Morris has sent his son Robert to peddle American lands abroad, supplementing the efforts of Temple Franklin. They both consult Gouverneur at every turn, but young Robert never faces the perils of revolutionary Paris. Constable had his own colossal acreage of New York State to unload in Europe. Morris's land correspondence makes a separate study, too bulky for this book.

[2] Written from London for greater safety, this letter sums up the Paris situation.

&c.ª, &c.ª. The Death of Mirabeau (who was beyond all Controversy one of the most unprincipled Scoundrels that ever lived)
left a great Chasm in the latter Party. He was then sold to the
Court and meant to bring back absolute Authority. The Chiefs
of the Jacobins were violent for two Reasons. First that the
Quatre vingt neufs would not join with them seriously and heartily, wherefore not being able to make Head alone, they were
obliged to use the Populace, and therefore to sacrifice to the
Populace. Secondly that the Objects of their Desire were much
greater tho more remote, than those of the other Party; for these
last had never sought in the Revolution any Thing else than to
place themselves comfortably, whereas the Jacobins did really at
first Desire to establish a free Constitution, in the Expectation
that sooner or later they should be at the Head of it. The Aristocrats you will observe were reduced to Insignificancy before the
others divided. That you know is a Thing of Course. You will
remember that the first Assembly had decreed that their Members could neither hold any Office under the Crown, nor yet be
chosen to represent the People. These Decrees were partly the
Fruit of Opposition between the two Parties, and partly the Result of Suspicions which they had both excited among the well
meaning Members of the Assembly. The first Decree was of
jacobine Parentage, to disappoint their Enemies who were upon
the Point of succeeding to Office. The second Decree was carried
against the secret Inclinations of both. But the Consequence was
that each was seriously disappointed; and as the Constitution
was clearly unable to support itself, they began to perceive that
its Ruin might involve their own, and therefore they formed a
Coalition in which each determined to make Use of the other for
its own Purposes. But you will say perhaps that both together
would be of little Use; and this is true in a Degree, for if the Constitution had been a practicable Thing those alone who were in
Power under it could have any real Authority. But that was not
the Case, and therefore the Plan of the *Allies* was to induce a
Belief in the Court that they alone had sufficient Popularity in
the Nation to preserve the monarchial Authority against the
republican Party, and on the other Hand to convince the Assembly that (having in their Hands the royal Authority) all

favors, Offices and Grants must come thro them. Thus they constituted themselves, if I may be allowed the Expression, the
Government Brokers of the Nation. I have mentioned the republican Party. This naturally grew up out of the old jacobine
Sect; for when the Chiefs, finding that all was nearly ruined by
the Want of *Authority*, had set themselves seriously to work to
correct their own Errors, many of their Disciples who believed
what their Apostles had preached, and many who saw in the
Establishment of Order the Loss of their Consequence, determined to throw off all Submission to crowned Heads as being
unworthy of a free People &cᵃ., &cᵃ. Add to this the Number of
'moody Beggars starving for a Time of Pell Mell Havock and
Confusion.'

It was this Coalition which prevented the King from accepting
the Constitution in a *manly* Manner, pointing out its capital
Faults, marking the probable Consequences, calling on them to
reconsider it and declaring that his Submission to their Decisions
arose from his Belief that it was the only Means to avoid the
Horrors of Civil War. They saw that this Conduct would render
them responsible and altho it was the most likely Means of obtaining a good Constitution at a future Day, and would have
bound the King down to the Principles he should then advance,
yet they opposed because such good Constitution would be established not only without but even against them and would of
Course deprive them of those Objects which they were in Pursuit
of. The King contended strongly for that kind of Acceptance
which I have just mentioned, but he was borne down, being
threatened with popular Commotions fatal to himself and his
Family, and with that civil War which he most wished to avoid as
the necessary Result of such fatal Commotions.

Shortly after his Acceptance it became necessary to appoint
another Minister of foreign Affairs, Monsieur de Montmorin having insisted so strongly on retiring that the King could no longer
with any Propriety ask him to stay. The State of the Ministry
was then as follows. Monsieur du Port the Keeper of the Seals a
Creature of, and sworn Adherent to the Triumvirate; which
Triumvirate is another Duport, Barnave and Alexander Lameth,
being the Chiefs of the old Jacobins. I say the *old* Jacobins, for

the present jacobins are the republican Party. This Keeper of the Seals constantly communicated every Thing that passed in Council to his Coadjutors. The Minister of the interior, Monsieur de Lessart, was a wavering Creature, one of those of whom Shakespeare says that they 'renege affirm and turn their Halcyon Beaks with every Gale and vary of their Masters.' He had been one of Mr Necker's Underlings, was brought forward by him, and had connected himself with the Triumvirate, Mr Necker's Enemies, as being the strongest Party, but still kept up a good Understanding with the Others. Duportail the Minister at War, of whom I formerly spoke to you when he was appointed, and foretold the Conduct he would pursue towards his Creator Monsieur de La Fayette, was also compleatly subservient to the Triumvirate. But at that Time he was so much embroiled with the Assembly that his speedy Resignation seemed unavoidable. Monsieur Bertrand had just been appointed to the Marine, an Office which Monsieur de Bougainville had refused to accept. *He* was pushed to it by the *Quatre vingt neufs* whom he despises, and told the King that he would not be Member of a Ministry many of whom he knew to be unfaithful to him. Monsieur Bertrand was brought forward by the same Influence, but he is really attached to the Crown, wishes ardently to obtain a good Constitution for his Country, is an intelligent sensible and laborious Man, formerly of the Robe and the particular Friend of Monsieur de Montmorin. I mentioned to you formerly that Monsieur de Choiseul had refused the Office of foreign Affairs. While it was in Question who should be appointed to succeed Monsieur de Montmorin, the King of his own Head named the Count de Moustiers and wrote him a Letter on the Subject which de Moustier has since shewn to me. He had the Prudence to write from Berlin to decline accepting untill after he should be in Paris. When he arrived in that City the King told him that he could not give him the Office because he was considered as an Aristocrat. You will observe that the Coalition had been at Work to get Rid of him, and here I must make a Digression. The Plan was that as soon as Circumstances would permit a Minister at War should be appointed faithful to the King, and then Bougainville take the Marine, Bertrand be appointed Keeper of the Seals, and de Lessart either kept in or turned out as he should behave. This Plan was not known to the Coalition at all, but they well knew that if de Moustiers got into Place it would be a Step towards the Destruction of their Influence and Authority; they therefore assured the King that they could not answer for Consequences, threatened him with popular Commotions, with Opposition in the Assembly and the like so that at last he gave up his Nomination and explained the Matter to de Moustiers. A long Interregnum ensued in that Office and as Monsieur de Montmorin absolutely refused to continue any longer, the *Portefeuille* was given to Monsieur de Lessart, and after some Time the Count de Ségur was appointed. He accepted in the Belief of two Things, in both of which he was mistaken. One that he had the Confidence of the King and Queen; but he had never taken the right Way to obtain either their Confidence or that of others. The second Article of his Creed was that the Triumvirate (his Patrons) commanded a Majority in the Assembly. He was undeceived as to the latter Point immediately and therefore threw up the Office and went out of Town. Under these Circumstances Monsieur de Narbonne tried hard to obtain that Place, and as I have mentioned his Name and that of Monsieur de Choiseul, I will in this Place mention that of the Abbé de Périgord, afterwards Bishop of Autun. These three are young Men of high Family, Men of Wit and Men of Pleasure: the two former were Men of Fortune but had spent it. They were intimates all three and had run the Career of Ambition together to retrieve their Affairs. On the Score of Morals neither of them is exemplary. The Bishop is particularly blamed on that Head. Not so much for Adultery, because that was common enough among the Clergy of high Rank, but for the Variety and Publicity of his Amours; for Gambling, and above all for Stock Jobbing during the Ministry of Monsieur de Calonne with whom he was on the best Terms, and therefore had Opportunities which his Enemies say he made no small Use of. However I do not believe in this, and I think that except his Galantries and a Mode of Thinking rather too liberal for a Churchman the Charges are unduly aggravated. It was by the bishop's Intrigues *principally* that Monsieur de Choiseul was formerly nominated to the Office of foreign Affairs, but he preferred staying at Constanti-

nople till he could see which Way Things would settle, and to that
Effect he prevailed on the Vizier, or rather the Reis Effendi, to
write that he thought it much for the Interest of France that he
should stay for three Years longer in that City. Monsieur de
Narbonne is said by some to be the Son of Louis the fifteenth by
Madame Adelaide his own Daughter and one of the present
King's Aunts. Certain it is that the old Lady, now at Rome, has
always protected and befriended him in the warmest Manner. In
the Begining of the Revolution he, a great Anti Neckarist tho the
Lover *en titre* of Madame de Stahl, Mr Neckar's Daughter, was
not a little opposed to the Revolution: and there was afterwards
some Coldness between him and the bishop, partly on political
Accounts, and partly because he (in Common with the Rest of
the World) believed the bishop to be well with his Mistress. By
the bye, she tells me that it is not true and of Course I who am a
charitable Man believe her. This Coldness was however at length
removed by the Interference of their common Friends, and the
bishop labored hard to get his friend de Narbonne appointed to
the Office of foreign Affairs but the King would not agree to this
because of the great Indiscretion of Madame de Stahl. Monsieur
de Lessart was therefore appointed, he being very glad to get rid
of the Department of the interior where he had every Thing to
apprehend from Want of Power, Want of Order, and Want of
Bread. The next Step was to bring Monsieur de Narbonne forward to fill the Place of Monsieur du Portail, and to this Mr de
Lessart gave his hearty Assistance by Way of compensating for
the Disappointment in the other Department. Finally the interior or Home Department was filled by a Monsieur Cahier de
Gerville of whom I know very little nor is it necessary that I
should. This Ministry stands then divided as follows. The
Keeper of the Seals and Mr Delessart are attached or supposed to
be so to the Lameth Faction, Monsieur de Narbonne and Mons.
Bertrand are supposed to be attached to the *Quatre vingt neufs*
and Mr de Gerville rather leaning to the latter. This Ministry,
extremely disjointed in itself and strongly opposed by the Assembly, possesses on the Whole but a moderate Share of Talents;
for tho the Count de Narbonne is a Man of Wit, and a very pleasant lively fellow, he is by no Means a Man of Business: and tho

Mr Bertrand has Talents, yet according to the old Proverb one Swallow never makes a Summer.

Such as it is, Every one of them is convinced that the Constitution is good for Nothing; and unfortunately they are many of them so indiscreet as to disclose that Opinion when at the same Time they declare their Determination to support and execute it, which is in Fact the only rational Mode (which now remains) of pointing out its Defects. It is unnecessary to tell you that some Members of the national Assembly are in the Pay of England, for that you will easily suppose. Brissot de Warville is said to be one of them, and indeed (whether from corrupt or other Motives I know not) his Conduct tends to injure his own Country and benefit that of their antient Foes in a very eminent Degree. The Situation of their Finances is such that every considerate Person sees the Impossibility of going on in the present Way; and as a Change of System after so many pompous Declamations is not a little dangerous among a People so wild and ungoverned, it has appeared to them that a War would furnish some plausible Pretext for Measures of a very decisive Nature, in which State Necessity will be urged in the Teeth of Policy, Humanity and Justice. Others consider a War as the Means of obtaining for the Government the eventual Command of disciplined military Force which may be used to restore Order, in other Words to bring back Despotism, and then they expect that the King will give the Nation a Constitution which they have neither the Wisdom to form nor the Virtue to adopt for themselves. Others again suppose that in Case of a War there will be such a leaning from the King towards his Brothers, from the Queen towards the Emperor, from the Nobility (the very few) who remain, towards the Mass of their Brethren who have left the Kingdom, that the bad Success naturally to arise from the Opposition of undisciplined Mobs to regular Armies, may be easily imputed to treasonable Counsels, and the People be prevailed on to banish them all together and set up a federal Republic. Lastly the Aristocrats, burning with the Lust of Vengeance, most of them poor, and all of them proud, hope that supported by foreign Armies they shall be able to return victorious and reestablish that Species of Despotism most suited to their own Cupidity. It happens therefore that the whole

Nation tho with different Views, are desirous of War, for it is proper in such general Statement to take in the Spirit of the Country, which has ever been warlike. I have told you long ago that the Emperor is by no Means an enterprizing or warlike Prince. I must now in Confirmation of that inform you that in the famous Conference at Pilnitz he was taken in by the King of Prussia for he came prepared to higgle about the Nature and Extent of the Succor to be given and Forces to be employed but the King cut the Matter short by telling him that the Difference in the Extent of their respective Dominions and a Variety of other Circumstances, would justify him in demanding greater Efforts on the Part of the Emperor, but that he would meet him on Ground of perfect Equality. In Consequence of this the Emperor was obliged to accede but he did so in the View and the Wish to do Nothing. When therefore the King accepted the Constitution, he chose to consider that as a Reason why foreign Powers should not interfere. The King of Prussia however gave to the King *personal* Assurances of his Good Will and *brotherly* Attachment and of this he offered *substantial Proofs*. The King's true Interest (and he thinks so) seems to consist in preserving the Peace, and leaving the Assembly to act as they may think proper which will demonstrate the Necessity of restoring in a great Degree the royal Authority. The Faction opposed to him are very sensible of this, which forms an additional Reason for driving every Thing to Extremity, and therefore with a View to destroy every Root and Fibre of antient Systems they have imagined to court the Alliance of Great Britain and of Prussia. In Consequence the Bishop d'Autun has been sent to this Country, and if my Information be good is authorized to propose the Cession of the Islands of France and Bourbon and the Island of Tobago as the Price of an Alliance against the Emperor. This has a direct Tendency to break the Family Compact with Spain, who has long been courted by Britain; for it is evident that this Country will not embark in a Contest which is to do France any good, and therefore the Game of Mr Pitt is as clear as the Sun and suits exactly his Temper and Disposition. He has only to receive the Offers made, and send Copies to Vienna and Madrid by way of supporting his Negotiations, particularly with the latter. He can offer them also the Guarantee of their Dominions and Rights against us, and by this Means we should find ourselves all at once surrounded by hostile Nations. The Minister of the Marine opposed violently in Council this Mission, stated the Consequences, & obtained some useful Restrictions. Mr de Warville proposed in the diplomatick Committee the Cession of Dunkirk and Calais to England as Pledges of the Fidelity of France to the Engagements which she might take. You will judge from this Specimen, of the Wisdom and Virtue of the Faction to which he belongs and I am sure the Integrity of your Heart will frown with indignant Contempt when I tell you that among the Chiefs of that Faction are Men who owe their all to the personal Bounty of the King.

This Mission of the Bishop d'Autun has produced Something like a Schism in the Coalition. The Party of Lameth and Barnave are strongly opposed to it. Monsieur de Lessart who had adopted the Scheme on the Representation of the Bishop (with whom it originated) and his Friends, abandoned it on the Representation of the others, and two Days before I left Paris an Express was sent to assure the Emperor that notwithstanding Appearances they meant him no Harm. In Effect they were again going to endeavor at an Alliance *of the Nation* with him, upon a Plan which was set on Foot about three Months ago by those who afterwards fell into the Plan of an Alliance with Britain. You may judge from hence how much dependence is to be placed on these newfangled Statesmen. The King and Queen are wounded to the Soul by these rash Measures. They have I believe given all needful Assurances to the Emperor and King of Spain: a confidential Person has desired me to assure you on their Behalf that they are very far from wishing to change the System of french Politics and abandon their old Allies, and therefore if any Advantage is taken of the present Advances to Britain that you will consider them as originating meerly in the Madness of the Moment, and not as proceeding from *them* or as meeting with *their* Approbation *but the contrary*. I shall send this Letter in such Way as promises the greatest Safety and I must entreat you my dear Sir to destroy it for Fear of Accidents: you will feel how important it is to them that this Communication be not disclosed. It is meerly personal from them to you and expressive of Sentiments which can have no Action untill they have some Authority. It is Time to close this too long Letter whose Object is to possess you of that interior Machinery by which outward Movements are directed. Believe always I pray in the Sincerity of those Sentiments with which I am yours

XI

SPRING IN LONDON

JANUARY 1792

Monday 30 *Jan?* — This Morning M.ʳ Constable calls on me and we have some Conversation. I go to Mark Lane where I see Inglis and Ellice. Go from thence to Ker and Co's and deliver a Watch for M.ʳ Stewart given into my Care by Lépine of Paris. I leave also an Almanack sent by Mad.ᵉ de Flahaut. Call on Count Woranzow ¹ and Count Rederen; leave for the first a Letter from M.ʳ Catchuby and for the second a Letter from the Countess d'Albani. Visit M.ʳˢ Phyn and sit with her a while. Visit the Count de Croix with whom I have some Conversation on the Politics of his Country. Visit the Dutchess of Gordon and Lord Landsdowne who are both abroad. Go to M.ʳˢ Church's and thence to R. M.'s Lodgings. He is abroad. Return Home and thence to the Oxford Coffee House where I meet him. He is to call on me Tomorrow. Dine at Church's. It is said that the Debts of the Prince of Wales and Duke of York are to be provided for this Session. I drink too much Wine this Day.

Tuesday 31 *Janu?* — This Morning R. M. calls on me and after him Constable. M.ʳ Boswell also. [sic]. R. M. tells me he expects to borrow Money from Pultney &c.ᵃ sufficient for present

---

¹ Count Semen Romanovich Woronzow (1744–1832), Russian Ambassador to George III, 1785–1806, a much-appreciated personality in London world. One sister, Countess Elisabeth Woronzow, had been mistress to Tsar Peter III, while a most erudite sister, Princess Daschkaw, devoted to Peter's wife, had played a prominent part in the 1762 revolution which overthrew him and established Catharine II as Empress of all the Russias. Woronzow is a hospitable widower who now and on later visits finds Morris congenial. His little daughter will marry the eleventh Earl of Pembroke. .

Purposes. M!. Constable desires me to apply to Wolfe to settle the Account of Stock sold him, taking the Deficiency at Par. I call on Ramsden the Optician and then visit the Count de La Luzerne who is come to Town with his Family. Returning I call on M!. Penn sen! who is abroad. On M!. Rogers who is also abroad but I find a Note from him and we dine together at the Piazza Coffee House. He urges for his Stock, on which he wants to raise Money to invest in Stock in France. After Dinner I visit M!.ˢ Penn and tell them that I expect to go out to America in the Spring. Mad!.ˡˡᵉ does not seem to like this Idea, from which I collect a great Deal. She tells me that a Quaker has been offering to buy her Estate near Phila?. Go with Penn to the Mount Coffee House where they discuss much Quidnunc Politics. The Weather was fine this Morning but rains again this Evening.

FEBRUARY 1792

Wednesday 1 *Feb.* — This Morning I stay at Home for M!. Rogers. R. M. calls and so does M!. J. Penn. I go to M!. Rogers's House but he is abroad, my Message was not delivered. Visit M!.ˢ Low who is also abroad. Return Home and wait some Time for M!. Francis, then go to dine with R. Penn. After Dinner call again on M!. Rogers who is not come Home, then come Home and sup on Oysters. Penn stays with me. Francis has been looking for his House and then been to tire himself at Covent Garden Theatre. The Weather has been pleasant to Day.

Thursday 2 *Feb.* — M!. Rogers calls and promises to procure if possible a Meeting of the Trustees for ToMorrow. I call on M!. Constable and converse with him, afterwards visit M!. R. Morris and read over all the Papers and Instructions from his Father. Visit M!. Colqhoun where we meet M!. Constable. Take him into the City. I call on M!. Wadeson twice but cannot find him. I call on M!. Baring but he also is abroad. Sit a little while with Mons!.

Chollet and then take M!̞ Constable to M!̞ Phyn's. Thence to dine at the Piazza Coffee House and after Dinner we go again to Phyn's. I sit late with him Tête à tête and talk of American Lands, which he seems to believe in much. The Wind blew very hard last Night from the Westward and blusters a good Deal all Day. The Air is warm.

Friday 3.̞ — Write a little while. M!̞ Ellice calls on me and as we are going out M!̞ Franklin comes in to press for his Stock. I go into the City and meet M!̞ Henchman at the American Fund Office. Nothing is done, but Things are in such Train that I shall get through speedily I think. See M!̞ Wadeson. He says that M!̞ Parker's Affairs are in a Train of Settlement. I am to see him on Sunday. Return Home and write, then take M!̞ Francis to M!̞ Penn's where we dine in Comp.̞ The Weather is cooler and the Wind very high from the Westward.

Saturday 4. — This Morning I write. R. M. calls on me and employs himself and me in prepar.̞ an Instrument of Writing. M!̞ Constable and M!̞ Colqhoun come in. The Count de Rederen, who leaves us as we are busy. The Count de Croix and M!̞ Bosville. At half past four I take Francis to dine with M!̞ᷤ R. Penn and after Dinner we go to the Play. M!̞ᷤ Siddons performs in the *Gamester* and very well. The Piece is very bad but her expressive Countenance draws Tears and even Groans from many of the Audience. The Weather has been pleasant this Day; this Evening there is a thick fog.

Sunday 5. — M!̞ Parker calls this Morning. He says he is very desirous of setling &c.̞ I read to him M!̞ Short's Letter and he says he is to do what is requisite ToMorrow Morning. I go to M!̞ Henchman's and meet there M!̞ Baring. They promise to do what I wish. Call on the Counts Rœderen and Woranzow who are both abroad. Visit the Count de La Luzerne [1] and sit with him a while. He has a fever. He tells me that in the War called the seven Years War, while the french were in Possession of Hanover, the great Frederick, who was a great Rogue, offered to leave France all the Country along the Rhine down to Holland & including Cleves and the prussian Guelderland, provided they

---

[1] Proud Minister of the Marine when Morris first knew Versailles, now an *émigré*.

would give him Hanover and let him be bound by the Wezel, and that in such Case he would agree to leave the Emperor in Possession of his antient Dominions in Silesia &c.ª. Leave my Name at Lady Tancred's & at Mͬ. Ellice's. Then visit Sir John Sinclair who tells me that Offers have been made to Charles Fox to come in, but he will not unless he can dictate, and particularly that he will exclude the Chancellor and Lᵈ. Hawkesbury. Call on Mͬ. & Mͬˢ. Church who are abroad. On Mͬ. & Mͬˢ. Penn, also abroad. Ride in the Park and walk in the Gardens, where I meet Lord Mountmorres. Dine at Mͬ. Phyn's. Constable tells me that a Paragraph is copied from a french Gazette in one of the Papers here, that I am come over Agent for the Aristocrats. Parker told me that Pinckney [1] is appᵈ. Minister from America to this Court. I come Home at nine to meet him but he does not come.

Monday 6. — This Morning write. Mͬ. Constable calls and tells me I am appᵈ. Minister plenipo: to the Court of France. I go to the Parliament Coffee House to meet Mͬ. Parker who gives me fair Promises of Payment. Call on Mͬ. Henry Drummond but do not meet with him. Afterwards on the bishop d'Autun who is abroad at the House of Commons. Then on Mͬˢ. Church and sit awhile with her. Tell her that Mͬ. Pinckney is appointed to this Court. She wished for her Father. [2] Go to Mͬ. John Penn's to Dinner. They congratulate me here on my Appointment but express their Regret that it is not to this Country. Return Home about ten oClock and sit up awhile with Mͬ. Francis who tells me that he is in Europe to qualify himself for public Office. The Weather this Day has been pleasant.

Tuesday 7. — Write this Morning. Mͬ. Franklin calls and Mͬ. John Penn junͬ. I dine with Mͬ. Colqhoun and stay the Evening. Mͬ. Franklin dines with us and a young Man who is going to settle on the Genesee Lands, also an Engineer who asks £900 Stᵍ. a Year to go out and superintend inland Navigations in America. I think it is a great Deal. Mͬ. Colqhoun is to send me the Papers ToMorrow. It has rained almost all Day and this Evening it rains hard.

Wednesday 8. — Write, then call on Mͬ. Constable and go

---

[1] Thomas Pinckney of South Carolina.
[2] General Philip Schuyler.

together into the City. I go to M.ᵣ Kapper's with M.ᵣ Inglis to settle the Terms of Agency in America by his Partner M.ᵣ Warder. Go to the American Fund Office but cannot find M.ᵣ Lane. Return Home and then go to M.ᵣ R. Penn's to Dinner. Return Home early and write till M.ᵣ Colqhoun comes in, who talks first Business and then Politics. He complains heavily of the Avarice and Meanness of Franklin. The Weather is pleasant.

Thursday 9. — Spend the Forenoon in the City to get the Trust Business finished. Call on M.ʳˢ Phyn who is abroad. At Ramsden's, as usual without Success, then go to dine at M.ᵣ Inglis's who shews me after Dinner the Basis of his Cotton Speculations. Return Home about ten. The Weather is pleasant again this Day. M.ᵣ Van Pradelles called on me this Morning.

Friday 10. — This Morning I write. R. M. calls on me. M.ᵣ Constable, Capt.ⁿ Truxton, M.ᵣ Jones, M.ᵣ Hinchcliff, Sir John Sinclair, M.ᵣ Bosville and M.ᵣ Colqhoun. Take R. Penn to dine at Grenier's Hotel à la française but the Bill is à l'holandaise. Spend the Evening at his House. The Weather is good this Day.

Morris to William Short

London 10 Feb.ʸ 1792

W.ᵐ Short Esq.ʳᵉ
         Paris

My dear Sir

... A Gentleman of my Acquaintance here shewed me the other Day a Letter from Mr King, one of the Senate, telling him that on the 22ᵈ of December you was nominated by the President to be resident Minister at the Hague. Mr Pinkney of Charlestown to be Minister here and I to be Minister in france. Believe me I sincerely participate in any Regret which this may occasion to you. I believe that after reflecting on the very precarious State of Things in France you will find your present Mission desirable. I sincerely hope it may in all Things be agreable and prosperous for I am very truly

        Yours

Since writing to you I have received Information that the Senate had not so late as the Morning of the tenth of January decided on the Nominations made by the President on the twenty second of December. It seems therefore very likely that the whole Business may fall thro. It has got, tho very lamely, into the public Prints of this City and I have by that Means been placed in the awkward Predicament of explaining to Congratulators my Position, which is not pleasant: for altho the Choice of the President is very flattering, the Rejection of the Senate would not be very grateful to any Man who has the common Feelings and yet I think it by no means improbable that this may happen to *me*. I make up my Mind however to meet that Event as well as I may and supposing always that those who are active on such Occasions are swayed by a Regard to the public Interest I forgive beforehand whatever they do against me. This does not arise entirely perhaps from Christian Charity. My Nomination has led me to take a nearer View of the Mission than I ever had done before and indeed I see so many untoward Circumstances attending it that I believe it would be better for me to pursue my original Design of going out to America this Summer. Let what will happen, I pray you to be assured of my sincere Regard and believe me to be your Friend.

Saturday 11. — This Morning M.ʳ Colqhoun calls and we visit together M.ʳ Pultney. I return Home and consult with R. M. about a Loan for his Father. Write. Visit at M.ʳ Drummond's but he is not at Home. Leave M.ʳ Pultney's Notes for his Consideration, then go to M.ʳ Constable and give him my Letters for America. Visit the bishop d'Autun. He tells me that the Duc de Biron is in Prison for 4500 £ St.ᵍ &c.ᵃ. I dine at the Piazza Coffee House and visit M.ʳ Phyn after Dinner. Sit with them pretty late. At my Return I receive unpleasant Letters.

Sunday 12. — Go this Morning by Appointment to M.ʳ Drummond's. He seems very cold upon my Propositions. Visit M.ʳ Constable and afterwards M.ʳ Franklin; take the latter with me to the Ring in Hyde Park. Dine with John Penn en famille, his Brother Richard and myself. John and his Wife intend going to America. Richard can't bear the Idea. Go to M.ʳ Colqhoun's and stay the Evening. Nothing.

Monday 13. — This Morning send for R. M. to bring with him the Materials for preparing the Plan of a Loan. The Count de Croix comes and tells me that by the last Accounts from Paris it would seem that Things could not continue long in their present Situation. Write all this Morning except while interrupted by him and by M.ʳ Henchman who calls about the Trust Business. Dine with M.ʳˢ Church. Mad.ᵉ de La Luzerne and her Family are here. The Count comes in afterw.ᵈˢ. At Dinner there is some Question about the Duc de Biron and after Dinner Church tells me that he was going forward to his Relief but discovered that Biron had not given a true and candid State of his Embarrassments, upon which he begged Leave to be off. Call on M.ʳ Rogers and then Return Home & write. The Weather has been very pleasant this Day.

Tuesday 14. — Write. R. Morris breakfasts with me. He cannot yet obtain all the Papers from M.ʳ Colqhoun. M.ʳ Constable calls. I go to Mess.ʳˢ Drummonds but no Answer is left for me on the Application to discount M.ʳ Pultney's Notes. Dine with M.ʳ Ellice and leave them (the Ladies yet at Table) to see *Othello* in which M.ʳˢ Siddons acts the Part of Desdemona. It is not well done in any one of the Characters. Young Banister in the *Citizen* out buffoons a low Character of low farce. The Weather has been very pleasant this Day.

Wednesday 15. — M.ʳ Rogers calls on me and M.ʳ Bosville. M.ʳ H. Drummond also comes. I then go into the City and pass the Morning at the Fund Office. We make some Progress. Dine with M.ʳ Inglis. Return Home about ten oClock. M.ʳ Francis comes in and sits awhile. He is as discontented a Man as need be. The Weather last Night was very foggy and this Morning it is worse; the Wind is got round to the Eastward and is as yet light but the Weather is grown colder.

Gouverneur Morris to Robert Morris

London 15 Feb.ʸ 1792

Robert Morris Esq.ʳ
Philadelphia

My dear friend

This Letter will be in Reply to what you have been so kind as to write respecting my Nomination as Minister to the Court of France. I feel as I ought the Honor conferred by the President in making it, and whatever may be its Fate in the Senate I shall always Count his Suffrage among the most flattering Events of my Life. I find that no Decision was made down to the Evening of the ninth of January tho the first Consideration was in the Morning of the twenty third of December, being in the whole eighteen Days that it had hung by the Eyelids. A mischievous Consequence of the Delay is that foreign Powers will suppose there is a great Division of Sentiment and of Course the Minister will have less Weight, at least for some Time, and if a bare Majority should eventually approve, that Circumstance also will operate in the same Way. To obviate this Evil, so far as the other Gentlemen may be concerned, I have declared here to those who have wondered at the Delay that I believe the Exceptions if any are against me. It has been reported that the Exception was to making any Appointment whatever, but I have declared my Belief that this was not the Case, for you will observe that such Opinion presupposes that the President was precipitate, whereas the Law passed on the Subject is of long Standing. On the whole I have thought it best to make myself the Scape Goat of the Flock, because if disapproved of it will then appear all natural enough and if appointed I must work thro the Difficulties as well as I can; they will be less important to my Country the other Side of the Channel, and my great Object is her Interest.

The Mission to France must be a stormy one let it fall on whom it may. You will have seen that every Character both in and out of their Country is very rudely handled by the Journalists. These Gentlemen stick not to declare that Monsieur de La Fayette is a mercenary Traitor sold to the aristocratic Faction. When such Things are said, read and believed by the vulgar you will judge what Likelyhood there is that Reason should be heard or Truth prevail. However as Mankind must in all Countries come to their Senses either sooner or later there is no Reason to doubt that a proper Conduct will at length succeed. You will observe that it was not in the Nature of Things possible to make an Appointment from *America* which would have been unexceptionable, and to have made none would have been offensive, for the Conclusion would have been that America looked with Contempt at their present Situation. That Kingdom is split up into Parties whose Inveteracy of Hatred is hardly conceivable and the Royalists and Aristocrats consider America and the Americans as having occasioned their Misfortunes. The former charge it upon us as Ingratitude seeing that it was the King who stepped forward to our Relief. Should this Party get the better in the Struggle there are very few Americans who would (for the present) be well received. On the other Hand the Republicans consider every Thing short of downright Democracy as an Abandonment of political Principle in an American. I could dwell minutely on both Sides of this Question but a Word to the Wise is sufficient. To stand *well* with all Parties is impossible but it is possible, and meerly so, to stand well with the best People in all Parties without greatly offending the others. . . .

Thursday 16. — Write a little this Morning. M.ʳ Constable comes and we go together to Charing Cross.¹ Mess.ʳˢ Drummonds will not discount M.ʳ Pultney's Notes. I go to M.ʳ Phyn's. M.ʳ Constable comes shortly after and then we go together to M.ʳ Lockart's the Bankers, to whom I propose the Discount of M.ʳ Pultney's Bills but they also decline for the present. We talk of some other Matters of Business. I visit the Dutchess of Gordon, M.ʳ John Penn & John Penn Jun.ʳ, M.ʳ Pultney, M.ʳˢ Church (who is brought to bed), Counts Rœderen and Voronzove; all except M.ʳˢ C. are abroad. Go to Mad.ᵉ de La Luzerne's, sit awhile with her and then visit her Daughter in Law. This last tells me that the bishop d'Autun has been very illy received and communicates the Particulars. Visit Lady Tancred and M.ʳˢ Low who are

---

¹ A century and a half later Drummond's bank is still at Charing Cross.

both abroad and then go to dine with Mrs R. Penn, who called on me this Morning. She shewed me the Draft of an Advertisement made by Francis to obtain a Loan on her Estate. Arrived at her House she asks me before him if he can mortgage that Estate. I tell her yes, but that the Mortgage will be good for nothing. Ask him what he wants to borrow for. He says he would buy Stock to sell out as he might want Cash; thus he would borrow at five p% and get 3 p% Interest, risquing the fall of Stocks. She says that he is mad and truly it would seem so. Return Home and read Payne's new Publication.[1] He visits Francis in the mean Time and the latter sends for me. I tell Payne that I am really affraid he will be punished. He seems to laugh at this and relies on the Force he has in the Nation. God knows what may happen but I should think the Example of France is not very inviting. He seems Cock Sure of bringing about a Revolution in Great Britain, and I think it quite as likely that he will be promoted to the Pilory. It is cold.

Friday 17. — This Morning write. John and Richard Penn call on me, also a Bird of the House of Bird, Savage and Bird. R. Morris comes, being sent for; he has not yet got the Paper I want. Mr Franklin comes and says he is willing to sell his 3 p% Stock at 15/ in the Pound, deliverable and payable next April so as to receive the Quarters dividend. He is a tight Hand. His Father calls shortly after. Dine with Mr Constable at the Piazza Coffee House. He wishes to speculate in Bank Stock, making Loans on it in Europe. I tell him that I am perswaded People will not lend beyond the Amount of the Capital on that Security. We return and take Tea. He leaves me at ten oClock. The Wind is high at North East with Flights of Snow. The Weather very cold.

Saturday 18. — Write this Morning. The younger Lockart calls on me and while here Mr Constable, whom he wants to see, comes in. He will do one of his Notes and probably the other. Mr Franklin comes in and when he is gone I talk to Mr Constable who seems to be high mounted with Respect to Bank Stock. Mr Paine calls and after him Mr Colqhoun. The latter seems desirous to get Hold of the Land which R. M. does not wish to sell.

---

[1] Second part of *Rights of Man*, which sends Paine into exile and gets him elected deputy to French Convention.

I go to R. Penn's and dine. After Dinner we go to see Mrs Siddons in Lady Macbeth but I cannot stay to the End of the Piece. It gives me very little Pleasure and I am now obliged to see either that it is badly acted or, which is perhaps equally true, that the Organization of Shakespeare's Plays is so barbarous that all the Force of his vast Genius will not compensate that capital Defect. Spend the Evening at Mr Phyn's. Madame kindly reproaches me for Neglect and I assure her truly that my Mind is not neglectful. Promise Amendment both to him and to her. The Wind is still high from the North East and the Weather very cold but it softens a little this Evening.

Sunday 19. — This Morning I call on Mr Constable, on R. Morris, on Sir John Sinclair, who are all at Home. Ask how Mrs Church does and go to Mr R. Penn's. Sit with them till five and then go to dine with the Count Woranzow. We have here Col.^{o} Miranda ^{1} who is I find very intimate, and Mr Paradise. After Dinner the Count tells me that he is perswaded Great Britain will court the United States in order to deprive France of the West India Islands. He says that Mr Pitt's Force consists in Finesse. That the Spanish Ambassador managed wretchedly in the Course of the Armament against his Country and that the Count de Florida Blanca, tho an able Courtier, is a wretched Minister, all which he promises to explain to me at another Time. He is a sensible well informed Man. He tells me it is impossible that the Emperor and King of Prussia should agree, that the Cabinet of the latter Power is deeply intriguing and will in Concert with Mr Pitt do every Thing that is possible to prevent the french Affairs from being settled. He speaks well of the Emperor and as he says from personal Acquaintance, and from Observance of his Administration in Milan and his Conduct since the Death of his Brother. Go from hence to Mrs Phyn's and sit till about ten oClock. Mr Francis sits with me afterwards till late. It has snowed all Day and is of Course mild but will I think become cold in Consequence.

Monday 20. — This Morning write. Visit Doctor Bancroft

---

^{1} After Miranda's visit to her Court, Empress Catharine had recommended the dashing South American to the special notice of all her foreign representatives.

and Mrs R. Penn. Take him to the Piazza Coffee House where half a dozen of us dine. Return Home about ten. The Weather is clear and very cold.

Tuesday 21. — This Morning Mr Drummond calls on me and Mr Constable. Mr Drummond declines the Propositions made to him on the Part of R. M. I call on Mr Donald and give him the Hint to apply to Opposition as a british Creditor of America. He seizes this Idea eagerly, being thereto prompted by his Vanity. I leave a Card with Mr Bird, then take up Mr Franklin and we dine together at the Bedford Coffee House. Go thence to his Father's to celebrate Temple's Birth Day. Col.^o Axtell is here who is a little tipsey but in very fine Preservation. M.^{rs} Le Mar is civil. We stay very late and I am heartily tired, being bored by Major Gamble who is drunkish, and a Deal of noisy singing and senseless Talk among the Rest of the Company. The Weather is calm, clear and very cold.

Wednesday 22. — Write a little. R. Morris calls and we consider what present Steps are to be taken in his father's Affairs. Go to visit Mrs Phyn, afterwards call on Mr Ellice and converse on the Situation of Banks, Money and Credit in America. I conclude that he means to go out and establish a Bank at Albany. Dine with Mr Phyn en famille, call after Dinner on Lady Anne Lindsay who is abroad and then sit some Time with Mad.^e de La Luzerne. Visit Mrs R.^d Penn and come Home at ten oClock. The Weather is calm, clear and cold. It snowed last Night. Mr Livingworth, recommended by Col.^o Wadsworth, sat with me some Time this Morning.

Thursday 23. — This Morning write. Mr Constable calls. After he is gone Payne comes in who seems to become every Hour more drunk with Self Conceit. It seems, however, that his Book excites but little Emotion and rather raises Indignation. I tell him that the disordered State of Things in France works against all Schemes of Reformation both here and elsewhere. He declares that the Riots and Outrages in France are Nothing at all. It is not worth while to contest such Declarations; I tell him therefore that as I am sure he does not believe what he says I shall not dispute it. Call to enquire after Mrs Church and then visit the Dutchess of Gordon. The Dutchess of Dorset comes in, but runs

COUNT WORONZOW
From the painting by Sir Thomas Lawrence

away at the Discussion of Gen! Gunning's Crim: Con: Cause.
Dutchess of Gordon tells me that she supposes I give Paine his
Information about America, and speaks very slightly of our Situation as being engaged in a *civil* War with the *Indians*. I smile
and tell her that Britain is also at War with *Indians*, tho in another Hemisphere. Gen! Murray observes that the Prosperity of
a Nation can best be determined by the State of the Funds and
that ours are very high. I confirm this Observation, which silences her Grace. She asks me afterwards what the Americans
think of M! Pitt. I tell her that there can be but one Opinion on
that Subject any where, viz that he is a very able Man. She says
she understands that is very high in France who even wish an
Alliance, but that cannot be; and then asks my Opinion of the
bishop d'Autun who is, as she is told, a very profligate Fellow. I
tell her he is a sensible pleasant Man. His Morals not exemplary
but that Matter much exagerated. Go to L⁴ Lansdowne's to enquire after his Health. Thence to R. Penn's where I write for M!ˢ
Masters a Letter to Abraham Ogden. Take Penn to Grenier's
Hotel where we dine with R. Morris, Jones and Franklin. After
Dinner go to a musical Party at M! John Penn's. He has the
Gout. The Music is very good. Come Home about twelve and
sit till two with M! Francis. The Weather seems to be about
changing. The Wind has hauled round to the South, tho very
feeble. The Air was soft about two oClock but grows colder towards Evening and freezes hard again at Night.

Friday 24. — This Morning write. A M! Masterman calls on
me about the Stock he possesses. While I am dressing M! Morris
and M! Jones call. I dine with R. Penn; after Dinner call on Doctor Warren who is abroad. Go to R. M.'s Lodgings and play
Chess at which I loose two Games. The Weather has grown very
mild, a light Wind from the Southward and a Thaw.

Saturday 25. — This Morning a young Man whom I dont know
calls to obtain Information about the Trust Stock. I visit M! ·
Constable. He wishes me to raise Money by a Circulation on
Amsterdam. I call on M! Wadeson who is I find gone over to
Amsterdam. Take up M! R. Penn and we go together to a Kind
of private Tavern in S! James Street where we meet M! Boswell
and M! Courtney; we dine well but the Wines are bad and our

Dinner is at 7/6 a Head; the Bill contains a Charge of 4/ for the Waiters, the first of the Kind that ever I met with. A sober Reckoning costs us just 20/ apiece. So much for London. We go to the Mount Coffee House and thence I set down Penn and Boswell each at his own House and return Home. The Weather is thick, rainy and warm.

Sunday 26. — Write. M.ʳ Colqhoun calls. He seems desirous of engaging his Friends more deeply in American Lands. I visit M.ʳ Constable to decide on the Answer to be given to M.ʳ De Wolfe's Letters. Call on M.ʳ & M.ʳˢ Phyn, then go to M.ʳ R. Penn's to Dinner. M.ʳ Francis shews here all his Father. Noisy, positive and wrong. Young M.ʳ Low called on me this Morning. The Weather was dull and rainy this Morning, the Afternoon fine and the Evening clear.

Monday 27. — Write. M.ʳ Ellice calls and after him M.ʳ Constable and then the Watch Maker. Dine at the Piazza Coffee House. After Dinner go to M.ʳˢ Phyn's. Sit a Part of the Evening with them and then visit M.ʳ Colqhoun with whom I stay till twelve. The Weather is pleasant.

Tuesday 28. — Write. Go into the City and meet M.ʳ Henchman at the City Chambers. Call on M.ʳ Levingworth who is abroad, on M.ʳˢ Low, also abroad. On M.ʳ Constable who is abroad. On M.ʳ R. Morris with whom I converse a few Minutes, then call to enquire after M.ʳˢ Church's Health. Dine at Mad.ᵉ de La Luzerne's. After Dinner visit M.ʳˢ Penn and then go to the Piazza Coffee House to meet the Americans. We sup together and stay very late. The Weather this Day has been pleasant. A Report of the Packet's Arrival, which is I believe unfounded.

Wednesday 29. — Write. M.ʳ Brown, who had been with me before on the same Business, comes and settles for some Stock. I go to dine with M.ʳ Gregory; a very pleasant Man is of this small Party. I propose to Gregory R. M.'s Loan and promise to give him a Note of it. After Dinner visit M.ʳ R. Morris for this Purpose but he is abroad. Call on M.ʳ Constable who is not at Home, then go to M.ʳˢ Phyn's where I spend the Evening. The Weather is warm and pleasant. R. Penn was with me this Morning.

MARCH 1792

Thursday 1 *March.* — M: Constable calls on me this Morning and afterwards M: Phyn. I go to the White Bear in Piccadilly where I meet M: Parker. He tells me that in Consequence of M: Wadeson's Journey to Amsterdam he expects soon to settle with me. This brings me no nearer *my* Journey's End than before. He shews me a Letter from Hasgill mentioning that he has Nothing in Hand. I go to M: John Penn's and sit awhile with them. Thence to ask after M:ʳˢ Church's Health. Thence to enquire of L:ᵈ Landsdowne's, thence to the Dutchess of Gordon's who is abroad. To the Count de Croix's with whom I stay awhile, then call on the Counts Woranzow and Rederen who are both abroad. Visit M:ʳˢ R. Penn and stay with her sometime, then call on Lady Tancred who is abroad, on the Mesdames La Luzerne who are also abroad. Look at the late french Embassador's Plate and Furniture, where I meet M:ʳˢ Rose and take her Home. Thence to dine with M: Bird. Bring Home R. Morris and sit a little while with him, then come Home. The Weather has been pleasant all Day but a drizling Evening.

Friday 2 *March.* — Write. The Watch Maker calls, R. M. having previously been with me and agreed for his friend George Harrison, I take his Watch and pay him for it. Payne calls on me. I go with M: Francis to see a Manufacture of lacquered Ware, or rather, the Shop where it is exposed for Sale. It is handsome. Thence we go thro a dirty Court to see a Piece of Mutton. It is salted, a Shoulder cut from a very smallboned Sheep that weighed 280ˡᵇˢ to the four Quarters. It is a solid Lump of Fat to all Appearance. Dine with R. Penn and go after Dinner to a Route at M:ʳˢ Phyn's where I spend the Evening. The Weather has been drisly and bad this Day but clears up before Midnight and it is very warm for the Season.

Saturday 3 *March.* — Write and then go into the City. M.ʳ Francis, who was to have gone with me, is out of the Way. I call on M.ʳ Gregory and give him a Note about opening a Loan for R. M. which he is to shew to his Partner M.ʳ Forbes. Go in Quest of M.ʳ Francis to the New York Coffee House and afterwards to the Pensilvania Coffee House but he is not to be found. I take up M.ʳ James Jones and we go to a China Shop which M.ʳ Francis had urged me to see, thence we go to M.ʳ R. Morris and proceed together to the British Coffee House where we dine. After Dinner I go to R. Penn's; they are all abroad. Go to the Mount Coffee House and kill a little Time, then return Home. When M.ʳ Francis comes in I enquire what became of him this Morning and he gives so strange and confused an Account that I cannot help being struck with that Obliquity of Temper and Mind which he has inherited. He says he is going to publish and [sic] Advertisement for a Loan on Acc.ᵗ of R. Penn. This leads to a Conversation in which I find it necessary to tell him that Penn cannot mortgage his Wife's Property and that she will not join in the Measure. It concludes by a Declaration on his Part that he will have Nothing more to do with it. He certainly had better mind his own Business than to meddle with Matters which he knows Nothing about and in which he must do Mischief. The Weather is pleasant this Morning but cloudy and damp this Afternoon. At Night it rains.

Sunday 4. — This Morning I visit Count Rœderen who is abroad and then Count Woranzow with whom I sit and converse some Time. He tells me of the absurd Manner in which the Marquis del Campo conducted the Negotiation about the Nootka Sound Affair, arising at first from the Insufficiency of the Count de Florida Blanca and afterwards from his own. Visit at M.ʳ Penn's who is abroad, then at Lady Tancred's with whom I sit awhile, then the Count de La Luzerne's; stay awhile with him; he says he has seen in one of the french Journals that my Appointment is confirmed by the Senate. *Quere.* Go to the Dutchess of Gordon's who is abroad and so is Sir John Sinclair. Call at M.ʳˢ Church's and then go again to R. Penn's. Speak to him in Consequence of what passed last Night with M.ʳ Francis. He says that he desires as much on Acc.ᵗ of Miss Masters as on his own to know

if Money can be borrowed on Estates near Philadelphia. I tell
him that unless he can procure a full State of his Affairs it is impossible to advise him. Dine with Doctor Bancroft and go
afterw.^{ds} to Governor Franklin's where we play Whist till very
late. The Weather this Day has been very rainy and disagreable.
It is warm with a Westerly Wind.

Monday 5. — This Morning I go to the Auction of the late
Marquis de La Luzerne and purchase some Plate. Return at four
and take up Mr Francis; we go together to dine with Mr Darby
and stay pretty late in the Evening. The Weather is warm and
damp. It was rather raw this Morning.

Tuesday 6. — Write. Mr Constable calls and tells me that he
has got Mr Pultney's Note discounted; in Part by Mr Pultney
himself. I call on Mr Rogers and he not being at Home go to the
City Chambers where I meet Mr Henchman and at his Request
write a Letter to Mr Baring and himself. Call on Mr Inglis whom
I afterwards meet at the New York Coffee House. He is to send
me the Money I want Tomorrow. Dine with the Count Woranzow *en famille*. After Dinner he tells me that it is impossible the
King of Prussia should join heartily with the Emperor. He had
informed me last Sunday that the King was offered by the Emi-
grant Princes a considerable Arrondissement on the lower Rhine
from the Elector Palatine's Dominions, and to make that Electorate whole by the Cession of Alsace. He sent immediately to the
Emperor and his Messenger Bischoffswerder offered to join in
procuring the Addition of french Flanders to the imperial low
Countries, but the Emperor replied that if he did interfere in the
Affairs of France, it should be as a Friend and not for the Spoil.
He tells me that the Bishop d'Autun has offered a Cession of the
Island of Tobago, the Demolition of Cherbourgh and an Extension of the Treaty of Commerce if England will, in Case of War
with the Emperor, preserve a strict Neutrality. He received for
Answer that England could not take any Engagements whatever
respecting the Affairs of France. He adds that the Bishop is not
now received, because he boasted of a Credit for £40,000 St.^g
which was to do Wonders and because he has frequented constantly the Dissenters and because he brought *Stephen Sayre*
over in his Suite. This last Circumstance is truly surprizing.

He tells me that young Laborde has written a Letter which he saw, mentioning that they would buy the Cabinets of London and Berlin. He says that the British Cabinet mean to establish the Independence of S.̣ Domingo and the other french Islands, wherefore the Offer of Tobago does not weigh; that they expect the Demolition of Cherbourg by the Sea in its present unfinished State and are at any Rate indifferent about it while the Marine of France remains in its present Condition; and as to a Treaty of Commerce, the Want of one is now supplied by Contraband which is vastly easy. But the Possession of the low Countries by France is an Object of the greatest Moment and not to be permitted. I go hence to M.̣ Phyn's and sit a little while with him. The Count de Woranzow inveighed against Mons.̣ de La Fayette in the strongest Terms I ever heard. He said that tho bred a military Man and obliged sometimes to order Punishments, he never could behold an Execution, his Nature recoiling from the View of human Misery, but yet if Lafayette and the Duke of Orleans were to be broken on the Wheel at Falmouth and he had no Means of seeing it done but by going thither on Foot he would set out immediately. This is strong Language. The Weather is pleasant this Day for some Time but then becomes cloudy, cold and rainy. The Wind is still, however, from the Westward.

Wednesday 7. — This Morning I call on M.̣ Rogers and give him the Accounts I received from the Trustees. He is to make the due Examinations and take other needful Arrangements. Go from thence to the late french Embassador's and purchase among other Things his Orders of the Cincinnatus which are put up at Auction. Dine with R. Penn and after Dinner call on M.̣ Morris, M.̣ Jones and M.̣ Constable. Find the two latter sitting with M.̣ Francis when I come Home. It has been a rainy disagreable Day.

Thursday 8. — This Morning I go to the Auction and buy a few Articles. Then go to M.̣ C. Jones's Lodgings and take him to the Lyceum where we see a Rhinoceros, Zebra and Hungarian Ram. We go from thence to Rakestraw's Museum which is well worth seeing. Among other Things an Egyptian Mummy and a Range of fœtus's from a few Days old to within a few Days of Maturity. There is a fine Collection of Subjects for obstetrical

Examination also. We step in for a few Minutes at the Exeter
Change where there is Nothing but what I had seen before at the
same Place. We dine at the Piazza Coffee House and then take
Tea together at my Appartments and play at Chess. The Weather
is very cold.

Friday 9. — This Morning I write. M.ʳ Constable calls and I
then go to the french Embassador's to bring away my Purchases
of Yesterday; meet Gov.ʳ Franklin and M.ʳˢ Franklin and M.ʳˢ
Twicross there. She asks me to dine *en famille* next Sunday. Return Home and from thence visit M.ʳˢ Church where I meet M.ʳˢ
Low. Go to dine with M.ʳ John Penn. Col.º Allen and M.ʳ Francis
are very near to a Dispute of a serious Nature on a Thing of no
Consequence. Go from hence to M.ʳ Franklin's and play at Whist
with him, Jones and Morris, till very late. This is Time very much
misspent. The Weather is cold with a North Easter and Flights of
Snow.

Saturday 10. — Write. M.ʳ Constable calls and sits with me a
long Time. After he is gone M.ʳ Levingworth comes and then the
Count de Croix to whom I read an enigmatical and unsigned
Letter from Mons.ʳ de Monciel with a Postscript from Brémond.
Call on M.ʳˢ Twycross to excuse myself from dining there Tomor-
row, then go to M.ʳ Phyn's where I dine and spend the Rest of the
Day and Evening. The Weather is very cold, the Wind still at
Northeast but not hard.

Sunday 11. — Write but am immediately interrupted. R. M.
comes in and before he goes away M.ʳ Bosville who stays a long
Time. M.ʳ Gregory comes shortly after and tells me that they have
been endeavoring to get Money on the Loan I proposed but without Success. Dine at Sir John Sinclair's where I learn the Death
of the Emperor,[1] very sudden and attributed to Poison. *Quere.*
Towards the Close of the Sitting I converse with Lord Hawke
who is pleased with that Conversation. Go from hence to R. M.'s
Lodgings and tell him what M.ʳ Gregory ment.ᵈ to me this Morning. The Weather is cold and the Wind still at North East.

Monday 12. — Go this Morning to the City Chambers and after waiting a long Time see M.ʳ Lane, who tells me the Powers I

---

[1] Emperor Leopold, younger brother of Queen Marie-Antoinette.

wished for are not gone. I must attend ToMorrow. Call on Lord
Hawke and Lady Affleck [1] and M.rs Low who are all abroad. Go
to M.r Franklin's and tell him that I cannot inform respecting the
Powers untill ToMorrow. Return Home and go from thence to
M.r Constable's. Sit a Minute and then leave my Name at the
Dutchess of Gordon's and M.r John Penn's. Visit L.d Landsdowne
and sit with him a while. Thence to R. Penn's where I stay Din-
ner. Return Home at eight and write. The Weather is still cold.

   Tuesday 13. — This Morning R. Morris shews me a Letter
from Amsterdam which is encouraging. M.r Constable calls;
M.r Colqhoun and M.r Inman who is going out to America. I afterwards go into the City and on my Representation to M.r
Hinchman they agree to send out Orders to invest in Fox's Name.
I return Home and write, then go to dine with R. Penn, C. Jones
and Francis at the Piazza Coffee House. Set Penn down at the
Mount and go to M.rs Ellice's Route where I stay Supper and untill two oClock. The Weather has changed this Day, the Wind
came to the Southward and about eight oClock it rained hard and
the Air is soft. This Morning M.r Jaubert breakfasted with me.
He came from Paris to consult me on the Part of Monsieur de
Monciel whether he should accept a Place in the Ministry, and
which. I opine for the foreign Affairs *comme la seule faisable.* He
tells me that De Narbonne has been guilty of notorious Peculation, and after having sold Contracts for the Army has allowed
to the Contractors the Depreciation of their Money. He is to be
turned out and Mons.r de Grave is among the Persons talked of to
replace him. Delessart will go out as the Price of his Duplicity
and Cahier de Gerville for Impotence. Monciel had refused any
Place untill thro M.r Bertrand he was certain that the King approved personally, and then he preferred rather the Department
of the Interior, but waits for my Opinion and Advice. We have a
good Deal of Conversation respecting the State of Parties &c.a.
He tells me that the Assembly is very low and would have been
quite down but that Narbonne's Intrigues have contributed to
give them a little Lift at the Expence of Order and good Government, in order to feather his Nest. He is well with Brissot and the
Rest of that wretched and pernicious Faction. They desire to

---

[1] Widow of Admiral Sir Edmund Affleck, Bart.

know of me what Conduct is to be pursued in order to arrive at a good Government. I do not chuse to enter deeply into this Subject for the present because so much must depend on Circumstances, but say in general that the first Step is to produce a general Conviction that the present Constitution is good for Nothing. He says that this is already done and that People in general seem to think that the Kingdom is ruined past Redemption. I do not however think that Opinion is even near to the needful Point. He is to write this Day and breakfast with me Tomorrow.

Wednesday 14. — This Morning Monsieur Jaubert again breakfasts with me. He had mentioned De Marbois Yesterday for the foreign Affairs, which I disapproved of, but this Morning I recommend him for the interior Department. We consider at great Length the State of Affairs and at his earnest Request I mark out in general what I conceive to be the proper Means of remedying the Evils complained of, observing that after all Circumstances must decide. I told him Yesterday and repeat this Day that they must have for Minister of War a very determined Fellow. That such a Man will, like any other, work his own Ruin but he will effect the Begining of Good. The Chevalier de Grave will do no Good in that Place, at least I think not. Write and go at half past four to dine with M.ͬ and M.ͬˢ Gregory. He tells me that he has not been able to get any Money. I give him the Information received from Holland and add that the Thing shall be left pending for a few Days, and then if Nothing can be done I will advise the young Gentleman to go to Holland. Go from hence to Sablonier's Hotel and visit M.ͬ Jaubert who sets off Tomorrow. Then return Home & as R. M. is sitting with M.ͬ Francis I communicate what M.ͬ Gregory told me. The Weather continues rainy and warm, Wind Westerly.

Thursday 15. — Write. M.ͬ Constable calls and while he is here the Count de Croix comes. M.ͬ J. Penn and Col.º Allen came before M.ͬ Constable and while he is here M.ͬ Payne comes in. Shortly after him the Count Rederen who tells me that the Son [1] of the

---

[1] Known as King of Hungary until elected at Frankfort Emperor Francis II of Germany. After Napoleon dissolves the Holy Roman Empire, 1806, this nephew of Marie-Antoinette, trained by his uncle Joseph, becomes Emperor Francis I of Austria.

late Emperor is of a feeble and consumptive Habit. That he was educated under Joseph and has acquired his Manner of thinking. He thinks that the Emperor would never have warred against France but in the last Necessity and that the intended Operations must now be postponed till Autumn at least. I dine at R. Penn's and in the Evening visit Mrs Church. The Weather is very fine again toNight but it rained a little in the Course of the Day. The Wind from the Westward.

Friday 16. — This Morning write. Afterwards call on Col.^? Allen who is abroad and then visit Lord Landsdowne. He speaks of Peculation in Ministers as a Thing of minor Importance, altho he himself detests it, and observes that even in my virtuous Country it prevailed to a great Extent. I assure him very seriously and very truly that he is misinformed. He says that Mr Pitt and the King are not well together and have not been so for a long Time past. The Cause is the Prince's Debts. He gives me the two Versions of that Story, one of which is that Mr Pitt, having been pressed by the Sovereign on this Subject, had declined with some offensive Expressions. This wounded the Father and the Mother who declares it to be the great and only Object of her Life to conciliate the Family Differences. Mr Pitt's Friends, on the contrary, declare the whole Story to be an abominable Falsehood and add that if there be any one Subject more particularly offensive to his Majesty it is the Mention of the Princes. That it never was a Question with the King to pay those Debts. That the Chancellor did indeed once say Something of the Kind but he is a strange Sort of Man and Nobody minds him. Dine at the Piazza Coffee House and afterwards take R. M. & Jones who dine with me to the Lodgings of the latter. Sit up there pretty late at Whist. The Weather was very pleasant this Morning, this Afternoon it rains.

Saturday 17 *March.* — This Morning write. Dine at Mr Phyn's and stay the Evening there. Mr Constable and R. M. were with me twice. The Weather is very warm and a little damp, the Wind from the Westward.

Morris to President Washington

London 17 March 1792

George Washington Esqr
                Philadelphia

Dear Sir

I had the Honor to write to you on the fourth of last Month. Two Days after I was informed that you had nominated me as Minister to the Court of France, but the latest Advices from America which come down to the tenth of January, shew that the Senate had not then made their Decision. Be that Decision what it may, I shall ever gratefully esteem and acknowlege this Mark of Confidence from the Person in the World whose good Opinion I consider as most estimable.

In my Letter of the fourth I gave you a Picture of the french Ministry, and a View of the Measures pursued by different Parties, including the Mission of the Bishop d'Autun. As he has now got back to Paris it may be well to communicate the Result. His Reception was bad for three Reasons. First that the Court looks with Horror and Apprehension at the Scenes acting in France, of which they consider him as a prime Mover. Secondly that his Reputation is offensive to Persons who pique themselves on Decency of Manners and Deportment, and lastly because he was so imprudent, when he first arrived, as to propogate the Idea that he should corrupt the Members of Administration and, afterwards, by keeping Company with leading Characters among the Dissenters, and other similar Circumstances, he renewed the Impression made before his Departure from Paris that he meant to intrigue with the discontented. His public Reception however furnishes no Clue to decide on the Success of his Mission; because the former might have been very bad and the latter very good. The Fact however is that he could offer Nothing worthy of their Acceptance, and that what he asked was of a Nature not to be granted. His offer was confined to a Session of Tobago, a Demolition of the Works of Cherburg, and an Extension of the commercial Treaty. He asked a strict Neutrality in Case of War with the Emperor. Now you will observe that no Court could prudently treat with France in her present Situation, seeing that

no Body can promise in her Name otherwise than as Godfathers
and Godmothers do at a Christening; and how such Promises are
kept every Body knows. Convinced of this, the bishop never told
his Errand to Lord Gower, the british Embassador at Paris, who
mentioned that Circumstance to me as extraordinary but yet so
far agreable in that he was glad not to have been called on for
Letters of Introduction. Respecting Tobago I must make a
Digression. It is now a long Time since it was mentioned to me,
in Paris, that some of the Colonists of St Domingo had come hither
to make Overtures to Mr Pitt. Since that Period, I learnt that the
french Ministry were in Possession of Documents to prove, not
only that he fomented the Disturbances in France, but that he was
in deep Intrigues with Regard to that Colony. The particular
Proofs were not shewn to me, so that I cannot speak positively.
Neither can I vouch for what I have learnt further on that Subject within this Month, but I am assured that it is Mr Pitt's Intention to bring about, if he can, the Independence of St Domingo. Mr Clarkson, the great Negro Advocate, is mentioned to
me as his Agent for this Business at Paris, and the Conduct of a
Part of the Assembly in opposing Succor to that Island seems cor-
roborative of such Idea. This then being the Case, or supposing
it to be so, the Offer of Tobago was too trifling to attract Mr Pitt's
Notice; even if unconnected with other Circumstances. By the
bye, my Informant tells me also that Mr Pitt means to coax us
into the Adoption of his Plan respecting St Domingo. And I learn
from another Quarter that he means to offer us his Mediation for
a Peace with the Indians. If all this be true, his Game is evident.
The Mediation is to be with *us* a Price for adopting his Plans, and
with the *Indian Tribes* a Means of constituting himself their
Patron and Protector. It may be proper to combine all this with
the late Division of Canada, and the present Measures for military Colonization of the upper Country, and above all with what
may come from Mr Hammond. I return to St Domingo. If such
be Mr Pitt's Scheme, altho we shall not I presume engage in, or
countenance it, yet the Success will be entirely for our Advantage, and a meer Preliminary to Something of the same Sort
which must happen to Jamaica on the first Change of Wind in the
political World. The Destruction of the Port of Cherburg is no

present Object with the british Ministry, because they suppose it will be ruined by the Elements before it can be compleated; and because the french Marine is, from the Want of Discipline, an Object more of Contempt than Apprehension. The proffered Extension of the commercial Treaty amounts to Nothing, because at present every Part of France is open to contraband Commerce; and because there is little Reason to believe that the Stipulations in a Treaty now made would be of any long Duration. Thus it happens that neither of the Objects offered were worthy of Notice. But the Neutrality required was of a most important Nature. By leaving the austrian low Countries exposed to french Invasion, it would have been a Violation both of antient and of recent Treaties. Nor is this all, for (as I have already had Occasion to remark) the Annexation of those Provinces to the french Monarchy would prove almost, if not altogether, fatal to Great Britain. And when we consider that they are almost in Revolt already, and that it is in Fact their Interest to become one with France, there is Reason to suppose that an Union might have been effected in Case of a War with the Emperor. So much then on the Ground of Good Faith, and good Policy. But there is still a farther Cause which, as the World goes, may be equal in its Operation to all others. It seems to be a moot Point whether it is the british or the prussian Cabinet which directs the other. Perhaps there may be a little of both, but be all that as it may, this much is certain, that neither feels disposed to counteract the Views of its Ally, in any open Manner. Now putting aside the personal Feelings which naturally agitate the Sovereign of this, as well as of other Kingdoms, in regard to the french Revolution, it is notorious, that from the very Dawn of it, Agents were employed to foment a Spirit of Revolt in other States, particularly in Prussia. The King of Prussia therefore feels for the french Revolutionists all the Enmity of a proud, passionate, and offended German Prince. Add to this that the Elector of Hanover, as such, cannot wish for a Change in the Government of Germany. If therefore it had been the Interest of Great Britain to establish a free Constitution in France (which it certainly is not) I am perfectly convinced that this Court would never have made a single Effort for the Purpose.

I stated to you, in my last, the french Ministry as being extremely disjointed. It was too much so for any durable Existence, besides which the Members took effectual Means to precipitate each other's Ruin. M.ʳ de Narbonne wished to get into the Office of foreign Affairs. This was desirable to him (it is said) on many Accounts, but particularly so because it gives the Command of large Sums without Account. Whatever may have been his Motives, the following seems to have been his Conduct. He stood forth the Advocate of all violent Measures. This would naturally have excited Suspicions with thinking Men, but not so with the Assembly. He associated himself to the Partizans of Democracy, and while by this Means he secured himself against their Clamors, he took great Care of his pecuniary Affairs. This at least is affirmed to me, and with the Addition that he had the Imprudence to pay off his Debts, altho it is notorious that his Estate (which is in Sᵗ Domingo) is among those which are laid Waste. It is further asserted, that in Order to quiet the Clamors of Contractors who had given him Money and found themselves in the Road to Ruin, he agreed to compensate the Depreciation of the Assignats. In Order to remove a great Obstacle to his Proceedings, he joined in the Intrigues against M.ʳ Bertrand, and at the same Time fostered other Intrigues against M.ʳ de Lessart with a View of getting his Place. The Proofs of all these Things are said to be in the King's Hands. M.ʳ de Lessart's Conduct I have already in Part communicated. I must add that, afterwards, imagining that Brissot de Warville and Condorcet were omnipotent in the Assembly, he violated his Engagements made with the Triumvirate and wrote some Dispatches conformably to the Views of those two Gentlemen. In Consequence of this, it was resolved to displace him, and they were looking out for a Successor. The person applied to was actually deliberating whether he should or should not accept, at the Moment when Brissot brought about his Impeachment and Arrest. In this same Moment M.ʳ de Narbonne was dismissed, & with him was to go Mons.ʳ de Gerville. The Chevalier de Graave succeeds M.ʳ de Narbonne. When I left Paris he was attached to the Triumvirate. He does not want for understanding, but I think it almost impossible that he should succeed. Monsieur Bertrand, against whom an Address from the Assembly was at length carried, has I find resigned. There is Something at the Bottom which I cannot discover, without being on the Spot, but you may rely on it he goes out with the full Confidence of the King and Queen.

My Informations from Paris were previous to the News of the Emperor's Death, which has probably occasioned the violent Proceedings against poor de Lessart, by removing the Fears of those who (in the Midst of all their big Words) were confoundedly frightened. What may be the Consequences of this Event it is impossible to determine, or even to conjecture. Much, very much, depends on the personal Character of his Successor, which I am not yet acquainted with.

It is supposed by some, here, that Mr Pitt is not strong in the Cabinet at present, altho the Majority in Parliament was never more decisive, and this is said to arise from his refusing to ask Money for Payment of the Prince of Wales's Debts, which the King (it is said) was desirous of, and which his Minister declined with some offensive Expressions. M.ʳ Pitt's Friends insist, on the other Hand, that the whole Story is false, from Begining to End. For my own Part, I do not think he will be turned out, because I believe him to be a very cunning Fellow; & altho he has conducted foreign Affairs but poorly, he manages all the little Court and parliamentary Intrigues with consummate Address.

Sunday 18 *March.* — This Morning I write a while and make some Calculations for M.ʳ Constable who sends me Word that the Packet is arrived from America. Dress and ride in the Park. Francis is with me and impressed with Amazement at the Show of Carriages, which is much inferior however to what I expected. M.ʳ Constable calls and we dine together at the Piazza Coffee House. After Dinner we go to visit M.ʳˢ Phyn and sit the Evening. My Stomach is out of Order and I know not why. The Weather is warm and very pleasant, showery with a Southwest Wind.

Monday 19 *March.* — This Morning I am suffering under nervous Affection from a diseased Stomach which is loaded with Phlegm. At half past two I walk with R. Penn to M.ʳ Barclay's Brewery in Southwark. He very politely shews and explains every Part of it and gives us a good Beef Steak afterwards. The

Steam Engine is on a pretty **Construction**. The Mode by which the Steam operates I do not readily understand but am informed that after Condensation it is thrown back into the Boiler, which is so far a Saving. The Force is equal to twelve Horses and the Consumption is one Bushel of Coals per Hour. There is a Cranck of very elegant Invention, being two Cog Wheels connected by a Bar from the one to the Axis of the other, and one of them is firmly fixed to a Piece of Timber which descends from the Beam of the Engine and which, having an Elbow equal to the Diameter of that Wheel, suffers it in ascending and descending to move round freely; and by Means of the Cogs the Motion which it communicates is steady and rendered still more so by a heavy Iron flier annexed to the Machinery of the Mill. This Engine performs the grinding, pumping &c^a. The large Vatts in which the Porter is kept are also very curious; they are of 800, 1600 and 2000 barrils. The Staves two Inches thick. The Porter is fermented three Times, once in a large Vessel, once in Barrils, and then it goes thro a small ripening ferment in these Vatts, in which it is continued from one to three Years. The Duties which this Company pay to the Government amount to about £70,000 St^g per Ann^t. After Dinner our Host tells me he is well informed that the Ministry were much hurt at Genl Washington's Declaration respecting the Intentions of this Court. I explain to him that, truly understood, it was strictly right. He says they are well pleased at Mr Hammond's [1] Reception and that he is convinced Mr Pitt means very well towards America and that if there be any Obstacles in the Cabinet they are thrown in by Ld Hawkesbury. Take Mr R. Penn Home and then take up R. Morris and Jones who drink Tea with me. The Weather has been prodigiously fine this Day.

Tuesday 20 *March.* — This Morning write. A Letter by the

---

[1] George Hammond (1763–1853) had been two years chargé d'affaires in Vienna before going out at 28 as first British Minister to the United States, where in 1793 he marries Margaret, daughter of Andrew Allen (Loyalist returned to Philadelphia). Socially a success, but insists that Loyalists should recover confiscated estates and be freed from restrictions, Jefferson equally firm about evacuation of American posts by British troops, questions only settled by Jay Treaty, 1794. Before Hammond leaves in 1795 he will come up against Genet. As Under-Secretary for Foreign Affairs Hammond will send reports about Morris to Lord Grenville from Berlin, 1796.

Packett informs me that my App.^t was confirmed by the Senate the 12 Jany last.[1] Dine with R. Penn and go to the Play afterwards with Mrs Penn and Miss Masters. Mrs Siddons acts well the Part of Lady Macbeth and Kemble is a tolerable McBeth. The other Parts are but badly done. Bring Mr Bird, of the House of Savage and Bird, home with me. He is a pleasant good humord little Fellow. The Weather was pleasant this Morning, a high Wind from the Westward rendered it very cool in the Day and this Evening it rains hard.

Wednesday 21. — Write this Morning till five in the Afternoon. R. Morris calls on me, to whom I make the Offer of becoming my private Secretary if, when his Business is over, he should wish it. W. Constable calls and I speak to him about the Offer to be made

---

[1] After eighteen days the Senate confirmed Washington's nomination of Gouverneur Morris by sixteen votes against eleven. Monroe thought Morris 'a monarchy man and not suitable to be employed by this country nor in France' although the 'monarch' he had always aimed at for the United States was a sovereign Congress. Sherman said Morris was no hypocrite, wrote a good draft, had never lacked integrity nor betrayed a trust, but opposed him as 'profane.' To the majority of Frenchmen now in power nothing could be less distasteful than lack of religion, real or supposed, but what must inevitably make Morris unwelcome is his approval of monarchy for France. England had introduced liberty, equality was America's contribution, in France's haste pulling the mighty down what seemed the quickest levelling. Morris thought: 'In Effect Time is needful to bring forward Slaves to the Enjoyment of Liberty. Time. Time. Education. But what is Education? It is not learning. It is more the Effect of Society on the Habits and Principles of each Individual, forming him at an early Period of Life to act afterwards the Part of a good Citizen and contribute in his Turn to the Formation of others. Hence it results that the Progress towards Freedom must be slow...' Contrary to Paris rumor he had never yet spoken with Louis XVI. He will find contact disillusioning — no snob could have penned such arid reports of attendances at Court; but pity for a bewildered victim will outweigh discretion, and trying to save the lives of kings is a reactionary pastime. As Minister to post-August France, Morris will be out of tune, out of date. But he will fly his country's colors mast-high through the two blackest years, claiming redress, at some risk to his life, for every insult, for every illegal capture at sea, every false imprisonment on land, yet respecting Washington's wish for twenty years of peace for the secure establishment of the American Constitution. Monroe will leave France much nearer war with the United States, although he will succeed Morris in full Thermidorean reaction, when the Marats, Dantons, Robespierres are as dead as their countless victims and a new decency is the order of the day. Approved by the Senate January 12, it is April 6 before Morris receives official notice, the Secretary of State's letter of January 23 having been delayed, overlooked, by some amateur postman!

of Lands to People in France. Dine with Church, who tells me after Dinner that he is determin'd to go to America when his Mother is buried. The Weather has been fine this Day.

Morris to Alexander Hamilton

London 21 March 1792

Alexander Hamilton Esqr
Philadelphia

Dear Hamilton

A Vessel just going to New York presents me an Opportunity of saying that I thank you for your Exertions to effect my Appointment. I know you too well, my good Friend, to make long Speeches on that Subject. I shall acknowlege the Services of my Friends properly on proper Occasions, and till then be silent. In patronizing this Appointment, you have incurred more Trouble than you was perhaps aware of, for you must water the Tree which you have planted. In plain English, I beg you to favor me with your Correspondence, and to give me Information *which otherwise I may not obtain.* In Return, I will apprize you of what is doing on this Side of the Water *confidentially*, which I will not do to every Body.

The other Day at an Auction of the late Marquis de La Luzerne's Effects, his various Orders were put up, and among them those of the Cincinati. These I bought, out of Respect to that Society, but as I have not the Honor of belonging to it, they are useless to me; and therefore if you know any worthy Member to whom they may be acceptable, I will with much Pleasure deliver them to your Order.

Hamilton to Morris

Philadelphia, June 22d, 1792.

My dear Sir,

I accept your challenge to meet you in the field of mutual *confidential* communication; though I cannot always promise punctuality, or copiousness. I will however do the best I can.

Will it not be a necessary preliminary to agree upon a cypher? One has been devised for me, which, though simple in execution, is tedious in preparation. I may shortly forward it.

In the mean time, let us settle some appellations for certain official characters. I will call,

The President, Scœvola.

The Vice President, Brutus.

Secretary of State, Scipio.

Secretary at War, Sempronius.

Sec'y of the Treasury, Paulus.

Attorney General, Lysander

Senators.

Robert Morris, Cato.

Oliver Ellsworth, Virginius.

Rufus King, Leonidas.

George Cabot, Portius.

Aaron Burr, Scœvius.

Richard Henry Lee, Marcus.

Monroe, Sydney.

Ralph Izard, Themistocles.

Representatives.

James Madison, Tarquin.

Ames, Valerius.

Abraham Baldwin, Hampden.

John Lawrence, Solon.

Mercer, Tacitus.

Murray, Livy.

Thomas Fitsimmons, Cicero.

Egbert Benson, Cromwell.

Jeremiah Wadsworth, Titius.

Jonathan Trumbull, Quintus.

Giles, Chronus.

You see that I have avoided characteristic names. In my next you shall have a sketch of the general state of the country, its politics and parties. I thank you for your calculations, as I will for every suggestion you shall make. I shall seldom fail to get either a new idea, or a new application of an old one. I shall endeavor to put in train, by this opportunity, the papers you advise to be sent to the Russian Ambassador. If your courage is not put to the test, by being put to *wear* what you have won, it will not be my fault. Do you know enough of the catechism in the vulgar tongue to fulfil what you have lately undertaken? Yours sincerely,

ALEXANDER HAMILTON.

Morris to President Washington

London 21 March 1792

George Washington Esqr
Philadelphia

Dear Sir

Yesterday I was informed that the Senate had agreed to your Nomination of diplomatic Servants. If I know my own Heart, this Intelligence is far less agreable to me on my own Acc^t than on that of the Public. I am sure that a Rejection from whatever Cause it may have arisen, would have been attributed to Disunion in our Counsels.

I find that the King of France has appointed to the office of foreign Affairs a Monsr de Mouriez, and that it is considered as a Sacrifice to the Jacobins. He is a bold determin'd Man. I am not acquainted with him personally but I know that he has long been seeking a Place in the Administration and was, about six Months ago, determined if appointed one of the Ministers, to destroy at the Peril of his Life, the jacobin and all other Clubs, and to effect a Change in the Government. How far he may have changed his Opinions since I really cannot tell, but I mention this to you *Now*, because when I know more I can refer to this Letter and say that *by coming into Office he has not changed his Sentiments*, if he persists in those his ancient Determinations. If not, I will tell you that *he is more prudent than was supposed*. And these Words will in either Case mean Nothing more than is here set down for them. The King consulted him (as I was told by his confidential Friend in the Middle of last October) on the State of Affairs when Mr de Montmorin went out; but the high-toned Measures he proposed were not adopted.

Morris to William Short

London 22ᵈ March 1792

William Short Esqʳ

Paris

My dear Sir

A gentleman of my Acquaintance has received a Letter by the Packet which mentions that the Senate have approved the Nominations made by the President in the diplomatic Line. I learn also, in the same Way, that you and our friend Carmichael are nominated and appointed Commissioners to treat with Spain respecting the Navigation of the Mississipi. On this Mark of public Confidence, honorable to you and in its Consequences useful to our Country, accept my hearty Congratulations. Neither I nor any other American of my Acquaintance have received Letters by the late New York Mail, which we all wonder at. There is nothing worthy of Communication here and Affairs are so changeable at Paris that Enquiries must be confined not to new but to newest Occurrences. The Ministerial Seats resemble electrical Chairs which give every Occupant a kick in the Breeches.

[A bitter disappointment to Short, who longed to stay in Paris. On the same day Morris adds his news to a letter on American land sales, written to Le Ray.]

This is the Time my dear Sir to strike, for the Iron is hot and it cannot long continue so. Indeed I never thought we should have so good a Chance but the Arrival of the Packet has brought forward some very unexpected Circumstances. She brings me Information that the Senate have confirmed my Appointment but I have nothing official on the Subject.

Thursday 22. — Write all the Morning. Mʳ Jones calls on me. I go with Mʳ Francis to dine at the Piazza Coffee House where we meet *par hazard* Mʳ Morris and Mʳ Jones. The two latter come Home with me and take Tea. Mʳ Franklin comes in afterwards and they stay late. The Weather is grown very warm this Evening; it was fair in the Day and pleasant. Payne called both this Day and Yesterday.

Friday 23. — This Morning I write. M.ʳ Church calls on me and we converse about a Proposal I made him to purchase land of R. M.. He offers for a considerable Tract at ¾ of what I had stated as the Price. Send for young Morris. M.ʳˢ Penn calls. M.ʳ Constable comes and while he is here M.ʳ Darby visits me. I dress and Morris calls, with whom I fix the Answer to be given to M.ʳ Church. M.ʳ Franklin & M.ʳ Jones call. I take a little airing and leave a Card for L.ᵈ Hawke, then go to dine with M.ʳˢ Low. M.ʳˢ Church comes in after Dinner and tells me she is thankful for my Offer to her Husband. *Tant mieux.* Come Home early and go to Bed. The Weather is windy from the Westward. This Morning it rained.

Saturday 24. — Write. Go at two oClock to see M.ʳ Philidore [1] play Chess. He played at three Games together of which he saw only one. He gained two of the three. This is a wonderful Instance of the Force of Memory. We go from hence to the Piazza Coffee House and dine together, M.ʳ Franklin, R. M. and M.ʳ Jones. Thence to Gov.ʳ Franklin's where we pass the Evening. The Wind has been high again from the Westward, this Night it blows hard with Rain. M.ʳ Constable and M.ʳ Paine called on me.

Sunday 25. — This Morning I write a little. Then call on M.ʳ Colqhoun and sit with him a while. He tells me that four Persons are employed in Germany to take in Subscriptions for the Purchase of Lands in America. To the Amount of 4,000,000 Acres. Go to R. M.'s Lodgings but he is abroad. Visit Sir John Sinclair, Lord Inchiquin, M.ʳ J. Penn & Lord Lansdowne who are all abroad. Go to M.ʳ Constable's by Appointment but he is abroad. Return Home and read, then take a Ride in the Park and dine with the Corps diplomatique at the Count de Rœderʹen's. The french Assembly have pardoned the Assassins of Avignon. This is dreadful. Go from hence to Mad.ᵉ de La Luzerne's and sit there some Time. The Society here, who are all *aristocrate*, say that not one in a hundred of the french Nation is attached to the pre-

---

[1] François-André Philidor (1726–1795), musician, greatest chessplayer of his day, learnt his game as choir-boy in King's Chapel, Versailles; cards forbidden, chess allowed in sanctuary. From 1772 the Salopian Coffee House subscribed for annual visits from Philidor, who advertised in London papers his famous three games blindfold.

sent Government. *Quere.* It is certain that many Priests who had taken the Oath retract, so that Religion seems to be embarked in the Quarrel, and if at the same Moment the Artillery of an Enemy and the Thunders of the Vatican shall be directed against them, many will be staggered. If, in Addition, a good Constitution be proposed it may work a wonderful and a happy Change, which God grant. The Weather this Day has been very windy from the Westward. I observe some Peach Trees in Blossom.

Monday 26. — Write all the Morning. M! Constable and young M! Phyn call on me. I dine with M! Church at half past Six and at ten go with her to Lady Affleck's Route where among other Americans or AntiAmericans I see and speak to M!ˢ Arnold.[1] Old M!ˢ Delancey is here who at seventy two plays well her Game of Whist and looks and moves very well. R. M. came this Morning on my Message to him and has accepted Church's Offer for Land but I find there will be some Difficulty about the Title. The Wind has been high all Day from the Westward and blows hard this Night.

Tuesday 27. — This Morning I write. M! Constable and M! Morris call on me; the former leaves Col? Hamilton's Report on the public Debt. The latter tells me that Colqhoun has expressed to him the Hope to obtain from Mess!ˢ Pultney and Hornby the Money they have in America and about which I wrote Yesterday. He offers me a Commission on the Sale to Church, which I decline, and also on the Bargain to be made with the others which I also decline. Visit M!ˢ Phyn and then dine at the Piazza Coffee House with R. M.. Take him after Dinner to visit M!ˢ Penn and we go thence to a Route at M!ˢ Franklin's. I see Galloway [2] here, and in Consequence make a speedy Retreat. The Weather is very windy this Day from the Westward with frequent Showers. M! Restiff called this Morning to get a Letter of Recommendation to the American Consul at Hull, if any there be.

---

[1] The Philadelphia toast, pretty Peggy Shippen, who in her belleship had married a national hero, Benedict Arnold, splendid soldier, who turned archtraitor.

[2] Joseph Galloway, born 1729 in Maryland, friend of Franklin, Speaker of Pennsylvania Assembly, member of first two American Congresses, who walked out, guided Sir William Howe across New Jersey, became his civil Governor of Philadelphia during British occupation, sailed to England to write against the United States and to testify to his friend Howe's incompetence.

Wednesday 28. — Write this Morning. M.ʳ Constable calls. He tells me that he does not leave Town ToMorrow but will wait for the french Mail. M.ʳ Jones (James Jones) calls on me. I dine with L.ᵈ Lansdowne, having visited the Dutchess of Gordon, M.ʳˢ Twycross, the Counts Rœderen and Woranzow who are all abroad. Saw M.ʳ & M.ʳˢ Ellice and M.ʳ & M.ʳˢ R. Penn. Take R. Penn to Dinner and thence to the Mount. Spend the Evening at M.ʳ Phyn's. The Weather is fine but with very high Wind from the Westward.

Thursday 29. — Write and then take M.ʳ Constable, who calls on me, into the City. Call at M.ʳ Wadeson's. He is not yet returnd but expected soon. The Attachment is withdrawn, of which M.ʳ Hardy gives me a Notice. I call on M.ʳ & M.ʳˢ Gregory who are both abroad. Go to M.ʳ Forbes's and converse with him on the Loan. Give him Information communicated by R. M. this Morning of Money in the Hands of Christie the Auctioneer. Call on M.ʳ Baring who is abroad. Leave the Notice for him with M.ʳ Inglis. Go in Pursuit of M.ʳ Lane but I cannot find him. Call at the Exchange where I see M.ʳ Phyn and M.ʳ Chollet. Tell the latter I am going to see Bourdieu, but he is not at Home. Go to the Piazza Coffee House where we dine; M.ʳ Penn, M.ʳ Bosville, M.ʳ Franklin, M.ʳ Constable & M.ʳ Morris. Go from thence to R. M.'s Lodgings. The Weather is windy but pleasant. Wind still from the Westward.

Friday 30. — Call this Morning on M.ʳ Darby who gives me some curled Maple; I leave it with a Cabinet Maker. Call at the City Chambers but cannot find M.ʳ Lane. Dine with M.ʳ Colqhoun who talks to me about the Proposition I made to him but I collect Nothing from what he says. Go from hence to M.ʳˢ Lestrange's Party. It is fullblooded Irish. The Weather is less windy than it was and very fine.

Saturday 31. — This Morning R. M. calls on me and I take him into the City. We call at different Places to find M.ʳ Lane who promises fair, then go to M.ʳ Wadeson's. He expects to come forward speedily from Amsterdam. D. P. is to call on me Tomorrow. I endeavor to find M.ʳ Gregory but without Success. Visit Mad.ᵉ de La Luzerne and go from thence to M.ʳ John Penn's. Dine with M.ʳ & M.ʳˢ Phyn *en famille* and stay the Evening. The Weather is

bad, tho tolerable enough this Morning. It blows very heavily
from the Southwest at Midnight.

APRIL 1792

Sunday 1 *April.* — M! Parker calls on me and promises fair
according to Custom. M! Hermanse comes and M! Constable. I
dine with M!ˢ R. Penn and go after Dinner to visit M!ˢ Church
who is abroad, thence to M!ˢ Phyn's where I spend the Evening.
The Weather is still blustering and damp, Wind from the Westward.

Monday 2. — M! Forsyth calls early this Morning and breakfasts. After breakfast we go to the Salopian Coffee House and
meet M! Constable with whom we proceed to the House of Commons, but cannot obtain Admittance. Walk with R. Morris, who
joins us, into S! James Park and then come Home. Take the Carriage and go to dine at Kew Bridge. Return Home and drink Tea
together, after which we play Chess. The Weather has been very
pleasant this Day. Wind from the Westward. R. M. says M!
Church told him this Morning that Le Couteulx had stopped
Payment.

Tuesday 3. — M! Colqhoun calls this Morning and I tell him
that R. M. must set off directly for Holland as it is in vain to wait
any longer here. That I suppose M! Pultney does not mean to
accept my Offer. He agrees with me, but I find that it is very
much against the Grain. I go into the City and there M! Henchman gives me a satisfactory Account of the Proceedings of the
Trustees. Call at M! Wadeson's but he is not yet come back. M!
Parker was with me this Morning. He expects a favorable Award
of the Arbitrators between him and Joy. I dine with Church who
is desirous of getting more Land in the Genesee and a better Bargain. *Sed qu?.* The Weather is fine this Morning but the Wind,
which is still from the Westward, brings up cold Clouds towards

Noon. In the Evening it rains and at Night it blows very hard.

Wednesday 4 April. — Write. Ld Wycombe calls and while he is here Mr Franklin comes and stays him out. Afterwards Mr Constable, with whom I agree on the Letters to be written to his Brother and Mr Fox. R. Morris calls. Mr Constable dines with me. R. Morris comes in afterwards and we take Tea together. I write after they are gone. Mr Constable told me at Dinner that Mr Dundas [1] has said the United States had asked the Mediation of G.^t Brit.ⁿ to make Peace with the Indians and that they consider the Line fixed in 69 as the proper Boundary. He tells me also that a Supply of Corn was given to the Indians in their late Expedition, that all the Powder of the Traders was distributed among them and that two Officers of the fifth Regiment, Captain —— and Captain Bunbury, passed the preceeding Winter in the Miami Towns. The Wind has blown very hard all last Night and all this Day from the N. West and West N. West. A very heavy Gale. Mr Ellice called to tell me he is going out of Town.

Thursday 5. — This Morning I write. Mr Constable calls. I dine with J. Penn and sit till ten in the Evening but not at the Bottle. The Wind blew hard last Night from the N. West. It lulld about six this Evening but is again very high at eleven. The Count de Croix called on me this Morning.

Friday 6. — Write all the Morning. Mr Johnson's Son or Clerk brings me a Letter from T. Jefferson Esqr, Secretary of State, containing my Credentials. I dine with Mrs R. Penn and go afterwards to Mr Phyn's where I stay a little while, then return Home and write. The Wind is at length lulld and the Weather looks quietly.

Jefferson to Morris

Philadelphia. January 23.^d 1792.

Dear Sir,

I have the pleasure to inform you that the President of the United States has appointed you Minister Plenipotentiary for the

---

[1] Henry Dundas (1742–1811), Treasurer of the Navy, manages India Board of Control; later Minister of War; trusted henchman of Pitt, makes lucid speeches in broad Scotch. Created Viscount Melville by Addington, 1802.

United States at the Court of France, which was approved by the Senate on the 12th instant, on which be pleased to accept my congratulations. You will receive herewith your Comission, a letter of credence for the King sealed and a copy of it open for your own satisfaction; as also a Cypher to be used on proper occasions in the correspondence between us.

To you it would be more than unneccessary for me to undertake a general delineation of the functions of the Office to which you are appointed. I shall therefore only express our desire, that they be constantly exercised in that spirit of sincere friendship and attachment which we bear to the French Nation; and that in all transactions with the Minister, his good dispositions be conciliated by whatever in language or attentions may tend to that effect. With respect to their Government, we are under no call to express opinions which might please or offend any party; and therefore it will be best to avoid them on all occasions, public or private. Could any circumstances require unavoidably such expressions, they would naturally be in conformity with the sentiments of the great mass of our countrymen, who having first, in modern times, taken the ground of Government founded on the will of the people, cannot but be delighted on seeing so distinguished and so esteemed a nation arrive on the same ground, and plant their standard by our side.

I feel myself particularly bound to recommend, as the most important of your charges, the patronage of our Commerce and the extension of its privileges, both in France and her Colonies, but most especially the latter. Our Consuls in France are under general instructions to correspond with the Minister of the United States at Paris; from them you may often receive interesting information. Joseph Fenwick is Consul at Bordeaux and Burrell Carnes at Nantz; M. de La Motte Vice Consul at Havre and M. Cathalan fils at Marseilles.

An act of Congress of July 1st 1790 has limited the allowance of a Minister plenipotentiary to 9,000 ^{1} dollars a year *for all his personal services and other expences*, a year's salary for his outfit,

---

^{1} Jefferson had found $10,000 wholly inadequate in his fine corner house in the Champs Élisées, but as Paris is no tourist centre under the Terror the reduction is less important than it might have been earlier.

and a quarter's salary for his return. It is understood that *the personal services and other expences* here meant, do not extend to the cost of gazettes and pamphletts transmitted to the Secretary of State's Office, to translating or printing necessary papers, postage, couriers, and necessary aids to poor American sailors. These additional charges therefore may be inserted in your accounts; but no other of any description, unless where they are expressly directed to be incurred. By an ancient rule of Congress, your salary will commence from the day you receive this Letter, if you be then at Paris, or from the day you set out for Paris from any other place at which it may find you: it ceases on receiving notice or permission to return, after which the additional quarter's allowance takes place. You are free to name your own private Secretary, who will receive from the public a salary of 1,350 dollars a year, without allowance for any extras. I have thought it best to state these things to you minutely, that you may be relieved from all doubt as to the matter of your accounts. I will beg leave to add a most earnest request, that on the 1st day of July next, and on the same day annually afterwards, you make out your account to that day and send it by the first vessel and by duplicates. In this I must be very urgent and particular, because at the meeting of the ensuing Congress always it is expected that I prepare for them a Statement of the disbursements from this fund from July to June inclusive. I shall give orders by the first opportunity to our Bankers in Amsterdam to answer your drafts for the allowances herein before mentioned, recruiting them at the same time by an adequate remitment, as I expect that by the time you receive this they will not have remaining on hand of this fund more than 7 or 8,000 dollars.

You shall receive from me from time to time the laws and journals of Congress, gazettes and other interesting papers; for whatever information is in possession of the public I shall leave you generally to the gazettes, and only undertake to communicate by letter such, relative to the business of your mission, as the gazettes cannot give. From you I shall ask, once or twice a month regularly, a communication of interesting occurrences in France, of the general affairs of Europe, and a transmission of the Leyden gazette, the *Journal logographe*, and the best paper of Paris for their Colonial affairs, with such other publications as may be important enough to be read by one who can spare little time to read anything, or which may contain matter proper to be turned to on interesting subjects and occasions. The English packet is the most certain channel for such epistolary communications as are not very secret, and by those packets I would wish always to receive a letter from you by way of corrective to the farrago of news they generally bring. Intermediate letters, secret communications, gazettes and other printed papers, had better come through the channel of M. de La Motte at Havre, to whom I shall also generally address my letters to you, and always the gazettes and other printed papers.

Mr Short will receive by this same conveyance, his appointment as Minister resident at the Hague.

I have the honour to be with great esteem & respect
Dear Sir   your most obedient & most humble serv.t
TH: JEFFERSON

Morris to Jefferson

London 6 April 1792

The hon.le Thomas Jefferson Esq.r
Philadelphia

Dear Sir,

I had the Honor to receive (this Morning) your Favor of the twenty third of January with its Enclosures, excepting the Cypher which seems accidentally to have been omitted in making up your Dispatches, or perhaps it has been put by Mistake in the Letter directed to Mr Short, which at Mr Johnson's Request I have taken Charge of. I shall deliver it as speedily as may be, intending to make my Arrangements for leaving this City as soon as the present Hollidays are over.

Nothing can be more just than your Observations respecting the Propriety of preserving Silence as to the Government of France; and they are peculiarly applicable to the present State of Things in that Country. Changes are now so frequent, and

Events seem fast ripening to such awful Catastrophe, that no Expressions on the Subject, however moderate, would be received with Indifference.

Feeling with you the Importance of our commercial Connections I shall of Course bend all my Attention to establish and extend them. Permit me to entreat, my dear Sir, that you will send me all the Informations which can be collected on the Subject. If at the same Time you could favor me with the particular Points which it is desired to carry I shall feel myself more at Ease than in a general Pursuit, which may perhaps be directed to Objects less important than I may suppose them.

I thank you for the accurate Statement you have been so kind as to make respecting my Salary &c.ª and you may rely that I shall exactly conform to your Wishes on that Head. And I take this Opportunity to say that you will never receive from me any Observations respecting the Amount. If it proves insufficient I will supply the Want from my own Funds, as far as they will permit, and the Ballance must be made up by Retrenchment.

As you have yourself ran thro the Career which I am now about to commence, you know much better than I do the Importance of early Information and therefore I feel more Confidence in acting under you than I should in any other Situation. If you would kindly afford me your good Counsel it would confer a great Obligation. Pardon me I pray you one Observation. The Distance of America is such that *probable* Events are almost of equal Importance with those which have actually happened because Measures must be squared in some Degree to the one as much as to the other. You will from hence infer my Desire to know on some Subjects the best Opinion which can be form'd, and I am sure I cannot better address myself for that Purpose than to you.

President Washington to Morris

Philadelphia Jany 28th 1792

My dear Sir,

Private

Your favor of the 30th of September came duly to hand, and I thank you for the important information contained in it.

The official communications from the Secretary of State, accompanying this letter, will convey to you the evidence of my *nomination*, and *appointment* of you to be Minister Plenipotentiary for the United States at the Court of France; and my assurances that both were made with *all my heart*, will, I am persuaded, satisfy you as to that fact. I wish I could add, that the *advice* & *consent* flowed from a similar source. — Candour forbids it — and friendship requires that I should assign the causes, as far as they have come to my knowledge. —

Whilst your abilities, knowledge in the affairs of this Country, & disposition to serve it were adduced, and asserted on one hand, you were charged on the other hand, with levity, and imprudence of conversation and conduct. — It was urged, that your habit of expression, indicated a hauteur disgusting to those who happen to differ from you in sentiment; and among a people who study civility and politeness more than any other nation, it must be displeasing. — That in France you were considered as a favourer of Aristocracy, & unfriendly to its Revolution — (I suppose they meant Constitution). — That under this impression you could not be an acceptable public character — of consequence, would not be able, however willing, to promote the interests of this Country in an essential degree.

— That in England you indiscreetely communicated the purport of your Mission, in the first instance to the Minister of France, at that Court; who, availing himself in the same moment of the occasion, gave it the appearance of a Movement through his Court. — This, and other circumstances of a cimilar Nature, joined to a closer intercourse with the opposition Members, occasioned distrust, & gave displeasure to the Ministry; which was the cause, it is said, of that reserve which you experienced in negotiating the business which had been entrusted to you. —

But not to go further into detail — I will place the ideas of your political adversaries in the light which their arguments have presented them to my view — viz — That the promptitude with wch your brilliant, & lively imagination is displayed, allow too little time for deliberation and correction; and is the primary cause of those sallies which too often offend, and of that ridicule of characters which begets enmity not easy to be forgotten, but which might easily be avoided if it was under the control of more caution and prudence. — In a word, that it is indispensably necessary that more circumspection should be observed by our Representatives abroad than they conceive you are disposed to adopt. —

In this statement you have the pros & the cons; by reciting them, I give you a proof of my friendship, if I give none of my policy or judgment. — I do it on the presumption that a mind conscious of its own rectitude, fears not what is said of it; but will bid defiance to and despise shafts that are not barbed with accusations against honor or integrity; — and because I have the fullest confidence (supposing the allegations to be founded in whole or part) that you would find no difficulty, being apprised of the exceptionable light in which they are received, and considering yourself as the representative of this Country, to effect a change; and thereby silence, in the most unequivocal and satisfactory manner, your political opponents. — Of my good opinion, & of my friendship & regard, you may be asured — and that

I am always —   Y.^{r} affect.^{e}

G.^{o} WASHINGTON

Morris to President Washington

London 6 April 1792

George Washington Esqr

Philadelphia

My dear Sir

I receive this Instant your Favor of the twenty eighth of January, and I do most sincerely thank you for the Information which you have been so kind as to communicate. I know how to value the Friendship by which they were dictated. I have always thought that the Counsel of our Enemies is wholesome, tho bitter, if we can but turn it to good Account & in Order that I may not fail to do so on the present Occasion *I now promise you* that Circumspection of Conduct which has hitherto I acknowlege form'd no Part of my Character. And I make the *Promise* that my Sense of Integrity may enforce what my Sense of Propriety dictates.

I have hitherto in my Letters communicated to you many Things which I should not willingly entrust to others, and in the Course of Events I may again possess Information which it might be well that you were acquainted with. At the same Time it is I presume expected that the public Servants will correspond fully and *freely* with the Office of foreign Affairs. It might therefore be deemed improper not to say *all* in my Letters to that Office. I wish therefore you would give me your candid Opinion on this Subject. I should be extremely sorry to offend or to give Pain but I cannot have the same unreserved Confidence in others that I have in you, and my Letter of the fourth of February will shew that Cases may occur in which I am not even Master of it.

I was told Yesterday that Mr Dundas has said that the United States have asked for the Mediation of this Country to bring about a Peace with the Indians. He told the same Person (a Mr Osgood, the new Chief Justice of the mid Province of upper Canada) that the Treaty made long since by Sir William Johnson seemed to be the proper Ground on which *to fix a Boundary* between the United States & the indian Tribes. I learn these Facts in such a Way that I am confident of the Truth, and therefore submit them without any Comment to your Consideration.

An Express arrived last Night brings an Account of the Assassination of the King of Sweden the twenty sixth of last Month at a Masquerade, and thus another Crown falls on the Head of a young Sovereign. Those who conceive the french Jacobins to be at the Bottom of a great king-killing Project approach the Deaths of the Emperor, the King of Sweden, and the Movements making against France, from whence they infer that the King of Prussia should take Care of himself ánd be cautious of his Cooks and Companions. Such sudden Deaths in so critical a Moment are extraordinary; but I do not usually believe in Enormities, and I cannot see how a Club can pursue a Path of Horrors where Secrecy is essential to Success.

The young King of Hungary has made such Reply to the peremptory Demands of France to cool a little the Extravagance of Joy manifested on his Father's Death. I am told that he is a Disciple rather of his Uncle Joseph than of his Father & if this be so he will not long remain idle. The Death of his Swedish Majesty will however make some Derangement in the Plan of Operations. How all these Things will end God only knows.

President Washington to Morris

Philadelphia June 21ˢᵗ 1792
(Private)

My dear Sir,

Since writing to you on the 28ᵗʰ of January, I have received your several favors of the 27ᵗʰ Decʳ from Paris — 4ᵗʰ of Febʸ, 17ᵗʰ & 21ˢᵗ of March, and 6ᵗʰ & 10ᵗʰ of April from London. — I thank you very much for the interesting and important information contained in several of these letters, particularly that of the 4ᵗʰ of Febʸ — If the last article, of which it is comprized, should, in your judgment, require an acknowledgment, I shall rely on your goodness to make it in suitable & respectful terms. — You can be at no loss to discover the paragraph to which I allude.

The plot thickens, and developement must have begun — but what the final issue will be, lyes too deep for human ken. — I will hope for the best, without allowing myself to wander in the field of conjecture for the result. —

Your letters, though exceedingly interesting in point of information, require but little to be said, in the way of reply. — The accounts given therein will be treasured up, to be acted upon as circumstances will warrant, and as occasions may present. — One thing, however, I must not pass over in silence, lest you should infer from it that Mr D[undas] had authority for reporting that, the United States had asked the mediation of Great Britain to bring about a peace between them and the Indians. — You may be *fully* assured, Sir, that no such mediation *ever* was asked;

— that the asking of it *never* was in contemplation; — and, I think I might go further & say, that it not only never *will* be asked, but would be rejected if offered. — The U. States will never have occasion, I hope, to ask for the interposition of that Power, or any other, to establish peace within their own territory. — That it is the wish of that government to intermeddle, & bring this measure to pass, many concurrent circumstances (small indeed when singly considered) had left no doubt on my mind before your letter of the 6th of April came to hand — What is there mentioned of the views of Mr P[itt] as well as of the assertions of Mr D[undas] is strong as "proof of holy writ" in confirmation thereof. — The attempt has, however, in its remotest movements, been so scouted as to have retarded, if it has not entirely done away, the idea. — But I do not hesitate to give it to you as my *private*, & decided opinion, that it is these interferences, and to the underhanded support which the Indians receive (notwithstanding the open disavowal of it) that all our difficulties with them proceed. — We are essaying every means in our power, to undeceive these hostile tribes with respect to the disposition of this Country towards them; and to convince them that we neither seek their exterpation, nor the occupancy of their lands (as they are taught to believe) except such of the latter as have been obtan'd by fair treaty, & purchase, bona fide made, & recognized by them in more instances than one. — If they will not, after this explanation (if we can get at them to make it) listen to the voice of peace, the sword must decide the dispute, and we are, though very reluctantly, vigorously preparing to meet the event.

In the course of last winter, I had some of the chiefs of the Cherokees in this City, and in the Spring I obtained (with some difficulty indeed) a full representation of the Six Nations, to come hither. — I have sent all of them away well satisfied, and fully convinced of the justice & good dispositions of this government towards the Indian Nations, *generally*. — The latter, that is the Six Nations, who, before, appeared to be divided, & distracted in their Councils, have given strong assurances of their friendship; and have resolved to send a deputation of *their* tribes to the hostile Indians with an acc! of all that has passed, accompanying it with advice to them, to desist from further hostilities. — With difficulty, *still* greater, I have brought the celebrated Capt.ⁿ Joseph Brandt to this City, with a view to impress him also with the equitable intentions of this government towards *all* the nations of his colour. — He only arrived last night, and I am to give him an audience at twelve this day. —

Nothing has yet been hinted on this side the water, to any of the Officers of government, of the other matter mentioned in your letter of the 6th of April; though suspicions of it have been entertained. —

Knowing from the letters of the Secretary of State to you, that you are advised in all matters of public concern, and will have transmitted to you the Laws as they are Enacted, and the Gazettes as they are published, I shall not trouble you with a detail of domestic occurrences. — The latter are *sur*-charged, and *some of them* indecently communicative of *charges* that need evidence for their support.

There can be but few things of public nature (likely to happen in your line, requiring to be acted upon by this government) that may not be freely communicated to the Department to which it belongs; because, in proceeding thereon, the head of the department will, necessarily, be made acquainted therewith. — But there may, in the course of events, be other matters, more remote in their consequence — of the utmost importance to be known, that not more than one intermediate person would be entrusted with; *here*, necessity as well as propriety will mark the line — Cases not altogether under the controul of necessity, may also arise, to render it advisable to do this, and your own good judgment will be the best director in these cases. —

With much truth & affection
I am always — Yours
G? WASHINGTON

Be so good as to give the enclosed letter a safe conveyance to Mr De La Fayette

Gouv. Morris Esq.

Morris to Rufus King

London 6 April 1792

Rufus King Esq.
                    New York

My dear Sir

I have received this Day my Credential to the Court of France; and am pleased to find that I am considerably indebted to you for effecting that Appointment. It is true that a Sense of Obligation is not generally agreable, but when a Favor received serves to strengthen the Connections we wish to preserve, and unite us to the deserving few with whom we wish to live, it never fails to excite the most pleasing Emotions....

As I have no Doubt that you urged my Appointment with a View to the public Service, it is incumbent on You to comply with my Request to be favor'd with your Correspondence. If I have not *good* Information and *early* Information, I can do little or Nothing. You will easily conceive that a Minister who knows not those Affairs of his Country which are known to many others is placed in an awkward Situation; besides there is always a kind of Traffic in Articles of Intelligence, among the Members of the diplomatic Body, in which Beads and Wampum are sometimes given for Gold to the Satisfaction of both Parties. It happens also not unfrequently that by knowing good or bad Tidings before any one else, we can make the most of the one, and obviate the worst of the other. For Instance, in poor Sinclair's Defeat, it might have been so handed out to the Public as to have look'd like Nothing and if a horrible Account had afterwards been publish'd by our Enemies, most People would not have been at the Trouble of reading it. On the other Hand, some of those gambling Operations in the Stocks which, however they may prejudice the Fortune or even Morals of Individuals, are clearly demonstrative of the public Prosperity, and of the Energy, Authority and Stability of Government; these I say may be so stated occasionally, as to give a just Idea of our Importance to those numerous Idlers whose Pursuit of Knowlege rarely extends beyond a Newspaper Paragraph. And yet this great Herd have more Influence on national Councils than is generally imagin'd, and especially in France, where every Thing is talked of and hardly any Thing is understood. Lastly it may happen that, from Ignorance of the real State of Things, a Minister may give up what his Country would wish to retain, or pursue what they would not acquire. You will tell me perhaps that there is a public Office for the Transmission of Intelligence and that is true, but the same Object strikes different People in a different Way, a Load of unexpected Business may distract the Attention of that Office, or Letters may be lost or long delayed, in Short considering the Distance, and other Circumstances, Accident may often obstruct, or Design totally stop that Channel of Communication. But why do I enter into this Detail? You will see my Solicitude, and you will believe I hope in the Sincerity of my Regard.

Gouverneur Morris to Robert Morris

London 10 April 1792

Robert Morris Esq!
                Philadelphia

My dear Friend
    ... As it is probable that I may be now some Time before I return to America let me entreat again that you would make out a State of the Accounts between us. Or if you please we will make a lumping Settlement. To that Effect you can tell me how much of the Genesee Land you think I should relinquish, or rather how much I may retain, and so pass mutual Release. In such Case you can authorize Robert to make Conveyance of a Tract of the Size required and not being in Lott N? 1, which you seem to consider as the best. He and I can agree on the Place. When I mention this it is with a View to extinguish every Claim from every Source which we or our Representatives may have on each other and I think it best that it be done in our Day and as I know how much your Time is engrossed, I mention a lumping Settlement as the Means of avoiding Labor, which perhaps you cannot conveniently bestow. I cannot quit this Subject without mentioning that when I think of your various Concerns, of the Characters of many with whom you have been connected, of the

Perplexity of Accounts during the Paper Money Time and of the Impossibility that your Wife and Children should ever go thro with the Adjustment; when I join to this Apprehension that should you fall during my Absence there is no Person I know of either able or willing to see that they have Justice done them, I say that very often when I think of these Things it makes me feel sick at Heart. I am sure that it is of the utmost Importance to you to wind up some Concerns *even with a Loss* rather than leave them to Posterity. I wish that all accounts between you and I may be closed that I may with more clear Propriety in Case of any Accident step forward to an Adjustment, in which I should then have no personal Interest.

. . . After saying so much to plague you I must now give you a further Trouble. I need not tell you the Importance of Intelligence to my public Situation. You will of Course conceive my anxiety to obtain the earliest and fullest. I apply to you for this Purpose as a Patriot and as a Friend. Not that I question Mr Jefferson's Care but he may be sick or absent or otherwise employed or his Letters may miscarry and I shall be blam'd perhaps for not acting conformably to Circumstances which I was not acquainted with. And when a Man's Enemies can fix a Charge on him the World is not over solicitous about the Justice of it. This we have often seen and experienced.

Saturday 7. — Write closely this Morning. M⸢r⸣ Hermanse calls on me but I make his Visit short. Dine with Lord Wycombe and go afterwards to M⸢r⸣ Phyn's where I stay till eleven. The Weather this Day is very fine.

Sunday 8 April. — This Morning I sit down to examine some Accounts but M⸢r⸣ Hermanse comes in and I dress and go out. Walk in Kensington Gardens where I meet M⸢r⸣ T. Moore of New York; he points out to me the extraordinary Effect of a Compost which, put on barked Trees, brings forward again the Bark on the bare Places and really infuses new Life into the sapless Trunk. I called on the Dutchess of Gordon who is denied but seems to be only *going* abroad. Visit at M⸢rs⸣ R. Penn's. Dine with the Count Woranzow. We are comme Tête à Tête. We have much Conversation after Dinner. He says that M⸢r⸣ Pitt was well enough inclin'd to a Connection with America but L^d. Sheffield's Book banish'd that Idea. He says that for a long Time he believd him to be an honest, candid Man but he had at last detected him in seriously asserting on his Honor Things absolutely false. That the British Government have spread over all Europe the most unfavorable Impressions respecting America. Desires to have Hamilton's Reports to Congress. He says the Object of L^d. McCartney's Mission to China is to get some exclusive Right to the Trade and that Money well employed at Pekin will ensure Success, the Chinese being the most corrupt as well as the most cowardly Wretches in Existence. He says that a leading Character in the Administration of India Affairs was heard to say in the Time when they expected to learn every Hour the Fall of Seringapatnam, that now was the Time to turn their Arms against China. He mentions the Insolence of M^r. Pitt's Menaces to him and the Meanness of his subsequent indirect Apologies. He says also that Marquis del Campo was so much a Tool of this Administration that he kept entirely secret from the French Embassador all his Proceedings, and that when the Spanish Minister at the Hague publish'd in the *Gazette of Leyden* some Observations which had in the Course of that Negotiation been made by del Campo, they gave him a severe Rap over the Knuckles and drove him to entreat of the Minister at the Hague that all further Publications should be suppress'd. He tells me that the Removal of Florida Blanca & Advancement of d'Aranda has given them very great Concern. He says that Lord Elgin is certainly sent over to France for the Purposes of Intrigue. The Conduct they have observed on the taking of the *Resolue* is, he says, the most impertinent imaginable. That Lord Grenville told M^r. Hertsinger [1] he must be sensible that they had a Right to act as they had done by the commercial Treaty. To which the latter replied only by expressing his Astonishment. The imperial Minister comes in, who is in Appearance a lively sensible Man. Shortly after, M^r. Katchuby comes in, but like every other Person immediately from a Journey he is too unsettled for serious Information.

Monday 9. — M^r. Morris and M^r. Constable call on me. I take

---

[1] Attached to French Embassy.

the latter into the City & after bespeaking some plated Ware and Cutlery go to Mark Lane where I leave him. Thence to Mr Wadeson's who is abroad. Mr Oliveira's, also abroad. Visit Mr Levingworth and Mrs Low and Mrs Phyn and Mrs Lestrange who are all abroad. Call on Lady Tancred and find there Lady Anne Lindsay and Lady E. Fordyce. Go to the Piazza Coffee House and dine with R. M.. Then take a long Walk and return Home. He sits with me till after eleven. The Weather is very fine.

Tuesday 10 *April.* — Write all the Morning. Mr Constable calls. I dine with Church and stand Godfather to his Child, christen'd Alexander.[1] Return Home at ten and sit writing till one. The Weather is very fine.

Wednesday 11. — Mr Constable calls and we go into the City together after I have finish'd my Letters. I leave my Plate with the plated Ware Manufacturer. I call on Mr Oliveira who is not at Home. On Mr Wadeson but he is detain'd in Amsterdam, having met with Obstacles in the Business. Go to Mark Lane and thence to the Exchange. Nothing. Dine with Mr Bourdieu and bring young Morris Home, after which I go to Mr Phyn's. Sit with them the Evening. The Weather is very fine.

Thursday 12. — Write a little while. The Count de Croix calls on me and we go together to look at several Places for Carriages. After he leaves me I visit Count Woranzow, Mr Catchuby, Count Rœderen, Mrs R. Penn who is at Home, the Rest abroad. Visit the Countess and VisCountess of La Luzerne to whom I pay short Visits. Lord Wycombe, who is in the Country. Go to Tattersal's where I see a handsome and cheap Coach. Thence to dine at the Piazza Coffee House. Afterwards go to Mr Church's to see the Children dance. The Marquis of Townshend is here. His Lady is very beautiful and I tell him so. Stay late and then set down Franklin and R. Morris. The Weather is very warm.

Friday 13. — Write. Mr Payne calls. Mr Oliveira came and I agreed with him for five Pipes Madeira and one of Malmsey. I go into Long Acre to look at Carriages and thence to Mr Phyn's to Dinner. Stay the Evening here. The Weather continues very warm and fine.

---

[1] Three years later young Alexander will step out with one-legged godpapa 'to see the Elephant and buy Toys.'

Saturday 14. — This Morning I call on M! Donald and we go to Greenwich where we examine the Hospital. It is a noble Building and extremely well kept, but I think the Food allow'd is too much considering the little Exercise which many of these disabled Men can possibly take. The daily Allowance, excepting on the Banyan Days, is a Pound of Flesh with the Broth made out of it, and on those Days, of which there are two in a Week, the Allowance is 1⅛ Pound of Cheese and one Ounce of Butter, with Pea Soup. They have also every Day one Pound of Bread and two Quarts of Table Beer. A Weekly Allowance of one Shilling Cash and a Proportionate Advance according to the Grades. Their Beds are sheeted once a Month in Winter and once ev'ry three Weeks in Summer. Cloathing is found for them and they have clean Shirts once a Week in Winter and twice a Week in Summer. We walk thro Greenwich Park and go on the Goff Ground of Black Heath where I observe some of the Greenwich Lads, of whom there are above 2300, attending the Players, for which they get each one Shilling. Our Dinner is not a good one, neither are our Wines of the best, but the Reception is very hospitable and flattering. We stay till nine when my friend and Introducer Donald is pretty well warm'd with Wine. I set him down and come Home where I find Letters. The Weather has been very fine this Day. There was a small Sprinkling of Rain while we were at Greenwich Hospital but the Wind came round to the Eastward about three oClock, and as long as it stands in that Quarter we must expect dry Weather.

Sunday 15. — Write. M! Morris calls on me. After him M! Colqhoun and M! R. Penn and his Son. I visit Sir John Sinclair and then go to dine at the british Coffee House. Make free Libations to the jolly god and then go to M! R. Penn's where I rather play the Fool than otherwise. The Wind is pretty high from the Eastward this Day and of Course the Weather is cooler than it was.

Monday 16. — Write. Call on M! Catchuby and we go together to Tattersal's and thence I go to another Livery Stable, then into Long Acre, then to Howard's Plate Manufactory, then to Mark Lane; give to Inglis Bills on the Bankers in Holland for f2200. Take M! Constable up and we dine together with M! Todd at the Piazza Coffee House. After Dinner come Home and go early to bed. The Wind is easterly but the Weather not cold.

Tuesday 17. — Write this Morning. R. Morris calls on me and afterwards Monsieur Bouinville. I take up R. Penn and we go to Spencer's to see Horses. Dine at the thatched House where according to Custom Mʳ Donald pushes the Bottle so as to make short Work. I set Penn down and go to Mʳ Phyn's where I become sensible of the Wine I had swallowed, and come Home. The Weather has been soft with Rain this Day.

Wednesday 18. — This Morning Mʳ Constable calls and we go to look at Carriages and Horses. I then take up R. Penn and we employ ourselves in the same Business. I buy a Coach and four Horses. Dine at Mʳ Phyn's and spend the Evening there. The Weather is very disagreable, Westerly Wind with cold Rain.

Thursday 19. — This Morning I write. The Harness Maker comes and I bespeak Harness for Leaders. Mʳ Spenser comes and introduces a Coachman who has been in Paris. His Demands are so extravagant that we cannot agree together. Mʳ Franklin and Mʳ R. Morris call on me. I dine with Mʳ Church and meet there Mʳ Beckwith, just arrived from America. Converse very little with him. Go from hence to R. Penn's. The Weather has been very disagreable all Day. Rain, with a North East Wind which blows hard; it clears about eleven oClock.

Friday 20. — Write. Thornhill calls. I go into the City and get Money. Call at Mʳ Wadeson's who is not yet return'd but hourly expected. Take up Mʳ Constable and go together to Mʳ Spencer's where I pay for my Horses. Set him down in Argyle Street and then dine at the Piazza Coffee House. R. Penn, Thornhill, R. Morris, Franklin and Jones. After Dinner, which is dull, the three last come Home with me and play Whist. The Wind is still from the North East and the Weather is colder.

Saturday 21. — This Morning I write a little. Mʳ Constable calls and after him Mʳ Hermans. While he is here R. Morris calls and converses about his Bargain with Mʳ Church which is continually changing for the worse. Mʳ John Penn comes in and I make a Note for R. Morris on which he is to ground a Letter to Church. Go to MᶜKenzie's and pay for my Coach. Thence to Madᵉ de La Luzerne's. Thence to a Bookseller's and afterwᵈˢ dine with Church. Go with her and Mad^e de La Luzerne jun^r to the Play of *Coriolanus* in which Mrs Siddons [1] acts perfectly well. Come Home and go early to bed, that is about one oClock, having spent some Time very unprofitably in looking over a Catalogue of Books. The Wind is very high from the Northwest; it has been very raw and cold this Day.

Sunday 22. April. — The Comte de Croix calls this Morning. R. M. breakfasted with me and I prepar'd the Draft of a Letter from him to Mr Church. Call on Inglis and we go together to dine with Mr Ellice at High Gate. Major Frazier is here who is a very pleasant agreable Man. He tells us how Baume was defeated at Bennington and lays the Blame entirely on him, but from his Account of the Matter it would seem that there was some Blame elsewhere. He gives me an Account of the Lands on the St Lawrence River which shews not so well for them as I formerly imagined. He was long stationed at Oswegatchee which he describes to be but a very small Stream and says the back Waters are stagnant, and dry up in the Autumn instead of running off. That in his Opinion that Part of the Country cannot be drained, the Surface being lower, he thinks, than the River, but this must be a Mistake. This drowned Country lies South and Southwest of Oswegatchee. The Wind continues very high from the Westward. The Weather threatned Rain in the Morning but it is clear this Afternoon and Evening.

Monday 23. — This Morning I write. Mr Constable calls to be off an Engagement. I go to see my Horses and shew them to my french Coachman who turns out very properly one of the Sett. R. Morris shewed me Church's Refusal to take the Genesee Land. I dine with Mr Inglis. The News is come by the Post which my Coachman brought over Express, viz that the King of France has propos'd to the Assembly a Declaration of War against the

---

[1] Mrs. Sarah Siddons (1755–1831). Her truly Roman Volumnia is played to the Coriolanus of her brother Kemble, who preserves the excessive dignity of his rôle on and off stage. June 4, 1791, the last curtain had fallen at 107-year-old Drury Lane, built by Inigo Jones, remodelled by Robert Adam. While Sheridan rebuilds it for more seating and bigger profits, he moves his company to Covent Garden, whose larger stage is having a bad effect on the acting. Main entrance then in angle of Piazza, under whose arcades cutpurses had been wont to mingle profitably with outcoming audiences.

Emperor. The Stocks have fallen a little in Consequence of it. Sit here till near ten and drink very good Madeira Wine. The Weather has been very windy all Day from the Westward and yet it is dry.

Tuesday 24. — This Morning R. Morris calls on me to take Leave. He goes for Amsterdam. I call on M.ʳˢ Church and we go together to visit M.ʳˢ Damer. She is at Work on her Statue of the King and it is a curious Spectacle to see a delicate and fine Woman with the Chissel and Mallet chipping a huge Block of Marble. She shews me two Heads which are very fine. Lady Lyttleton had formerly condemn[ed] in strong Terms her Pursuit, and dwelt on the Indecency of those Nudities which form a necessary Appendage of every Statuary's Study. I thought then of a few Lines on the Subject, and with a very bad Pen now write them:

> Why so sternly condemn my Pursuits, noble Dame,
> And say that my Cheeks should be crimson'd with Shame?
> Can the learned or lovely object to a Plan
> Whose Motive is Taste and whose Subject is Man?
> A numerous Offspring all Sages declare
> Are the Gems the most precious a Matron can wear,
> And you, once so blest by connubial Love
> The Truth of that Maxim will surely approve.
> Since, then, tis your Praise the live Subject to bear
> Need I blush who in Stone the cold Copy prepare?

Go to the Bookseller's and leave a List of Books to be sent to me in Paris. Call on M.ʳ Faden for Maps, which according to his Custom are not yet finished.

Call at the Cabinet Maker's who still puts off a Trifle which should have been compleated long ago. Visit M.ʳ Johnson who tells me that young Seton brought M.ʳ Jefferson's Dispatches and detaind them twenty Days. Bespeak four Groce of Burton Ale and eight Groce of Porter of Blew and Hippart. Visit at M.ʳ Gregory's and call to see if M.ʳ Wadeson is come Home but he has not. Visit at M.ʳ Phyn's and find her oppressed with an intermittent. Call at M.ʳ Spencer's Livery Stables and then at M.ᶜ Kenzie's Rhedarium. Dine with M.ʳ and M.ʳˢ Church *en famille* and sit with him after Dinner. He says that immediately on

Lord Elgin's Return, Dispatches were sent off to inform the King of Hungary that, let the Declaration of War come from whichever Side it may, He is the Aggressor; and therefore, notwithstanding the Treaty of Guarantee, this Country will remain neuter. *Quere.* Church tells me, which indeed I suspected before, that he was concern'd with the late french Embassador in Stock Speculations during the Spanish Armament. He says that del Campo made regular Communication of all his Dispatches to La Luzerne. But yet they made little or nothing by the Speculation and should have made a Plumb apiece if the Thing had ended in the Time and Manner which was expected. He says that Mr Pitt is a very great Rascal, as great as his Father tho not by any Means so great a Man. That far from being a daring Minister He is timid and therefore false. That he is an unblushing Promise breaker and will descend to any Meanness in order to carry a favorite Point. The Weather has this Day been damp and foul, Wind from the Southward and then from the Westward. In the Afternoon it is raw but drier.

Wednesday 25. — This Morning Mr Spencer calls and with him the Man who is to take on my Horses to Paris. Settle with them. A Sailor comes who had been with me before to get a Passage to New York. Capt.ⁿ Bunyan, to whom I recommended him, is gone. Send him to Mr Johnson. I write. Mr Constable calls and Mr Gregory. I endeavor to put them together. Thornhill comes in. After they are gone I continue my writing, then dress and call on Mr Colqhoun. He shews me Capt.ⁿ Williamson's Letters from New York respecting the Genesee Country. Dine at the Bedford Coffee House with R. Penn, Thornhill and several of their Acquaintance quite *à l'anglois.* As I come off Thornhill introduces me to one of the Company who is a Stockbroker, saying that we may perhaps be useful to each other. His Friend is to send me his Address &c.^a. I call on Mrs Phyn who is but just risen and is very much indisposed. Perswade her to retire as there is too much Company and Conversation for a sick Person. Constable tells me there are Advices from New York that Duer has blown up and that several others must follow, in Consequence of which the Funds were down amazingly. Bring Forsyth Home, who on my mentioning that I had now quitted Business, says he hopes not for that I may perhaps give them useful Hints. The Weather has this Day been very fine. The Wind still from the Westward but light.

Thursday 26. — This Morning I write and then go into the City. Call on M.ʳ Silk the Cabinet Maker who disappoints me again. He promises to send Home my Wood. Call at Mark Lane and see M.ʳ Ellice, M.ʳ Inglis being out of the Way. Go to M.ʳ Wadeson's who is at length return'd. Call at Argyle Street and enquire after M.ʳˢ Phyn's Health. Leave there some Books and Papers for W. C.. Visit M.ʳˢ Low who is abroad. Sit one Minute with Doctor Bancroft. Call on Gov.ʳ Franklin who is abroad. On M.ʳ Rogers who has din'd and is in good Spirits. Go to the Bookseller's and then to dine with Count Woranzow. After Dinner go to Mad.ᵉ de La Luzerne's and sit awhile with her, thence to M.ʳ Hertsinger's who is abroad. Then go to Lady Tancred's and M.ʳˢ L'Estrange's, both abroad. Return Home earlier than usual. The Weather is very pleasant this Day.

Friday 27. — This Morning I write. M.ʳ Constable calls on me and also M.ʳ Colqhoun. Take M.ʳ Constable into the City. M.ʳ Ellice tells me he has consulted with M.ʳ Inglis and that I may rely on Secrecy and Attention if I make to them any Communications. Return Home and go thence to the Bookseller's, then to M.ʳ John Penn's and Lord Lansdowne's and Count Rœderen's, thence tow.ᵈˢ M.ʳ Franklin's. Meet him in the Street. Call at Sir John Sinclair's who is abroad, then visit M.ʳ Jones, who to shew his Wit talks Nonsense, a very common Case. Dine at R. Penn's, his Brother John of the Party. The Leave taking here affects my Feelings much. Go to Argyle Street and visit M.ʳˢ Phyn who is a little better but still indispos'd. The Weather has been very pleasant this Day but rather cool.

Saturday 28. — Write this Morning. M.ʳ Constable calls on me and M.ʳ Wadeson and Lord Wycombe and Doctor Bancroft and Gov.ʳ Franklin and M.ʳ Franklin and Sir John Sinclair. I dine with M.ʳ Church and after Dinner visit Mad.ᵉ de La Luzerne who is in Bed, then go to the french Minister's and then to M.ʳ Phyn's. She is gone to Bed, being much indispos'd. The Weather is good and warm. Col.º Smith and his Wife are arriv'd from New York but not yet got up to Town.

Sunday 29. — Write this Morning and pay my Bills. M.
Franklin calls and makes a short Visit. Count Woranzow and
M. Catchubey call and make a pretty long Visit. M. Parker
comes and while he is here Count Rœderen pays me a short
Visit. Settle with M. Parker and take his Notes. He dines with
me. After Dinner I go to Mark Lane and leave a Letter for M.
Inglis who is abroad. Go to Argyle Street to visit M.ˢ Phyn who
is in bed indispos'd. Bring M. Constable Home with me and we
take Tea. Deliver to him my Letters with a Memorandum and
then bid good bye and pack up for Departure. The Weather this
Day has been pleasant, the Wind light from the Eastward.

Monday 30. — This Morning at ½past six I leave London and
at six I reach Dover. Observe on the Road that the Fall of Water
has been considerable and injured many Fields. Col? Smith calls
on me at Dover and sits some Time. He gives me a Detail of
American Parties and Politics. I embark at eleven. The Weather
this Day has been very fine.

MAY 1792

Tuesday 1 *May*. — At half past four this Morning we began
to move and at half past eight we are moor'd at the Key of
Calais. Dine; wait on the Municipality and obtain my Passport.
The Officers at the Custom House insist on my paying the Duties
sauf à les reprendre &cᵃ. The Chevalier d'Orléans arrives this
Evening. He is on his Route *comme Émigrant*. The Wind blows
fresh from the Westward this Day and it is cold.

Wednesday 2.ᵈ *May*. — This Morning at twenty Minutes after
eight I leave Calais and reach Boulogne at one. Dine here and
set off at three. Get in at Montreuil at eight. The Weather has
been very fine this Day.

Thursday 3.ᵈ — This Morning at half past seven we leave the
Hôtel la Cour de France at Montreuil, which has fallen off from

what it was when I first knew it. The Wind is still from the North-west and is cold. On the Road to Abbeville, which we reach at twenty Minutes after one, the Ostler tells me in very bad French that there was Ice formed last Night, that he expects it will be still colder toNight and that much of the Rye is already blighted. We dine at Abbeville at the Tête de Bœuf; *la Cave est meileur que la Cuisine.* At a Quarter after three we leave Abbeville and arrive at Half past six at Flixecourt. This is very slow travelling. The Country, which from the Clods in the tilled Land seems to have been much moistened some Time ago, is now again thirsty and this Westerly Wind is parchingly dry as well as cold.

Friday 4 *May.* — This Morning at ten Minutes after six we leave the Post House at Flixecourt, a bad Inn and a dear one; in two Hours and three Quarters we reach Amiens and breakfast there. We go from Amiens to Breteuil in four Hours and three Quarters. It is ten Minutes after three when we arrive and the Intention was to stay all Night but every Thing is so dirty and there is such a Crowd of Militia that I hire two additional Horses and leave it at five after a very bad Dinner and worse Wine, both dear. Go to St Juste in two Hours, where we must stay tho Appearances are not flattering. The Weather is still cold tho the Wind has got round to Southward and after some Mist and some Shower it sets in to Rain this Evening very hard.

Saturday 5. — This Morning we leave St Juste at ten Minutes before nine and in six Hours and three Quarters we reach Chantilly where I stay the Remainder of the Day. The Wind is at North East and very cold.

G. Morris to his nephew

London 29 April 1792

James Morris Esqr

New York

My dear Sir

I have receiv'd your Letter of the thirteenth of Novr and thank you for the Assurance that my Wishes shall be attended to in laying off the proposed Road when the Bridge over the Harlem

River shall have been compleated. I consider that as an Event by no Means desirable to the Owners of Morrisania and so they will find whenever it takes Place, for the Idea of feeding Cattle on their Route to New York Market is illusory and for every Thing else a Bridge will bring Trouble and Cost instead of Pleasure and Profit, not to mention the Danger of being robb'd by Straglers.[1] ...

You tell me that my Farm looks well and others tell me the same Thing. I am glad of it for good Looks are good Things, but I should be glad to hear a little of some resulting Income to repay my great Advances, which have been constant for a long Time past, and I have receiv'd from Morrisania in above three Years which have elapsed since I left it just one Apple. I think you will agree with me that it ought to have been a golden one.

Jefferson to Morris

Philadelphia Mar. 10. 1792

Dear Sir

My letter of Jan. 23. put under cover to Mr Johnson in London & sent by a passenger in the British packet of February will have conveyed to you your appointment as Min. Plen. to the U.S. at the court of France. By the Pennsylvania Capt. Harding, bound to Havre de Grace, & plying pretty regularly between this place & that, you will receive the present letter, with the laws of the U.S. journals of Congress, & gazettes to this day, addressed to the care of M. de La Motte. You will also receive a letter from the President to the King of France in answer to his announcing the acceptance of the constitution, which came to hand only a week ago. A copy of this letter is sent for your own use. You will be pleased to deliver the sealed one (to the Minister I presume according to the antient etiquette of the court) accompanying it

---

[1] Alas! what would Morris say of the Tri-Borough Bridge which runs past the ghost of his vanished windows, of the taming of the clear, swirling khyll in which he fished as it raced past his salt meadows. Only with tight-shut eyes can a lover of Morrisania conjure back its beauties, now levelled, built over, degraded.   (1937.)

with those assurances of friendship which the occasion may permit you to express, and which are cordially felt by the President & the great body of our nation. We wish no occasion to be omitted of impressing the national assembly with this truth. We had expected ere this that in consequence of the recommendation of their predecessors, some overtures would have been made to us on the subject of a treaty of commerce. An authentic copy of the recommendation was delivered but nothing said about carrying it into effect; perhaps they expect that we should declare our readiness to meet them on the ground of treaty; if they do we have no hesitation to declare it. In the mean time if the present communications produce any sensation, perhaps it may furnish a good occasion to endeavour to have matters replaced in *statu quo* by repealing the late innovation as to our ships, tob? & whale oil. It is right that things should be on their antient footing at opening the treaty. Mons! Ternant has applied here for 400,000 dollars for the succour of the French colonies. The Secretary of the Treasury has reason to believe that the late loan at Antwerp has paid up all our arrearages to France both of principal & interest, & consequently that there is no part of our debt exigible at this time. However the legislature having authorised the President to proceed in borrowing to pay off the residue, provided it can be done to the *advantage* of the U.S. it is thought the law will be satisfied with *avoiding loss* to the U.S. This has obliged the Secretary of the Treasury to require some conditions which may remove from us that loss which we encountered, from an unfavorable exchange, to pay what was *exigible*, and to transfer it to France as to payments not exigible; these shall be fully detailed to you when settled. In the meantime the money will be furnished as fast as it can be done, indeed our wishes are cordial to the reestablishment of peace & commerce in those colonies, and to give such proofs of our good faith both to them & the Mother country, as to suppress all that jealousy which might oppose itself to the free exchange of *our mutual productions*, so essential to the prosperity of those colonies, and to the preservation of *our agricultural* interests. This is our true interest & our true object, & we have no reason to conceal views so justifiable, tho' the expression of them may require that the occasions be proper

& the terms chosen with delicacy. The gazettes will inform you of the proceedings of Congress, the laws past & proposed, & generally speaking of all public transactions. You will perceive that the Indian war calls for sensible exertions; it would have been a trifle had we only avowed enemies to contend with. The British Court has disavowed all aid to the Indians. Whatever may have been their orders in that direction, the Indians are fully & notoriously supplied by their agents with every thing necessary to carry on the war. Time will show how all this is to end. Besides the laws, journals & newspapers before mentioned, you will receive herewith the State Constitution, the Census, an almanac and an answer to L.ᵈ Sheffield [1] on our commerce. A cypher is ready for you, but cannot be sent till we can find a trusty passenger going to Paris.   I am with great respect & esteem Dear Sir

Your most obed.ᵗ

& most humble serv.ᵗ

TH: JEFFERSON

Mar. 14. Since writing the preceeding, the two houses have come to resolutions on the King's letter which are inclosed in the president's; and copies of them accompany this for your use.

Jefferson to Morris

Philadelphia. Apr. 28. 1792.

Dear Sir,

My last letter to you was of the 10ᵗʰ of March. The preceding one of Jan. 23 had conveyed to you your appointment as Minister Plenipotentiary to the court of France; the present will, I hope, find you there. I now inclose you the correspondence between the Secretary of the Treasury & Minister of France on the subject of the monies furnished to the distresses of their Colonies. You will perceive that the Minister chose to leave the adjustment of the terms to be settled at Paris between yourself & the King's ministers; this you will therefore be pleased to do on this prin-

---

[1] In 1783 Pitt's bill for relaxing navigation laws in favor of the United States was answered and defeated by Lord Sheffield's book, *Observations on the Commerce of the American States*, which his friend Gibbon thought had saved the 'Navigation Act, the palladium of Britain.'

ciple that we wish to avoid any loss by the mode of payment, but would not chuse to make a gain which should throw loss on them. But the letters of the Secretary of the Treasury will sufficiently explain the desire of the Government, & be a sufficient guide to you. I now inclose the act passed by Congress for facilitating the execution of the consular Convention with France in a bill which has passed the H. of Representatives for raising monies for the support of the Indian war; while the duties on every other species of wine are raised from one to three fourths more than they were, the best wines of France will pay little more than the worst of any other country, to wit between 6. & 7. cents a bottle, & where this exceeds 40. per cent on their cost, they will pay but the 40. per cent. I consider this latter provision as likely to introduce in abundance the cheaper wines of France, and the more so as the tax on ardent spirits is considerably raised. I hope that these manifestations of friendly dispositions towards that country will induce them to repeal the very obnoxious laws respecting our commerce, which were passed by the preceding national assembly. The present session of Congress will pass over without any other notice of them than the friendly preferences before mentioned; but if these should not produce a retaliation of good on their part, a retaliation of evil must follow on ours. It will be impossible to defer longer than the next session of Congress, some counter-regulations for the protection of our navigation & commerce. I must entreat you therefore to avail yourself of every occasion of friendly remonstrance on this subject. If they wish an equal & cordial treaty with us, we are ready to enter into it. We would wish that this could be the scene of negotiation, from considerations suggested by the nature of our government which will readily occur to you. Congress will rise on this day sennight. I inclose you a letter from Mrs Greene who asks your aid in getting her son forwarded by the Diligence to London on his way to America. The letter will explain to you the mode & the means, and the parentage and genius of the young gentleman will ensure your aid to him. As this goes by the French packet, I send no newspapers, laws or other articles of that kind, the postage of which would be high. I am with great & sincere esteem Dear Sir, Your most obed.t & most hble serv.t

TH: JEFFERSON

XII

UNITED STATES MINISTER TO FRANCE

MONARCHY TRANSITION REPUBLIC

MAY 1792

Sunday 6. — This Morning at twenty Minutes before six we leave Chantilly and reach the Hôtel du Roi in Paris at twelve. After sorting my Papers a little I dress and wait a long Time for a Fiacre which I cannot get and therefore am oblig'd to walk to the Louvre where I dine. After Dinner Monsr de Favernay and Mad.^{lle} Duplessis go out to see her Mother and Monsr de Flahaut to bring Home Madame de Boursac. We then celebrate. She tells me she has promised the Bishop to go and visit him in London, and begs my Permission and Approbation. I give the former but tell her that the latter is impossible. In the Evening a good Deal of Company comes in and among them Monsr Hermans who brings me Home and sits with me some Time. He tells me that an Offer has been made to the Duke of Brunswick to command the Armies of France and this accompanied with a View to the Crown. He speaks of Dumouriez as likely to go out very soon and as being a great Rascal. Mad.^e de Flahaut told me the same Thing. He tells me the Conduct of the German Army in the low Countries, which has been perfect; he adds that there is a Report of the Duc de Biron's being pursued by his own Troops and that every Thing at and about Valenciennes is in Confusion.

Mons! de La Fayette has stopped a little Way beyond Givet, having receiv'd Intelligence of the Check receiv'd by the french Troops on his left. The Weather is still cold but it rains this Evening, from whence it would seem that the Wind has got round to the Westward.

Monday 7. — This Morning I go out pretty early and visit M! Short who receives me drily. He tells me many Propositions have been made respecting the Debt from America, which he has deferred answering untill my Arrival. After some Conversation I leave him and call at the british Embassador's with a Package for Lady Sutherland. Go from thence to Monsieur de Montmorin's and visit the several Members of the Family. Go from thence to the Louvre and take up my friend. We go together to look for a House and then I set her down and go to dine with Madame Foucault. After Dinner call on M! Bertrand who gives me much Information. Go from thence to the Louvre where I spend the Evening. Monsieur de Graave has resign'd. The Weather is dirty this Day but warmer.

Tuesday 8. — This Morning M! Swan calls on me and Brémond. M! Swan shews me a Memoire about furnishing the Marine. M! Jaubert makes a Visit. After they are gone I dress, go to the Louvre... then go to look for a House but without Success. Dine with Mad? de Montmorin. After Dinner visit Mad? de Ségur who is abroad and then spend a few Hours at the Louvre. Go to Mad? Foucault's and after sitting a little while, leave them. The Weather is raw this Day and rains in the Evening.

Wednesday 9. — This Morning M! Monciel calls and immediately after him M! Chaumont, then Mons! de Ségur, then Admiral Jones and then M! Short who stays till near three. I dine at the Louvre and we go after Dinner a House hunting. After setting my friend down I visit Mad? de Corney and then the Countess d'Albani and then M! Perigaux the Banker to know the Rent of a House and Conditions. After which I return Home. The Weather lours but it does not rain. M! Hertsinger was with me this Morning and shew'd me a Letter from Lord Grenville to him expressive of the King's Satisfaction at his Conduct. He tells me that [sic] He tells me that their new Minister Mons!

de Chauvelin [1] has been receiv'd with very great Disrespect and even Contempt and that he has return'd a List of ten Persons, with the Bishop d'Autun at their Head, as annex'd to the Embassy.

Thursday 10. — This Morning M! Hermans [2] calls on me and repeats all that Hertsinger had previously told me. I go to M! Short's and sit with him a long Time considering the Affairs of the United States. Then go to the Louvre to dine and squabble a little with my Friend whom at last I quit in Wrath. Go to the british Embassador's where my Reception is flattering. From thence to the Place Vendôme where I leave a Card for Mons! & Mad? Le Couteulx and then to Mad? d'Albani's. Sit awhile here in a large Circle and return Home early.

Friday 11. — M! Brémond calls on me this Morning and brings the Plan of a Memoire for supplying the Marine with Provisions, in which he offers me a Share, but I decline it, telling him that I cannot in my present Situation do any Thing of that Sort. Go to M! Grand's and give them Bills on Amsterdam, thence to M! Hertzinger's who is abroad. Thence to the Louvre where I take up my Friend and we go to examine a House in the Rue de la Planche, after which we take up Mad.!!e Duplessis and ride; in the Way I stop at M! Perigaux's and agree for the House at 3500# [francs] per Annum. Dine at the Restorateur's and return to the Louvre. My Friend tells me that Crèvecœur informs her Monsieur de Mouriez will not receive me as Minister from America, so at

---

[1] Twenty-six-year-old Marquis de Chauvelin, good revolutionary, as figurehead because of Talleyrand's four-year disability as ex-deputy; Mirabeau's Duroveray, councillor; as secretary of legation Reinhard, future Minister to Hamburg, called by *Morning Chronicle* vicar-general to Bishop Talleyrand. French invasion of Netherlands shatters hopes of alliance, but Chauvelin's 25 May *communiqué* to Dumouriez announcing British neutrality is considered diplomatic triumph for Talleyrand. After June 20 invasion of Tuileries the mission is cold-shouldered, at Ranelagh treated like lepers, space pointedly left round the group. Imperturbable Talleyrand will be in Paris for 14 July celebrations, this time as onlooker, his next central rôle under Directoire. Hertzinger had presented him to Pitt in January, his only interview with the Premier. Socially he had disappointed, his reserved silences not the stock idea of a gay, wicked Parisian.

[2] Herman, esteemed official of Comté d'Artois, has for son the Terror's correct, ice-cold prosecutor who will preside at trial of Marie-Antoinette, now a lawyer in Robespierre's native Arras.

least he is told by a Member of the Assembly. We shall see. Go
to the Manufacture of Angoulême and order some porcelaine.
Thence to the Louvre and thence to Mad. de Witt's. It seems
pretty certain that the King of Prussia will act in Concert with
the King of Hungary. The Weather is pleasant but cool.

Saturday 12. — This Morning I write but am expos'd to Interruptions. M. Monciel and M. Jaubert call on me and in the
Course of Conversation I tell them what M. Crèvecœur had told
me this Morning, that the Minister wishes not to receive me.
They determine to pump La Sonde on this Subject. M. Jones the
Admiral calls and after he is gone M. Swan comes who insists
that the Idea of not receiving me was started by Short, but I do
not believe it. He tells me that La Forêt has written to the Ministry to be on their Guard lest I should outwit them. I dine at
Mad. Foucault's where there is a large Company of Aristocrats.
They have Letters from the different Armies which all concur in
stating the Indiscipline to be compleat. After Dinner I visit
Mad. de Guibert who is just going abroad, and then Mad.
Tronchin. As I come away Tronchan, who is a great Revolution-
ist, expresses to me his Apprehensions and asks my Opinion. I
tell him that it seems probable that Despotism will be reestab-
lished as the necessary Consequence of Anarchy. Call on M.
Short who is abroad, and on Mad. de Flahaut with whom I pass
the Evening, conversing with Madame d'Albani who tells me
among other Things that her Relation Mad. de Tarente is glad I
am got back. It is the Gladness in that Quarter which indisposes
the others to receive me, at least such is my Interpretation. The
Weather is grown very cold and sour.

Sunday 13. — This Morning I write. The Architect calls from
M. Perigaux and goes to examine the House I have hired. M.
Swan comes in. Martin tells me that he cannot serve me as
Maître d'hôtel unless I will take a frotteur under him, and wishes
his Account, which I make out. Go out, but the Baron de Grand
Cour stops me to tell the News. He says two and an Half Regiments of Cavalry are gone over to the Enemy. That the Troops
are every where in Mutiny and La Fayette's Army without Necessaries of every Kind. The Horses dead, the Soldiers sick and
weary, and the Officers apprehensive and discontented. Go to

Mad.ᵉ de Flahaut's where I find Madame d'Albani & while there Mons.ʳ de Molleville gives us a Denunciation he has made against the Jacobins. Call on M.ʳ Short who has not yet rec.ᵈ an Answer from M.ʳ de Mouriez and has written a second Letter. Short tells me that Rochambeau resigns decidedly unless de Mouriez is turn'd out. We go together to M.ʳ Grand's to Dinner and meet there the Abbé Raynal. After Dinner I go to the British Embassador's. They consider the Affairs of France as brought to a Close almost, and that a few Weeks must terminate the Business. Take M.ʳ Hertsinger from hence to Monsieur de Montmorin's. She expresses the Wish that Mons.ʳ de La Fayette's Army may be thoroughly beaten, which she considers as necessary to destroy the Hopes of the Revolutionists. Go to the Louvre where there is a good Deal of Company. I stay but a little while. The Weather is grown warmer and promises to be pleasant.

Monday 14. — This Morning I rise early and write. M.ʳ de Favernay breakfasts with me. He asks my Advice as to his future Conduct, which I decline giving. He says there are a great Number of staunch friends to the King in Paris who wait the favorable Moment to act. I tell him they had better be quiet for the People will certainly oppose the Measures which they espouse. Go to Madame de Tarente's who has been foolishly playing the Aristocrate at her Section. She wishes very much to have my Sentiments and I thereupon tell her that I have form'd none. She wishes some Kind of Advice for the Queen. I tell her that in my present Situation I can give none, but further, I think their Majesties should not only march in the Line of the Constitution but should not permit any Person in their Presence to jest on that Subject, much less seriously to blame the Ministers or their Measures. Go from hence to my newly hired House and thence to the Louvre where I dine. My friend takes me aside to tell me as a happy Thing just learnt from Mons.ʳ de Ricé that the old Jacobins are willing to adopt a second Chamber. I tell her that it is too late. They are now of no Sort of Consequence. Arms must decide the Controversy. She is convinced at last and thereby much distressed. We ride together and call on some Goldsmiths of whom I make Purchases. Spend the Evening here. It is true that the two and an Half Regiments of Cavalry have deserted, and

Monsr de Favernay tells me that the Regiment of Cavalry which he belongs to have signified to their Officers at Coblentz that they are ready to join them at the first Word. He mentions another which was in the Affair of Biron and which ran away on Purpose. It is whisper'd that the Corps under Gouvion has had a Dressing and Monsieur de Flahaut tells me that a Commissary is come from the Département du Bas Rhin to tell the Ministers that there is such a Scene of Plunder and Disorder there that he cannot answer for the Supply of the Army. The Weather has at length grown warm.

Tuesday 15. — This Morning my Horses arrive. Mr Brémond calls and stays till I go to Mr Short's, from whence we go together to the Minister of foreign Affairs.[1] The Interview here is very short. I tell him that I have a small favor to ask of the King, which is that he will receive me without a Sword because of my wooden Leg. He says there will be no Difficulty as to that Matter and adds that I am already acquainted with the King. I reply that I never saw his Majesty but in public nor ever exchanged a Word with him in my Life, altho some of their Gazettes have made of me one of his Ministers; and that I am perswaded he would not know me if he should see me. Upon this he says that since I have mention'd it he will acknowlege that such is the general Idea. I tell him that I am naturally frank and open and therefore do not hesitate to say that in the Time of the Constituent Assembly I endeavor'd, being then a private Individual and prompted by my Regard for this Nation, to effect certain Changes in the Constitution which appear'd to me essential to its' Existence. That I was not successful, and being at present a public Man I consider it as my Duty not to meddle with their Affairs. I ask him then when I shall wait upon him to be presented and he

---

[1] Charles-François Duperrier Dumouriez (1739–1823), soldier of fortune, had offered his sword to Paoli in Corsica, had sponsored new harbor works at Cherbourg and been made its commandant, had succeeded his benefactor de Lessart, 15 March, as Minister of Foreign Affairs. For the moment it pays him to appear at Jacobin Club in red Phrygian cap; he becomes the Gironde's martial hero, his desertion in 1793 helps pull them down; intriguing with Brunswick, deserting because he fails to re-establish monarchy; and Morris will find him in Hamburg itching to strike a blow for the new Duke of Orleans. A soldier of fortune, but a fine, successful general.

says he will let me know but he thinks the sooner it is done the better. Go from thence with M.ʳ Short to the Stable to see my Horses which he considers as indifferent and the House as having but a poor Appearance. Go from thence to the Louvre. Abroad. Come Home and settle with the Person who brought on my Horses. Dine at the Louvre. Take my friend to the Comedy. Call on some Tradesmen, leave my Name with Mad.ᵉ du Bourg and visit the Montmorin Family. Converse some Time with him. He wishes me to prepare a Form of Constitution for this Country, which I evade speaking about. He tells me that he has several *Projets* of Dumouriez and among others for a Counter Revolution. Spend the Evening at the Louvre. There is a Report of further Desertions of whole Regiments. The Weather is very fine.

Wednesday 16. — M.ʳ Brémond calls this Morning with the Exordium of his Work on the Finances. This will give me a great Deal of Trouble and be of little Use, if any. Visit my Friend and as we are sure of being alone . . . She mentions again her *Projet* of going to England. Dine at the british Embassador's and call after Dinner at Madame du Bourg's. She is abroad. Go to the french Comedy and there take up my friend and her Companion whom I bring Home. Thence to Madame Tronchin's and thence again to the Louvre where I pass the Remainder of the Evening. There are several Stories in Circulation of capital Defeats but I do not believe a Word of the Matter. The Weather is very warm with Rain in Showers.

Thursday 17. — Write. Monsieur Vic d'Azyr calls and we have a long Conversation. After he is gone I finish what I was about, dress and go abroad. When I arrive at the Louvre I perceive to my great Surprize that they are at Dinner. I join the Party and go afterwards to visit Mons.ʳ de Moustiers. Mad.ᵉ de Bréhan tells me that by taking away his Appointments they have reduced him to his own 2000# per Annum, in Consequence of which he has turn'd off his Household. Go from hence to Mad.ᵉ d'Albani's and pass the Evening. Bring my friend from thence to the Louvre and amuse ourselves en Route. It is said here that the prussian Troops move very slowly and will not arrive at Coblentz before the first of July. De Moustiers calculates on a sincere Coopera-

tion of Prussia and states at 160,000 Men the combined Army.
He says further that the Prince of Condé has a Corps of 7000
Cavalry which is excellent. This Evening I have a long Conversa-
tion with Monsieur de S!ᵉ Croix who says he does not believe the
Foreign Powers will attempt Paris but confine their Efforts to
Alsace and Lorraine. According to him the Army will be very
great. He calculates the Austrian Troops now in the low Countries at *60,000* and the Prussians in that Neighbourhood at *20,000*.
He states the prussian Army in March at *56,000* and the Troops of
Hesse and Brunswick at *14,000*. He supposes in the Brisgau, with
those now near that Destination, *20,000*, and states the Contingent of the Empire, which ought to be *50,000*, at *30,000*. Thus he
says there is an Army of *200,000* Men without counting the second Line of Austrian Troops or the french Emigrants which last
may amount to *20,000* Men. The Weather has grown much cooler
and threatens Rain.

Friday 18. — This Morning M.ʳ Brémond calls again with his
Work. I go to the Louvre and take up my friend . . . We then go
to the Linnen Merchants and agree for what I want. Thence to
the Louvre and afterwards I dine with Madame d'Albani and
pass the Evening there. The Weather has grown warm. M.ʳ
Hertzinger called this Morning and I wrote under his Dictée
a Note to M.ʳ de Mouriez enclosing a Copy of my Letters of Credence and asking when I am to be presented.

Saturday 19. — This Morning M.ʳ Swan and M.ʳ Brémond call.
After the former has left me the latter tells the Success of his
Work with Monsieur de La Meth. It contains too much Truth.
M.ʳ Chaumont calls and after him M.ʳ Cambray. When he is gone
Chaumont and I converse on Business and then dine together at
the Restorateur's. After Dinner I go to several Places of Sale to
look at furniture and then pass the Evening at the Louvre.
The Weather is very warm. I hear Nothing from Monsieur de
Mouriez. It is said this Evening that he is about to quit his Post.

Sunday 20. — Write this Morning. Go by Appointment to the
Louvre but instead of friendly Converse we have Altercation. I
leave her with much Coldness. Call on M.ʳ Short who complains
that he hears Nothing from Monsieur de Mouriez about his Passport. Look at my Horses and then go to Monsieur de Mont-

morin's where I dine. The Count de Goltz comes in, who is to
leave this City in a few Days with M.ʳ Bloomendorf, the Imperial
Chargé d'Affaires, and others of the Corps diplomatique. He
says the prussian Troops will be all arriv'd by the Middle of June.
Go from hence to the british Embassador's where we learn that
the good News from India was fabricated in the Alley. We learn
also that the Assembly has accused the Juge de paix who has in
the Course of his Duty brought forward some of the Members.
I leave my Name with Madame de Guibert and then go to the
Louvre for an Instant, thence Home and write.

Monday 21. — This Morning M.ʳ Brémond calls and gives me
the News. Go to the Louvre and thence to sundry Shops. Dine
at the Restorateur's. Go afterw.ᵈˢ with my friend to Shops and
thence to the Louvre and thence to Madame d'Albani's. It is
very warm Weather but less so than it was. We call'd this Morning on M.ʳ Bertrand. I gave him the News and took back the Constitution formerly deliver'd to him.

Tuesday 22. — This Morning I write a little but am interrupted.
I go to the Louvre and settle the Difference with my friend in the
Manner most amicable. Go to see some Tradesmen, dine at the
Restorateur's. Visit Mad.ᵉ de Chaumont after Dinner, then go to
the Opera and thence to the Louvre where I spend the Evening.
The Weather is pleasant.

Wednesday 23. — Write. Dine at Home. M.ʳ Short breakfasted with me and left the Accounts of De Wolf to be examined.
I go to the Louvre and pass a little Time in secure Tête à tête
with my friend. We ride together and afterwards walk in the
Bois de Boulogne. Then take up Mad.ˡˡᵉ Duplessis. Spend the
Evening at the Louvre. The Weather is grown cooler and is very
pleasant.

Thursday 24. — This Morning I write. M.ʳ Brémond and M.ʳ
Chaumont and M.ʳ Short call on me. I visit Madame de Mont-
boisier and M.ʳ de Grand Cour. Call at the Louvre. My friend
is ill. Dine at the british Embassador's. We visit after Dinner at
Monsieur de Montmorin's. Thence to the Louvre. Sit a while
there and go to Madame d'Albani's where I spend the Evening.
The Weather is pleasant, rather cool.

Friday 25. — This Morning M.ʳ Brémond calls and tells me the

News. Roubet the Taylor brings Livery Lace and as he is an Officer in the Garde Nationale he talks Politics. He says the Garde is *très montée.* He speaks of the present Administration as a Set of Scoundrels and the Jacobine Club as being the most abominable Tyranny. The ancien Régime so much complained of never, he says, affected him or others in his Line of Life, but the present System renders the whole Community miserable either by real Injury or the constant Apprehension of Evil. I go to the Louvre where I see my friend in Bed *et souffrante.* Go to the House I have hired, meet the Gardener here and Monsieur Périgaux the Banker, finish the Business which brought me hither and then take up Mad.ᴵˡᵉ Duplessis. Dine at the Louvre and after Dinner visit M.ᵣ Wilcocks and M.ᵣ Russell and M.ᵣ Newton, the friend, Relation and Companion of M.ᵣ Wilcocks. Call on Mad.ᵉ de La Borde and sit a little while with her. Leave my Name for Col.ᵒ Gordon and then go to Mons.ᵣ de Montmorin's. He shews me the Defence which he has begun and the Letters from which Brissot quoted Extracts. These prove fully in his Favor. He ought to publish them immediately. The Weather is cool and it rains. I come Home, take Tea and write.

Saturday 26. — This Morning I write a little. Call at the Louvre. Go to the Caisse D'Escompte. Dine at the Restorateur's. Go to the Théâtre des Vaudevilles where the new Tragedy of *Lucrèce* is very well ridiculed by Harlequin Tarquin. Spend the Evening at the Louvre. The Weather is very pleasant.

Sunday 27. — This Morning I write and read. Then go to the Louvre and thence to the Luxembourg where I meet Mons.ᵣ Malouette. Call on M.ᵣ Short who is abroad. Dine at the Louvre. After Dinner we embrace *amicalement.* I visit the british Embassadress and then at Mons.ᵣ de Montmorin's. Call on M.ᵣ Chaumont and converse on our Business which is in good Train, as he says. Spend the Evening at the Louvre. The News of a Victory gain'd by Monsieur Gouvion turns out unluckily to be a Defeat. The Weather is pleasant with light Showers.

Monday 28. — M.ᵣ Chaumont breakfasts with me this Morning and we go thro a Part of our Business. M.ᵣ Short comes in at one and while he is here a Gentleman from North Carolina, recommended by M.ᵣ Jefferson. M.ᵣ Swan arrives afterwards. I go to my House and thence to dine with the british Embassador. After Dinner leave my Name with Mad.ᵉ de Guibert and go to Madame d'Albani's. The Assembly has decreed a permanent Session and it is thought will dismiss the King's Life Guard and overturn the Constitution. I think they are actuated more by Fear than by any regular Plan or Principle. The Officers of the Northern Army have it is said all resigned and every Thing seems to be falling into Confusion. Take Home Mad.ˡˡᵉ Duplessis and my Friend. Monsieur is at the Tuilleries. Send for him and in his Absence sacrifice on the cyprian Altar. The Weather is sour and cold with a little Rain.

Tuesday 29. — This Morning M.ʳ de Monciel calls and tells me that M.ʳ de Mouriez is to go out soon and that he will be replaced by Mons.ʳ Semonville. M.ʳ Swan calls and M.ʳ Ducher. I go to the Louvre and thence to my House to meet some Workmen. After that I take Mad.ˡˡᵉ Duplessis to the Louvre where we dine. After Dinner accompany my friend to Mad.ᵉ de Montmorin's and Madame La Borde's, thence to the Louvre where we spend the Evening. My friend tells me that S.ᵗ Foi says all is lost, that the Bishop d'Autun and Monsieur de Chauvelin will soon return, that the former would be willing to make his Peace. I tell her that as to that I have no Doubt. Monsieur de Favernay tells me that Luckner has written to the Minister at War that the Disorder is so great in his Army that, join'd to the absolute Want of Necessaries, he thinks it impossible to do any Thing. The Weather is very cool and cloudy.

Wednesday 30. — M.ʳ Brémond calls and reads me an intended Publication. After he is gone I dress and go to M.ʳ Short's. Take Leave of him and then go to the Post Office and to Mess.ʳˢ Doerner & Co's to get Bills accepted. Thence to Mad.ˡˡᵉ Duplessis and thence to the Louvre. Take my friend and her son to M.ʳ de Faverney's where we dine and after Dinner I take Mons.ʳ to the Tuileries. Call on the british Embassador who is abroad and then go to my House. Come back to the Louvre where I meet my friend and we embrace. Spend the Evening here. The Assembly have reformed the King's Guard and accused Mons.ʳ de Brissac, the Commander of it. The Weather is fine.

Thursday 31. — This Morning M.ʳ Chaumont calls on me and

we agree on our Business, to be equally concern'd in the Purchase
and Resale of some Lands, and I write in Consequence offering a
sixth Interest to W.ᵐ Constable. I call on M.ʳ Le Couteulx who is
not at Home. Ride and take up my friend at the Convent.
Bring her Home and embrace. Dine at Mad.ᵉ du Bourg's, pass the
Evening at Mad.ᵉ d'Albani's, take my friend and Mad.ᵉ de La
Luzerne Home and set Mons.ʳ down at the Tuileries. The Weather
is fine.

JUNE 1792

Friday 1 *June.* — M.ʳ Brémond and M.ʳ Monciel call on me this
Morning and tell me that M.ʳ de Mouriez, in order to shew his
Sincerity, read in the Council a Plan for overturning the Jacobines, but was outvoted. He has since promised to turn out Clavière and Servan. This latter is to be replaced by a Mons.ʳ ——, a
Jacobin. They are on the look out for a Minister of Contributions
and they think Mons.ʳ Semonville is to be the Successor of de
Mouriez. I urge Monciel to put himself in that Place. They are
to let me know ToMorrow what Train they are in. They are to
forward the Advice not to reinstate the King's Guard &c.ᵃ, according to a Plan which I give them. The Justices of the Peace are
to pursue the Plaint of Mess.ʳˢ de Montmorin and Bertrand. I
go to the Louvre and thence to Mad.ᵉ de Ségur's. I was at the
Caisse d'Escompte but could not get my Business done, being a
few Minutes too late. Dine with Mad.ᵉ d'Albani and in the Evening go to the Louvre. The King's Guard were disarm'd this Day
by his Majesty's Order. The Weather is cool and indeed coldish.
It threatens Rain.

Saturday 2.ᵈ — This Morning M.ʳ Short breakfasts with me.
He met with an Accident to his Carriage on the Way and is return'd to get another. He complains heavily of the Persecutions
of Fortune and indeed seems to be penetrated with the Idea that

Heaven has mark'd him as an Object of Desolation. I cannot help smiling at this Affliction. Go to the Caisse d'Escompte and then to the Louvre and then to the Flint Glass Manufacture and then to my House and then to the british Embassador's where I dine. In the Evening go to the Louvre. The Weather is cloudy but pleasant.

Sunday 3. — This Morning M⸢r⸣ Monciel, M⸢r⸣ Brémond and M⸢r⸣ Swan call. The two former give me some Intelligence. M⸢r⸣ S⸢t⸣ Pardou breakfasts with me and we go together to the Château of the Tuilleries. Lord Gower tells me that Lady Sutherland has a Boy and is very well. I am presented to the King, who on receiving my Letter of Credence says: '*C'est de la Part des États Unis*' and his Tone of Voice and his Embarrassment mark well the Feebleness of his Disposition. I reply: '*Oui, Sire, et ils m'ont chargé de témoigner à votre Majesté leur Attachement pour elle et pour la Nation française.*' I am afterwards presented to the Queen who shews me her Son and says: '*Il n'est pas encore grand.*' I reply: '*J'espère, Madame, qu'il sera bien grand et véritablement grand.*' — '*Nous y travaillons, Monsieur*'.[1] I then go to Mass; and afterwards visit Madame de La Borde and then Madame de Flahaut. Dine at the Venetian Embassador's where I arrive too late. After Dinner visit Madame de Witt and spend the Evening at the Louvre. The Weather is pleasant. There has been a *fête civique* this Day in Honor of the Mayor d'Étampes, massacred by a Mob in doing his Duty.

Monday 4. — This Morning M⸢r⸣ Brémond and M⸢r⸣ Wilcox and M⸢r⸣ Chaumont and M⸢r⸣ Lalive call on me. They keep me till late. I go to the Cabinet Makers & Upholsterers and thence to the Louvre an Instant in my Way to Mons⸢r⸣ de Mouriez where I dine. The Society is noisy and in a bad Style. The Dinner is still worse. After Dinner I converse with M⸢r⸣ Boncarère and give him Reasons why they should repeal the Decrees respecting our Commerce. He says he is fully in Opinion with me but nothing

---

[1] 'He is not very big.' — 'I hope, Ma'am, that he will grow great and *truly* great.' — 'We are working for it, Sir.' (Training which will be destroyed in the Temple deliberately and to order by an illiterate cobbler and drunken sentinels, turning the gay little boy into a shrivelled, perverted wreck before he is nine; perhaps the ugliest note in this discord of revolution.)

can be done till they have brought the Assembly into greater Consistence &cᵃ, &cᵃ. I observe that Du Mouriez is anxious to converse. Give him the Opportunity and begin by delivering the Letter from the President of the United States to the King on his Acceptance of the Constitution. He says that he cannot attend to the Affairs of the United States untill after his Return from the Frontiers. He says the King of Prussia will not act against France. That he is quite easy on that Head. He says that if the Negotiators in England have made any considerable Offers since he came into the Administration it is without Authority. He is against all Treaties other than those of Commerce. He thinks there is no Danger to the Constitution at present, that it will triumph over every Obstacle and must amend itself. I think he cannot believe one Half of what he says. I take my friend to the Upholsterer's where I buy Furniture for the Salon. Then go to the Louvre and thence to Madame d'Albani's; in my Way visit and stay awhile with Madᵉ de Guibert. The Weather is pleasant.

The President of the United States to the King of France

Very great, good, and dear Friend and Ally.

I receive as a new proof of friendship to the United States, the letter wherein you inform me that you have accepted the Constitution presented to you in the name of your nation, and according to which it is henceforth to be governed. On an event so important to your Kingdom, and so honorable to yourself, accept the offering of my sincere congratulations,[1] and of the Sentiments of the Senate and Representatives of the United States expressed in their resolutions now enclosed.

We have watched, with the most friendly solicitude, the movements of your nation for the advancement of their happiness: we have regarded this great spectacle with the feelings natural to those who have themselves passed through like perils, and, with sincere satisfaction, we have seen this second occasion proclaim your Majesty, a second time, the friend and patron of the rights of mankind.

---

[1] A substance congratulating a shadow!

That yourself, your family and people, under the edifice which you have now completed, may repose at length in freedom, happiness and safety, shall be our constant prayer; and that God may ever have you, Great and dear friend and Ally in his safe and holy keeping.

Written at Philadelphia, this fourteenth day of March 1792, and of our Independence the sixteenth.

Your faithful friend and Ally

By the President.   GEORGE WASHINGTON.

THOMAS JEFFERSON.

Morris to Jefferson

No. 1.   Paris 10 June 1792

Thomas Jefferson Esqr

Secretary of State

Dear Sir

I have the Honor to acknowlege your Favors of the tenth of March and twenty eighth of April. My last was of the twenty fifth of April. As Mr Short remain'd here untill the second Instant and was better acquainted with the current Transactions I relied on him for the Communication of them. He inform'd you that we obtain'd an Interview with Mr de Mourier on the fifteenth of May. In this Interview he told me that he thought it was best I should be presented to the King immediately, but yet my first Audience did not take Place untill the third of this Month. He apologiz'd for this Delay as proceeding from the State of public Affairs which kept him continually occupied and agitated. I shall have Occasion presently to say Something about them. In our first Conversation as a fair Opportunity presented itself I made Use of it to tell him that during my Residence here in a private Character I had, as well from my Attachment to the Cause of Liberty in general as to the Interests of France in particular, endeavored to effectuate some Changes in the Constitution which appeared to me essential to its Existence. That being now in a public Character I thought it my Duty to avoid all Interference in their Affairs, of which from henceforth I should be a meer Spectator. I will not trouble you with repeating what pass'd at my Reception by the King and Queen.

On the next Day I din'd with Mr Demourier and delivered the Letter from the President to the King on his Acceptance of the Constitution, of which Letter I had previously made a Translation to avoid Mistakes of their Agents, which are not uncommon. By the bye, several Members of the *Corps diplomatique* have spoken to me on the Subject of this Letter which has given them a high Idea of the President's Wisdom. I took Occasion according to your Instructions to mention the obnoxious Acts of the late Assembly both to Mr de Mourier and to Mr Boncarère his confidential Secretary. The latter told me that he coincided with me in Opinion fully on that Subject but that Nothing could be done till they brought the Assembly into more Consistency. That they could indeed command a Majority but that they could not bring that Majority into a Support of other Measures than those of the Moment. That (however) we might digest the Business and put it in Train. Mr de Mourier told me that his System of politics was extremely simple. That a Power so great as France stood in no Need of Alliances and therefore he was against all Treaties other than those of Commerce. That he would very readily enter with me into the Consideration of a Treaty of Commerce but wish'd me to defer it untill he should return from the Frontiers.

In order that you may fully understand the Facts which I shall have Occasion to communicate, I think it most advisable to mention the State of Affairs in this Country such as it appears to me. I shall avoid speaking of Characters for evident Reasons. You are already inform'd I suppose of the Reasons which led to a Declaration of War against the King of Hungary, and you know that the Hope of an Insurrection in the austrian Flanders was among those Reasons. Indeed the Intention to excite it and the Efforts made to that Effect have (for the first Time I believe in modern Days) been publickly avowed. This Hope has hitherto prov'd fallacious and indeed as far as can be judg'd from the Temper and Character of the Flemish People and from the Information I have been able to collect, it seems to be the better Opinion that however they may feel an Aversion to the Austrian Government they are still less dispos'd to that of France. There is there-

fore no Probability of any capital Diversion in that Quarter, &
the Chance of it is daily decreasing from two natural Causes.
First that the french Troops are extremely undisciplin'd, and
secondly that the Force of their Enemies will soon receive very
considerable Additions. On the first of these Heads I need say
Nothing since you will receive from various Quarters the sufficient Evidences. In Respect to the latter, having combind all
the Intelligence which can be relied on it results that about the
middle of next Month the allied Armies will be one hundred and
eighty thousand strong exclusive of the french Emigrants. It is
doubtful whether these last will be permitted to act, and for the
following Reasons. First it is not to be supposed that twenty
thousand Gentlemen Volunteers serving at their own Expence can
be well disciplin'd, consequently it is to be apprehended that
they will be more injurious to their Friends than to their Enemies. Secondly it is next to impossible that in such a Number,
all irritated by Injuries either real or supposed, there should not be
some who will act more from Motives of private Vengeance than
Regard to public Good and it is certain that Acts of Cruelty and
Injustice will rather tend to prolong than terminate the Contest,
at least to give it that Termination which they wish for. Thirdly
it is notorious that the great Mass of the french Nation is less
solicitous to preserve the present Order of Things than to prevent
the Return of the antient Oppressions, and of Course would
more readily submit to a pure Despotism than to that kind of
Monarchy whose only Limits were found in those noble, legal and
clerical Corps by which the People were alternately oppressed and
insulted. And this Observation leads naturally to the Object
of the combined Powers, which I conceive to be the Establishment of a military Government on the Ruins of that anarchic
System which now prevails, and in the Continuance of which no
Power but England has any Interest. The others seeing that
without a Counterpoise in the marine Scale Britain must possess
the Empire of the Ocean (which in the present commercial State
of the World is a kind of universal Empire) cannot but wish to
reestablish this Kingdom. But a great Question occurs. What
kind of Government shall be establish'd. The Emigrants hope
for their Darling Aristocracy: but it can hardly be suppos'd that

Kings will exert themselves to raise abroad what they labor incessantly to destroy at Home, and more especially as the french Revolution having been begun by the Nobles, the Example will be so much the more striking if they become the Victims of it. But if the allied Monarchs have an Interest in destroying the Aristocracy, they have a much stronger and a more evident Interest in preventing a free and well poiz'd System from being adopted. Such System must inevitably extend itself, and force the neighbouring Powers to relax from their Tyranny. If the Court of Berlin could have been insensible to this Truth, in which it is so deeply interested, the zealous Reformers here would not have permitted the prussian Ministers to slumber over their Danger. The Desire to propagate and make Converts to their Opinions has led them so far that the Quarrel which might have been only political has become personal, and I have good Reason to believe, notwithstanding the profound Secrecy which is preserv'd respecting the Designs of the grand Alliance, that it is in Contemplation to put all Power into the Hands of the King. Things have been prepar'd for that Event by the inconsiderate Partizans of Liberty. In their Eagerness to abolish antient Institutions they forgot that a *Monarchy* without intermediate Ranks is but another Name for Anarchy or Despotism. The first, unhappily, exists to a Degree scarcely to be parrallelled; and such is the Horror and Apprehension which Licentious Societies have universally inspir'd that there is some Reason to believe the great Mass of french Population would consider even Despotism as a Blessing, if accompanied with Security to Person and Property such as is experienced under the worst Governments in Europe. Another great Means of establishing Despotism here is to be found in that national Bankruptcy which seems to be inevitable. The Expence of the last Month exceeded the Income by about ten Millions of Dollars. This Expence continues to encrease and the Revenue to diminish. The Estate of the Clergy is consum'd and the Debt is as great as at the Opening of the States General. The current Expence has, by taking away the Property of the Church, been increased about a sixth. The Dilapidation in every Department is unexampled, and they have, to crown all, an encreasing Paper Money which already amounts to above three hundred Millions of Dollars. From such Facts it is impossible not to draw the most sinister Presages. The Country People have hitherto been actuated in a great Measure by the Hope of Gain. The Abolition of Tythes, of feudal Rights, and burthensome Taxes, was so pleasant that a cold Examination of Consequences could not be admitted; still less an Enquiry into the strict Measure of Justice. Next to the Abolition came on those philosophical and mathematical Arrangements of the Fisc which are very beautiful and satisfactory, and to which there lies but one Objection of any Consequence which is that they are inexecutable. Now I have frequently observed that when Men are brought to abandon the Paths of Justice it is not easy to arrest their Progress at any particular Point, and therefore as the whole Kingdom (Paris excepted) is interested in the non-payment of Taxes, the Question will be decided without much Difficulty if once the Legislature get out of this City.

They are already preparing for a March, and it is intended to take the King with them, to which Effect a Decree has already passed to disband his Life Guards, and another to collect 20,000 Men to the Northward of this City. An Opposition will be made by the parisian Militia to the latter Decree, because they begin to perceive the Object: and as it seems to be a pretty general Opinion among them that no capital Opposition will be made to the austrian and prussian Troops, they consider the Person of Louis the sixteenth as forming the most solid Reliance they have to protect them from Plunder and Outrage. This Decree may therefore occasion either a Schism between the Militia and the Assembly, or among the Inhabitants of Paris, or both. Already there exists a serious Breach between the Members of the present Administration, and a Part of them must go out. I have the best Reason to believe that the whole will be changed before many Weeks and some of them within a few Days. There exists also a mortal Enmity between different Parties in the Assembly. At the Head of the Jacobine Faction is the Deputation of Bourdeaux, and that City is (as you know) particularly indispos'd to our commercial Interests. It is this State of universal Hostility or rather Confusion, to which Demourier alluded when he apologized for delaying my Audience. And it was this also which his

Confidant had in View when he mention'd the Necessity of waiting for a greater Consistency in the Legislature before any Thing could be done.

I mention'd to you above that Mr Dumourier had it in Contemplation to visit the Frontiers. This was in his Quality of principal Minister and certainly not as a Minister of foreign Affairs. One of his principal Advisers tells me that he has dissuaded him from taking that Step. The Object was to bring the Army to Action; for having brought on a State of Hostility for which he is personally responsible, he is deeply concerned in the Success, and he has little Hope unless from a *Coup de Main* before the Armies of the Enemy are collected. In Consequence, he has given repeated Orders to fight, both to Monsieur Luckner and Monsieur de La Fayette. The former has declin'd, and the latter peremptorily refus'd; the Situation of their respective Armies not permitting any well grounded Expectations. At present the two Armies are in March to form a Junction, when the whole will be commanded by Monsieur Luckner. It is expected that he will be at the Head of 60,000 pick'd Troops, and the Austrians cannot well oppose above 35,000. It is said that they are to act immediately but I have pretty good Reason to believe that the Stroke will be about the twentieth to the twenty fifth.

Mr de Mourier told me that he was perfectly easy in Respect to Prussia whose only Object was to get the House of Austria fairly engag'd and then to take Advantage of its Embarrassments. I told him that he must of Course be well inform'd on that Subject but that since the Departure of the prussian Minister without taking Leave I could not but suppose the Intentions of that Court were more serious than he imagin'd. He gave me many Reasons for his Opinion, which I should have suppos'd to be only an ostensible one if his Intimates had not on another Occasion quoted it to me, and if I did not know the principal Channel thro which he derives his Intelligence. A late Circumstance will tend rather to establish than remove his Opinion. I mean the Attack of Poland by the Empress of Russia to overturn the new Constitution. Whether this Movement be in Concert with the austrian and prussian Cabinets or not is doubtful. I cannot as yet make up any tolerable Judgment on the Subject, but I believe that in either Case those Cabinets will pursue their Object in Regard to this Country.

The Details I have entered into and the Informations which you will collect from the public Prints will shew that in the present Moment it will be very difficult to excite Attention to other Objects than those by which they are so strongly agitated. The best Picture I can give of the french Nation, is that of Cattle before a Thunder Storm. And as to the Government, every Member of it is engag'd in the Defence of himself or the Attack of his Neighbor. I shall notwithstanding pursue the Objects which you recommend. The Obstacles to Success form but Incitements to the Attempt. It must however be made with Caution because any sudden Change of Affairs may bring forward Persons who would oppose a Measure merely because their Predecessor had approv'd of it.

You desir'd me among other Things to send you the *Moniteur*, but the Editor of that Paper does not give so faithful a Report of what passes in the Assembly as you will find in the *Logographe*. If there be any one of the Gazetteers who is impartial it is the Author or rather Transcriber of this. I send you of Course the *Gazette of France*, which says you know whatever the Ministry order it to say. The *Patriote français* written by Mr Brissot will give you the Republican Side of the Question as the *Gazette universelle* does that of the kind of Monarchy propos'd by the Constitution. The Paper call'd the *Indicateur* is written by a Party who wish a more vigorous executive, altho (strange to tell) this Party consists of the Persons who in the Begining of the late Assembly did every Thing to bring the Kingdom into the Situation now experienced. The Journal of the Jacobines will give you what passes in that Society. The *Gazette of Leyden*, which I transmit according to your Request, will convey a kind of Digest of all these different Sentiments and Opinions. Thus Sir if you have the Patience to look over these several Papers you will have a clear View not only of what is done but of what is intended.

For the present I take my Leave with the Assurances of that sincere Respect and Esteem with which I am yours.

Tuesday 5. — This Morning I pay my Visits to the Corps dip-

lomatique. Call at the Louvre between three and four; eat a light
Dinner. Sit with my friend the Afternoon and Evening. We are
Part of the Time alone and of Course —— The Weather is cool
but pleasant.

Wednesday 6. — This Morning I write. M.ʳ Wilcox calls on me.
I dine at Home and go at four oClock to the Louvre. We embrace and then I take my friend up to my House. We afterwards
ride. Set her down and go to M.ʳ Chaumont's. Stay till ten here
and then pass an Hour at the Louvre. The Weather is pleasant
but cool.

Thursday 7. — This Morning I go to Court and am detained a
long Time. Thence to Madame de La Borde's and to the Louvre.
M.ʳ Bertrand de Molleville interrupts us here in a Moment little
desir'd. I take him to Mons.ʳ de Montmorin's. He mentions there
that a Pole who is appointed to command the Advance of Mons.ʳ
Lukner's Army has offered him to cause a Defeat, which he expects to be paid for. Mons.ʳ de Montmorin tells us that this Man
is one of the greatest Rascals in Existence and gives many Proofs.
Bertrand tells me that La Fayette has the Plan of coming to
Paris to drive away the Assembly. If this is true he will ruin himself and injure the royal Family. I dine with the Venetian Embassador who has a very good Cellar and a very good Cook.
Visit Madame de Stahl after Dinner with Lord Gower. She is
abroad. I go to Madame de La Borde and take her to Madame
d'Albani's. Pass the Evening here. The Weather is cool, very
cool. This Morning it rain'd hard.

Friday 8. — This Morning M.ʳ Brémond and M.ʳ Monciel call
on me and give me the News. After they are gone I write. M.ʳ
Newton and M.ʳ Wilcox call on me. M.ʳ Chaumont dines with me
and after Dinner we work till eight oClock. I go to the Louvre
and thence to Madame d'Albani's. Take Home Mad.ˡˡᵉ Duplessis
and Mad.ᵉ de Flahaut who has taken Offence this Evening improperly. It rains this Afternoon; the Morning was dull and raw.

Saturday 9. — This Morning I write. At a little after three I
visit my friend who has the Air of Affliction. She is alone and
wishes me to stay, which I decline. She owns that she was in the
wrong, but I continue firm to my Point. Go to Monsieur de Montmorin's where I see Mons.ʳ Lally Tolendal. La Fayette has joined

Luckner and it is supposed they will soon attack. After Dinner I go to the Pension at Chaillot and give George Greene [1] a Letter from his Mother. Spend the Evening at Mad.ᵉ de Witt's. The Weather is somewhat warmer but still it is very cool for the Season.

Sunday 10. — Young Greene breakfasts with me this Morning. I go to Court. The King seems to be less afflicted. After the Levée is over I go to the Pension and speak with the Preceptor who says that Greene is of a Temper which requires Attention and M.ʳ Barlow, with whom he proposed to go to England, is in his Opinion too negligent. Go to Madame Tronchin's and thence with Madame d'Albani to see my Horses. Then to the Venetian Embassador's to Dinner. Call upon Chaumont after Dinner and then pass the Evening at the Louvre. Tell Vic d'Azyr that the King and Queen must perswade themselves that they are out of Danger. He asks if that is my Opinion. I assure him that it is and that the present Troubles are but the Corruscations which succeed a Storm. Ask S.ᵗ Croix if he knows any very good Military Man. He tells me that he does, that it is a Baron La Fort who commanded at Avignon. He offers himself for any Thing I may judge proper and wishes to wait on me, which for the present I decline. The Weather is wet and disagreable.

Monday 11. — This Morning Brémond calls and I write after he is gone. M.ʳ Wilcox comes and I give him a Passport. Dine at the Louvre. Go to my House after Dinner to see a sick Horse. Visit the Rochefoucault family & sit some Time. Call on Madame du Bourg. Give some Orders to my *Tapissier* and *Ébéniste*, then visit Madame de La Borde. Afterwards spend the Evening at Madame d'Albani's. The Weather is showery and too cool for the Season.

Tuesday 12. — Write, then go out to receive Money and look at a Lustre which I purchase. Visit my House and Horses. I shall be a long Time yet I fear before I come into Possession of my new Habitation. Dine at the Restorateur's. Call after Dinner at the Louvre and then leave my Name at Madame de Staahl's. Call at the *Tapissier's* and go from thence to the Luxembourg.

---

[1] Son of the revolutionary hero, General Nathanael Greene of Rhode Island.

Walk round the Garden and then visit Madame de La Borde in my Way Home. The Weather is cold, very cold for the Season.

Wednesday 13. — Write all the Morning. Chaumont dines with me. After Dinner I go to the House to see how the Workmen go on, which is but badly; indeed the Weather is bad. Go to the Louvre. Visit Madame Tronchin and Madame du Bourg. Spend the Evening at the Louvre. Three of the Ministers [1] are dismissed this Day and Brissot attacks de Mouriez in Consequence.

Thursday 14. — Write this Morning. Young Greene and his Preceptor come and breakfast with me. The latter wants to prevent his Departure with M! Barlow but the young Gentleman seems to be the Master. *Quere* as to the Pasports. I call at the Louvre and dine with M! Dumouriez. He is more at his Ease than usual, having opened himself to the King and Queen and given them Assurances of his Attachment. This my friend has learnt thro S!ᵗᵉ Foi. I say many Things to him *avec Connaissance de Cause* which the other Members of the Corp diplomatique cannot comprehend and which they are therefore surpriz'd at. Visit Monsieur de Montmorin in the Afternoon and then spend the Evening at Madame d'Albani's. The Weather has been wretched this Morning but clears up in the Afternoon. I was at Court and observ'd that both the King and Queen were more at Ease than usual.

Friday 15. — This Morning Brémond and Monciel call on me. I write and then go up to my new House for a Minute. Dine at the Louvre tête à tête with my friend and after Dinner we embrace to mutual Satisfaction and in a few Minutes... We take up Mad!ˡˡᵉ Duplessis and go to the Muette, walk across the Bois de Boulogne and then return to the Louvre where I spend the Evening. The Change of Ministry has gone off very quietly, notwithstanding the Noise of the Moment.

---

[1] Roland, Interior; Clavière, Contributions; Servan, Minister for War, proposer of camp of 20,000 *fédérés* to be assembled near Paris for 14 July celebrations. The King had vetoed this decree of 6 June and one of 25 May, which allowed any twenty voters to order the deporting of any non-juror priest. Manon Roland had written the King just what she thought of him, threatening explosion unless he sanctioned the decrees. The *journée* of 20 June is planned, a Liberty Tree to be planted at Tuileries, crowds to demand recall of the three 'good ministers' and sanction of both decrees.

Saturday 16. — This Morning I write. Call at the Louvre. Go up to my House and thence to M![r] Spinola's to dine. M![r] de Mourier has resigned and in Consequence of it M![r] de Mourgue. M![r] Lajarre is app[d] Minister of War. I call at M![r] de Montmorin's after Dinner. He tells me that Dumourier and Brissot had a Conversation and were about to unite together. In Consequence the Decrees for 20,000 Men and for Transportation of the Priests were to be sanctioned and M![r] de Clavière was to be brought back into the Administration. The King refus'd to sanction these Decrees and thereupon de Mourier resign'd. Take M![r] de Montmorin to the Louvre and go thence to Mad![e] de Witt's where I spend the Evening. The Weather has grown warm.

Sunday 17. — This Morning M![r] Monciel calls and tells me that the Lameth Party have pressed him hard to accept the Place of Minister of the interior. I advise him to take Nothing but the Office of foreign Affairs and he quits me with that Intention but says they have offered him the interior as a Step towards the other Office. I dress and go to Court; we have here a List of Ministers in which Monciel stands for the interior. *Quere.* The Assembly have receiv'd and referr'd a Petition of the jacobine Society for suspending the King. I go to the Louvre where instead of Love and Love's Delights we have a Sparring without Reason or Measure. I come Home and write; receive a Repentant Message — Cold — Go to the Venetian Ambassador's to Dinner. After Dinner visit Lady Sutherland who is a little pale from her Delivery. Go with Lord Gower to the Jeu de la reine which is a mighty stupid Kind of Amusement to all Parties. Go to Madame Tronchin's where I meet Madame Martinville. Call at Madame de Staahl's. She had invited me to Supper and is not at Home. This is some Mistake but it is fortunate because it gives me Room to be off another Time. Call at the Louvre and stay a few Minutes only. Come Home. The Weather is very warm and at the same Time louring.

Morris to Jefferson

No. 2   Paris 17 June 1792

Thomas Jefferson Esqr Secretary of State
                   Philadelphia

My dear Sir

I had the Honor to write to you (N.º 1) on the tenth Instant. The Ministry is chang'd rather sooner than I expected, that is to say as to the Totality. Messieurs Servan, Roland & Claviere were dismiss'd by Mr de Mouriez. He fill'd the Places of the two former with his particular Friends, and as this Step was decisive and would certainly bring on very serious Quarrels it was suppos'd that he had prepar'd himself before Hand for all Consequences. It would seem however that he was less firmly fix'd than he had imagin'd, for as the Reason for sending away the other Ministers was that they insisted on the royal Sanction to the two obnoxious and unconstitutional Decrees, it was in the natural Order of Things that they should be immediately sent back to the Assembly. Instead of that it is said that Monsieur de Mouriez insisted on passing both and in Case of Refusal threatened Resignation. To his Surprize the King accepted the Resignation, and in Consequence his Friends newly appointed go out with him. As the present Sett have not all taken the Oaths I will defer giving you the List for the present but put at the Foot of my Letter the Names and Places of such as may finally be fixed on. The Jacobines were busy all last Night to excite a Tumult in the City but the Precautions taken to prevent it have as yet prov'd successful. I am told that Mr Luckner and Mr de La Fayette still persist in their Determination not to risque an Action. If so the present State of Uncertainty may continue some Time. If they fight and gain a Victory it is not improbable that we may witness some Outrages of the most flagitious kind. If on the Contrary there is any capital Defeat the jacobine Faction will be a little moderated. On the whole, Sir, we stand on a vast Volcano, we feel it tremble and we hear it roar but how and when and where it will burst and who may be destroy'd by its Eruptions it is beyond the Ken of mortal Foresight to discover.

While I am writing I learn the following to be the Arrangement for the new Ministry. Of the old Sett two remain, Mr Duranthon and Mr Lacoste. The former is said to be a pretty honest Man but rather too much attach'd to the *Faction bordeloise*. The latter is considered as an honest Man well acquainted with the Business of his Department, the Marine. Mr Lajar is appointed to the Department of War. He is a Creature of Monsieur de La Fayette. His Ability doubtful but his Principles sound. Mr Chambonas is appointed to the Office of foreign Affairs. He is *un homme d'esprit* but *une mauvaise tête, un mauvais Sujet* and ignorant of the Business, at least so says my Informant & he is well inform'd. Mr de Monciel, a very worthy Man, is nam'd to the Department of the interior but his Acceptance is very doubtful. The Minister of Impositions is not yet fix'd on. He will I believe be a Cypher, for two or three such have been applied to.

This new Ministry will be purg'd (at any Rate) of some of its Members but one great Doubt exists, whether it will not be driven off the jacobine Faction. It is in Contemplation to make a serious Effort against that Faction in favor of the Constitution and Mr de La Fayette will begin the Attack. I own to you that I am not sanguine as to the Success. Very much is to be done and there is very little Time to do it, for the foreign Enemy will soon be greatly superior in Number and it seems now to be ascertain'd that Alsace and Lorraine are dispos'd to join the Invaders. Thus while a great Part of the Nation is desirous of overturning the present Government in order to restore the antient Form, and while another Part still more dangerous from Position and Numbers are desirous of introducing the Form of a federal Republic, the moderate Men, attack'd on all Sides, have to contend alone against an immense Force. I cannot go on with the Picture for my Heart bleeds when I reflect that the finest Opportunity which ever presented itself for establishing the Rights of Mankind throughout the civilized World is perhaps lost and forever. I write on as Events arise and shall continue to do so untill the Opportunity to send my Letters shall present itself.

Lord George Gordon to Morris

London, Newgate Prison, June 18th, 1792

Sir,

Seeing your arrival in Paris announced in the English papers, as Ambassador from America, I use the freedom of a very old acquaintance to enclose a little publication,[1] touching on the situation of these kingdoms, for your perusal; and I shall be happy to hear it has come safe to hand, and that you enjoy your health in Europe. The General never calls upon me; to say the truth, we differed so much, in my mother's lifetime, about the American war, that he has never forgotten it. I hope Lewis Morris is well, and Richard and his family.

I am, Sir, with great respect, &c.

GEORGE GORDON.

---

[1] Lord George Gordon (1751–1793), a well-known British oddity, youngest son of General Morris's late wife, sends him an anti-popery propaganda pamphlet and elicits a valuable pronouncement of Morris's own views. They were the same age and the 'old acquaintance' must have begun as boys in America, which Lord George had visited as a midshipman, the War of Independence soon breaking off any intercourse. He had been in his voluble twenties before the public eye as an independent Member of Parliament, declaiming against war with America, against Tories, against Whigs, until the House of Commons of the seventies was popularly said to hold three parties, 'Ministry, Opposition, and Lord George Gordon.' The fourth bugbear of this highly strung fanatic was the Pope, so the Acts for removing Roman Catholic disabilities excited his Protestantism to monomaniac pitch. In June, 1780, he had led a mob in procession to Westminster to protest against the Acts, these 'No Popery' Gordon Riots lasting several days. Four hundred and fifty lives, burnt houses and chapels of Papists, partly burnt Bank of England, Newgate and other prisons, was the toll, high treason the charge, from which the skill of Erskine got him acquitted. Exile, libel actions, getting himself initiated as a Jew, filled his troubled days. Sentenced in 1788 to five years' imprisonment in Newgate, this eccentric's apostleship will soon find peace through the horrors of a delirious jail fever, in November 1793.

Morris to Lord George Gordon

Paris 28 June 1792

Lord George Gordon
New Gate

I have had the Honor to receive, my Lord, your favor of the eighteenth and observe with Concern that it is written from a Prison. Accept my Thanks for the Communication of your printed Letter. My Mind has now for many Years been employ'd in considering national Objects but yet I must confess to you that I am not able to estimate the Operation of religious Sentiment on the political System of your Country. I believe that Religion is the only solid Base of Morals and that Morals are the only possible Support of free governments. But when I come to apply these general Ideas it is necessary to possess all Facts and Circumstances which relate to the Question. Such copious Information I have not, and if I had I should greatly distrust my own Judgment. Every Day of my Life gives me Reason to question my own Infallability and of Course leads me farther from confiding in that of the Pope. But I have liv'd to see a new Religion arise. It consists in a Denial of all Religion and its Votaries have the Superstition of not being superstitious. They have with this as much Zeal as any other Sect and are as ready to lay Waste the World in order to make Proselytes.

My last News from America announce that the various Members of my Family were well. Accept I pray my Thanks for your Remembrance of them and believe me with Respect &c.ª.

Monday 18. — This Morning M.ʳ Brémond calls to tell me that Monciel has accepted. Young Green and his Tutor call. He goes by the Way of Havre. I dine with Madame du Bourg at Marli. Spend the Evening with Madame d'Albani. Tell M.ʳ de S.ᵗ Croix that I think of mentioning him as Minister of the Civil List. The Weather is pleasant. Mons.ʳ de La Fayette's Letter ¹ to the

---

¹ Sent by La Colombe, La Fayette's letter pointed out to the Assembly that all disorder arose from the Jacobin faction organized as a separate empire within the kingdom, that it preached indiscipline to the army and called anything law-abiding aristocratic and anything law-breaking patriotic. Read to an astonished, loudly protesting *Législative*, outside the Assembly it sets Robespierre, Danton, and Camille Desmoulins roaring for his head.

Assembly has been read and has produced some little Effect. In going out to Marli this Morning I observed some Fishermen who had thrown a Net across the River and let it float down a considerable Distance, they being at one End in a Boat to keep the land End clear. I stop to see the Success and find that they have taken a small shining Fish. I ask the Use of this Fish and am told that of the Scales they make false Pearl and Mother of Pearl.

Tuesday 19. — M. Crèvecœur and young Greene breakfast with me. A Vessel is going soon from Havre for New York in which he is to embark. I have Brémond with me before Breakfast who tells me that Monciel will call on me early Tomorrow. He has had a long Conversation with the King and is well pleas'd with him. There is to be a Sort of Riot Tomorrow about fixing a Maypole before the Château. I call at the Louvre, then go to Réveillon's paper Manufactory and purchase some Hangings for M.ʳˢ Morris. Dine at the Restorateur's and return to the Louvre. ... Set her down at the Venetian Embassador's and return Home to write. The Weather is tolerably pleasant but rather cool.

Wednesday 20. — This Morning Ailly de Crèvecœur calls on me and urges me to let them go Post on Horseback to Havre, which I consent to. A M. Denison calls to obtain a Passport. There is a great Movement in Paris and the Guard is paraded. I dine with the Baron de Blome. After Dinner we learn that the Deputation of the Fauxbourgs has forced the unresisting Guard, filled the Château and grossly insulted the King and Queen. His Majesty has put on the Bonnet rouge but he persists in refusing to sanction the Decrees.[1] I spend the Evening at the Louvre. The Constitution has this Day I think given its last Groan. The Weather is again very cool and indeed almost cold.

Thursday 21. — This Morning M. Monciel and M. Brémond

---

[1] To multitudes swarming through grand rooms ordering the King to choose between Coblentz and Paris, his gesture of accepting the red cap of liberty from a patriot head and perching it on his powdered hair, was disconcerting, not in the programme; nor his tossing down the wine they offered, a corpulent King as overheated as any one of them. Vergniaud tried eloquence, only got a laugh. Mayor Pétion strolled in at six, said he had only just heard of this all-day disturbance, said it was unseemly to extract promises from the King by force, persuaded tired rioters to go home; leaving a trail of smashed-open doors.

call on me. The former asks my Advice in this critical Situation of Affairs. I recommend the Suspension of Péthion and the Prosecution of the Ringleaders of Yesterday's Tumult. He leaves me. After Breakfast Brémond calls again and shews me a Letter from the Victualling Department by which it appears that the Resources of Paris for Butcher's Meat will be soon curtail'd very much. Go to Court. M.ʳ Swan came in just as I went out and told me that the National Guards are outrageous about Yesterday's Business. The King behav'd perfectly well Yesterday. This Morning a M.ʳ Sergans, one of the Municipality, is kick'd and cuff'd by the Garde nationale in the Court of the Château for his vile Conduct of Yesterday. M.ʳ Péthion also is received with very contumelious Language. Thus the Riot turns out differently from what its Authors expected. Call at the Louvre and dine with the british Embassador. Visit after Dinner at Monsieur de Montmorin's. He takes the Merit of what is done and doing for, says he, Duport call'd on me and went from my House to see Monciel &c.ª. Now Brémond told me that he found Duport fast asleep and made him get up and go to Monciel's after they left me this Morning. I go to the Louvre and embrace my friend, after which we go together to Madame d'Albani's. The Weather is pleasant.

Friday 22. — This Morning a Gentleman calls to know if there are any Orders to pay the foreign Officers.[1] I desire that a Letter may be written to me on that Subject. I write all the Morning. Brémond called. Dine at Madame d'Albani's. Take my friend and Mademoiselle Duplessis to the Bois de Boulogne which we traverse on Foot. Spend the Evening at the Louvre. The Weather is pleasant but very cool.

Saturday 23. — Brémond calls this Morning and tells me what is going. Mons.ʳ de Favernay also comes. I visit Madame de Tarente who is abroad and Mad.ᵉ de Spinola, but I meet her Husband instead of her. Go to the Tapissier's and thence to the Louvre. My friend abroad. Go to the Glass Shop & thence to the Cabinet Maker's. Go to my House and thence to Mons.ʳ de Montmorin's. They are at Dinner. After Dinner we walk in the

---

[1] The United States were still pensioning French officers who had fought in their service.

Garden and he, Mallouette and Bertrand meditating on the State of Things, in order to see what Stuff they are made of I tell them what Measures would put an End to all Troubles; but these Measures are deep and dangerous and when we go into M.ʳ de Montmorin's Closet he sickens. Go from hence to the Louvre but am disappointed. Visit Mad.ᵉ du Bourg but she being abroad I walk in the Garden of the Luxembourg and then return Home.

Sunday 24 *June.* — Brémond calls this Morning and tells me his Conversation with Servan, the late Minister of War, who is about to take the Command in the South of France. He expects that a great Republic will be establish'd there & invites Brémond to manage its' Finances. Brémond expects by Degrees to become Master of their Secrets. Digest an Answer to the Assembly for Monciel. Their Order is captious and if they do not blush at the Inconsistency of their Conduct they will push the Ministers hard. Go to Court. The King receives this Day a Part of the Militia. The Dauphin is in the Uniform of the Garde nationale. Go to the Louvre and embrace my friend. Dine at Madame de Guibert's. After Dinner visit the Embassador of Venice and of England. Return to the Louvre and spend the Evening. The Weather is damp and coldish.

Monday 25. — This Morning write. Brémond comes early and tells me what he has pick'd up from Servan. The King has receiv'd an Offer of Assistance from Picardy. Give Brémond some Hints. I call at the Louvre but I find there a Music Master. Dine with Madame du Bourg. Call again for a Moment at the Louvre and then return Home. Brémond comes and writes under my Dictation a Plan to be submitted by the King to the Assembly. He does not finish till after Midnight. The Weather is very warm.

Tuesday 26. — This Morning Brémond calls and tells me that Monciel will give the Note prepar'd last Night to the King this Morning. I write a little but am interrupted. My Taylor, who is a Captain in the Militia, tells me that Things go very badly. That the Militia is much divided in Opinion. I go to the Minister of foreign Affairs and mention to him sundry Things which I had to communicate. Am to make Notes thereof. While I am here Monciel comes in but we do not know each other. I go to the Louvre but my friend is abroad. Thence to my House to speak to the Gardner and Workmen. Dine at the Louvre tête à tête and embrace most cordially after Dinner. Then visit Mad.^{lle} Duplessis and the british Embassadress. Take a Ride afterwards, taking with me the Abbé Dillon, and then come Home. The Weather is very cool.

Wednesday 27. — This Morning write. Mr Terasson, Mr Chaumont and Mr Swan call. Brémond brings me the Draft of Tomorrow's Report from the Ministry to the Assembly. Paul Jones comes but I send him away. Mr Gardoqui's Brother brings me a Letter from Carmichael. Jones dines with me. After Dinner I go to my House to see what they are doing and then take my friend to ride and walk in the Bois de Boulogne. Call first at the Pension to announce to young Green his Departure on the sixth.[1] Come Home early and write. The Weather is very pleasant.

Thursday 28. — This Morning Monsieur de Monciel calls on me before I am up and tells me that Monsieur de La Fayette is arriv'd and is to go this Morning to the Assembly. The King, on receiving the *Projet* prepared for him, said it would be very good if they could count on the Gardes nationales. I tell him that La Fayette's Visit can produce Nothing and therefore he must exert himself to bring forward the Picards. He thinks La Fayette may be rendered instrumental to the *Sortie* of the King

---

[1] Morris had written to Delamotte, consul for United States at Havre: 'You tell me, Sir, that Vessels offer daily for Philadelphia. There is in this Place a young Gentleman of about sixteen Years of Age, son of the late General Greene, whose Mother has requested me to send him out to America, he having been here some Time [since 1785] under the Protection of Monsieur de La Fayette for the Sake of Education.... It would be desirable that the Captain had a Mattrass and Sheets because these Objects cost and seldom answer any Purpose on Shore. I shall not send the young Gentleman forward untill about the Time that he is to depart because he is better here under the Care of his Tutor than he would be in a Seaport Town.' The consul recommends ship *Aerial*, Captain Decature: 'the passage will cost 500 livres payable in assignats to have on board all the comforts of life.' ... 'I cannot tell you with any precision dates of sailing. Captains often change their plans, one says he will go to such a place who three days later goes elsewhere, another counts on leaving in ten days who finds himself detained for a month, others lack wine today and water tomorrow; I invite you, Sir, for the safe expedition of your mail to address it to me and let it take its chance.' [Trans.] July 20 young George Washington Greene embarks, passage 600 livres, mattress, blanket, pillow 94.7. Little *Aerial* carries him safe across the ocean, only to drown two years later in Savannah River, with all his French learning and knowledge of the world.

from Paris and he counts on the Success. This latter Part of the
Plan is the most reasonable. M.ʳ Chaumont comes and shews me
what he has written to M.ʳ Constable. I dress and go to Court
but find that the Reception of the Corps diplomatique is postponed till ToMorrow. Visit Monsieur Gardoqui and Madame de
Reichteren. Go to the Louvre ... Come Home and change my
Dress. Go to a Shop and buy some Articles of Dress as a Present
to M.ʳˢ Greene's Daughters. Go to my House to see how Things
go on there; it is but slowly. Dine at the british Embassador's
where I meet Madame de Staahl. She gives me an Account of
Mons.ʳ de La Fayette's Reception and address to the Assembly.
She is not satisfied but says that this may be owing to her Fond-
ness for Eloquence. I go to Madame du Bourg's and thence to
Madame d'Albani's. I visited this Morning Mad.ᵉ de La Borde.
The Weather is very warm.

   Friday 29. — Brémond calls this Morning. M.ʳ Howell also
comes. I go to Court. Madame Elizabeth and the Queen remark
to me that I came Yesterday. I tell the latter that it was the
Fault of the Post, for so Sequeville told me, and the Remark seems
directed against him and Lalive. La Fayette speaks to me at
Court on the Ton of antient Familiarity. I tell him I should be
glad to see him for a few Minutes. He says he is going out of
Town this Evening, but gives me Rendezvous at Mons.ʳ de
Montmorin's. I tell him he must return soon to his Army or go to
Orleans.[1] And that he must determine to fight for a good Consti-
tution or for that wretched Piece of Paper which bears the Name.
That in six Weeks it will be too late. He asks what I mean by a
good Constitution, whether it is an aristocratic one. I tell him
Yes, and that I presume he has lived long enough in the present
Style to see that a popular Government is good for Nothing in
France. He says he wishes the American Constitution, but an
hereditary Executive. I tell him that in such Case the Monarch
will be too strong and must be check'd by an hereditary Senate.
He says it goes hard with him to give up that Point. Here ends
our Colloquy. Return Home and undress. Visit at the Louvre

---

[1] Cases of high treason were still being tried at Orleans; the creation of the
infamous Revolutionary Tribunal will soon be transferring them to Paris. La
Fayette had left his army, had rushed to Paris to protest against the June 20

but my friend is abroad; at Madame Alex.ᵉ de La Rochefoucault's, She is also abroad. Call on Madame de Guibert and sit with her a while. Go to the pension at Chaillot and speak to Greene's Tutor about his Departure. Go to my House which goes on slowly. Dine with Madame d'Albani. I call'd en route on my friend who expected me for the Afternoon. Tell her I cannot stay nor spend the Evening in her Company. Luckner has adhered to La Fayette's Measures. I call again for a few Minutes at the Louvre and then return Home. Dictate to Brémond a further Counsel to be given by Monciel to the King. The principal Object is to get a Decision. The Weather is very warm.

Saturday 30. — Brémond calls. I write and then go abroad. Call at the Louvre and go thence, nobody being at Home, to visit Madame Chaumont. Sit a while with her Husband. Return to the Louvre and pass a half an Hour in setling our Differences. Go with M.ʳ Bertrand to dine at the Restorateur's, and thence to the Rue de la Planche from whence we go together to Réveillon's paper Manufactory and after.ᵈˢ return with what we had purchased to the Rue de la Planche. Come together to the Louvre where I spend the Evening. The Weather is warm but pleasant, there being a fine Breeze from the Westward.

---

invasion of the Tuileries. Having spoken his mind, implored the Assembly to punish its instigators as criminals and to suppress the Jacobin Club, La Fayette strode out of the *Manège* leaving the deputies gaping. At Court next day the Queen's reception is frigid, Madame Élisabeth and the King seem friendly. He arranges to ride with the King to review National Guards, to make a speech to rekindle their loyalty. It is said the Queen thinks any fate better than being saved by La Fayette, that she quite incredibly warns Pétion of the plan. Somehow he gets wind of it, cancels the review. La Fayette, discouraged, rides back to his frontier command. All desperately gallant and quite fatal to himself and to his sovereign. And he and Morris could still argue about constitutions!

JULY 1792

Sunday 1 *July.*[1] — Brémond breakfasts with me and gives me the Bulletins of the Day. He tells me that the Queen and Madame Elizabeth have sent to Monciel a Hint to beware of Duranthon. Go to Court. Nothing new. Return Home and sort some Papers, then go to my House and for the first Time examine the Cellars, which begin to be furnished. They are good. Dine tête à tête with my friend and of Course we are well together. Then take her to see Monsieur de St Prés who may perhaps answer for a Minister of the Marine. Thence to Mad.[lle] Duplessis. Leave them at the Louvre and return Home. The Bishop d'Autun is coming to Paris, in which he does wrong. The Weather is very cool.

Monday 2. — Write this Morning. Brémond calls. Gardoqui comes with Mr de Munoz who is appointed Chargé des Affaires of Spain in the United States. I dine with Madame du Bourg and walk after Dinner in the Garden of the Luxembourg. Then call on my friend at the Louvre. She complains of nervous Affection ... I come Home and write. Monciel and Brémond call on me. The King has neither Plans, Money nor Means. The Lameth Faction are all as naked as he. Monciel says he is afraid of falling into the Hands of the Constitutionalists. The French (says Monciel) are I am afraid too rotten for a free Government. I tell him that the Experiment may nevertheless be tried and

---

[1] July 1 Morris writes to Jefferson: 'I left London on the last Day of April, wherefore my Salary to the last Day of June, being for two Months, was fifteen hundred dollars. My outfitt is nine thousand, making together ten thousand five hundred dollars which I have drawn for on the Bankers of the United States at Amsterdam.... My Secretary's Salary will now commence.' — A lucky find, twenty-four-year-old New York lawyer Henry Walter Livingston, born at Livingston Manor on Hudson. Part of his job will be taking really important letters to mail in England, from where packets to America could be trusted.

Despotism still remains as a last Shift. Brémond stays till after twelve oClock and my Time is consum'd for Nothing. The Weather is warm and pleasant.

Tuesday 3. — Write. Captain Decatur calls and tells me that he shall not sail till the fifteenth. I give him my Letters and a Box of Papers for M.ʳ Jefferson. Take him with me to the Pension where I introduce him to young Green. Go to the Office of foreign Affairs, M.ʳ Chambonas tells me that he will in a Day or two attend to the Objects I have mention'd. I ask him for the Passeport for my Effects and it turns out that the Letter has been mislaid. Call on Madame d'Albani. She is not at Home. Call on M.ʳ de Munoz who is also abroad. At the Louvre, my friend is gone out. Go to my House which is *en train*. Mad.ᵉ de F——'s Maid calls to request I will be at the Louvre at half past two. Take Mad.ˡˡᵉ Duplessis thither. She is not come in. I visit Mad.ᵉ de Montmorin who tells me that the Bishop d'Autun is return'd. Dine at the british Embassador's. His Secretary tells me that Monciel ¹ was an Œconomiste and a Magnetiste. This is much against him. I go to my House for a Moment, thence to the Tapissier's, thence to Mad.ᵉ du Bourg's. About ten I call at the Louvre; still abroad. I come Home and read. The Weather is very pleasant this Day.

Wednesday 4 *July*. — This Morning Brémond breakfasts with me and reads a Piece intended for Publication. I write all the Morning. My Countrymen dine with me and some of them stay till nine oClock. I then go to the Louvre where I sit an Hour and come Home. The Weather has been blustering this Day with some Showers.

Thursday 5. — Brémond comes in while Chaumont is at Breakfast. Agree with the latter on the Letters to be written. The

---

¹ Terrier de Monciel (1757–1831), of old family from Franche-Comté, had in 1790 been President of Department of the Jura before his mission to Elector of Mainz. Howled down whenever he appeared in Assembly as Roland's successor in Interior. After June 20 invasion of Tuileries, Monciel broadcast all over the kingdom appeals to the better feelings of Frenchmen, to which several big towns responded favorably. He was able to hide, August Tenth, and to get back to his native province, emerging, 1814, with the Bourbons. Dies on his *terre* near Besançon. His efforts to get the King away from Paris must have remained secret.

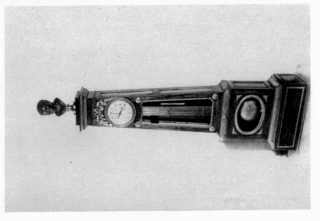

TALL CLOCK BY LÉPINE AND LOUIS XVI WRITING BUREAU,
USED BY MORRIS IN PARIS AND AT MORRISANIA

former is to bring me a full State of Things this Evening. Go to
Court. Call on my friend who is abroad. Go to my House and
thence to the Tapissier's. Call again at the Louvre and wait till
Madame comes in. Cold. Dine at the Minister of foreign Affairs.
Go afterwards with Lord Gower to Houdon's and then come Home
and write. The Weather is cloudy but pleasant.

Friday 6. — Write all the Morning. Brémond gives me an
Account of what is doing. Suggest to him a Decree to be adopted
respecting the foreign Ministers. I dine at the Restorateur's; go
between four and five to the Louvre where I embrace my Friend.
Then ride together and go to the Convent of Chaillot, afterwards
to the Convent of St Gervais to speak for Sweetmeats. Return and
again embrace. The Weather is pleasant. I spend the Evening here
and sup. Danton has said to Day publicly, à propos of the Intrigues
of the Court, that they would get Rid of the whole the 14th.

Saturday 7 *July*. — This Morning I write, then go to Mr
Lépine's and order home my Clocks; thence to Mr Le Couteulx's
and thence to the Porcelaine Manufacture. Buy here Dishes and
ornamental China to a too large Amount.[1] Call at the Louvre.
My friend has Company but excuses herself. . . . The Different
Parts of the Assembly are united and all is Love and Kindness.[2]
This arises from Fear among the Republicans. I dine with
Monsieur de Montmorin and visit after Dinner Lady Sutherland.
Thence to the Louvre. I see Vic d'Azyr and tell him I had pre-

---

[1] Chiefly white with delicate Bourbon Sprig (cornflower) decoration.

[2] Reconciliation farce known as *baiser Lamourette*, after the Bishop of Lyons
who made moving appeal for unity in face of danger hammering at the frontier.
The Assembly's nerves manifested in sudden ecstasy of goodwill. Informed of
this wave of emotion the King appeared; smiles, sobs, kisses among deputies
who had recently been slapping faces. King blesses deputies through happy
tears. July 10 by a majority forgiveness is voted to La Fayette. July 11 they
declare '*la Patrie en danger.*' Assembly's idyll not reflected in the streets. July
13 Pétion is released to be hero of Feast of Federation next day. Perhaps purposely ignored in this diary; King and Queen attend, are booed, hustled, stoical,
but Madame de Staël saw tears in the Queen's eyes. *Fédérés* already arrived
refuse to fight the King's battles unless he is suspended; suspension July
catchword, hardening to deposition. Marseilles deputy, beautiful Barbaroux,
had asked for men who knew how to die. Six hundred are marching north
through midsummer dust, bawling a new song written by Rouget de Lisle at
Strasbourg to hearten the Army of the Rhine. When the southern contingent
swings into Paris, 30 July, to the music of their voices, it becomes forever the
Marseillaise.

par'd a Letter for his Mistress but I will not send it. He urges me but I refuse. The King has been to the Assembly which I disapprove of. Spend the Evening at Mad⁰ de Witt's. The Weather is very warm Today.

Sunday 8. — Brémond calls this Morning and tells me that Monciel intends to resign. He oppos'd in Council what was done Yesterday and spoke privately both to the King and Queen but without Effect. Go to Court. Her Majesty is in good Spirits and very affable. I am not pleas'd, however, with her Conduct. Go to the Louvre, but my Friend not being ready I go up to my House. No Workmen this Day. Take up my friend and carry her to Chaillot. Thence to the Pension to desire M⁰ Lemoine to let me have George Greene's Accounts; thence to Madame de Damas's where I leave my Friend and go to dine with the Embassador of Venice. After Dinner I take a solitary Ride and call (in the Country) on M⁰ Grand who is abroad walking. Come back and spend the Evening at the Louvre where the Abbé de L'Isle recites some charming Verses. The Weather this Day is very warm and indeed hot.

Monday 9. — This Morning young Crève Cœur and Greene call on me; they are to leave Paris to Morrow. I desire them to dine with me. I go at half past three to my House and thence to the british Embassador's to Dinner. The Weather is very sultry. After Dinner I go to the Louvre and take up my friend. We ride and return to the Louvre. She corrects for me a Letter I had written to the Minister of foreign Affairs. Spend the Evening at Madame d'Albani's. The Venetian Embassador, who had exprest great Hopes and Expectations Yesterday from the Reconciliation Scene, is quite done over to Day. Brissot has pronounced a fiery Discourse against the King. Tronchin is heartily sick of the Revolution.

Tuesday 10. — This Morning I write. Brémond breakfasts with me and we digest a Discourse for the King. Young Greene and Lamoine his Tutor, and Crèvecœur dine with me. After Dinner I call on the Minister of the Marine, who is gone to Court. At the Louvre, Nobody at Home. Chaumont calls on me after Dinner. I spend the Evening at the Louvre. The Ministers have all resign'd. The Weather is very hot.

Morris to Jefferson

No. 4   Paris 10 July 1792
Thomas Jefferson Esq?
Secretary of State

Dear Sir

I had the Honor to write to you (N? 3) on the first Instant.
On the seventeenth of the last Month I mention'd the Plans then
in Contemplation, and gave a short View of the existent State of
Things. I did not communicate those Events which have since
taken Place, because you will find the most ample Details in the
several Gazettes. On Saturday the seventh a Farce was acted
in the Assembly in which the principal Performers played well
their Parts, and the King was dup'd according to Custom. Things
are now urging fast to the Catastrophe of the Play. For some
Weeks the adverse Parties, I mean the Court and jacobines, have
been laboring each to cast on the other the Odium of violating
entirely the Constitution and commencing the civil War. The
Party which calls itself independent, and which in Fact is the
fearful Party, begs hard for Peace, and seizes eagerly whatever
bears the Appearance or the Name. It was to catch these Gud-
geons that the Scene of Saturday was exhibited. The King and
Queen believing that the Actors were in earnest, and knowing
that their Lives had been at Stake, were overjoy'd: and their
timid Counsellors, trembling under the tyrannous Powers of the
Assembly, seiz'd with Eagerness the Bait of Reconciliation which
had been thrown out without any Hope that they would swallow
it. One of them, whom I have already mention'd to you as a very
worthy Man, saw thro the thin Veil of Deception, and oppos'd
the Opinion of the others, but in Vain. Events in justifying him
have fix'd his Predominance. This Day the King will commence
a new Career and if he goes *thorough,* I think he will succeed. I
have every Reason to believe that this Letter will go safely, but
yet I cannot justify saying more on the Subject, because otherwise the Confidence repos'd in me might in the Course of Events
prove fatal to my Informant.

The present Intention of the King is to secure the Liberty of
France; but whether he will preserve the steady Purpose thro

those varying Events which must soon take Place, to me appears uncertain. Indeed I doubt whether he will be sufficiently Master of his own Party to execute such Purpose even if it be not chang'd. Whether he will live thro the Storm is also uncertain. It will blow hard.

The exterior Enemy hovers over his Prey, and only seems to wait the Moment which he has fix'd to himself for his own Stroke. New Parties to the Grand Alliance daily shew themselves. The Palatinate has declar'd, Holland seems on the Point of adhering, and Doubts in Regard to England begin to appear. The Force which France can oppose to her numerous Assailants does not exceed 180,000 undisciplin'd Men; some of whom wait but the Opportunity to desert. Against her are collected two hundred and fifty thousand of the best Troops in Europe, under the Command of the ablest General in this Hemisphere. The Intention was not to enter before the Harvest, in order that Subsistence might be easily procur'd. Whether this Plan will be chang'd in Consequence of what is like to happen here, I cannot say. I rather think it will. I understand that the Manifesto which precedes Attack, will disavow the Constitution and claim for the King (what it calls) his Rights; for the Clergy its *Possessions*. That this City will be rendered responsible for the royal Family. That the *Gardes nationales* will be consider'd as arm'd Peasants, medling with Business not their own, and therefore not under the Protection of the Laws of War. The allied Monarchs are to declare themselves in Arms not against France, but against the *Revoltés*. You will easily see that these broad Terms will mean whatever Power may chuse to explain them to.

I have repeatedly pressed the Minister of foreign Affairs to come to a Settlement of Accounts, which he has promised to do and I think I shall accomplish my Purpose, because the marine Department is to treat with me for Supplies to St Domingo. I mean to be generous in the Terms of Exchange for this Supply, obtaining at the same Time a beneficial Liquidation of past Payments; for you will observe, Sir, that the whole Account is open. Two Reasons operate with me on this Occasion. First I think that we ought to encourage our own Agriculture and Arts, and secondly I think that what is paid here goes into a Gulph of unbottom'd Profusion, and can but little advance the real Interests of the Nation.

I have also repeatedly call'd the Minister's Attention to the obnoxious Acts of the late Assembly, and to their Proposition of a new commercial Treaty. He has replied very candidly that for himself he should be glad to settle every Thing to my Satisfaction, but that his ministerial Existence is too precarious to undertake any extensive Plan, that the Attention of Government is turn'd too strongly towards itself (in the present Moment) to think of its exterior Interests, and that the Assembly, at open War with the executive, would certainly reject whatever should now be presented to them. These are Truths which I knew before, and therefore I thought it best not to urge too strongly for a Decision, in the unpropitious Moment. The apparent Reconciliation of Saturday seem'd to give a better Prospect. The Court on Sunday had an Air less embarrassed, and therefore (altho the Dictate of my Judgment was different from that of others) I thought it my Duty to make a formal Application, which I did Yesterday in a Letter Copy of which shall be transmitted. My Intelligence of this Morning justifies the Opinion I had form'd, and proves that the Matter must be yet for some Time suspended.

Wednesday 11. — Brémond comes this Morning and tells me that their Majesties flash'd in the Pan Yesterday Morning, which occasion'd the Resignation of the Ministry. This I suspected. He says they have reproach'd Monciel who retorted smartly. On the Ground of these Reproaches we prepare Heads of a Discourse for Monciel in the View, if their Majesties come round, to strike a still more important Stroke. I think there is a Want of Mettle which will ever prevent them from being truly royal. I go to Lépine's this Morning, taking with me M. Mountflorence. Thence to de Lange's the Lamp Manufacturer, thence to Réveillon's, thence to a Cabinet Maker's, Fauxbourg S. Antoine, thence to my House, thence to Beauvillier's where I dine. Return Home to my House and begin the placing of my Papers which I shall endeavour to compleat Tomorrow. Return Home from hence, take Tea and go to bed early. The Weather is very hot.

Thursday 12. — This Morning Brémond comes and tells me

that he has seen Pellin who blames Monciel for Precipitation and says that Things may yet be arranged. Monciel is to have an Interview with the King and Queen this Morning. I go to Court. The Countenances of their Majesties are a little down. Go from the Tuileries to my new House where I intend to sleep this Evening. Dine with M.ʳ Perregaux who says that Luckner and La Fayette are to be in Town Tomorrow. Drink too much here. After Dinner I go to a Silver Smith's and borrow a Pair of Ladles and Candlesticks.¹ Thence to Madame d'Albani's where I take Tea and fall asleep. Return Home much heated.

Friday 13. — Last Night was sleepless and in Consequence I am tormented with nervous Heaviness this Morning. Monsieur and Madame de Flahaut dine with me. Also Monsieur Bertrand, Monsieur S.ᵗ Pardoux and Mad.ˡˡᵉ Duplessis. Madame d'Albani comes after Dinner and then we take a small Ride and go to the Louvre where I pass an Hour and come Home. The Weather is more pleasant than it was. My friend and I found Means to enjoy en passant. Monsieur Pétion the Mayor is restored by the Assembly.

Saturday 14. — This Morning I employ in sorting my Papers. Monsieur Sully calls on me to converse about Land Speculations in America. I give him all the Information in my Power. My friend comes to dine with me tête à tête at half past five. We embrace and then walk in the Garden. At seven she leaves me. I go to the british Embassador's and leave my Name, thence to Madame de Montmorin's where I pass an Hour. Thence to the Louvre where I stay till after eleven. The Weather is pleas-

---

¹ Thus equipped Morris is ready for his first guests at 488 rue de La Planche, Faubourg Saint-Germain, across the river from the Louvre, not far from the then Swedish Embassy in the rue du Bac. In the spring of 1792 it had still seemed worth while to take a good house and furnish it with lovely things. By September Morris himself is about the whole of the Diplomatic Corps, his colleagues dispersed, his friends emigrated, the Ministers too insecure to think of giving official dinners, having barely time to put their desks in order before they are replaced. The Revolution soon descends to the gutter before rising purified by war to dominate the Continent of Europe, under the dictator Morris had long foretold. As he wrote to Jefferson: 'You will perceive at a Glance that this is not a Moment for making commercial Treaties. I shall however do all which I can without seriously compromising our *future Interest*.' The United States are not on the frontier, nothing else is important this summer, Morris has to mark time.

ant. Brémond was with me this Morning. He says that a Conference has taken Place and that Monciel understands a little
now with Monsieur de Montmorin.

Sunday 15. — Brémond does not call as he had promis'd. I
go to Court. Nothing new. Visit M.ʳ Bon Carère to put him in
Mind of the Letter I had written and to which I receive no
Answer. Call on Mad.ᵉ d'Albani and go thence to Madame
Tronchin's. Afterwards to the Louvre and then pass at the Door
of my former Lodgings where I take up some Effects I had left
behind me. Dine tête à tête at Home with Monsieur Vic d'Azyr.
Go at five to the Louvre where we embrace and then take up
Mad.ˡˡᵉ Duplessis and ride. After setting them down I go to Lady
Sutherland's and find her alone. We talk of Love and Love's
Disport till an old Man comes in to give the History of his Gout.
I leave her in this Society so as to make a Relief of his Ennui
and come Home to work. The Weather is warm.

Monday 16. — Brémond calls this Morning but I send him
away and write. Dine at the Louvre. Go after Dinner to the
Comédie française. Thence to Madame d'Albani's where a M.ʳ
Latille talks plenty of Absurdity. Take up Mad.ˡˡᵉ Duplessis at the
Louvre and come Home at eleven.

Tuesday 17. — M.ʳ Brémond calls this Morning. He gives but
a melancholy Account of the Situation of Affairs. I write this
Day. Monsieur and Madame de Montmorin and Madame de
Beaumont, Lord Gower and Lady Sutherland and Huskisson,[1]
Sec.ʸ to L.ᵈ Gower, Venetian Embassador and Spanish Chargé
d'Affaires, dine with me. In the Evening Monsieur de Montmorin takes me into the Garden to communicate the Situation of
Things and ask my Opinion. I tell him that I think the King
should quit Paris. He thinks otherwise and fosters a thousand
empty Hopes and vain Expectations. The Weather is very warm.
We had last Night a most severe Thunder Storm.

Wednesday 18 *July*. — This Morning I write. Having slept
ill I have nervous Affections. M.ʳ Brémond does not come and
his Friend Monciel is fairly out of the Administration. M.ʳ Russel

---

[1] William Huskisson (1770–1830), educated in Paris, is on eve of long successful parliamentary and ministerial career. Killed, run over, at opening of
Manchester and Liverpool railway.

calls on me and Mʳ. Van Staphorst and Mʳ. Swan, all to excuse themselves for not dining with me on Friday. A Message from Paul Jones that he is dying. I go thither and make his Will which the frenchmen will not witness. Send for a Notary and leave him strugling with his Enemy between four and five. Dine *en famille* with Lord Gower and Lady Sutherland. Go to the Minister of the Marine's. He is at Council. I go to the Louvre. My friend formalizes. She is *un peu jalouse de l'Ambassadrice*. Take her and Vic d'Azyr to Jones's Lodgings but he is dead, not yet cold.[1] The People of the House ask me if they must put the Scellé on his Papers and I answer in the Affirmative. The Weather is very warm.

[Nearly a year later, 26 May, 1793, Morris writes to Robert Morris about this hero's lonely death, the letter, perhaps, of a man nettled by criticism. To a living Jones he had always been warmer-hearted.]

'It is rather late now to mention Paul Jones. But I should have written to you about his Death immediately if I could have gotten a Copy of his Will to transmit. I was promis'd from Day to Day and at length the Matter lay over and since his Relations have been here and have written to you. I drew the Heads of his

---

[1] 'A dropsy in his breast' is the contemporary definition of his illness, probably too far gone when the message first reached Morris for the eighteenth-century equipment of Vic d'Azyr to have saved him. A commission from Congress empowering Jones to treat with Algiers about peace and ransoms arrives too late to remove from the Chevalier his sense of being shelved, frustrated. Ready to fight with or against any power to get the decks of a fine ship again under his feet, his plans against the Turk, promises of high employ by Denmark, service to Catharine of Russia petering out under jealousy of her naval captains, everything had gone wrong for this brilliant sailor ever since *America*, largest of 74-gun ships of the line, slender as a frigate, was wrested from his command almost at her launching and presented to the French. His body will lie 113 years in the then suburban cemetery, corner rue de La Grange aux Belles and rue des Écluses Saint-Martin, before being heaped with honors at Annapolis Naval Academy. In connection with his first too modest funeral Morris has been blamed. *Freeman's Journal* for December, 1792, says the American Minister had friends to dinner and did not attend it. The dinner is borne out in his diary. One account says there was no priest nor service, only a volley of muskets; another says a French pastor, Marron, pronounced a discourse; the Assembly sent twelve deputies, Simmoneau, Commissary of the Section, paying the expenses, 432 francs.

Will, poor fellow, the Day he died and when his Extremities were already cold. I calld on him in the Afternoon with Monsieur Vic d'Azyr, first Phisician to the Queen, and he was then a Corpse. It was somewhat singular that he who detested the french Revolution and all those concerned in it should have been follow'd to the Grave by a Deputation from the National Assembly. And that I should read in one of your Gazettes something very like a severe Reflection on me for not paying him due Respect, I who during his Life had rendered him all possible Service and possess'd his Confidence to the last so that he wish'd to name me with you for Executor. But such is the World, whose Mistakes frequently amuse me and on more serious Occasions. Before I quit poor Jones I must tell you that some People here who like Raree Shows wish'd him to have a pompous Funeral and I was applied to on the Subject, but as I had no Right to spend on such Follies either the Money of his Heirs or that of the United States, I desird that he might be buried in a private and œconomical Manner. I have since had Reason to be glad that I did not agree to waste Money of which he had no great Abundance and for which his Relatives entertain a tender Regard. I promisd them to entreat your Attention to their Requests, which will no Doubt be somewhat troublesome and consume the Moments you can badly spare. A preview of this made me desire Jones to think of some other Executor, but the poor fellow was so anxious, telling me that as we alone possess'd his full Confidence he could not think of loosing the Aid of both &c^a. And as what he said besides his natural Stammering was interrupted by the Strugglings against Death I was oblig'd to quit my Opposition. Thus, my dear friend, I have given you a History which ought to have been communicated long ago. You will probably find it somewhat tedious now; for the Delay then and the Prolixity now I beg your Pardon.'

Morris to the heirs of Paul Jones

Paris 22.ᵈ October 1792

M.ʳˢ Taylor and M.ʳˢ Lowden
Dumfries.

I had the honor to receive the letter which you did me the honor to write and I desired M.ʳ Livingston to answer it from London, as he had been in Quest of the Copy of the late Admiral's Will. Since that Period the Seals have been broken by regular Course of Justice at the Instance of some Persons who had Demands on his Estate. This has enabled me at length to get a Copy of his Will, which you will find enclosed. A necessary Consequence of the Proceedings was a Sale of his Effects, which took Place two days ago and in which, as I learn, the various Articles went off at a good Price. I desired a Gentleman to attend and bid for the different Effects, which he did and thereby raised the Prices considerably. The Sword given to him by the King of France was not put up but is reserved for you. A Mourning [sic] Sword, that which he wore in the Action of the Serapis, His Order of Merit and Cincinnatus I caused to be bought and you can have them when you please at the Cost, or if you prefer the Price I will keep them, so that I pray you in this Respect to act without any Regard to the Circumstance of the Purchase or to my Intention in making it. I did hope to have been able to send you an Account of the Sale but I have not as yet been able to obtain it. I shall now write to M.ʳ Morris [1] and send him a Copy of the Will. — You may rely on it that he will, if he undertakes the Management of the Estate committed to him, do every Thing which is proper on the Occasion.

Thursday 19. — This Morning go to Court and afterwards call on the Minister of the Marine who is abroad. Go to the Office of foreign Affairs and get a Passport for the interior of the Kingdom. Go to M.ʳ Grand's but he is abroad. Call on Le Couteulx, then go to the Louvre and take up my friend and her

---

[1] Robert Morris's preoccupations with his own difficulties make him a most negligent executor. The sword of honor is given to Barry, America's ranking naval officer.

Husband who dine with me. Madame d'Albani, the Count Alfieri, Mad.^{lle} Duplessis, Monsieur Bertrand and Monsieur de Favernay. After Dinner I take my friend to the Convent at Chaillot and thence to the Louvre where we embrace. Thence to Mad.^e d'Albani's and she brings me back to the Louvre. I have quarrelled a little and remain cold, which must last for some Days. The Weather is pleasant tho warm.

Friday 20. — This Morning Mr Brémond calls and tells me that in Consequence of the Memoire which he made up from my Hints and which Monciel presented to the King, a Conversation has taken Place between him and Monsieur de Montmorin and M. de Bertrand. He gives me the Heads of the Manifesto which is to appear and desires to know what Step the King is to take in Consequence of it. He tells me that Mallet du Pin is sent by Bertrand to be the Secretary of the Duke of Brunswick. I have a large Company to Dinner. After Dinner go to visit Madame de Narbonne who is my Neighbour, thence to the British Embassador's; Madame is abroad. Thence to visit Madame de Guibert, sit with her a little while and go afterwards to Madame Le Couteulx's. Chat with her and to my Surprize she declares for Gallantry without the least Scruple so that I conjecture rather the Reverse. Return Home early. The Weather is pleasant this Evening but we had a Storm in which the Lightning struck very near me about seven oClock.

Saturday 21. — Brémond calls this Morning to know my Determination; I give it to him in general Terms. Write. At three take a Ride. Dine with Mad.^e de Montmorin. Malouette is here and of Course I do not as I intended confer with Montmorin and Bertrand. Call on the british Embassadress who is abroad and then go to the Louvre. My friend is in Bed and struck with Melancholy. She is too proud to complain. I speak tenderly and must endeavor to obliterate the Impressions. The Weather is quite cool. The Fœdérés begin to insult the Assembly.

Sunday 22. — Brémond comes this Morning to tell me that Monciel will be with me ToMorrow. Dress and go to Court. There are fresh Accounts of Murders and Assassinations from the South of France. After the Levée is over I go to the Louvre but the Bishop arriving at the same Time I make my Visit short & go to Le Couteulx's; thence to Beaulieu, the Minister of the Contributions, but he is abroad. Call on Mr Gauthier and then on La Caze. Go to the Louvre again and make a Reconciliation. She has had a Fever for two Days in Consequence of our Quarrel. We embrace and then I go to dine with the Venetian Embassador. After Dinner I take my Friend a short Tour to take up Mad.^{lle} Duplessis and then, having set her down, go to the Jeu de la Reine where I am ennuiéed for half an Hour and return to the Louvre. Come Home early. The Weather is very pleasant.

Monday 23. — This Morning write, having risen for the Purpose at Half past four oClock. Mr Brémond calls and after him Mr de Monciel who is to bring about a Meeting with Mr Bertrand. Mr Constable comes a little before three. Mr de Flahaut and his Wife and Mad.^{lle} Duplessis and Mr de St Pardou dine with me. After Dinner we ride and having set down Mr Constable go to the Louvre. From thence I go to Madame d'Albani's and pass the Evening. The Weather is cool.

Tuesday 24. — Brémond comes this Morning and after him Monciel. This last brings me the King's Money at his Majesty's Request, who tells him at the same Time that I have always given him good Advice and he has the greatest Confidence in me. We consider what is to be done in the Case of a Suspension. Monciel is to dine with me. Constable comes just after the Count de Croix has left me and he dines with me. Hold with him the needful Conversation respecting Lands. Monciel and I go after Dinner to Bertrand and bring him a good Deal into our Views. He is to dine with me Tomorrow. Call on Mr Constable. Go thence to the british Embassador's and sit a long Time. Thence to the Louvre. My friend is in Bed. I leave her to play at Drafts with Mr de Ste Croix. The Weather is pleasant.

[Alas! for Morris's promise to Washington to preserve a 'Circumspection of Conduct.' He was accredited, not to Girondins or Jacobins, but to Louis XVI. Convinced that an innocent man's life was in danger, Morris, with Ministers, ex-Ministers and would-be Ministers once more buzzing round him, is up to his neck in a plan to get the royal family away, not from France but from

Paris; this explains his hopefulness, otherwise unaccountable in a man so astute. Unknown to Morris or to each other escape plans were being showered on the King; Molleville sent one; Madame de Staël offered services of Narbonne; unknown to each other handfuls of loyalist troops were waiting at various stations; the stumbling-block was his Majesty's inherent indecision, perhaps his longing for some more dignified solution. This summer's diary needs the key of the following document, unsigned, undated, addressed 'Son Altesse Royale,' obviously written in Vienna, 1796, when Morris restores to Madame Royale, not yet married to the Duc d'Angoulême, the remnants of her father's secret service money. Copied from 1888 edition and re-translated:]

... Sa position affreuse l'avait pourtant mise dans la nécessité de se servir de personnes qui lui étaient à peine connues. Parmi ceux que les circonstances avaient portés au ministère, se trouvait M. Terrier de Monciel, un homme que M. M—— avait connu pour être fidèle au roi, quoiqu'il eût des liaisons à juste titre suspectes. Il crut donc devoir dire à Sa Majesté qu'elle pouvait s'y fier. Il en résulta qu'il fut chargé par elle de l'affaire la plus importante, c'est à dire, d'aviser aux moyens de tirer le roi de sa périlleuse situation. Il eut à cet effet des consultations fréquentes avec M. M——, et parmi les différents moyens qui se présentèrent, celui qui leur parut le plus essentiel fut de faire sortir la famille royale de Paris. Les mesures étaient si bien prises à cet effet que le succés en était presque immanquable, mais le roi (pour des raisons qu'il est inutile de détailler ici) renonça au projet le matin même fixé pour son départ, alors que les gardes suisses étaient déjà partis de Courbevoie pour couvrir sa retraite. Ses ministres, qui se trouvaient gravement compromis, donnèrent tous leur démission. Le moment était d'autant plus critique que Sa Majesté tenait déjà les preuves de la conspiration tramée contre sa personne. Il ne lui restait alors qu'un seul moyen. Il fallait remporter la victoire dans le combat qu'on allait lui livrer aussitôt que les conspirateurs se trouveraient en force. M. de Monciel, après avoir eu une explication avec Leurs Majestés, consentit à les servir encore, quoiqu'il ne fut plus au ministère.

On s'occupa de lever à la hâte une espèce d'armée royale, chose extrêmement délicate, et qui ne pouvait que compromettre ceux qui s'en étaient mêlés, si les ennemis du roi avaient le dessus. M. de Monciel associa à ses travaux M. Brémond, un homme courageux, zélé, fidèle, mais emporté, bavard et imprudent. Cette dernière qualité était presque essentielle, puisque la situation de la famille royale éloignait ceux dont le zèle pouvait être refroidi par les dangers. Vers la fin du mois de juillet, Sa Majesté fit remercier M. M—— des conseils qu'il lui avait donnés, et lui témoigna son regret de ne les avoir pas suivis — enfin le pria de surveiller ce qu'on faisait pour son service et de devenir dépositaire de ses papiers et de son argent. Il répondit que Sa Majesté pouvait toujours compter sur tous ses efforts, que sa maison ne lui paraissait pas plus sûre que le palais des Tuileries, puisqu'il était en but depuis longtemps à la haine des conspirateurs, qu'ainsi ni les papiers ni l'argent du roi ne seraient en sûreté chez lui. Mais comme cet argent ne portait aucune marque de propriété il consentirait, si Sa Majesté ne pouvait pas trouver une autre personne, à en devenir le dépositaire et à en faire l'emploi qu'elle voudrait bien lui indiquer. En conséquence du consentement ainsi donné, M. de Monciel lui apporta, le 22 juillet, 547,000 livres, dont 539,005 livres étaient déjà là, le deux août, en train d'être employées conformément aux ordres du roi. La somme de 449,750 livres, payée le deux août, devait être convertie par Brémond en louis d'or. Il en acheta effectivement 5,000, et les mit en bourses de 20 louis, car il s'agissait d'en faire la distribution à des personnes qui devaient se transporter avec des affidés aux endroits qui leur seraient indiqués et s'y battre sous leurs chefs. Et pour rendre ces contre-conspirateurs encore plus utiles, il s'agissait de prendre par préférence des Marseillais et autres agents des conspirateurs. Aussi, afin que le roi ne fût pas trompé, il était convenu que le paiement ne se ferait que lorsque les services auraient été rendus. En attendant, les 5,000 louis restèrent chez M. M——. Les événements du dix août sont trop connus pour qu'on puisse se permettre d'en faire le pénible récit. Ce jour-là, M. de Monciel apporta 200,000 livres, en se réfugiant avec sa famille chez M. M——, ainsi que plusieurs autres personnes. Après quelques jours, il se trouva dans la nécessité de se cacher. Brémond l'avait déjà fait quelque part ailleurs, et Madame de Monciel fut chargée de faire les démarches nécessaires pour sauver les personnes qui étaient compromises, et qui pouvaient d'autant plus compromettre le roi qu'elles étaient connues et que leurs opérations étaient fortement soupçonnées.

D'Angrémont fut pris et sacrifié, mais il eut le courage de se taire. À force d'argent, on trouva moyen de faire évader les uns et cacher les autres. Sur ces entrefaites Brémond envoya une personne, qu'il avait initiée au secret, chercher les 5,000 louis, qui lui furent payés, d'abord parce qu'il ne fallait pas donner occasion à un homme du caractère de Brémond de dire ou de faire des folies, mais principalement parce qu'on croyait que de concert avec M. de Monciel, il allait employer cette somme à quelque service essentiel, mais il n'y avait aucun projet de cette espèce. Au contraire, Brémond, avec une légèreté inconcevable, avait trahi un secret important, afin de mettre une assez forte somme entre des mains d'où, jusqu'à présent, on n'a pas pu en tirer un sou. Lorsque le duc de Brunswick fut entré en France, M. M——, persuadé que s'il arrivait jusqu'à Paris les assignats ne seraient que d'une mince valeur, et sachant d'ailleurs les projets extravagants de ceux qui régentaient la France, fit la remise, en Angleterre, de 104,800 livres, valant alors £2,518, afin de mettre cette somme à l'abri des événements. Il en fit payer à peu près le quart (600 livres sterling) à M. de Monciel, qui se trouvait alors à Londres, et négotia des traites pour le reste, afin de faire face à une demande que lui faisait Madame de Monciel. Enfin il resta la somme de 6,715 livres, qu'il conserva toujours à sa disposition jusqu'à ce qu'il eût enfin la satisfaction d'apprendre que tous ceux dont les aveux auraient pu être employés par les ennemis du roi pour motiver leur inculpation, étaient en lieu de sûreté. Il est vrai que ces accusations étaient fausses et calomnieuses, puisque le roi n'avait eu d'autre objet que celui de se défendre. Mais le succès était pour eux, et les conspirateurs n'auraient pas manqué de faire valoir les faits ci-dessus énoncés. L'appoint de 6,715 livres a subi le sort des assignats et a perdu de sa valeur, mais on peut estimer le change à raison de ——; et c'est cette somme que M. M—— aura l'honneur de payer à la personne que Son Altesse Royale voudra bien avoir la bonté de lui désigner. Au moment de la remise, le change était 17½. Il était parti de Londres pour aller en Suisse y travailler à la rentrée des 5,000 louis, pour venir les verser entre les mains de Son Altesse Royale. Mais les circonstances lui bouchèrent le chemin de la Suisse. Il est donc venu à Vienne, n'y ayant d'autre objet que de communiquer les faits ci-dessus mentionnés. Il vit avec regret, non seulement que les démarches faites pour la restitution ont été jusqu'à présent infructueuses, mais aussi qu'on commence à manifester, à ce sujet, des prétentions extraordinaires. Le récit minutieux en serait trop volumineux, d'ailleurs, le résumé d'une partie de ce que M. M—— désirait dire à la princesse, se trouve écrit ci-dessus et son bon esprit en devinera le reste. Elle apprendra facilement combien il est essentiel de tenir secret, autant que possible, des faits qui regardent de si prés le meilleur et le plus malheureux des rois. Il supplie Son Altesse Royale d'agréer l'hommage de son inviolable attachement.

[Translation:]

... [The King's] frightful position had however made it necessary for him to make use of people whom he hardly knew. Among those brought by the circumstances into the Ministry was M. Terrier de Monciel, a man with connections rightly considered suspect, but whose fidelity to the King was known to Mr M[orris]. He therefore believed he should tell his Majesty he could trust him. As a result he was charged by the King with the most important affair, to devise means of rescuing him from his perilous situation. To this end he had frequent consultations with Mr M[orris] and among the different steps which suggested themselves the one that seemed to them most essential was to get the royal family away from Paris. Measures were so well taken for this that success was almost assured, but the King (for reasons useless to detail here) renounced the project on the very morning fixed for his departure, when the Swiss Guards had already left Courbevoie to cover his retreat. His ministers, who found themselves seriously compromised, all resigned. The moment was all the more critical because the King already held the proofs of a conspiracy against his person.

Only one course remained to him; he had to be victorious in the attack that would be made against him as soon as the conspirators found themselves in force. M. de Monciel, after an explanation with their Majesties, consented still to serve them, altho no longer in office. Steps were taken to raise in haste a sort of royal army, an extremely delicate proceeding which could not fail to compromise those mixed up with it if the enemies of the King were to get the upper hand. M. de Monciel shared his labors with M. Brémond, a man who was courageous, zealous and faithful, but impetuous, garrulous and imprudent. This last characteristic was almost essential, for the situation of the royal family did not attract those whose zeal could be cooled by danger. Towards the end of July his Majesty sent his thanks to Mr M[orris] for the advice he had given him and his regrets for not having followed it, and finally begged him to supervise what was being done in his service and to become guardian of his papers and of his money. He replied that his Majesty might always count on all his efforts, but that his house did not strike him as any safer than the palace of the Tuileries, since he had long been an object of hatred to the conspirators, so that neither the papers nor the money of the King would be safe in his keeping. But as the money bore no mark of ownership, if his Majesty could find no other person to take charge of it he would consent to do so and to put it to the use he would be good enough to indicate. In consequence of the consent thus given M. de Monciel brought to him on 22d July, 547,000 livres [francs] of which by the second of August 539,005 livres were already being used according to the orders of the King. The sum of 449,750 livres paid on August second was to be converted by Brémond into louis d'or. He bought 5000 of these and divided them into purses of twenty louis, for it was a question of distributing them to individuals who, with other trustworthy people, were to repair to certain places and there to fight under their chiefs. And to make these counter-conspirators still more useful it was decided to take preferably Marseillais and other agents of the conspirators. Moreover, so that the King should not be betrayed, it was agreed that payment would not be made until services had been rendered. Meanwhile the 5000 louis remained at Mr M[orris]'s. The events of August tenth are too well known to admit of repeating their painful story. On that day M. de Monciel brought 200,000 livres to the house of Mr M[orris] where he and his family, as well as several other people, took refuge. After several days he found it necessary to hide. Brémond had already hidden elsewhere and Madame de Monciel was entrusted with the task of saving the compromised men who, being known and their operations strongly suspected, might further compromise the King.

D'Angrémont was caught and sacrificed but he had the courage to be silent. By spending much money ways of escape were found for some and hiding places for others. Meanwhile Brémond sent someone to whom he had divulged the secret, to fetch the 5000 louis, which were paid to him partly because a man of Brémond's character must not be given occasion for foolish speech or action, but principally because it was believed that he, together with M. de Monciel, was going to employ this sum for some essential service. But there was no such project. On the contrary, Brémond, with an inconceivable levity, had betrayed an important secret so as to place a considerable sum in hands from which up to the present hour he has been unable to recover a penny. When the Duke of Brunswick invaded France, Mr M[orris], convinced that if he reached Paris assignats would have but slender value, and knowing moreover the extravagant plans of those ruling over France, sent to England the 104,800 livres, then worth £2,518, so as to protect this sum against eventualities. He had about a quarter of it (600 pounds sterling) paid over to M. de Monciel, then in London, and negotiated drafts for the remainder to meet a demand made on him by Madame de Monciel. 6,715 livres were left, which he held always at his disposition until at last he had the satisfaction to hear that all those whose confessions might have been used by the King's enemies to inculpate them, were in a place of safety. It is true that these accusations were false

and calumnious, since the King had had no object but self
defence. But success was their's and the conspirators would
not have failed to make capital of the above mentioned facts.
This residue of 6,715 francs has shared the fate of assignats
and has lost in value, but the exchange may be reckoned at
       ; and it is this sum which Mr M[orris] will have the
honor to pay to the person her Royal Highness will have the
goodness to designate. At the time of the remittance exchange was at 17½. He had left London to go to Switzerland
and make efforts to collect the 5000 louis so as to pay them
into the hands of her Royal Highness. But his road to
Switzerland was blocked by circumstances. He therefore
came on to Vienna, having no other object there but to communicate these facts. He has seen with regret, not only that
efforts to obtain restitution have so far proved ineffectual,
but that on this subject extraordinary claims are being advanced. The detailed recital would be too voluminous, and
in any case the summary of part of what Mr M[orris] wished
to tell the Princess is written above and her own mind will
conjecture the rest. She will easily appreciate how essential
it is to keep secret as much as possible facts which so closely
concern the best and most unfortunate of Kings.

[Mr. Morris] begs Her Royal Highness to accept the
homage of his inviolable attachment.

[Brémond, rash Provençal, might have done better to return
the five thousand golden louis to the American Minister, rather
than confide them with compromising data to the bankers
Schweizer et Jeanneret before his escape from Paris to London
in October; that he did not attempt to take the money in any
form with him showed some wisdom, when his chances of reaching open sea unmolested were so slender. The mischief was that,
although these bankers outlived the Terror, their reluctance to
refund the 5000 louis increased with every exasperated demand
Brémond wrote them. A thick *dossier* cataloguing this correspondence will reach Morris from Switzerland two years later,
with offers to give Brémond first charge on pictures and furniture
the bankers were hoping to get out of France for sale, and with at

least one threat to blow out Brémond's brains if he wrote one
more letter. The impressive Morris might have dealt with them
more successfully by word of mouth if army movements had not
cut him off from Switzerland when taking to Vienna the small
residue left in his own hands. There he will be presented at Court
to Madame de France, Madame Royale, betrothed but not yet
married to her cousin the Duc d'Angoulême. Whether obeying
her own instinct or some ruling of the Emperor's government to
keep her from becoming a centre of French intrigue, the daughter
of Louis XVI will be granting no private audiences, not even to
her mother's adoring Fersen. So Morris will deliver to her Mem-
oir and money by the hand of La Fare, Bishop of Nancy, chargé
d'affaires at the Imperial Court from the make-believe Court of
her uncle Louis XVIII, then perching uneasily at Verona, with
the rumble of Bonaparte's evicting cannon growing daily louder
across Italy.]

Wednesday 25 *July.* — Brémond calls this Morning and gives
me all the Information which he has. I have several Visitors,
among the Rest M.ʳ Francis who is just arriv'd by the Way of
Valenciennes. He says that Things are in a most deplorable Situation. That the Austrians speak of spending their Winter at
Paris with the utmost Confidence. That the French seem totally
discouraged. I go to the Louvre for a Moment. Find there Monsieur de Schomberg, and the Bishop d'Autun comes in soon after.
I meet him on the Stairs and he expresses politely his Misfortune
to come always as I go away. He will have frequently that Misfortune. At a little after two M.ʳ Monciel and then M.ʳ Bertrand
come. I read the Memoire written for the King at the Time of
his Acceptance of the Constitution. We dine and after Dinner
read the Plan of a Constitution, then discuss the Steps which the
King is to take. M.ʳ Bertrand is a Stickler for the ancien Régime
but we drive him a little out of his Opinion which he will I think
come back to again. He is to prepare ToMorrow the Form of a
Letter to accompany the Manifest. Monciel is to be with him,
which is right. Go pretty late in the Evening to the Louvre and
sit there some Time. The Weather is pleasant.

Thursday 26. — Brémond calls this Morning. I go to Court

and thence to the Louvre; take my Friend to ride. Stop at the
Pension of Chaillot to get young Greene's Account which is not
yet made out. Dine at the Louvre. My friend mentions a Con-
spiracy against the Life of the King but will not name her Infor-
mant. I talk to her very seriously and near to scolding. Come
Home at six and meet Monciel who tells me that Bertrand has
begun his Work by Mention of the Cahiers, which is idle enough.
He is to see the King at eleven and give him the Result of the
Measures which I have propos'd and which we have discussed.
Call on the british Embassadress and sit some Time. Then go to
Madame d'Albani's where I stay till after eleven. The Weather
is pleasant.

Friday 27. — This Morning Brémond calls and afterwards
Monciel. We work all the Morning to prepare some Memoirs for
the King. I have a large Company to dine with me and after
Dinner I take my friend to her Convent where we embrace *en
attendant la Religieuse*. Afterwards go to the Louvre and spend
the Evening there. The Weather is pleasant.

Saturday 28. — Brémond comes this Morning and after him
Monciel who stays till three oClock; we finish the Form of a Letter from the King to the Assembly. I have a large Company to
Dinner. After Dinner ride to S.ᵗ Clou and having set my friend
down at the Louvre return Home. The Weather is pleasant.

Sunday 29. — This Morning M.ʳ Chaumont calls and after
him Brémond. Communicate to Chaumont the State of Things
respecting the Purchase to be made of Constable.¹ Brémond tells
me that he is to accept the Place of Minister of foreign Affairs.
I go to Court and afterwards call at the Louvre. Return Home to
Dinner expecting Monciel, who does not come till after six. We
make an Addition to the Letter for the King and then Part. I
visit Lady Sutherland and then spend an Hour at the Louvre.
Pleasant Weather.

Monday 30. — This Morning I write by the Post. M.ʳ Constable
calls. I go to the Louvre but we cannot be sure of our Moments.

---

¹ Which results in Chaumont forming the Paris New York Land Company of
Castorville while the guns are bombarding the Tuileries, that unlucky French
settlement on 'la Black' which Morris will be asked to wind up on his return
home.

M.̲ Monciel call'd to tell me that he has delivered to the King the Letter and one from M.̲ Bertrand on which he has communicated his Observations. I dine with Madame de Narbonne where there is a Host of Aristocrats. After Dinner I visit the british Embassadress. M.̲ Livingston calls on me. I go in the Evening to Madame d'Albani's. When I arrive there I find them all terrified at a Riot in which the Marseillois have kill'd one or two of the Gardes nationales. There is much Stir in Paris but I think the Business is over for this Evening. The Weather is very pleasant.

Tuesday 31. — This Morning M.̲ Monciel and M.̲ Brémond call to tell me what passed Yesterday and what is doing for to Day. Brémond is furious but after he is gone we agree not to permit any of those horrible Things which his Indignation would lead him to. Go to the Minister's. M.̲ Swan call'd. There is nothing new. I went according to Promise to the Louvre but there is no Chance of being alone. Come Home and meet Monciel who gives me the Bulletins of last Evening. Agree on what is to be done and on the Message to be sent by Monsieur Bureau de Puzy to Monsieur de La Fayette. Dine at the british Embassador's and go after Dinner to the Louvre. We embrace hastily. I go with my friend to Madame de La Blaydoière's & spend the Evening. The Weather is fine.

Morris to Jefferson

No. 5   Paris 1 August 1792

Thomas Jefferson Esq.̲ Sec.ʸ of State

Dear Sir

My last was of the tenth of July. Mr Livingston, who is on his Way to America, presents an Opportunity of writing which must not be neglected altho I am engag'd at present in Examination of the Account receiv'd from the Commissioners of the Treasury. I have already mention'd to you, Sir, that the whole of this Account is open and I must now observe that I do not find myself particularly authoriz'd to make the final Adjustment. If it becomes necessary I will do it but I shall avoid it as long as I can.

In Respect to the Pay.^{ts} made and making in America I am at
Ease because there I have your Orders, but not in Regard to those
made by Mr Short. I shall hope however to be favor'd with your
Instructions in Consequence of his Communications. I shall write
particularly respecting the Account when I have gone thro it.

In my Letter N.º 2 I mention'd that Monsieur de La Fayette
was about to commence an Attack upon the jacobine Faction. I
have not follow'd that Business in my Correspondence because
the Gazettes will furnish the most ample Intelligence. I mention'd my Apprehension that it would not be successful and it
furnishes a new Instance of the instability of human Affairs,
especially of those which depend on the Opinion of an ignorant
Populace. I verily believe that if M.^r de La Fayette were to appear just now in Paris unattended by his Army he would be torn
to Pieces. Thank God we have no Populace in America and I hope
the Education and Manners will long prevent that Evil. In the
present State of Things it seems evident that if the King be
not destroy'd he must soon become absolute. I think the Prime-
Movers of the Revolution see no other Mode of establishing the
Affairs of their Country on any tolerable Footing and will therefore declare their Adherence to his Majesty grounded on the
Abolition of the Constitution by the Assembly and their Masters
the Jacobine Club.

In my last I told you that the King would that Day commence
a new Career, but while I was writing all was chang'd and my
Letter was gone off a few Minutes before I was inform'd that the
Ministry had given in their Resignation. I will not communicate
the Reasons because they would be uninteresting to you and
should my Letter miscarry it would occasion much of that Noise
and Nonsense in which it is unpleasant to find one's Name. And
the wrongheaded People who get hold of such Things cannot distinguish between a Person who has obtain'd exact Information of
what is doing and those who are Actors in the Business. For the
same Reason I must decline mentioning the Plans in Agitation at
present to establish a good Constitution. I dare not say that I
hope this will take Place. I ardently *wish* it but I have Doubts
and Fears because I have no Confidence in the Morals of the
People. The King is anxious to secure their permanent Happiness

but Alas they are not in a State of Mind to receive Good from his Hands. Suspicion, that constant Companion of Vice and Weakness, has loosened every Band of social Union and blasts every honest Hope in the Moment of its budding.

You will have seen in the Report of the Minister of foreign Affairs to the Assembly, that the Impressions are made which you desire respecting the Dispositions of the United States. After this Report was made some Persons spoke to me of those Dispositions in a Tone of Irony, but I assur'd them very seriously that our grateful Sentiments for the Conduct of this Nation would be demonstrated by our Conduct whenever Occasion should require. That the Changes they might make in their own Administration would by no Means affect our Regard for them nor diminish our Attachment. As this Language was not ministerial but held in the Sincerity of social Life it surpriz'd those who, unfortunately for them, can find for the Conduct of Nations no Motive but Interest and are so Short Sighted as not to perceive that a virtuous and honorable Conduct is the truest Interest which a Nation can pursue.

In Respect to other Objects which are committed to me it is hardly necessary to say that Nothing can be done in the present Moment. Such Time as the Assembly can spare from the Discussion of Party Disputes is necessarily engrossed by the Departments of War and Finance. The Determination to suspend the King has been a little palled by the Information that their Armies would immediately revolt, and particularly the Southern Army on which they made their greatest Reliance. This Circumstance has greatly derang'd the Plan of Operations and the more so as many Instruments specially conven'd and collected for that grand Stroke, are at present no small Encumbrance to the Contrivers of it. Among these are the Bretons and Marseillois [1] now in this City. . . .

---

[1] Within ten days a most congenial use will be found for the 'Marseillois in this City,' speeded up by the Brunswick Manifesto, which Morris says 'may be rendered in a few Words: "Be all against me, for I am against you all; and make a good Resistance, for there is no longer any Hope."' Written by French *émigré* Limon, approved by the Bourbon princes, it reaches Paris August 3 and sends men crowding to enlist, with its threat to destroy Paris and treat her citizens with 'exemplary and unforgettable vengeance' if there were any fur-

Madame du Bourg to Morris

Rouen 9 Août 1792

... c'est assés d'être privée du plaisir de vous voir, sans ajouter à ce regret celui d'en être oublié. Je vous plains d'être obligé de rester dans cette *maudite babilone* où l'on ne peut que prévoir et que craindre chaque jour des malheurs, je ne crois cependant pas à la *déchéance*; le suplément au manifeste du duc de Brunswick pourra bien leur faire faire quelques réflexions, il me paroit bien utile et bien sagement vu dans les circonstances; les événemens semblent tout à la fois se précipiter et se ralentir, les autrichiens ne peuvent, dit on, être avant le 13 sur la frontiere, que de maux peuvent arriver d'ici là! je vois plus en *noir* que jamais; les jours paraissent des années, et j'aurois bien besoin pour calmer ma tête une longue conversation avec vous, car votre raison, avec laquelle j'aime encore mieux causer qu'avec votre esprit, m'a été souvent d'un grand secours pour rappeller la mienne; au reste, je suis fort contente d'avoir choisi Rouen pour le lieu de ma retraite, on y est dans la plus parfaite tranquillité; touts les autorités constitués sont animés du meilleur esprit, et le marchand, tres occupé de son commerce, ne s'embarrasse guerre de la révolution; comme personne n'a intérêt de remuer le peuple, il est fort calme, et les jacobins sont sans influence en cette ville. je vois fort peu de monde, et je mene absolument la vie de la campagne; rendés moi mon *exil* agréable en me donnant quelquefois de vos nouvelles; croyés vous que les jours du Roy soyent en sureté? dans quelle position grand dieu est ce malheureux prince? et comment n'en être pas touché jusqu'au fond de l'ame. j'ima-

---

ther violations of the Tuileries; to shoot down the National Guard as armed civilians if they dared make any defence. The Manifesto disclaims all idea of conquest, but summons the French nation to declare against its revolutionary oppressors. The calm of Rouen is a commentary on Paris methods, whose people, while Madame du Bourg is penning her letter, are being incited to the red horrors of the very next dawn, August Tenth.

August 9 sees the last of those familiar entries: 'Call at Mons.ʳ de Montmorin's.' Within a week the Count will be one of those aristocrat inmates of the Abbaye whose only interest in September's bloody week will be studying the best position for meeting death; watching from a turret window the agony of friends, it is seen that those who raise their hands suffer longer, swords reaching head or throat with less direct impact.

gine que vous êtes actuellement dans votre nouvelle maison, et c'est une grande raison pour moi de regretter le luxembourg. écrivés moi je vous prie le plus tot que vous pouvés, et recevés les plus sinceres et les plus tendres assurances de mon attachement

du B du B

[*Translation:*]

... it is enough to be deprived of the pleasure of seeing you, without adding to such a regret that of being forgotten. I pity you, obliged to stay on in that *cursed Babylon*, where one can but foresee and dread every day some fresh misfortune. I do not, however, believe in *dethronement*; the supplement to the Duke of Brunswick's manifesto may well make them pause and reflect, it strikes me as very useful, and wisely conceived for present circumstances; events seem to be rushing on and yet at the same time slowing down, it is said that the Austrians cannot reach the frontier before the 13th, what disasters might not happen between then and now. I am seeing things more than ever in *black*, days seem like years, and to calm my head what I need is a long talk with you, for your judgment, which I enjoy even more than your wit, has often done me the service of steadying my own. I am pleased at my choice of Rouen for my retreat; one is in perfect tranquillity here, all the constituted authorities are animated by the best intentions and the merchant, absorbed in his commerce, does not trouble himself about the revolution; as nobody has any interest in stirring up the people they remain quite calm, and the jacobins are without influence in this town. I hardly see anyone and lead in every way the life of the country; make my *exile* pleasant by sending me now and then news of you. Do you think the King's life is in safety? in what a situation, great God, is this unhappy prince! and how can one help being touched by it to the depths of one's soul. I imagine that you are now in your new house, and this makes me regret the Luxembourg. I beg you to write to me as soon as you can, and pray accept the most sincere and the most tender assurances of my attachment.

du B du B

AUGUST 1792

Wednesday 1 August. — This Morning M̲ṛ Brémond calls for a Moment to tell me what is doing. M̲ṛ Chaumont also calls and I answer his Letter. The Count de Croix pays me a Visit and sends to taste a Bottle of Claret from the Owner of the Lafite Vineyard. The Wine is very indifferent indeed. I have Company to Dinner and after Dinner take a Ride; call on Mad̲ẹ de Montmorin and sit with her a little while, then go to the Louvre. Nothing new this Day. The Wind has got round to the Eastward and the Weather is fine and dry.

Thursday 2. — This Morning M̲ṛ de Monciel calls on me and tells me that they are trying to send him to Orleans. We agree on the Conversion of the King's Paper into Specie. I go to Court. Afterwards call on the Minister of the Marine who is gone abroad altho he promised to be at Home. S̲ṭe Croix is appointed Minister of foreign Affairs. Return Home and undress. I have Company to dine with me. M̲ṛ Constable comes before Dinner and I shew him that he had better comply with Chaumont's Views. Chaumont dines with me and tells me the State of that Affair. After Dinner go with Mons̲ṛ Bertrand and the Ladies to the Bois de Boulogne. At the Place Louis XV returning, my friend and I get into my Chariot and en Route to Mad̲ẹ d'Albani's we with Difficulty embrace. The Weather is very hot.

Friday 3. — Monsieur de Monciel calls this Morning and so does the Count d'Estaing, also a young Quaker from Philadelphia. Monciel dines with me and we prepare an Address to the Marseillois. I complain of the Appointment of Bon Carère to Philadelphia and he promises to speak to the King on the Subject. I go after Dinner to the Louvre and my Friend tells me that the King propos'd this Embassy by Way of getting Rid of Monsieur Bon Carère. That S̲ṭe Croix objected he would not be received but his Majesty said so much the better, let us but get

Rid of him. We embrace and I stay till after ten. The Weather is very warm.

Saturday 4. — M.ʳ Brémond brings me this Morning 5000 louis d'ors which he has purchased. He is to have the Correspondence of the Jacobins for 1000. M.ʳ de Monciel calls and we compleat a Letter to be written by the King to the President of the Section of the Fauxbourg S.ᵗ Marceau about the River Bièvre which will, it is supposed, give his Majesty that Fauxbourg. Monciel tells me that the King and Queen are much distressed and in great Apprehension. I call at the Louvre and dine at the British Embassador's. We walk after Dinner to the Champs de Mars where we see a few Raggamuffins who are signing the Petition for the *Déchéance.* I call at Monsieur de Montmorin's where I find a Family in deep Distress. Go to the Louvre and stay only a few Minutes. Then go to M.ʳ Constable's. He has agreed with Chaumont. At my Return Home I find Lady Sutherland at my Door; she comes to obtain an Interview between me and the Chevalier de Coigny. I tell her that I will be at Home if he will call on me tomorrow. He wishes to give my Ideas direct to the Queen without passing thro the Medium of Monsieur de Montmorin. They expect all to be murdered this Evening at the Château. The Weather is very warm.

Sunday 5. — Go to Court this Morning. Nothing remarkable, only that they were up all Night expecting to be murdered. Go to the Louvre for a Moment. My friend is much hurt that I will not dine with her. Pacify her and come Home to meet M.ʳ de S.ᵗᵉ Croix. He comes late. Tells me what he is about. M.ʳ Constable dines with me and M.ʳ Livingston, whom I have taken as my private Secretary. After Dinner I go to visit Lady Sutherland and stay some Time conversing with Lord Gower. Thence to the Louvre for a little while. The Weather is still hot.

Monday 6. — This Morning I write. M.ʳ Constable, M.ʳ Francis and M.ʳ —— his Companion call on me. M.ʳ de Monciel comes and tells me how Things are. M.ʳ & Mad.ᵉ de Flahaut &c.ᵃ, dine with me. M.ʳ Chaumont calls and we decide what is to be done. I go to Madame d'Albani's and then call at the Louvre. M.ʳ de S.ᵗᵉ Croix comes in with whom I have some Conversation. The Bishop d'Autun and M.ʳ de Beaumetz are the Party. The Weather continues very hot.

Tuesday 7. — This Morning I write. M.ʳ de Monciel calls and the Chevalier de Coigny with whom I have a long Conversation on the State of Affairs. MonCiel tells me that the King would not listen to the entrusting his Secret to S.ᵗᵉ Croix. The public Mind is much better than it was and will mend. We digest a Petition for the Marseillois calculated to make the King declare himself.¹ Monsieur de Coigny is to push the same Point with the Queen. Chaumont comes and Constable, who was to have met him, sends an Excuse that John Phyn is arriv'd. This is a bad Reason for neglecting Business. After Dinner I go to the Louvre. My friend tells me that her Husband has behav'd brutally and threatned Separation. We ride, and having taken up Mad.ˡˡᵉ spend the Evening at Madame de La Blédoyère's. The Weather continues hot and dry which is excellent for the Harvest.

Wednesday 8. — Monsieur de Monciel calls this Morning. M.ʳ Phyn also comes to visit me. M.ʳ de Monciel tells me that Things are going on well. The King seems to hold the proper Opinions also, which is a desirable Thing. I dine with Madame de Stahl and after Dinner, the Gentlemen desiring to drink, I send for Wine and let them get preciously drunk. Go to the Louvre and take my friend to ride; after I set her down I go to Lady Sutherland's and pay her a pretty long Visit. She will be at Court To-morrow. The Weather is very warm still.

Thursday 9. — This Morning M.ʳ de Monciel calls and brings me some Money. I dress and go to Court. Afterwards go to M.ʳ Constable's and converse with him and M.ʳ Chaumont respecting their Agreement. Thence to the Louvre where I pass a happy Moment with my Friend, then go to dine with the british Embassador. Afterwards call at Mon.ʳ Montmorin's and go thence to Madame d'Albani's, where I stay till near twelve. Paris is in great Agitation.

Friday 10 *August*. — This Morning M.ʳ de Monciel calls and his Report is tranquilizing but shortly after he leaves me the Cannon begin, and Musquetry mingled with them announce a warm Day.

---

¹ These busy gentlemen have not readjusted their values. What King and Ministers think is now of little account; what matters is what Danton from the Cordeliers, Robespierre from the Jacobins, are concerting with Commune, *fédérés*, and the man in the street.

The Château, undefended but by the Swiss, is carried and the Swiss wherever found are murder'd. The King & Queen are in the National Assembly who have decreed the Suspension of his Authority. Madame de Flahaut sends her Son and comes afterwards to take Refuge.[1] I have Company to dine but many of those which were invited do not come. M.r Huskisson, the Secretary to the british Embassador, comes in the Evening. He gives a sad Account of Things. The Weather continues very warm or rather, extremely hot.

Saturday 11. — A sleepless Night renders me heavy during this Day. The King & Queen remain yet at the Assembly which goes on rapidly under the *Dictée* of the Tribunes. We are quiet here. Things are taking on their new Order. The Weather continues to be very hot. M.r de S.t Pardou calls in the Evening and seems torn to Pieces by Affliction. I desire him, if he sees the royal Family, to tell them that Relief must soon arrive.

Sunday 12. — This Morning Monsieur de Monciel and his Wife come before I am up. I have my House full all Day and am heartily fatigued this Evening. I calld in the Morning on Lady Sutherland who is *un peu abbattue*. The Venetian Ambassador, who was abroad, and so was Madame d'Albani. She & the Count Alfieri come about three oClock. She is violently affected and afflicted. The Weather is very warm still and even oppressive.[2] The State of the Air is evidenced by some Perch which, alive in the Morning at six oClock, are spoil'd at Dinner. So rapid a State of putrefaction I never yet saw.

Monday 13. — Write this Morning. M.r Constable calls and M.r Phyn and M.r Swan with M.r Ingram, M.r Price and M.r Jarvis and a naturalized frenchman. These four want Passports. M.r Amory calls for the same Purpose and M.r Mountflorence to get a Passport for M.rs Blagden. Madame d'Albani dines with me and requests me to ask a Passport for her from the british Embassador. I go after Dinner and he, as I expected, refuses to grant it. The Weather is somewhat cooler this Evening, having had Rain.

Tuesday 14. — Write this Morning. But I have many Inter-

---

[1] See footnote on page 519.

[2] Crowded into the reporters' box at the Assembly the royal family was stifling without even a change of clothes except what Lady Sutherland sent for the Dauphin, her son Lord Strathnaver being about the same age.

ruptions. Among others who call on me M.ʳ Francis gives a dreadful Account of what he saw on the tenth and says that he shall not dare to tell it in America. Gen.ˡ du Portail calls on me. He wishes to get away from hence should Things grow more serious. M.ʳ Chaumont comes just before Dinner. M.ʳ Constable and M.ʳ Phyn dine with me and so does M.ʳ Chaumont. The Weather is more pleasant than it was but still it is very warm.

Wednesday 15. — This Morning M.ʳ Chaumont comes and we at length get thro our Business but in the Midst of many Interruptions. L.ᵈ Gower and M.ʳ [Lindsay] the british Minister call on me respecting some Points which he wishes to elucidate, and to obtain my Opinion without formally asking it. In this I comply. After Dinner I ride to the Bois de Boulogne with my distressed friend and walk till she is tir'd. At my Return pay a short Visit to Lady Sutherland. After I get Home Mad.ᵉ de Narbonne comes and sits the Evening. The Weather is grown more mild but still warm.

Thursday 16. — This Morning I write. Americans to dine with me. Stay at Home the Evening. Weather still warm.

Morris to Jefferson

No. 6   Paris 16 August 1792

Thomas Jefferson Esq.ʳ
        Philadelphia

Dear Sir

My last was of the first Instant N.º 5. Since that period another Revolution has been effected in this City. It was bloody. Success, which always makes Friends, gives to the present Order an Air of greater unanimity than really exists. A very considerable Party is deeply interested to overturn it but what may be their Conduct is uncertain. Whether they will confine themselves to idle vows and empty wishes, or whether they will break out into Action is doubtful. Some of them are Men of Enterprize, but it is rather small than great Enterprise. As you know well this Kingdom it may perhaps be sufficient to mention the kind of persons which compose this party. They are those who call'd themselves the moderate or middle men, and who hoped to ballance the two Extremes and govern the Kingdom by playing off one sett against the other. This in quiet Times requires great Talents, as well as great Address, and they had more of the latter than the former. In times of Turbulence it is necessary that those who play this game should have a considerable armed force, because neither Argument nor persuasion can then avail. It remains to be prov'd by the Fact whether they possess such force. If they do, it must be in the hands of Monsieur de La Fayette; and as all must depend on an immediate exercise of it I rather think that the precious moment will be suffered to pass away. I have long been convinced that this middle party, who by the bye were the prime movers of the revolution, must fall to the Ground, and that those who compose it must join one of the great factions. The Aristocratic Faction is still split into two or more. Some are for absolute Monarchy, some for the ancient régime, some, and those but few, desire a mix'd Government. The framers of the late Constitution had got up to this last Ground, but the Idea of an *hereditary* Senate stuck in their Throats. The King, who has an uncommon firmness in suffering but who has not the Talents for Action and who is besides a very religious Man, found himself fettered by his Oaths to the Constitution which he in his conscience believed to be a bad one; and about which indeed there is now but one opinion in this Country, because Experience, that great parent of Wisdom, has brought it already to trial & Condemnation. The King, from the Causes just mentioned, would not step forward and of course there was no Standard to which the adherents of the two Chambers could repair. The Republicans had the good Sense to march boldly and openly to their object, and as they took care not to mince matters nor embarrass themselves by legal or Constitutional niceties, they had the Advantage of Union, Concert, and Design, against the disjointed Members of a body without a head. If under these Circumstances the foreign Force were out of question, I should have no Doubt that the republican Form would take place quietly enough, and continue as long as the morals of the country would permit. You know the State of morals here, and can of course (if it be necessary) form the Calculation for yourself. The Circumstance of foreign force is however, on the present occasion, a preponderant Object, and I think its Effect will depend on its Activity. Should the Duke of Brunswick advance rapidly, he will be join'd by great numbers, even of the Armies opposed to him; because the late change will furnish to some a reason and to others a pretext, for abandoning the cause they had espoused. If on the contrary his progress be cautious and slow, it is probable that those who are now silent from fear, will habituate themselves by Degrees to speak favorably of the present Government, in order to lull Suspicion; and that thus a public Opinion will appear, which when once pronounced governs the generality of mankind. If by this means the new republic takes a little root, foreign powers will I believe find it a difficult matter to shake it to the ground, for the French Nation is an immense Mass which it is not easy either to move or to oppose.

You will observe Sir that matters are now brought to a simple Question between an absolute Monarchy and a Republic, for all middle Terms are done away. This Question also must be decided by Force, because on one Side it is in the hands of the people who cannot treat for themselves, and who will not permit others to treat for them in respect to the important interests which are now at Stake. If, as in former times, some factious Nobles were at the head of a party, they would (as formerly) take the first Opportunity to stipulate for themselves at the expence of their party; but without entering here into a Question of relative Integrity, I do not think that the People are so attach'd to any particular Men as to have what may be called Leaders; and those who appear as such are in my opinion rather Instruments than Agents.

I do not go into the History of Things, nor trouble you with a recapitulation of Events. I enclose and shall send by the present Opportunity the Gazettes since my last, which will communicate all particulars which you may desire to know. Since the Operations of the tenth the *Logographe*, *Gazette Universelle*, and *Indicateur*, are suppressed, as indeed are all those who were guilty of *Feuillantisme*, that is, Adherence to the *Club des Feuillans soi disant Constitutionel*. You must therefore make Allowances for what you find in the other Gazettes, written not only in the Spirit of a party, but under the Eye of a party. The first must influence the most honest Printer in the coloring of some facts, and the second will restrain the boldest printer in the publishing of other facts. If it were necessary, or could be useful, I should communicate all the particulars which come to my Knowledge; but this invidious task would answer no good end, and long before my letters could reach you, changes must inevitably take place.

One particular however it is becoming to note. You will find that the Assembly immediately superseded the appointment of a Mons. Bon Carère as Minister to the United States. This Man's Character is as bad as need be, and stain'd by infamous vices. By what Influence he was introduced into the Office of Foreign Affairs I know not, for I was then in England; but I have reason to believe that it was the poor Expedient of the *Feuillans*, to watch, and check, and perhaps to betray the Jacobine Ministry. While the King was pressing Mr Ste Croix (an eight day Minister) to accept the Department of Foreign Affairs, this last declared that he would not serve if Bon Carère was retain'd; and to get rid of him they invented the Expedient of sending him to AMERICA. I considered this Step as a kind of insult, and transmitted my Sentiments on the Subject to the King, who thereupon told Mons. de Ste Croix that I was angry at that Appointment and he must arrange the Matter with me. That he wished I would prevent his being receiv'd. The Minister apologized for himself by saying the Nomination had taken place before he came into Office, and that he had remonstrated against it. He apologized for the thing, as well as he could, admitting always that it was wrong; and added that his Embarkation should be delayed, and I was at liberty to prevent his being receiv'd. To this I replied that he must not embark at all, but be removed: and that would have been done, for when he presented the *Bon* for his Appointments the Minister refused to sign it. In the mean time the new Revolution took place, and the History of Mr Bon Carère's Ministry is at an End. It may perhaps be misrepresented, and therefore having stated the facts I think it right to add that it proceeded from downright weakness. He was supposed to possess the Confidence of a great many of the Nobility, and therefore they were afraid to turn him about his business. Perhaps also he had been trusted so far that he knew too much. This was the case with some others, not better than him as to Essentials, tho not so much abas'd; for this Man was (as I am told) the friend of a noted Procuress of this City, and Superintendant of her Brothel.

I shall send herewith a Packet containing my Correspondence with the Commissioners of the Treasury, relative to our Debt; and in the same Packet you will find a letter from Mr Cathalan to you relative to a Riot at Marseilles, and his conduct therein. He has written two long Letters to me on that Subject, and I have replied by one of the thirteenth Instant which you will also find enclos'd with his letter to you.

I have already had Occasion to mention to you, Sir, that I did not find myself authorized to go into the Settlement of the Account *finally* with the Commissioners of the Treasury. This Observation I must again in this place repeat, and add that notwithstanding my utmost Efforts I have not been able to bring the Minister of Foreign Affairs to consider for a Moment the Question referr'd to me respecting the Sums paid and paying in America. What is still more surprising is that the Minister of the Marine, altho' authorized to treat with me for Supplies to the Colony of St Domingo, has done nothing in that Affair. Two Ministers have occupied that Place since the Decree. Each has given me various *rendez vous* but neither has appeared at the time and Place, because Circumstances of the Moment have obliged them to attend to something else. Indeed the executive of the late Constitution has been at the last Agony for this three months, and of course has thought more of saving its life than of doing its Business. The present Executive is just born, and may perhaps be stifled in the Cradle. If a general Arrangement could have been made with the late Government for paying the whole of our Debt at some fix'd Exchange so as to do Justice and fulfil the honorable Intentions of the United States, I should have been well pleased, and altho not exactly authorized should probably have taken on me to make the needful Engagements: and in so doing I should have made a great sacrifice to the public, because I wish of all Things to be free from any pecuniary Transactions; for I know by Experience that the utmost possible

Purity will not prevent malicious Insinuations, which however unfounded will always find some believers. It appears however a probable event that before our Debt be paid we may experience some considerable losses on Exchange, not to mention the dead charges which are considerable too. It has therefore appeared to me most advisable to make one general Statement and Settlement of the Whole; and if it shall appear that we have gain'd and that they have lost by the modes of Payment, then to give a good round Sum as a Compensation, and as it were gratuitously, because by that means we have the Reputation of the good we do and the Sacrifice we make; and because otherwise the Agents of this Government might attribute to their address an advantage gain'd, instead of giving Credit to our Generosity for a Compensation granted. And it seems important to establish the latter idea, because it cannot fail to extend our Credit throughout the World; and consequently to facilitate all pecuniary Operations which hereafter we may have occasion to make.

Before I conclude this letter, permit me my dear Sir to request the orders of the President respecting my line of conduct in the Circumstances about to arise. Perhaps these Orders may not reach me until the Circumstances are past, but even then they may serve as a Ground to reason on in the Circumstances which succeed. If they arrive in Season they will relieve my mind from a great Weight. At present I feel myself in a State of contingent responsibility of the most delicate kind. I am far from wishing to avoid any fair and reasonable risque and I rely on the justice of Government at the same time to mark out as exactly as possible the Conduct to be pursued, as well as on its goodness to judge favorably of cases unforeseen.

Morris to Jefferson

No. 7   Paris 17 August 1792

Thomas Jefferson Esq.
                    Philadelphia

Dear Sir,

If I have not hitherto mentioned the Application made to me by the foreign Officers who have Certificates whereof the Interest is payable in this City, it has not been for want of sufficient Cause but because I did daily hope to have received some Orders on that Subject. Many have spoken to me, written to me, and call'd upon me. I have given to all the general Assurances that Justice would be done, that I would transmit their Claims, and the like. I now enclose a Letter from the Polish Envoy relative to the Claims of Brigadier General Koskiusko, and I have told the Count d'Oraczewski that I daily expect dispatches from you on this Subject. I did this because General du Portail told me that he has Information from Col? Ternant that these Claims are all honorably provided for. In the uncertainty as to what may have been done I feel it my duty to bring the Matter to your recollection, persuaded that you will do every thing which may be proper on the Occasion.

I enclose in like Manner a Letter I have receiv'd from Mr Francis Coffyn of Dunkirk, respecting the Consular Office in that City. I tell him in Answer to it that I shall enquire of Mr de La Motte as to the Appointment he complains of and will transmit his letter to you and take your Orders. These you will I trust be so kind as to give me. I know not Mr Coffyn and consequently can say nothing either for or against him.

[Here is a specimen of the appeals from French officers. In days of remote antiquity, viscounts of Lomagne had enjoyed the privilege of coining money. Not the least sign of their descendant's bravery was writing in English.]

Sir

I have the honour to apply myself to your excellency and most humbly to represent that i have been during the Last War, as a field officer in the Service of the United States of America; in wich Service i have made great Losses wich have not yet been repaired; but what affected me most sensibly was a heavy Sickness wich setled me in the year 1781 at Philadelphia at the foot of my grave, for, by this unlucky event, i was obliged to Leave the Service, and consequently to Loose the fruit of my military Labours.

i had Leave from Congress to return to france for the recovery of my health, according to the prescription of the phisicians; i had during my passage at home the misfortune to be taken twice; first by a privateer on the coast of St. Domingo; and Lastly, being in the Ship Anne, Cap.ᵗ Ashmead, from Philadelphia, and another privateer being in chace of us, we did run aground near bermuda and we were forced to surrender ourselves prisoners of war to the inhabitans of that island; i was nevertheless soon after this unhappy event exchanged, and arrived at Last at the port so much wished; i reached my home most naked; for the privateer and the bermudians had appropriated themselves of all, very little excepted, that did belong to me and to the unfortunate crew; however i had the good luck to safe from the naufrage a Loan office certificate of the Sum of one thousand and thirty two dollars bearing interest at 6 per cent and given to me by order of congress. it is partly on that Subject that i have the honour to write to your excellency that i might know if the payment of these certificates has been yet performed, and if i may be in hopes of soon receiving and upon due aplication the amount of mine; i have also the honour to ask your excellency if my services during the Last War, of whom I have the best attestations from the congress and from several generals namely gen.ᵗ Stuben, Muhlenburgh, and Hand do not entitle me to ask to the united States that some Land in any part setled of the continent may be granted to me, in reward of my services and Losses; i am, in some way, under the necessity of asking you this, on account of the body of nobility of whom i was a member having been, as you know it, Lately Suppressed, according to the new Constitution of this Kingdom, and their property so much reduced by it and especially that one of my parents, that it is almost out of their power to help their Large family with any thing else but the breeding; it is in this critical situation that i am applying to your excellency being sure that you'll grieve at my fate and that you'll endeavour to sweaten it by making use, at my humble request, of your ascendant upon the Chiefs of North America whom you represent at the court of france, that i may obtain from them the reward i am now requiring as well as the payment of the Loan Office certificate....

i have the honour to be

your excellency   Most humble and

Most obedient Servant

LOMAGNE TARRIDE L'aîné.

bereux prés d'orthes en bearn

  le 28 juillet 1792

Alexander Hamilton to Morris

[Received end of November]   Philadelphia, September 13th, 1792.

Sir,

The legislature at their last session having made provision for paying off the debt due to foreign officers, the interest of which is payable at the house of Mr Grand, banker at Paris, and the President having authorised me to carry that provision into effect, I have concluded to commit such part of the business, as is to be transacted at Paris, to your management, not doubting of the cheerfulness with which you will render this service to the public, and to my particular department.

The object not regarding your diplomatic mission, and Mr Jefferson being absent from the seat of government, I open without scruple a direct communication with you on the subject.

By the tenor of the certificates, which were issued, the stipulation to pay at Paris is confined to the interest. The principal is of course payable in the United States.

To enable you to make payment of this interest, Mr Short is directed to subject to your order, in the hands of our Commissioners in Holland, the sum of one hundred and five thousand guilders.

Enclosed is a list, showing the names of the persons to be paid, and the amount of principal and interest due to each; computing interest from the first of January, 1789, up to the last of the present year.

The reason for beginning at the first of January, 1789, is that Congress placed a fund in the disposition of their then Minister Plenipotentiary, to make payments up to that time, and though an account of the application of that fund has not been rendered, it is understood that the payment provided for was made.

By the list referred to, you will find, that the sum directed to be placed to your order is adequate to the object.

The instruction of the President to me is, to cause the payment to be made in a 'mode which will exempt the parties from the loss attendant on the depreciation of the Assignats, and at the same time occasion no loss to the United States.'

The line of conduct, which has appeared to me proper to fulfil the spirit of this instruction, is to give to each creditor his option, either to receive payment in bills on Amsterdam, dollar for dollar, according to the intrinsic par of the metals at Paris and Amsterdam, or to receive an equivalent in Assignats, according to the current rate of exchange between Paris and Holland at the time.

To exemplify what is meant by an equivalent, suppose the following data.

1. That two and a half guilders are equal to a dollar, according to the intrinsic par of the metals at Paris and Amsterdam.

2. That the current rate of exchange between the two places is twenty per cent against Paris; that is, one hundred guilders at Paris will bring only eighty at Amsterdam.

3. That the sum to be paid for principal and interest is one hundred dollars.

The computation to ascertain the equivalent will then stand thus;

If 80 be equal to 100, so will 100 be equal to 125; $125 \times 2\frac{1}{2}$ is $= 312\frac{1}{2}$ guilders, which being converted into livres, at par, will be to be paid in Assignats, at their nominal value, *livre* for *livre*.

I have made an arrangement to begin the discharge of the principal here, at any time after the fifteenth of October next, upon demand, and the production of the certificate by the party or his legal representative, or Attorney duly constituted and authorised. Notice will be given, that after the last of December next interest will cease, as to all those, who shall not have made application for their principal by that day.

I request, that you will also cause some proper notification of this arrangement to be given in France.

As the certificates will be required to be produced here, the payment of interest at Paris must be made without the production of them. Especial care must of course be taken to ascertain, that the payments are made to the identical creditors, or their certain Attornies. It will be well that duplicate or triplicate receipts may be taken for such payments, in order that one or more sets may be transmitted with the accounts current.

Should there be any, who may prefer receiving their whole dues, interest as well as principal, here, they may have the option of doing it; but in this case, they must make known their election to you, or to some person, whom you shall appoint, and must obtain a certificate from you, or the person appointed by you, of their having made and communicated that election. Should you authorise another person for the purpose, you will please to inform me, without delay, who he is, and send me his signature.

The payments are stipulated to be made at the house of Mr Grand; and those which have been heretofore made have passed through his hands. The same course will be proper, unless there are good reasons to the contrary. You, who are on the spot, will judge how far any such reasons may have resulted from the tempests, which have of late agitated the kingdom; and you will act accordingly. Nobody knows better than you, how important it is to make no misteps in money concerns.

With the most respectful consideration, I have the honor to be, &c..

ALEXANDER HAMILTON.

[September 21, the Convention, 780 strong, will begin its sittings; 25th it abolishes royalty and declares a Republic 'one and indivisible.' Gironde the Right. Extremist new Left soon known as the 'Mountain.' Centre the 'Plain or Marsh,' moderates who lack a leader, although Sieyès will be once more a deputy and sit among them.

These dates show how precarious any Franco-American debt transactions were in August, 1792, results of the elections not known, France no longer a kingdom and not yet a republic, when it meant handing over public money to a bunch of Ministers who from day to day might lose all substance and official existence; and yet, owing to the delays of nervous Crown officials, an engagement of some magnitude taken with them between July 30 and August 5 had to be honored to the Executive Committee of the interregnum. No wonder that Short was in agony about paying this instalment of America's debt to France, agony partly made up of remorse that he had not himself completed the payment due, when the transaction had been specifically put into his hands, when the money was lying ready and idle in Amsterdam banks, and when delay added to the interest the United States was paying to France and to the dead interest on the loans raised in Holland and Belgium chiefly for the purpose of these repayments. Into his appointment as Resident Minister at The Hague instead of Minister Plenipotentiary at Paris, Short had chosen to read a lack of government confidence in his talents, and had made a point of leaving the payment in question to whoever should be appointed to Paris, whose 'superior abilities' might make a better bargain about exchange and depreciation. If Jefferson ever turned the business over to Short's successor, such a letter from the Secretary of State never reached Morris; and as several American official letters urging a settlement were sent to Short months after Morris's appointment, the implication is that he was right in thinking the matter was still considered to be in Short's hands. For paying pensions to French officers of the American War, Morris will receive instructions from Hamilton, Secretary of the Treasury; that will be clear sailing; and the difficulties that arose at the end of August about payments for provisioning the French sugar islands out of the American debt were not so much because Morris felt a lack of authority as because the new Ministers Le Brun and Clavière were trying to bully him into making these payments to them in France, when the whole point of the agreement was that they should be made to the French Minister in America, for him to spend there on American commodities for the French Colonies. Paying instalments of interest and instalments of principal to diminish the original 34,000,000 livres of America's war debt to France was a separate and much larger affair. It might automatically fall into the province of the new American Minister at Paris without a word of instruction from his government, or it might still be considered as belonging entirely to the duties of Mr. Short. Before leaving Paris, Short arranged with Morris to back up his negotiations. They were used to working together, officially on one side only, for Short had seldom carried out a loan without bombarding Morris with questions and with letters asking for advice; he had placed one loan for three million florins with De Wolf at Antwerp solely on Morris's recommendation that De Wolf was a sound man and that creating some rivalry with the Amsterdam monopoly would lower the rate of interest the United States had to pay. Having done so, Short wrote by every post asking Morris if he really was sure of De Wolf. That belongs to 1791. In the ministerial uncertainties of 1792's cataclysmic summer, Morris found it hard work nailing the constantly superseded officials to so much as keeping an appointment. It was August 5 before he could finally get them to arrange that the six million livres then falling due should be paid at the equivalent of 1,625,000 florins banco. Morris's letter announcing this to Short was posted the 6th; by some mistake of Short's servants it wandered back and forth between The Hague and Amsterdam, not meeting up with that Minister until the 16th. Even without accidents, Short could hardly have ordered the money to Paris in time to be receipted for by Ministers of the Crown. News of the August Tenth Revolution flew north before the money had started and threw Short into passionate uncertainty. He bitterly regretted not having paid the instalment to the government which had created *assignats*, fearing that a new government might repudiate them or fatally depreciate them. He tried to devise a form of receipt that would guard the United States against any questions and demands at 'the resurrection.' To Morris on the spot, a Bourbon resurrection looked too remote to have any effect on his transaction; the calm confidence of his attitude that his arrangement with France must be honored, and could be safely honored, to any government France chose to live under, drove Short nearly over the borderline of hysteria. Yet Morris's confidence was justified by the event. This payment of six million livres was duly credited by the French Treasury to the United States Treasury, and no future government ever questioned that the amount had been paid and received with due regularity. When news of the King's suspension reached America, instructions were sent to suspend payments.[1] The adherence of Morris to his agreement with the late King's late government had at least the advantage of saving interest on the debt, and no harm ever came of it. He felt that the United States was safeguarded by portions of the debt still owing, from which this six millions could always be deducted. Part of Short's panic was that France would receipt in terms of florins, leaving room for future argument about exchange. In spite of Morris's assurances that livres were understood and arranged, Short grumbled away about this until he heard from America that 'The commissioners have some time ago rec.d a letter from the commissaries of the treasury, confirming them in answer to the letter they wrote, that the credit was given 6,000,000#,' [livres]. On November 27 he passes this on to Morris as news. Extracts from the two Ministers' letters supply details.]

Short to Morris

The Hague, July 6

... You inform me that the Assembly has authoriz'd the minister to concert with you the means of supplying the colonies out of the American debt – ... It may be proper to mention to you also that the Sec.y of the Treasury has informed me of his having paid to M. de Ternant or le Forest on acc.t of the French debt 100,000 dollars, on the 12.th of March, – & engaged to make three further payments of 100,000 dollars each, on June 1, – Sep. 1, – & Dec. 1, – & also inclosed me an acc.t of articles furnished

---

[1] A letter to that effect from Hamilton to Short hangs on a wall of the new Museum of New York City (1937).

on same acc.ᵗ to the amount of 8962 dollars. He had formerly
paid two sums, one of 8325 dollars & the other of 22,000 dollars.

Morris to Short

Paris 9 August 1792

William Short Esq.ʳ
          Hague.

... In my last of the sixth I requested you to cause ᵇᶠ · 1,625,000
to be paid to Messieurs Hoguer Grand & Com.ʸ, which I now
confirm. By a strange fatality it happens that until the present
hour I have not had the desired Meeting with the Minister of
the Marine. Many Appointments have been made, in every one
of which he has failed. But the Attention of Ministers is so
strongly call'd to the Objects round them that those which are
distant either in Time or Space make but a feeble, too feeble
Impression. It seems to me that in moral as in phisical Action,
Objects influence each other in proportion inverse as the Squares
of their Distances. Let it not be so with us, but preserve me a
place in your friendly Sentiments and believe me always —

Paris 13 August 1792

William Short Esq.ʳ
          Hague

Dear Sir,
    Common Fame will make to you her report of the Scenes which
have lately passed in this Capital. I shall not enter into details
which sooner or later must appear in the Gazettes. Neither will
I consume Time in Reflections since they would all resolve themselves into this single one, that a Ship badly ballasted has overset.
Experienced Seamen knew that it must happen, before she went
out of Port. The fresh Water Sailors by whom she was fitted and
equipt are many of them drown'd and more of them will be
drown'd. They would not be advised and they pay for their
Presumption. The Tyranny of deceased Monarchs is expiated
on their Progeny. The Ambition of those who sought rather than

the public Good their private Glory, meets what it merits and the rage of the present Hour, as it is greater than those which precede, will of course precipitate the Actors with more Rapidity towards their Fate, for there is nothing eternal but that which is founded on and supported by Justice and Truth.

Paris 20 August.

Yours of the seventh was long in coming; probably mine of the 6.th was equally delayed. You will find by it that I had agreed with the Commissioners for a considerable Payment on that Day. The Events of the Tenth ought not I think to make any Change in that Disposition.... if I could have brought the Minister of Foreign Affairs to treat about it, I would have strained a point and concluded a general Bargain for the whole of what is yet due by us to be paid by Delivery of Obligations for florins, because I think with you that the Moment was favorable; but the Commissioners could not settle this Matter and the Minister of Foreign Affairs could not find Time to think of it, so that unless I had bargain'd with myself, all Agreement was impossible. Add to this that in these same Money Matters I do not like to step out of the Line prescribed to me unless I can render effectual Service and compleatly.

Paris 27 August.

... By the account they sent me, the Ballance due was L. 6,560,145$^{\#}$ on the first of July. I have made some Observations to them on that Account, which will I think reduce the Ballance, but as we are paying 300,000 Dollars in America, it is evident that on the broadest basis the whole of the Installments now due is paid. The Question of Depreciation and consequent Compensation remains entire. I have written to Mr Jefferson that I cannot, consistently with my Instructions, treat it untill I receive further Orders, unless Necessity should compel me.

Now as to future Questions, I am quite tranquil. What was done was done by Consent both of King and Country so that all is well done, let whichever of them get the better which Fate or Fortune may chuse. If, as is very possible, we lose our future Payments, it will be a sufficient reason to withold Compensation on the past. If we do not lose, then we can come forward with a

gratuitous Sum, and let who will be King or Minister, those who
bring Money will be well receiv'd: therefore I think you may rest
in Peace as to that Affair. I do suppose however that you will be
considered here as an Aristocrat for having directed the Receipt
to be given in Part of a Debt to *his most Christian Majesty and
to be held subject to his Orders*. I doubt whether Hoguer will give it.

Paris 6 September 1792.

I did not answer yours of the eighth of August by the last post.
The Scenes then acting in Paris were the Reason of and not the
Excuse for this Omission. The same Reason still exists. I have
ordered a Subscription to be made for the *patriote français* to be
sent to you. I did not undertake to send it, and at another Time
I will tell you why. I do not go into a recital of what has lately
pass'd here. It is too shocking and among the Victims are some
whose Fate will much affect you. I must not conceal from you
that (as I am told) the venerable Made d'Amville and Monsieur
de La Rochefoucault are on their way to this City under Guard.
The Dutchess de La Rochefoucault remains I am told at La
Rocheguyon. Poor Charles Chabot [1] is no more. Knowing how
much you interest yourself in the Fate of this worthy family I
feel obliged to tell these unhappy tidings.

Extracts from Short's answers

The Hague, July 17.

... My own opinion of your superior knowlege on all subjects
– & particularly money subjects – & my knowlege of your possessing a greater degree of the confidence of government – would
necessarily make me consider it as their wish & my duty to assent to what you shall judge most advantageous for the public
interests....

The Hague, August 17.

... I determined to await the arrival of this day's French post,
not knowing but that the present change of government in

---

[1] Short's Duchess was born Alexandrine de Rohan-Chabot.

France, by the suspension of the King, might effect some change in your dispositions on this subject. Your letter of the 13.th is this moment rec.^d & seeing that you say nothing relative thereto I shall give the orders this evening conformably to your letters of Aug. 6.th & 9.th, taking it for granted you have taken such precautions in having this sum carried properly to the credit of the U.S. that there can be no dispute or difficulty hereafter, with the government which may come.... No subject ever gave me more uneasiness, as I fear I shall be blamed in America for having suffered so long delay, & yet I think the motives which influenced me cannot but be approved by everybody & particularly the President. I should infer from your letter that the compensation for depreciation was not finally settled, & if so it must be by a future government, which is what I wished above all things to be avoided.... I do not see how I could with delicacy have acted otherwise than I did in postponing the business for your zeal & abilities to take it up – & as you have not done it, the proper conclusion is that it cannot be done.... Arrange the matter finally before their final death if possible, & yet I sh.^d fear what they do posterior to the King's suspension will be regarded as illegal – or at least unconstitutional.

The Hague, Aug. 28.

... Another difficulty now proceeds from Hogguer – he wishes it to be stated in the rec.^t que le dit Sr Short le requiert à ne se désaisir de cet argent qu'avec le plein et libre consentement de S.M.T.C.ⁿ, wch I dont think w.^d be proper, for several considerations.[1] The rec.^t sh.^d be so worded as to include what is right & what is our wish, without any requisition being expressed by us – I have rec.^d this morning only the model of the rec.^t he proposes, & am to give the orders this evening –. the bankers think it a proper one & request the orders to pay – they say they have purchased the bank money requisite – I shall direct them however to insist on the kind of rec.^t mentioned, & as Hogguer wishes of course this money to pass through his hands, I cannot help thinking he will come into it – had your letters been rec.^d here before

---

[1] The said Mr Short requires him, the banker Hogguer, to hand over this money only with the full and free consent of His Most Christian Majesty.

the intelligence of the suspension there w^d have been less difficulty. As it is, I really cannot help thinking there might & w^d
be difficulty if this money was p^d to & expended by the present
reigning powers.... You say the business is straight as to us —
but dont you think if it were paid after the known suspension of
the King & expended during the *interregnum*, that there might
& w^d be difficulties with respect to it? for we sh^d certainly have
made the payment to persons whom we are not as yet authorized
to acknowlege as the government of France to whom we owe the
money.... According to the acc^t lately transmitted to me by the
Sec. of the treasury it stands thus: 34,000,000$^{\#}$ the original debt —
14,000,000$^{\#}$ of this principal due Jan. 1. 92. – & 13,953,611$^{\#}$ of
interest from w^{ch}, deducting pay^{ts} made by M. Grand on acc^t of
interest 1,600,000$^{\#}$, leaves the balance due on acc^t of interest
Jan. 1. 92, – 12,353,611$^{\#}$; the pay^{ts} made from Amsterdam &
Antwerp are to be deducted from the 26,352,611 of principal &
interest due Jan. 1792, the remaining 20,000,000$^{\#}$ falling due
successively to 1802. The debt to the farmers general & other
articles contained in the acc^t of the commissaries are questionable
& to be settled by our government, who think they have been
already paid.

The Hague, Sep. 4.

... Hogguer refuses to accept the money any other way than
as has hitherto been practised, viz, by giving a draught or bill
on the commissaries of the treasury for the am^t – or on a receipt
where it shall be expressed that at my requisition he engages
himself to hold the money until the King's free consent can be
obtained for its disposal.... you seem to have no doubt as to
the propriety of the payment, insomuch as w^d make me suppose
my doubts without foundation – if it were possible to shut my
eyes on its being neither more or less than the case of a bond given
to A. being robbed by B., or obtained by fraudulent or violent
methods – now would you or could you, knowing that, pay the
money to B. & consider yourself honestly discharged from A.?
– This manner of viewing the subject by me, on one hand —
your making no question on the other – added to its being
important for us to save an interest on six millions of livres, all

together embarrass me beyond measure. . . . I should wait still to hear from you if the time w^d admit of it — but I fear the commissaries might in that case be no more — or be removed from Paris. I shall accordingly relying on your judgment & from confidence in your knowlege of such matters direct the bankers to make the pay^{ts} to Hogguer.[1] I cannot describe to you my anxiety on this subject — but as you have made the engagement with the commissaries, & as you seem to see no danger, & even have no doubt on the subject, I cannot but subscribe thereto. . . . Such parts of the principal of the debt for instance as have been paid, would it not be proper to withdraw the original obligations given therefor, & wch are deposited in the national treasury?

Morris to Short

Paris 23 & 24 September.

. . . I come now to the Idea you express of making our adjustment with the Commissaries, and *taking up our Obligations*. . . . The Obligations are for large Sums,[2] and therefore large Sums are needful to acquit them. The two first are payable by Installments of Which one Half are due the thirty first of December 1791. The last is payable by Installments of which the first is due on the first of January 1797. Now a previous Point is to adjust the Value of those Payments, for you know that your Ideas differ very much from those entertained by Monsieur de Clavière. . .

[Morris had already written:]

Paris 9 September 1792

William Short Esq.

Hague

Dear Sir,

Yours of the fourth Instant arrived yesterday afternoon and I write now that I may be in time for the Post tomorrow. I believe the Delay of my Letter was not in this City. As the six Millions

---

[1] Then agent in Amsterdam for the Treasury in Paris.

[2] One for 18 millions, one for 10 millions and one for 6 millions of livres.

are I suppose paid, it is not necessary to dilate on that Subject. In regard to the extent of my Powers I will explain to you my Ideas thereon. At first I supposed that the management of what relates to our Debt was in some sort a needful appendage to this Mission. Mr Jefferson's Letter committing to me *expressly* an incidental Negotiation respecting a small part of it undeceiv'd me. Counting however on your Concurrence in such Measures as might appear proper I should have gone on to prepare with the Minister a Plan for the final liquidation of this Object, could I have prevail'd on him to attend to it. I have since had Occasion when I treated with the Commissaries of the Treasury, to examine a little more minutely into my Powers so far as they relate to the Debt and I found that the Management of it was committed entirely and of Course exclusively to you. Whether the knowledge they must have acquired before the present moment that nothing final is done, join'd to the Idea that you are in Spain, will induce them to address their Orders to me I know not and you will I trust excuse me for adding that I hope not. Of all things I wish to steer clear of pecuniary Transactions because they involve a Species of Responsability which is most irksome and exposes the Agent to the Chance of being call'd by every Calumniator to answer at the Bar of Public Opinion.

You tell me, in the very moment that you express an Apprehension as to the Validity of Transactions with the present Government, that you would be glad that I took up certain of our Obligations &c &c. On this head I must observe to you that the Information you have receiv'd and communicated to me respecting the State of the Account and the Objections made by the Secretary of the Treasury prove beyond a possibility of Doubt that our Government do not mean or wish that I should meddle therein. I have not receiv'd a Line from the Secretary of the Treasury of any kind. To return however to your wish, you will doubtless see with me that our Obligations do not *constitute* but only *evidence* our debt. To possess ourselves of them (therefore) otherwise than by due payment would not cancel or alter the Debt. And from the moment that you impeach the right of the present Government to receive the Money, you invalidate any Transactions respecting it which they may make.

This Observation I make for your Consideration, it cannot in any wise affect my Conduct because I am, for the reasons already mention'd, quite unauthoriz'd and indeed *indirectly* prohibited from Acting in that behalf.

Among the many Scenes of Bloodshed which have of late been exhibited you will lament the Fate of the Duke de La Rochefoucault, kill'd in the presence of his aged Mother.

[Short must have heard this tragic news with mixed feelings. It set free the lady of his dreams, but although it is said the duchess welcomed and shared his devotion she dedicates her life to the care of her mother-in-law, Duchesse d'Anville, instead of marrying her faithful American. Poor Short, engaging person and valuable public servant, this disappointment adds color to his conviction that for him nothing ever goes entirely right.]

Morris to Short

William Short Esq?   Paris 20 September 1792
              Hague
Dear Sir,

I have receiv'd your two letters of the eleventh and the fourteenth. I certainly do not mean to withdraw myself from any Situation in which either Duty or Propriety may bid me to remain. This is a general maxim which will I hope govern me thro Life. I proceed now to take up again the Payment made on Account of our Debt. I did hope that there was an End of our Correspondence on that Subject, and when you reflect that Observations respecting the legality of a Government should not be committed to Post Offices subject to its inspection, you will be sensible how disagreable it is to me to be forced into such questions, and that too about an Affair which is done and which cannot be altered unless for the worse. If you will read over my letter of the twenty third of July you will see that my doubt as to the Power of treating for the Debt with the Government of this Country is not new. Recollect also that I never saw your Instructions. I proceed to state the Facts.

On the thirtieth of July (having receiv'd on the evening of the twenty ninth a Copy of the Account from the Treasury) I informed the Commissaries that the United States had Money at Amsterdam and desired them *in order to avoid unnecessary Delay* to fix a Rate at which they would be willing to receive it. that if that Rate were convenient I would write in consequence *to make the Payment to their Agent*, and if not that I would take measures to pay them here. On the same thirtieth of July I wrote to you that I would that Day write &c. It was Post Day and therefore the letter to you was first written, and of course could not contain a Copy of the other. From a Similar Cause my letter to you of the sixth of August preceeded that of the same date to the Commissaries. I tell you '*I have agreed* with the Commissioners of the Treasury (for the present) and in Consequence I pray you will give our Bankers an Order to pay to Messieurs *Hoguer Grand and Company* the Sum of ^{b}f. 1,625,000.' Immediately after I wrote to the Commissaries 'I have given the necessary Directions for Payment of ^{b}f. 1,625,000 to Messrs H.G. & Co which at the Exchange you have mentioned is equal to 6,000,000$^{#}$. I hope that my letters may arrive in Season to prevent any other Appropriation and you will of Course cause the above Sum of 6,000,000$^{#}$ *to be carried to the Credit of the United States this Day*, saving always the Right of Counter Entry should the Payment not be compleated *instanter* at Amsterdam.' Here ended my Agency. After the Solicitude which you had expressed I could not doubt that you would cause immediate Payment to be made. I wrote however on the ninth as follows. 'In my last of the sixth I requested you to cause ^{b}f. 1,625,000 to be paid to Messieurs Hoguer Grand & Company which I now confirm.' On the tenth a Revolution in the Government took Place. Now observe that if in Consequence of my letter of the sixth you had paid the Sum mentioned, no Question could afterwards arise in the Contingency you suppose that the Present Government should be overturned and its Acts annulled. On the twenty third of August I wrote to you. 'It occurs to me that Hoguers House may feel themselves Embarrassed about this Payment, and therefore may not incline to receive the Money, *but if they do all is strait as to us.*' This letter was in Answer to yours of the seventeenth in which you express your Fears that what the Commissaries may do posterior to the King's Suspension will be regarded as illegal. On the twenty first you mention to me the kind of receipt which you had desired from Mr Hoguer, viz, that the money was paid *On Account of the Debt due his Most Christian Majesty and to be held at his Orders.* And you tell me that you supposed he would be glad of such a Clause *to have saved him from the Orders of the new unconstitutional Ministry.* In mine of the twenty seventh of August I tell you that 'I am quite tranquil as to future Questions because that what was done was done by consent both of King and Country so that all is well done.' And I express to you my Doubt whether Hoguer would give the Receipt which you had desired. On the twenty eighth of August you inform me that you have still Difficulties respecting the *receipt.* Hoguer proposing one Thing and you another, viz, that which you had before directed. On the fourth of September you inform me that you shall direct the payment to be made taking *Hoguer's Bill on the Commissaries* for the Amount. This was accordingly done on the fifth of September, a month after my letter of the sixth of August. Such are the facts. I now proceed to consider these facts under the Hypothesis first, that the present Government should continue, and in that case there is *now* no Difficulty, but if the money had been accepted by Hoguer on the terms you held out I think the Difficulty would have been very great. Secondly, if the present Government should be overturn'd; and here two possible Cases occur; first that their Acts should be deem'd valid, secondly that they should be annulled. In the first case there is still no Difficulty. In the second Case there would (as I have already said) have been none had the Payment been readily made: and the Questions which may hereafter arise have been created in Amsterdam. First you will observe that the Receipt you required was as inconsistent with the late Government as it is with the present. By the laws and Constitution, such as they existed on the ninth of August, the Debt from the United States was to the *Nation* and not to the *King* of the French, much less to *his most Christian Majesty.* Consequently it could in no wise be considered as the Completion of a Transaction which I had begun, but was a new and different Transaction, and as I (acting without Authority from our Government) could only be considered in this behalf as the Agent of you who possessed that Authority, it would follow perhaps that by your Act mine was suspended if not annulled. The Receipt which you asked was not given, and therefore the Question above stated may not perhaps be stirred; but at length instead of a Receipt, or of a payment without a receipt and which could have been establish'd by the Books of our Bankers, you have *taken a Bill on the Commissaries*. Certainly a question may be raised on this Ground whether that be the payment which I had stipulated. Thus you will see, my dear Sir, that while you were doubting of the Legality of the present Government you changed the form of what had been done with the former Government, and it gave the Air of a Payment to those whose Authority you denied. And then you desire me to do certain other things respecting this same Transaction with those same Persons whose Authority you still deny.

Now I will not enter into any question respecting the Competency of the present Government. The Corner Stone of our own Constitution is the right of the People to establish such Government as they think proper. In this Country, Reason may perhaps say one thing and Force another, but putting all that aside I think it proper to adhere to the original Nature and Form of the present Payment. First, because the Exchange is much more favorable than that which now rules, and secondly because, as is above hinted, there is a Difference of one Month's Interest on the sum paid of 6.000.000$^{\#}$.

I must before I close this too long Letter inform you that the present Ministers of this Country complain much of your intention to place the Sum in Question out of their reach, which Conduct they consider as evincing a hostile Disposition.

I wish I could give you agreable Intelligence of the State of things in this Quarter and of your Friends, but we must wait with Patience for more quiet Times. The Consequences of Anarchy begin to be felt, and that is always a preRequisite to the Establishment of Order.

Friday 17. — This Morning write. Mr Chaumont calls and he and Mr Constable dine with me, their Affairs not yet finish'd.

After Dinner I visit Lady Sutherland and when her *Monde* is gone we take Tea. It rains this Evening and is somewhat cooler. M.̃ de S.ᵗᵉ Foi, who was here this Morning, says that the Treatment of the King, Queen and royal Family is extremely ignominious. He gives Details which are painful.

Saturday 18. — Write this Day, a small Company to Dinner. Visit in the Afternoon the british Embassadress. Lord Gower is abundantly cautious. Several of the Corps diplomatique are going off. The Weather is grown cooler.

Sunday 19. — This Morning I take Mad.ᵉ de Flahaut to see her Sister in Law at Versailles. I have some Difficulties as to a Passport. Go to the Municipality of Versailles which is very polite. Company at Dinner. Chaumont on Business. Company again in the Evening. Nothing new of Importance. The Weather is pleasant.

Monday 20. — Write this Morning. Company at Dinner. Visit Lady Sutherland in the Afternoon. They have rec'd Orders to come Home and at the End of the Dispatch is a Threat if they injure the King. Some English are brought back, who were on their Way. The Weather is pleasant.

Tuesday 21. — This Morning write a little but I am incommoded. Visit Lady Sutherland to take Leave. They cant get as yet their Passport. The Venetian Embassador has been brought back and very ignominiously treated. Even his Papers examin'd as it is said *by him*. This is strong and raises in my Mind a Question whether I ought not to shew Resentment by leaving the Country. I have Company at Dinner & in the Evening I go to sup with Lady Sutherland. They can't get Passports. He is in a tearing Passion. He has burnt his Papers, which I will not do. They give me broad Hints that Honor requires of me to quit the Country. The Weather is pleasant and I am very gay, which he can hardly bear.

Wednesday 22. — Write this Morning. Dine without Company except Mons.̃ de Flahaut. In the Afternoon visit Lady Sutherland. They have receiv'd a polite Note from Monsieur Le Brun and expect to get their Passports speedily. He is so cautious that if it be not the Timidity of which he is accused it is Something very like it. The Weather was pleasant this Morning. This Evening it rains.

Thursday 23. — Write this Morning. M.ʳ Hinchman of Boston calls on me. He says the Accounts transmitted to England of what is doing here have created such Alarm that he did not dare bring to me the Dispatches with which M.ʳ Pinkney wish'd to charge him. He has receiv'd, however, along the Road all Kind of civil Treatment. He says that the Judgment I have form'd as to the Conduct which I ought to pursue is just, and that if I should quit France without just Cause it would excite much Illwill in America. I dine with the british Embassador and after Dinner the Venetian Embassador comes with M.ʳ Tronchin. This last says the Assembly have permitted the Corps diplomatique to depart, but not other Strangers. I laugh a little too much at the Distresses of the Baron Grand Cour and L.ᵈ Gower gets a little too much in a Passion with L.ᵈ Stair.¹ I visit M.ʳˢ Redwood and M.ʳˢ Blagden. Return Home later than I intended. The Weather is pleasant.

Friday 24. — This Morning I write a little; walk afterwards and then go to pay Visits, first to Madame Le Couteulx who wishes me to give her a Passport which I refuse. Next to the Dutch Embassador who is not at Home, then to the Venetian Embassador who relates his Woes, then to the british Embassador with whom I sit a little while. Lady Sutherland comes in but so late that I am oblig'd to leave her soon. I am very very sorry that she is going and she is convinced that I am. I have a large Company to Dinner. Richard calls in the Afternoon and tells me that Monsieur de La Porte is on his Way to the Place of Execution. The Weather is very pleasant.

Saturday 25. — This Morning I write and then go to see L.ᵈʸ Sutherland. They have not yet got Passports. Another Man is beheaded this Evening for *Crime de lèze Nation*. He publish'd a Newspaper against the Jacobines. This is severe at least. The Weather is pleasant.

Sunday 2I. — Write. Visit the Minister of the Marine at his Request. I have some Scruples about the Business which he proposes. He wishes me to meet the Ministers of foreign Affairs and of Contributions, which I promise to do. Call on Lady

¹ This triumph of nerves over manners paints with a master stroke the general tension.

Sutherland. They are busy packing up. Small Company at Dinner. The Weather is pleasant. Autumnal.

Monday 27. — Write. Chaumont and his friend Mori dine with me. After Dinner I go to the british Embassador's and bid them Adieu. A long Adieu perhaps. It is said here that the former bishop of Châlons has received a Letter on the Part of the Duke of Brunswick desiring him to mention whether he wishes the Episcopal Palace &c.ª to be respected. They expect soon to be there. If Verdun surrenders as Longwi has done the foreign Troops will soon be here. The Weather is warm with small Rain. I find Company at Home which stays late. One of them, S.ᵗᵉ Croix, comes after I am in Bed to ask an Asylum. The Municipality are in Pursuit of him.

Tuesday 28 August. — Write. Stay at Home all Day. It is said that Verdun and Metz are both taken. That the prussian Army is at S.ᵗ Menehoud and that the Couriers are all confin'd which bring the News. I think there can be little Use in confining them because the taking of Towns can't be kept secret. We shall know more by & bye. The Weather is pleasant in the Afternoon. This Morning it rain'd.

Wednesday 29. — Go this Morning to Monsieur Lebrun's.[1] The Minister of Contributions Monsieur Clavière, and Monsieur Monge the Minister of the Marine meet me here at the Hôtel of foreign Affairs. They wish me to enter into a Contract to furnish $400,000 in America for the Use of S.ᵗ Domingo. I shew them many Reasons why I cannot and among others tell them that I am not authoriz'd to treat with them. This touches them unpleasantly. I add that I will write and recommend the Matter strongly to the Ministers of the United States but that is not what they want. Clavière is much vexed. I have Company to Dinner. The Dutch Embassador tells me he has receiv'd his Orders and shall ask for his Passports Tomorrow. In the Evening a Number of Persons enter, upon an Order to examine my House for Arms said to be hidden in it. I tell them that they shall not examine — that there are no Arms and that they must seize the Informer that I may bring him to Punishment. I am oblig'd to

---

[1] New Minister of Foreign Affairs.

be very peremptory and at length get Rid of them. Just after
they are gone Monsieur de Ste Croix ^{1} comes in. He is a lucky
Man. He was hidden, but the Order to search all Houses brings
him hither. We are it seems to have another Visit this Night.
The Weather is pleasant.

Thursday 30. — This Morning I write. Dine at Home. The
News of the Aristocrats is that the Troops of the Duke of Brunswic
make Excursions as far as Châlons. That Luckner's Army is
surrounded, Verdun taken. Ste Foi, who comes in the Evening,
tells me that the Bombardment of Verdun has been heard in the
Neighbourhood. St Pardou says that 600 Men are ordered for a
secret Expedition as on Saturday next and he fears that it is to
carry off the royal Family. The Commissaire de Section call'd
on me this Morning and behav'd very well. The Weather is
pleasant. I learn that many People have been taken up last
Night.

Morris to Jefferson

No. 9   Paris 30 August 1792

Thomas Jefferson Esqr.
                        Philadelphia

Dear Sir,

My last (N° 8) was of the twenty second Instant. In (N° 6)
I mention'd to you that I had not been able to adjust with the
Minister of foreign Affairs the Rate of Exchange which should

---

^{1} August Tenth, first, not last crisis in history when distracted foreigners
will seek American aid. Diplomatic immunity of an Envoy's roof, limited
to household and staff, does not include other French nationals. Old Flahaut
is not the only one in deadly peril who risks compromising the American
Minister. Sainte-Croix, eight days Minister of the Crown, too terrified for
tact, is more fortunate than considerate when he rushes in for asylum. Bal-
timorean Thomas Waters Griffith reports that he found Morris after the Tuileries earthquake surrounded by weeping women and by men like d'Estaing who
had fought for America. Aware of the risk to himself, of a gay courage, fatal-
ist, believer in Providence, Morris is not a man to panic and has too much
heart to throw other men to the head-hunters. Cool, courtly, sententious, a
restorative to frantic fears and intense emotions of his uninvited guests.

govern the Payments made & making in America on Account of our Debt to France. And that I had not been able to see the Minister of Marine to adjust with him the Sums which the Assembly had determin'd to apply out of that Debt to the Use of St Domingo. You will have seen by my correspondence with the Commissioners of the Treasury that the last payment of six Millions will nearly ballance the Account, according even to their Statement of it, over and above the 400,000 Dollars which are to be paid at Philadelphia during the current Year.

A few Days since, Mr Monge, the present Minister of the Marine, desir'd an Interview and at our Meeting presented me a regular Contract for Payment of 800,000 Dollars as being equivalent to the 4,000,000[#] of livres which the Assembly had appropriated as abovemention'd. I will not trouble you with the Conversation, because it ended in a Request on his Part to meet Mr Le Brun, the Minister of Foreign Affairs, and Mr Clavière, the Minister of Public Contributions. This Meeting took Place yesterday by their Appointment. The same form of Agreement was again produced and Mr Clavière, who was principal Spokesman, mentioned my signing it as a thing of course. I told him that I had been authorized to settle with the late Government the Exchange of one half of that Sum already paid & paying on this very Account. He spoke of such Settlement as the easiest thing in the World, and advanc'd on the Subject exactly those Principles which Mr Short had refus'd to be govern'd by, and rejected as visionary those which Mr Short had stated as just, and which I think are reasonable and right. The great object however was to get the Money, and *Congress* was to fix the Exchange. I told them (which is very true) that I felt a very sincere desire to furnish Aid to that unhappy Colony, and had done every Thing in my Power to comply with the wish of the Legislature in that respect, but in vain. That at last our Bankers in Holland, being extremely anxious to discharge themselves of the large Sums which had for Months been lying in their Hands, their own Commissaries of the Treasury being also desirous to receive, Mr Short (to whom the management of that business had been committed by the United States) being also solicitous that the Payments should be made, I had desired him to place in the Hands of the

Bankers nam'd by the Commissaries an Equivalent of 6,000,000 livres by which means the Instalments of our Debt already due were overpaid. That of course any Advances now made must be on Account of those Installments which are to become due hereafter. That I have no Instructions respecting them, for reasons I had already assign'd, and that of consequence if I should enter into the Agreement they wish'd I should probably be blam'd for exceeding the line prescribed to me. That there remain'd however another Point worthy of their Attention, which was that my Agreement would be in itself void because I had no Powers to treat with the present Government. It follow'd therefore that the Ministers of the United States would feel themselves as much at Liberty as if nothing had been done, and act according to their own Ideas of the Object, distinctly from my Engagements; that it would be equally useful to them and more proper in me, to state the whole matter to you in the first Instance, and that I would add my earnest request to make the desired Payment. This however did not at all suit their Ideas. Mr Clavière made many observations on the Nature of our Debt and the manner in which it had accrued. He said that the United States would certainly act in a different Manner towards the present Government than the Monarchs of Europe did. That it was impossible I should have any Difficulty if I inclin'd to do what they ask'd, and then concluded by asking me peremptorily whether I would or would not. His Language and Manner was such as naturally to excite some little Indignation, and altho I would pardon much to a Man whose Stockjobbing Life had not much qualified him for a Station in which Delicacy of Manner and Expression are almost essential, yet I could not submit to an Indignity in my Person towards the Country I represent. I told him therefore that I did not understand what he meant to say. My Countenance I believe spoke the Rest of my Statement and led him to say, in Explanation, that it was necessary for them to have some positive Engagement because otherwise they must make provision for the Service from another Source, and then he again express'd his conviction that the United States would recognize them, and at any rate would not disavow the Engagements which I might make. I told him that it was not proper for me (a Servant) to pretend to decide on what would be the opinion of my Masters. That I should wait their Orders and obey them when receiv'd. That the present Government might collect my Sentiments from my Conduct. That I could not possibly take on me to judge questions of such Importance. That I would do every thing I could with propriety and again repeated my Offer which they would not listen to and I left them not a little displeas'd, if I may judge from Appearances by no means equivocal.

The Dutch Embassador, who din'd with me, told me that he had receiv'd his Orders, and should ask for Passports this Day. The British Embassador went off two days ago and Mr Lindsay, their Minister, intends going tomorrow. He offers to take my letters to Mr Pinkney to whom I shall enclose this to be forwarded to you.

Last Evening between ten and eleven I receiv'd a Visit from some *Commissaires de Section* who came in Consequence of a Denunciation made by some Blockhead or Rascal that I had Arms conceal'd in my House. I made them sensible of the Impropriety of their Conduct, told them that I had no Arms and that if I had they should not touch one of them. That in such case they must apply to me thro' their Minister of foreign Affairs, and ask me to cede them. I insisted that the Man who had presum'd to make this Denunciation should be seized, and then I would demonstrate the falsehood that he might be punish'd. The Scene finish'd by Apologies on their Part. Last night there was a general Visit and Search throughout the Town for Arms, and I presume for Persons also. It still continues. Between nine and ten, the Commissary call'd on me with many Apologies and took a Note of my Reply so that we met and parted good friends.

You will see by all this my dear Sir that I have sufficient Cause to take Offence and depart if I were so inclin'd; but I will stay, if possible, so as to preserve to you the most perfect Liberty of Action. I do not indeed feel offended at what is done by the People, because they cannot be supposed to understand the Law of Nations and because they are in a State of fury which is inconceivable and which leaves them liable to all Impressions and renders them capable of all Excesses. I shall endeavour nevertheless to preserve the proper firmness and let what will happen I hope that tho' my Friends should have Occasion to lament my Fate, they will never be oblig'd to blush for my Conduct.

[The explanation is graft, a word not yet invented. Morris's reluctance to fall in with the proposals of the French Ministers was largely because he smelt a peculative rat in their extreme urgency, and so it turned out. The whole plan was based on handing this portion of the debt over to French agents in America, to be spent there on American goods and provisions for the distressed islands; but what Clavière and his friends wanted was to get the money into their own hands in France and feather their nests with odds and ends of bribes and commissions. With Ministries falling like ninepins they had little time to lose in discussion.

Here is the letter which excited Morris's indignation, followed by his reply:]

Lebrun to Morris

Paris le 30 Août 1792
L'an 4ᵉ de la Liberté.

Je ne vous rappelle, Monsieur, aujourdhui le point essentiel sur lequel nous nous sommes entretenus dans notre conférence d'hier, que pour vous convaincre de la nécessité de prévenir les inconvéniens majeurs qui résulteraient de la prétendue insuffisance de vos pouvoirs. En partant du principe que vous n'êtes pas autorisé par vos instructions à traiter avec le nouveau Gouvernement françois, vos fonctions seroient nulles dans ce moment ci, et nos colonies dont l'urgence des approvisionnemens exige notre Sollicitude, notre activité et notre Zèle, seroient dans le cas d'en manquer.

J'ai l'honneur de vous observer, Monsieur, que nous avons une trop haute idée des Sentiments d'Amitié et d'attachement que portent les États Unis à la france, pour croire que leur représentant pût et dût hésiter sous quelque prétexte que ce puisse être, à contribuer au Succès d'un arrangement entamé par Mr Short et dont la continuation a été confiée à vos Soins.

La Suspension du Roi de ses fonctions ne dois rien changer,

Monsieur, aux dispositions d'une nation avec qui nous avons des liaisons d'amitié et d'intérêt, et dont l'indépendance est notre ouvrage. Elle connoit tous les efforts et les sacrifices que nous avons fait pour la lui procurer; nous ne le disons point pour émouvoir votre reconnoissance mais pour exciter votre bonne Volonté: Je crois Monsieur, que vous la deviez à la nation françoise avant l'évènement actuel, et que si vous la manifestiez dans ce moment-ci vous rempliriez assurément le Voeu de vos Commettans.

Pour me résumer, Monsieur, je dois vous dire que le Roi n'est que suspendu; D'ailleurs le Gouvernement étant immuable et devant toujours subsister, aucun représentant ne peut, sans un ordre exprès de sa Cour ou de ses Commettants, se refuser à traiter directement avec lui. Depuis l'établissement du nouveau Gouvernement, vous n'avez point reçu de vos Commettants aucun ordre qui pût rompre cette mesure; vous pouvez donc, Monsieur, faire remplir l'engagement pris par Mr Short relativement aux huit cent mille dollars qui seront tenus dans l'amérique septentrionale à notre disposition pour les achats nécessaires à l'approvisionnement de nos Colonies. Si les faits que je viens de vous détailler ne vous engagent point à changer la détermination que vous nous fites connoître hier, je vous prie de vouloir bien motiver votre refus dans la réponse que j'attendrai de votre part, et qui me servira de direction.

Le Ministre des affaires étrangères

LE BRUN

A Paris le 1 Septembre 1792

Monsieur
       Le Brun.

Monsieur,

Votre lettre du 30 Août ne m'a été rendue qu'hier à quatre heures. Je vais y répondre avec les plus grands détails, et dans le plus court délai possible. Vous me faites l'honneur de me dire *que je puis faire remplir l'engagement pris par Monsieur Short relativement aux huit cent mille Dollars qui seront tenus dans l'Amérique Septentrionale à votre Disposition pour les Achats nécessaires à l'approvisionnement de vos Colonies.* Je vous ai déjà observé,

Monsieur, et je vous repète dans ce Moment, que le Soin de faire les paiemens de notre dette à la france a été confié à Monsieur Short, et *que jamais je n'ai été autorisé à m'en mêler.* J'ose ajouter Monsieur, que vous avez dans vos propres Bureaux les preuves de ce que je viens de vous avancer. Vos prédecesseurs m'ont dit avoir reçu du Ministre de la France à Philadelphie la Copie d'une lettre que Monsieur Hamilton, Ministre de nos finances, lui avoit écrit en datte du huit Mars. Vous verrez Monsieur, que Monsieur Hamilton y dit. 'D'après les Instructions qui ont été données à Monsieur Short, d'après les progrès connus de ces Opérations, et par quelques Passages d'une de ses lettres du douze novembre dernier, *Je conclus avec Certitude* qu'il a payé tous les Intérêts arriérés et remboursemens de Capitaux échus jusqu'a la fin de l'année 1791.' Il ajoute (a l'égard des quatre cent mille Dollars qu'il est convenu de payer pendant l'Année 1792) '*que cette Somme sera une Anticipation de ce qui doit écheoir à l'avenir.*' C'est ici que je crois devoir vous observer Monsieur que tous les Engagemens pris par Monsieur Short seront remplis par les états unis avec la plus grande exactitude.

Je dois aussi Monsieur vous prier de fixer votre Attention sur un autre fait très important que j'ai eu l'honneur de vous exposer. Monsieur Short avoit laissé entre les mains de nos Banquiers à Amsterdam de très fortes Sommes pendant plusieurs mois, en attendant toujours les Arrangemens définitifs à l'égard des paiemens; Arrangemens qui n'ont pas eu lieu pendant sa mission. Le 30 Juillet dernier j'ai exposé aux Commissaires de la Trésorerie nationale l'impossibilité où je me trouvois de rien conclure à cet égard, jusqu'à ce que j'eusse reçu les Ordres de ma Cour. À cet époque Monsieur Short, de son côté, me pressoit de faire recevoir par les Commissaires de la Trésorerie l'argent qui étoit à sa Disposition, et Messieurs les Commissaires me pressoient aussi de faire ce même paiement. En Conséquence, ayant convenu avec eux du Change auquel il devoit être réglé pour le Moment, et sauf toujours les Arrangemens définitifs à faire avec la personne qui seroit autorisée à cet Effet par les États Unis, j'ai prié Monsieur Short par une lettre du 6 Août de donner Ordre à nos Banquiers de payer à Messieurs Hoguer Grand et Compagnie, Banquiers designés par Messieurs les Commissaires de la

Trésorerie, la Somme d'un Million six cents vingt cinq mille florins de banque, laquelle au dit Change revient à six Millions Argent de france.

Vous aurez la bonté d'observer Monsieur que selon le Compte de Messieurs les Commissaires il étoit dû à la France au premier Juillet dernier une Somme de six Millions et demi. Que dans cette Somme se trouvoit comprise celle de £3,157.758# qui n'entroit pas dans les Calculs de Monsieur Hamilton, et dont une partie au moins est encore à vérifier. Vous voudrez bien remarquer aussi que dans ce même compte les paiemens qu'on fait actuellement en Amérique ne sont point compris, ce qui fait encore un Objet de plus de deux Millions. Il en résulte que dans tout état de Choses les Remboursemens à faire jusqu'à présent, sont tous acquittés. Je vous observerai encore Monsieur, que je ne suis nullement autorisé de disposer des sommes qui étoient ou qui pourroient être entre les Mains de nos Banquiers à Amsterdam, et que tout ce que j'ai fait, ou que j'ai pu faire, a été de m'addresser à Monsieur Short, qui seul reste toujours le Maître à cet égard.

Il me reste encore Monsieur à vous rapeller un autre fait très important et qui se trouve constaté dans cette même lettre de Monsieur Hamilton, qui est que, vu les dépenses extraordinaires qu'occasionne notre guerre contre les Sauvages, il lui étoit impossible de promettre le paiement de la Somme de 400000 Dollars à des Époques plus rapprochées que celles qui y sont marquées, et dont la dernière est au premier Décembre 1792. Vous pouvez juger Monsieur d'après l'exposée que je viens de vous faire, s'il m'est possible d'aller plus loin que l'offre que je vous ai faite, de faire auprès de ma Cour les plus vives Solicitations pour l'engager à vous accorder le Secours que vous me demandez. Offre que vous avez refusé d'accepter.

Quant à la Suspension du Roi, Monsieur, vous sentirez sûrement, comme moi, qu'un Ministre n'a pas le droit d'exprimer un Sentiment quelconque sans les Ordres préalables de sa Nation. Et lorsque je vous en ai parlé je n'ai voulu vous en exprimer aucun, mais seulement, lorsque vous insistates, vous faire appercevoir que s'il eut été possible que j'eusse risqué de me compromettre en consentant aux Arrangemens pécuniaires que vous désiriez et qui ne m'ont pas été confiés par ma Cour, vous ne pour-

riez pas réclamer auprès d'elle l'exécution de mes engagemens,
parceque, tout en reconnoissant votre Autorité, elle pourroit vous
répondre que vous auriez dû attendre mes nouvelles lettres de
Créance.

Dans la lettre que j'ai eu l'honneur de vous écrire le 21 Août,
je vous ai prévenu Monsieur que mon Intention étoit de rester à
Paris, mais le Style de la votre du 30 Août m'impose la nécessité
de vous demander un passeport pour sortir de la France. Je
voyagerai avec mes Chevaux à petite Journée et je prendrai la
route de l'Angleterre par Calais. Je laisse ici ma Maison, mon
Secrétaire & une partie de mes Gens en attendant les Ordres des
États Unis.

[*Le Brun to Morris*]   [*Translations:*]

Paris, August 30, 1792
4th year of Liberty.

I remind you, Sir, today of the essential point which we discussed in our conference of yesterday, only to convince you
of the necessity of obviating the major inconveniences which
would result from the pretended insufficiency of your powers.
According to the principle that you are not authorized by
your instructions to treat with the new French Government
your functions would be nil at this moment and our colonies,
whose urgent need of supplies demands our solicitude, our
activity and our zeal, would risk being left unprovided.

I have the honor to observe to you, Sir, that we have too
high an idea of the sentiments of friendship and attachment
which the United States bear to France to believe that their
representative could or should hesitate under any pretext
whatsoever to contribute to the success of an arrangement
begun by Mr Short and whose continuation has been confided to your care.

The King being suspended from his functions must change
nothing, Sir, in the dispositions of a nation with which we
have links of friendship and of interest and whose independence is our work. She knows all the efforts and sacrifices we
made to procure it for her; we do not say this to stir your
gratitude but to excite your goodwill. I think Sir, that you

owed it to the French Nation before the present event and that if you were to manifest it at this moment you would be surely carrying out the wishes of your constituents.

To sum up, Sir, I must tell you that the King is only suspended; moreover, the Government being immutable and always existent no representative may, without an express order from his Court or his constituents, refuse to treat directly with it. Since the establishment of the new Government you have not received from your employers any order which could break off this measure; you can then Sir, cause the engagement to be fulfilled that was entered into by Mr Short concerning the eight hundred thousand dollars to be held in North America at our disposal for the purchases necessary to the provisioning of our Colonies. If the facts which I have just detailed do not lead you to alter the determination which you made known to us yesterday, I beg you to state the motives of your refusal in the answer which I shall expect from you and which will serve me as a guide.

The Minister of Foreign Affairs,
Le Brun.

Paris 1 September, 1792.

Monsieur Le Brun
Sir,

Your letter of August 30th was not delivered to me until yesterday at four o'clock. I answer it in great detail and with the shortest possible delay. You do me the honor to tell me *that I can cause the engagement to be fulfilled that was entered into by Mr Short concerning the eight hundred thousand dollars to be held in North America at your disposal for the purchases necessary to the provisioning of your Colonies.* I have already observed to you Sir, and now repeat, that the charge of making the payments on our debt to France has been entrusted to Mr Short and *that I have never been authorized to act in the matter.* I venture to add, Sir, that you have in your own offices proof of what I have just asserted. Your predecessors told me they had received from the Minister of France at Philadelphia copy of a letter which Mr Hamilton, Minister of our Finances, had written to him, dated eighth of March. You will see Sir, that Mr Hamilton therein says: 'From the instructions given to Mr Short, from the known progress of these operations and by some passages in one of his letters of twelfth November last, I conclude with certainty that he has paid off all the back interest and reimbursements of capital due up to the end of the year 1791.' He adds (in regard to the four hundred thousand dollars agreed to be paid during the year 1792) 'that this sum will be an anticipation of what will fall due in future.' And here I feel obliged to observe to you Sir, that all engagements taken by Mr Short will be met by the United States with the utmost exactitude.

I must also, Sir, beg you to turn your attention to another very important fact which I had the honor to communicate to you. Mr Short left in the hands of our bankers at Amsterdam during several months very substantial sums, pending the final arrangements in regard to payments, arrangements not made during the period of his Mission. On the 30th of last July I explained to the Commissioners of the National Treasury the impossibility in which I found myself of concluding anything in that respect until I had received orders from my Court. At that time Mr Short, on his side, was urging me to get the Commissioners of the Treasury to receive the money which lay at his disposal and those gentlemen were also urging me to make this payment. Consequently, having agreed with them on the exchange at which it should for the moment be settled and saving always the final arrangements to be made with the person who should be authorized to that effect by the United States, I begged Mr Short in a letter of August 6th to give orders to our bankers to pay Messrs Hoguer Grand and Company, bankers designated by the Commissioners of the Treasury, the sum of one million six hundred and twenty-five thousand florins banco, which at the said exchange comes to six millions, French money.

You will have the goodness to observe Sir, that according to the accounts of the Commissioners there was due to France on the first of last July a sum of six million and a half. That in this sum was included one of £3,157,758 which did not enter into the calculation of Mr Hamilton and of which a portion at least remains to be verified. You will be pleased also to remark that in these same accounts the payments now being made in America are not included, a matter of more than two million. It results that in any case the repayments due up to date are all discharged. I will point out to you once more Sir, that I am by no means authorized to dispose of sums which have been or may again be in the hands of our bankers at Amsterdam and that all I have done or could do was to refer to Mr Short who alone is still master in this respect.

There remains Sir, another fact to remind you of, very important, which is stated in this same letter from Mr Hamilton; that considering the extraordinary expense occasioned by our war against the Indians it was impossible for him to provide payment of the sum of 400,000 dollars any sooner than the designated epochs, of which the last is December first, 1792. You can judge Sir, by this recital of facts, whether it be possible for me to go beyond my offer to you to make strong representations to my Court urging it to grant the succor you ask. An offer which you have refused to accept.

As to the suspension of the King, Sir, you will surely feel, as I do, that a Minister has no right to express any sentiment whatever without the previous orders of his Nation. And when I spoke of it to you I was expressing none but only, when you insisted, wished to make you see that even if I could risk compromising myself by consenting to the pecuniary arrangements you desired and which had not been confided to me by my Court,[1] you would be unable to claim from

[1] Lebrun's 'no representative may without express order from his court or his constituents refuse to treat directly,' etc., may have been only echoed in Morris's 'pecuniary arrangements not confided to me by my court.' Quotation marks would have made this clear. Or, jealously upholding the dignity of his infant nation as a great Sovereign State with Congress, from whom he took his orders, as the sovereign power within that State, he may have written 'Court' not in quotation, bravado, or inadvertence, but in all good faith. The slip pursues him and on both sides the Atlantic capital is made of such an unre-

her the fulfillment of engagements taken by me because, while acknowledging your authority, she might have answered that you should have waited for my new credentials.

In the letter I had the honor to write you on August 21st I informed you Sir, that it was my intention to remain in Paris, but the tone of yours of the 30th August imposes on me the necessity of asking for a passport to take me out of France. I shall travel with my own horses by short stages and shall take the route to England via Calais. I leave here my house, my Secretary and some of my servants while awaiting the orders of the United States.

Morris to Jefferson

No. 8   Paris 22ᵈ August 1792
Thomas Jefferson Esqʳ
                    Philadelphia
Dear Sir

My last (Nº 7) was of the seventeenth Instant. In Nº 6 of the 16ᵗʰ I mention'd the Revolution of the tenth. I suggested my Idea that the Force commanded by Monsieur de La Fayette would not be brought to immediate Action, and that in such Case he and his friends had Nothing to hope for. He, as you will learn, encamp'd at Sedan and Official Accounts of last Night inform us that he has taken Refuge with the Enemy. Thus his circle is compleated. He has spent his fortune on a Revolution and is now crush'd by the wheel which he put in motion. He lasted longer than I expected. Some other Officers tried to influence their Troops in favor of the late Constitution but without Effect. They are, it seems, yet to learn that an Officer has never compleat possession of his Soldiers till rigid Discipline has led them by the Hand over Fields of Glory in which he has

---

publican utterance. Was his friend the Venetian Ambassador using 'Court' as a conventional term for 'government'? He represented a free Republic which will finish a six-hundred-year run five years later when Bonaparte hands it over gagged and bound to Austria. Meanwhile, by demanding his passports, he had shown the Venetian Republic's disapproval of August Tenth.

shar'd in their Danger and pointed them the Path which leads
to Triumph. These Scenes are yet remote but if the combin'd
Powers cannot succeed in the present Plans, they must hereafter
take Place. In the mean time much Suspicion, much Jealousy
and many victims are all in the natural Order of Things. I do
not find that the Prince of Brunswic has made those rapid Movements which the existent State of things required, and he looses
much by Delay. He probably understands too well the business
of War and his high Station requires a Man in whom the accomplish'd General should be but a secondary Talent. I cannot for a
Moment suppose a possibility of beating him with the french
Army, if Army it can be call'd where there is no discipline, but
if he will not commit himself a little to Fortune it appears to
me a very easy Matter to wear away the Time till Winter shuts
the Theatre. We are now far advanc'd in August and he has at
most three Months before him.

The Day before Yesterday the British Embassador receiv'd
a Dispatch from his Court which he immediately transmitted to
the present Minister of Foreign Affairs and at the same Time ask'd
for Passports. This Dispatch has not yet been communicated
to the Assembly because it runs rather Counter to Expectations
which had been rais'd, and of course the public mind is not duly
prepared. The purport of this Dispatch is that Britain has determin'd on a strict Neutrality, that she means to preserve it,
and therefore as his letters of Credence are to the King now
dethron'd he had best come away. To this is subjoin'd a Hope
that nothing will happen to the King or his Family *because that
would excite the Indignation of all Europe.* This Dispatch turn'd
into plain English is shortly, that the British Court resent what
is already done and will make War immediately if the Treatment
of the King be such as to call for or to justify Measures of
Extremity.

The different Embassadors and Ministers are all taking their
Flight and if I stay I shall be alone. I mean however to stay
unless circumstances should command me away because in the
admitted Case that my letters of Credence are to the Monarchy
and not to the Republic of France it becomes a Matter of indifference whether I remain in this Country or go to England during

the Time which may be needful to obtain your Orders or to produce a Settlement of Affairs here. Going hence, however, would look like taking part against the late Revolution, and I am not only unauthoriz'd in this respect, but I am bound to suppose that if the great Majority of the Nation adhere to the new form the United States will approve thereof; because in the first place we have no right to prescribe to this Country the Government they shall adopt, and next because the Basis of our own Constitution is the indefeasible Right of the People to establish it.

Among those who are leaving Paris is the Venetian Embassador. He was furnish'd with Passports from the Office of Foreign Affairs, but he was nevertheless stopp'd at the Barrier, was conducted to the Hôtel de Ville, was there question'd for Hours and his Carriages examin'd and search'd. This Violation of the Rights of Embassadors could not fail (as you may suppose) to make Impression. It has been broadly hinted to me that the Honor of my Country and my own require that I should go away. But I am of a different Opinion, and rather think that those who give such Hints are somewhat influenc'd by Fear. It is true that the Position is not without Danger, but I presume that when the President did me the honor of naming me to this Embassy it was not for my personal Pleasure or Safety, but to promote the Interests of my Country. These therefore I shall continue to pursue to the best of my Judgment, and as to Consequences they are in the Hand of God.

[The American Minister to Portugal now unburdened himself of a big idea; even had it been practicable, French soil was clear of the enemy before his letter got to Paris. Discretion makes disappointing newsmongers, and the vagueness of Morris's answer, essential to its safe passage, must have exasperated in out-of-the-way Lisbon.]

David Humphreys to Morris

Lisbon. Augt 17th 1792

My dear Sir

As I have had no direct occasion of troubling you with any letter since you were placed in a public Character at the Court of France I have foreborne to offer ceremoneous congratulations on the subject. Even now I am determined to make no formal affair of it. So take in the simplicity of Soul, with which they are offered, my best wishes for your happiness wherever you may be, together with assurances on my part of a desire to co-operate with you in any thing that may be useful to the Public or yourself while we may remain abroad. An idea lately suggested itself to me, that, if the Austrian & Prussian armies should really enter France, they might be very much weakened & perhaps ruined by desertion, if suitable, secure & alluring measures could be taken to encourage it. Nothing, in my judgment, would be so likely to effect this as for the Government of France to provide passages, at its own Expense for all such non commissioned officers & soldiers as should chuse to go & settle in America. I forbear to enter into any details of a Plan, since easy & cheap means will occur, if the Project should be deemed feasible. The Experiment, at least, would cost little. Addresses, or Proclamations, in their own language, might be spread among them in spite of all the Efforts of their officers to hinder it. In these, the hardships of their situation in being dragged from home to fight against innocent People with whom they have no quarrel, might be contrasted with the benefits they will enjoy in becoming free Citizens of the U.S. They might be told what numbers of Germans chose to remain in America after the last war. They might be told how many of their Countrymen, & perhaps acquaintances & relations, once in no better circumstances than themselves, are now happy, independent & rich in Pensylvania & other parts of the U.S. Perhaps that project being known to the Austrian & Prussian Cabinets, might have some influence in deterring them from sending, or at least continuing Armies in France. For they must inevitably be under some apprehensions lest their Troops should take the French political fever either the natural way or by inoculation. The idea is just hinted in the enclosed letters to the Mar. de La Fayette & the D. de Rochefoucault, as merely a Provisional Project, to be mentioned or not, as circumstances may justify. I beg you will have the goodness to cause these letters to be delivered to their address.

You are now in a Theatre of the most important action, that can easily be conceived. Every thing seems hastening to a Crisis. Every Post, every Packet, every moment, we expect to hear of great events. The confusions & parties in Paris appear more alarming than the danger from foreign force; but I hope better things from the Provinces & People at large. We have here but too few well wishers to the French Revolution. There are, however, several of the English in public office, as well as in the Factory, who entertain liberal & just ideas on the Subject. Of the French in public Character here, I can say nothing. etc. etc. etc.

My dear Sir,
        Your most obedient humble Servant.
                       D. HUMPHREYS.

Morris to David Humphreys

                              Paris 6 Dec.[r] 1792
David Humphreys Esq.

My dear Sir,
Your Letter of the 17.th of August has been very long coming to me. Before its Arrival the Duke de La Rochefoucault had perish'd and Monsieur de La Fayette had been obliged to fly. I therefore have not forwarded to him the Letter but still hold it subject to your Order. That for the Duc de La Rochefoucault I committed to the Flames.

In respect to the State of public Affairs here, I can say nothing which would gratify common Curiosity, much less convey useful Information. Things of a public Nature are very public. As to such as are kept or attempted to be kept secret, every different Person has a different Tale and a different Opinion, which last depends more on the Observer than on the Thing itself. In a misty Morning Objects appear not in their true Shape, and every Eye beholds the Thing it pleases, because Imagination comes in to supply the Defect of Vision. I wish my Expectations with respect to this Country could keep pace with my Wishes, for I wish them all Manner of Honor and Felicity and that from the Bottom of my Heart, but yet that Heart has many sinister bodings and reason would strive in vain to dispel the Gloom which always thickens when she exerts her Sway. — Farewell, my dear Sir, continue to me your good will and when occasion offers express it by the Conveyance of such Tidings as may meet your Notice.

Friday 31. — Write. Just before Dinner I receive an insulting Letter from the Minister of foreign Affairs. In the Evening the bishop d'Autun tells me it is written by Brissot and that their Intention is to force me into an Acknowlegement of the present Governm^{t}. He urges me to go away because all others of the Corps diplomatique go and because I shall in staying be exposed to all the insidious Malevolence of bad Men. He recites a Scene which past in his Presence and which is alike shocking and ridiculous. He tells me that there is a Division already among the Rulers here. He communicates the Views of those who in the natural Course of Things must become strongest. I give him my Reasons for thinking that they pursue an impracticable Object.

SEPTEMBER 1792

Saturday September 1. — I employ the greater Part of this Morning in making a Reply to the Letter of Mr Lebrun and copying it. In the Evening I read both, or rather, shew them to the Bishop d'Autun who approves much of my Answer and observes that the Letter is both absurd and impertinent. I had sent for Swan and told him that his friend Brissot, instead of promoting, had spoilt his Business and would drive me out of the Country. He

says he laments this last Point much, as a few Days must overset
the present Establishment. I rather think he is mistaken as to
the Time at least, and there may be yet many Overturns before
there is a settled Government.

Sunday 2.^d — This Morning I go out on Business. Mad.^e de
Flahaut takes the same Opportunity to visit her Friends; on our
Return we hear, or rather see, a Proclamation. She enquires into
it and learns that the Enemy are at the Gates of Paris,[1] which
cannot be true. She is taken ill, being affected for the Fate of
her Friends. I observe that this Proclamation produces Terror
and Despair among the People. This Afternoon they announce
the Murder of Priests who had been shut up in the *Carmes*. They
then go to the Abbaie and murder the Prisoners there. This is
horrible.

Monday 3.^d — The murdering continues all Day. I am told
that there are about eight hundred Men concerned in it. The
Minister of Parma and Embassadress of Sweden have been
stopped as they were going away.

Tuesday 4. — The Murders continue. The Prisoners in the
Bicêtre defend themselves and the Assailants try to stifle and
drown them. A certain Mr Bertrand of the Cavalry comes here.
Mad.^e had sent for him to give him a Compensation for his
Kindness in saving her Husband. I collect from him that Paris
waits but the Moment to surrender. He does not say so, but if
I may judge from strong Indications, the Cavalry mean to join
the Invader. Several Strangers who call on me complain that
they cannot get Passports. It is said that as soon as the Prisoners
are demolish'd the Party now employ'd in executing them mean
to attack the Shop Keepers. The Assembly have official Accounts

---

[1] This proclamation helps create desired panic; three days of domiciliary
visits have crammed the prisons; Danton makes his '*Toujours de l'audace*'
speech, but a fantastic question, politically inspired, is going the rounds: 'Shall
we march to the frontier and leave our families at the mercy of priests and
aristocrats who may break prison and kill them all?' Hence the prison massacres without which Collot d'Herbois declared the Convention could never
have been elected — meaning his own type of deputy who will sit on its 'Mountain,' for the fight is on between Commune and Gironde. Sixteen hundred and
fourteen defenceless prisoners victimized and recorded, 438 more missing;
the actual murderers reckoned at 150, centre of savage crowds among whom
move heroic rescuers in disguise.

that Verdun is taken and, it is said, Stenay also. The Weather is grown very cool and this Afternoon and Evening it rains hard.

Wednesday 5. — Mr P. tells me that the Ministry and secret Committee are in Amaze. Verdun, Stenai and Clermont are taken. The Country submits and joins the Enemy. The Party of Robespierre has vowed the Destruction of Brissot. The Bishop d'Autun tells me that he has seen one of the Commission extraordinaire (i.e.) secret Committee, who tells him that there is the most imminent Danger. I was told that one of the principal Jacobines had exprest his Fears, or rather Despair, not so much on Account of the Enemy Force as of their internal Divisions.

Thursday 6. — There is Nothing new this Day. The Murders continue and the Magistrates swear to protect Persons and Property. The Weather is pleas.^t.

Friday 7. — I write this Morning. The News from the Armies are rather encourag.^g to the new Government. The bishop d'Autun tells me that he hopes to get his Passport and urges me to procure one for myself and quit Paris. He says he is perswaded that those who now rule mean to quit Paris and take off the King, that their Intention is to destroy the City before they leave it. I learn that the Commune have shut the Barriers because they suspect the Assembly of an Intention to retreat. The Weather is very pleasant.

[One of the Revolution's most hideous deeds brings haunting sorrow to the old Duc de Penthièvre and his daughter, Duchesse d'Orléans, whose sister-in-law Princesse de Lamballe had been in safe exile, returning on her own initiative to comfort the Queen in the Tuileries, re-entering the service of that royal cousin whose first playmate she had been in France.]

Morris to the Duchess of Orleans

[Copied from Sparks, these may both be translations.]

September 7

The letter of the good Princess reached me at the moment when the horrors were beginning. They have not yet reached their limit. The vengeance of Heaven will, sooner or later, strike the wretches, who have escaped from human justice; and the God of peace and mercy will, I hope, have pity on this people, pardon them, and give them at last repose and tranquillity. Ah! Princess, if virtue and goodness like yours were found in all, the exterminating angel would very soon sheathe his sword. I pray you to present my homage to Monseigneur, your father, and to believe always in the sentiments of respect and affection which animate me.

Duchess of Orleans to Morris

September 12.

Your attentions touch me deeply. You share, I am persuaded, my father's grief and mine, and conceive in what affliction we are plunged. All the circumstances of this death are heart-rending; we are overwhelmed by it. To my affliction is added my maternal anxiety, which increases every day. My children were well on the sixth. They were at Toul. But how many events may have taken place since that time! Alas! We know but too well how many may happen in a very brief space. My father is always grateful for your remembrance. He charges me to thank you sincerely, and to speak well of him to you. Our good Mr Morris knows the value I attach to his friendship, and merits the sentiments which I have devoted to him forever.[1]

---

[1] In August the Duchess had written to Morris: ' No more agreeable idea ever presented itself to my mind than that of the tea-table, where the administration of liberty and equality is so well established'; but their Palais-Royal tea with gossip is over forever.

No. 10   *Morris to Jefferson*

Paris 10 September 1792

Thomas Jefferson Esqr
                Philadelphia

Dear Sir,
    ... We have had one Week of uncheck'd Murders in which
some thousands have perish'd in this City. It began with between two and three hundred of the Clergy who had been shut
up because they would not take the Oath prescrib'd by Law and
which they said was contrary to their Conscience. Thence *these
Executors of speedy Justice* went to the Abbaye where the persons
were confin'd who were at Court on the Tenth. These were dispatch'd also, and afterwards they visited the other prisons. All
those who were confin'd, either on the accusation or Suspicion of
Crimes, were destroy'd. Madame de Lamballe was I believe the
only woman kill'd and she was beheaded and emboweled, the
Head and entrails paraded on Pikes thro' the Street, and the
body dragg'd after them. They continu'd I am told in the Neighbourhood of the Temple until the Queen look'd out at this horrid
Spectacle. Yesterday the Prisoners from Orleans were put to
death at Versailles. The destruction began here about five in
the afternoon on Sunday the second Instant. A Guard had been
sent a few days since to make the Duke de La Rochefoucault
prisoner. He was on his way to Paris under their Escort with
his wife and Mother when he was taken out of his Carriage and
killed. The Ladies were taken back to La Roche Guyonne where
they are now in a State of Arrestation. Monsieur de Montmorin
was among those slain at the Abbaye. You will recollect that a
petition was sign'd by many thousands to displace the Mayor on
account of his Conduct on the twentieth of June. The signing of
this Petition is considered as a sufficient proof of the Crime of
Feuillantisme and it was in contemplation with some to put all
those who were guilty of signing that Petition to Death. This
Measure seems however to be suspended (for the present at
least) but as there is no real executive Authority the Plan may
be easily resum'd should it suit the views of those who enjoy
the Confidence of that part of the People who are now active.

Saturday 8. — The bishop d'Autun has got his Passport. He tells me that he does not think the Duke of Brunswick will be able to reach Paris and he urges me strongly to leave it. I have, however, receiv'd from the Minister an indirect Apology for his impertinent Letter and therefore I shall stay. The Weather is very pleasant. M.ʳ Constable has got his Passport but tells me that M.ʳ Phyn [being English] finds great Difficulty.

Sunday 9. — Lord Wycombe calls on me this Morning and Chaumont comes in the Afternoon to take Leave. The Weather is pleasant.

Monday 10. — The Prisoners were kill'd Yesterday at Versailles. The Number of Troops to be oppos'd to the combin'd Armies seems now to be as inferior as the Discipline and Appointments. L.ᵈ Wycombe dines with me. He says that he hopes the End of the french Affairs will cure other Nations of the Rage for Revolutions. The Weather is grown much cooler but it is very pleasant.

Tuesday 11. — Nothing new this Day except that the Camp of Maulde is rais'd after sending a Detachment to Dumouriez. The Troops are retir'd to Valenciennes. This opens the northern frontier. Thionville is beseiged and so *perhaps* is Metz. The nonjuring Priests are murdered at Rheims. The Weather is grown cool.

Wednesday 12. — Nothing new this Day. The Duke of Brunswic seems to be waiting awhile for the Operations of others. It is said that Champaigne in general waits the Opportunity of joining the Enemy. And it is said also that every Man is turning out against them. In this Case as in other Cases *Medio tuttissimus ibis*. The Weather grows cool.

Thursday 13. — Nothing new this Day. A Battle is said to be in Agitation between Dumouriez and the Duke of Brunswic. We shall know more of this hereafter. The Inactivity of the Enemy is so extraordinary that it must have an unknown Cause. Confessedly the Forces opposed were inferior and it would be extraordinary that great Manœuvre should under such Circumstances be needful.

Friday 14. — This Morning I visit Madame de Ségur and afterwards take an Airing on the Boulevards. There is Nothing from the Armies except a Confirmation of the raising of the Camp de Maulde with some Circumstances to shew that the french have been roughly handled in that Quarter. Some People have amus'd themselves this Day in tearing the Earings out of People's Ears and taking their Watches. It is said that some of the Violators have been put to Death. The Factions seem to be daily more embittered against each other and notwithstanding the common Danger they are far from a Disposition to unite. It seems probable that those who possess Paris will dictate to the others. The Weather is pleasant.

Saturday 15. — This Day we have an Account that the Enemy have been repulsed in an Attack upon Thionville. I think it is but a trifling Affair, much exagerated. There are Accounts also of an Action between the Army of Dumouriez and the Duke of Brunswick. No Details, but I conjecture that it is only a Feint to draw the French to their left in order to turn their Right. The Weather is very cool.

Sunday 16. — Nothing new except what I do not believe, that the Army of Dumouriez has repulsed the Enemy with considerable Execution. The Weather very pleasant.

Le Brun to Morris

Paris le 16 Septembre 1792
l'an 4ᵉ de la liberté

J'ai vu, Monsieur, dans la réponse que vous avez Faite à la lettre que j'ai eu l'honneur de vous écrire, le 30 du Mois d'Août dernier, que vous n'avez point saisi le vrai Sens de certaines expressions qu'elle contient, et qui sont rélatives aux circonstances. Mon objet, en vous parlant du Gouvernement actuel, était de vous prouver qu'en France, il n'a jamais pû être dissoût, ni rien perdre de sa gravité, tant que la nation existera. D'après ce principe juste et incontestable, j'ai jugé que vous pouviez résider à paris, y attendre de nouvelles Lettres de créance, et de nouvelles instructions de vos commettans; enfin continuer à traiter sans interruption ni retard les affaires qui intéressent les deux peuples.

Vous deviez être persuadé, Monsieur, que vous nous eussiez trouvés très empressés à vous donner satisfaction sur tous les points qui auraient eu pour base la justice et la raison. Et comme sans doute vous n'en eussiez jamais présenté d'autres, le résultat de nos conférences et de vos démarches auprès de nous, auroit été suivi du succés que vous eussiez desiré.

Quant à l'éloignement que vous paraissez avoir pour notre Gouvernement actuel, je crois être en droit de vous rappeler un Fait qui vient à l'appui du principe que je viens de vous citer plus haut: Le voici: Lors que les habitans de l'Amérique Septentrionale résolurent de se séparer de l'Angleterre et de conquérir leur Liberté, ils envoyèrent en France des Représentans pour négocier avec le Gouvernement, qui ne fit aucune difficulté d'entrer en pourparler, et de conclure même avec eux un Traité d'amitié et de commerce, ainsi qu'un traité d'alliance. À peine les provinces unies eurent-elles nommé un Congrès, que le Docteur Francklin fut reconnu par nous en sa qualité de Ministre-plénipotentiaire. Il fut admis avec tout le corps diplomatique aux audiences de la Cour, et du Ministre. La France envoya et accrédita aussi de sa part un Ministre auprès du Congrès.

Cependant, Monsieur, vous savez qu'à cette époque, on n'avait pas encore pris de mesures fixes pour l'établissement d'un Gouvernement en Amérique; et il n'en pouvait exister de Solide, puisque l'on continuait encore à y faire la guerre pour la cause de l'indépendance et de la Liberté. Notre position actuelle et celle de votre pays alors sont bien différentes: vous en serez convaincu par le Fait suivant.

Avant notre Révolution, nous avions un Gouvernement qui depuis toujours a Subsisté. Il a pris à la verité une autre Forme; mais la Liberté, le salut de la patrie ont ainsi déterminé sa création. D'ailleurs, vous, Monsieur, qui êtes né au milieu d'un peuple libre, deviez envisager les affaires présentes de la France sous un autre point de vue que celui de tous les Ministres étrangers résidans à paris. Nous soutenons la même cause que celle de votre pays: donc nos principes et les votre doivent être les mêmes; et par une Suite de conséquences naturelles, aucune raison ne peut s'opposer à votre résidence à paris.

Je souhaite, Monsieur, que cette exposition de Faits qui vous sont aussi connus qu'à moi, vous engage à faire de nouvelles réflexions, et puisse vous déterminer à changer de résolution.

Quoi qu'il en soit, Monsieur; j'ai fait expédier le passeport que vous m'avez demandé; il est actuellement à la Municipalité pour remplir les Formalités. Je compte pouvoir vous l'envoyer demain.

Vous verrez, Monsieur, par l'extrait ci joint de la réponse du Ministre des contributions publiques, que vous avez une Satisfaction presqu'entière sur tous les points contenus dans votre lettre du 21 Août dernier. J'ai l'honneur de vous observer que les petits accidens personnels que vous avez éprouvés rélativement à vos effets, vos vins et vos comestibles, sont une suite, comme vous le savez, de l'agitation inséparable d'une grande révolution.

J'ai l'honneur d'être avec un sincère attachement, Monsieur, votre très-humble et très obéissant Serviteur

Le Ministre des affaires étrangères./.

LE BRUN

[*Translation:*]

Paris 16 September 1792
4th Year of Liberty.

I have seen, Sir, in your answer to the letter I had the honor to write you on the 30th of August last, that you have not seized the true meaning of certain expressions contained in it and which are relevant to the circumstances. My object in speaking to you of the present Government was to prove that in France it can never have been dissolved nor have lost any of its weight so long as the Nation exists. On this just and incontestable principle I consider that you can reside in Paris and await here new letters of credence and new instructions from your constituents; in fact continue to treat without interruption or delay the affairs that interest both peoples.

You should have felt sure, Sir, of finding us eager to give you satisfaction on all points based on justice and reason. And as you would doubtless never have brought forward any others, the result of our conferences and of your applications would have been followed by all the success you could have wished.

As to the aversion you appear to have towards our present Government I feel justified in recalling to you a fact which bears out the principle I have just cited. It is this. When the inhabitants of North America resolved to separate from England and to conquer their liberty they sent representatives to France to negotiate with the Government, which made no difficulty whatever about entering into parley, even concluding with them a treaty of amity and commerce as well as a treaty of alliance. The united provinces had but just nominated a Congress when Doctor Franklin was recognized by us in his quality of Minister Plenipotentiary. He was admitted with the Diplomatic Corps to the audiences of the Court and of the Ministers. On her side France sent a Minister accredited to Congress.

And this although as you know Sir, at that time no regular measures had yet been taken to establish a Government in America, and no solid one could exist as war was still being waged for the cause of independence and liberty. Our present position and that of your country at that time are very different; you will be convinced of this by the following fact.

Before our Revolution we had a Government which had always existed. It is true that it has taken another form; but Liberty, the welfare of our fatherland, have thus determined its creation. Besides, you Sir who were born in the midst of a free people, should regard the present affairs of France from a different point of view to all the foreign Ministers resident in Paris. We uphold the same cause as that of your country, therefore our principles and yours should be the same and by a chain of natural consequences no reason can oppose your residence in Paris.

I trust Sir, that this exposition of facts which are as well known to you as to me, will induce you to reflect anew, and may lead you to alter your decision.

However this may be, Sir, I have had the passport forwarded which you asked for; it is at this moment at the

Municipality to fulfil the formalities. I expect to send it to you tomorrow.

You will see Sir, by the enclosed extract from the answer of the Minister of Public Contributions, that you have an almost complete satisfaction on the points contained in your letter of 21 August ultimo. I have the honor to observe that the small personal annoyances which you have suffered in connection with your effects, your wines and your comestibles, are the result, as you know, of the disorganization inseparable from a great revolution.

I have the honor to be with a sincere attachment, Sir,
Your most humble and most obedient Servant
LE BRUN.

Morris to Monsieur Le Brun

À Paris le 17 Septembre 1792

Monsieur Le Brun

Monsieur,

J'ai eu l'honneur de recevoir vos lettres du 8 et du 16. D'Après les explications que contient la dernière je ne reviendrai plus sur celle du trente Août et comme c'étoit elle qui m'avait decidée à quitter la France, je reprends ma Détermination d'y rester et d'y attendre les Ordres de ma Cour. Quant à mes opinions personelles Monsieur, elles ne sont d'aucune importance dans une Affaire aussi grave, mais vous pouvez être persuadé que jamais je n'ai mis en doutte le droit qu'a tout peuple de se faire gouverner de la manière qui lui plait. Depuis bien des années j'ai fait des voeux sincères pour que la France jouît de toute la liberté et de tout le bonheur possibles: et je suis sûr de remplir les Intentions des États Unis en vous assurant que ces voeux sont partagés par tous mes Compatriots.

J'ai l'honneur de vous renouveller, Monsieur, ma Demande d'un Passeport pour l'intérieur. En constatant mon état il me garantira des interruptions qu'on éprouve dans le moment actuel.

[*Translation:*]

Sir,

I had the honor to receive your letters of the 8th and 16th. In consideration of the explanations contained in the latter I will not again refer to yours of August thirtieth, and as it was that which decided me to leave France I resume my intention of staying on and awaiting the orders of my Court. As to my personal opinions, Sir, they are of no importance in so grave a matter, but you may rest assured that I have never questioned the right of every People to be governed as they please. For many years I have sincerely wished that France should enjoy all possible liberty and happiness, and I am certain of carrying out the intentions of the United States in assuring you that these wishes are shared by all my compatriots.

I have the honor to renew to you Sir, my request for a Passport for the interior. By indicating my status it will guarantee me against the obstructions met with under present circumstances.

Monday 17. — This Day Accounts arrive from the Army to shew that Dumouriez has been defeated or Something very like it. The Weather cool for the Season but pleasant.

Tuesday 18. — By the official Reports of this Day Paris is in a State of imminent Danger from the internal Movements. The Factions grow daily more inveterate. The Weather is very cool.

Wednesday 19. — Every Thing still wears an Appearance of Confusion. No Authority any where. The Weather is pleasant.

Thursday 20. — M.ʳ Payne calls on me. I find from various Channels that the brissotine Faction is desirous of doing me Mischief if they can. I am inform'd that the Powers of Barbary are about to cut off all Communication with this Country. If so the southern Provinces will starve. The Weather lowers and this Evening it rains hard.

Friday 21. — Nothing new this Day except that the Convention has met and declar'd they will have no King in France. The Weather is foul.

Saturday 22. — This Day News are receiv'd of the March of

the prussian Army towards Rheims after a long Action with the Advance of Dumouriez' Army under Kellerman, which was I presume to amuse him. The Weather is pleasant but cool.

Sunday 23. — Nothing new this Day. We have some Details of the Action of Kellerman but too vague to conclude any Thing. The Weather is clear and cool but feels like Change.

Monday 24. — A vague Report is current that the Enemy are at Rheims. I presume that a Junction is meditated with the northern Army at Soissons. The Weather is raw and rainy.

Tuesday 25. — I am told that the suppos'd Action with Kellerman is all a Fiction. The Weather is foul. I dine at Boulogne with Madame de Narbonne. Nothing new this Day.

Wednesday 26. — I am told that the King of Prussia has made Overtures for Accomodation with the Assembly. This is I presume a military Trick. The Weather is very pleasant.

Thursday 27. — This Morning I am inform'd from unquestionable Authority that the supposed Overtures from the King of Prussia are in Effect Overtures from Dumouriez to him. Rainy Weather.

Friday 28. — This Day the News arrive that Montesquiou has broken into Savoy and is carrying all before him. The Weather is variable and frequently foul.

Saturday 29. — Yesterday I sent off my Dispatches by M.ʳ Mountflorence and wrote also to London by M.ʳ Livingston. This Day we have Nothing new. Lord Wycombe tells me that he has direct Information of a Desire of the King of Prussia to treat. I think his Informant is duped for the Thing appears impossible, except as a Manœuvre perhaps. The Weather is still variable. Mad.ᵉ de Valence dined with me this Day.

Sunday 30. — Nothing extraordinary this Day except a Confirmation of the Account that the King of Prussia wishes to treat and which Account I cannot believe. The Weather is foul but warm.

Morris to Jefferson

No. 12   Paris 27 September 1792

Thomas Jefferson Esqr

Philadelphia

Dear Sir,

My last, N°. 11, was of the 19th. I therein transmitted Copies
of my Correspondence with the Minister respecting the Subject
of the Conversation mentioned in mine of the thirtieth of last
Month, of which as well as of those of the seventeenth and twenty
second, Copies are here inclosed. I think it is proper to mention
to you now a circumstance relating to that Conversation. I had
good reasons to believe that a private Speculation was at the
Bottom of the Proposals made to me, and the extreme urgency
which was exhibited by one of the Conferees, who had been
designated to me as being concerned therein, tended not a little
to confirm the Information I had received. The wrath excited
by the unwillingness on my Part to jump over all the bounds of
my powers and Instructions, did by no means lessen, but came
in support of the same Idea. Since that Period I have been asked
by a Person who said he was offered a Bill drawn by the Government here on the Treasury of the United States, whether such
Bill would be paid. I expressed my surprise thereat, and was
told that this Bill would be for the Sum decreed by the Assembly
to be employed in purchasing supplies for the Colony of S^t.
Domingo. I observed thereon that it seemed a strange proceedure
either to sell or buy such a Bill: because the Vendor could only
employ the Money in America, and of course need not risque a
Draft; and the purchaser, who must make the expenditure thereof
could not I supposed find his Account in the Transaction. This
led to an Explanation. The Bill was to be paid for in Assignats
at Par six or nine Months hence, and the Produce was to be
employed in purchasing Manufactures suitable to the Colony in
this Country. I told the Person who applied to me that I did
not think this would be considered in America as falling within
the Decree, and that no good reason could be assigned for paying
under great *Disadvantages* in Philadelphia, what could be paid

with great *Advantage* in Paris, when the Sum paid was not to be expended in the United States but in France. At length the true Object of this Application to me came out. I discovered that it was merely a Scheme of Speculation to be carried into Effect if I could be induced to recommend the payment, under what was known to be a favorite Idea with me, viz the expending *in America* what we owe to France, and *for the Support of the Colony of S.ʰ Domingo*. As my concurrence could not be hoped for I believe that the Plan is abandoned, but perhaps it is only abandoned in Appearance.

I also take the liberty to enclose the Extract of a letter from Mr Short respecting Monsieur de La Fayette, with my answer thereto. I understand that he was forwarded from Luxemburg (privately) on the Route to Vienna, and had got as far as Brisgaw several days ago. I presume that his treatment will depend very much on the success of the military Operations. If the allied Monarchs, finding themselves disappointed in their Expectations from the present Campaign are obliged to look forward to more extensive and more permanent Efforts, they will probably endeavour to gain one of the great Parties in this Country: and should they turn their Eyes towards the *quatre vingt neufs or Feuillans* they will naturally consider Monsieur de La Fayette as the most fitting Instrument to be employed. And he will, as naturally, desire to aid in the Establishment of the Party and the principles which he considers as true Supporters of liberty in this Country. For you will observe that in like manner as the Cleric and Aristocratic Parties considered the Assembly in 1789 as an Usurper, the leaders of that Assembly affixed on the Jacobins the same Charge of usurpation, and now the leaders of the last Revolution are charged by some of their Brethren with *Feuillantism*. You will see by the Gazettes that there is the same Enmity between the present Chiefs which prevailed heretofore against those whom they considered as their common Enemies, and if either of the present parties should get the better, they would probably again divide, for Party, like Matter, is divisable *ad infinitum*, because things which depend on human opinion can never be tried by any common Standard. And not only is it unavoidable that there should be Differences among different

Men, but it is even uncommon to find in the same Man the same
Sentiments for a continued length of time, tho upon the same
Subject, for either the Circumstances change or else the Man.

[Three American Legations were soon simmering with impotent
indignation at Allied treatment of their 'fellow citizen' La Fayette.
Hoping to save their proscribed heads to be of later use to France,
the General and a small group of officers, three La Tour-Mau-
bourgs, three Romeufs, Bureaux de Pusy, La Colombe, a Gouvion,
a Laumoy, had cast the die and started north on Sunday morning,
August 19. Soon joined by Alexandre de Lameth, an old adver-
sary of La Fayette's, by Monsieur d'Arblay, whose destiny was
leading him to an English village and Fanny Burney, and by
other chance-met officers, they amounted with orderlies to fifty-
three horsemen, a somewhat noticeable party to thread unchal-
lenged between the armies. An Austrian outpost near Rochefort
put an abrupt end to La Fayette's individual plan of reaching
neutral Holland, of getting his wife and daughters to meet him
in England, of sailing with them to a welcoming America; so
William Short, by nature a worrying young man, cautious, not
impulsive, was spared the perplexity of befriending him at The
Hague. Short soon received the following letter from the prisoner,
dated 26 August from Nivelle, near the not yet famous Waterloo.
It comes via Sparks, who does not label it a translation:]

My dear Friend,
    You have been acquainted with the atrocious events which
have taken place in Paris, when the Jacobin faction on the tenth
of August overthrew the Constitution, enslaved both the Assembly and the King, the one by terror, the other by destitution and
confinement, and gave a signal for pillage and massacre.
    I could have found a high station in the new order of things,
without even having meddled with the plot. But my feelings did
not admit of such an idea. I raised an opposition to Jacobin
tyranny; but you know the weakness of our *honnêtes gens*. I was
abandoned; the army gave way to clubish acts. Nothing was
left for me but to leave France. We have been stopped on our
road and detained by an Austrian detachment, which is absolutely

contrary to the *droits des gens*, as may appear from the enclosed
Declaration, which I request you to have published. You will
greatly oblige me, my dear Sir, by setting out for Brussels as soon
as this reaches you, and insist on seeing me. I am an American
citizen, an American officer, no more in the French service. That
is your right, and I do not doubt of your urgent and immediate
arrival. God bless you.

LAFAYETTE.

[Short got the Declaration published free in the *Leyden Gazette*,
whose pro American editor Luzac said he was happy to do it in
homage of La Fayette, but Short did not hurry to Brussels. He
felt he lacked authority to interfere, there was no American representative at Vienna or at Berlin, he begged the Austrian Minister
at The Hague to write for information, and meanwhile himself
wrote to Morris:]

The Hague, Sep. 7. 1792

... I have now to communicate one to you of a very different
nature − & although I have no idea myself of what can be done
in it by us with any hope of success, yet I lose no time in informing you of it as I have been requested to do in order to concert
with you & M. Pinkney, conformably likewise to request, the
measures to be pursued. You are no doubt informed of the circumstances of M. de la fayette's arrestation & confinement. —
He & his companions were first sent to Nivelles near Brussels —
everybody supposed (& even the persons at Brussels the most
acquainted with the dispositions of the government there, &
the best informed here among others) that they would be released
immediately on an answer's being rec.d from Vienna. − On the
contrary, before that answer could have been received, orders
were given for sending M. de la fayette & the three members of
the former Assembly accompanying him, to Luxemburg − for
detaining the others at Nivelles − & releasing such as had been
made prisoners the day after M. de la fayette, & who had also
been brought to Nivelles. Under these circumstances, which
would seem to indicate no intention in the government to release
those whom they now detain manifestly in contravention to the

principle existing of allowing the peaceable & unarmed citizens to
pass as travellers through the two countries, I have been pressed
to concert with you & M: Pinckney means of our jointly reclaiming
M. de la fayette in the name of the U.S. as a citizen thereof. —
I am urged to this by some officers his friends, & former companions who arrived here, & by a letter from himself which is
short but pressing in the extreme. – Whatever is done should be
done immediately for numberless reasons – & whatever is possible in a case of this kind will no doubt be considered as proper
– I therefore submit it to you as I shall do to M: Pinckney under
the urging request above mentioned. – I am persuaded you will
both weigh the matter as it ought to be & suggest some means of
acting with propriety & efficacity if there be any. – I shall be
anxious to hear from you – & to prevent delay imagine you will
find it proper to communicate directly with M: Pinckney on the
subject.   I can add nothing to the considerations which will
naturally occur to you on this distressing occasion, & which the
companions of M. de la fayette who are here, represent as dangerous to him.   I trust however that their fears are exagerated by the
interest they take in what concerns him. – I cannot help flattering myself that the Austrian Government, from a regard to
their own character will not extend this violation of the most
sacred principle of right & justice, further than to a meer deten-
tion of those gentlemen who fled from their country because they
would not partake of the atrocities which the same government
have held up as the motives for their interfering & endeavouring
to suppress the factions which have occasioned them – which
factions the persons now detained prisoners notoriously combated
& are exiles for their having so done – in this exile & proscrip-
tion they abandoned their arms & asking only a peaceable passage
through the country whose government had taken the engagement in the eyes of Europe to extend protection to all they found
in that situation, instead of receiving this passage to which every
right entitled them, were arrested, imprisoned & are still detained.
– History & posterity, the supreme tribunal of sovereigns, will
no doubt avenge such a violation of the solemn promise made
by the allied sovereigns & by those who proclaimed it in their
name. – – Being persuaded myself however of the enlightened

mind & love of justice which those who possess the Emperor's confidence both at Vienna & in the low countries have given so many proofs, & of the moderation also which directs these councils, I cannot allow myself to believe that the passage to neutral territory which was asked by these gentlemen after having quitted their arms & determined to leave their country, can be long refused them – yet lest I sh.ᵈ have mistaken the character of the Imperial government, I join my request to that already made — that you will weigh well this matter & communicate to M.ʳ Pinckney & myself your sentiments.

Y.ʳˢ

W. Short

[These multiple citizenships were the very dickens for setting puzzles. While La Fayette was running the Revolution, the most prominent Frenchman in France, his Americanship can have had only a sentimental, complimentary value; from his first Austrian guardroom it seemed to have practical possibilities. American hearts might melt with sympathetic anguish at the senseless savagery of La Fayette's treatment; American minds had to jerk themselves into remembering that the United States were allied to France in whose eyes he was a French deserter, fleeing from the so-called justice of the governing faction; and that they were at peace with Prussian King and Austrian Emperor in whose eyes he was a much-dreaded throne-breaker. Europe was in danger of being swept by the 'French disease'; princely thrones big and little were in an ague of apprehension; what more reprehensible and threatening than a polished, fanatical aristocratic republican who might become a focus of discontents, an apostle of deliverance! This may explain their not letting him go free, but supplies neither motive nor excuse for the dripping underground dungeons of Wesel, for the knife-and-forklessness of Olmütz, for the torture of dark solitary confinement without books, pens, or news, for the unsanitary conditions which brought the Marquis de La Fayette, the Comte César de La Tour-Maubourg, the devoted aide-de-camp Bureaux de Puzy, and Comte Alexandre de Lameth separately and at different times within a breath of dying. Rumor shattered their families' hopes by reporting them insane, dead, but will-power brought them out alive five years later. Fear had driven Prussian King and Austrian Emperor back to the mentality and methods of the Middle Ages. Morris consults his London colleague:]

Paris 23 September 1792

Thomas Pinckney Esq.
London

Dear Sir,

I am to acknowledge your favors of the eleventh and eighteenth,[1] the former ... was brought by M.r Paine *Membre de la Convention nationale*, who call'd on me the Day after his Arrival, and the next Day gave his Voice for the Abolition of Monarchy here which was determined on Nem: Con:

I have received a Letter from M.r Short of the eighteenth in which he tells me that he had not yet received an Answer from you. By yours I perceive that our Sentiments on the Question he proposed are coincident with each other, at which I am much flattered. I have every possible wish to be useful, but I really apprehend that we might do more Harm than Good. I have also some Reason to believe that the Person is now far removed. If however you can strike out any Plan likely to produce the desired Effect, you may rely on my Concurrence.

---

[1] Pinckney's letter of September 18 is missing from the package, but his ideas on the La Fayette dilemma appear in his answer to Short of the 14th, sent on to Morris and remaining with his papers. Pinckney's tentative 'Note' was not forwarded to the Powers who were holding La Fayette and his three friends as hostages for Louis XVI and who offered liberation to La Fayette only at the price of leading their armies against his country. His disdainful refusal was a thing of course and the horrors of Magdeburg are piled on the miseries of Wesel till Prussia hands him over to Austria and Olmütz with the fellow sufferers he so seldom sees.

Morris to Short

Paris 12 September 1792

William Short Esqr

Hague

Dear Sir,

... The Situation of Monsieur de La Fayette I have long lamented and since these last disasters I feel more than ever a Desire to alleviate his Distress. I had already meditated on the Circumstances in which he might be plac'd and his Imprisonment was among those Events which appear'd not improbable. The Enemy may consider him as a Prisoner of War, as a Deserter, or as a Spy. In the first Capacity he might be delivered up to be sacrific'd by his Countrymen. In the last he might be made the Victim of Resentments excited by his former Conduct. As a Deserter he is entitled to Protection but I doubt whether he would chuse to be so protected.

I incline however to the Opinion that the Enemy mean to use him in a different Capacity, and that his future Treatment will depend entirely on himself, but at the same time I fear that the Employment they would give him is not such as he will chuse to engage in. Be all this however as it may, he is in their power and they will do as they please. The reasons you urge for his liberation are cogent, and I hope they will be attended to; but Power sometimes makes Law for itself, and in such Cases it cares but little for History or Posterity.

Supposing that Monsieur de La Fayette were a natural born Subject of America, and taken under the Circumstances in which he was plac'd, I do not exactly see how the United States could claim him. He was not in their Service. If he had been made a Prisoner of War and they claim him as their Citizen? If claim'd and delivered up, would they not be bound to put him to death for having attack'd a neutral power, or else by the very Act of acquitting him declare War against those who had taken him? Can the United States interfere in an Affair of this Sort without making themselves Parties in the Quarrel? But Monsieur de La Fayette is a Frenchman, and it is as a Frenchman that he is taken and is to be treated. Again, supposing the right as clear as it is questionable, I presume that before the United

States made such Demand they would determine to go all lengths to establish their right in case it should be refused; for otherwise by advancing the Claim and then receeding they would sit down quietly under an Insult. Consequently they would consider well before they plac'd themselves in a Situation to be dishonored or else drawn into a War.

These are Points of such Magnitude that I do not feel myself competent to decide on them in Behalf of my Country; and therefore if I were Minister to his Imperial Majesty I should (I think) confine myself to Prayer and Solicitation until I received express orders from the President of the United States. But as I am not Minister to the Emperor I rather think that my interference would prove offensive and do more Harm than good to Monsieur de La Fayette. And not only the Emperor, and perhaps the King of Prussia too, might complain if they thought it worth while to take any notice of such unauthoriz'd application, but the Government of this Country also might feel itself offended, and that in either of those Events which are now at the Issue of the Sword. If there was however any probability that a Demand on our part would liberate him, it might be well to attempt it. You may perhaps find out how that Matter stands thro the Medium of the Court at which you are, and this it would I think be well to do. If the Austrian Ministry should wish an Excuse to deliver him from Bondage, they may admit of that which you mention, but certainly they will not consider it as a reason.

Morris to Thomas Pinckney

Paris 13 September 1792

Thomas Pinckney Esq:
London

Dear Sir,

I received yesterday a letter from Mr Short respecting Monsieur de La Fayette of which I enclose you an Extract and also a Copy of that Part of my Answer which relates to the same Subject. My opinion is that the less we meddle in the great Quarrel which agitates Europe the better will it be for us, and altho the private feelings of friendship or Humanity might properly sway us as private Men we have in our public Character higher Duties to fulfil than those which may be dictated by Sentiments of Affection towards an Individual. I may view this Affair thro' a false medium and therefore I shall wait with Impatience for your Opinion and listen to it with Deference and Attention.

Thomas Pinckney to William Short

London 14th Sept. 1792

Dear Sir

Among the afflicting considerations which have impressed themselves on my mind from the moment I heard of the misfortune of our friend and fellow Citizen the Marquis la Fayette, none have afflicted me with such painful Sensations, as the conviction that no exertions of his American friends can be of utility to him in his present Situation: and since the receipt of your favor of the 7th which did not reach me till yesterday this Subject has scarcely been a moment out of my thought; but I search in vain some foundation whereon to establish a right to demand his liberation; and to demand it with a certainty of refusal, & with a consciousness that such refusal may be founded on principles of propriety would without Benefitting our friend commit our Country and ourselves. I feel myself however so much interested in this business that it will afford me real pleasure to find that Mr Morris or you upon more mature reflexion have discovered any plan to which my concurrence can add efficacy. And in order to evince the readiness with which I contribute my endeavor to strike out some expedient which may be serviceable I venture to inclose for the deliberation of Mr Morris & yourself a rough sketch of a note to which however I perceive forcible objections: and only submit it as the least exceptionable of such ideas as have suggested themselves to me. A claim of the rights of an American Citizen to a person in the Marquiss's circumstances appears to me to be claiming nothing, & it can only I fear at best serve as a testimonial of national gratitude, and may be a consolatory tribute to the feelings of a man of whose services and zeal for our country there is I believe but one sentiment in America. If a measure of that or any other nature should be adopted, it ought I conceive to be so conducted as to avoid involving any discussion of principle & should be the joint act of all the American Ministers in Europe, if distance of situation will permit their uniting within the time necessary to render it serviceable.

I fear I shall not have time to transmit to you the statement you desire by this mail, but will forward it by the next opportunity. With sentiments of sincere attachment I have the honor to be
                    Dear Sir
                              Your most obedient
                                humble Servant
                                    THOMAS PINCKNEY
Mr Short.

Short to Morris

                              The Hague. Sept 18. 1792
... Your sentiments with respect to the affair of M. de la fayette I consider as perfectly conformable to reason & policy — so far as they regard us — I will endeavour to acquire the information you consider as proper to be aimed at. I have been wishing for an opportunity which may perhaps present itself from the Imperial minister lately arrived here. I have not as yet received an answer from M͞r Pinckney which however I dont doubt will be conformable to yours....

                              The Hague. Nov. 13. 1792
... The success of the French arms has thrown everything into consternation at Brussels — & produced visible uneasiness here. Precautions are taken to prevent the retiring into these provinces of the unhappy French emigrants, who are flying in crowds from the Austrian Netherlands & who have nothing left for them but despair & death. — All doors seem to be shut against them except those of England. — The officers who were arrested with M. de la fayette & imprisoned in the chateau D'Anvers have been released within these few days, except two who found means to

escape from their confinement some time ago, & went to England.
– The treatment of M. de la fayette & his companions of misfortune at Wesel is cruel & rigorous in the extreme. – They are
separated – & have no communication with each other – or
without doors. – One of them Bureau de Puzy, is dead, as I
am told by the Imperial Minister here. . . .

The Hague. Dec 7. 1792

. . . As to our fellow citizen in confinement & of whom you desire to be fully informed, I can only tell you that the most im-
penetrable secrecy has been observed with respect to him & his
fellow sufferers. It is certain that he is the individual of all France
that both Austrians & Prussians hate the most cordially – the
desire of revenge & determination to punish them made them
commit the most flagrant act of injustice – & the most shameful
violation of the *droit des gens* – they are probably sensible of it &
therefore wish to smother the whole business & the victims also.
It is certain the agents of the Emperor & Prussia here are ignorant
of what passes; which is probably confined to the walls of the *donjon* of Wesel. It has been reported that our fellow citizen has
lost his reason & is in a state of insanity – Although I cannot assure that it is not so, yet I should suppose it was not from what
these gentlemen have told me, though they can only speak from
conjecture. In fine I have never been able to learn a single word
with certainty respecting these prisoners since their transfer to
Wesel – nor has any body else here been able to do it. . . .[1]

[Early in the new year Morris had a call from La Fayette's
gentle sister-in-law Louise, married to a cousin and still a Noailles,
who came to say that scarcely any funds stood between him and
prison diet; so the American Minister took practical steps and
chanced the approval of his Government.]

---

[1] Morris wrote to Washington: 'In reading my Correspondence with M:
Short, you must consider that I wrote to the French and Austrian Government,
as each would take the Liberty to read my Letters. . . . I had very good Reason
to apprehend that our Interference at that Time would have been injurious
to him, but I hope that a Moment will soon offer in which Something may be
done for his Relief.'

Paris 27 January 1793

Messrs W & J Willink, N & I⎫
Van Staphorst & Hubbard   ⎭
Amsterdam

Gentlemen

I learn from the Friends of Monsieur de la fayette (who is now Prisoner at Magdeburg) that altho kept in close Confinement no Provision is made for his comfortable Subsistence. I own that I do not believe this Assertion, but should it be true I think no Moment is to be lost in administering Relief. You will therefore be pleased to write to your Correspondents at Magdeburg on the Subject, and desire them to supply the Sums needful for him. You can extend your Credit to the Sum of ten thousand florins, which you will please to charge as paid by my Order, in your Accounts with the United States. Observe also that it is not in my Contemplation to furnish the Means of Escape, for I cannot enter into Intrigues of that Sort directly nor indirectly, because it is not becoming the Dignity of the United States to act in an underhand Manner; but they would hear with great Concern that a Person who has been eminently useful to them should be in Want of those Necessaries which it is in their Power to bestow.[1]

---

[1] From London, July, 1794, Pinckney will write: 'I am directed to replace the money you lodged for a Friend at Amsterdam a year and a half ago.' This by the United States Government. Morris's loan of 100,000 livres to Madame de La Fayette to pay her husband's debts of honor in June, 1793, will be repaid by her ten years later, scaled down to 53,500. In June, 1794, he hits off the right psychology in his appeal to rough Buchot when she is threatened with the guillotine, but the honor of getting her out of jail is reserved for Monroe under a change of policy. Her sisters and Madame de Staël give Morris full credit for saving her life.

OCTOBER 1792

Monday 1 *Oct*.. — Attended the breaking of the Seals on Commodore Jones's Effects. Nothing new this Day, but the Information begins to leak out respecting the suppos'd Treaty with Prussia. Paine offers a Bet that the King of Prussia will soon be oblig'd to treat for the Surrender of his Army or for Leave to retire. The Weather is pleasant.

Tuesday 2. — Nothing new this Day but in the Evening we learn that the prussian Army is retreating. This appears very extraordinary. They are said to be sickly. The Weather is mild but lowering.

Wednesday 3. — This Morning I have Details respecting the Retreat of the Prussians. Great Sickness and the crafty Policy of Austria account for it. This Retreat gives Room for a long War should the Allies persist, unless the national Levity of the French should induce them to abandon their young Republic in the Cradle. Every Reason to apprehend a Famine.

Thursday 4. — Accounts arrive this Day of the taking of Spire by Gen! Custine; 3,000 Prisoners of War. Dumouriez seems extravagantly rejoiced at the Retreat of the prussian Army.

Friday 5. — Reinforcements are thrown into Lisle so that in all Probability that Place is saved. The rainy Weather is very unfavorable to the sickly Troops under the Duke of Brunswick.

Saturday 6. — Write all the Morning, as I have done for several preceeding Days. Every Thing looks favorably to the Cause of the new Republic. The Weather is mild and pleasant.

Sunday 7. — Write this Morning till two, then call on the Cabinet Maker and the Baron de Blome. The Weather is very pleasant. The Siege of Lisle is said to be rais'd.

Monday 8. — Write this Morning. Confirmations arrive of the taking of Nice and from every Quarter Success pours in. 'Oh! Mortals impotent and blind to Fate, too soon dejected and too soon elate.' The Weather is **very foul**. Dumouriez is seriously occupied by the Plan of marching into Flanders. He says he will take up his Winter Quarters at Brussels.

Tuesday 9 *Oct*.. — Write all the Morning. Worms is taken, in which, by the bye, there was no Garrison. The Weather is foul.

Wednesday 10. — Write. M:̣ Livingson arrives from London this Morning. The Weather still lours.

Thursday 11. — Nothing new this Day. The Weather is more pleasant but unpromising.

Friday 12. — Go to Versailles this Morning. The Weather is foul and threatning. This Night it blows hard from the Southward with Rain.

Saturday 13. — Write this Day, or rather, examine Accounts. A Storm from the South. Further Progress of the french Arms. Verdun is evacuated by Capitulation.

Sunday 14. — Nothing new this Day. Weather unpleasant, high Winds from the South.

Monday 15. — The Wind still blows hard from the Southern board. The Air is mild but damp.

Tuesday 16. — This Morning I am much indisposed but it is I think my own Fault. *Nous verrons*. There is nothing new.

Wednesday 17. — Fine Weather, my Health somewhat better but not well. Nothing new.

Thursday 18. — This Morning it rains, at Noon it clears up. My Health is a little better but not much. Nothing new.

Friday 19. — Pleasant Weather this Day. In the Afternoon I visit the Baron de Blome. He tells me that the french Troops are very ill.

Saturday 20. — Pleasant Weather. Nothing new except a Convention to evacuate Longwi.

Saturday [sic] *Sunday* 21 *Oct*.. — Fine Weather to Day. No News.

Monday 22. — Fine Weather. Some Dispatches, taken by the Carelessness of Monsieur, the King's Brother, open up Scenes of french good Faith, or rather of aristocratic Folly.

Tuesday 23. — My Health is still unconfirm'd. The Weather is pleasant.

Morris to Jefferson

Paris 23 October 1792.

Extracts from No. 13

The unexpected Events which have taken place in this Country since your Letter was written and of which you will have been informed before this reaches you, will show you that I cannot, untill I receive the President's further Orders, take up any of the Objects to which it alludes, not having indeed the proper Powers. I apprehend also the United States will wish to see a little into the Establishment of the new Republic before they take any decided Steps in Relation thereto. In this Case I may be yet a long Time without such Orders, which is to me a distressing Circumstance because it involves a Degree of Responsibility for Events which no human Being can foresee. It may indeed be replied that in a Position like mine the proper Conduct is to preserve a strict Neutrality and of Course to do Nothing, but Cases often arise in which to do Nothing is taking a Part. I need not state the many Situations of that Sort which occur. I had it in Contemplation to leave Paris and visit Bourdeaux and Marseilles but I found it necessary to continue here for the Sake of such of my Countrymen as were in this City and who might in the Madness of the Moment be exposed to Danger, but certainly to Inconvenience. . . .

With Respect to the present Temper of the People of this Country I am clearly of Opinion that the great decided effective Majority is now for the Republic. What may be the Temper and Opinion six Months hence, no prudent sensible Man would I think take upon him to declare. . . . whether they can establish an Authority which does not exist, as a Substitute (and always a dangerous Substitute) for that Respect which cannot be restored after so much has been done to destroy it; whether in crying down and even ridiculing Religion they will be able on the tottering and uncertain Base of Metaphisic Philosophy to establish a solid Edifice of Morals; these are Questions which Time must solve.

Morris to President Washington

Paris 23^d October 1792

George Washington Esqr
     Philadelphia

My dear Sir

Yours of the twenty first of June is at length safely arrived. Poor La Fayette. Your Letter for him must remain with me yet some Time. His Enemies here are as virulent as ever and I can give you no better Proof than this. Among the King's Papers was found nothing of what his Enemies wish'd and expected except his Correspondence with Monsieur de La Fayette, which breathes from Begining to End the purest Sentiments of Freedom. It is therefore kept Secret while he stands accus'd of Designs in Conjunction with the dethron'd Monarch, to enslave his Country. The Fact respecting this Correspondence is communicated to me by a Person to whom it was related confidentially by one of the Parties who examin'd it. You will have seen in my Letters to Mr Jefferson a Proposition made by Mr Short respecting Monsieur de La Fayette, with my Reply. I had very good Reason to apprehend that our Interference at that Time would have been injurious to him, but I hope that a Moment will soon offer in which Something may be done for his Relief. In reading my Correspondence with Mr Short you must consider that I wrote to the French and austrian Government, as each would take the Liberty to read my Letters. You will have seen also that in my Letters to Mr Jefferson I hint at the Dangers attending a Residence in this City. Some of the sanguinary Events which have taken Place and which were partial Executions of great Plans will point to a natural Interpretation thereof, but these were not what I contemplated. Should we ever meet I will entertain you with the Recital of many Things which it would be improper to commit to Paper, at least for the present. You will have seen that the King is accus'd of high Crimes and Misdemeanors, but I verily believe that he wish'd sincerely for this Nation the Enjoyment of the utmost Degree of Liberty which their Situation and Circumstances will permit. He wish'd for a good Constitution, but unfortunately he had not the Means to obtain it, or if he had he was thwarted by those about him. What may be his Fate God only knows, but History informs us that the Passage of dethron'd Monarchs is short from the Prison to the Grave.

I have mention'd to Mr Jefferson repeatedly my Wish to have positive Instructions and Orders for my Government. I need not tell you Sir how agreable this would be to me and what a Load it would take from my Mind. At the same Time I am fully sensible that it may be inconvenient to give me such Orders. The United States may wish to temporize and see how Things are like to end, and in such Case, leaving me at large with the Right reserv'd to avow or disavow me according to Circumstances and Events is, for the Government, an eligible Position. My Part in the Play is not quite so eligible, but altho I wish the Senate to be sensible of this, I am far from wishing that any precipitate Step be taken to relieve me from it, for I know how contemptible is every private Consideration when compar'd with the public Interests. One Step however seems natural, viz to say that before any new Letters of Credence are given it will be proper to know to whom they are to be directed because the Convention, a meer temporary Body, is to be succeeded by some fix'd Form and it may be a long Time before any such Form is adopted. . . .

Rufus King to Morris

New York 1 Sep? 1792

I presume that you are furnished with our news-papers and with the Journals of congress, from them you will be able to form a pretty good opinion of the State of parties here. The gazette of the U.S. published at Philadelphia by Fenno [1] is on one side, and the national Gazette published at the same place by Freneau, a clerk in Jefferson's Office, is on the other — in this paper every measure of the Government is censured, and if you believe the accounts it publishes the country is generally dissatisfied — the

---

[1] Fenno, launched and financed by Hamilton and King, reported official and social doings with a Court-circular unction. Freneau, poet of the Revolution, had a more brilliantly slashing pen and was for Jefferson educating the nation to democracy.

contrary however is the Truth — we are, and have reason to be, the happiest people in the world — our Government is established, it performs as much as its friends promised, and its administration has evidently advanced the prosperity of our Citizens.

The Opposition that now exists, arises from other principles than those which produced an opposition to the Constitution, and proceeds from that Rivalry which always has & will prevail in a free country.

The Revenues are abundant, and are collected with unexampled Fidelity. The branch called Excise will soon be productive — the northern states are satisfied with this Tax, and new Distilleries are building for the distillation of Corn & Fruit — this Tax has been complained of in the back counties of Pennsylvania, Virginia & the Carolinas, but as the law is better understood, the objections are overcome and by the mild and steady measures of Government all opposition will soon disappear — add to this the Tax will work a Reform in these Districts, since it will destroy a great many small Distilleries, and make the Business a branch of Labor, instead of being as it hitherto has been, a ruinous employment pursued by every family.

The national judiciary without having been much employed, has been the means of settling a large proportion of our foreign Debts — from the Potomack east nothing remains to be settled — in South Carolina where immense sums were due, they are doing well, and in a few years will be in a very prosperous condition. Virginia will be the last to do, what her own interest required her long since to have performed.

The settlement of our new lands is only equalled by the increase of our population — you hear of companies formed & forming in all the States for the improvement of our inland navigation, and thus the most distant lands will become almost as valuable as those nearest to our principal markets.

Our commerce & navigation continue to increase, & what is of still more consequence, the capital employed is in a good degree an American, instead of a British one — the sound state of public credit and the Establishment of Banks have already given aids to commerce, and will soon afford assistance to manufactures and agriculture — the national Bank have established Branches at

Boston, New York, Baltimore, Richmond, & Charleston, and will go on to place others in such situations as will best promote their own, & the public interest — the Facilities which this institution gives to Trade, and to the collection of the Taxes, is generally acknowledged; and by establishing a connexion in Holland & London (which is in contemplation) it may deal profitably in exchange, as well as place itself in a situation to avoid the Dangers to which Banks are exposed by the exportation of Coin.

Though we are preparing a respectable Force to oppose the Indians, still we have taken every measure to conclude a Peace — and from the Characters of the Agents engaged in this Business there is reason to expect Success — at any rate we shall make no Campaign this year — the season will be spent in disciplining the Army, and in Efforts to establish Peace — the Frontiers are quiet, and well guarded against incursions. Washington & Adams will be rechosen this winter — the first without opposition; whether the opponents of Mr Adams will combine their Opposition I consider as uncertain; should this be the case Clinton will be their man.

We are in a singular situation respecting our Governor — a majority of the Votes at the last Election was given to Mr Jay — a majority of the Canvassers rejected the Votes of three Counties under the pretence of a Defect in the Form of the Returns, & declared Mr Clinton elected — the minority of the Canvassers protested and it is very probable that a majority of the State disapprove of the Decision of the Canvassers — the Legislature will meet in November, and it will be attempted to procure a Resolve for the calling of a Convention for the sole purpose of annulling the canvassers' Decision, and ordering a new Election — Mr Clinton qualified and is in the Exercise of the Office.

Thus my dear Sir, I comply with the proposal that you made me in your Letter from London, and give you an outline of our situation. I will hereafter do more by furnishing you with those incidents which from time to time may occur, and which may serve to explain the views of the persons engaged in our public Affairs — our information respecting France comes principally through England, and is so confused and coloured, that we are unable to form a rational opinion of their Affairs — you are in the best possible

situation to obtain & give exact intelligence, and you will do me a
Favor to gratify me on this subject.

   With sincere Esteem
     I am Dear Sir
       Your ob.^t Servt

           RUFUS KING

G. Morris Esqr.
 &c &c

Morris to Rufus King

         Paris 23.^d Octr 1792

Rufus King Esqr
   New York

Dear Sir
 Yours of the first of September reach'd me a few days ago.
Accept my sincere Thanks for the Information it contains which
is precious and highly pleasing. I might Comment on what you
say respecting a Print which answers every measure of Government but you will readily anticipate all which I might say on that
Subject. I cannot give you such desirable Intelligence respecting
the State of Things here as I might have done if the late revolution
had not taken place, because I find my Intercourse of necessity
suspended, and until I have Orders respecting the new Government I am bound to preserve a neutrality of Conduct so that I
cannot as heretofore peep behind the Scenes. Add to this that
there is at present no very certain March anywhere, each feeling
himself obliged to deviate according to Circumstances from the
Course which he might wish. I will attempt however to give you
an Abbreviation of the late Events and in my Letters to Mr Jefferson, which may perhaps be communicated to the Senate, and
at any rate from the Gazettes preceding and subsequent to the
tenth of August, you will be able to fill up the outlines of the
Sketch.
 The late revolution has for its remote Cause that Excess in the
human Temper which drives men always to Extremes if not
checked and controled. For its proximate Cause it has the Vices

and Defects of the late Constitution and particularly that an Executive without power was rendered responsible for Events and that a Legislature composed of a single Chamber of representatives was secured by every precaution, and under no Control except some paper Maxims and popular Opinion. That the People or rather the Populace, a Thing which thank God is unknown in America, flattered with the Idea that they are omnipotent and disappointed from necessity in the golden prospects originally held out to them, were under no restraint except such as might be imposed by Magistrates of their own Choice. It resulted inevitably that the Executive must be in the power of the legislative and this last at the mercy of such Men as could influence the Mob. By reducing the Royal Authority below all reasonable measure the Constitution makers had created a moral Impossibility that the People should believe the King sincere in his Acceptance even if it had been possible that he should without regret have beheld himself reduced from the first Place allotted to Man, to a State so low as to be exposed to insult from the lowest. It was evident that the Constitution could not last and in the overturn three Things might happen viz The Establishment of Despotism, the Establishment of a good Constitution or the institution of a Democracy. The first under an able and ambitious Prince was inevitable. The second was extremely difficult, not in itself but because the Chiefs of different parties all found themselves committed to different Points and Opinions. The last was only a natural Continuation of the progress of Men's minds in a necessary succession of Ideas from the Bill of Rights. The Advocates for republican Government therefore had an easy Task altho both to themselves and others it appeared difficult. From the moment that the second Assembly met a Plan was formed among several of the Members and others to overturn the Constitution they had just sworn to observe, and establish a republic. This arose in Part from the desire of placing themselves better than they could otherwise do and in part from a conviction that the System could not last and that they would have no Share in the Administration under a pure Monarchy. As they had a strong hold upon the lowest class of people, as the aristocratic and constitutional Parties were at open War, as these last avowed openly their Wish to amend, in other words to change the Constitution which at the same Time they assumed to venerate, it was not a difficult Matter to assault a Monarch who adhered to that Form which he could not be supposed to approve and whose Faults became daily more and more apparent. Add to this that the Court was involved in a Spirit of little paltry Intrigue unworthy of any Thing above the Rank of Footmen and Chambermaids. Everyone had his and her little project and every little project had some Abettors. Strong manly Councils frightened the Weak, alarm'd the envious and wounded the enervate mind of the lazy and luxurious. Such Counsels therefore (if perchance any such appear'd) were approved but not adopted, certainly not followed. The Palace was always filled with People whose Language, whose Conduct and whose Manner was so diametrically opposite to every Thing like Liberty that it was easy to persuade the People that the Court meant to destroy the Constitution by observing strictly the Constitution. Some Persons avowed this Tactick, which from the moment of such avowal was no longer worth a Doit. The King, whose Integrity would never listen to anything like the violation of his Oath, had nevertheless the weakness to permit those who openly avowed unconstitutional Sentiments to approach his person and enjoy his Intimacy. The Queen was still more imprudent. The Republicans (who had also their Plan to destroy the Constitution by the Constitution) founded on the King's personal Integrity their Operation to destroy his Reputation for Integrity, and hold him out to the world as a Traitor to the Nation whom he was sworn to protect. They in Consequence seized every Occasion to pass popular Decrees which were unconstitutional. If the King exercised his Veto he was accused of wishing a Counter Revolution. If he sanctioned the Decree he was so far lost with those who were injured by the Decree, and of course became daily more and more unprotected. The Success of his Enemies was beyond their own Expectation. His Palace was assaulted. He took Refuge with the Assembly and is now a Prisoner of State with his Family. But now the Ideas of Revolt which had been fostered for his overthrow are grown very troublesome to those who have possessed themselves of the Authority. It is not possible to say either to the people or to the Sea, so far shalt thou go and no farther, and we shall have I think some sharp struggles which will make many men repent of what they have done when they find with Macbeth that they have but taught bloody Instructions which return to plague the Inventor.

Morris to Alexander Hamilton

Paris 24 October 1792

Alexander Hamilton Esqr
           Philadelphia

My dear Sir,

I have receiv'd yours of the twenty second of June & am in the hourly Hope to hear farther from you. I need not tell you that it will give me Pleasure. Enclosed you will find the Copy of a Letter which I wrote to Mr Jefferson the seventh of November 1791. This with some other Communications at the same Epocha he never acknowledged, I know not why, but I think the Paper enclos'd in that Letter will be agreable to you tho not very amusing. It would seem that your Friend Scipio is not much attach'd to Paulus, at least if I may judge from some Things which I see. However there is a great Chasm in my News Papers which breaks the Thread of my Conjectures as well as of my Information for I have little, I might almost say none, of the latter except from the Gazettes: of Course I know what passes about two Months after every Body else. Tell me I pray you how Scævola stands affected between the Parties just nam'd. I think he never had a very high Opinion of the first mention'd but he was attach'd to Tarquin immeasurably and that with some local Circumstances may have form'd a stronger Chain than I should otherwise suppose.

You will have seen that the late Constitution of this Country has overset. A natural Accident to a Thing which was all Sail and no Ballast. I desire much, very much, to know the State of Opinions with us on that Subject. Some Gentlemen who considered it as the Achmé of human Wisdom must I suppose find out Causes which Persons on the Spot never dreamt of. But in seeking or inventing these Causes what will be their Opinion of present Powers, what the Conduct they wish to pursue. These are to me impor-

tant Questions. Brutus will doubtless triumph but I wish to feel
the Pulse of Opinion with you, or rather to know before Hand how
it is like to beat. There are pros and cons whose Action I cannot
estimate. The Flight of Monsieur de La Fayette, the Murder of
the Duc de la Rochefoucault and others with many similar Circumstances have I know affected the Ideas of some. But what
will be the republican Sense as to the new Republic? Will it be
taken for granted that Louis the sixteenth was guilty of all possible Crimes and particularly of the enormous one of not suffering
his Throat to be cut which was certainly a nefarious Plot against
the People and a manifest Violation of the Bill of Rights. Paulus
who is no Enemy to Kings will not believe that they are all Tygers
but I am not certain that if he were here he would not consider
them as Monkeys. However, we are done with them in France, at
least for the present. There are two Parties here. The one consists of about half a dozen and the other of fifteen or twenty who
are at Daggers' Drawing. Each claims the Merit of having be-
gotten the young Republic upon the Body of the Jacobine Club
and notwithstanding the Dispute is very loud and open the People is as fond of the Child as if it were its own. But this has a
Relation to antient Manners for there has been a Practise here
from Time whereof there is no Memory of Man to the contrary,
viz that one Sett of Men were employ'd in getting Children for another Sett. My public Letters and the Gazettes will bring you acquainted with Things here as fully as I can in any Way communicate them. It is not worth While to detail the Characters of those
now on the Stage because they must soon give Place to others.[1]

Wednesday 24. — I am still indispos'd. The Weather tolerable.
Thursday 25. — This Morning I am in the Enjoyment of Health
but this Evening feverish. The Weather pleasant.

[1] Interpreting the American side of this letter with the key sent to Morris
by Hamilton, it means that democratic Secretary of State *Scipio* Jefferson was
not devoted to his fellow Cabinet Minister federalist Secretary of the Treasury
Paulus Hamilton; that Morris wonders how President *Scævola* Washington
stands with both, and thinks *Tarquin* Madison may be a connecting and en-
dearing link between the other two great Virginians. *Paulus* Alexander Hamilton, 'who is no enemy to Kings,' had seemed, at the making of the Constitution, to want a United States monarchy. Morris thinks that *Brutus* John
Adams will triumph in the election, so that he and not Clinton, will be Vice-
President in Washington's second administration.

Friday 26. — This Day I am very much indispos'd. Ride out. Consult Monsieur Dessault who is to take me in Hand.

Saturday 27. — Still indispos'd. The Weather foul.

Sunday 28. — Somewhat better. Much Rain. Francfort is taken like Mayence by Capitulation.

Monday 29. — I am still indispos'd. The Weather is better.

Tuesday 30. — My Health mends. Go out in the Evening. The Parties here drive hard at each other. The Weather is pleasant.

Wednesday 31. — The Exchange keeps rising. No Demand for Bills. My Health is better. The Weather is bad all the Morning. In the Evening it clears. Mild.

NOVEMBER 1792

Morris to Carmichael

Paris 5 November 1792

M! Carmichael
            Madrid.

My dear Carmichael,

... As to the State of Things here, I can give you no very satisfactory nor flattering Accounts. True it is that the French Arms are crowned with great Success. Towns fall before them without a Blow, and the Declaration of Rights produces an Effect equal at least to the Trumpets of Joshua: but as on the one Hand I never questioned the Force of France if united and her natural Enthusiasm warm'd by the Ardor of New Born Freedom, so on the other I was always apprehensive that they would be deficient in that cool reflection which appears needful to consolidate a free Government. We read in the History of Man as it is developed in the great Books of Nature, that Empires do by no means depend on their Success in Arms but on their civil, religious and political Constitutions, and that in the framing of these it is an useless

Question what kind are best in themselves. The more so as good and bad in most things here below, but especially in that which we now contemplate, are meer relative Terms. The true Object of a great Statesman is to give to any particular Nation the kind of Laws which is suitable to them and the best Constitution which they are capable of. Now by as much as it is an easy thing and within the Compass of every School Boy to deal in generals and abstractions, pursuing Demonstrations which in moral Subjects are frequently least exact when they appear to be most evident, by so much is it of high and almost unsurmountable Difficulty to descend into the nice Estimates of Manners, Habits and Sentiments, and amid the Discord of loud and contradictory Passions and Interests to discover the means of establishing an harmonious System where each part has the needful Relation to every other and to the great whole. These Observations are I know familiar to you, and to every other sensible Man who has had much Experience in human Affairs, but they are heathen Greek or, if you will, flat nonsense when addressed to those new fledged Statesmen who are always positive and peremptory in Proportion to their Ignorance of Politics. . . . Before the People will assent to the Form of Government which in Hypothesis shall be supposed the most fitting for them, they must be convinced of the Fitness. No easy Task, believe me, even if Man were a reasonable Creature. But he is not. He is a sensible Creature and governed invariably by his Feelings. Now you can easily make him feel that in Point of Right he is equal to every other Man. Vanity may even whisper to him that he is so in Point of Talent, and if Vanity were remiss the Prompter Flattery is at Hand: but the more he feels his Equality of Rights and Talents, the more must he feel his Inequality in Point of Possessions. Where these are wanting, he has Rights which he cannot exercise, Talents which he cannot employ, Desires which he cannot allay. Now the severe Law of Property is that in any well settled Country a few must soon possess all, and the Majority, the great Majority, nothing. Between the Œconomy which constitutes the Tyranny of the rich, and that Misery which enslaves the poor, let the Form of Government be what it may there is a constant Struggle, which forms great Men, and great Men are generally ambitious Men.

Their equals in Property are as much enslaved by their pleasures as the poorer kind can possibly be by their wants. In such a State of Things, where the Constitution is not ballanced in its Structure and supported by strong Props of private Interest, it must be overturned.

I quit these Investigations to tell you that all here is in a State of uncertainty. Time will disclose the Events with which he is charged in their due Season. Some of them will I think be of sable Hue.

Thursday 1 *Nov*. — Write this Morning, then ride. The Weather is very pleasant.

Friday 2. — My Health is better, the Weather is good. Nothing new. It is confirm'd to me that the Government have written to America urging my Recall.

Saturday 3. — I am tolerably well and that is Something. The Weather is fine. Nothing new.

Sunday 4. — Good Weather. Calm. Heavy Dews. Nothing new.

Monday 5. — Write all this Morning. Very fine Weather. There seems to be much Movement in Paris.

Tuesday 6. — Pleasant Weather. Robespierre has got thro his Affair with *Éclat*.[1]

---

[1] 'Robespierre has got thro his Affair with Éclat.' On October 29 Louvet, one of Madame Roland's Girondins, journalist of her group, had electrified the Convention by a *robespierride*; he had dared accuse the Candle of Arras of accusing everybody else; of having long calumniated the purest patriots, of putting himself constantly forward as an object of idolatry, of aiming evidently at supreme power; each charge beginning with the dread *Je t'accuse!* Robespierre went into a week's retreat to secrete enough venom and wrap it up in hypocritical modesty; his come-back was a personal triumph. Some magnetism, which certainly his printed words cannot convey, was giving him an ever-increasing ascendancy. Nothing in his speeches explains it, unless their lack of eloquence gave an impression of great sincerity to audiences overfed on revolutionary bombast. Girondins loudly accused him of *tartuferie*. He fostered his smug self-satisfaction, his valuable self-esteem, by associating with men of less education, for he required incense, but sometimes in public he took pains to disguise his conviction of superiority under a measured reasonableness. Mocked in the cultivated *Constituante*, applauded at the Jacobin Club, from the Mountain he will make the Convention tremble, this immaculately neat small-town lawyer, correct, cold, self-controlled, whose patriotism will lead him to view life and death through lenses of ever-increasing distortion.

Wednesday 7. — Every Thing quiet.

Thursday 8. — The Weather is good; this Evening arrives the News of the taking of Mons.

Friday 9. — The Weather is pleasant, at Times some Rain.

Saturday 10. — A little Rain this Day.

Sunday 11. — Pleasant Weather but damp.

Monday 12. — This Morning the Weather is very fine. After writing my Letters I go to see Gen! Washington's Statue at Houdon's. P. calls and gives me Information.

Tuesday 13. — Fine Weather. Nothing new.

Wednesday 14. — The Weather is still fine. A vague Report that Brussels is taken.

Thursday 15. — This Morning write, then walk, the Weather being very fine. This Evening the News arrives that Dumouriez took Possession of Brussels the 14.th.

Friday 16. — The Weather continues to be very fine. Nothing new.

Saturday 17. — The Weather is very pleasant. Montesquiou is gone off into Switzerland.

Sunday 18. — Good Weather. Nothing new.

Monday 19. — The Weather continues good.

Hugon de Basseville to Morris

Naples le 20 Octobre 1792

Monsieur

Je suis arrivé dans ce pays, l'un des plus beaux et des plus agréables de notre hémisphère, vers la fin du mois d'Août. Vous imaginez facilement, et vous scavez sans doute, que nous n'y avons pas marché sur des roses. On nous fuit et on nous craint comme des Lépreux qui charient le mal immonde.[1] . . . il faut pren-

---

[1] Carrying credentials from Louis XVI, the new French mission to Ferdinand IV was being aggressively Girondist. De Mackau, aristocrat-revolutionary, was subtly pouring vinegar into existing dissensions between Naples and the Papal States, while in Rome his secretary Basseville was calling the aunts of his King *les demoiselles Capet* and the cardinals of His Holiness 'purple geese of the Capitol.' One version says that his substituting tricolor for Bourbon lilies on the Villa Medici, home of the French Academy, was the Romans' excuse for tear-

dre patience, c'est ce que je fais. J'ai parcouru, autant que ma santé me l'a permis, les environs de Naples un Virgile à la main : je me suis promené dans la partie de la ville de Pompeia, qui est découverte ; j'ai été admirer le riche museum de Portici qui est unique dans son espèce ; ce qu'on y trouve ne se voit nulle part, et les autres Souverains ne pourraient, même avec des sommes immenses, se procurer les mêmes curiosités : c'est une mine qui appartient au roi de Naples, il faut encore bien du tems et bien de l'argent pour arriver au terme de son exploitation entière, à peine est-elle entamée.

Je ne vous demande pas, Monsieur, si vous avez plus d'une fois regretté les bords tranquilles de la Delaware ; c'est bien assez pour un philosophe, d'avoir vu une révolution dans sa patrie... pour quoi la notre n'a-t-elle pas été en tout semblable à la votre?... *gens humana vicit per Vetotum nefas.*

Je ne sais ce que je vais devenir, ni ce que je vais faire. Nous n'avons des nouvelles de France que par ricochet, rien de direct. Notre correspondance est arretée et depuis 4 Couriers nous n'avons reçu ni gazettes ni lettres du ministre, et je n'ai reçu depuis le 10 juin que j'ai quitté Paris, que 2 lettres, quoique j'en ai écrit environ 72. Je ne scais si celle ci vous parviendra, je le désire bien ardemment, ainsi que la continuation des marques de Bienveillance et d'Amitié, dont vous m'avez comblé en toutes rencontres.

Tels sont les Sentimens avec lesquels j'ai l'honneur d'être Monsieur

> votre très humble et très obéissant
> Serviteur
> N. J. HUGON (DE BASSEVILLE)
> Secrétaire d'Ambassade à Naples

Comme je ne scais pas l'addresse de M.ʳ Robert Morris le jeune j'espère que vous voudrez bien lui faire parvenir l'incluse.

---

ing Basseville limb from limb. Mackau will refuse to wear mourning for Louis XVI when ordered to by Acton, Prime Minister of Bourbon Ferdinand and favorite of his Queen Caroline, a sister of Marie-Antoinette. His mission ends in war.

[Translation:]

Naples 20 October 1792

Sir,

I arrived in this country, one of the most beautiful and one of the most agreeable in our hemisphere, towards the end of August. You can easily imagine, and you doubtless know, that we have not been walking on roses; we are shunned and feared as lepers who spread the unclean disease.... One must cultivate patience and so I do. As much as my health would allow I have explored the surroundings of Naples Virgil in hand; I have walked through the excavated part of the town of Pompeii, I have admired the rich museum at Portici which is unique of its kind; what one sees there could be found nowhere else, and other Sovereigns could not even with immense expense procure the same curiosities: it is a mine belonging to the King of Naples, much time and money will be needed before coming to the end of its exploitation, as yet hardly touched.

I do not ask you, Sir, if you have not more than once regretted the tranquil banks of the Delaware; it is enough for a philosopher to have seen a revolution in his own country... why has ours not resembled yours in every way?... *gens humana vicit per vetotum nefas.*

I know neither what will become of me nor what I shall do. News from France reaches us only by ricochet, nothing direct. Our correspondence is stopped and for the last 4 posts we have received nothing, neither gazettes nor letters from the Minister, and I myself since leaving Paris on the tenth of June have received but 2 letters though I have written about 72. I cannot tell whether this will reach you but I wish it ardently, as well as a continuation of the signs of goodwill and friendship with which you have favored me at every interview.

Such are the sentiments with which I have the honor to be, Sir,

Your very humble and very obedient Servant
N. J. HUGON (DE BASSEVILLE)
Secretary of Embassy at Naples.

As I do not know the address of Mr Robert Morris junior, I hope you will be good enough to forward to him the enclosed.[1]

Tuesday 20. — Still fair. The french Arms are still triumphant.

Wednesday 21. — The Weather wet. No News. Dine with Madame de Narbonne.

Thursday 22. — Go this Morning by Appointment to M.[r] Lebrun's Office and urge an Exception in the Law against Emigrants favorable to those who are in the United States. Pleasant Weather as yet but threatning. Dine with La Caze.

Friday 23. — The Weather seems inclinable to change for Cold. The Wind hangs to the Eastward.

Saturday 24. — Pay some Visits this Day. Weather cold and clear.

Sunday 25. — Write all Day. Wind at North East. Cloudy and cold.

Monday 26. — Cold Weather. Wind at North East.

Tuesday 27. — Weather continues cold. I have several Bankers to dine with me. Troubles in the Departments.

Wednesday 28. — Still cold. The Papers discovered at the Tuilleries [2] affect sundry Persons who supposed themselves safe.

---

[1] This letter shows the attitude of foreign courts towards French diplomats after news of August Tenth had come through. On January 13, 1793, a few weeks after writing it, Nicolas-Jean Hugon de Basseville was set upon and killed by a Roman mob for making his servants wear the tricolor cockade. The French Government adopted his son and in 1797 extracted an indemnity of 300,000 livres from the Papal Court. How he would have enjoyed that 300,000 as a man, not a memory! for Gouverneur had set him down as an extravagant fellow, always plaguing him for more pay from Robert Morris, whose sons Robert and Thomas he had tutored between 1781 and 1788 when the 'Financier' had sent the little boys abroad because the War of Independence had dislocated education in America. Basseville had been writing for the *Mercure Nationale*, had published a mythology, some fugitive verses, and in 1790 a history, somewhat premature, of the French Revolution.

[2] May, 1791, Louis XVI scooped out a recess behind panelling of a dark passage, valet Derey holding a candle, dumping rubbish in the Seine. The King, accomplished blacksmith, made a little iron door, sent for locksmith Gamain, who had taught him at Versailles, to add staples, lock, hinges. Filling the hidden cupboard with papers the King felt ready for flight. His trial ends Gamain's months of indecision; too terrified for further loyalty he takes his secret to Roland, who spends some hours combing this find before sharing it with the

A Dinner to french People this Day.

Thursday 29. — Cold Weather still. Americans to dine with me.

Friday 30. — The Weather continues cold and clear.

Morris to Thomas Pinckney

Paris 3 December 1792

Thomas Pinckney Esq.
          London

... Success as you will see continues to crown the French Arms, but it is not our Trade to judge from Success. We must observe the civil, moral, religious and political Institutions. These have a steady and lasting Effect, and these only. You will soon learn that the patriots hitherto adored were but little worthy of the Incense they received. The Enemies of those who now reign treat them as they did their Predecessors, and as their Successors will be treated. Since I have been in this Country I have seen the worship of many Idols and but little of the true God. I have seen many of those Idols broken and some of them beaten to dust. I have seen the late Constitution in one short Year admired as a stupendous Monument of human Wisdom and ridiculed as an egregious Production of Folly and Vice. I wish much, very much, the Happiness of this inconstant People. I love them. I feel grateful for their Efforts in our Cause and I consider the Establishment of a good Constitution here as the principal Means, under divine Providence, of extending the Blessings of Freedom to the many millions of my fellow Men who groan in Bondage on the Continent of Europe. But I do not greatly indulge the flattering Illusions of Hope, because I do not yet perceive that Reformation of Morals without which Liberty is but an empty Sound.

[In less earnest vein Morris expounds to Lord Gower's pretty wife how the threats of the crass Brunswick Manifesto had welded the French into a nation of patriots against the world, in spite of faction hatreds.]

Convention. La Fayette's patriotism comes out unspotted; there is little evidence against the King; his prosecutors make ingenious, disingenuous use of scattered phrases robbed of context.

Morris to the Countess of Sutherland

Paris 19 January 1793

Lady Sutherland
   London

 The Science of Politics is at best a dry one. The French there-fore discuss it with the Ladies, and indeed the Presence of a fine Woman is so pleasant that it diffuses general Gladness. In this View of the Subject, I am now about to converse with one of the loveliest I know and thus begins our Conversation.

> When Brunswic hither came express to
> Restore the King, his Manifesto
> Denouncing widely War and Vengeance
> Was one of those destructive Engines
> Which if we do not sagely chuse them
> Prove hurtful to the Men who use them.
> No Wonder that he missed his Aim.

Here you reply

> An easy Task it is to blame
> And when a General's Measures fail
> The World is privileg'd to rail.
> But would you, whilst Men wound & curse you
> Present them nought but Christian Mercy?
> Mildness to those abandon'd Wretches
> The Men of Paris without Breeches,
> With due Submission to your Meekness
> Deserves no better Name than Weakness.

Now tis my turn

> I grant you that the *Sans Culottes*
> Who please themselves by cutting Throats
> Might well expect, if Times should alter,
> To be rewarded with a Halter.
> But they who lov'd the Constitution

You come in here pat

> Prepar'd the second Revolution;
> Twas they who led their hapless Nation

Out of the Road of her Salvation
To follow that fantastic Scheme
The Rights of Man. A boyish Dream
Where Words of vague ambiguous Sense
Conduct to bloodiest Consequence.
They pull'd unhappy Louis down,
Then mock'd him with a paper Crown
Which any Breath might blow away
And leave him bare. In short twas they
Who with a Rage perverse and blind
Would fain have ruin'd all Mankind.

To this I answer

Admitting what you say were true,
Yet Punishments most justly due
May be deferr'd when hasty Zeal
Would rather lead to Woe than Weal.
Those who contend against a Foe
Of great Resources, strive to sow
Dissention in his State; make Friends
Who may contribute to their Ends,
And, easier Conquests to obtain
Adopt the Rule — *Divide and reign.*
If Brunswic had this line pursued
He had not now his Fortune rued,
For this you safely may rely on,
He would have taken Town of Thion
Without a Stroke, as well as Metz.
But when the Fate of La fayette's
Companions was proclaimed here,
Each Bosom was appall'd with Fear.
The Constitutionals elate
Before, in his beheld their Fate,
And found, in Arms 'twas better die
Than to surrender or to fly.
Thus Brunswic was oblig'd to fight
Both with the Party Jacobite
And with the Feuillantins their Foes

Who, but for him, had come to Blows
Before this Hour; and thus the Nation,
United by his Proclamation,
Display'd at once uncommon Force.
But had he ta'en a diff'rent Course
He would have found a num'rous Party
Who in the royal Cause were hearty
And wish'd sincerely to restore
The Power they destroy'd before.

And hereon charming Lady I greet you; and I would have you to consider that all this Rhyme is not without some Reason. So pray ask your Lord to give the Gentleman who bears this Letter an Interview. And sometimes when you have Nothing else to do, think of a lone Man who thinks very often of you and never without wishing you were again establish'd in Paris. Adieu —

President Washington to Morris

Philadelphia, October 20th, 1792.

My Dear Sir,

Although your letter of the tenth of June, which I have received, did not paint the prospects of France in the most pleasing colors, yet the events which have since taken place give a more gloomy aspect to the public affairs of that kingdom, than your letter gave reason to apprehend.

A thousand circumstances, besides our distance from the theatre of action, made it improbable that we should have, in this country, a fair statement of facts and causes through the medium of the public prints; and I have received no other accounts, than what have come in that channel. But taking up the most favorable of these, gloomy indeed appears the situation of France at this juncture. But it is hardly probable that even you, who are on the spot, can say with any precision how these things will terminate; much less can we, at this distance, pretend to augur the event. We can only repeat the sincere wish that much happiness may arise to the French nation, and to mankind in general, out of the severe evils which are inseparable from so important a revolution.

In the present state of things we cannot expect, that any commercial treaty can now be formed with France; but I have no doubt of your embracing the proper moment of arrangement, and of doing whatever may be in your power for the substantial interest of our country.

The affairs of the United States go on well. There are some few clouds in our political hemisphere, but I trust that the bright sun of our prosperity will disperse them.

The Indians on our western and southern frontiers are still troublesome, but such measures are taken as will, I presume, prevent any serious mischief from them; I confess, however, that I do not believe these tribes will ever be brought to a quiescent state, so long as they may be under an influence which is hostile to the rising greatness of these states.

From the complexion of some of our newspapers, foreigners would be led to believe, that inveterate political dissensions exist among us, and that we are on the very verge of disunion; but the fact is otherwise. The great body of the people now feel the advantages of the general government, and would not, I am persuaded, do anything that should destroy it; but this kind of representations is an evil, which must be placed in opposition to the infinite benefits resulting from a free press; and I am sure you need not be told, that in this country a personal difference in political sentiments is often made to take the garb of general dissensions.

From the Department of State you are, I am informed, furnished with such papers and documents from time to time, as will keep you more particularly informed of the state of our affairs. I shall therefore add nothing further to this letter, than assurances of being always and sincerely yours, &c.

G? WASHINGTON.

DECEMBER 1792

Saturday 1 *Dec*.. — Still cold.

Sunday 2. — Cold Weather. Dine with the Count de Ségur who gives us a greek Wine after Oysters, and by Mistake as a second Bottle of the same, some of the best Tokay I ever tasted. I drink the greater Part of it, praising always his greek Wine, till his Brother in Law, astonish'd at my Choice, tastes it and then all is discover'd.

Monday 3. — Dine this Day with Mons! Greffeuille. A Madame Simon who is here is handsome. The Weather still continues cold. The Convention this Day determine to try the King.

Tuesday 4. — The Weather still cold but softens. Le Couteulx and his Wife dine with me, and Greffeuille, who gets a little tipsy. It grows every Day more probable that England will declare War.

Wednesday 5. — Dine with the Maréchal de Ségur. Rainy damp Weather.

Thursday 6 *Dec*.. — Dine with Mad? Alex? de La Rochefoucault. Soft nasty Weather.

Friday 7. — The Weather is warm and wet, it has given me a very serious Cold.

Saturday 8. — Disagreable Weather for the Season. I am much indispos'd.

Sunday 9. — This Day we have the News that Francfort is taken by the King of Prussia. The Weather still disagreable.

Monday 10. — Nothing new. The Weather is fair and pleasant.

Tuesday 11. — This Afternoon the Weather is foul. The King was this Day question'd before the Assembly and answered well. Some who saw him conducted tell me that the People seemed rather sorrowful than triumphant.

Wednesday 12. — I am told this Day that the Committee think they have been pushed too far against the King by the Orleans Faction. The Weather is variable, my Cold somewhat better.

Thursday 13. — Write this Morning, bad Weather. The Army of Dumouriez wants many Things, particularly Forage.

Friday 14. — Nothing new. Disagreable Weather.

Saturday 15. — The Weather is still bad. I visit the Baron de Blome and Madame de Ségur this Morning. Am told that Dumouriez is in Town. Also that Agents from the Cabinet of S.t James are come to claim the King.

Sunday 16. — I am told that Yesterday's News is all false. I did not believe it and had ventur'd to contradict the latter Part. The Weather is damp. This Day the Convention banish the Bourbon Family.

Monday 17. — Nothing new. Mild Weather but damp.

Tuesday 18. — Nothing new. Weather as before.

Wednesday 19. — Weather still damp. All Accounts from England shew a Design to engage in the War. Dine with Perrégaux and some Deputies. The Decree against the Bourbons is suspended.

Thursday 20. — Several Americans to dine with me. Payne looks a little down at the News from England. He has been burnt in Effigy. Piquet promises to help Nicolls in the Sale of his Flour. I receive a Letter from M.r Jefferson by Express from Bordeaux.

Friday 21. — A Company of french to dine with me. The Weather pleasant.

Saturday 22. — Nothing new to Day. Foul Weather, particularly this Evening.

Sunday 23. — Still bad Weather. Sleet but cold. P. tells me that the Ministry will make Sacrifices for Peace with England.

Monday 24. — Bad Weather still.

Tuesday 25. — M.r Nicolls, who dines with me, says there is a Report that Custine and his Army are taken Prisoners. I doubt this. Count d'Estaing told me this Morning that a Majority of the Convention would give M.r Pitt the french West Indias to keep him quiet. He spoke to me also on a Subject which Paine had communicated confidentially.

Wednesday 26. — Bad Weather.

Thursday 27. — Bad Weather.

Friday 28. — M.r Short arrives this Day from Holland and goes to Rocheguyon Tomorrow.

Saturday 29. — Company of Americans this Day.
Sunday 30. — Bad Weather.
Monday 31 *Dec*. — Bad Weather.

Jefferson to Morris

Philadelphia Oct. 15. 1792

Monsieur
  Monsieur Morris
    Ministre Plenipotentiaire
      des E. U. d'Amerique
        à Paris

Sir

I have duly received your favor of July 10. N.° 4. but no other N.° preceding or subsequent. I fear therefore that some miscarriage has taken place. The present goes to Bordeaux under cover to Mr Fenwick who I hope will be able to give it a safe conveyance to you. I observe that you say in your letter that 'the marine department is to treat with you for supplies to S. Domingo.' I presume you mean 'supplies of *money*' and not that our government is to furnish Supplies of *provisions* &c. specifically, or employ others to do it; this being a business into which they could not enter. The payment of money here to be employed by *their own agents* in purchasing the produce of our soil is a desirable thing. We are informed by the public papers that the late Constitution of France *formally notified to us*, is suspended, and a new Convention called; during the time of this suspension, & while no legitimate Government exists, we apprehend we cannot continue the payments of our debt to France because there is no person authorised to receive it, and to give us an unobjectionable acquittal. You are therefore desired to consider the paiment as suspended until further orders. Should circumstances oblige you to mention this (which it is better to avoid if you can) do it with such solid reasons as will occur to yourself & accompany it with the most friendly declarations that the suspension does not proceed from any wish in us to delay the paiment, the contrary being our wish, nor from any desire to embarrass or oppose the settlement of their government in that way in which their nation shall desire it: but from our anxiety to pay this debt justly & honorably, and to the persons really authorised by the nation (to whom we owe it) to receive it for their use; nor shall this Suspension be continued one moment after we can see our way clear out of the difficulty into which their situation has thrown us. That they may speedily obtain liberty, peace & tranquillity is our sincere prayer. The present summer is employed by us in endeavors to persuade the Indians to peace, and to prepare for the ensuing campaign if our endeavors for peace should fail. That they will fail, we have reason to expect; and consequently that the expences of our armament are to continue for some time. Another plentiful year added to the several others which we have successively had is some consolation under these expences. Very early frosts indeed have somewhat shortened the productions of the autumn.

I have the honor to be with great respect & esteem Dear Sir

Your most obed!

& most humble serv!

TH: JEFFERSON

Morris to Jefferson [1]

No. 14   Paris 21 Dec! 1792

Thomas Jefferson Esq!

Philadelphia.

Dear Sir,

I have received your favors of the twelfth of July and fifteenth of October. The last reach'd me yesterday by Express from Bordeaux. I am astonish'd to find that so late as the middle of October you had received but one of my Letters. I had taken every precaution against *Miscarriages* but there is no answering for the

---

[1] In this letter Morris comments to Jefferson on the superlative qualities of French artillery. Compared to cavalry and the line, hardly any officers had emigrated from the scientific branches of the service; more interested in technical problems than in dancing attendance at Court, gunners and sappers had always been soldiers in earnest, and now combined the discipline of the old army with a new efficiency.

Negligence of those one is obliged to employ in the Ports. I shall transmit you herewith the Copies of N.º 1. 2. & 3. altho the Time which has elapsed will have reduc'd them to the value of waste-paper, excepting the last. I have written to Monsieur Merlino but have receiv'd no Answer and really know not where to find him. I shall however keep a Look out.

When I mention'd Supplies to S.º Domingo I certainly meant that such Supplies should be purchased by French agents in the United States and that the Money should be advanc'd by us in Diminution of our Debt upon such Terms as that the United States should not loose in the Mode of Payment but the contrary; besides the Advantage of expending such large Sums in the purchase of objects the Growth Produce and Manufacture of our Country, and of its industrious Inhabitants. As to Specific Supplies I had declared in pointed Terms that the American Government would by no means enter into Stipulation of any kind with relation thereto. I am happy to find that on this Occasion my Sentiments have so fully coincided with yours.

It gives me also great Relief to be inform'd that until further Orders the Payments are suspended. You will have seen that on this Point I have been hard run, and I do assure you that if Fear or Interest would have induc'd me to swerve from the Line of Duty, there were not wanting sufficient Motives. But it is not needful to relate such particulars, and you may rely that I shall not communicate your present Instruction respecting our Debt unless I shall be of Opinion that it will become serviceable to the Honor & Interest of the United States.

I see with concern that the Indian War is like to continue. This War prevents the Investments of European Money in the Purchase of our Waste Lands, and I have already expressed to you my Conviction that this species of Investment would be as salutary as the Engrossing of our domestic Debt is pernicious. The distress'd State of Things here induces many to turn their Attention towards us and consequently occasions numerous Applications to me. I endeavour as far as Propriety will admit to lead People to a Preference of American Lands but am sorry to observe that the Disposition to invest in our Funds is predominant and that we shall thereby become tributary to those who obtain,

below its Value, a Share of those Funds. I think it my duty to
mention this to you to the End that if any measures can be de-
vis'd to enhance the Value with you and thereby lessen the Negotiations, or at least obtain thereon the compleat Value, such
Measures may be adopted. . . .

The Brissotins, finding themselves hard push'd towards the
killing of the King, and apprehensive (not without reason) that
this might be a Signal for their own Destruction, determin'd on a
Measure not a little hazardous, but decisive. This was the Ex-
pulsion of the Bourbons, a Blow principally levelled at the Duke
of Orleans. The Motion was carried, but the Convention have
been oblig'd to suspend the Decree, and that is I think equivalent
to a Repeal. The Suspension was pronounc'd under the Influence
of the Tribunes, evidently. Many Members have talked of leaving Paris, but the same Fear which controls them while in this
City will prevent them from quitting it. At least such is my
Opinion.

I come now to the Trial of the King, and the Circumstances
connected therewith. To a Person less intimately acquainted than
you are with the History of human Affairs, it would seem strange
that the mildest monarch who ever fill'd the french Throne, one
who is precipitated from it precisely because he would not adopt
the harsh Measures of his Predecessors, a Man whom none can
charge with a Criminal or cruel Act, should be prosecuted as one
of the most nefarious Tyrants that ever disgraced the Annals of
human nature. That he, Louis the sixteenth, should be prosecuted even to the Death. Yet such is the Fact. I think it highly
probable that he may suffer, and that for the following Causes.
The Majority of the Assembly found it necessary to raise, against
this unhappy Prince, the national Odium, in order to justify the
dethroning him (which after what he had suffer'd appeared to be
necessary even to their Safety) and to induce the ready Adoption
of a republican Form of Government. Being in Possession of his
Papers, and those of his Servants, it was easy (if they would permit themselves to extract, to comment, to suppress and to muti-
late) it was *very* easy to create such Opinions as they might think
proper. The Rage which has been excited was terrible, and altho
it begins to subside, the Convention are still in great Streights;

fearing to acquit, fearing to condemn, and yet urg'd to destroy their Captive Monarch. The violent Party are clamourous against him for Reasons which I will presently state. The Monarchic and Aristocratic Parties wish his Death, in the Belief that such Catastrophe would shock the national Feelings, awaken their hereditary Attachments, and turn into the Channels of Loyalty the impetuous Tide of Opinion. Thus he has become the common Object of Hatred to all Parties, because he has never been the decided Patron of any one. If he is saved it will be by the Justice of his Cause, which will have some little Effect, and by the Pity which is universally felt (tho none dare express it openly) for the very harsh Treatment which he has endur'd. I come now to the Motives of the violent Party. You will see that Louvet (whose Pamphlet with many others I send you) has charg'd on this Party the Design to restore Royalty in the Person of the Duke of Orleans. This Man's Character and Conduct give but too much Room to suspect him of criminal Intentions. In general I doubt the public Virtue of a Profligate, and cannot help suspecting Appearances put on by such Persons. I have besides many particular Circumstances which lead me to believe that he has, from the begining, play'd a deep and doubtful Game, but I believe also that on the present Occasion as on some preceeding, he is the Dupe. Shortly after the tenth of August, I had Information on which you may rely, that the Plan of Danton was to obtain the Resignation of the King, and get himself appointed Chief of a Council of Regency (composed of his Creatures) during the Minority of the Dauphin. This Idea has never, I believe, been wholly abandon'd. *The Cordeliers* (or privy Council which directs the Jacobine Movements) know well the Danger of interverting the Order of Succession. They know how to appreciate the fluctuating Opinions of their Countrymen, and tho they are willing to employ the Duke of Orleans in their Work, I am much mistaken if they will consent to elevate him to the Throne. So that, for his Share of the Guilt, he may probably be rewarded with the Shame of it, and the mortifying Reflection that after all the Conflicts of his political Warfare, he has gained no Victory but over his own Conscience.

It is worthy of Remark that altho the Convention has been now

THE MARQUESS OF LANSDOWNE
Gainsborough pinx:, Bartolozzi sc:

THE SAME PLATE ALTERED BY MARIANO BOVI INTO
A PORTRAIT OF LOUIS XVI AS PAINTED BY CALEIS

near four Months in Session, no Plan of a Constitution is yet produced. Nevertheless the special Authority committed to them by
the People, and the only Authority perhaps which cannot be con-
tested, was to prepare such Plan. . . .

Extract, Morris to Washington

Paris December 28, 1792.

I did myself the Honor to write to you on the twenty third
October. Since that Date the exterior Affairs of this Country
have put on a more steady Appearance. My Letter of the twenty
first instant to M. Jefferson will communicate my View of Things,
to which I could add but little at this Day. I have not mention'd
to him the Appointment of M. Genet [1] as Minister to the United
States. In Fact, this Appointment has never been announced to
me. Perhaps the Ministry think it is a Trait of Republicanism to
omit those Forms which were antiently us'd to express Good Will.
In the Letter which is addressed to you is a Strain of Adulation
which your Good Sense will easily expound. Let it be compar'd
with M. Le Brun's Letter to me of 30th of August. Fact is, that
they begin to open their Eyes to their true Situation; and besides,
they wish to bring forward into Acts our Guarantee of their Islands, if the War with Britain should actually take Place. A
propos of that War, I am told that the British Ultimatum is as
follows. France shall deliver the royal Family to such reigning
Branch of the Bourbons as the King may chuse, and shall recall

---

[1] Edmond Charles Genet (1765–1834) now appears. Red-headed young
brother of Madame Campan, chief waiting-woman to Marie-Antoinette and
writer of *Mémoires*, his youth was spent playing in the Queen's rooms at Versailles or working in his father's Bureau of Interpreters, succeeding to that post,
1781. Stayed on as chargé d'affaires in St. Petersburg when Ségur left, 1789.
After Varennes Catherine II sent French subjects packing, her Ministry politely ejecting a defiant Genet in July 1792. Revolutionary enthusiasm of his
dispatches ensured his welcome by the Gironde. Of great education and old
Burgundian lineage, 'opportunist' describes Genet better than Morris's 'upstart,' which has been seized upon and criticized. Within a year Morris will be
ordered to cut short Genet's fantastic career as Minister from France, by demanding his recall, granted without question by a government which had overturned Genet's patrons. As an act of reciprocity this leads to Morris's recall,
welcome news in the grim summer of 1794.

her Troops from the Countries they now occupy. In this Event, Britain will send hither a Minister, and acknowlege the Republic, and mediate a Peace with the Emperor and King of Prussia. . . .

I have not yet seen Mr Genet, but Mr Paine is to introduce him to me; in the mean Time I have enquired a little what kind of Person it is: and I find that he is a Man of good Parts and very good Education, Brother of the Queen's first Woman; from whence his fortune originates. He was, thro the Queen's Influence, appointed as Chargé d'affaires at Petersburgh, and (when there) in Consequence of Dispatches from Mr de Montmorin, written in the Sense of the Revolution and which he interpreted too literally, he made some Representations in a much higher Tone than was wish'd or expected. It was not convenient either to approve or disapprove of his Conduct, under the then Circumstances, and his Dispatches lay unnoticed. This to a young Man of ardent Temper, and who, feeling Genius and Talents, may perhaps have rated himself a little too high, was mortifying in the extreme. He felt himself insulted and wrote in a style of petulance to his Chief, believing always that, if the royal Party prevail'd, his Sister would easily make fair Weather for him at Court: which I doubt not. At the overturn of the Monarchy, these Letters were so many Credentials in his Favor to the new Government, and their Dearth of Men has opened his Way to whatever he might wish. He chose America, *as being the best Harbor during the Storm*, and if my Informant be right, *he will not put to Sea again untill it is fair Weather*, let what will happen.

In addition to what I have said respecting the King to Mr Jefferson, it is well to mention to you that the Majority have it in Contemplation not only to refer the Judgment to the Electors of France (that is to the People) but also to send him and his Family to America, which Payne is to move for. He mentioned this to me in Confidence but I have since heard it from another Quarter. Adieu, my dear Sir, I wish you many and happy Years —

JANUARY 1793

[This new year was to bring little enough happiness to France! On the 6th of January Morris again reports to Washington:]

Since I had the Pleasure of writing to you on the twenty eighth of last Month I have seen Mr Genet and he has din'd with me. He has I think more of Genius than of Ability and you will see in him at the first Blush the Manner and Look of an Upstart. My friend the Maréchal de Ségur had told me that Mr Genet was a Clerk at £50 p.an. in his Office while Secretary at War. I turned the Conversation therefore on the Maréchal and Mr Genet told me that he knew him very well, having been in the Ministry with him. After Dinner he entered into Dispute with a Merchant who came in and as the Question turn'd chiefly on Facts the Merchant was rather an Over Match for the Minister. I think that in the Business he is charg'd with, he will talk so much as to furnish sufficient Matter for putting him on one Side of his Object should that be convenient. If he writes he will I believe do better.

I have endeavor'd to shew him that this is the worst possible Season to put to Sea for America. If he delays there is some Room to suppose that Events may happen to prevent the Mission; perhaps a british Ship may intercept that which takes him out. And I incline to think that untill Matters are more steady here you would be as well content with some Delay as with remarkable Dispatch.

[*Paine is to move to send the King and his family to America. A way out for the Gironde, who wished to abolish royalty without burdening their conscience with royal executions. Brissot, Tom Paine, the Rolands, and Genet had devised the plan; Genet was to escort the banished Bourbons in the frigate taking him to his new post, and American gratitude was expected to do the rest. But they had all reckoned without the Mountain. The Decree of Banishment of December 16 was suspended three days later; the visionary, theoretical Girondists were about to find their masters, and nothing short of the King's trial and execution would satisfy*

the Jacobins and the Paris Commune. Genet or Genest, the mute
s still wanders in and out of his name, was to sail alone. But not
without Morris's usual mark of goodwill to westward-bound
Frenchmen, a letter of introduction to Robert Morris, powerful
Senator in spite of tangled fortunes. The Minister offered to
carry dispatches for Morris, but why add fresh risks to existing
uncertainties? — somehow those dispatches failed to be prepared
in time.]

Mr Morris a l'honneur de faire ses Complimens à Monsieur
Genest et de lui souhaiter un bon Voyage. Il n'a pas eu un Moment à lui pour préparer ses lettres mais il n'a pas pu omettre
une Occasion de présenter Monsieur Genest à son ami intime. Il
prie en Conséquence Monsieur Genest de se charger de la lettre
ci jointe pour Mons.ʳ Robert Morris de Philadelphia.

Paris 15 January 1793

Robert Morris Esq.ʳ

Philadelphia

My dear Friend,

This Letter will be delivered to you by M.ʳ Genest who goes
hence in quality of Minister Plenipotentiary to the United
States. He presses his Departure at this unfavorable Season on
account of important Business, the Nature of which I am not acquainted with. I think it possible that notwithstanding the Information which he has acquired respecting our Country, it may
happen that your Advice may become useful to him and I trust
that if ask'd, your Regard for the french Nation will induce you to
grant it. Your Civilities as a Gentleman he will in Course receive. I would to both of these Objects request your Attention if
I did not know it to be unnecessary.

[On February 13 and March 26 Morris speaks of him to Jefferson:]

I ought also to mention to you, which I omitted in its due Season, that Monsieur Genest before he went hence called to take
Leave, and apologized for M.ʳ Lebrun on Account of his constant
Business for not calling on me to present M.ʳ Genest. [That
much he had the grace to do to mitigate] the Slight put on me by

sending out M.ʳ Genest without mentioning to me a Syllable either of his Mission or his errand, both of which nevertheless I was early and sufficiently informed of.

[But the frigate *Embuscade* had not been long at sea before Morris made a disconcerting discovery, which for greater safety he transmitted through the American Minister in London, to whom he wrote:]

I think it well that you should be acquainted with a Fact which it is very important to communicate to our Secretary of State as soon as may be. I am inform'd in a Way that precludes Doubt that the Executive Council here sent out by M.ʳ Genest three hundred blank Commissions for Privateers to be given clandestinely to such Persons as he might find in America inclin'd to take them. They suppose that the Avidity of some Adventurers may lead them into Measures which would involve Altercations with Great Britain and terminate finally in a War. This appears to me (waving all Question of Honesty) no very sound measure politically speaking, since they may as a Nation derive greater Advantage from our Neutrality than from our Alliance. But whatever light it may be viewed in as to them, it is in Respect to us a detestable Project.

... I have no late News from America and none of any Date which you would wish to know. Our Secretary of State seems much attach'd to Brevity.

Gouverneur Morris to Robert Morris

24 December 1792

You will long ere the present Day have learnt that the Scenes which have past in this Country and particularly in this City have been horrible. They were more so than you can imagine. Some Days ago a Man applied to the Convention for Damages done to his Quarry. The Quarries here are deep Pitts dug thro several Feet of Earth into the Bed of Stone and then extended along the Bed of Stone under the Surface. The Damage done to him was by the Number of dead Bodies thrown into his Pitt and which choakd it up so that he could not get Men to work at it. Think of the

Destruction of hundreds who had long been the first People of a Country, without Form of Trial, and their Bodies thrown like dead Dogs into the first Hole that offered. At least two hundred of these unhappy Victims had committed no other Crime than that of being Ecclesiastics of irreproacheable Lives who were conscientiously scrupulous of taking an Oath prescribed to them. I am much mistaken if we do not experience similar Scenes before the present Revolution is finished.

Adieu my dear Friend. I heartily present to you and yours the Compliments of this, which is with you a festive Season. I write from a Place deserted by its former Inhabitants where in almost every Countenance you can mark the Traces of present Woe and of dismal Forebodings.

Tuesday 1 *Jan*? 1793. — All Accounts from England seem to announce War.

Wednesday 2. — The Weather Yesterday was cold and this Day it snows.

Thursday 3. — M⸢ Genest, who is appointed Minister to the United States, dines with me. M⸢ Short calls in the Evening and I give him his Passport. The Weather is soft.

Friday 4. — M⸢ Short, the Maréchal de Ségur, M⸢ Grefeuille and the Chevalier de La Tremblai dine with me. The Weather grows colder.

Saturday 5. — I go out this Morning but am glad to get Home. The Streets are in a Glare of Ice. Horses tumbling down and some killed. Mine come off tolerably. —

The Situation of Things is such that to continue this Journal would compromise many People, unless I go on in the Way I have done since the End of August, in which Case it must be insipid and useless. I prefer therefore the more simple Measure of putting an End to it.

[In the handwriting of Morris's widow:[1]] 'Surely this justifies my shewing the journal to the Biographer of M⸢ Morris, having obtained his promise not to put it in any other hands. To avoid neglecting my exemplary Son's comfort I have read this after he was in bed. Old age and business have ruined my eyes.'

---

[1] Ann Cary Randolph, married to Morris on Christmas Day, 1809. Their only child, Gouverneur, born at Morrisania 9 February 1813.

Morris to Jefferson

No. 16   Paris 6 January 1793

Thomas Jefferson Esq⁝
                        Philadelphia

Dear Sir,

Mr Short, who is so kind as to take Charge of my Letters as far as Bordeaux, will go he says this Day. I therefore take the latest Opportunity to write, and to inform you that the Appearances have not at all changed since mine of the first. Dumouriez has been some Days in Paris. He stays at Home under Pretence of Illness, but in Fact to receive and consider the Propositions of the different Parties. It would seem that he is not reconciled to Pache the Minister of War. Pache is very strong in Paris, and that Circumstance renders him formidable both to his Colleagues and to the Convention. I am told that the Majority of the latter Body expect soon to be supported by a considerable Number of Volunteers from the Departments. I am also told that it cannot be long before the Bursting of the Storm which has been so long brewing. This last Intelligence is from one of those who, tho a Promoter of the last Revolution, is now marked as one of the Victims. He says he will die hard but laments the Feebleness of Temper which he experiences among those who, like him, are doom'd to Destruction. On the other Hand a Person of cool discerning Temper and Understanding, who is in the Confidence of those who direct the Jacobines, told me when I last saw him that *they* are determined to rule or perish. You will easily suppose that this Prevision of Horrors is far from pleasant. I have, I assure you, been not a little Tempted to spend a few Days with some of my friends in the Country during the festive Season, which would render such an Excursion natural, but the critical State of Things with Great Britain might take a Turn which it would be important for you to know and therefore it is right that I stay here.

[In November France had formulated two excuses for invading her neighbors, the decree of the 19th, that 'France will accord help to all nations who wish to recover their liberty,' and Danton's more frank doctrine of 'natural frontiers': Ocean, Rhine, Alps,

Pyrenees. November saw Dumouriez's victory of Jemmappes in his rapid conquest of Belgium; he preached a simple recognition of its independence, but the Convention decided to annex it and in the name of liberty to invade Holland, risking war with England, who would not meekly tolerate French control of Antwerp, the Scheldt, and Amsterdam. This new invasion was to be entrusted to Dumouriez, but with attention focussed on the King's trial the hero of Jemmappes was kept waiting.

Having settled her young son, the future charmer Charles de Flahaut, at school in England, finding Talleyrand more occupied with the galaxy of *émigré* wit centred round Madame de Staël at Juniper Hall than with his old flame, finding also that he refused her any financial help and was himself living on the sale in England of his collection of fine books, the Comtesse de Flahaut was contemplating a return to Paris, and was thinking it worth while to divorce the soon-to-be guillotined husband hiding somewhere near Boulogne. Her plans hung on the verdict in the King's trial. On January 18 she writes: 'I was on the point of starting when *all that I know here* made it clear to me that it was extravagant to travel at the moment of the King's affair, to risk being imprisoned as an *émigrée* in spite of my status as an English woman; so here I am, waiting to hear the result of what may have happened on Monday.' As the King was condemned, prudence triumphed over her nostalgia, and over the divorce idea. She will see Morris at Hamburg in 1795, but Bonaparte will be in power before she dares attempt Paris. From London, 4 January, she had given Morris some idea of English feeling about revolution and the ordeal of Louis XVI:]

'Not a line from you and yet I write, and will even always write. Soon I shall be arriving, however, for my mind is made up and the end of next week will not see me in London. I have done all I should and even more than I should; I don't know whether you owe me any gratitude, but I don't feel guilty in the least for having abandoned you for so long. I claim the right of sacrificing you as much as myself when serious misfortunes call me. I complain to you, and with you, but it seems to me there can be no question of excuses between us because, on my side at least, there can be no wrongs.

'I am deeply anxious over the affair of the King; everybody here is wishing him well; and those who thought England ready for democracy were far from being good judges of the national spirit; the people, down to the last street urchin [*petit Savoyard*], sing "God Save the King" with as much enthusiasm as we intone the hymn of the Marseillais.

'Let this be your New Year gift, you who were separated from this little island by a true Republicanism; I will once more make you a present of the lovely blue cup which I offer you every year with renewed pleasure; you will find it among the china sent to Martin's care. Good-bye, my dear and good friend; I am in the best of spirits at the thought of seeing you soon.

'Cabagne says she sends you a New Year kiss. My compliments to Mr. Livingston.'[1]

Morris to Jefferson

No. 18   Paris 25 January 1793.

Thomas Jefferson Esq[r].
                        Philadelphia

Dear Sir,
My last N° 17 was of the seventeenth Instant. The late King of this Country has been publicly executed. He died in a manner

---

[1] Translated now from three little letters in French, of such slight historical value that they seem to have escaped Mr. Sparks. Her 'status as an English woman' remains unexplained; it would have been a flimsy protection against the constantly tightened up restrictions against *émigrés*.

The poor King was so much in the news that an enterprising Piccadilly publisher made capital of the similarity of portly figure in his portrait by Caleis with that in Gainsborough's painting of the first Marquess of Lansdowne, father of Madame de Flahaut's Lord Wycombe. Mariano Bovi was set to scratching the face from Bartolozzi's plate of the Gainsborough, to engraving in its place the Bourbon features of doomed Louis, to reversing the direction of the broad ribbon, substituting the Star of the Saint Esprit for that of the Garter and dangling the Golden Fleece from the neck of the new print, ready for sale in January, 1793. This press-photographer instinct for the topical, combining speed and profit with economy in means, was nothing new; skilful strokes had once turned Queen Elizabeth into James I, one equestrian plate had in turn worn the countenance of Louis XIV, Charles I, and Oliver Cromwell, according to the market, and young Queen Victoria's riding companion in a popular nineteenth-century engraving will exchange the mature face of her Minister Melbourne for the whiskered good looks of her consort Albert.

becoming his Dignity. Mounting the Scaffold he express'd anew his Forgiveness of those who persecuted him and a Prayer that his deluded people might be benefited by his Death. On the Scaffold he attempted to speak but the commanding Officer, Santerre, ordered the Drums to be beat. The King made two unavailing Efforts but with the same bad Success. The Executioners threw him down and were in such haste as to let fall the Axe before his Neck was properly plac'd so that he was mangled. It would be needless to give you an affecting narrative of Particulars. I proceed to what is more important having but a few Minutes to write by the present good Opportunity.

The greatest Care was taken to prevent an Affluence of People. This proves a Conviction that the majority was not favorable to that severe measure. In Effect the great Mass of the parisian Citizens mourn'd the Fate of their unhappy Prince. I have seen Grief such as for the untimely death of a beloved Parent. Every Thing wears an appearance of Solemnity which is awfully distressing. I have been told by a Gentleman from the Spot that putting the King to Death would be a Signal for disbanding the Army in Flanders. I do not believe this but incline to think it will have some Effect on that Army, already perishing by want and mouldering fast away. . . .

[The Diary has petered out, the King has been beheaded, these two volumes must hold no more. But Morris's mail-bag for the next two years is well worthy of a third, not only for diversity of human interest, but to correct an impression of Morris's work for his country's merchant marine given through Thomas Paine by biographers of Paine who have never seen the American Minister's correspondence with injured sea captains, or with United States consuls at Dunkirk, Havre, Marseilles, and Bordeaux.]

THE END

INDEX

INDEX